Asia Pacific Regionalism

Asia Pacific Regionalism

Readings in International Economic Relations

edited by

Ross Garnaut and Peter Drysdale

Australian National University

with

John Kunkel

HarperEducational
A Division of HarperCollins *Publishers*

in association with

The Australia–Japan Research Centre
The Australian National University

© HarperEducational*Publishers* 1994

Published 1994

HarperEducational*Publishers*
A Division of HarperCollins*Publishers*
25 Ryde Road, Pymble, NSW 2073, Australia
in association with
The Australia–Japan Research Centre
The Australian National University

National Library of Australia
Cataloguing-in-Publication information:

Garnaut, Ross.
Asia Pacific regionalism: readings in international economic relations

Bibliography.
Includes index.
ISBN 0 06 312140 9
1. International economic relations 2. Pacific Area — Foreign economic relations
3. Asia — Foreign economic relations I. Asia Pacific regionalism: readings in
international economic relations. I. Drysdale, Peter. II. Title.

337.5

Copy edited by Gary Anson
Cover design by Neil Carlyle
Index by Suzanne Ridley
Typeset by Minni Reis
Printed in Australia by Australian Print Group

Contents

Ten: CHINA: THE REGION'S EMERGING
GIANT   409

Tables

Figures

Contributors

Mangat Ram Aggarwal
Professor of Economics, Department of Economics, Panjab University, Chandigarh.

Narongchai Akrasanee
Chairman and Chief Executive Officer, General Finance and Securities Public Company Ltd, Bangkok, and Thai representative to the APEC Eminent Persons Group.

Torsten Amelung
Acting Head, Communication, Economics and Energy Economics Department, RAG Führungsgesellschaft, Essen.

Kym Anderson
Professor of Economics and Director of the Centre for International Economic Studies, University of Adelaide, South Australia.

H. W. Arndt
Emeritus Professor and Visiting Fellow, National Centre for Development Studies, Research School of Pacific and Asian Studies, Australian National University, Canberra.

C. Fred Bergsten
Director of the Institute for International Economics, Washington DC, and Chairman of the APEC Eminent Persons Group.

Jagdish Bhagwati
Arthur Lehman Professor of Economics and Professor of Political Science, Columbia University, New York.

Chia Siow Yue
Associate Professor of Economics and Acting Head of the Department of Economics and Statistics, National University of Singapore.

Richard Cooper
Boas Professor of International Economics, Harvard University, Cambridge, MA.

Peter Drysdale
Executive Director, Australia–Japan Research Centre and Professor of Economics, Research School of Pacific and Asian Studies, Australian National University, Canberra.

Andrew Elek
Formerly Head of the Economic and Trade Development Division of Australia's Department of Foreign Affairs and Trade (1987 to 1990) and Senior Research Fellow at the Australian National University (1990 to 1994), Canberra.

Jeffrey A. Frankel
Professor of Economics, University of California, Berkeley, Director of the National Bureau of Economic Research's program in International Finance and Macroeconomics, and Senior Fellow, Institute for International Economics, Washington DC.

Ross Garnaut
Professor of Economics and Convenor, Economics Division, Research School of Pacific and Asian Studies, Australian National University, Canberra.

Gary C. Hufbauer
Reginald Jones Senior Fellow, Institute for International Economics, Washington DC.

Paul Krugman
Professor of Economics, Stanford University, Stanford, CA.

Lee Tsao Yuan
Deputy Director, Institute of Policy Studies, Singapore, and representative of Singapore to the APEC Eminent Persons Group.

P. J. Lloyd
Professor of Economics, Institute of Applied Economic and Social Research, University of Melbourne, Victoria.

Hege Norheim
Formerly (at the time the paper was written) Research Intern at the GATT Secretariat, Geneva.

Posh Raj Pandey
Research Fellow, Department of Economics, Panjab University, Chandigarh.

Peter A. Petri
Carl Shapiro Professor of International Finance and Director of the Lemberg Program in International Economics and Finance, Brandeis University, Waltham, MA.

Gary R. Saxonhouse
Professor of Economics and Director of the Japan Economy Program, University of Michigan, Ann Arbor, MI.

Jeffrey J. Schott
Senior Fellow, Institute for International Economics, Washington DC.

Hadi Soesastro
Executive Director, Centre for Strategic and International Studies, Jakarta.

David Stifel
Research Consultant to General Finance and Securities Public Company Ltd, Bangkok.

Lawrence H. Summers
Under Secretary for International Affairs, US Department of the Treasury, Washington DC.

Yun-Wing Sung
Reader in Economics and Co-director of the Hong Kong and Asia-Pacific Economies Research Programme, Chinese University of Hong Kong.

Shujiro Urata
Professor of Economics, School of Social Sciences, Waseda University, Tokyo.

Ippei Yamazawa
Professor of Economics, Hitotsubashi University, Tokyo, and Japanese representative to the APEC Eminent Persons Group.

Soogil Young
President, Korea Transport Institute, Seoul.

Preface

This book of readings brings together a representative part and much of the best of the considerable literature that has emerged from analysis of Asia Pacific regionalism over the past two decades. The Asia Pacific literature, like the phenomenon from which it has grown, is distinctive. The importance of the literature was recognised by few in the North Atlantic community of economists until the realisation in these last few years that the centre of gravity of the world economy has moved decisively to the Pacific region, and is moving towards the Western Pacific. The distinction of the literature is still little recognised.

These readings will make the Asia Pacific literature on regionalism accessible to the large community of people who now recognise the importance of Asia Pacific regionalism: economists, business people, government officials, and participants in discussion of the grand events of our lives and times. The reader of this book will have access to all of the main strands of discussion — the main channels of ideas, some of the tributaries that entered and changed the mainstream, and maybe even a stream or two that is destined to end its course in shallows and in miseries.

Most of the readings are extracted from longer papers and chapters of books. The original source, and whether it is an extract from a longer piece, is noted at the bottom of the first page of each reading. We have tried to include enough of each reading to make the major ideas intelligible within the piece itself, but some readers may wish to follow some extracts in full in their original places of publication.

We, and the authors, have resisted the temptation to update in any substantial way, correct or vary the original pieces. In a few places we have made adjustments of style or nomenclature for consistency within this volume.

Jim Davidson, on behalf of the publishers, urged us into the enterprise, over our initial protestations that we were too heavily committed at this time. We, and we hope the readers and users of the book, are glad that we did. That we were able to deliver on our commitments is due mainly to the excellent professional support that we received from John Kunkel. John's knowledge of the literature, good judgement, diligence and hard work are responsible for a large part of what is admirable in the book. We alone are responsible for any weaknesses that remain. We are grateful for John's professional quality and good humour.

We are grateful, too, for excellent preparation of the manuscript by Gary Anson working within the Australia–Japan Research Centre. Minni Reis, of the Centre's publications staff, has done a fine job with typesetting the manuscript. The Australia–Japan Research Centre, since its establishment in the late 1970s, has provided much of the intellectual and communications infrastructure of Asia Pacific economic cooperation, and the work in the production of this book continues that role.

Ross Garnaut and Peter Drysdale
Canberra
May 1994

1 Asia Pacific regionalism: the issues

Ross Garnaut and Peter Drysdale

It is now a commonplace that the Asia Pacific is the world's most dynamic centre of growth in trade and economic output. The phenomenon of Asia Pacific dynamism, with national strategies built on the powerful use of opportunities for international specialisation in production, has been associated with the intensification of international economic ties within the region. With no formal, inter-governmental structures for promoting intra-regional trade and specialisation, and no region-wide trade discrimination, intra-regional trade shares are higher than those within the European Community.

The unusual phenomenon of high regional concentration of trade, with neither official trade discrimination nor formal institutional support, challenged old ideas of regional development, and inspired a new literature. The new literature is informed by but distinct from the theory and lines of empirical inquiry that supported and grew from the emergence of the European Community (EC) in the 1960s. It led to the advocacy and eventually to the establishment of Asia Pacific-wide institutional arrangements that, it was argued, could consolidate and extend the gains from non-discriminatory expansion of regional trade.

This book presents readings from major elements of the literature of Asia Pacific regionalism. It reproduces mostly extracts from major papers over the past two decades, concentrating more strongly on the policy-focused discussion that preceded and accompanied the emergence of formal Asia Pacific Economic Cooperation (APEC) in 1989.

There are some consistent themes in the literature that distinguish it from its counterparts in Europe and North America. The differences are sometimes subtle, and sometimes missed by analysts who have grown up in the older traditions of regionalism and analysis of the nature of regionalism. The new themes include the high importance of market processes in producing economic integration — requiring relative freedom from official controls on international trade and payments, but, in the right circumstances, proceeding powerfully in the absence of special official measures to promote regional trade. The focus on market integration draws attention to the importance of non-official institutions in achieving gains from trade and the distinction between market integration and institutional integration (Cooper, Chapter 2). Trade-promoting institutions do contain elements of 'public goods' which assist in overcoming the difficulties faced by private investors in appropriating fully the benefits of international specialisation. How this occurs is a powerful interest related to the role of governments in providing regional public goods to promote trade.

The defining concept of Asia Pacific regionalism is *open regionalism*. Open regionalism encompasses integrative processes that contain no element of exclusion or discrimination against outsiders. The concept of open regionalism grows naturally out of the themes of *market integration*, and government support for public goods that facilitate international trade within a region. From this perspective, the policy focus is on the agenda set out by Elek (Chapter 17).

Some elements of the literature have sought to push the concept of open regionalism further, to encompass regional cooperation on mutual reduction of barriers to trade within the Asia Pacific region without discrimination against outsiders. This dimension of open regionalism would encompass agreements on trade liberalisation, extended to others on an *unconditional* most-favoured-nation (MFN) basis (see Drysdale, Chapter 4). This element of open regionalism has collided with support in the Americas for concepts of *discriminatory regionalism*. The resolution of this clash of concepts is for the future of discussion of regionalism in the Asia Pacific.

The boundaries of the region

The 'region' of Asia Pacific trade expansion has defined itself as the set of East Asian and Pacific countries joined by intense trade and investment ties. In the early discussion of Asia Pacific regionalism, in the 1960s, this placed the spotlight on the region's five advanced economies: the United States, Canada, Japan, Australia and New Zealand. Successful internationally-oriented economic growth in the newly industrialised economies and several Association of South East Nation (ASEAN) economies in the 1970s broadened the self-selection to include the substantial developing 'market economies' of the Western Pacific. This, with some representation from Southwest Pacific developing countries, but with Taiwan excluded because of ambiguity in its diplomatic status, was the limit of full participation in the original Pacific Economic Cooperation Conference (PECC) in 1980.

China's adoption of an internationally-oriented development strategy in the late 1970s soon propelled it into the Asia Pacific economy. Formal diplomatic recognition by the United States in 1979, the Sino-British agreement on the future of Hong Kong in 1984, the Taiwan government's lifting of major restrictions on contact with the mainland in 1987, and the establishment of diplomatic relations between Seoul and Beijing in 1992 — all progressively removed official inhibitions to China's full participation in Asia Pacific dynamism.

New candidates for membership of the Asia Pacific economy have emerged in recent years. Market-oriented and internationally-oriented reform in Vietnam (and elsewhere in Indochina), reflected eventually in the lifting of US restrictions on economic relations in 1994, and Vietnam's strong response in expansion of production and trade have turned it quickly into an Asia Pacific economy. Mexico's deep integration into the North American economy, with the movement to internationally-oriented policies and membership of the North American Free Trade Agreement (NAFTA) made it a necessary participant in regional integration joined by the United States. Papua New Guinea is linked to the region through intense economic relations with Australia and has also been brought into regional arrangements, in a manner analogous to Mexico through the United States, but without any reciprocal free trade agreement.

The spreading through South Asia and Latin America of more internationally-oriented policies in the East Asian style has raised new and difficult questions about the natural boundaries of the economic region. The continuation of momentum of internationally-oriented economic reform in India and South Asia would integrate these economies deeply into the web of Asia Pacific regionalism, unless retreat into old-style discriminatory regionalism in the established Asia Pacific economies came to limit the opportunities for newcomers.

The spread of more internationally-oriented development strategies in Latin America has an uncertain impact on the natural boundaries of Asia Pacific dynamism. Latin America historically has been a realm of commitment to discriminatory regionalism in the old style that became important with the formation of the European Community. This commitment was an early complement to Latin American protectionism. The new legitimacy of discriminatory regionalism in the Americas following the formation of NAFTA has laid an ideological basis for integration of the Latin into the North American economies, and therefore indirectly into an Asia Pacific economy. Such a basis of Latin American participation — integration through discriminatory trade ties with the United States — would come to challenge open regionalism as the ordering idea of Asia Pacific regionalism. The one possible exception is the case of Chile, where open and market-oriented policies have spurred a pace and pattern of development that shares much with the East Asian style.

The emergence of Asia Pacific regionalism

The web of intense economic ties that bind the Asia Pacific region emerged from market processes (see Drysdale and Garnaut, Chapter 5; Petri, Chapter 10; Anderson and Norheim, Chapter 11; and Yamazawa, Chapter 16).

The role of government was first of all facilitating: the removal of barriers to trade and payments at the borders of participating economies created opportunities that were developed creatively by business enterprises. These steps were taken in the

United States, Canada and Japan to a considerable extent through successive rounds of multilateral trade negotiations under the auspices of the General Agreement on Tariffs and Trade (GATT). In Japan, two other forces were important. After the mid-1970s, and especially through the 1980s, some major liberalising steps were taken in relation to manufacturing activities as part of domestic economic strategy — to promote adjustment out of energy-using, polluting, low technology and labour-intensive products that had been left behind by changes in Japan's resource endowments and comparative advantage. In Japan, some liberalising steps were taken also to resolve bilateral trade disputes with the United States, including early steps in liberalising some trade in services and farm products.

In the rest of the Western Pacific — in the developing countries of East Asia, including China, in Australia and New Zealand, and now in the economies of Indochina — liberalisation of manufactured goods trade was overwhelmingly guided by domestic economic strategy. Hong Kong and Singapore were virtually free trade economies from the beginning, and their deep integration into neighbouring economies was a powerful factor in Asia Pacific trade expansion.

It was the adoption of the policy in the early 1960s to liberalise payments and trade, and especially to bring incentives for export and import-competing production more closely together, that marked the beginning of the long periods of sustained, internationally-oriented growth in Taiwan and the Republic of Korea. Several of the ASEAN economies — Malaysia, Thailand, and later Indonesia — took similar if less decisive steps successively in the early 1970s and through the 1980s. The Philippines' weak progress in liberalisation programs of similar intent was one factor in that country's poor growth performance. Australia and New Zealand embarked upon gradual but radical import liberalisation after the mid-1980s, deepening integration into the international, especially the Asia Pacific, economies. China from the late 1970s and Vietnam from the mid-1980s chose to replace old central planning systems with greater use of markets and integration into the national and international economies.

US pressures on Korea and Taiwan from the early 1980s increased momentum for trade liberalisation, and helped extend it from the manufacturing sector to politically more sensitive areas in agriculture and services. American pressure was reinforcing tendencies that had their origins in domestic economic strategy, and it is difficult to be precise about its undoubted influence over this period (Smith 1994).

Rapid, internationally-oriented economic growth in East Asia and the Pacific was associated with high intensity in and rapid expansion of intra-regional trade (see Frankel, Chapter 19; and Saxonhouse, Chapter 20).

In early years, only tiny proportions of this trade were promoted by trade discrimination in favour of regional partners. Economically important remnants of the old imperial discrimination in US–Philippines and intra-Commonwealth trade had been removed by the mid-1970s. Trade discrimination — in US–Canada and later North American trade relations, in Australia–New Zealand trade under the Closer Economic Relations (CER) Agreement, and within ASEAN, especially after the announcement in 1991 of commitment to establish an ASEAN Free Trade Area

(AFTA) — increased in importance in the early 1990s, but remained a relatively minor influence on regional trade flows. Similarly, the elements of pan-China discrimination in favour of the mainland's economic relations with Taiwan were minor sources of the explosive growth of trade across the Straits after 1987.

Indeed, official discrimination in several potentially important trade relationships inhibited expansion of Asia Pacific intra-regional trade ties until the legacy of the Cold War had been put to rest in the Western Pacific. The development of US economic relations with the People's Republic of China awaited diplomatic recognition in 1979. The Sino-British agreement of 1984 on the future of Hong Kong was the trigger for rapid expansion of investment and trade across the border. Realisation of the huge potential for trade across the Straits of Taiwan was delayed until the government in Taipei lifted many restrictions on contact with the mainland in 1987. Sino-Korean trade expanded rapidly with mutual diplomatic recognition in 1992. Normalisation of US economic relations with Vietnam was delayed until 1994. The new international orientation in Indian economic policy from the early 1990s was partly a response to the geo-political realignment associated with the collapse of the Soviet Union and the end of the Cold War.

Perhaps the most important impact of official trade discrimination in promoting intra-regional trade in the Asia Pacific was associated with the formation of the EC. As a matter of arithmetic, trade creation within the EC increased the intensity of trade among other economies (see Anderson and Norheim, Chapter 11). Of more economic significance, common exclusion from European markets and the associated trade diversion made Asia Pacific economies more competitive in each other's markets, and expanded intra-regional trade (see Drysdale, Chapter 4).

Overwhelmingly, it was market forces acting in a more open general trade and investment environment that spurred the rapid expansion of trade among Asia Pacific economies. Intra-regional trade shares rose to levels higher than those in Europe, without institutional promotion and without trade discrimination — although statistical techniques developed in the Western Pacific cautioned against the use of trade shares as indicators of trade intensity (see Drysdale and Garnaut, Chapter 3).

The literature on *open regionalism*

The extent and dynamism of market integration in East Asia and the Pacific encouraged new lines of economic analysis directed at its measurement, analysis and policy implications.

The Asia Pacific literature on regional economic integration has emphasised the role of transactions costs of varying kinds in determining the intensity of bilateral and regional trade. Some elements of transactions costs are closely related to distance, or relative distance, between trading partners. Transactions costs are affected by the activities of multinational companies, and by many factors affecting ease of communications (see Amelung, Chapter 6).

One determinant of transactions costs is the effectiveness of institutions in internalising the full costs of establishing and maintaining trading relationships. This is where cross-border cultural and investment ties are particularly important.

Where private institutions are inadequate in internalising externalities, there can be large gains from provision by governments of the 'public goods' required to maintain high levels of trade (see Elek, Chapter 17). Recognition of this reality has been one spur to the search for regional institutions to promote trade expansion. In this context, 'institutionalisation' of regional economic cooperation means something very different from the old-style institutions of the free trade area and the customs union.

These are the first two elements of Asia Pacific 'open regionalism': recognition of the power of market forces in promoting high intensity in intra-regional trade; and acceptance in principle that there is a role for governments in provision of public goods to promote regional trade expansion. These are on the original agreed and secured agenda of the Asia Pacific Economic Cooperation (APEC) forum. Neither of these elements of open regionalism lends itself to mutually exclusive or discriminatory trading relationships. Each element lends itself to more rapid and deeper integration in some trading relationships than others within a region of intense trade, and even to especially intense trading relationships between parts of economies (see Chia and Lee, Chapter 27; and Sung, Chapter 28).

Consistently with open regionalism and the avoidance of discrimination in international trade, but beyond the original and secure agenda of APEC, there has been a search for mechanisms to promote trade liberalisation on an MFN basis in regional economies. The literature observes the tendency for individual Western Pacific economies to choose in their own interest unilateral trade liberalisation. This is the world of the 'prisoner's delight' in which each economy in its own interests liberalises foreign trade, coincidentally raising the gains to third countries associated with their own liberalisation, and therefore facilitating the third countries' liberalisation. How much greater the gain from each country's liberalisation if there were concerted action from a number of members of a region? There has been recognition that the prospects for unilateral non-discriminatory liberalisation are greater in commodities in which the world's most competitive suppliers are members of the region.

To this point, the discussion of trade liberalisation remains within the boundaries of open regionalism. But there have been recent pressures to retreat from this point, back into discriminatory regionalism in the old style. The pressure for discriminatory regionalism has been increased by the recent, new legitimacy of regionalism based upon the NAFTA model and by the increased American interest and role in APEC, combined with the dominance of the old models in North American and now pan-American perceptions of regional cooperation.

The American pressures for discriminatory trade in the Asia Pacific have been given enhanced leverage by American leadership of APEC's Eminent Persons Group since early 1993 (see Bergsten, Chapter 18). They are being resisted strongly in the Western Pacific. But the importance of US participation in APEC cannot be denied; nor the increased weight of Latin America as discriminatory regionalism in the

Americas spreads south. But it is more difficult to judge how this contest of philosophies and strategies will be resolved.

The clash between 'open' and 'discriminatory' visions of regionalism in the Asia Pacific is of fateful dimension in its process and outcome. One possible outcome is that Asia Pacific-wide negotiations on trade liberalisation will fail to gain momentum in any form, so that APEC continues to concentrate on its original agreed agenda. APEC could still play a useful role as a force for multilateral liberalisation through the new World Trade Organization. Discussion within APEC could still play a role in encouraging unilateral liberalisation within member economies, by increasing confidence that this is the trend of trade policy within the region. But the clash of visions could also block any efforts in APEC to negotiate a process of regional trade liberalisation on either an open or a discriminatory basis.

This is among the big issues that will be addressed in future literature on Asia Pacific economic regionalism.

Reference

Smith, Heather 1994, *The Role of Government in the Industrialisation of Taiwan and Korea in the 1980s*, Unpublished PhD thesis, Australian National University, Canberra.

Part One

Some Developments in the Theory of Regionalism

2 Worldwide regional integration: is there an optimal size of the integrated area?

Richard Cooper

The historical origins of the question posed in the title are clear enough. There has been a running debate since the Second World War (with antecedents in the 1930s) over whether the world economy would be better served by full multilateralism or by regional groupings that 'discriminate' in favour of members and against non-members. This question arose especially with respect to customs unions and free trade areas, where the principal instrument of discrimination was the import tariff. But it also arose with respect to balance-of-payments policy (with the Sterling Area and the European Payments Union representing the leading examples of regional groupings) and later with respect to the domain appropriate for fixed exchange rates among currencies or even for a common currency. As usually posed, the questions concern groupings among *nations*. However, similar questions, deriving from a different starting point, have been asked with increasing force about the optimal provision of public goods and services *within* nations — particularly those with a federal structure, which have shown increasing strain in trying to provide public goods both efficiently and with sufficient regard for local variations in preferences of the public.

Thus, from a theoretical point of view, the issue posed in the title goes beyond possible regional relationships among nations. Put more generally, we can ask what is the optimal combination of communities or regions for an integrated area. In some cases the answer may involve grouping existing nations into a larger region; in others it might involve subdividing existing nations. Before proceeding further we should make a few distinctions about the meaning of 'integrated area'.

Reprinted from *Economic Integration Worldwide, Regional, Sectoral*, edited by Fritz Machlup, pp. 41–53 (with deletions). Copyright © 1976 by the International Economic Association. This work originally appeared, and is referenced elsewhere in this volume, as *Yale Economic Growth Center Discussion Paper*, No. 220, November 1974. Reprinted with permission from Macmillan Press Ltd.

Some important distinctions concerning 'integration'

Several distinctions are necessary before we proceed to a discussion of optimal integrated areas. First, 'integration' can refer to the legal and institutional relationships within a region in which economic transactions take place, or it can refer to the market relationships among goods and factors within the region. This distinction becomes clear when we imagine a nineteenth-century *laissez-faire* economy with no government barriers to inter-regional transactions but with markets not linked because of ignorance or high transportation costs. A region can be integrated in the first sense but not in the second. If there are institutional or legal barriers to trade and capital movements, on the other hand, markets of course cannot be fully integrated either, at least in the sense of equal product and factor prices. But even then prices may move in parallel with one another, indicating market integration at the margin — in other words, high sensitivity to developments elsewhere in the region.

Before we return to this distinction between institutional and market integration, it is useful to draw a second distinction: between integration as an end in itself or as a state of affairs and integration as a process. Much of the post-war debate on regionalism versus globalism was concerned with process rather than with state of affairs; the advocates of economic regionalism saw it as an effective route to some other objective — either economic globalism or regional political unification. The universalism of the Bretton Woods agreement and the GATT, both laid down in the 1940s, stood in sharp contrast to the regionalism of the Sterling Area, the European Payments Union, the European Coal and Steel Community (ECSC), and the European Economic Community (EEC). Each of the latter institutions was hotly resisted in its early stages as an undesirable retreat from the universalism which the architects of the post-war international economic system hoped to achieve. The regional institutions, for their part, were rarely justified as ends in themselves, although occasionally that strand of thought was present. Rather, they were regarded as superior means to more far-reaching ends. Thus Robert Triffin argued persistently that the European Payments Union, with its implied discrimination against the US dollar, represented much the most effective way to achieve currency convertibility and to restore a truly multilateral system of international payments.[1]

Like-minded countries with similar problems would move more quickly together than they could either separately or when grouped with countries facing very different problems. To try everything at once would stymie progress, as the failure of the International Trade Organisation seemed to suggest. On this formulation, the objective of both parties to the debate is the same, namely a multilateral world economy; judgments differed only on the best way to achieve it.

Unfortunately for clarity in the debate, another group, associated with Jean Monnet, had quite different objectives and sought to use the same instruments of economic regionalism to attain their objective of regional political unification. So a confusion was introduced; the probability that economic regionalism would eventually lead to economic universalism was reduced to the extent that it would lead to regional political integration.

Integration as a process on either basis involves establishing a situation that is not in long-run equilibrium; partial integration creates new problems, which in turn call for further integrative measures, and so on.[2] On the first version of integration as process, success among a limited group of countries breeds a willingness by others to join in, and eventually the regional approach becomes global. On the second version, one thing leads to another, and eventually political integration captures the minds of the people, creating durable political bonds within the region. In either of these frames of reference, the 'optimal' region for integration is that which best achieves the desired objective rapidly and securely.

We return to economic integration as a state of affairs, rather than as a process. Markets are integrated if one price prevails for each product or factor, after allowance for transportation cost. On this market formulation, the optimum integrated area is the world as a whole, for any artificial interference with price equilibration (except those designed to eliminate market imperfections) will *ipso facto* represent a source of inefficiency in the allocation of resources. What then is the case for regionalism? It lies, I believe, not in the realm of private goods, but in the realm of public or collective goods, where these are defined broadly to include the nature of the economic regime itself — that is, the system of property ownership, of contract, of risk-bearing, of resource allocation, and the like. Some individuals may not want an economic regime based on markets and may be willing to pay the economic price for that decision. Viewed from the perspective of public goods, 'regions' really means governmental jurisdictions, and the enquiry must begin with the economic functions of government. The standard list calls on governments to provide public goods, to stabilise the level and growth of income, to redistribute income, and above all to provide a regulatory framework for economic and social transactions. Whether a region is 'optimal' then depends on its optimal suitability for performing these various functions. 'Optimal' means best able to serve the various social objectives, where 'best' is in the Pareto sense of not permitting closer achievement of one objective without compromising the attainment of some other objective.

The perspective adopted here thus renders irrelevant Viner's (1950) classic distinction between trade-creating and trade-diverting customs unions, and their analogue in the monetary area. As Cooper and Massel (1965a, 1965b) showed, in terms of raising real national income, a unilateral tariff reduction is superior to the formation of a discriminatory trading bloc, and the formation of customs unions must therefore be rationalised along different lines. Johnson (1965) has provided a more general framework for regarding protection in general and customs unions in particular as devices (perhaps inefficient ones) for the attainment of public goods — features from which the public at large derives some satisfaction, whether they be nationalism, redistribution of income, or a level of industrial production above what could be sustained by the operation of unimpeded market forces. In this context the formation of regional groupings on a discriminatory basis might represent the most efficient method of attaining a given objective; but the results would have to be shown in each specific case, for the general optimality of discriminatory trade or payments arrangements cannot be assumed.

The optimal provision of collective goods

The optimal provision of public goods involves both technological considerations and the accommodation of public preferences. We will first consider the technological considerations, which generally (but not always) press for enlargement of governmental jurisdiction, while accommodation of public preferences generally (but not always) presses for relatively small governmental jurisdictions.

Three technical factors have a bearing on the provision of public goods: economies of scale, the presence of externalities (including the important special case in which some of the objects of regulation are mobile), and the possibilities for reducing economic disturbances through integrating markets.[3]

Economies of scale

Scale economies offer a traditional argument for increasing the size of jurisdictions, at least up to a point. Certain public goods, especially those requiring for efficiency a high degree of specialisation, experience strong economies of scale. Examples would be certain forms of scientific research, public health, police investigatory work, the penal system, some aspects of national defense, and flood control and irrigation. Where scale economies are substantial, the governmental jurisdiction (or its functional equivalent in facilities shared among jurisdictions) must be large enough to encompass the scale required, or else its residents will either enjoy lower-quality services or pay more than is technically necessary for those services.

The optimum scale for governmental jurisdiction will of course vary from public good to public good. Where jurisdictions can be effectively separated along functional lines, they can be tailored to the requirements of each different good. (Los Angeles and London both offer examples of urban areas with many overlapping jurisdictions, drawn in part along functional lines.) Where as a practical matter that is not possible, the choice of scale of a jurisdiction should (other things being equal) be governed by the minimum cost of the package of public goods that is to be offered. Because of organisational, managerial and informational costs, the optimal jurisdiction will be well below the global level, in contrast to the optimal market area.

External effects

External effects arise when activities within one jurisdiction affect directly the welfare of residents of another jurisdiction, other than through market prices. External effects can be either positive, as in the case of malarial control, or negative, as in the case of downstream water pollution. In one respect, external effects can be thought of as a more general case of economies (or diseconomies) of scale: once a service (such as malarial control) is provided, the marginal cost of additional consumption (enjoyment) of that service is low or zero, and therefore the average cost to citizens is lower the larger the jurisdiction is in terms of taxable population. It is worthwhile to preserve the distinction between the two considerations, however, since economies of scale normally refer to technical input–output relationships in the production of a well-defined good or service, not to the consumption effects.

A special kind of externality arises from the mobility of the objects of policy action. Here the problem is that a 'public good' by community preference may involve unwelcome restraints on certain elements of the community, such as its business firms, its radio stations, or its high-income members. Activation of these regulatory or redistributional policies will then drive the adversely affected parties out of a jurisdiction that is too small relative to their domain of mobility. They will escape the onerous action by leaving the jurisdiction in question.[4] To prevent this, the jurisdiction must either inhibit the mobility of its business activities or become large enough to encompass their entire domain of mobility. The latter course does not necessarily involve enlargement to the global level, because as a practical matter persons and firms are not globally mobile. Considerations of economics, geography, language and culture all limit the actual domain of mobility.

The mobility of factors beyond a government jurisdiction limits the capacity of that jurisdiction to redistribute income. The heavily taxed will move out, and those who are subsidised will move in. Both movements undercut the fiscal viability of redistributional policies. Even trade in goods and services will affect the rewards to factors of production, as is underlined by the Heckscher–Ohlin–Samuelson theorem concerning factor–price equalisation. But the imposition of tariffs can alter the free trade distribution of income, and in any case the resulting factor rewards are *before* allowance for income taxes, which can serve redistributive objectives. It is factor mobility, not commodity movement, that really limits the possibilities for redistribution.

Similar considerations apply to attempts by jurisdictions to regulate business activity, such as capital structure, financial disclosure, safety, pollution, and so on. Once the regulations go beyond what is acceptable to the mobile firm, where 'acceptability' will be influenced by the competitive environment in which the firm operates, it will depart for a jurisdiction with less onerous regulations.[5] Thus, mobility presses for the enlargement of jurisdictions to make policy effective.

Diversity of preferences

Individuals differ greatly in their preferences for collective goods, both of the systemic type (fundamental nature of regime, capitalist or socialist; strong preference for order; high respect for individualism) and of the specific public type (flood control, parks, scientific research). These strong differences are conditioned by differences in cultural background and in income level. The greater the diversity of preferences within a given jurisdiction, the more difficult it will be, obviously, to satisfy all the demands for public goods by the residents even approximately, since by their nature public goods are provided in roughly equal amount to all residents of the relevant area. There are, therefore, large consumption losses in jurisdictions with a wide diversity of tastes, relative to what would be possible with different jurisdictions each catering more precisely to the preferences of its residents. This consideration pushes strongly towards relatively small communities that are homogeneous in their preferences for collective goods; it underlies much of the pressure for greater decentralisation of government and more local control.

Dahl and Tufte (1973) pose the trade-off in a slightly different way. They point to the conflict between 'system capacity' and 'citizen effectiveness' (that is, the capacity of the governmental system to deliver public goods efficiently as against the ability of citizens to participate effectively in making governmental decisions affecting the level and composition of public goods to be provided). They do at one point seem to suggest a positive value to diversity among the citizenship and to pluralism as such, however, particularly to provide an environment favourable to the dissenting citizen (which on one issue or another will be all of them), and this would suggest enlarging the jurisdiction despite the advantages cited above for having communities with homogeneous tastes. They do not, however, attempt to weigh this desire for pluralism against the necessary consumption loss on other public goods that arises from diversity in tastes (Dahl and Tufte 1973, esp. pp. 22–5, 138).

Considerations of liberty, however, press for smaller, more numerous jurisdictions, provided that individuals are free to move from one jurisdiction to another. Breton (1970, p. 114) has put the point strongly: 'The number of levels and sizes of units [of government] should be such that for any level of costs, the power of politicians — defined as their capacity to depart from the preferences of citizens — should be minimised'. Those fearful of the coercive powers of the state would set the scale of jurisdictions at a low level, even if that meant sacrificing some economic efficiency, for the sake of keeping politicians under check through competition with other jurisdictions.

What is the optimal area?

How are these conflicting considerations to be weighed against one another? That itself is an issue involving the diversity of preferences, for different individuals will be willing to sacrifice differing amounts of income (as taxes) in the form of less efficient provision of conventional public goods in order to purchase some given amount of liberty or national prestige or sense of cultural identity. It is necessary, as Samuelson told us years ago, to have a social-welfare function that weights not only the provision of goods and services but also the individuals that make up the community. But to say we need a social-welfare function, while formally correct, merely passes the question to the agent who specifies that function.

Functional federalism

Compromise among the various considerations is possible. Under a system of functional federalism, the trade-off between scale economies and diversity of tastes is made for each public good separately, leading to many overlapping governmental jurisdictions, each dealing with its own set of highly specialised and closely related problems: police protection, weather forecasting and control, flood control, economic management. Each has its own autonomous decision-making structure and its own citizenry, which may differ from issue to issue. This in a way is the method of specialised international organisations, each established by separate treaties on civil aviation, tariffs, monetary arrangements, world public health, and so on, and it can also be seen in federal countries.[6] It is an attractive idea, and in practice it will be necessary, at least in some degree. The notion of sovereignty inevitably becomes ambiguous under a system of functional federalism, for there is no sovereign, only a series of partial sovereignties. But that ambiguity is necessary to achieve the objective of the optimal provision of public goods, unless of course the existence of an unambiguous sovereignty is itself regarded as the overriding public good.

However, a system of functional federalism with partial sovereignties has its disadvantages as well. In the first place, both technology and tastes are in flux. A particular organisation that is optimal now will in general not be optimal ten years from now. Yet an ongoing bureaucracy develops vested interests of its own and is very difficult to change. Every country is living with outdated but durable — not to say tenacious — governmental institutions. Flexibility would be lost through a proliferation of jurisdictions, none with overriding authority.

In the second place, a system of functional federalism would inhibit bargaining and political compromise across functional jurisdictional boundaries in the absence of a higher authority willing and able to sacrifice the vested interests in particular jurisdictions. For much of the time it is useful to have each issue operate on its own track, with its own set of conventions and sanctions to influence behaviour. But from time to time the inability to bargain across issue areas would prevent communities from reaching an optimal configuration of public goods.

In the third place, decision-making groups drawn up along specialised lines seem often as a matter of experience to become dominated by the specialised producer interests, so broad consumer interests receive less attention than they should and than they would with more broadly based decision-making bodies.

Contemporary relevance

I will close with some comments on the contemporary relevance of what are otherwise broad and largely inconclusive generalisations.

The pressures for enlargement of governmental jurisdictions are strong and growing in the modern world. Activities in each jurisdiction have impacts on other jurisdictions in an increasing number of areas. Economies of scale and externalities in some activities have been growing as well, so to the extent that those activities are desired as public goods, the jurisdiction required to carry them with any efficiency has also increased in size. Not the least of the sources of 'spillouts' in the modern world is the fact that governments have become active in pursuing a variety of social objectives, and these pursuits often vary from country to country, setting up strains, including those arising from the mobility of firms and persons, between different jurisdictions. Even when factor mobility is not present, one hears charges of 'unfair' competition from a country that pursues practices somewhat different from one's own. Economic stabilisation and income redistribution have become more difficult for countries to achieve acting alone. On all these grounds, therefore, an argument can be made for increasing the size of jurisdictions — for forming regional groupings out of nations.

The EEC is one response to these pressures. The motivations behind the formation of the Community are many, and are mainly political, but at their root was a perception that European nations acting one by one would have a diminishing influence on the course of world events and hence even on their own welfare; thus they joined together to pool their influence and to try to restore some autonomy to their evolution.

The EEC is relatively homogeneous by global standards, so the welfare loss associated with 'harmonising' various policies will be less than it would be for a larger and more diverse group of countries. The United States has been relatively successful in part because, while very large, it is relatively homogeneous in taste and outlook, and it has a system of decentralised government capable of catering to variations in local preferences. Indeed, the greatest internal difficulties within the United States have arisen when local preferences, such as on racial discrimination, have offended a national norm.

Growing centralisation and bureaucratisation in response to pressures for enlargement have created counterpressures for greater decentralisation in governmental decision-making. These arise partly out of psychological revulsion at the growing distance between the average citizen and his government, and partly out of the perception that centralisation really reduces responsiveness to local preferences.

For these various reasons, therefore, regional integration regarding public goods seems to be a more promising route than global integration. (I emphasise that I am writing here about public goods — not private goods, for which the optimum region is the world.) Indeed, there should be no objection to groups of countries getting together to pursue their common interests, so long as neither their intent nor their effect is to gain at the expense of other countries. There are numerous opportunities for such 'clubs' to form which are not at the expense of other countries, and indeed their activities may be beneficial to others.

I conclude, therefore, the same way Cairncross (1972) did in his discussion of the optimal firm: there is no such thing. Nor is there such a thing as an optimal region, at least at the high level of generality that has been considered here. Not the least of the difficulties is that close cooperation among nations or within regions *builds* close ties and more homogeneous preferences as well as reflecting them, a point well perceived by the advocates of the economic route to political unification of Europe. Rather, optimality calls for a much more complex array of jurisdictions, compromising between the desire for greater decentralisation and the technical need for greater centralisation.

Notes

1   For a selection of Triffin's numerous articles and memoranda written in the early post-war era, see his *World Money Maze* (1966, esp. pp. 376–405).

2   On the theory underlying the neo-functionalist approach to political integration, see Haas (1958) and Nye (1971, esp. pp. 48–54).

3   Discussion of the last consideration relating to economic stabilisation has been deleted from this extract due to its minimal bearing on the other literature in this volume.

4   An example of this process was the proposal by the Labour government in Britain in 1974 to tax the total income of foreign residents in Britain. The proposal was greeted with howls of protest, some foreign residents made their plans to leave, and the British government backed away from its initial position.

5   For a further discussion of these issues and of the influence of mobility on the formulation of government policy, see Cooper (1974).

6   For a stimulating discussion of the division of labour among different levels of government, see Olson (1969).

References

Breton, A. 1970, 'Theoretical problems of federalism', *Recherches Economiques de Louvain*, 32, September.

Cairncross, A. K. 1972, 'The optimal firm reconsidered', *The Economic Journal*, 82 (suppl.), March, pp. 312–20.

Cooper, R. N. 1974, 'Economic mobility and national economic policy', Wicksell Lectures 1973, Uppsala, Sweden: Almqvist & Wicksell.

Cooper, C. A. and B. V. E. Massell 1965a, 'A new look at customs union theory', *Economic Journal*, 75, December, pp. 742–7.

—————— 1965b, 'Toward a general theory of customs unions', *Journal of Political Economy*, 73, October, pp. 461–76.

Dahl, R. A. and E. R. Tufte 1973, *Size and Democracy*, Stanford: Stanford University Press.

Haas, E. B. 1958, *The Uniting of Europe*, Stanford: Stanford University Press.

Johnson, H. G. 1965, 'An economic theory of protectionism, tariff bargaining, and the formation of customs unions', *Journal of Political Economy*, 73, June, pp. 256–83.

Nye, J. S. 1971, *Peace in Parts*, Boston: Little, Brown.

Olson, M. Jr. 1969, 'The principles of "fiscal equivalence": the division of responsibilities among different levels of government', *American Economic Review*, 59, May, pp. 479–87.

Triffin, Robert 1966, *World Money Maze*, New Haven: Yale University Press.

Viner, J. 1950, *The Customs Union Issue*, New York: Carnegie Endowment for International Peace.

3 Trade intensities and the analysis of bilateral trade flows in a many-country world: a survey ———

Peter Drysdale and Ross Garnaut

Introduction

There is now scattered through the journals a considerable literature on the analysis and measurement of the various determinants of bilateral trade levels. The literature has identified a number of barriers, or *resistances*, to trade that, together with the various factors analysed in the pure theory of international trade, determine the size, commodity composition and welfare effects of bilateral trade flows.

The literature on the analysis of bilateral trade flows has proceeded along a number of independent paths, with some major contributions having been developed apparently in ignorance of other, closely related publications. This suggests the need for an integrating survey. This survey of the literature on the determinants of bilateral trade levels discusses the various methods that have been applied to the analysis of resistances to bilateral trade flows, and assesses evidence on the importance of these resistances in the determination of trade flows in a many-country world.

The concept of obstacles or resistances to bilateral trade flows is central to the survey. We can define resistances to bilateral trade as any factors which prevent or retard the immediate international movement of commodities in response to price differentials. Recent theory distinguishes two basic types of resistance: *objective* resistances, which an individual firm can overcome only at some cost; and *subjective* resistances, which derive from the imperfect information available to businesspeople, from internal constraints on profit-maximising behaviour and from the particular processes through which firms engaged in international trade take decisions that effect the volume or commodity composition of trade. Objective resistances can be further decomposed into transport and other costs of overcoming geographic distance, and the costs of overcoming official barriers to trade (for example, protection). [1]

Reprinted with permission from the *Hitotsubashi Journal of Economics*, Vol. 22, No. 2 , 1982, pp. 62–84 (with deletions). Copyright © 1982 by the Hitotsubashi Academy, Tokyo, Japan.

The presence of resistances to bilateral trade causes absolute prices for given commodities (converted at some appropriate exchange rate) and also relative prices of commodities to vary from country to country. The cost of overcoming resistances varies across bilateral trading relationships. As a result, the prices at which commodities are offered for international sale or purchase vary with the bilateral trading relationship within which the transaction is to be made. The reality that the price a country receives for its exports varies with the market to which it is sold, and the price of imports varies with the market in which it is purchased, has profound implications for determination of the volume and commodity composition of foreign trade and for assessment of the gains from trade.

Mainstream trade theory has been developed to analyse the effects of one important type of resistance on bilateral trade levels: tariffs, quotas and other obstacles imposed by governments on trade. The theory of protection examines systematically the effects of obstacles imposed by one or both governments in a two-country world upon the volume, commodity composition and welfare effects of trade.[2] The theory of customs unions explores the effects of official constraints on trade being more costly to overcome in some bilateral trading relationships than in others.[3]

The pure theory of international trade has developed with little reference to trade resistances beyond official barriers to trade. But many authors have been impressed by casual empirical evidence on the importance of several other types of resistances to bilateral trade levels in determining the volume and composition of countries' foreign trade. The two-country models, so important in the pure theory of international trade, assume away all interesting questions about the determination of bilateral trade levels.[4] Evidence that an economy's aggregate export performance is correlated with the rate of growth of total imports into the particular foreign economies with which it has close ties cannot be understood in terms of the two-country model.[5] Equally challenging to established theory was evidence that, for some pairs of countries, resource endowments relative to each other provided a better guide to the commodity composition of bilateral trade than each country's resource endowment relative to the world as a whole.[6]

In response to the accumulation of evidence on the importance of bilateral trading relations in the determination of the volume and commodity composition of total foreign trade, Bhagwati (1964, p. 20) in his important survey states that established trade theory provides no *a priori* grounds for deciding whether bilateral trade is of no importance, of some importance or all-important.

There have been a few attempts to integrate the concept of trade resistances into the general corpus of trade theory, most notably by Johnson (1968). Much more must be done before there is a satisfactory general trade theory that incorporates the reality of differential costs of overcoming resistances in different bilateral trading relationships, a theory which can explain simultaneously bilateral trade flows and countries' total foreign trade. This survey has the more limited objective, outlined above, of laying out the literature on the nature, determinants, measurement and use of the resistances concept.

Much of the statistical analysis of trade flows in a many-country world that has been undertaken over the years has been applied to the attempt to understand the nature of resistances to bilateral trade flows and their importance in the determination of trade patterns. Some has been applied further to the projection of bilateral trade flows into the future, on the assumption that there is some predictability over time in patterns of resistances as measured by various statistical indexes.

Two approaches can be identified among systematic studies of the determinants of bilateral trade levels. The gravity model approach seeks to explain each bilateral trade flow independently, by reference to measures of the 'trade potential' of the two economies and to resistances to bilateral trade. The assumption of independent bilateral trade flows gives rise to attempts at estimation of countries' total imports and exports as the sum of these bilateral trade flows. The intensity approach, on the other hand, does not seek to explain countries' total imports and exports. It takes total imports and exports as given and measures and seeks to explain deviations from bilateral trade flows that would obtain if resistances to trade were equal on all bilateral routes. In some applications of the intensity approach, the measures of deviations from randomly established patterns of trade are assumed to be more or less stable over time and are used to project bilateral trade flows on given assumptions about the growth of individual countries' and total world trade.

The next two sections of the paper survey the major contributions that have been made to the analysis of trade resistances and the determination of bilateral trade flows within the gravity model approach and the intensity approach. The final section of the paper then summarises what has come to be understood about the nature of various resistances and their quantitative importance in determining trade flows.

The gravity model approach to trade analysis

Tinbergen's (1962, pp. 262–93) pioneering use of the *gravity model* made bilateral trade levels a function of two potential trade variables (gross national product of importing and exporting countries) and three resistance variables (distance, a dummy variable for adjacent countries and a dummy variable for common membership of a preferential area). Linnemann (1966) elaborated the Tinbergen model by introducing additional potential trade and resistance variables into the analysis. The most important was a complementarity variable, measured by the scalar product of the two vectors representing the commodity composition of the exporting country's total exports and the commodity composition of the importing country's total imports.

Two interesting features of the Linnemann results were the tendency for the distance coefficient to take on a higher value for more isolated countries, and the absence of any clear association between the importance of transport costs as an explanator of trade flows and the importance of high transport cost bulk commodities in countries' trade.[7] The latter phenomenon suggests that the effect of distance in lowering trade levels may operate through factors other than transport costs.

The gravity model is a very ambitious approach to analysis of the effects of trade resistances, and its ambition raises two important problems. Difficulties in measuring 'potential trade' affect the levels of trade explained by reference to resistance variables and so obscure the relationship between resistances and bilateral trade levels. Of more fundamental importance, the assumption of independent bilateral trade flows is extreme.

Several characteristics of Linnemann's own results seem to be explained best in terms of interdependence among bilateral flows. The tendency for the distance coefficient in the Linnemann regressions to take higher values for countries in more isolated locations suggests that *relative* distance is important in the determination of trade levels. Two close countries at the periphery of the world economy (say, Australia and New Zealand) *relatively* are closer to each other than two similarly proximate countries in Western Europe. The discontinuity in the bilateral trade data observed by Linnemann, with parameter values that were consistent with larger trade flows overestimating smaller flows, is open to the possible explanation that scale factors raise larger trade flows partly by diverting trade from smaller flows. But Linnemann discussed the possibility of interdependence among variances of trade flows (or diversion of trade from high resistance to low resistance routes) in relation to the effects of membership of preferential areas. Evidence presented on this question does not allay doubts that the high levels of trade observed on intra-area trade routes have resulted in considerable part from diversion of trade from non-preferential routes (Linnemann 1966, pp. 91–2).

Linnemann did not publish individual countries' coefficients for the commodity composition variable. However, there is no *a priori* reason why the coefficients as he defined them should take on more extreme values for countries whose foreign trade was concentrated in commodities that held small shares in world trade. His complementarity index, like the distance variable, fails to take account of relative 'closeness'. Yet it is clear that the likelihood of country i exporting a given shipment of commodity k to country j depends on the availability of alternative supplies: the smaller country j's share in world exports, the less likely it is that a particular export consignment of commodity k from country i would be sent to j. Leamer and Stern (1970, p. 165) err in arguing that the Linnemann complementarity index C_{ij} may be close to a weighted inner product C^*_{ij} where the weight of each commodity is in inverse proportion to its share of world trade.

Indeed, a weighting of commodities in the complementarity index according to their uniqueness in world trade would contradict the independence assumption of the gravity model.

Wolf and Weinschrott (1973) have applied the gravity model to identify bilateral trading arrangements which are characterised by high potential for, and low resistances to, trade, with a view to assessing the benefits from trading partners' incorporation within a free trade area or other multi-country association. Their model is distinguished by the incorporation of several variables designed to measure differences in 'natural' comparative advantage, and of a variable designed to measure socio-cultural 'distance'. They conclude that the structural relations in the model (as measured by the various coefficients) are stable in the short and medium term; that the proxy variables included to capture differences in 'natural' comparative advantage have some explanatory power; and the socio-cultural dummy variables are in most cases significant. One interesting further conclusion is that the largest negative residuals are usually found in trading relationships between countries that are separated by great distance.

Bryan (1974) has estimated parameters for a gravity model by examining the experience of Canada's bilateral trade with various countries disaggregated by commodity. The relative importance of various trade potential and resistance factors varied considerably across commodities, with special attention being given to international transport costs. Transport costs are more significant determinants of bilateral trade levels in some commodities (especially primary, simply processed and other more homogeneous products) than in others (especially highly differentiated manufactured goods). One interesting conclusion is that international transport costs are generally more important determinants of bilateral trade flows than tariffs.

Leamer (1974) uses the framework laid out in his earlier work with Stern to test the adequacy of traditional trade theory, alongside more recent theory which stresses the importance of scale economies, and resistances in determining the commodity composition of trade in manufactures. He concludes that trade dependence ratios are best explained by the development variables, GNP and population, but that when the development group is constrained to *per capita* GNP, 'resistance factors of tariffs and distance offer nearly the same predictive accuracy for many commodities' (p. 372). Resource endowment variables do not perform well as explanators of import dependence ratios in the manufactured goods trade.

In another contribution in the gravity model tradition, Geraci and Prewo (1977) use a sophisticated version of the familiar model to demonstrate that the use of an estimate of actual transport costs gives significantly better results than the use of a distance proxy.

Analysis of trade intensity

Intensity indexes

A separate line of analysis was pioneered by Brown (1949) and developed and popularised by Kojima (1964), using an *intensity of trade* index which concentrates attention on variations in bilateral trade levels that results from differential resistances, by abstracting from the effects of the size of the exporting and importing countries. As modified by Kojima, the index I_{ij} takes the form:

$$I_{ij} = \frac{X_{ij}}{X_i} \bigg/ \frac{M_j}{M_w - M_i} \qquad (1)$$

where X_{ij} is country i's exports to country j,
  X_i is i's total exports,
  M_j is j's total imports, and
  M_i is i's total imports, and
  M_w is total world imports.

M_i is subtracted from M_w in the above expression because a country cannot export goods to itself, and the only share it can meaningfully have in total world trade is a share in the imports of all countries other than itself.[8]

The intensity of trade index is a crude index of relative resistances because it fails to make allowance for the varying commodity composition of countries' foreign trade. Where commodities are not substitutable for each other, opportunities for bilateral trade are limited by the degree of complementarity in the commodity composition of one country's exports and the other's imports. Drysdale (1967, 1969) refined the intensity of trade indexes by developing new indexes that separate the effects of the commodity composition of countries' foreign trade (complementarity) from other factors influencing the intensity of trade. The complementarity index, unlike that of Linnemann, takes account of the closeness of countries' commodity trade structures *relative* to world trade structure.

Drysdale's index of *complementarity* in country i's exports to country j, C_{ij}, is the weighted sum of the products of each commodity's share in country i's exports and in country j's imports, with commodities weighted by the inverse of their shares in world trade. The weighting reflects the increased probability of country j drawing a consignment of commodity k from country i when alternative sources of supply are more limited.

$$C_{ij} = \sum_k \left(\frac{X_i^k}{X_i} \cdot \frac{M_w - M_i}{M_w^k - M_i^k} \cdot \frac{M_j^k}{M_j} \right) \qquad (2)$$

where X_i^k is country i's exports of commodity k,
  M_j^k is country j's imports of commodity k, and
  M_w^k is world imports of commodity k.

The complementarity index C_{ij} indicates the value that the intensity index I_{ij} would take if i's exports of each commodity k were distributed among world import markets exactly in proportion to each market's share of world imports of commodity k.

Drysdale defined an index of *country bias*, B_{ij}^k in trade for each commodity analogously to the intensity index.

$$B_{ij}^k = \frac{X_{ij}^k}{X_i^k} \bigg/ \frac{M_j^k}{M_w^k - M_i^k} \qquad (3)$$

where X_{ij}^k is country i's exports of commodity k to country j.

A weighted average of indexes of country bias for all commodities k yields an index B_{ij} of country bias in i's aggregate export trade with j.

$$B_{ij} = \sum_k \left(B_{ij}{}^k \frac{\overline{X}_{ij}{}^k}{\overline{X}_{ij}} \right) \tag{4}$$

where $\overline{X}_{ij}{}^k$ is the hypothetical value of $X_{ij}{}^k$ obtaining when $B_{ij}{}^k$ equals unity, and $\overline{X}_{ij}$ is the hypothetical value of X_{ij} obtaining when all $B_{ij}{}^k$ equal unity. The ratio $X_{ij}{}^k / \overline{X}_{ij}$ is equal to the percentage contribution of commodity k to complementarity in i's exports to j. The indexes C_{ij} and B_{ij} are so defined that their product equals I_{ij}.

$$I_{ij} = C_{ij} \cdot B_{ij} \tag{5}$$

The effect of the commodity composition of countries' trade on intensity of trade is measured by the complementarity index. The country bias index B_{ij} measures the *average* effect of differential resistances on intensity in bilateral trade. Among the difficulties associated with Drysdale's decomposition of trade intensity into complementarity and country bias elements is the assumption that the commodity composition of each country's global trade is, in the extreme, independent of influences affecting bilateral trade. It is quite conceivable that, for example, changes in a tariff or the structure of transport costs would have effects on import specialisation and complementarity as well as country bias in trade. If there were many such cases, the distinction between country bias and complementarity would be blurred.

The importance of different resistances varies from commodity to commodity and it is not uncommon for a certain resistance (say, transport costs) to be relatively high for exports of one commodity from country i to country j, but to be relatively low for other commodities in the same bilateral flow. Thus, although the aggregate country bias index B_{ij} is a useful summary of the effects of a range of resistance influences, it needs to be supplemented by the disaggregated indexes $B_{ij}{}^k$ in a detailed study of the nature of resistances to bilateral trade flows. Country bias indexes for individual commodities are a reliable reflection of the ordering of relative resistances in various bilateral trade flows so long as the commodity classification used identifies homogeneous commodities that are not substitutable for each other.

Kunimoto (1975, 1977) has attempted a taxonomy of trade intensity measures using statistical contingency table analysis as an integrating framework. In describing the logic of the various indexes that have been used in the work on the analysis of bilateral trade flows, he makes no comment on their economic meaning or analytic value but observes that 'it is not possible *a priori* to say which index is best suited for the analysis of international trade flows . . . [and] therefore, the choice of index hinges on the nature of the problem to be tackled' (1977, p. 30). However, in his work Kunimoto introduces what he considers to be a new index of trade intensity, which is in fact a contingency table formulation of Drysdale's complementarity index.

The intensity approach acknowledges the interdependence of levels of bilateral trade on different routes. Although it does not seek to answer important questions about the effects of resistances on countries' total exports and imports, it has major advantages as a starting point for analysis of the nature of resistances to trade flows. Country export and import totals are given, in aggregate or by commodity, and so the intensity approach abstracts from the effects of excluded variables and random fluctuations on 'potential trade', which distort the magnitudes to be explained by resistances in the gravity model.

An assumption that all countries' imports and exports are made up of large numbers of independent consignments underlies the intensity approach. Let country i have a share in world exports x_i. This equals X_i / W where X_i is country i's total exports and W is total world trade. The probability that any trade transaction in the world involves country i as exporter is x_i. Similarly, the probability that j is the home of the importer is m_j, the ratio that j's imports bear to total world trade.

The probability that a particular transaction will involve two given countries is negatively related to relative resistances to bilateral trade. Deviations from 'expected' levels of bilateral trade occur because resistances vary among bilateral trading relationships. Ratios of actual to expected levels of bilateral trade below unity are associated with high relative resistances and ratios above unity with low relative resistances. Where they are expressed in volumes or value of trade, positive deviations are associated with low relative resistances and negative deviations with high relative resistances.

Intensity indexes and the analysis of trade resistances

Several studies have employed forms of the intensity indexes introduced above as indicators of relative resistances to bilateral trade flows, and have analysed the nature and importance of various resistance factors by explaining variations in the indexes over time and across bilateral trading relationships. Other studies have employed the intensity of trade concept for this purpose, without using explicitly an intensity index. Here we survey some conclusions about the nature of resistances that have emerged from this literature.

Drysdale (1967) examined variations in the complementarity and country bias index in trade between Australia and Japan over the half century from 1913 to 1962. Large variations in the country bias index through this period were associated with major changes in the external political relationships of one or other country and, significantly with the increase in mutual knowledge of each other's markets and trading institutions through the post-war period.

Two publications by Yamazawa (1970, 1971) explored characteristics of the complementarity and country bias indexes. The first of these studies observed changes over time and association between levels taken by the two indexes. The second tested the relationship between intensity of trade and resistance variables and complementarity by the use of least squares regression techniques.

Yamazawa's second study estimated parameters of a log-linear equation relating complementarity as measured by the Drysdale index and a large number of resistance variables to intensity of trade. Apart from the use of the complementarity index, unique features of the analysis included the use of a relative distance variable, inclusion of a variable representing official aid flows, and inclusion of a wider range of trading blocs.

The overall fit between the estimated equation and the data was disappointing, especially since a large part of the multiple correlation was accounted for by the complementarity variable. Only a small fraction of the variance of country bias appears to be explained by the measures or indexes of resistances incorporated in the Yamazawa study. Five of the nine independent variables were significant and all of these showed the sign expected from *a priori* reasoning: complementarity, relative distance, the dummy variable representing common membership of colonial trading blocs, the dummy variable representing common membership of the socialist trading bloc, and the dummy variable that was assigned a non-zero value if one trading partner was a socialist and one a capitalist country. The coefficient of the dummy variable representing common membership of colonial trading blocs took on a lower value in 1965–67 than in earlier years, indicating the declining importance of such ties over time.

Some of the Yamazawa variables could be refined so as to reflect more faithfully the levels of the relative resistances they represent. Yamazawa's relative distance variable is not weighted by the weighted sum of the distance between all pairs of trading partners, as is necessary to preserve the logic of the intensity approach. The index of 'aid' flows covers only the less important types of international capital flows, and it is not surprising that it was swamped by other influences. However, these and other refinements of the variables are likely to raise the correlation coefficient only marginally. As an analysis of trade resistances, the Yamazawa study employed more satisfactory concepts than those used in any other econometric work to that time,[9] yet the analysed variables accounted for a very small part of the variance in country bias in trade.

Garnaut (1972) used the aggregate and commodity-specific country bias index to generate an ordering of relative resistances across the bilateral trade relationships between Australia and each of the five ASEAN member countries. Despite the similar geographic location of the five Southeast Asian countries, there were large differences in the total and disaggregated indexes across the five trading relationships. The effects of the objective resistances, transport costs and protection, were calculated by statistical methods. The case study method, involving interviews with company executives involved in trading decisions, was then employed to attribute the unexplained variation in country bias to various subjective resistances. This study revealed that the preferences of ultimate users were important in determining bilateral trade patterns in highly differentiated commodities, but not in more homogeneous commodities. For the latter, biases in the trade decision-making processes of companies were of considerable importance. For affiliates of multinational enterprises, which accounted for a substantial part of Australian and Southeast Asian foreign trade, there was a high degree of intra-company trade, so that the location of affiliates was a major determinant of bilateral trade patterns. For independent enterprises, the particular order in which pioneering trading firms searched the international environment for trading opportunities was of considerable importance, especially since many firms relied heavily upon other trading firms in their own country for leads on new markets. Explicit internal constraints on profit maximising behaviour appeared relatively unimportant in the determination of trading patterns.

Interactions among the various types of resistances, and between complementarity and country size, were analysed and appeared to be very important to the explanation of variations in country bias. In most cases, subjective resistances tended to reinforce the effects of objective resistances, with the former being of greater direct importance for more differentiated commodities and the latter for more homogeneous commodities. The presence of economies of scale in overcoming all resistances to bilateral trade meant that there was considerable multicollinearity among values taken by the various resistance variables. These economies of scale, together with high external costs of pioneering new trade links, were seen to be major factors in explaining the observed stability in country bias over time.

Two factors seem to have been of particular importance in determining country bias levels: distance, and common former membership of imperial trading blocs. Both influenced the order in which traders searched the international market, patterns of multinational investment and transport costs. Preferential import restrictions dating mainly from the 1930s promoted intra-imperial trade, which continued with high intensity after the cessation of the preference, but increasingly less powerfully over time. The decline in importance of the old imperial blocs caused relative distance to emerge more powerfully as a determinant of country bias in trade.

In analysing the effects of international ownership ties on bilateral trade flows, an index of ownership compatibility was developed, consistent with the logic of the intensity approach. This index explained a high proportion of variations in country bias in those commodities in which a high proportion of trade was conducted within multinational corporations, notably the petroleum trade.

Three later studies applied the intensity of trade and one of them a modified intensity of trade index, to the analysis of the effects of political blocs on levels of bilateral trade. The method of these studies was pioneered by Girgis (1973), who sought to answer the question whether trade between Arab countries and various external countries was more or less intense than might be expected *a priori* from the countries' position in world trade.

Girgis recognised that the particular commodity composition of two countries' foreign trade might cause the index of trade intensity between them to take values away from unity, independently of the effects of those factors which we have described as resistances, although he does not control for this by the use of a precise measure of complementarity. Girgis is interested in intensity in bilateral trading relationships which involve one developed and one developing country. He argues that there are consistent differences between the commodity composition of the trade of less developed countries and that of the world as a whole. Deviations from unity in the aggregate intensity of trade index can then be expected simply as a result of these variations in 'complementarity'. Thus he employs as an index of intensity of trade between one developed and one developing country the product of the bilateral trade level's share of the developing country's total trade, and the developed country's share of the total trade of developing countries. The Girgis index of trade intensity compares the developed country's share of the trade of the particular developing country with its share of the trade of developing countries as a whole.

The diversity of developing countries' patterns of export specialisation creates difficulties for the use of this method. Take the important case of a developed country that has large domestic oil production (perhaps the United Kingdom) and a developing country heavily specialised in oil exports (one of the Organisation of Petroleum Exporting Countries [OPEC]). Trade intensity measured by the aggregate index will be very low because of very low complementarity. The Girgis correction will yield an even lower intensity value in the common case (again, the United Kingdom) where the developed country's share of the exports of developing countries is greater than its share of total world exports. This is not to argue that the Girgis index is not more satisfactory on average as an index of relative resistances in developed-developing country trade than an aggregate intensity index. But it is certainly less satisfactory than the country bias index, which adjusts precisely for any peculiarities of the two countries' commodity specialisation in world trade.

Kleiman (1976, 1978) has applied a similar approach in analysing the impact of colonial political relationships on bilateral trade patterns. Kleiman compares the metropolitan country's share of the colony's (or ex-colony's) trade with that of a control group of countries, the metropole's trade share of which could have been expected to be similar to that of the colony in the absence of the colonial tie. In one case, he uses the metropole's share in the trade of African dependencies as a whole as his control group (Kleiman 1976). An identical approach, with similar advantages and disadvantages, was employed in a study of the effects of the residual ex-colonial cultural ties on trade between Spain and the former Spanish Latin America (Kleiman 1978). In this case, the ex-Portuguese colony of Brazil was used as the control group. This approach suffers from its failure to allow precisely for differing complementarity in trade, and introduces a new consistent bias in the comparisons to the extent that colonialism caused each of the metropolitan countries' trade with Africa as a whole to be more intense than it would otherwise have been. However, it does have advantages as an approach to the identification of the effects of one particular source of relatively low resistances to bilateral trade, colonial ties, to the extent that its use of adjacent territories (in Africa) as a control group reduces the differential effect on trade intensity of one other source of relatively low resistances, geographic distance.

The approach used by Girgis and Kleiman is in fact very similar to Kojima's (1962) earlier use of intensity indexes to analyse the factors underlying resistances to regional trade flows in Asia and the Pacific.

The substantive conclusions of the Girgis and Kleiman papers are of some interest, despite some lack of precision of their method. Girgis observed some tendency over time towards multilateralisation of Arab countries' trade relations, although political conflicts between pairs of countries were a source of sudden large falls from time to time in values of the indexes. Kleiman observed in his *Economic Journal* article that colonial ties raised the volume of trade between metropole and colony by at least several times, and that this remains with diminishing effect over about two decades from independence. In this later article, Kleiman concluded that the residual cultural heritage of Spanish colonialism now has very little effect in promoting trade between Spain and former Spanish colonies in Latin America.

The use of more precise methods and a more complete conceptual framework of analysis would change the magnitudes associated with these conclusions as well as encourage more qualified judgements about the dominance of particular resistance factors, for example Kleiman's conclusions on Spain's trade with Latin America, but it would not affect their general thrust.

A number of studies have measured changes in trade intensities simply to demonstrate the changes in the geographic structure of trade in the post-war period (see Wilford and Christou 1976) or the effects of customs union and free trade associations on the value of intensities (see Carney 1970; Wilford and Christou 1973). A more ambitious study by Roemer (1977) employs the intensity, complementarity and country bias concepts to explore the effects of 'sphere of influence' and economic distance on the commodity composition of trade in manufactures. He observes that exporters of manufactured goods tend to market their less competitive manufactures disproportionately in the geographic areas of strongest relative market share, and that this phenomenon cannot be accounted for entirely by transportation costs. He suggests that it is due largely to 'sphere of influence factors: supra-market, historical factors that give exporters trading advantages in some areas that other exporters do not have . . . ' (p. 327). Importantly, Roemer notes the difficulty of separating 'sphere of influence' factors from distance factors in the explanation of country bias in manufactured goods trade although no attempt is made to theorise about the interaction between the two factors.

Another area of research within the intensity approach (that is, analysing the determinants of bilateral trade given country totals), but incorporating some of the method of the gravity model, was opened up by Tilton. Tilton (1966, p. 419) used linear programming techniques to test association between actual patterns of bilateral trade, null (equal resistance) patterns of trade and the pattern of trade that would minimise total 'transport costs', for a range of minerals and metals. Focus on individual commodities rather than total trade abstracted from the effects of commodity composition on trade intensity. The effect of differentiation of the individual commodities was very slight, since the minerals and metals studies were relatively homogeneous. Transport costs were a significant determinant of bilateral trade flows. Other resistances (ownership ties, trading blocs) commonly exercised significant pressures in a direction opposite to those of transport costs.

Tilton supplemented his linear programming analysis with an econometric study that incorporated characteristics of both gravity and intensity approaches. The study had several unsatisfactory features, but it did point to ownership ties between exporting and importing firms in different countries as having a very important influence on trade patterns.

Tilton and his associates have refined the original work in a series of papers employing the gravity model methodology, surveyed by Demler and Tilton (1978). All of these studies find that ownership ties greatly influence minerals and metals trade flows, especially at the ores and concentrates stage of metals production. There has been some decline over time in the importance of ownership ties, but they remain very significant. The old colonial blocs continue to have a significant effect on bilateral trade in minerals. Distance has an important effect, but one that is uneven across commodities, and that is clearly less significant than ownership ties.

Conclusions

This survey has sought to digest the considerable literature on the measurement and analysis of bilateral trade flows. It has identified two basic approaches to the question: the gravity model approach, which seeks to explain the level of trade conducted between two countries in terms only of the characteristics of the two countries and the strength of obstacles to trade between them; and the intensity approach which takes each country's total imports and exports as given, and seeks to explain levels of bilateral trade in terms of the strength of obstacles to trade between other pairs of countries in the world economy.

Each of the two approaches is useful for particular purposes. The gravity model approach provides some indication of the importance of resistances to bilateral trade as determinates of the total size of a country's foreign trade. The intensity approach identifies differentials in resistances across various bilateral trade relationships, and the examination of these differentials provides fertile ground for analysis of the nature and relative importance of the various types of resistance to trade. The literature covered by this survey demonstrates that resistances to trade are substantial determinants of bilateral trade flows, and indicates the most important resistance factors.

The relative importance of various resistances varies across commodities and with the particular characteristics of a bilateral trading relationship. Studies in both the gravity model and intensity traditions demonstrate the importance of distance and common membership of imperial trading blocs to bilateral trade flows, and also the declining importance of the latter influence over time. Early studies tended to see distance and common membership of politico-economic blocs as proxies for relatively low transport costs and commercial policy barriers to trade but it has since been shown that these variables are correlated with the cost of overcoming a wide range of objective and subjective resistances. Several studies with widely differing approaches have demonstrated important effects of international ownership ties in determining trade patterns. There is considerable evidence of the interdependence of trade levels across bilateral trading relationships and of the interdependence of the costs of overcoming various types of resistance within a single bilateral trading relationship. Patterns of resistances to trade, and hence patterns of bilateral trade, tend to be relatively stable over time, and there are important economic reasons why this is so. However, they can change markedly over time in some circumstances, and there is considerable interest in the analysis of the pressures which can generate such change.

Resistances to bilateral trade flows affect the size, commodity composition and gains of foreign trade, and so warrant integration into the pure theory of international trade. This important task has not been attempted in this survey, although a clear view of the nature of resistances may assist this development in trade theory.

Notes

1   See Garnaut (1972, pp. 25–6 and ch. 6 *passim*) and Garnaut (1980, ch. 13). Johnson (1968) suggested a slightly different categorisation, distinguishing 'geographic distance and the transport cost of overcoming it', 'differences of political and legal systems, culture and language that differentiate nations from one another as market areas', and 'protection'.

2   See Corden (1971) and (1974) for thorough treatments of the theory.

3   There is a large literature on the theory of customs unions. For useful surveys, see Lipsey (1960) and Vanek (1965).

4   Jones (1977) reviews the limited discussion of many-country trade specialisation, in a world of zero transaction costs.

5   Some of the literature on this point is discussed in Leamer and Stern (1970, ch. 7).

6   See, for example, Tatemoto and Ichimura (1959), which was the first in a series of Leontief-type studies to draw attention to this phenomenon.

7   The latter conclusion should be treated with extreme caution because of the high degree of aggregation in commodity classes defined for the test.

8   The calculations of trade intensity indexes in Petri (Chapter 10) and Petri (Chapter 23) are based on an intensity equation which does not subtract M_i from M_w. The variability in the indexes which results from this is only minor.

9   Higher correlation coefficients in the gravity model studies are misleading, because much of the variance of total bilateral trade flows 'explained' by the independent variables is accounted for by variation in the size of the trading partners.

References

Bhagwati, J. 1964, 'The pure theory of international trade: a survey', *The Economic Journal*, 74(293), pp. 1–84.

Brown, A. J. 1949, *Applied Economics, Aspects of the World Economy in War and Peace*, London: George Allen and Unwin.

Bryan, I. A. 1974, 'The effect of ocean transport costs on the demand for some Canadian exports', *Weltwirtschaftliches Archiv*, 110(4), pp. 643–62.

Carney, M. K. 1970, 'Development in trading patterns in the common market and EFTA', *Journal of the American Statistical Association*, 65(332), December, pp. 1455–9.

Corden, W. M. 1971, *Protection*, Oxford: Clarendon Press.

—————— 1974, *Trade Policy and Economic Welfare*, Oxford: Clarendon Press.

Demler, F. R. and J. E. Tilton 1978, 'Modelling international trade flows in mineral markets', Paper presented to the Conference on Commodity Markets, Models and Policies in Latin America, Lima, Peru, 11–13 May.

Drysdale, P. D. 1967, 'Japan, Australia and New Zealand: the prospects for Western Pacific integration', *Economic Record*, 45(111), September, pp. 321–42.

—————— 1969, *Japanese–Australian Trade*, PhD dissertation, Australian National University, Canberra.

Garnaut, R. G. (ed.) 1972, *Australian Trade with Southeast Asia: A Study of Resistances to Bilateral Trade Flows*, PhD dissertation, Australian National University, Canberra.

—————— 1980, *ASEAN in a Changing Pacific and World Economy*, Canberra: Australian National University Press.

Geraci, V. J. and W. Prewo 1977, 'Bilateral trade flows and transport costs', *Review of Economics and Statistics*, 59(1), February, pp. 67–74.

Girgis, M. 1973, 'Development and trade patterns in the Arab world', *Weltwirtschaftliches Archiv*, 109, pp. 121–68.

Johnson, H. G. 1968, 'Comparative cost and commercial policy theory for a developing world economy', Wicksell Lectures, Stockholm.

Jones, R W. 1977, 'Two-ness in trade theory', *Special Papers in International Economics*, Princeton: Princeton University Press.

Kleiman, E. 1976, 'Trade and the decline of colonialism', *Economic Journal*, 86, September, pp. 459–80.

—————— 1978, 'Cultural ties and trade: Spain's role in Latin America', *Kyklos*, 31(2), pp. 275–90.

Kojima, K. 1962, *Sekai Keizai to Nihon Boeki* [The World Economy and Japan's Foreign Trade], Tokyo: Keiso Shobo.

—————— 1964, 'The pattern of international trade among advanced countries', *Hitotsubashi Journal of Economics*, 5(1), June.

Kunimoto, K. 1975, *The Contingency-Table Analysis of International Trade Flows: An Approach to Methodology*, PhD dissertation, Yale University, New Haven.

—————— 1977, 'Typology of trade intensity indices', *Hitotsubashi Journal of Economics*, 17(2), February, pp. 15–32.

Leamer, E. L. 1974, 'The commodity composition of international trade in manufactures: an empirical analysis', *Oxford Economic Papers*, 26(3), November, pp. 350–74.

Leamer, E. L. and R. M. Stern 1970, *Quantitative International Economics*, Boston: Allyn and Bacon.

Linnemann, H. 1966, *An Econometric Study of World Trade Flows*, Amsterdam: North-Holland.

Lipsey, R. G. 1960, 'The theory of customs unions: a general survey', *The Economic Journal*, 70(279), September, pp. 496–513.

Roemer, J. E. 1977, 'The effect of sphere of influence and economic distance on the commodity composition of trade in manufactures', *Review of Economics and Statistics*, 59(3), August, pp. 318–27.

Tatemoto, M. and S. Ichimura 1959, 'Factor propositions and foreign trade: the case of Japan', *Review of Economics and Statistics*, 41(4), November, pp. 442–6.

Tilton, J. E. 1966, 'The choice of trading partners: an analysis of international trade in aluminium bauxite, copper, lead, manganese, tin and zinc', *Yale Economic Essays*, 6(2), pp. 419–74 (taken from a PhD dissertation, Yale University, New Haven, 1966, microfilm).

Tinbergen, J. 1962, *Shaping the World Economy — Suggestions for an International Economic Policy*, New York: Twentieth Century Fund.

Vanek, J. 1965, *General Equilibrium of International Discrimination: The Case of Customs Unions*, Cambridge: Harvard University Press.

Wilford, W. T. and G. C. Christou 1973, 'A sectoral analysis of disaggregated trade flows in the Central American Common Market 1962–1970', *Journal of Common Market Studies*, 12(2), pp. 159–75.

_____ 1976, 'Directional intensities of world trade flows, 1957–1968', *Journal of Developing Areas*, 10(2), January, pp. 181–92.

Wolf, C. Jr. and D. Weinschrott 1973, 'International transactions and regionalism: distinguishing "insiders" from "outsiders"', *American Economic Review*, 63(2), May, pp. 52–60.

Yamazawa, I. 1970, 'Intensity analysis of world trade flows', *Hitotsubashi Journal of Economics*, 10(2), February, pp. 61–90.

_____ 1971, 'Structural change in world trade flows', *Hitotsubashi Journal of Economics*, 11(2), February, pp. 11–21.

4 International economic pluralism

Peter Drysdale

Domains for international collective action

International agreements and understandings are important pillars on which gainful economic interdependence is built. Growing world economic interdependence over the past several decades is certainly in part the result of both technological developments in industrial countries favouring specialisation within larger and larger international markets and the lowering of transportation and communications costs. But, importantly, it is also a consequence of the various institutional and policy commitments that followed the Second World War and built a stronger framework for international exchange and financial settlements (see Dam 1970).

The process of international economic integration is far from complete, nor has its progress been in any sense uniform throughout the world economy. The levels of integration within the international economy reflect, among other factors, the framework of tacit or explicit arrangements and understandings within which cooperative economic exchange has occurred. Trade among industrial countries generally grew much more rapidly than among other countries in the earlier post-war period. Integration also proceeded much more rapidly among these countries. The Atlantic community and the EC have taken economic integration further than most groups of countries, the latter within the framework of a customs union arrangement and measures encouraging broader economic and political union.

A central question is what criteria can be elicited to determine appropriate domains in which to further collective action aimed at strengthening the arrangements for cooperative international economic exchange and the gains from closer economic integration.

Closer economic integration has many possible roots. It can originate through commitments — multilateral, regional, bilateral — which are simply based upon a

Reprinted from *International Economic Pluralism: Economic Policy in East Asia and the Pacific,* by Peter Drysdale, pp. 32–42 (with minor editing). Copyright © 1988 by Peter Drysdale. Reprinted with permission from Allen & Unwin Pty Ltd, Sydney, Australia.

recognition of the gains to be had from closer international economic cooperation and interaction. The great post-war multilateral institutions, such as the GATT, were based on such commitments. It can germinate within a system of common cultures and social institutions; historically the close commercial ties among the British Empire countries had such origins. It may spring from ideological alignments, as among the former Council for Mutual Economic Assistance (Comecon) countries and, more broadly, among the countries of the Western bloc. It may be encouraged by the advantages that contiguity presents in economic exchange. Or it may grow out of other non-economic interaction among nation states, such as membership of a common political alliance. Both relative contiguity and membership of a common political alliance provided starting points for closer Pacific economic integration. In Europe a commonly felt threat to external security prompted the formation of the EEC (Cooper 1968, p. 7). Any of these factors, separately or in some combination, can provide the impetus and rationale for collective action which effectively promotes closer economic integration within the international community of nations. A wide range of studies of international political and economic systems reveals a great diversity of approaches over time and in different circumstances towards developing institutional frameworks aimed at fostering economic integration. The classic literature on the shaping of the Atlantic community stresses the relationship between the preconditions for integration and the feasibility of alternative approaches to integration (Deutsch et al. 1957). The relative homogeneity among European nations and their common security interests, for example, were critical factors in encouraging the elaboration of a comprehensive framework for economic and, later, political union. Heterogeneity limits the scope for comprehensive union among many countries. However, a heterogeneous group of highly complementary economies can develop an intensive pattern of economic transactions fostered by propinquity, common political associations and a strong coalition of interests, which both encourages and requires closer policy coordination and economic association. Just such an intensive pattern of economic exchange has developed among the diverse countries of the Pacific.

Complete integration among a group of nations might be thought to require not just 'common' commodity markets or 'common' factor markets but also a tendency towards the equalisation of commodity prices and of the prices of the factors of production within them (Cooper 1968, pp. 10–11). Common cultural and institutional factors offer one avenue to encouraging international market integration in this sense, and to creating the increased sensitivity of one nation's markets to developments in the markets of other countries, which is one of the important consequences of integration. Another avenue is presented by the low resistances to bilateral or regional trade which arise from geographic proximity. This is a particularly important factor inducing geographic concentration in trade for whole classes of commodities, such as minerals and raw materials, which are bulky in relation to their value and costly to transport.

The systematic study of international trade resistances is, surprisingly, a new branch of economic enquiry, but it yields some useful general observations.[1] The cost of overcoming resistances to international trade varies across bilateral trading relationships, and as a result the price at which commodities are offered for international sale or purchase also varies according to the bilateral trading relationship within which the transaction is made. The effect of resistances on relative commodity prices provides incentives for the development of close trading ties among particular groups of trading nations. Low resistances are commonly associated with proximity. But other factors are also influential in determining the structure of trade resistances. In addition to objective trade resistances, which are the product of distance and transport costs or government policies that discriminate between trading partners, traders face various subjective resistances to trade, including imperfect knowledge of trading opportunities and the absence of confident and established business relationships. Low transport and communications resistances interact with institutional, political and other resistances to generate high intensities in trade and other economic relations, such as have developed among the economies of the Pacific. Low resistances to trade on some trading routes encourage the processes of market and institutional integration more strongly among some groups of countries than among others. These discontinuities and fragmentations in otherwise more or less interconnected world markets are important in the management of foreign economic relations within the relevant policy horizons.[2] Indeed, within a multilateral set of economic relationships, their contours define important domains for international collective action to secure agreements among groups of countries about a framework for economic exchange, as well as agreement on the policy coordination that is required, in one form or another, to manage the development of closer economic integration.[3]

The distinction between institutional and market integration throws further light on what determines an appropriate domain for international action on the trade regime (Cooper 1974, pp. 2–4, also Chapter 2, this volume). Institutional integration refers to the legal agreements and institutional arrangements which facilitate economic exchange among a community of nations. Market integration refers to the intensity of transactions in the markets for goods and factors of production within the community. If a circumstance exists where there are no governmental or direct institutional barriers to intra-community transactions, but markets are in fact not linked because of either high transportation costs or the ignorance of trading opportunities, then institutional integration exists but market integration is underdeveloped. If, however, there are institutional and legal barriers to trade and capital movements but market ties survive, market integration is frustrated by the lack of institutional integration. This distinction is useful, not so much to draw attention to these different processes in integration as to underline the interaction between them. Institutional and market integration involve an important two-way interaction, in which close economic ties and common economic problems set the requirements for institutional arrangements, and institutional arrangements influence the degree of economic and political cohesion. Institution-building can usually neither wholly precede nor wholly follow the integration of economic markets.

The distinction between institutional and market integration also highlights the scope for advancing integration arrangements on several fronts and at different levels. The literature in international economic theory might seem to take another position: that international economic policy should generally be multilateral in focus to be efficient and constructive. An argument which stresses the importance of the institutional framework within which international economic exchange is to take place prescribes no such automatic policy guideline. From this perspective, multilateral action, regional action and bilateral collective action all provide fertile and potentially efficient routes to elevating exchange possibilities. Multilateral collective action can establish a minimum set of acceptable and sustainable rules for cooperative exchange among the widest and most diverse group of nations. Collective action among smaller (regional) groupings may promise fuller agreement and more intensive economic ties based on the common interests growing out of proximity, common political associations or whatever. Bilateral collective action may allow the development of cooperative exchange arrangements further and faster than is possible within a broader regional and multilateral setting.

It is important to note that collective action directed at shaping international economic regimes cannot, of its nature, be 'unilateral', so that the individual nation state is foreclosed from policy action to secure these important effects, except in the sense that it may be able to implement such policy by exercising hegemony over some other nation or nations, thereby imposing conformity to its preferred rules for economic exchange. In fact, the theory of international relations has given consider-able attention to the character and stability of hegemonic systems. It tends to suggest that hegemonies play a crucial role in supplying the collective goods that are necessary to the existence and effectiveness of international regimes. However, as Keohane (1982, pp. 325–56) argues, following Coase's theorem, regimes are also demanded and sustained by incentives to collaborate in the establishment of frameworks for the negotiation of international agreements (thereby reducing transactions costs), and for the coordination of actor expectations (thus improving the quality and quantity of the information available to nation states).

It is significant that agreements at the regional or bilateral level, which are consistent with non-discriminatory principles in international trade, may well be an effective means of building and extending confidence in international exchange. It is arguable, for example, that the 1957 Agreement on Commerce between Australia and Japan, which incorporated MFN principles and was non-discriminatory in its thrust, effected the most significant elevation of Australia's specialisation in the international economy in post-war years (Crawford and Okita 1978, pp. 47–51; Drysdale 1981). However, many bilateral and regional agreements do embody elements of commercial policy discrimination. Some of these agreements may well be effective in serving the objective of promoting and extending confidence in international exchange despite their embodying discriminatory elements. It is arguable, for example, that the New Zealand–Australia CER Agreement serves that purpose effectively for New Zealand. The efficiency or inefficiency of such discrimination in trade arrangements is a matter that needs separate judgement, although an important conclusion is that discriminatory trade regimes are likely to be damaging to the interests of East Asian and Pacific countries.

The nature of regional economic cooperation

The intensive network of trade and other economic exchange that has grown up within the Pacific region has developed without a firm framework of institutional ties at the regional level and despite the persistence of significant discontinuities between the commodity markets of the national economies involved. There are no comprehensive trade or economic agreements or understandings within the region. Multilateral arrangements and involvements only partially cover the trade and economic exchanges among Pacific countries. High levels of trade protection and other commercial barriers persist. Purposeful action to reduce these barriers and uncertainties associated with trading within the region, even with only vague and tacit commitments to regional economic cooperation, may have the potential to yield important gains to the countries of the Pacific.

The development of overlapping economic relationships and interests among the nations of the Pacific over the past two decades or so can be illustrated by reference to Figure 4.1. Figure 4.1(a) depicts the pattern of economic interaction between North America, Japan and other Western Pacific countries in the earlier post-war period, while Figure 4.1(b) shows the strong three-way interdependence in recent years. In the earlier period the dominance of the bilateral relationships of Japan and the Western Pacific with North America is represented. Japan is now much more important to other Western Pacific countries and the United States, and the shaded areas reflect the vastly enlarged intersection of regional economic interests. The diagram provides a highly stylised but essentially accurate picture of the development of overlapping economic relations within the Pacific, and suggests the interests that might encourage the development of regional cooperative agreements, institutional arrangements and organisations to define and supervise choices within growing spheres of mutual economic interest.

Regional economic cooperation which strengthens the trade regime has a sound basis in such patterns of trade and economic interaction. What form of regional economic cooperation and what structure of economic association might be adopted are matters taken up in detail in Drysdale (1988). But some of the possibilities, and the characteristics of the more important among alternative forms of economic cooperation, need to be introduced here.

In the field of commercial policy the range of possible commitments to regional economic cooperation include: agreements to consult on commercial policy action; the adoption of codes of trade and investment policy behaviour to maintain open markets; agreements to lower commercial barriers on an MFN basis; the establishment of a limited or complete free trade area; sectoral agreements to free trade; or the

Figure 4.1   Patterns of economic interaction

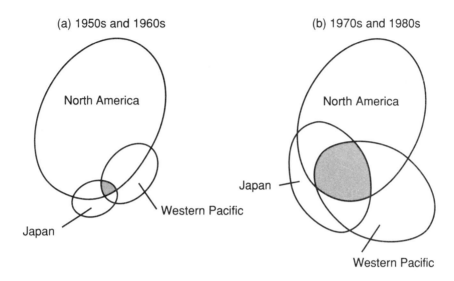

(a) 1950s and 1960s

North America

Japan

Western Pacific

(b) 1970s and 1980s

North America

Japan

Western Pacific

formation of a customs union. The last three forms of economic cooperation involve discrimination against third parties, and are not generally desirable on grounds of economic efficiency (Lipsey 1957, pp. 40–6). Regional economic cooperation can also take the form of macroeconomic policy coordination; arrangements for partial or complete pooling of foreign exchange reserves; monetary union; or broader economic union, including institutional changes to facilitate integration of the markets for factors of production (Cooper 1968).

The case for regional economic cooperation which incorporates discrimination against third parties in commercial or other foreign economic policies (as do customs or payments unions) is said to hinge on whether, on balance, the economic 'liberalisation effects' dominate the 'withdrawal effects' of such arrangements for the world as a whole. Johnson (1962), however, has argued that discriminatory arrangements, such as customs unions, should be regarded as devices for the attainment of collective goods such as political alliance, cultural alliance, or higher levels of industrial production than those that would be achieved with the operation of unimpeded market forces. The issue can then be stated in terms of whether a regional grouping that discriminates against third parties (and carries the economic cost of that) is the most efficient means of attaining a given collective aim; and this has to be demonstrated in each specific case, for there is no general presumption that it will be so (Lipsey and Lancaster 1956, pp. 11–33).

But the argument for regional economic cooperation offered here does not depend on whatever case can be made for arrangements which discriminate against third parties. Rather, it identifies the value of regional arrangements which serve collective ends but not at the price of discrimination in commercial policy. The core of economic theory suggests that the optimum integrated area is the world as a whole, since any 'unnatural' interference with the process of equalising international commodity and factor prices (except that designed to eliminate monopoly power or market imperfections) will cause an inefficient allocation of resources.[4] However, the point is that a priority in international economic policy directed at attaining the full benefits from exchange in a world divided by political boundaries has to be the joint securing of the regime within which exchange takes place. It does not follow that multilateral collective action to secure the regime for economic exchange is the only feasible or efficient route to closer economic integration. Regional economic cooperation, within a framework of multilateral economic relations, offers the potential for joint provision of a stronger trade regime — a trade regime which also raises confidence in international economic specialisation and promotes closer world economic integration.

There is another rationale for regional economic cooperation based on the provision of the specific alongside the systemic collective good of rules and agreements governing exchange. While the highest priority is clearly securing the trade regime for countries with sufficiently strong common interests, the objects of collective action can also be a wide array of specific public goods — research and information services, communications systems, health systems and environmental controls, as well as military security (see, for example, Olson and Zeckhauser 1976). Within nation states the provision of specific collective or public goods is more or less coterminous with the collective action which sustains the regime for exchange itself. This may also be so within associations of nation states, as in Europe. However, the diversity in social preferences within the international community and the different technological considerations for different types of collective goods both suggest that a variety of overlapping jurisdictions — multilateral, regional, bilateral — will serve in the most rational and sensible way the international provision of systemic and specific collective goods.

The shape of international economic cooperation is not just a technical matter; it is also a political question. The determination of an optimal jurisdiction in the realm of international economic policy-making requires, among other ingredients, careful weighing of the political elements in the various alternative arrangements that might be considered, since they represent potential constraints on the nature of progress towards, as well as forces which can be mobilised more effectively to achieve, international economic goals.

The logic of collective choice

It is evident that the domain for international collective action to achieve economic goals is neither single nor disjoint, in the sense that nation states will have an interest in membership of several groups or levels of international organisation. Moreover, the different domains within which collective action sustains a regime for economic exchange or the international provision of specific collective goods have a wide variety of possible origins — economic, geographic, technological, cultural, political and strategic. In turn, these origins shape the choice of regime and the nature of the specific public goods that are provided internationally. If the sovereignty of the nation state is accepted as an initial condition and, by implication, some kind of equality is accorded among nation states, complex questions of collective choice arise within the international economic system.

Diversity among national preferences in respect of regimes for international economic exchange and the provision of other collective goods is an important influence on the feasibility of collective action. Agreement to collective action is likely to be achieved most readily among countries which do not differ greatly in their preferences for the international economic system or for specific public goods (Cooper 1968, pp. 227–8; 1974, pp. 9–10, also Chapter 2, this volume). On the other hand, differences in these preferences limit the scope for international economic cooperation and are often the cause of considerable international conflict.

If a pluralist international community is one which accommodates a non-homogeneous set of social preferences among its members — on matters to do with how trade and commerce should be organised, commercial policies managed, monetary arrangements operated, or the whole range of social institutions ordered — a fundamental question is whether and by what principles collective choice can be exercised effectively. Within democratic and pluralistic nation states (which acknowledge the 'equal value' and 'right to differ' principles), more or less satisfactory mechanisms have evolved which allow some measure of reconciliation among divergent positions or some measure of tolerance for collective action which does not have a completely unanimous basis. Between sovereign and independent nation states such mechanisms are by no means fully developed.

A practice of reconciliation and tolerance has built up among some countries in certain fields, and priorities have been established within the international economic community — such as through the GATT, the International Monetary Fund (IMF), within the Organisation for Economic Cooperation and Development (OECD), and among the Group of Seven; but the basis for this cooperation is only tenuously founded on the principles of international pluralism. This question needs to be addressed at some length, since it is at the heart of defining an appropriate framework for economic cooperation among a group of nations such as those within the Pacific community.

The problem of international choice and collective action is complex. It almost always involves multi-dimensional decisions, rather than one-dimensional decisions that can be scaled along a single measure, such as the level of expenditure, without a simultaneous consideration of other values. A group of independent nations about to settle on the nature of a regime for cooperative economic exchange is confronted with just such complexity of choice. The nature and difficulty of this kind of choice can be illustrated by a simple example.[5]

Consider a world in which there are three sovereign nation states whose preferences are accorded equal value. They wish to cooperate to secure an agreement to foster trade under a regime which just sufficiently eliminates arbitrary action that would damage their principal trading interests. Assume that the three countries are, respectively, an industrial economy, a newly industrialising economy (NIE) and an agricultural economy. Further, assume that there are three broad classes of commodities: capital-intensive goods, produced most efficiently by the industrial country according to the principle of comparative advantage; labour-intensive goods, produced most efficiently by the NIE; and land-intensive goods, produced most efficiently by the agricultural nation. Each country harbours feelings of insecurity, which are not totally overcome by the will to cooperate rationally with its partners through economic specialisation. Moreover, these feelings are given effective expression through protectionist pressures, justified on the grounds of national interest and revealed in a national preference for some measure of diversification unattainable under free trade but felt necessary for security's sake (Johnson 1965).

Preferences for protection in each country are so ordered that the strongest preference for protection is revealed for the good which has the most comparative disadvantage, there is a less strong preference for protection of the good of intermediate comparative advantage, and, of course, the weakest preference for protection (zero levels are desired) applies for the good with the greatest comparative advantage. A viable trade regime is taken to require a guarantee of freedom to trade in at least two goods, while allowing arbitrary protection of the third. The choice of trade regime can be styled in terms of the good for which arbitrary protection is allowed. There are three possible trading regimes: one in which arbitrary intervention is allowed against capital-intensive goods (the 'capital protected' regime); one in which arbitrary intervention is allowed against labour-intensive goods (the 'labour protected' regime); and one in which arbitrary intervention is allowed against land-intensive goods (the 'land protected' regime).

Each country's preferences for each of these three trade regimes (or states of the world that might be achieved through cooperative agreement) are ranked in Table 4.1.

If each country's order of preference counts equally, the logic of collective choice reveals that it is impossible for the group to make a consistent decision by majority rule. Take first the choice between the 'land protected' regime and the 'labour protected' regime. Only the agricultural country prefers the 'labour protected' to the 'land protected' regime, so that majority rule puts the 'land protected' regime ahead. On the next choice, between a 'labour protected' regime and a 'capital protected'

Table 4.1   Choice of trade regime

	Industrial country	NIE	Agricultural country
Land protected	1	2	3
Labour protected	2	3	1
Capital protected	3	1	2

regime, only the industrialising country prefers the latter, so that the 'labour protected' is put ahead of the 'capital protected' regime. This would seem to imply that the group preferred a 'land protected' over a 'capital protected' regime, but the reverse turns out to be true! Indeed, the preferences of the group as a whole are cyclically inconsistent. Pairwise choice leads to an endless cycle which cannot be resolved other than arbitrarily.

This is no trivial application of Arrow's insight into the theory of collective choice (Johnson 1965). Simple as it is, this example typifies the hard choices of international politics and political economy. Indeed, the example is a quite plausible, if partial, representation of the conflicting interests that faced the international community in the establishment of the post-war trade regime. The resolution of such conflicts of choice in international politics is frequently found in the exercise of a decisive role by one or more members of the group. After the Second World War, industrial countries effectively dictated the exclusion of agricultural trading nations from the full benefits of the GATT. The preferences of stronger and larger parties for a choice, such as the one described here, are given fuller rein and are often allowed to dominate when no independent rules or principles can be addressed to effect a decision.

The question arises whether such problems of collective choice are as readily resolved within nation states as has been assumed thus far. Certainly nation states are characterised by the presence of mechanisms which allow some measure of reconciliation among divergent positions, and these mechanisms have more authority and are more fully developed than any such mechanisms among nation states. But the contest of preferences or priorities is sometimes open and commonly vigorous. How this contest is resolved in each individual nation state is a matter of considerable interest and importance in the context of trade and foreign economic policy formation. It will affect, for example, whether and how reliably a particular country can deliver a 'cooperative trade strategy' — that is, maintain a commitment to trade without restrictions or penalties.

Indeed, a prolific literature has developed around the analysis of the political market for protection within nation states. It seeks to explain why countries protect domestic production and restrict external trade when trade theory would suggest that the alternative policy approach would improve national welfare. In this literature there are some elegant analyses of the determination and structure of tariffs and trade restrictions built upon the presence of competing domestic interests (Krueger 1974; Pincus 1977; Findlay and Wellisz 1983).

Nonetheless, conflict in preference ordering or priority setting within nation states suggests that, for any given country, it is important to have information about the domestic collective choice problems of its economic partners, since that information will affect its assessment of the probable pay-off from whatever international strategy it may choose. International consultative institutions provide an effective method of acquiring and disseminating such information. Certainly, private traders acting alone are unlikely to be able to undertake adequately the role of acquiring such information. Hence, there is an important rationale for the development of consultative mechanisms within the Pacific.

The conflicts of collective choice are endemic in a genuinely pluralist community. They can be resolved in a number of ways: the exercise of authority by a decisive group member; the weighting of some preferences or priorities over others; and the transformation or shaping of preferences so that they become more homogeneous and consistent. All are possible ways of resolving conflicts of collective choice and attaining cooperative outcomes (Mueller 1976, pp. 403–15). In practice, pluralist communities incorporate all three solutions, although the exercise of decisive authority would only seem compatible with the notion of pluralism if it were seen to be in some combination with the other two elements — some weighting of priorities and an openness to persuasion. Hence, agreement to a minimal ordering of priorities and the opportunity for communication and persuasion regarding orders of preference would appear to be two essential conditions to a robust pluralist community. These are evidently two basic requirements for successful economic cooperation among the heterogeneous nations of the Pacific region.

Notes

1   For a review of the analysis of these issues, see Drysdale and Garnaut (1982, also Chapter 3, this volume).

2   Crawford and Okita (1978, pp. 41–7) justify the strong bilateral policy interest in the Australia–Japan economic relationship on these grounds.

3   The trade relations among Pacific countries are analysed in detail in Drysdale (1988, ch. 4) in order to explore the extent to which they provide such a domain for international collective action.

4   Cooper (1974, p. 4, also Chapter 2, this volume) makes the point that these allocative issues cannot easily be separated from distributional issues.

5   The modern theory of complex choice was developed by Arrow (1951). In the literature there are a vast number of explanations of the Arrowian 'impossibility theorem', of which an example follows.

References

Arrow, Kenneth 1951, *Social Choice and Individual Values*, New York: Witary.

Cooper, Richard 1968, *The Economics of Interdependence: Economic Policy in the Atlantic Community*, New York: McGraw–Hill.

_____ 1974, 'Worldwide versus regional integration: is there an optimal size of the integrated area?, *Yale Economic Growth Center Discussion Paper*, No. 220, November.

Crawford, J. G., S. Okita et al. 1976, *Australia, Japan and Western Pacific Economic Relations*, Report presented to the Australian and Japanese Governments, Canberra: Australian Government Publishing Service (also referred to as the Crawford–Okita Report).

_____ 1978, *Raw Materials and Pacific Economic Integration*, London: Croom Helm (revised version of Crawford and Okita 1976).

Dam, Kenneth 1970, *The GATT: Law and International Economic Organisation*, Chicago: University of Chicago Press.

Deutsch, Karl et al. 1957, *Political Community and the North Atlantic Area*, Princeton: Princeton University Press.

Drysdale, Peter 1981, 'Australia and Japan in the Pacific and world economy' in Peter Drysdale and Hironobu Kitaoji (eds), *Japan and Australia: Two Societies and Their Interaction*, Canberra: Australian National University Press.

_____ 1988, *International Economic Pluralism: Economic Policy in East Asia and the Pacific*, New York: Columbia University Press/Sydney: Allen and Unwin.

Drysdale, Peter and Ross Garnaut 1982, 'Trade intensities and the analysis of bilateral trade flows in a many-country world', *Hitotsubashi Journal of Economics*, 22, February.

Findlay, R. and S. Wellisz 1983, 'Some aspects of the political economy of trade restrictions', *Kyklos*, 36.

Johnson, Harry 1962, 'The economic theory of customs unions', in Harry Johnson (ed.), *Money, Trade and Economic Growth*, London: George Allen & Unwin.

_____ 1965, 'An economic theory of protectionism, tariff bargaining, and the formation of customs unions', *Journal of Political Economy*, 73, June.

Keohane, Robert O. 1982, 'The demand for international regimes', *International Organization*, 36(2).

Krueger, Anne O. 1974, 'The political economy of the rent-seeking society', *American Economic Review*, 64, June.

Lipsey, R. 1957, 'The theory of customs unions: trade diversion and welfare', *Economica*, 24, February.

Lipsey, R. and K. Lancaster 1956, 'The general theory of second best', *Review of Economic Studies*, 24.

Mueller, Dennis 1976, 'Public choice: a survey', *Journal of Economic Literature*, 14(2), June.

Olson, Mancur and Richard Zeckhauser 1976, 'An economic theory of alliances', *Review of Economics and Statistics*, 8(3), August.

Pincus, J. J. 1977, *Pressure Groups and Politics in Antebellum Tariffs*, New York: Columbia University Press.

5   Principles of Pacific economic integration

Peter Drysdale and Ross Garnaut

The Asia Pacific trade model

East Asian and Asia Pacific regional trade expansion is very different in nature from that which is emerging in North America and from what has been established and is continuing to develop in Europe (Table 5.1). There has been no economically important trade-expanding discrimination in East Asia:[1] trade preferences within the ASEAN region so far have had trivial effects (Garnaut 1980), although the 1991 commitment by the ASEAN heads of government to move towards an ASEAN Free Trade Area will have future significance. The two most rapidly expanding intra-East Asian bilateral trading relationships over the past several years, those between mainland China and Taiwan, and between China and the Republic of Korea, have developed around and despite discriminatory restrictions on bilateral trade. Trade discrimination in Australia–New Zealand and North America has been associated with relatively small parts of the total Asia Pacific trade expansion.

East Asian and Asia Pacific trade expansion has nevertheless been associated with reductions in barriers to international, including intra-regional, trade. All the Western Pacific member economies of the APEC group, except Hong Kong and Singapore, have substantially reduced official border restrictions over the past decade, and especially since the mid-1980s. Hong Kong and Singapore have, throughout the period under discussion, been the world's most important examples of free trading economies. There has been major import liberalisation in Japan, Korea, Taiwan, mainland China, Thailand, Malaysia, Indonesia, Australia and New Zealand. Political weakness has meant slower progress in the Philippines, although recent official commitments are impressive. Trade liberalisation has been mostly

Table 5.1   Asia Pacific and world trade flows, 1970 and 1990 (per cent)

Trading country / Partner country	Western Pacific	Austral-asia	East Asia	North America	Asia Pacific	Western Europe	European Community	Rest of World
1970								
Western Pacific								
Exports	34.99	3.63	31.36	27.88	62.85	18.18	13.64	18.97
Imports	34.09	6.51	27.58	26.52	60.62	18.39	13.90	20.99
Australasia								
Exports	39.06	5.93	33.13	16.33	55.39	27.54	26.38	17.07
Imports	22.92	5.84	17.08	26.98	49.91	39.61	29.35	10.48
East Asia								
Exports	34.22	3.19	31.02	30.04	64.26	16.41	10.27	19.33
Imports	36.10	6.63	29.47	26.44	62.54	14.58	11.13	22.88
North America								
Exports	16.17	2.25	13.92	32.50	48.67	28.61	27.42	22.72
Imports	19.53	1.88	17.65	38.31	57.84	24.02	19.42	18.14
Asia Pacific								
Exports	23.52	2.79	20.73	30.69	54.21	24.53	22.04	21.26
Imports	25.57	3.80	21.77	33.42	58.99	21.68	17.13	19.33
Western Europe								
Exports	4.81	1.47	3.35	9.31	14.13	66.75	53.85	19.12
Imports	4.79	1.34	3.45	12.30	17.09	61.90	50.97	21.01
European Community								
Exports	4.97	1.57	3.41	9.63	14.61	66.24	53.10	19.15
Imports	5.00	1.54	3.46	13.19	18.19	59.62	50.24	22.19
Rest of World								
Exports	21.83	1.16	20.67	17.64	39.47	40.41	38.64	20.12
Imports	8.89	0.79	8.10	31.19	40.08	37.93	32.96	21.99
World								
Exports	12.53	1.76	10.77	16.98	29.51	47.04	40.59	23.45
Imports	12.40	2.11	10.29	20.11	32.50	43.97	36.19	23.53
1990								
Western Pacific								
Exports	42.71	2.63	40.08	27.55	70.26	18.48	19.93	11.26
Imports	47.35	4.39	42.96	21.17	68.52	16.58	16.11	14.90
Australasia								
Exports	57.12	7.25	49.87	12.44	69.56	15.83	15.11	14.61

(Table 5.1 continued)

	Western Pacific	Austral-asia	East Asia	North America	Asia Pacific	Western Europe	European Community	Rest of World
Imports	42.54	7.29	35.25	23.15	65.68	27.61	21.53	6.70
East Asia								
Exports	41.67	2.30	39.37	28.65	70.32	18.67	16.24	11.02
Imports	47.76	4.14	43.62	21.00	68.76	15.64	14.12	15.60
North America								
Exports	24.50	2.02	22.48	33.98	58.48	23.34	20.55	18.18
Imports	34.81	1.03	33.78	27.49	62.30	20.93	17.18	16.77
Asia Pacific								
Exports	35.23	2.38	32.85	30.19	65.43	20.47	17.97	14.10
Imports	40.95	2.67	38.27	24.39	65.34	18.80	15.97	15.85
Western Europe								
Exports	6.70	0.77	5.93	7.90	14.60	71.66	55.24	13.73
Imports	9.77	0.64	9.12	8.00	17.77	68.99	67.38	13.24
European Community								
Exports	5.99	0.69	5.29	7.29	13.27	66.19	55.77	20.54
Imports	8.21	0.52	7.69	7.27	15.47	59.96	51.18	24.57
Rest of World								
Exports	17.68	0.65	17.03	18.55	36.23	35.22	32.29	28.55
Imports	13.65	1.36	12.29	13.98	27.63	35.89	33.59	36.49
World								
Exports	19.06	1.35	17.71	17.89	36.95	46.79	37.71	16.25
Imports	22.50	1.55	20.95	15.39	37.89	43.78	42.84	18.33

Source: International Economic Databank, Australian National University, compiled from United Nations, International Monetary Fund and national statistics.

non-discriminatory and unilateral, and sometimes influenced by the multilateral disciplines of the GATT. The main exceptions, sometimes temporary, have favoured the United States, following pressure from that country to reduce bilateral trade imbalances. Even more important has been the reduction of non-official barriers to trade of many kinds, as part of the process of deep integration into the international economy.

The new model of regional and international trade expansion that has developed in the Asia Pacific region, and especially in the Western Pacific economies, is consistent with the spirit of the GATT as it was conceived in the 1940s and as it developed in the early post-war decades. Three crucial features distinguish Asia Pacific trade expansion, and take it beyond the GATT's constitution, rules and practice, and beyond the GATT's framework for the encouragement of regional trade expansion under Article XXIV.

The first distinguishing feature derives from the fact that GATT negotiations in practice have assumed that liberalisation is a concession, the withholding of which has value for a member country. The trade negotiations 'game' therefore has elements of the 'prisoner's dilemma', in which, in the absence of deliberate communication and cooperation, the most unfavourable outcome for each participating country is the one that occurs. In contrast, the trade expansion 'game' that has emerged in the Western Pacific can be characterised as 'prisoner's delight'. Observation of the highly beneficial effect of one country's liberalisation on its own trade expansion has led each Western Pacific economy to calculate that, whatever policies others follow, it will benefit more from keeping its own borders open to trade than from protection. Each country's liberalisation in its own interests has increased the benefits that trading partners receive from their own liberalisation. This 'prisoner's delight game' consists of a series of movements towards sets of trade policies that are more favourable for all countries. There are gaps and exceptions (notably in East Asian agriculture), reflecting the domestic political economy of industry policy in most of these economies. It is in these excepted areas that outside pressure plays an important role in each individual country's trade liberalisation, so far most effectively through multilateral negotiations and other fora of the GATT, and sometimes in bilateral negotiations influenced by GATT disciplines.

The 'pay-offs' from unilateral trade liberalisation, across the range of trade policy stances of other countries, that generate the 'prisoner's delight' are recognisable as the outcomes predicted by standard trade theory. What is new in East Asia and the Western Pacific is that close observation in neighbouring country after neighbouring country that trade liberalisation enhances economic performance has changed political perceptions of the pay-off matrix. Any perceived disadvantages in changes in income distribution associated with trade liberalisation are judged by the political process to be less important than the gains for the nation as a whole — helped along by the obviously favourable effects on the incomes of the relatively poor of labour-intensive manufactured export expansion in labour-abundant economies.

Second, Asia Pacific trade expansion has not been associated with substantial discrimination in trade policy. Official barriers have not been lower for intra-regional than for extra-regional trade expansion.

Third, the East Asian and Pacific experience demonstrates powerfully the importance of non-official barriers to trade, and the role that their reduction plays in trade expansion and economic development.

'Market' integration and 'discriminatory' integration

Analysis of the unusual character of Asia Pacific trade expansion has been advancing over the past quarter century. It is, however, only in the past few years, when the United States and the EC have been seeking to understand and respond to an East Asian presence of obviously large proportions in the international economy, that many trans-Atlantic mainstream economists have turned their attention to the character of Asia Pacific trade expansion. Much of the recent American and trans-Atlantic discussion of East Asian and Asia Pacific trade expansion has made little use of the insights that have emerged from a quarter century of analysis of the different trade phenomenon across the Pacific.

Cooper (1974, also Chapter 2, this volume) was one of the first to draw attention to the various origins of regional trade expansion with his identification of 'market integration' around institutional and legal barriers to trade, involving capital movements and other forms of economic interchange. In contrast to this form of integration, economic integration in Europe has flourished within the institutional arrangements of the EC. European 'institutional integration' discriminates against economies outside the region: the removal of internal barriers to trade has been accompanied by the maintenance of external barriers, while others, such as those affecting agricultural trade, have become a greater encumbrance to global trade growth.

The terms 'market integration' and 'institutional integration' have been useful in drawing attention to the difference between European and Asia Pacific economic integration. But they are misleading to the extent that they are interpreted literally. The emergence of new institutions — to a considerable extent private but increasingly inter-governmental — to reduce the costs of trade expansion has been important in the Asia Pacific region. Meanwhile, the important role of integrative institutions embodying large elements of official discrimination in Europe and now North America has not excluded market pressures from a major role in trade expansion (Milner 1991, p. 7).

On balance, we have found it useful to retain Cooper's term 'market integration' for the case where the initiative has remained primarily with enterprises acting separately from state decisions, and where official encouragement of regional integration does not include major elements of trade discrimination. We prefer the term 'discriminatory' integration to 'institutional' integration for arrangements of the EC and NAFTA kind.

A general theory of economic integration

We define 'economic' integration as movement towards one price for any single piece of merchandise, service, or factor of production. The global economy is, in this sense, considerably disintegrated. The price for an undifferentiated item may vary greatly between a store on 49th Street and another on 120th Street in New York, between a market in East Java and another in North Sumatra, or between Tokyo and Paris.

Disintegration persists because of barriers, or resistances, to trade. We define resistances to trade as phenomena that prevent or retard the immediate movement of commodities in response to price differentials.

One line of literature that has developed out of analysis of the Asia Pacific experience distinguishes two basic types of resistances: objective and subjective.[2]

Trade resistances and economic integration

Objective resistances can be overcome by firms only at some objectively determined minimum cost. They comprise principally transport, communications and other costs of overcoming distance, and official barriers to trade (principally protection).

Subjective resistances comprise a range of social, psychological, and institutional factors that cause prices to vary across geographic space by larger margins than can be explained by the necessary costs of overcoming objective resistances. Subjective resistances derive from perceptions of risk and uncertainty about property rights and valuations at various stages of trade transactions, from imperfection in the information available to firms, and from the processes through which firms engaged in trade make decisions that affect the volume, geographic direction, or commodity composition of trade.

Johnson has suggested a slightly different categorisation of the same phenomena, distinguishing 'geographic distance and the transport cost of overcoming it', 'differences of political and legal systems, culture and language that differentiate nations from one another as market areas' and 'protection' (Johnson 1968). We think that it is more useful analytically to see Johnson's second category as factors affecting the costs of overcoming subjective resistances to trade, rather than as separate resistances in themselves.

Resistances are present in all economic transactions, whether domestic or international. They are commonly, although far from universally, lower within than between countries. This difference is one of the factors distinguishing international from inter-regional trade. There are, however, important exceptions to the common pattern. Regional price disparities within some large, weakly integrated economies (say, Indonesia and China) can exceed disparities, at least for many commodities, between major cities exposed to trade between countries (Arndt and Sundrum 1975). Border trade occurs between adjacent regions of two countries when the cost of overcoming intra-national resistances exceeds the cost of overcoming international resistances.

The costs of overcoming various resistances vary across bilateral trading relation-ships. The divergences from the law of one price associated with resistances to international trade are typically very large. Among objective resistances, while official barriers have received the most consideration in public discussion and the literature, these are probably less important than transport costs today, at least in relation to imports of most manufactured goods into advanced industrial economies. There are exceptions, of which restrictions on the import of textiles and clothing into the OECD countries are the most important.

There is some evidence to suggest that subjective resistance can be quantitatively more important than objective resistances (Garnaut 1972). Sung (1992, also Chapter 28, this volume) underlines the importance of these considerations in his discussion of the large and increasing role that Hong Kong is playing in China's trade — a role that contributes a major part of Hong Kong's *raison d'être* today. Interestingly, Hong Kong's role in the China trade has expanded as China has opened to the outside world, despite reductions in resistances to direct trade between established enterprises in China and in the rest of the world. The resolution of this paradox can be found in the effect of China's internationalisation in increasing the range of firms and commodities participating in foreign trade, and therefore the transaction costs in dealing with them.

The costs of overcoming various types of resistance to bilateral trade, objective and subjective, are closely interrelated. Economies of scale affect the cost of overcoming all except official resistances: objective transport and communications costs up to quite large levels of bilateral trade, and subjective resistance of all kinds. There are externalities stemming from one firm's investment to reduce the cost of overcoming resistances to trade: investment in the organisation of a new pattern of transport or communication will reduce costs for other firms in the bilateral trading relationship; and investment in information to support a new pattern of trade provides information to others — including through observation of the resulting trade expansion itself.

These two characteristics of the costs of overcoming resistances to trade together introduce a conservative bias and stability in bilateral trade patterns. They increase the time lags in the adjustment of trade patterns to new relative cost relationships, which in any case would be as long as the time needed for enterprises to search for information, process that information and respond to it. They cause trade expansion associated with reduction in one type of resistance to trade to reduce the cost of overcoming all other resistances to trade. And they demonstrate the importance of institutions, private or public, from the internally integrated multinational enterprise to mechanisms to enforce contracts in international trade, in determining the costs of overcoming resistances to trade.

Resistances and trade discrimination

The cost of overcoming trade resistances has not been treated systematically in the theory of international trade. Subjective resistances make a cameo appearance in the theory of the product cycle (Vernon 1966), but disappear without influencing the whole corpus of theory.

The exceptions are the theory of protection (Corden 1971,1974) and the theory of customs unions (Lipsey 1960; Vanek 1965), which analyse the impact of official barriers to trade that are, respectively, uniform and differentiated across countries. Insights from the theories of protection and of customs unions are of considerable value in understanding the impact of resistances more generally on trade and welfare.

'Multilateral' reductions in resistances to a country's international trade unambiguously expand the welfare of the country itself, and the rest of the world. However, reductions in resistances in some bilateral relationships but not in others may raise or lower the welfare of countries involved in the resulting bilateral trade expansion, depending on the balance of trade creation and trade diversion. Such differentiated reductions in resistances in some bilateral trading relationships unambiguously reduce trade with, and the welfare of, countries in the rest of the world, outside the trade-expanding bilateral relationships, unless the income-increasing effects of trade creation are very large compared with other economic effects.

There may be a shift of trade from established channels resulting from reduction in subjective resistances to trade, resulting from investment by private firms in information about opportunities in a new bilateral trading relationship, or in building business relationships to support a new pattern of bilateral trade. In the case of subjective resistances, however, the new knowledge of superior gains from trade with a new partner is more likely to be analogous to the removal of trade discrimination against the new partner than to classical trade diversion. Trade may indeed be 'diverted' from old channels to new. It could be 'trade diversion' in the classical sense, for example if the investment in information and business ties with the new partner is associated with an absolute decline in effort in maintaining the old relationships. It is more likely, however, that the switch will 'divert' trade from a less profitable to a more profitable partner, in the case in which the initiative lies with non-state businesses rather than governments. The latter is not classical 'trade diversion', and has different economic effects.

Let us illustrate the point with one example of considerable contemporary significance. As Taiwan enterprises have put more effort into trade and investment with mainland China in recent years, they have, perforce, devoted less managerial time to identifying and exploiting business ties in the rest of the world. This may have increased absolutely resistances to trade between Taiwan and (parts of) the rest of the world, especially when economies of scale in overcoming resistances to bilateral trade are taken into account. But even if it has not, the reduction of resistances to trade between Taiwan and mainland China, in, say, labour-intensive electronic components, will have had some effect in diverting trade in these components from other bilateral relationships. This tends to reduce welfare in the rest of the world, unless incomes growth associated with trade creation in Taiwan and China makes these two economies much larger participants in trade with the world as a whole.

Such a change in the pattern of subjective resistances is more likely to raise the welfare of the new trading partners, Taiwan and mainland China, than is a discriminatory reduction in official barriers. It is therefore more likely to be associated with a preponderance of classical trade creation over trade diversion, a net increase in the economic welfare of the bilateral trading partners, and welfare gains for the world as a whole and the rest of the world.

The discussion in the preceding paragraphs of 'trade diversion' and 'trade creation' associated with the reductions in resistances in some but not all bilateral trading relationships exemplifies a general difference between differential reduction in official and other resistances to trade. Reductions in other resistances result from independent firms' search for lower-cost and more profitable patterns of trade. While the reduction in the gap between minimum possible and actual transport costs may divert trade from old relationships, it is unlikely to divert trade from lower-cost to higher-cost sources and destinations. Unlike discriminatory reduction in official barriers, it is highly unlikely to reduce welfare in the trading partners experiencing trade expansion or in the world as a whole, although it may still reduce welfare in the rest of the world outside the trading partners.

The presence of externalities in investment to reduce subjective resistances to trade, and to bring transport and communications costs closer to their objective minima, introduces the possibility of economically efficient roles of government, quite separate from those associated with the imposition of official barriers to trade. These are the roles of governments in providing public goods that are relevant to the efficient operation of an international market: improving transport and communications infra-structures, including through regulatory regimes; reducing perceptions of risk in international contracts; and disseminating information on profitable trade opportunities (Garnaut 1993). The impact of these roles of government on trade and welfare is best analysed in a framework analogous to that applied to independent enterprises' efforts to reduce the cost of resistances, rather than that developed in the pure theory of customs unions for analysis of differentiated reduction in official barriers.

In this section we have articulated elements of a general theory of economic integration. Within this theory, disintegration is the normal condition of inter-regional and international trade in goods and services. The reduction of resistances takes investment and time, and is affected by the whole range of cultural, linguistic, legal, and other factors that affect the cost of trade transactions. Much of the dynamism in Asia Pacific trade expansion derives from the progressive reduction of subjective and objective but non-official resistances to trade. The process has been driven by independent enterprises' search for more profitable patterns of trade, sometimes assisted by provision by governments of 'public goods' that affect the operation of private markets.

The general theory of economic integration brings out the crucial distinction between reductions in resistances in some trading relationships through a process of official discrimination, on the one hand, and reductions in resistances through a process of 'market' and non-discriminatory integration, on the other. Discriminatory integration blocks the economic processes of search for more profitable patterns of trade.

Where discrimination favours trading relationships that would in any case, through market processes, be large relative to the partner countries' total trade, the chances of economic loss in the partner countries and the world as a whole are correspondingly reduced. These conditions reduce the magnitude of economic loss in the rest of the world.

Krugman (1991, 1992, also Chapter 13, this volume) makes the point that discrimination in favour of trade between naturally close states is less likely to reduce world welfare, but takes it too far. Summers (1991, also Chapter 15, this volume) asserts a similar point more strongly, and does not attempt to justify his strong arguments in support of discriminatory liberalisation.

The reality that 'optimal' patterns of trade are different across commodities, increases the costs of general official discrimination in bilateral trading relationships, for the bilateral partners and the rest of the world. The presence of economies of scale and externalities in overcoming many resistances compounds the effect of trade discrimination in promoting welfare-reducing trade. Discriminatory official barriers block the role of market pressures, in reducing trade resistances in new trading relationships when changing economic circumstances and opportunities justify the effort.

Problems with a Pacific Free Trade Area

What does this analysis mean for assessment of proposals to form a comprehensive Pacific Free Trade Area (PAFTA), based on discriminatory approaches to trade policy?

The reality of free trade areas and customs unions in practice is that exceptions have been important, at least in their early years; and where they have not, the establishment of the area has been associated with increased barriers to trade with the rest of the world. This outcome is driven by an important asymmetry in the political economy of protection policy, between the highly focused opposition to trade creation by established interests in protected industries, together with the highly focused support of established interests in trade diversion, on the one hand, and the diffuse beneficiaries from trade creation on the other (Anderson and Garnaut 1987, ch. 4). Hence the tendencies towards higher protection against the rest of the world that can be observed early in the lives of the US–Canadian, Australian and European customs unions, and the proliferation of exceptions early in the lives of the Australia–New Zealand and Canada–US free trade areas.

One would be blind to the realities of the political economy of protection to ignore the likelihood that, in a PAFTA, the process of negotiation and compromise would favour trade diversion over trade creation.

Neither can we presume that all Pacific countries would seek to participate in negotiations to establish a free trade area. China, with its partially reformed prices system, is not now in a position to accept the obligations of participation in a clean free trade area. It would be possible in principle to negotiate a range of commitments to open trade by China that led in the direction of more open and even free trade. But the presence of special rules to govern China's trade relations with the Pacific would invite the proliferation of commitments short of free trade by other participants, especially (but not only) in developing countries. Yet to exclude China would carry considerable costs. It could retard China's progress towards more open trade relations, thus reducing the chances of ultimate success in the whole modernisation program. Trade diversion from China within a smaller PAFTA would generate tensions and retaliation that would carry costs of their own. And if China continued to grow strongly despite these new obstacles, over time a progressively smaller proportion of opportunities for profitable intra-Pacific trade would be covered by the free trade area, thus weakening the presumption of net benefits for members and the world as a whole.

Nor is it likely that the ASEAN countries would accept membership of a clean free trade area. Governments in Indonesia, the Philippines, Malaysia and even Thailand have all compromised heavily in implementing trade liberalisation programs over the past decade (Findlay and Garnaut 1987, pp. 271–3). Attempts at intra-ASEAN liberalisation have yielded much more trade diversion than trade creation. Despite the attraction of open access to North American and Australasian markets, it is unlikely that the ASEAN states would agree to participate fully. To exclude ASEAN and to expose its members to trade diversion in favour of other Pacific economies would reduce the gains from Pacific integration, and set back the hesitant process of trade liberalisation in the ASEAN economies themselves. To welcome ASEAN membership on a non-reciprocal or incompletely reciprocal basis would invite pressures elsewhere for the proliferation of exceptions.

We defined our first objective as the preservation of the relatively but imperfectly open trading environment that had supported the productive extension of rapid growth in East Asia in recent decades. This objective seems to us to rule out embarkation on an integration process that runs a severe risk of setting back severely the prospects for internationally-oriented growth in China and the ASEAN states. Now let us presume for analytic purposes that it was possible to wave a magic diplomatic wand and embark on a process of negotiation that actually delivers a clean and comprehensive PAFTA. Would such a process help or hinder the reduction of barriers to trade between Pacific countries and trading partners in the rest of the world?

The process of establishment of a PAFTA would require a huge concentration of political and administrative effort within all member countries. This would inevitably divert attention from wider trade policy objectives in the international system.

It is not clear to us how a commitment to a PAFTA, involving substantial trade diversion away from the rest of the world in the best of scenarios, would facilitate the negotiations of lower trade barriers with the EC. Action to implement such a commitment would have the effect of, at best, suspending progress on the negotiation of reciprocal liberalisation with Europe during a long transitional process.

5) Similarly, the diversion of trade policy-making resources into the development of a PAFTA, and the diversion of trade from the rest of the world, would weaken the region's capacity to respond to early stirrings of interest in internationally-oriented development in the former Soviet Union and Indochina, and the tentative signs of possible future stirrings in North Korea. For the foreseeable future, the expansion of trade relations between the Pacific countries and these centrally planned economies is of minor importance in narrowly economic terms. But it would be foolish to diminish the potential for reduction in political tension and the threat of war, and eventually reduction in military expenditure, that would over time be associated with constructive Pacific responses to these centrally planned economies' interest in closer economic relations.

6) The United States at least would be mindful of Mexican and other Latin American interests in the process of Pacific integration. The accommodation of these interests would further increase the likelihood of special arrangements and exceptions within a PAFTA.

It may seem that the liberalisation of access to trade in services appears more likely to be susceptible to treatment under the aegis of the 'free trade area' approach. The obstacles to international competition in services do not arise mainly through fiscal mechanisms as they do with tariffs on commodities. They take the form of government monopoly of service (communications); government controls on entry or capacity (aviation); prescriptions of qualifications for entry (professional services); or rules on domestic content (media). Some of the restrictions involve international agreements on rights or conditions of operation. These issues may appear easier to press through arrangements such as the Australia–New Zealand CER Agreement. However, while their multilateral negotiation may be difficult at this point, they are not likely to be treated easily within the framework of a Pacific-wide free trade area (as United States–Canada experience attests). Indeed, the complexities of service trade liberalisation would seem equally amenable to negotiation within the framework of broader MFN-type trade and commerce agreements, alongside commodity trade issues.

conclusion: We conclude that efforts to establish a PAFTA are not consistent with Pacific countries' interests in more effective movement towards global trade liberalisation. Discriminatory trade arrangements within the Pacific region, and discriminatory treatment of Japan by the United States and other Western Pacific countries, or of other Western Pacific countries by Japan and the United States, are inconsistent with East Asian and Pacific trade policy interests and are likely to damage the growth performance of other countries in the region. If, on the other hand, the 'free trade area' suggestion were not intended to involve trade discrimination within the Pacific, it may provide an impetus for accelerating movement towards liberalisation on an MFN basis, and reinforcement of the 'prisoner's delight' process, both in the region and more broadly. The important requirement in such discussions would be to avoid *open regionalism".*

any acceptance of the discrimination against non-Pacific countries implied by the term 'free trade area', and to work towards finding areas of reciprocal concession that can be offered on an MFN basis.

Notes

1   East Asia includes China, Japan, Hong Kong, Korea, Taiwan, Brunei, Indonesia, Malaysia, the Philippines, Singapore and Thailand. The APEC group (at the time of writing) additionally includes Canada, the United States, Australia and New Zealand.

2   For background to the discussion in this and subsequent paragraphs, see Garnaut (1972), Drysdale and Garnaut (1982, also Chapter 3, this volume) and Drysdale (1988).

References

Anderson, Kym and Ross Garnaut 1987, *Australian Protection: Extent, Causes and Effects*, Sydney: Allen & Unwin.

Arndt, H. W. and R. M. Sundrum 1975, 'Regional price disparities', *Bulletin of Indonesian Economic Studies*, 11(2), July.

Cooper, Richard 1974, 'Worldwide versus regional integration: is there an optimal size of the integrated area?', *Yale Economic Growth Center Discussion Paper*, No. 220, November.

Corden W. M. 1971, *Protection*, Oxford: Clarendon Press.

––––––––––– 1974, *Trade Policy and Economic Welfare*, Oxford: Clarendon Press.

Drysdale, Peter 1988, *International Economic Pluralism: Economic Policy in East Asia and the Pacific*, New York: Columbia University Press/Sydney: Allen and Unwin.

Drysdale, Peter and Ross Garnaut 1982, 'Trade intensities and the analysis of bilateral trade flows in a many-country world', *Hitotsubashi Journal of Economics*, 22(2), pp. 62–84.

Findlay, Christopher and Ross Garnaut (eds) 1987, *The Political Economy of Manufacturing Protection: Experiences of ASEAN and Australia*, Sydney: Allen & Unwin.

Garnaut, Ross 1972, *Australian Trade with Southeast Asia: A Study of Resistances to Bilateral Trade Flows*, PhD thesis, Australian National University, Canberra.

––––––––––– (ed.) 1980, *ASEAN in a Changing Pacific and World Economy*, Canberra: Australian National University Press.

––––––––––– 1993, 'The market and the state in economic development: applications to the international system', *Singapore Economic Review*, 36(2), March, pp. 13–26.

Johnson, H. G. 1968, 'Comparative cost and commercial policy theory for a developing world economy', Wicksell Lectures, Stockholm.

Krugman, Paul 1991, 'The move to free trade zones', Federal Reserve Bank of Kansas, *Review*, December.

––––––––––– 1992, 'Regionalism vs. multilateralism: analytical notes', Paper presented at the World Bank–CPER Conference on Regional Integration, 2–3 April, Washington, DC.

Lipsey, R. G. 1960, 'The theory of customs unions: a general theory', *The Economic Journal*, 70(279).

Milner, Helen 1991, 'A three bloc trading system', Paper presented at the IPSA Conference, Buenos Aires, Argentina, 20–25 July.

Summers, Lawrence H. 1991, 'Regionalism and the world trading system', Paper presented at the Jackson Hole Conference on Free Trade Areas, Federal Reserve Bank of Kansas City, August.

Sung, Yun-Wing 1992, 'The economic integration of Hong Kong, Taiwan and South Korea with the mainland of China', in Ross Garnaut and Liu Guoguang (eds), *Economic Reform and Internationalisation: China and the Pacific Region*, Sydney: Allen and Unwin.

Vanek, J. 1965, *General Equilibrium of International Discrimination: The Case of Customs Unions*, Cambridge, Mass.: Harvard University Press.

Vernon, R. 1966, 'International investment and international trade in the product cycle', *Quarterly Journal of Economics*, 79, May.

6   The impact of transaction costs on trade flows in the Asia Pacific

Torsten Amelung

Introduction

An empirical analysis of foreign trade flows among countries reveals that there has always been a tendency towards regionalisation of foreign trade, in the sense that some countries maintain more intensive trade links with particular trading partners relative to the rest of the world. This phenomenon is in line with mainstream trade theories, which show that differences in factor endowments, comparative cost advantages as well as similarity of demand patterns may have an impact on the volume and the direction of trade between particular countries.

Moreover, trade barriers can cause the evolution of regions that are characterised by a higher degree of trade integration within the region as compared to outsiders (Balassa and Stoutjesdijk 1984; El-Agraa 1988; Amelung 1989). Following Viner's (1950) customs union theory, regionalisation is likely to evolve as a result of legal trade barriers which discriminate against countries not belonging to preferential trading areas. In addition, natural trade barriers such as transport costs have been identified as major factors affecting the regional pattern as well as the composition of foreign trade (Lösch 1954; Yeats 1981; Deardorff 1987).

Yet there is another category of obstacles to foreign trade. According to Johnson (1968), information costs can be regarded as a trade barrier, since there are differences in the availability and costs of acquiring information about national markets in different countries. To the extent that these information costs hinder contracting between individuals, they have been also termed 'transaction costs' in the theoretical literature (Caves 1982; Johanson and Mattsson 1987; Schmidtchen and Schmidt-Trenz 1990a, 1990b; Alam 1990).

While the impact of differences in factor endowments, transport costs and the effects of legal trade barriers on the volume and the direction of trade have been analysed empirically,[1] the role of transaction or information costs has been neglected in these empirical models.

This paper will attempt to provide a tentative empirical approach showing that transaction cost differences among countries are an important determinant of trade regionalisation. The following section focuses on the definition of transaction costs in foreign trade and discusses major problems of measuring these costs. The third section presents an empirical model that includes various determinants of transaction costs as explanatory variables. This approach is tested for the Asia Pacific region.

Transaction costs in foreign trade

Basically, foreign trade involves transactions of goods, services and capital between two individuals belonging to different countries and thus to different legal systems (Schmidt-Trenz and Schmidtchen 1990). The specification and initiation of these transactions is due to contracts that have to be negotiated between the trading partners before the transaction can take place. Basically, transaction costs comprise all costs of contracting — namely, transaction costs of the initiation of cooperation as well as transaction costs arising from deficient cooperation (Schmidtchen and Schmidt-Trenz 1990a).

Although this definition of transaction costs is a useful theoretical device, it does not yield a clear delineation of cost components that can be classified as transaction costs. In fact, foreign trade involves a large set of different costs that can be regarded as transaction costs — for example, costs of contract-making via search or advertisement, costs of gathering information on foreign markets, costs of monitoring (especially screening of quality, metering of quantity, timing of instalments), costs of export guarantees, factoring and swaps, as well as costs of information-gathering on foreign markets (Casson 1982). However, these cost components cannot be used as an input for an empirical analysis of transaction costs on foreign trade. There are two main reasons for this. Firstly, it is impossible to derive a data set featuring the sum of transaction costs for the export sector of one country, since the costs listed above can only be quantified by using firm-specific data that are not publicly available. Secondly, these firm-specific costs reveal only contracting costs due to transactions that have been actually finalised. However, contracting costs can be prohibitive, so that contracts and thus foreign trade cannot develop. Such transaction costs that actually prohibit cooperation between trading partners must be brought into the analysis in order to assess the impact of transaction costs of foreign trade.

Since it is not possible to measure transaction costs directly, this paper will attempt to quantify some of the determinants of transaction costs. These determinants will be used as exogenous variables in the empirical analysis. Basically, all transaction costs can be traced back to the fact that information is not freely available, so that transactions due to foreign trade incur costs of information (Johanson and Mattsson

1987). The costs and requirements of information — namely, checking the credibility of trading partners — are much higher in foreign than in domestic trade, because foreign trade involves transactions between trading partners belonging to different legal systems. Hence the respective property rights cannot be enforced on the international level, thus adding incentives for contract default to international transactions (North 1987, 1989). Since international transactions involve a change in property rights, trading partners run the risk of expropriation and default. This uncertainty, which in international transactions has been termed 'sovereign risk' (see, for instance, Stüven 1988) or 'constitutional uncertainty' (Schmidtchen and Schmidt-Trenz 1989, p. 23), gives rise to coordination problems which impose transaction costs on the trading partners.

So far as the default risk is concerned, individuals engaging in international trade must run this risk, unless they can acquire an export guarantee, make use of document-against-payment schemes or sell their claims to an export factoring service. If the frequency of transactions increases, it can be profitable to engage in foreign direct investment, so that there is a hierarchical link between the exporters and the importers (Schmidtchen and Schmidt-Trenz 1990a; Schmidt-Trenz and Schmidtchen 1990). Irrespective of whether one of the trading partners engages in such institutional arrangements or exposes himself to the risk of expropriation and contract default, the uncertainty prevailing in foreign trade increases transaction costs. Costs due to this default risk can be proxied by using an index which assesses the risk of debt default of the respective trading partners.

Another coordination problem which is due to a lack of information goods and constitutional uncertainty involves currency risk. If the trading partners use a legal tender other than the invoicing currency, they must expose themselves to exchange rate fluctuations or insure themselves by buying foreign currency on the forward exchange market, if such an institution exists in the home country of the trading partners. The transaction costs due to the currency risk can be proxied by the variance of exchange rate fluctuations, as is shown in the next section.

In addition, transaction costs are incurred as firms enter foreign markets, since there are considerable information requirements. These requirements have to be met in order to facilitate contracting and monitoring. In general, it has been argued that exporting firms will prefer those foreign markets where they can rely on a comparative advantage in information costs *vis-à-vis* firms from other countries (Bilkey and Tesar 1977; Bilkey 1978). Following Johnson (1968), culture and language among other factors differentiate nations from one another as market areas and determine the level of information costs in foreign trade. Hence, it has been hypothesised that information costs are higher when the trading partners have a completely different cultural background (Caves 1971, p. 5; Herrmann et al. 1982, p. 16). According to the business administration literature, marketing costs are substantially higher if the potential foreign market displays cultural characteristics that are completely different to those prevailing in the home country of the exporter (Vahlne and Wiedersheim-Paul 1977). Moreover, Carlson (1977) has asserted that cultural factors impact on the sequence of foreign market entry; entry is likely to begin with countries where information costs are lower due to cultural affinity with the country of the exporter. Furthermore, North (1987) has argued that cultural homogeneity of trading reduces costs of contracting and control, if the trade relationship involves a personal exchange relying on personal ties between trading partners, namely friendship or family membership. Accordingly, the resemblance of moral attitudes resulting from similar cultural roots adds to the reliability of trading partners. Hence, the cultural similarity of trading partners is likely to reduce transaction costs on foreign trade. Cultural homogeneity as a determinant of transaction costs can be estimated by using various indices, as is shown in the next section.

Finally, it must be noted that the existence of transaction costs in international trade introduces an inertia element into the geographical distribution of trade flows. There are several reasons for this. Firstly, a change of trading partners causes considerable information costs and risks to the transactor. This fosters a tendency towards stable and long-term partnerships engaging in repeat dealings (see, for instance, Carlson 1977, p. 2; Johanson and Mattsson 1987, p. 2; North 1989, p. 1320). New partnerships evolve as a slow process starting off with small and few transactions, as both trading partners have to prove their reliability (Johanson and Mattsson 1987, p. 5). Hence, the cost of changing trading partners involves barriers-to-entry in foreign trade.

Secondly, some cost components that can be termed transaction costs involve fixed cost elements, so that exporters can realise economies of scale if they increase the frequency of transactions and their volume of trade (Picot 1981, p. 284). Moreover, foreign trade involves country-specific learning effects that can be utilised by the exporter, as he increases his foreign trade volumes and the number of transactions. Both effects lend support to the hypothesis that exporters are inclined to intensify existing trade relations in countries to which they have already been exporting rather than enter new markets. The resulting inertia element in international trade can be proxied by using the historical trade relations as an explanatory variable.

Summing up, there are four factors that are expected to determine the level of transaction costs in foreign trade between two countries: exchange rate fluctuations, risk of default, cultural homogeneity and historical trade relationships. As transaction costs constitute natural trade barriers, there is reason to assume that they affect the quantity of trade between particular countries. This has been shown by Alam (1990) in a partial equilibrium framework. Transaction costs, however, are not equivalent across all possible combinations of trading partners but are likely to be different depending on the countries engaging in bilateral trade. Furthermore, it seems likely that there are groups of countries displaying relatively low transaction costs in their bilateral trade compared to countries that do not belong to that particular group. In such a case, transaction costs may have a discriminatory effect on outsiders, similar to non-members in Viner's (1950) customs union theory or remote areas in Deardorff's (1987) transport cost approach.

Hence, the transaction cost differential may, among other factors, have an impact on the direction and the regionalisation of international trade. To test this hypothesis empirically, the next section attempts to explain geographical distribution of exports, (that is, the share of exports to one trading partner in total exports) for a set of countries in the Asia Pacific region by using the determinants of transaction costs mentioned above.

The empirical impact of transaction costs on the direction of trade in the Asia Pacific

As was shown in the last section, transaction costs are not uniform for all pairs of countries. It is therefore very likely that differences in these costs may affect the direction of trade.

This leads to the question of how bilateral trade links — that is the variable to be explained in the following — can be measured. In an earlier fact-finding study on regionalisation in the Asia Pacific region (Amelung 1990), the export shares (EXP) — namely, the share of export from country i to country j in total exports of country i, were calculated in order to correct for the differences in size among countries and to show the relative importance of bilateral trade links. On the basis of these export shares, it has been shown that there are clear trends of regionalisation in the Asia Pacific region. Using regression analysis, we test whether it is possible to establish a causal relationship between these export shares and transaction costs for bilateral trade in seventeen Asia Pacific countries.[2] Since the endogenous variable is subject to fluctuation because of changes in export prices and quantities, export shares have been averaged on the basis of export values for the 1981–87 period.

As far as the exogenous variables are concerned, there is a striking lack of data on transaction costs that enter into the cost calculations of transactors engaging in international trade. For this reason, resort must be had to proxies that can be derived from the hypotheses discussed in the last section. The model to be tested for the Asia Pacific region comprises the following variables (the signs in parentheses yield the expected signs of the coefficient):

$$EXP = a + \overset{(+)}{b_1 \, HIST} + \overset{(+)}{b_2 \, CRED} + \overset{(+)}{b_3 \, CUL} + \overset{(+)}{b_4 \, EXST} + \overset{(+)}{b_5 \, LAB}$$

$$+ \overset{(-)}{b_6 \, DIS} + \overset{(-)}{b_7 \, CAP} + \overset{(+)}{b_8 \, BOR} + \overset{(+)}{b_9 \, PCI} + \overset{(-)}{b_{10} \, PROT}$$

$$+ \overset{(+)}{b_{11} \, SIZE} + \overset{(+)}{b_{12} \, DASEAN} + \overset{(+)}{b_{13} \, DBANG} + \overset{(+)}{b_{14} \, DSPFT}$$

The first variable is the historical level of export shares (HIST). It can be hypothesised that this variable is positively related to EXP. HIST is meant to capture the inertia element in international trading partnerships resulting from transaction costs involved in international trade. In an earlier study by Herrmann et al. (1982), trade data of 1900 have been used in order to explain the trade flows between OECD countries in the 1970s. The measurement of historical trade flows is somewhat difficult, since many developing countries in the Asia Pacific region achieved their independence only after the Second World War. Statistical data reaching back to the colonial period are either not available or not reliable. For this reason, export shares for 1966 have been calculated, as they can be obtained from the IMF's *Direction of Trade Statistics*.

The second variable (CRED) refers to sovereign risk or constitutional uncertainty involved in international trade. The higher the reliability in transactions, the more trade can be expected to grow between two trading partners. The credibility of trading partners can be proxied by the debt default risk of the particular countries. Hence, only risks due to export credits or project financing are considered in the analysis, while contract default in the form of delayed delivery or payment and expropriation are neglected. The respective country ratings ranging from zero for bad debtors to 100 for good ones have been derived from the publications of the Institutional Investor. The CRED variable features the sum of these ratings for the two trading partners in 1985.

Another risk component in foreign trade is due to exchange rate fluctuations. The variable EXST measures the correlation coefficient of the two trading partners' exchange rate *vis-à-vis* the US dollar, which is the most frequently used invoicing currency in the Asia Pacific region. A high positive correlation coefficient would imply relative stability in the exchange rate movements of the trading partners. The opposite is true for negative exchange rate fluctuations, since in this case an appreciation of one currency is accompanied by a depreciation of the other.

The CUL variable measures the cultural homogeneity of countries. As was discussed in the last section, cultural homogeneity of trading partners reduces risks, costs of information, marketing and bargaining. Hence the regression coefficient is expected to yield a positive sign. The index of cultural similarity used in the regression was calculated as follows:

$$\text{CUL}_{ij} = \sum_{k=1}^{n} \min \left[\frac{e_{ik}}{P_i}, \frac{e_{jk}}{P_j} \right],$$

where e_{i1} (e_{i2}) is the number of the population belonging to the ethnic group k in country i (j) while P_i (P_j) is the number of total population in country $i(j)$. The data for the calculation of the index have been obtained from the *Fischer Weltalmanach* (see Haffs 1985) and refer to 1981 and 1982, depending on the particular countries.

Earlier studies by Herrmann et al. (1982), Abebe (1980) and others, have tested the linguistic affinity by analysing whether the official languages in pairs of countries are identified. Since English is a widely accepted language in the Asia Pacific region, it seems unnecessary to test for linguistic similarity, since communication costs are not likely to evolve because of language problems. For this reason, in this study the ethnic origin of the population was taken as a yardstick in order to assess whether cultural similarity can impact on personal ties, resemblance of customs, habits, and so on.

Apart from transaction costs, tariffs and non-tariff barriers may impact on the direction of trade. Since data on the implicit protection for our sample of countries was not available, a dummy variable PROT was taken in order to capture the effect of protectionism on foreign trade. These dummies have been derived from classifications of countries with respect to their degree of outward orientation, made available in the *World Development Report 1987* for the period 1973–85. In this report, a broad sample of developing countries have been classified into various categories — strongly outward-oriented, moderately outward-oriented and strongly inward-oriented. The PROT variable shows the degree of inward orientation for the importing country. The dummy equals 0 (1) for strongly (moderately) outward-oriented countries and 3 (2) for strongly (moderately) inward-oriented countries.

Preferential tariff treatment resulting from institutional integration schemes was proxied by introducing dummies for their member countries. DBANG equals 1 for the member countries of the Bangkok Agreement in the sample (Bangladesh, Sri Lanka, India, South Korea). In the same vein, dummies were introduced for the ASEAN countries (DASEAN: Malaysia, Singapore, the Philippines, Indonesia, Thailand), the South Pacific Free Trade Arrangement (DSPFT: Australia, New Zealand, Papua New Guinea), and the South Asian Association for Regional Cooperation (DSAARC: Bangladesh, India, Sri Lanka, Pakistan).

Beside trade barriers, regulations on the foreign exchange market may hinder trade between two countries. In order to capture the effects of barriers to capital transfers, the percentage difference between the official and the black market exchange rate was averaged on the basis of yearly data from *Pick's Currency Yearbook* (now called the *World Currency Yearbook*) for the period 1981–86. It can be argued that this percentage difference is higher the more exchange controls are implemented. The CAP variable proxying the extent of capital transfer barriers between trading partners are calculated as follows:

$$\mathrm{CAP}_{ij} = \frac{1}{7} \sum_{t=1980}^{1986} \frac{b_{jt} - e_{jt}}{e_{jt}},$$

where b_{jt} is the black market rate in the year t for the importing country j and e_{jt} is the respective official or effective exchange rate.

Next, two variables with a geographical dimension enter the equation. The first one, DIS, measures the distance between the main ports of the respective trading partners and thus serves as a proxy for freight costs. The distance variable has been measured by using the Reeds Marine Distance Table.

The other geographical variable, BOR, attempts to proxy the relevance of border trade due to geographical conditions. If two nations share a border which is very long relative to their size, there is a high potential for regional trade, since road and rail transport is more important. The proxy for geographical conditions facilitating such border trade is defined as follows:

$$\text{BOR}_{ij} = \frac{L_{ij}}{A_i},$$

where L_{ij} is the length of the border line between the two trading partners (countries 1 and 2), while A_i is the total area of exporting country i.

Then there are two variables that refer to mainstream trade theories. LAB proxies the difference in factor endowments according to the Heckscher–Ohlin–Samuelson model. Accordingly, trade between countries is a result of differences in factor endowments. A simple proxy for the differences in the endowments with human capital and physical capital is per capita income (Havrylyshyn 1987). A low per capita income is supposed to reveal a rather poor endowment with physical and human capital. In order to have a control variable, a similar proxy was used in this study:

$$\text{LAB} = \frac{L_i / \text{GDP}_i}{L_j / \text{GDP}_j}.$$

Moreover, there is a potential for intra-industry trade (Linder-type trade) when both trading partners have reached a high stage of development, allowing for the diversification of the demand structure. To capture this phenomenon, the per capita income of the trading partner with the lower income was included as an additional variable PCI.

Finally, the SIZE variable corrects for the size of the countries. The export shares that constitute the endogenous variable can be expected to be higher when the importing country reveals a higher demand because of a large domestic market, high GDP per capita and a free import regime. The SIZE variable features the total imports of the importing country in the period 1981–87.

The results of the stepwise cross-sector regressions can be obtained from Table 6.1. Altogether three equations were tested. This was necessary because there is a high degree of multicollinearity between some variables. As a consequence, some coefficients are not significant in some equations depending on the selection of variables included. As can be seen from the equations, the credibility (CRED) of trading partners is a significant variable in all equations explaining the direction of trade in the Asia Pacific area. CUL yields a significant coefficient in equations 2 and 3, whereas EXST attaches significance only to equation 1. Moreover, past trade flows as reflected in the HIST variable in equation 3 are highly significant. This points to the fact that trade relations reveal a large element of inertia in the geographical concentration of international trade. This supports earlier findings on the stability of regional trade in the Asia Pacific region (Amelung 1990).

The degree of inward orientation (PROT) attached significance to all equations. By contrast, the CAP variable does not add any explanatory value. This can be explained by the high correlation between CAP and PROT and the fact that, in most

Table 6.1   **Estimation results (N=272)**

	Eq.1	Eq.2	Eq.3
CUL	0.038	0.061	0.063
	(1.44)	(3.19)***	(3.79)***
HIST	-	-	0.274
			(8.07)***
CRED	0.082	0.029	0.022
	(5.34)***	(2.45)**	(2.11)**
EXST	1.607	-0.498	-0.056
	(2.30)**	(0.94)	(0.13)
LAB	0.074	-0.004	-
	(2.29)**	(0.15)	
DIS	$6.1 \cdot 10^{-5}$	$-2.9 \cdot 10^{-4}$	$-2.0 \cdot 10^{-4}$
	(0.55)	(3.39)***	(2.78)***
SIZE	-	$9.4 \cdot 10^{-6}$	$7.1 \cdot 10^{-6}$
		(15.71)***	(11.45)***
DSPFT	0.783	1.129	-
	(0.30)	(0.58)	
CAP	1.566	0.405	0.661
	(0.49)	(0.23)	(0.46)
BOR	-	-0.123	-0.049
		(0.43)	(0.21)
PROT	-1.726	-	-0.105
	(3.55)***	-	(3.46)***
DSAARC	4.752	1.212	-
	(2.19)**	(0.73)	
DASEAN	1.922	0.858	-
	(1.25)	(0.75)	
DBANG		-4.711	-
	(0.64)	(0.30)	
Constant	-5.468	-0.739	-0.613
	(2.71)***	(0.51)	(0.49)
$\bar{R}^2$	0.232	0.586	0.671
F	8.46	33.03	62.41

Note: ** and *** denote significance at the 95 and 99 per cent levels, respectively. T ratios appear in parentheses.

Source: IMF, *Direction of Trade Statistics*, various issues; Amelung (1990); World Bank, *World Development Report*, various issues; Institutional Investor, *Country Ratings*, various issues; *Fischer Weltalmanach*, various issues; *Pick's Currency Yearbook*, various issues; *National Geographic Magazine*, 1957 World Map; own calculations.

strongly inward-oriented countries, both import markets and foreign exchange markets are equally distorted.

The dummy variables indicating the existence of preferential trading arrangements fail to add explanatory power to the equations, except for DSAARC in equation 3 and DSPFT in equation 1. However, the significance of DSAARC in equation 1 can be attributed to the omission of SIZE. As India is the major trading partner in South Asia, the DSAARC captures the effect of the control variable. Accordingly, the inclusion of SIZE reduced the significance of DSAARC. The performance of these dummies in the regressions confirm earlier studies by Wong (1988), Amelung (1989) and Brockmann, Hofmann and Rieger (1990), showing that these institutional arrangements have had little impact on regional trade flows in the Asia Pacific region.

The geographical distance of trading partners, DIS, seems to impact on the direction of trade, as shown by equations 2 and 3. By contrast, the BOR variable does not seem to do so. This can be explained by the relevance of sea traffic in the Asia Pacific and the lack of data on regional border trade, which is only partly registered in the national statistics on foreign trade.

Finally, the LAB variable yields significant results in equation 1, thus confirming earlier studies analysing differences in factor endowments. By contrast, PCI turns out to be insignificant in all equations. Since PCI did not even reach the threshold value for the inclusion in the stepwise regression process, it is not included in Table 6.1.

The rather low explanatory value of equation 1 points to the fact that a better specification of transaction costs is required, since it is mainly the SIZE and HIST variables that add to the significance of the other equations. The availability of so-called 'market-making activities', in particular, which are meant to reduce transaction costs, would be tested as an additional determinant of transaction costs. Also, a better indicator for protectionism between countries should be calculated, with a more careful estimation of differences in factor endowments perhaps adding to the significance of the equations. These extensions of the model together with a more direct specification of transaction costs provide opportunities for further research.

Conclusions

The formation of regional entities characterised by strong bilateral trade links has been attributed to differences in factor endowments, preferential trade agreements and differences in freight costs in the recent literature. In this paper a broader concept has been applied, as many other obstacles to international trade incurring transaction costs were included in the analysis. Given such transaction costs — for instance, costs of information, bargaining and insurance — the direction of trade is not merely a function of relative differences in factor endowments and production costs as well as of trade barriers and transport costs; it is also a function of differences in transaction costs across countries.

In order to assess the extent to which these transaction cost differentials affect trade flows, the bilateral trade between seventeen countries in the Asia Pacific region was empirically analysed. Summing up, it can be concluded that the determinants of transaction costs between trading partners have a considerable impact on the direction of trade in the Asia Pacific region. Cultural similarity among trading partners seems to enhance trade, as it eases communication and thus reduces costs of information, bargaining and marketing. In addition, the credibility of trading partners and exchange risks involved in international trade have affected the direction of trade among countries. Moreover, policy variables seem to impact on the direction of trade. A coordination of monetary policies reducing exchange rate fluctuations between countries can help to lower transaction costs and enhance trade, as has already been asserted by Nsouli (1984).

The existence of transaction costs in foreign trade consequently seems to affect both the quantity of trade between two countries as well as its geographical distribution between countries. Thus, institutional integration schemes should not focus on the costs created by trade barriers, since the latter are only one of several obstacles to foreign trade. If costs of information and costs of default add to these obstacles, there is reason to assume that international institutional arrangements that help to reduce transaction costs may enhance foreign trade. However, the design and analysis of such potential institutional arrangements, already initiated by Schmidtchen and Schmidt-Trenz (1990b), reveal a need for further research.

Notes

1   For instance, Sautter (1983), Havrylyshyn (1987) and Lal, Khanna and Alikhani (1987) provide extensive analyses of the impact of resource endowments and comparative cost advantages on the direction of trade. Empirical studies with respect to the role of transport costs include Yeats (1982) and Langhammer (1987).

2   This set of countries includes the United States, Australia, Japan, New Zealand, Bangladesh, China, Hong Kong, India, Indonesia, South Korea, Malaysia, Pakistan, Papua New Guinea, the Philippines, Singapore, Sri Lanka and Thailand.

References

Abebe, T. 1980, *An Economic Study of the Determinants of International Patterns of Trade: OECD and Africa*, PhD thesis, North Illinois University, Dekalb Illinois: University Microfilms International, Dissertation Information Service, Ann Arbor.

Alam, S. M. 1990, 'Transaction costs of trade: some partial equilibrium results', *Southern Economic Journal*, 57(2), pp. 323–9.

Amelung, T. 1989, 'Wirtschaftsgemeinschaften', in K. Macharzina and M. Welfe (eds), *Handwörterbuch und Internationale Unternehmung*, Stuttgart: C. E. Poeschel, pp. 2285–94.

_____ 1990, 'Economic regions in Asia Pacific: an exercise in regional delimitation', *Kiel Working Papers*, 409, Kiel Institute of World Economics, Kiel.

Balassa, B. and A. Stoutjesdijk 1984, 'Economic integration among developing countries', in P. K. Gosh (ed.), *Economic Integration and Third World Development*, London: Greenwood, pp. 33–50.

Bilkey, W. J. 1978, 'An attempted integration of the literature of the export behavior of firms', *Journal of International Business Studies*, 9, pp. 33–6.

Bilkey, W. J. and G. Tesar 1977, 'The export behavior of smaller-sized Wisconsin manufacturing firms', *Journal of International Business Studies*, 8, pp. 93–8.

Brockmann, K. L., A. Hofmann and H. C. Rieger 1990, 'Market integration in the Asia Pacific: measures and institutions of national governments', Paper presented at the Interim Researchers' Meeting on Regional Economic Integration in Asia Pacific at the Institute of Southeast Asian Studies, Singapore.

Carlson, S. 1977, *Swedish Industry Goes Abroad: An Essay on Industrialization and Internationalization*, Lund: Studentliteratur.

Casson, M. C. 1982, 'Transaction costs and the theory of the multinational enterprise', in A. M. Rugman (ed.), *New Theories of the Multinational Enterprises*, London: Croom Helm, pp. 17–34.

Caves, R. E. 1971, 'International corporation: the industrial economics of foreign direct investment', *Economica*, 38, pp. 1–27.

_____ 1982, *Multinational Enterprise and Economic Analysis*, London: Cambridge University Press.

Deardorff, A. V. 1987, 'The direction of developing-country trade: examples of pure theory', in O. Havrylyshyn (ed.), *Exports of Developing Countries: How Direction Affects Performance*, World Bank Symposium, IBRD, Washington, DC, pp. 9–21.

El-Agraa, A. M. 1988, 'The theory of economic integration', in A. M. El-Agraa (ed.), *International Economic Integration*, London: Macmillan, pp. 16–41.

Haffs, H. (ed.) 1985, *Fischer Weltalmanach*, Frankfurt: Fischer.

Havrylyshyn, O. 1987, 'Evidence of differences between South–South and South–North trade', in O. Havrylyshyn (ed.), *Exports of Developing Countries: How Direction Affects Performance*, World Bank Symposium, IBRD, Washington, DC, pp. 67–84.

Herrmann, H. et al. 1982, *Kommunikationskosten und Internationaler Handel*, Schriften des Instituts für Regionalforschung der Universität Kiel, Munich: Florentz.

Institutional Investor, *Country Ratings*, New York, various issues.

Johanson, J. and L.-G. Mattsson 1987, *Interorganisational Relations in Industrial Systems — A Network Approach Compared with the Transaction Cost Approach*, University of Uppsala, Uppsala.

Johnson, H. G. 1968, *Comparative Cost and Commercial Policy Theory for a Developing World Economy*, Stockholm: Almquist & Wicksell.

Lal, S., A. Khanna and I. Alikhani 1987, 'Determinants of manufactured export performance in low-income Africa: Kenya and Tanzania', *World Development*, 17(9), pp. 1219–24.

Langhammer, R. J. 1987, 'Transport costs differentials and competitive advantages of industrial countries' exports to ASEAN countries', *Economic Bulletin*, 12, pp. 379–87.

Lösch, A. 1954, *The Economics of Location*, New Haven: Yale University Press.

Nsouli, S. 1984, 'Monetary integration in developing countries', in P. K. Gosh (ed.), *Economic Integration and Third World Development*, London: Greenwood, pp. 153–8.

North, D. C. 1987, 'Institutions, transaction costs and economic growth', *Economic Inquiry*, 25(3), pp. 419–28.

_____ 1989, 'Institutions and economic growth: an historical introduction', *World Development*, 17(9), pp. 1319–32.

Picot, A. 1981, 'Unternehmensorganisation und Unternehmensentwicklung im Lichte der Transaktionskostentheorie', in E. Streissler (ed.), *Information in der Wirtschaft*, Berlin: Duncker & Humblot, pp. 282–6.

Sautter, H. 1983, *Regionalisierung und Komparative Vorteile im Internationalen Handel*, Tübingen: J. C. Mohr.

Schmidtchen, D. and H.-J. Schmidt-Trenz 1989, 'Private law, the world production possibility frontier and the need for an international private law community: German theory of order and constitutional economics at work', *Department of Economics Discussion Paper*, No. B8901,University of Saarland, Saarbrücken.

_____ 1990a, 'New institutional economics of international transactions', *Jahrbuch für Neue Politische Ökonomie*, 9, pp. 3–34.

_____ 1990b, 'The division of labor is limited by the extent of the law: a constitutional approach to international private law', *Constitutional Political Economy*, 1(3), pp. 49–71.

Schmidt-Trenz, H.-J. and D. Schmidtchen 1990, 'Private international trade in the shadow of the territorality of law — Why does it work?', *Southern Economic Journal*, 58.

Stüven, V. 1988, 'Zur Risikoaufteilung bei Krediten an Entwicklungsländer ein Vertragssytem zur Reduzierung des Souveränitätsrisikos', *Die Weltwirtschaft*, 1, pp. 150–64.

Vahlne, J. E. and F. Wiedersheim-Paul 1977, 'Psychic distance — An inhibiting factor in international trade', *Department of Business Administration Working Paper*, No. 2, University of Uppsala, Uppsala.

Viner, J. 1950, *The Customs Union Issue*, New York: Carnegie Endowment for International Peace.

Wong, J. 1988, 'The Association of Southeast Asian Nations', in A. M. El-Agraa (ed.), *International Economic Integration*, London: Macmillan, pp. 314–26.

World Currency Yearbook (formerly *Pick's Currency Yearbook*), International Currency Analysis Inc., New York, various issues.

Yeats, A. J. 1981, *Shipping and Development Policy: An Integrated Assessment*, New York: Praeger.

_____ 1982, 'Market access and transport problems as constraints to Asian regional integration', Paper presented at the International Symposium on Two Decades of Asian Development and Outlook for the 1980s, Institute of Developing Economies, Tokyo, 8–11 March.

Part Two

The Context of Asia Pacific Regionalism

7   Pacific economic cooperation: the history of an idea

Hadi Soesastro

Over the past two to three decades, a number of proposals have been made to create various Asian regional organisations. These will be examined here by employing different frames of reference, or approaches. For example, a concept-oriented approach would recognise that the pan-Pacific idea which is of relevance today is derived from the fact and implications of regional economic interdependence. Such ideas began to emerge only in the mid-1960s and found their more elaborate expression in the 1970s. The rationale given for an institutionalised arrangement in the Pacific rested on the realisation that the growing economic interdependence of the region requires new mechanisms for more effective communication and association, and the recognition that 'bilateralism is no longer adequate, while regional rather than global considerations are more suited to the circumstances' (Fifield 1981, pp. 14–15).

Alternatively, an event-oriented frame of reference can be employed to identify the origin of an idea. However, since a concept might emerge as a response to a particular event, this approach often would converge with a concept-oriented approach. For example, it was pointed out that the early concerns in post-war Japan with schemes for broader regional economic cooperation occurred at a time when Japan was far from sure that it would achieve an economic miracle (Gordon 1981). However, a different view suggested that 'the notion that the Pacific Basin can be made a world economic center by promoting freer flow of trade and capital among the nations on its periphery did not come into fashion until the rise of Japan as a major economic world power' (Chung 1981, p. 4).

A third orientation focuses on the actors involved. Actors can be nations, institutions, or individuals, depending on the preferred level of analysis. The role played by Robert Schuman and Jean Monnet in the formation of the ECSC was a decisive one, although other factors also contributed favourably to that end. With such actors in mind, Han Sung-joo observed that 'in the Pacific region today, it is simply very difficult to find leaders who carry much weight either among the developing or developed countries, let alone among countries in both of the groups, and who are committed to the idea of Pacific Community' (Han 1983, p. 65). Nonetheless, a person such as the late Saburo Okita comes to mind as one of the most important actors in the pan-Pacific movement. Individual actors are important because they develop ideas or modify concepts to changing circumstances by virtue of their ability to interpret or foresee events.

However, ideas on cooperation in the Pacific often are scrutinised not on the basis of the soundness of the concept itself but with reference to the originators or actors involved. Because of historical factors, ideas for a broader regional cooperation that originate from Japan tend to arouse a great deal of suspicion. It is unfortunate that Japan often finds itself in such a situation.

Since the early 1960s the Japanese have been in the vanguard of the development of pan-Pacific ideas. Japanese proposals to form regional cooperation arrangements were certainly made with the view to promoting Japan's national interest. In fact, all nations must clearly see their interests in their pursuit of particular objectives. The various pan-Pacific ideas, be they of Japanese origin or otherwise, must be assessed by all the respective countries on that same basis. Discussions on pan-Pacific ideas, especially in the late 1970s and early 1980s, were not free from misperceptions, which themselves were often motivated by a search for hidden motives. Perhaps the lack of a proper perspective on the historical evolution of the ideas has contributed greatly to the widespread misunderstanding.

The history of the ideas for regional economic cooperation in the Pacific has not yet been well researched. Evolution of the concepts has been written about mainly to demonstrate the growth of interest in pan-Pacific ideas, especially Pacific economic cooperation (Drysdale 1978). The following examination of the evolution of pan-Pacific ideas seeks to describe the various proposals that were made, and the circumstances in which they were presented, and to identify the main factors that influenced the development of the concepts and the efforts to translate them into action.[1] This study identifies three consecutive periods in the development of Pacific economic cooperation ideas. The first is from the early 1960s to around 1967, a period marked by efforts made almost exclusively in Japan to initiate and develop Pacific economic cooperation ideas and schemes. The second period, from 1968 to 1977, saw a process of 'internationalisation' of the idea, whereby persons and institutions from many other countries became actively involved in the idea, though activity was still confined mainly to academic and business circles. The third period, starting in 1978, was marked by serious attempts to translate ideas into action. This process saw increased involvement by governments. The period also witnessed the emergence of a regional consensus, albeit still weak, on the main principles for organising Pacific economic cooperation. This process is expected to be followed in the early 1990s by a more urgent task of further consolidating the process of cooperation in a changed international political and economic environment.

The period 1960 to 1967

In the first period, three different developments in the idea of Asia Pacific regional cooperation can be identified in Japan. The first involved a concept of cooperation to promote regional cohesion, an idea that originated with Morinosuke Kajima, a businessman and Liberal Democratic Party (LDP) politician who raised the question in 1960 in the Upper House of the Diet about the possibility of creating a pan-Pacific organisation. Kajima's proposal was based on the idea of pan-Asianism rather than on a pan-Pacific concept, and the proposal could have been motivated by Japan's broader regional interests, which became apparent as Japan vigorously pursued its economic development. Kajima saw the importance of a Japanese role in promoting regional consolidation, namely the improvement of the political and economic situation in Asia. He therefore proposed a Marshall Plan-type Asia Development Fund that would provide grants — rather than credits — which were deemed necessary for development. He took great pains to explain that his proposed scheme of cooperation was based on an entirely different concept than that of the Greater East Asia Co-Prosperity Sphere. This suggests his clear understanding of the sensitivities involved. Nonetheless, Kajima's pan-Asianism was not free from charges of being another form of Japanese hegemonism (Bandura 1980).

The second idea developed independently of Kajima's proposal and was manifested in a series of studies and research on regional economic cooperation undertaken by leading Japanese economists such as Saburo Okita and Kiyoshi Kojima. The underlying concept was the promotion of regional economic integration that began to develop in the early 1960s. While Morinosuke Kajima's proposals seem to have gotten nowhere, the works by Okita and Kojima have contributed significantly to the subsequent development of the concept of Pacific economic cooperation.

In the early 1960s the establishment of the Japan Economic Research Center (JERC) provided an institutional vehicle in Japan for studies on Pacific economic cooperation by leading Japanese economists. This proved to be of great importance to subsequent development of the Pacific economic cooperation idea. The Center's first report, entitled 'Economic Cooperation in the Pacific Area', proposed that annual meetings be held among representatives from the five developed Pacific nations — Australia, Canada, Japan, New Zealand and the United States — to discuss issues of common interest in the fields of economic relations, transportation and communication, as well as cultural exchanges. The questions of the status of representatives — whether they should be ministers, government officials or private business — was left open (Morris-Suzuki 1981). In November 1965, at JERC's first international conference on 'Measures for Trade Expansion of Developing Countries', Kiyoshi Kojima and Hiroshi Kurimoto of Hitotsubashi University presented a paper entitled 'A Pacific

Economic Community and Asian Developing Countries', in which the idea of a PAFTA was proposed (JERC 1966). In their proposal, Kojima and Kurimoto argued that a PAFTA, comprising the five developed Pacific countries, possessed the conditions necessary for effective regional integration. Moreover, if they were willing to welcome developing countries that might wish to join as associate members with preferential treatment, the result would be a vast Pacific trade expansion.

This led to the third development in May 1967, when the idea of regional consultations was first espoused by the Japanese at an official level. With Prime Minister Sato's encouragement, Foreign Minister Miki formally endorsed the notion of an 'Asia Pacific policy' for Japan. This foreign policy initiative could be seen as the first attempt by Japan to play a greater role in Asia in the post-war era. Miki's policy focused on the fact that the central issue for all Asian nations was the problem of poverty and suggested that any solution to this problem must be predicated upon a combined effort by both the developed Pacific nations and the developing countries in Asia.

Another quite notable development during the period 1960–67 occurred in the business world. In April 1967, at a meeting of the Japan–Australia Business Cooperation Committee, the respective business groups established the Pacific Basin Economic Council (PBEC), a private organisation with five national committees (Australia, Canada, Japan, New Zealand and the United States). PBEC's objectives were to promote the study and discussion of issues raised in regional trade and investment and greater cooperation between public and private interests.

In addition to this initiative, Japan and Australia implemented other important regional initiatives in subsequent periods. Beginning in the mid-1960s, Japan and Australia's bilateral economic relations expanded rapidly, primarily in response to external factors. As explained by Drysdale (1978, pp. 613–14), the reactions of those two countries to the changing international environment moved them towards closer involvement with each other. In view of the emergence of a discriminatory bloc within Western Europe, Japan and Australia each sought 'to encourage closer economic relations with its major Pacific trading partners and pursue a commercial diplomacy designed to counter the effects of intensification of European protectionism by developing an alignment of interests within the Pacific economic community'. Therefore, it is not surprising to see that these two countries have become active proponents of the Pacific economic cooperation idea. As suggested elsewhere, the main accomplishment of Japan and Australia in these efforts was to bring the Pacific Basin concept into the agenda of national and international discourse (Gordon 1981, p. 270).

The period 1968 to 1977

The second period of development of the Pacific economic cooperation idea saw it become internationalised, although largely in academic circles only. With the support of Foreign Minister Miki, the first Pacific Trade and Development (PAFTAD) conference was convened by Kiyoshi Kojima in January 1968 in Tokyo under the auspices of JERC, headed by Saburo Okita. This gathering of academics and the next PAFTAD conference in the following year actively discussed the pros and cons of a PAFTA among the five developed Pacific countries. These conferences involved an ever increasing number of policy-oriented economists in the discussion of regional foreign economic policy issues and became an important vehicle for the development of Pacific economic cooperation ideas. Discussions in PAFTAD conferences, however, revealed a lack of support for the idea of a PAFTA, and indeed Kojima also later withdrew his support.

In Japan no new ideas on Pacific economic cooperation were developed in the late 1960s and early 1970s, although a number studies were commissioned. In 1970 the Japan Institute of International Affairs (JIIA), a Foreign Ministry-related research organisation, commissioned Okita and Kojima to study the prospects for Pacific economic cooperation. In the same year, the Institute of Developing Economies, which is allied to the Ministry of International Trade and Industry (MITI), published a collection of studies on the Pacific economic region (Morley 1983). The second wave of public interest in Pacific economic cooperation ideas in Japan came only in the late 1970s with the publication of studies conducted by the Nomura Research Institute, beginning in 1977, one of which was entitled 'International Environment and Japan's Grand Strategy for the 21st Century'. This report proposed that Japan's future security interests lay within the framework of a Pacific regional organisation. It put forward plans for a US$20 billion 'Pacific Cooperation Fund', an expanded program of personnel exchanges, and a regular series of ministerial or summit meetings (Morley 1983).

Outside Japan, studies on the Pacific economic cooperation idea were initially sporadic, with the majority being undertaken in the United States at the Brookings Institution, the Hudson Institute, the Asia Society, the Pacific Forum, the East–West Center, and various universities (Morley 1983). In addition, the end of this period saw the beginning of a series of international meetings and conferences that were specifically convened to examine the Pacific economic cooperation idea. Such meetings brought about a greater awareness of the idea on the part of policy-makers in the region.

In addition to the unofficial international meetings, there were also important developments at the official level, primarily initiated by Japan. In May 1968, following his 'Asia Pacific policy' of the previous year, Foreign Minister Miki outlined a four-point 'Asia Pacific bloc establishment plan' after summoning together all Japanese ambassadors to the Asia Pacific area for a four-day conference. As described by Gordon, 'one of its points is the critical role which he [Miki] hopes Japan will play as a bridge between the developed Pacific nations . . . and the States of Southeast Asia. Miki hoped to press for a greater Japanese role as the Vietnam war subsided' (Gordon 1969, p. 6 footnote). Miki's plan manifested the gradual revival of Japanese interests in Southeast Asia.

However, Japan's leaders were not sure at the time as to how they should promote relations with Southeast Asia. The emergence of ASEAN as an effective institution helped to resolve the uncertainty. With ASEAN's successful conclusion of its first summit meeting in Bali in 1976, it appeared to have definitely proved itself in Japan's eyes.

As ASEAN became better organised, the group sought greater cooperation from Japan. This was met by a Japanese initiative in the summer of 1977. Only months after his inauguration as Prime Minister, Fukuda undertook a major tour of ASEAN and announced in Manila the so-called Fukuda Doctrine of 'heart-to-heart' diplomacy. Fukuda pledged to contribute to projects that would strengthen ASEAN cooperation. In addition, this initiative also was to put to rest Southeast Asian fear of Japan's possible domination. Seen from the point of view of relations within the Asia Pacific community, Fukuda's diplomacy represented a significant step. In fact, this period can be regarded as an important one from a political–diplomatic perspective, with attempts made to develop one of the most crucial relationships in Pacific regional building — the relationship between Japan and the ASEAN countries.

In this period, another important initiative was jointly undertaken by Japan and Australia. In October 1972, at the first ministerial conference between Australia and Japan, the two governments agreed to finance 'The Australia, Japan and Western Pacific Economic Relations Research Project' to be conducted jointly by JERC and the Research School of Pacific Studies of the Australian National University (ANU). The project was headed by Saburo Okita and Sir John Crawford, and research was led by Kiyoshi Kojima and Peter Drysdale, all leading figures in the PAFTAD circle. One of the earlier outcomes of this research program was a report to the governments of Australia and Japan presented by Sir John Crawford and Saburo Okita in 1976.[2]

Up to this point, perhaps the most significant achievement in the development of the Pacific economic cooperation idea was the evolution of the concept of cooperation and its institutional arrangements. Kojima's original PAFTA proposal, which involved institutional integration as in the case of the EEC, was abandoned and modified, initially by Kojima himself, and the concept of cooperation evolved into a more loosely structured type of arrangement, similar to the OECD.

The period since 1978

The year 1978 saw the beginning of a new era in the development of Pacific economic cooperation ideas, marked by greater interest and activity at the official and policy levels in a number of countries. Two important events took place in that year. The first was the request made in April 1978 by Senator John Glenn, Chairman of the Sub-committee on East Asian and Pacific Affairs, Committee on Foreign Relations of the US Senate, to the Congressional Research Service (CRS) of the Library of Congress to examine the feasibility of a regional economic organisation. The CRS in turn commissioned a study by Hugh Patrick of Yale University and Peter Drysdale of the

Australian National University. Submitted in May 1979, their report, 'Evaluation of a Proposed Asian–Pacific Regional Economic Organization', examined the interest and participation of the United States in an Organisation for Pacific Trade and Development (OPTAD) (Congressional Research Service, Library of Congress 1979).

The importance of this event was twofold. First, the idea was taken up by the United States and given serious consideration at the policy level. Interest in the United States in the Pacific economic cooperation idea has for a long time been confined to groups and individuals and has had a very limited audience (Morrison 1980). In fact, without the interest and participation of the United States — the largest economy in the region — a Pacific regional economic association of any form would have been less meaningful. And second, examination of the idea at the policy level made use of intellectual input of considerable credibility.

The second important event in 1978 was the official support in Japan for a 'Pan-Pacific Association' announced — and in fact initiated — by the then newly elected Prime Minister Masayoshi Ohira in December. Ohira formed the Pacific Basin Cooperation Study Group, an advisory group to Prime Minister Ohira, to study ways to enhance regional cooperation and harmonious relations among Pacific countries as well as to construct a regional community within the Pacific Basin region.

The Pacific Community Seminar, held at the Australian National University on 15–17 September 1980, was a crucial step in the development of cooperative institutions in the Pacific. This seminar was directly sponsored by the Australian government, following discussions with Japanese Prime Minister Ohira. Discussions focused not only on the forces promoting the Pacific Community idea, the issues for substantive cooperation, and the interest of countries in participating, but also (as explicit in the agenda) on the next steps that might be taken. Deliberations at the seminar led to a recommendation to establish a standing committee, the Pacific Cooperation Committee (PCC), with the task of coordinating an expanded information exchange within the region and setting up task forces to undertake major studies of issues for regional cooperation.

Despite some short-term setbacks following the Pacific Community Seminar in Canberra, in particular, a degree of wariness in the ASEAN countries, the attempt at translating the idea into action was a valuable one. For example, discussions at the Canberra meeting noted the desirability of a 'tripartite' involvement of academics, business people and other professionals, and government officials, from both the developed and developing countries, not only as part of the efforts to realise the Pacific economic cooperation idea but also in the emerging (and ultimate) structure of Pacific cooperation itself. Indeed, the period from 1978 witnessed a much greater interest and involvement in the development of the Pacific economic cooperation idea by a much larger and diversified group of people and institutions.

As a consequence, discussions about Pacific economic cooperation were no longer confined to issues of desirability and the designing of neatly structured technocratic blueprints. They were now obliged to confront the issue of feasibility.

Political scientists and practitioners — including government officials in their private capacity — who joined in the discussion strongly argued for greater understanding of the political aspects of cooperation and the political conditions and sensitivities involved in community building (Han 1983, p. 8). Since then, a greater realism has been introduced in examination of the Pacific economic cooperation idea. The Canberra seminar showed that while there was increasing support for the idea of Pacific economic cooperation, there was still no consensus on the actions that should follow. The following years saw the gradual emergence of regional consensus on the principles of cooperation and the direction of its development, and also a slow but gradual involvement of governments in the process. The most important vehicle for this consensus building and government involvement became known as PECC.

PECC's members comprise national committees, or representatives of countries or regional institutions. PECC has twenty member committees representing the following economies: Australia, Brunei Darussalam, Canada, Chile, China, Hong Kong, Indonesia, Japan, Korea, Malaysia, Mexico, New Zealand, Peru, the Philippines, Russia, Singapore, Chinese Taipei, Thailand, the United States and the Pacific Island nations. In addition, two international organisations — PBEC and PAFTAD — are 'institutional members' of PECC. As such, they participate in all PECC activities but have no vote on the standing committee.

It is also widely believed that the unofficial Pacific economic cooperation process which started in Canberra has survived primarily because of subsequent official initiatives taken by ASEAN countries, particularly by Thailand and Indonesia (Kaneko 1988, p. 73). In July 1984 the first initiative was undertaken at the official level, and is known today as the '6 plus 5' meeting or ASEAN Post-Ministerial Conference. The cooperation formula calls for the foreign ministers of the five developed Pacific countries to join their ASEAN counterparts at the time of the regular ASEAN foreign ministers meeting for an exchange of views on Pacific economic development and cooperation. Its importance as a means to increase ASEAN's confidence rests on the fact that the terms of the exercise are set by ASEAN itself. While there was some apprehension about this formula, the '6 plus 5' scheme was seen at the time as the only viable one at the official level.

The series of meetings of the PECC and the many task force activities and other regional study groups and fora under its auspices are often criticised for their lack of real action. However, they should be seen as a necessary part of the process of getting to know each other, which is immensely time and energy-consuming in view of the region's diversity. It is claimed that the influence of PECC meetings on the progress of efforts towards Pacific economic cooperation 'is ambivalent: they have destroyed many illusions concerning any kind of rapid formation of a Pacific cooperation organisation, but on the other hand — and this may be due to the mere fact of their existence — they have indeed been able to reinforce the feeling of solidarity among the Pacific nations' (Kraus and Luetkenhorst 1986, p. 109).

In 1989 PECC was strengthened and the Pacific economic cooperation process extended to the ministerial level by the formation of an inter-governmental forum,

APEC, led by Australian Prime Minister Bob Hawke. Initially a response to Australia's need for deeper integration intra-regionally into the dynamic Asia Pacific area, APEC soon captured the interest of eastern Pacific countries, including Canada and the United States. This in turn led to the formation of a 12-nation forum comprising the six ASEAN countries and Australia, Canada, Japan, Korea, New Zealand and the United States. Since then, membership has been enlarged to include China, Hong Kong and Taiwan (under a formula like that used to determine their membership in PECC) and more recently Mexico and Papua New Guinea. Agreement has also been reached to extend APEC membership to Chile with its first participation being in the APEC meetings in Indonesia in late 1994.

In June 1989 US Secretary of State James Baker endorsed Hawke's APEC initiative and at the G-7 Summit in July 1993 President Clinton announced his administration's support of the APEC Ministerial Meeting in Seattle in November 1993, emphasising the importance of APEC principles to US policy in the Asia Pacific and referring to a 'new Pacific community'.

APEC has thus emerged in the aftermath of the epoch-making events in Eastern Europe, the former Soviet Union and the Persian Gulf since 1989 as the leading policy-making group to move economic regional cooperation forward in the Asia Pacific. Its key aims are to encourage regional institution-building (including Japan and the United States in this process), to avert subregional trade wars and protectionism and to stimulate trade creation.

APEC was created out of a perceived need for a more comprehensive regional dialogue than that afforded by PECC. It has been guided by the same principles that have enabled PECC to succeed in its objectives: openness, equality and gradual evolution. So far, a positive and interdependent relationship has evolved between APEC and PECC. PECC can generate issues based on the practical problems of the private sector in the Asia Pacific region on which APEC can make policy decisions at the ministerial level. The 'work projects' undertaken by APEC have already produced benefits for the member economies and for the region as a whole, and cover areas such as trade promotion, expansion of investment and technology transfer, human resources development, energy cooperation, marine resources conservation, fisheries, and telecommunications.

APEC and PECC have become, perhaps by default, the most important 'actors' in the development and realisation of the Pacific economic cooperation idea. They are a substitute for the individual (or individuals), like Jean Monnet in the case of the EC, or perhaps even for a country (or countries) that would be expected to take the lead.

Future prospects

The development of regional economic cooperation in the Asia Pacific region in general, and the APEC process in particular, has been guided by the wisdom that processes are more important than structures. This does not mean that the institutional structure is unimportant, but rather that it should be dictated by what is required by the process.

It is clear that APEC's institutional structure will continue to evolve. It is equally clear that while APEC should be based on pragmatic approaches, it needs also to develop a vision for itself. The beauty of the APEC process is the injection of fresh leadership in each succeeding cycle by having the host of the ministerial meeting chair APEC. The host can, and indeed should, project its interest in and vision of APEC.

It is hoped that the combined force of APEC and PECC will prove effective in dealing with the North–South problems emerging in the Asia Pacific region, as well as with other issues relating to East–West relations in the expanding Pacific Rim region. With respect to North–South problems, the main focus is the relationship between the ASEAN countries and Japan. In terms of East–West relations, there is continued uneasiness about the security implications of the movement towards closer regional economic cooperation. Are these concerns still valid when the region is currently experiencing a shift from alliances to alignments? The genesis of the new Pacific regionalism is the development of regional economic interdependence; the problem is that such development has led to the emergence of a functional region rather than a geographic region. In essence, this defines who would be included and who would be excluded. APEC and PECC advocate the principle of openness or non-exclusiveness.

Yet another issue for the future is the trend towards subregional arrangements. This may be a natural tendency in view of the vastness and diversity of the Pacific region. The Canada–US Free Trade Agreement and NAFTA can be seen as special cases. By the same token, the CER Agreement between Australia and New Zealand is also a special case; as is ASEAN; not to mention the recent proliferation of subregional special economic development zones involving several countries. A case in point is the three-nation 'growth triangle' project undertaken by Thailand, Malaysia and Indonesia that aims to promote trade and economic development. It is not clear how these subregional agreements affect the realisation of the Pacific economic cooperation idea and the principles of APEC and PECC. They can become building blocks for Pacific economic cooperation, but they could also lead to regional fragmentation. Increased concern about the possibility of such fragmentation has led to increased pressures upon APEC and PECC to move more rapidly towards greater institutional integration.

This, indeed, is of much greater relevance today compared to the recent past in view of the great uncertainties in the development of the international political economy. As Borthwick (1986) suggested, 'progress toward regional cooperation will respond to more than just an internal Pacific Basin dynamic. Global economic and political forces will play an equal if not greater role in determining the pace and future direction of any cooperation arrangements'. However, the ability of governments and other socio-political forces in the various countries to properly assess the importance of their ability to anticipate and meet such challenges and to see the merit of a Pacific focus in their responses starts at home. Therefore, the agendas of APEC and PECC in the years to come will need to emphasise the importance of strengthening the national or local committees that are the real focal points in the region. A systematic regional effort to undertake this task must be based on a continuous identification and examination of the basic interests, positions and conditions of all the respective countries.

Notes

1   For earlier attempts, see Soesastro (1983) and Morley (1983).
2   The report was published as a book edited by Sir John Crawford and Saburo Okita, *Raw Materials and Pacific Economic Integration* (Crawford and Okita 1978).

References

Bandura, Y. 1980, 'The Pacific Community — a brainchild of imperialist diplomacy', *International Affairs* (Moscow), June, pp. 63–70.

Borthwick, Mark 1986, 'Pacific Basin institutions: current directions and future possibilities', *Pacific Basin: Concept and Challenges, Alternatives for the 1980s*, No. 20, Washington, DC: Centre for National Policy.

Congressional Research Service, Library of Congress 1979, 'An Asian Pacific regional economic organization: an exploratory concept paper', Paper prepared for the Committee on Foreign Relations, United States Senate, Washington, DC: US Government Printing Office.

Crawford, Sir John and Saburo Okita (eds) 1978, *Raw Materials and Pacific Economic Integration*, Canberra: Australian National University Press.

Drysdale, Peter 1978, 'An organization for Pacific trade, aid and development: regional arrangements and the resource trade', in Lawrence Krause and Hugh Patrick (eds), *Mineral Resources in the Pacific Area*, San Francisco: Federal Reserve Bank of San Francisco.

Fifield, Russell H. 1981, 'ASEAN and the Pacific community', *Asia Pacific Community*, Winter.

Gordon, Bernard K. 1969, *Towards Disengagement in Asia*, Englewood Cliffs, NJ: Prentice Hall.

———— 1981, 'Japan and the Pacific Basin proposal', *Korea & World Affairs*, Summer, pp. 268–88.

Han Sung-joo 1983, 'Political conditions of Pacific regional cooperation: theoretical and practical considerations', in Hadi Soesastro and Han Sung-joo (eds), *Pacific Economic Cooperation: The Next Phase*, Jakarta: Centre for Strategic and International Studies.

Hoon-mok Chung 1981, 'Economic integration in the Pacific Basin: a historical review', in Hang Sung-joo (ed.), *Community Building in the Pacific Region: Issues and Opportunities*, Seoul: Asiatic Research Centre, Korea University.

JERC 1966, *Measures for Trade Expansion of Developing Countries*, Tokyo: Japan Economic Research Center, October, pp. 93–134.

Kaneko, Kumao 1988, 'A new Pacific initiative: strengthening the PECC process', *Japan Review of International Affairs*, Spring/Summer.

Kraus, Willy and Wilfred Luetkenhorst 1986, *Economic Development in the Pacific Basin*, New York: St. Martin's Press.

Morley, James W. 1983, 'The Pacific Basin Movement and Japan', *Roundtable Reports*, No. 7, East Asian Institute, Columbia University.

Morris-Suzuki, Tessa 1981, 'Japan and the Pacific Basin community', *The World Today*, December, pp. 454–61.

Morrison, Charles E. 1980, 'American interest in the Pacific Community concept', *The Pacific Community Concept: Views from Eight Nations*, JCIE Papers No. 1, Tokyo: Japan Center for International Exchange, pp. 17–31.

Soesastro, Hadi 1983, 'Institutional aspects of Pacific economic cooperation', in Hadi Soesastro and Han Sung-joo (eds), *Pacific Economic Cooperation: The Next Phase*, Jakarta: Centre for Strategic and International Studies.

8   Anatomy of regionalism —————

H. W. Arndt

Regionalism is in fashion. Some years ago, Dr Saburo Okita declared 'globalism and regionalism' to be 'the two main currents in the world today' (Okita 1989). Globalism has somewhat lost its glamour since then (cf. Arndt 1992). But regionalism is still near the top of the agenda.

One reason for its almost universal popularity is that it means almost all things to all people. Before we can really decide whether to welcome or fear it, we need to define which kind of 'regionalism' we have in mind. The object of this paper is to distinguish the various meanings of 'regionalism' currently in vogue, to identify what they have in common and how they differ and in passing to say something about potential benefits and costs.

Kinds of regionalism

Preferential trading arrangements

When Okita identified regionalism as one of the two main currents in the world today he had in mind the EC and the Canada–US Free Trade Agreement. He expressed concern about 'inward-looking regionalism in Europe and North America' which 'could well be divisive' (Okita 1989, p. 10). This is perhaps the most common use of the term. Snape (1992, p. 2), for example, speaks of 'moves towards regionalism' which involve 'trade barriers and harassment against countries not in trading blocs'. Lloyd (1992, p. 3) refers to the 'growth of regional blocs' as a 'threat to the multilateral trading system'. Some authors use 'regionalisation' instead of 'regionalism'. Dutta (1992, pp. 67, 69), for instance, refers to the 'EC paradigm of economic regionalisation' though he also envisages 'continent-based regionalism'. But 'regionalisation', as

Reprinted with permission from the *Journal of Asian Economics*, Vol. 4, No. 2, 1993, pp. 271–82 (with minor editing). Copyright © 1993 by JAI Press, Inc., Greenwich, Connecticut, USA.

Lorenz (1991) has suggested, is probably better reserved for the process of regional market integration without government-initiated regional trading arrangements (RTAs).

Growth triangles

Another 'example of regionalism' in the literature is the 'growth triangle' ... linking Singapore with the neighbouring sub-national economies of Johor in Malaysia and Riau in Indonesia (Parsonage 1992). This kind of regionalism, which also goes by the name of 'de facto economic integration' (Edward Chen, cited in Howes and Bollard 1992) in a 'transnational economic zone' (Lee 1991) and of which China's southern provinces, increasingly integrated with Hong Kong and Taiwan, are even more striking examples, is clearly very different from the first.

'Open regionalism'

Drysdale and Garnaut (1993) have for some years expounded a concept of 'open regionalism' which differs from NAFTA and other RTAs in being non-discriminatory, essentially aimed at regional economic cooperation by Pacific Rim countries for reduction of barriers to trade, both official, such as tariffs and non-tariff barriers (NTBs), and others such as transport and transaction costs, and in this and other ways at the maintenance of an open world trading system in the pure GATT spirit. They see the APEC forum as embodying this notion of regionalism.

Sub-national regionalism

The notion that economic planning should concern itself with sub-national regions, assembling 'national plans by aggregating a series of regional plans' (Higgins 1989, p. 169), attained some prominence in the 1970s, without ever presenting itself as a form of 'regionalism'. As national planning has declined in favour, one hears less of it, though there is still a United Nations Centre for Regional Planning which promotes studies of rural and urban problems at the regional level. Recently, however, some commentators, observing the disintegration of the USSR and Yugoslavia, demands for secession or at least regional autonomy in Scotland, Brittany, Catalonia and Lombardy and the establishment by German state governments such as Baden–Württemberg of their own offices in Brussels, have begun to speak of a tendency towards 'sub-national regionalism' in Europe: 'The Europe of the national state seems to be moving towards a Europe of the regions' (Clark 1992). They suggest that 'the regional trend may provide a new impetus for Quebec and Kashmiri separatists, others in west China and on the Horn of Africa' (Clark 1992).

Here then are four very different notions of regionalism. All four in varying degrees imply rejection of the national economy as the sole module of the world economic system. But this is where the resemblance ends. The first three have in common that they refer to supra-national regions; they involve regional economic integration. The fourth, in contrast, involves sub-national disintegration, politically and probably economically. The first and fourth which depend on government initiative, largely aim at political objectives and involve discrimination in trade policy against non-members. Economic integration in the second and third is market driven and is, at least in principle, consistent with the GATT postulate of non-discrimination. In the first three, economic integration can vary in 'depth' from liberalisation of intra-regional product markets (trade in goods and services) to liberalisation of factor markets (capital, labour, information), harmonisation and functional cooperation, to monetary and ultimately political union. What is the significance of these differences?

Economic integration

The essential common feature of the three supra-national kinds of regionalism — we can for the moment ignore the fourth — is economic integration. Drysdale and Garnaut (1993, p. 189) define economic integration as:

> movement toward one price for any piece of merchandise, service or factor of production . . . Dis-integration persists because of barriers, or resistances, to trade. We define resistances to trade as phenomena that prevent or retard the immediate movement of commodities [service or factors] in response to price differentials.

They further distinguish 'objective resistances', which include official barriers to trade (principally protection) as well as transport and other transaction costs, and 'subjective resistances', in which they include psychological and institutional factors such as perceptions of risk and uncertainty and imperfections in the information available to firms (Drysdale and Garnaut 1993). One might object that information costs are as objective as transport costs and risk reflects information costs; the subjective category therefore seems unnecessary. But with this qualification, the Drysdale–Garnaut definition of economic integration is extremely helpful.

There is a presumption that economic integration, the reduction of resistances, improves welfare through more efficient static resource allocation (Pareto optimality). It may also make even more important contributions to welfare by increasing dynamic efficiency through economies of scale, through the encouragement of investment and technological advance and other external economies in a widening market and through the spur of competition. But the welfare-enhancing effect of economic integration, as Viner (1950) pointed out, is only presumptive. It is unambiguous if the reduction in resistances is non-discriminatory. If it favours some sections of the market over others, the net effect on welfare depends on the balance between trade creation and trade diversion. Integration in the product market is the subject matter of the theory of protection and customs unions and it covers much of the economics of regionalism.

The economic aspects of human welfare, of course, are not everything. Many of the contentious aspects of regionalism have to do with shares, the distribution of the benefits of economic efficiency and growth among groups, especially regional groups, and with cultural values. But the economic theory of integration addresses what most would regard as the important issues.

'Internationalisation of protection'

With the important exception of the EC, which from the beginning was motivated by the political objective of peace through a United Europe, regionalism in the first sense of preferential regional trading arrangements aims at what Harry Johnson (1967, p. 28) called the 'internationalisation of protection'. It was Raul Prebisch who, as Executive Secretary of the UN Economic Commission for Latin America, concerned about the failure of small national markets to induce significant industrial development in Latin America, in 1959 floated the idea of free trade areas for groups of developing countries: 'Preferential treatment is needed inside the area to promote specialisation in industrial products and primary commodities' (Prebisch 1959, p. 267). The following years saw a flurry of such schemes: the Central American Common Market and Latin American Free Trade Association (LAFTA) in Latin America, the Arab Common Market in the Middle East, another in East Africa (Robson 1968). None of these for long survived political and economic friction among their member countries. The two that did, the European Free Trade Association (EFTA) in Europe and ASEAN in Asia, owed their survival to different motivation — defensive cooperation among north European non-members of the EC in the case of the former, political and security motives for cohesion in the case of the latter. There is little reason to believe that in any of these schemes the gains from trade creation would have outweighed the losses of trade diversion had intra-regional, and therefore discriminatory, trade liberalisation been carried very far.

The free trade area schemes initiated by the United States in recent years, the Canada–US Free Trade Agreement, and NAFTA, with its possible extension to the whole hemisphere, also have an ingredient of internationalisation of protection, as does the CER Agreement between Australia and New Zealand. All three involve intra-regional trade liberalisation which discriminates against outsiders. But the risk of serious trade diversion through the Canada–US Free Trade Agreement and the CER is relatively slight because the pairs of national economies were already closely integrated, and trade liberalisation was largely based on the MFN principle. How far NAFTA, with its incorporation of Mexico within the US protective system and possible 'hub and spoke' links further afield, will damage the trade of third countries remains to be seen. A US policy of bilateral preferential links with individual countries in the Asia Pacific region would inevitably give rise to concern in others, especially China, of being left out and discriminated against.

Deep integration in Europe

The EC, with its Common Agricultural Policy (CAP), its role in the Multifibre Arrangement (MFA) and its use of NTBs to protect its steel and textile industries, among others, has also from the start constituted an exercise in the internationalisation of protection. There is still some anxiety in the rest of the world that the EC may yet turn into a 'Fortress Europe'. Statements such as that by the President of the Commission, Jacques Delors, in his introduction to the Cecchini Report——'it cannot be the purpose of an economic union to surrender its internal market to foreign competition' (Delors 1988) —are not calculated to allay such fears. What distinguishes the EC from all other regional trading arrangements is its objective of political union and the 'deep' integration it has pursued with this objective in mind.

The predominant motive which led Robert Schuman and others at the end of the Second World War to envisage the creation of a European Common Market and Economic Community, and to work for this objective for thirty years, was to secure peace. While obviously appreciative of the potential economic benefits, they saw these as stepping stones towards a United Europe. After the collapse of the USSR and German reunification, the political imperative of binding a resurgent Germany into Europe has seemed even more urgent.

The distinguishing feature of economic integration in the EC is its 'depth'. Beyond the creation of a common product market through intra-regional liberalisation of trade in goods and services, the EC has pursued a program of 'deep integration' in various forms: far-reaching liberalisation of factor markets (for capital, information and, less completely, labour); harmonisation of social welfare, environmental and other policies and of legal rules and standards; functional cooperation in transport, energy, education and other aspects of infrastructure; and, most ambitiously, monetary union and a single currency, with political union as the ultimate goal approached through the operation of the European Commission, Council and Parliament, serviced by a large secretariat in Brussels.

Considerable sections of public opinion, especially but not only in Britain, remain unreconciled to the surrender of national sovereignty required by a United Europe. There is widespread resentment of the Brussels bureaucracy, of what is seen as 'nit-picking interference in national standards and ways of doing things, lack of responsibility to the people of the community, and determined centralism' (McGuinness 1992). There are concerns, in France and elsewhere, that a United Europe, rather than contain German domination, may merely serve to reinforce it.

There is a range of dilemmas with which the EC has been faced by the collapse of the USSR: on the one hand, the opportunities of 'European economic space', a second enlargement east as well as south; on the other hand, the potential problems of a greatly widened membership, including much more diverse economies; the huge financial burden of reconstruction in east Germany and in the Commonwealth of Independent States; and the flood of refugees. No less worrying is the flaring up, in response to the inflow of refugees and non-European migrants, of xenophobia and race prejudice, and of the petty ethnic nationalism which manifests itself in demands for sub-national regional autonomy if not independence. It is the latter that constitutes our fourth category of regionalism. It goes beyond 'subsidiarity' (decentralisation of decision-making from Brussels to national governments within the EC) to devolution of power from national to sub-national regional governments.

Finally, there is the question mark which now hangs over monetary union. The difficulties of bringing within a single currency area national economies as different in financial strength and macroeconomic policy stance as Germany and Britain, or even France and Italy, were underlined by the financial crisis of September 1992. It is not obvious that the benefits of economic integration in the sense of liberalisation of product and factor markets cannot be obtained without monetary union. The 'resistances' to trade and factor mobility arising from exchange risk may be less than those resulting from drastic macroeconomic imbalances and corrective measures. 'Microeconomic optimisation', to use Dutta's terminology, may be obtainable without a 'macroeconomic core' (Dutta 1992). Monetary union is necessary for political union, but probably not for economic integration.

Deep integration in Asia

The possibility of economic integration without monetary union is being demonstrated in Asia. There could hardly be a more striking contrast than that between 'regionalism' in Europe and 'regionalism' in Asia. What has been happening in recent years in the coastal provinces of China and in the Johor–Singapore–Riau Growth Triangle is deep integration. Official resistances are largely ignored and transaction cost resistances are overcome by factor mobility. The process is market driven, initiated by business enterprise, not by inter-governmental negotiation. There are no plans for monetary union, and little if any functional cooperation or formal harmonisation by national governments.

During the decades of relative economic isolation of Maoist China from the world market economy, Hong Kong served as China's 'window', as an entrepôt trade centre and, with the inflow of refugee capital and labour, as industrial trade partner. Political barriers meanwhile precluded economic relations of the mainland with Taiwan and South Korea. In the last ten years this situation has been dramatically transformed. To quote the author of a recent account of the economic integration of Hong Kong, Taiwan and South Korea with the mainland of China:

> China's inauguration of its open-door policy in 1979 coincided with the need of the East Asian NIEs to change their economic structures. Wages had been rising rapidly in the NIEs, forcing a shift from labour-intensive manufacturing to capital-intensive and skill-intensive activities. The East Asian NIEs have

taken advantage of China's open-door policy through international trade and investment channels. Hong Kong and Taiwan, for their part, have moved their labour-intensive processes to the mainland on a large scale (Sung 1992, p. 149).

There are few, if any, parallels to the contribution that market driven economic integration is making to economic growth in the coastal regions of south China. The stimulus of deregulation and opening-up and the advantages of geographical proximity have been powerfully reinforced by the lubricant of cultural affinity between the business people, large and small, of the 'three Chinas'.

This process of economic integration, moreover, has occurred despite an array of formal obstacles. China has had no diplomatic relations with Taiwan and (until recently) with South Korea. Trade, investment and travel links with China have remained formally illegal in Taiwan. Hong Kong, under the Sino-British agreement, remains a separate customs territory with its own currency and is to continue to do so beyond 1997. Immigration from China to Hong Kong and Taiwan is strictly controlled. Although China abolished tariffs on Taiwanese goods in 1980 in an attempt to promote trade links, they were replaced by an 'adjustment tax' in 1983. But none of these obstacles has significantly restrained the flow of trade, investment and people across national boundaries. Tariffs are evaded by extensive smuggling, migration controls by illegal movements of people. The Hong Kong dollar circulates widely — unofficially — in Guangdong province. Besides its own massive investments in China, Hong Kong serves as an entrepôt for Taiwanese and Korean trade and investment flows to the mainland.

The Tiananmen incident has, paradoxically, further contributed to the regionalisation of the Chinese economy. As the authority of the central government has diminished, the regional development of the coastal provinces by newly industrialising economy (NIE) enterprise has become easier and is said to be spreading further north into the central provinces. At the same time, direct economic links between Taiwan and Fujian province are coming to be more openly accepted on both sides, and there are now prospects of direct links between South Korea and the east coast of China in a 'Yellow Sea Economic Region'.

A parallel development on a small scale is under way in the growth triangle formed by Singapore with the Malaysian state of Johor to the north and Indonesia's Riau province, and especially the island of Batam, to the south. Singapore industry needs land and labour, Indonesia and (less enthusiastically) Malaysia are keen to attract investment for industrial development, for the promotion of financial and tourist services, for infrastructure and skill formation. Here, again, the creation of a 'transnational economic zone' is primarily market driven, with Singapore and multinational companies riding the wave. There is already talk about other such growth triangles being formed further north, for instance, linking Medan, Penang, Northwest Malaysia and South Thailand (Lee 1991, p. 24).

To call Asian economic regionalism market driven is not to deny that national governments have played an important role. Soon after the announcement of the open-door policy, the Chinese government took the initiative in 1979 of authorising Guangdong and Fujian provinces to form Special Economic Zones (SEZs), with autonomy in trade and investment, aimed at inflow from Hong Kong and Taiwan in particular. In 1988 the Liaoning and Shandong peninsulas were designated open areas, with an eye to closer economic links with South Korea. China has at various times made trade overtures to Taiwan, and the Taiwan government from 1987 eased its trade and exchange controls with the mainland, if only in recognition of its inability to stem the flow. Regular, almost routine, talks between Beijing and Taipei are now held on economic, cultural, legal, environmental and other matters (Klintworth 1992).

National governments were even more conspicuous at the inception of the Johor–Singapore–Riau Growth Triangle. The concept was announced by Goh Chok Tong, then Singapore's Deputy Prime Minister, in December 1989, following an initiative in 1988 by the Johor state government for a policy of 'twinning' with Singapore to promote the state's industrial development through relocation of labour-intensive Singapore industry and in 1989 by agreement between Singapore and Indonesia on liberalisation of investment on Batam. The concept was endorsed by Indonesia's President Suharto and Malaysia's Prime Minister Mahathir in June 1990. All three governments have cooperated in various ways. There is a Singapore–Indonesia agreement for the development of tourism, water resources and industry in Riau and a joint venture to construct the Batam Industrial Park involving Singapore state and Indonesian conglomerate capital. On the Indonesian side, government is indirectly involved in the Batam Industrial Development Authority through its chairman, the Indonesian Minister for Research and Technology, Dr Habibie. Nonetheless, even here, the role of government is seen as secondary, to facilitate regional economic integration through trade and factor flows, 'to assist the private sector to maximise the opportunities, and to reduce the political, social, equity and federal-versus-state problems that are sometimes encountered' (Lee 1991, p. x).

Regionalism in substance, though not in name, may also be seen in operation in such projects for transnational economic cooperation as that sponsored by the Asian Development Bank among the economies of mainland Southeast Asia, Burma, Thailand, the three countries of Indochina and Yunnan province in China (Asian Development Bank 1992). As economic policy in all of them is becoming increasingly outward-looking, trade and investment across national borders is getting under way spontaneously, but governments see advantage in assisting this process by cooperative improvement of infrastructure — roads, railways, airlines, bridges, ports, river navigation and electric power.

Asian economic regionalism is economic (commercial, financial, developmental) not political in its motivation. It does not aim at political unity. There is no plan to turn any of the transnational economic regions into customs unions or free trade areas or into monetary unions with a single currency, a central bank or macroeconomic policy coordination. In all of these respects it is very different indeed from the EC or NAFTA.

The regionalism of the Asian growth triangles is not without political risks and costs. Over the Chinese coastal ones hangs uncertainty about China's political development and about the 'one country, two systems' compromise for Hong Kong and Taiwan. In relation to the Johor–Singapore–Riau Growth Triangle there are reservations in Malaysia about Singapore–Chinese domination and 'cheap-labour' industrial development in Johor and worries in Indonesia about the social effects of mass tourism and of concentration of large numbers of women workers brought to Batam from other parts of Indonesia (Lee 1991, p. 104). But, for the present, this kind of regionalism is an almost unqualified success story.

Pacific 'open regionalism'

The 'open regionalism' described by Drysdale and Garnaut and embodied in APEC is quite another kind. Like the EC–NAFTA version, and unlike the Asian growth triangles, it is a cooperative enterprise of national governments and its primary concern is intra-regional trade liberalisation. But like the Asian kind of economic regionalism, and unlike the EC (though not NAFTA), it has economic rather than political objectives; it aims at neither political nor monetary union; and, above all, it is emphatically and deliberately non-discriminatory. Its chief object is trade liberalisation, but while supportive of the GATT process of multilateral trade negotiations it seeks to promote unilateral non-discriminatory (MFN-based) liberalisation, rather than bilateral or multilateral trade deals. As Drysdale and Garnaut have put it, the hope is that national governments, rather than being caught in the prisoner's dilemma of negotiated 'concessions', will generate the 'prisoner's delight' of observing the highly beneficial effects of each country's liberalisation on its own trade expansion (Drysdale and Garnaut 1993, p. 187).

APEC is not wholly inter-governmental. It is associated with private cooperative initiatives in the Pacific region, such as the regular PAFTAD conferences and PBEC, and itself developed from the trilateral PECC (cf. Harris 1991). The objective is economic integration, freeing product and factor markets from official and unofficial resistances. In this respect, APEC is quite consistent with the market driven process of regionalisation that is occurring in the growth triangles. Indeed, APEC spokesmen like to envisage a gradual coalescence of these two approaches to economic integration, allowing latitude for differences of focus, pace and procedure. As Elek (1992, p. 1) has put it, 'APEC's guiding principles stipulate that cooperation should be outward-looking, building consensus on a gradually broader range of issues'.

But APEC is on the way to becoming an inter-governmental institution, with a ministerial council and a secretariat (in Singapore). It is planning to extend cooperation from trade liberalisation to various fields of functional cooperation in the Asia Pacific region, such as improvements in transport and telecommunications to reduce transaction costs, streamlining of dispute settlement procedures and even harmonisation of domestic legislation relating to environmental and other standards (Elek 1992). In this respect, APEC looks like following in the footsteps of the EC, with the risk of similar pitfalls. Like the EC, it also confronts the dilemma of enlargement, how many members can be added without making the institution too cumbersome and exposing it to the hazard of politicisation. The UN Regional Commission — the Economic and Social Commission for Asia and the Pacific (ESCAP) — serves as a warning example in both respects.

What distinguishes APEC, at least in the minds of its smaller members like Australia which have most to lose from the EC, NAFTA and other preferential arrangements, is the emphasis on non-discrimination and defence of the open multilateral world trading system which was created after the Second World War, primarily through US vision and drive. The system is now in danger of fracturing, not least because the United States appears to have weakened in its faith in it. Many see a world economy divided into three contending trade blocs, centred on Washington, Berlin and Tokyo, or at any rate into regional groupings indulging in varying degrees of trade discrimination. In so far as APEC seeks to counter this threat to open multilateralism it could be described as anti-regional, opposed to discriminatory, divisive regionalism. In so far as a major *raison d'être* of APEC is to bind the United States and Japan in the same cooperative trade liberalisation process, and thus minimise the risk of bloc formation, it could even be said to have a political purpose — trade diplomacy at the highest level.

Conclusion

The purpose of this paper has not been to put forward specific policies or measures. It has been analytical, to dissect and differentiate the various kinds of regionalism in the current large literature on the subject and thus to warn against facile support for, or opposition to, 'regionalism' in general. But I suspect my prejudices have not remained entirely below the surface. I favour economic integration in the sense of liberalisation of product and factor markets (subject only to concern about the risk of conflict engendered by complete freedom of international movements of labour); and I hope that the domestic political pressures behind protectionist and discriminatory trade policies can be contained.

But this still leaves a question in my mind. If integration of markets is unambiguously desirable, manna from heaven when it is market driven and a public good when promoted by governments, why stop at regions? Why not go beyond regionalisation to globalisation, beyond regionalism to globalism?

One answer is that globalism is unrealistic. Even regionalism, as we have seen, runs into political obstacles, resistance by vested interests, from French farmers and Australian manufacturers to nationalist politicians and entrenched bureaucrats, who see themselves threatened by uncontrolled market forces. But this answer merely questions the feasibility, not the desirability, of a totally integrated world market economy, without national or regional economic boundaries. Would it be desirable if the single market of the EC were extended to embrace all of Europe and beyond into Africa and Asia, if NAFTA became the all-American free trade area, if APEC membership were widened indefinitely to include all comers?

I suspect that the ideal of a worldwide integrated market economy abstracts unduly from all the various kinds of market failure which even libertarians admit require government intervention. And once the need for government is conceded, the diseconomies of scale in political and bureaucratic management which are already in evidence in the EC, and which within the EC are giving rise to demands for more citizen participation in decentralised decision-making, would probably counsel against anything like a single world government of a single world market.

The idealist's reply to such scepticism is presumably that this is a bridge we can think about crossing when we come to it. Meanwhile, there is a long way to go in liberalisation of markets where the benefits clearly outweigh the costs.

References

Arndt, H .W. 1992, 'The economics of globalism', *Quarterly Review*, Banca Nazionale del Lavoro, March.

Asian Development Bank (ADB) 1992, *Subregional Economic Cooperation: Framework Report*, Manila, October.

Clark, A. 1992, 'Europe looks for its roots', *Australian Financial Review*, 4 September.

Delors, J. 1988, 'Introduction to Cecchini Report', *Europa '92—Der Vorteil des Binnenmarktes*, Baden-Baden Nomos Verlag.

Drysdale, P. and R. Garnaut 1993, 'The Pacific: an application of a general theory of economic integration', in C. Fred Bergsten and Marcus Noland (eds), *Pacific Dynamism and the International Economic System*, Washington, DC: Institute for International Economics.

Dutta, M. 1992, 'Economic regionalisation in Western Europe: Asia Pacific economics (macroeconomic core: microeconomic optimisation)', *American Economic Review*, 82(2), May.

Elek, A. 1992, 'Pacific economic cooperation: policy choices for the 1990s', *Asian-Pacific Economic Literature*, 6(1).

Harris, S. F. 1991, 'Varieties of Pacific economic cooperation', *Pacific Review*, 4(4).

Higgins, B. 1989, *The Road Less Travelled: A Development Economist's Quest*, Canberra: Australian National University Press.

Howes, S. and A. Bollard 1992, 'Economic reform and internationalisation: China and the Pacific region', *Pacific Economic Papers*, No. 208, June, Australia–Japan Research Centre, Canberra.

Johnson, H. G. 1967, *Economic Policies towards Less Developed Countries*, Washington, DC: The Brookings Institution.

Klintworth, G. 1992, 'Taiwan winning with sugar-coated bullets', *Canberra Times*, 22 September.

Lee Tsao Yuan (ed.) 1991, *Growth Triangle: The Johor–Singapore–Riau Experience*, Singapore: Institute of Southeast Asian Studies.

Lloyd, P. J. 1992, 'Regionalisation and world trade', *OECD Economic Studies*, 18, Spring.

Lorenz, D. 1991, 'Regionalisation versus regionalism — problems of change in the world economy', *Intereconomics*, 26, pp. 3–10.

McGuinness, P. P. 1992, 'Europe finds a whipping boy', *The Australian*, 20 September.

Okita, S. 1989, *Emerging Forms of Global Markets and the Nature of Interdependence in an Increasingly Multipolar World*, Paris: OECD Development Centre.

Parsonage, J. 1992, 'Southeast Asia's "growth triangle": a subregional response to global transformation', *International Journal of Urban and Regional Research*, 16(2), pp. 307–17.

Prebisch, R. 1959, 'Commercial policy in underdeveloped countries', *American Economic Review*, May.

Robson, P. 1968, *Economic Integration in Africa*, London: Allen and Unwin.

Snape, R. H. 1992, 'Bilateral initiatives: should Australia join?', mimeo, Conference on Regionalism in the World Economy, Glenelg, South Australia, July.

Sung, Yun-wing 1992, 'The economic integration of Hong Kong Taiwan and South Korea with the mainland of China', in Ross Garnaut and Liu Guogang (eds), *Economic Reform and Internationalisation*, Sydney: Allen and Unwin.

Viner, J. 1950, *The Customs Union Issue*, New York: Carnegie Endowment for International Peace.

9 Origins of the Pacific Community ——————

This Summary Report was based on the discussions at the Pacific Community Seminar and the conclusions reached at the Round-Up and Closing session of the seminar on 17 September 1980. It was presented by the Chairman to a public session of the seminar on 18 September 1980. This Seminar, chaired by the Chancellor of the Australian National University, Professor Sir John Crawford, in response to a request from Australian Prime Minister Fraser and Japanese Prime Minister Ohira, was the origin and the first of the PECC conferences.

The prime motivating force serving to promote the idea of a Pacific Community has been the rapid economic growth in the region, combined with the trend towards increasing economic 'interdependence' and the increasing significance of the region in global economic terms. Notable in this connection has been the rise of Japan as a major economic power and the major expansion of its exports, the striking growth in many of the developing countries of the region as well as the relatively slower growth, over the same period, in the Western European economies. The role of private enterprise as a major contributor to growth in the region was recognised. This has given rise to a situation in which economic progress in the Pacific region is of major importance to all the countries represented at the seminar.

The huge expansion of trade and investment flows within the region in recent decades caused the meeting to agree that something of a Pacific Community already existed. It was present within and in the contacts of many large corporations within the region, in the role played by regional groupings of businesspeople and scholars, and in the interests of institutions in many countries in the region.

However, despite the considerable growth of a sense of community in the Pacific area, there were important problems in the economic relations of Pacific countries which blocked the full realisation of the region's potential for productive economic exchange. Many of these problems derived from a failure of mutual understanding between the countries of the region, based on historical, racial, cultural, linguistic and ideological differences as well as disparities of economic development.

While expanding all Pacific countries' economic opportunities, there were some ways in which increased economic 'interdependence' in itself had given rise to

Reprinted with permission from *Pacific Economic Cooperation: Suggestions for Action*, edited by Sir John Crawford (assisted by Greg Seow), pp. 27–32 (with minor editing). Copyright © 1981 by Heinemann Educational Books (Asia) Ltd, Singapore; Pacific Community Seminar 1981.

problems in the Pacific region, for example when some countries within the region reacted to pressures for structural adjustment by introducing policies that brought about a retreat from 'interdependence'. There were also problems if the content of 'interdependence' did not seem to lead to an equitable distribution of benefits among countries.

There were signs, too, that the sense of community in the Pacific may be under great stress in the more difficult climate of the 1980s than in the 1960s and 1970s. The 1980s are bringing greater protectionist pressures in many countries, increased competition in international trade, a trend towards regionalism elsewhere in the world and heightened problems with access to resources.

There have also been a number of political forces giving rise to an interest in enhanced cooperation in the Pacific region, including the ending of colonial ties of many regional countries since the Second World War, the remarkable economic development of Japan, the birth of ASEAN as a grouping and its economic progress, as well as the emergence of more outward-looking policies in the People's Republic of China in recent years.

There was a considerable body of opinion that the establishment of new institutional arrangements to promote consultation, including among governments, would help to manage these problems. There was unanimous approval of the idea that the exploration of this possibility was worthy of continued effort.

In spite of the great expansion of economic contacts that had occurred, some participants thought that there was still a major need for Pacific countries to 'get to know each other' better before steps were taken towards creation of new, formal inter-governmental institutions for regional cooperation. There was a need for greater 'socialisation' among the peoples and countries of the region. Some participants considered that this was a necessary 'pre-condition' for further progress on substantive questions of economic cooperation. Others considered that this was more likely to develop out of the practice of cooperation on substantive issues. Nevertheless, there was a widespread recognition that the present lack of mutual understanding was a constraint on building a sense of community in the Pacific and that, as a result, it would be necessary to work on a cautious, and gradual basis, in trying to develop areas of fruitful cooperation through a process of consensus among regional countries, similar to that by which ASEAN itself has developed.

In this regard, special emphasis was placed on the need to satisfy the concerns of the developing countries, including members of ASEAN and the South Pacific Forum, that their particular interests would be fully taken into account in any new wider regional arrangement, and to ensure that it offers advantages to them. Indeed, the need to meet these interests should be taken as a premise of any future developments.

Participants from ASEAN countries expressed a number of concerns about a Pacific Community which they would want to see overcome, including:

1   that it must not undermine the strength and cohesion of ASEAN;

2   that it should not have hidden political motivations which could conflict *inter alia* with its non-aligned approach;

3   that it must not result in new forms of neo-colonialism;

4   that it should not lead to increased dependence on or domination by the major industrialised economies of the region at the expense of important extra-regional relationships, but should result instead in the latter taking greater account of ASEAN interests especially in the field of trade liberalisation;

5   that it must not involve 'divide and rule' tactics so far as broad developing country interests in the North–South dialogue are concerned;

6   that it must not undermine existing regional and multilateral arrangements;

7   that it must not lead to increased rigidity which might hinder the operation of the principle of comparative advantage, but rather it should have the opposite effect;

8   that it should strengthen ASEAN's bargaining position in commercial negotiations; and

9   that it must bring about more meaningful results than have been achieved thus far on a bilateral basis. It was generally felt that there was scope for pursuing these interests among ASEAN and Pacific countries in a pragmatic and constructive way.

In the case of the South Pacific island developing countries, concern was expressed about the need for a cautious and unhurried approach; about whether a multilateral arrangement would facilitate the achievement of comparative advantage; about their limited resource bases and the consequent need for their special interests to be taken into account; and about the possibility that greater concessions could be won by dealing with the major industrialised economies of the region bilaterally. In this latter context, it was noted that the pooling of industrialised countries' efforts to assist the South Pacific countries may help the South Pacific on some issues.

There was some discussion of the need to accommodate in some way the interests of those South Pacific countries whose citizens were not present at the seminar, and South Pacific participants suggested that something like the method of representation at the seminar, including the presence of the Director of the South Pacific Bureau for Economic Cooperation, would be appropriate at future meetings.

Participants thought that it was natural that ASEAN and the South Pacific Forum would wish to ensure that their integrity was not impaired by any new Pacific regional organisation. The nature and form of any Pacific Community needed to be designed to meet this requirement. Participants recognised the importance of accommodating the global interests of the United States, Japan and other Pacific countries within any Pacific Community and of strengthening the resistance to protectionism to accommodate dynamic industrial development within the region. Attention was drawn to the interest of all Pacific countries in a cooperative economic relationship between the United States and Japan.

There was considerable discussion of the desirability of keeping participation in Pacific economic cooperation open. While countries participating in the seminar would comprise the core for the Pacific Cooperation Committee (described later in the recommendations), it was considered desirable for the Pacific Latin American and socialist countries to participate in the activities of the proposed task forces on substantive issues of interest to them. Wider participation in the Pacific Cooperation Committee itself could be considered in due course.

Participants were of the view that given the particular conditions facing the Pacific region, it would not be sufficient to rely on existing models of cooperation applying elsewhere in the world. A new approach was required. A new set of objectives and 'rules of the game' were required for the Pacific Community. Among the special features identified were the need to avoid military/security issues to create a sense of community without creating a sense of threat; that EEC-style discriminatory trading arrangements were inappropriate in the Pacific; and that it was necessary to 'hasten slowly', to see the full blossoming of the Pacific Community idea as a longer term objective, and to proceed towards long-term goals step-by-step, with each intermediate step being useful in itself, and not dependent for success on further steps being taken.

It was also necessary to ensure that existing bilateral, regional and global mechanisms for cooperation are not undermined by any new wider regional arrangement and that it be complementary with them; that arrangements should be outward-looking; that there was a need for an 'organic approach', building up private arrangements already in existence in the Pacific, including such bodies as PBEC, the PAFTAD conference series and other privately-based activities; and a need to involve academics, businesspeople and governments jointly in this cooperative enterprise.

Other special features of Pacific cooperation include the need to avoid unnecessarily bureaucratic structures; the need for a fairly loose and as far as possible non-institutionalised structure, recognising that while disputes settlement may prove difficult in sensitive areas, discussion of problems may contribute towards ameliorating them; the need for all members to be placed on an equal footing (that is, no EEC-style associate membership); the need to concentrate attention on areas of mutual regional interest; and the need to make substantive progress in improving upon the benefits emanating from existing bilateral, global and regional arrangements.

There was considerable discussion of the characteristics of issues which lent themselves to substantive cooperation among Pacific countries. They should be issues with some prospect of rendering gains to all participants. They should be important issues and so, unavoidably, they would sometimes be controversial. They should be issues that are not being managed effectively, and are not likely to be managed effectively, through bilateral consultations and negotiations, or through the established multilateral mechanisms.

Three areas that received widespread endorsement as proper subjects for further cooperation and consultation among Pacific countries were industrialisation, trade expansion, structural adjustment and related questions of protection and trade liberalisation; energy production, use and trade; and direct investment, including codes of behaviour in international investment. Structural adjustment and trade liberalisation were clearly the highest priority issues for participants from developing countries.

Among the more commonly favoured of the other issues suggested were cultural and educational exchanges; communications; transport (including civil aviation and shipping); agriculture; food security and agricultural commodity issues; mineral security, trade and commodity issues; Pacific fisheries and ocean resources, including scientific study on the Pacific Ocean; capital markets and financial flows; relations between China and other Pacific countries; and, finally, population movements (including refugees). It was thought to be important to include some issues of importance to the South Pacific, and here the transport and communications issues were considered relevant.

Not all of these issues could be immediately incorporated into a program of increased regional cooperation. This is reflected in the following recommendations. There was a general consensus that existing bilateral, regional and multilateral institutions need to be supplemented to deal with important issues that arise in Pacific regional economic cooperation. It was recognised that considerable regional exchanges have developed among the business and academic communities, but there was a need to strengthen the involvement of governments in this process. This fact points to a need for a new forum for consultation on major regional policy issues. Such an arrangement would be designed to promote mutual understanding and a habit of cooperation among Pacific countries, enabling them to take advantage of opportunities, and to solve problems that could be damaging to the expansion of economic relations as they emerge.

Advance must be step-by-step. The first goal should be to build arrangements that are loosely structured but purposeful and which are worthwhile in themselves and encourage the practice of substantive cooperation on a regional basis. A special characteristic would be the involvement of academics, businesspeople, and government personalities. It is useful to continue to explore the merits of a formal institutional structure, and important to ensure that other efforts are consistent with, but not dependent on, the eventual emergence of such an organisation.

An essential element in Pacific regional cooperation is the furthering of the economic aims and interests of the ASEAN group of countries and the South Pacific Forum. One of the useful means to promote this Pacific cooperative process is to focus priorities around the development of regional issues, including global issues in the regional context. Regional issues means issues which have regional causes and/or implications, and which can best be tackled through regional approaches. A number of regional issues which can be usefully developed and which can serve as the means to promote further Pacific regional cooperation were identified.

The seminar therefore recommended that a standing committee of about twenty-five persons be established to coordinate an expansion of information exchange within the region and to set up task forces to undertake major studies of a number of issues for regional cooperation. The committee, which could usefully be called the Pacific Cooperation Committee (PCC), would be unofficial, private and informal. It would advantageously have a designated contact institution in each country. The committee should include a mixed group of business, academic, professional and government persons of considerable authority. The seminar noted, in this context, the contribution of Dr Thanat Khoman, Dr Saburo Okita and Mr Richard Holbrooke to its own deliberations.

The committee would require secretarial assistance. An existing institution could be invited and assisted to provide support for the committee. A prime responsibility of the PCC would be to establish task forces in agreed areas to explore substantive issues for regional economic cooperation, to review their reports and transmit them to governments, with such comments as they may wish to make. The committee would also usefully continue the exploration, begun in this seminar, of a possible future permanent institutional structure for Pacific cooperation. The members of the committee would be drawn initially from North American and Western Pacific market economies.

Participation in each task force may sensibly involve countries of the wider Pacific region who are interested in and share the objectives of the exercise.

The committee would establish task forces to undertake studies and to report to it upon some of the following issues: trade (including market access problems and structural adjustment associated with industrialisation in the developing countries); direct investment (including guidelines for investors and harmonisation of foreign investment policies); energy (including access to markets, assurance of continued supply, alternative forms, conservation and research exchanges); Pacific marine resources; and international services such as transportation, communication, and education exchanges.

In the work of the task forces we would expect considerable support from established research institutions. In addition, an existing institution or institutions would be strengthened to facilitate an enhanced exchange of information among the various private bodies concerned with regional affairs, including business sector organisations such as PBEC, and to provide a basis for continuity in the activities for the PAFTAD conference series among Pacific scholars.

The final recommendation was that the Chairman of the seminar should, when he reports to governments, advise interested governments on arrangements necessary to establish the PCC, its secretariat, and questions of funding, including their need to consult with non-governmental groups.

10 The East Asian trading bloc: an analytical history

Peter A. Petri

Three major historical developments are important for understanding East Asian [1] interdependence. The first is the development of Asian treaty ports in the nineteenth century, which established a network of trade driven by major ports such as Singapore, Hong Kong, Manila and Shanghai. A second is Japan's imperial expansion, which created a very high level of economic integration among the economies of northern East Asia. Finally, the spectacular growth of the region's economies is emerging as a new force for integration today: as East Asian countries are becoming increasingly important to each other, they are beginning to invest heavily in linkages that are very likely to increase their intra-regional bias.

It is also possible to identify forces that have worked against regional integration in the post-war period. These include the central role of the United States in the post-war Pacific economy, the rapid economic development of the region, which enabled its economies to enter many new global markets, and the general integration of the world economy due to trade liberalisation and improvements in transport and communications. This paper attempts to trace how the changing balance of these pro- and anti-regional forces has led to the complex pattern of rises and declines that have characterised East Asian economic integration.

Determinants of interdependence

Bilateral trade patterns and their determinants usually receive little attention in the economic analysis of international trade flows. Economists usually chide non-economists for concerning themselves with bilateral or regional trade flows when, at least according to some popular theoretical works, bilateral trade flows are analytically

Reprinted from *Regionalism and Rivalry: Japan and the United States in Pacific Asia*, edited by Jeffrey A. Frankel and Miles Kahler, pp. 21–48 (with deletions). Copyright © 1993 by the National Bureau of Economic Research. Reprinted with permission from the University of Chicago Press, Chicago, USA.

uninteresting and even indeterminate. [2] Yet the pattern of bilateral flows is far from random and exhibits remarkable stability over time. It would be difficult to understand this stability without reference to large differences in transaction costs across alternative bilateral linkages.

The most obvious candidate for explaining the differential intensity of bilateral linkages is transport cost. Studies of bilateral trade patterns typically show that bilateral trade is negatively related to the distance separating the partners (see, for example, Linnemann 1966; and Frankel 1993, also Chapter 19, this volume). Yet the strong empirical effect of distance is hard to reconcile with the facts of transport technology. Transport costs amount to only a few percentage points of the value of international trade, with much of the cost accounted for in arranging for shipment and the loading and unloading of products (Leontief 1973). Thus, while transport costs can vary greatly across products and modes of transport, they do not vary much with distance itself. Nor is there evidence that bilateral flows were much affected by the large fluctuations in transport costs that took place during the oil price shocks of the 1970s, for example.

So the empirical importance of distance is most likely due, not to distance itself, but to factors correlated with distance. Important among these may be human and physical assets that facilitate trade, on both sides of a trading relationship. Investments in such assets are more likely to be made among physically and culturally proximate trade partners. These assets may include knowledge about the partner's language, culture, markets and business practices. They may also include a network of personal or business relationships and business reputations abroad.

The importance of these factors is underscored by the pervasive role of institutions that economise on transactions costs in international trade. International trade is often intra-firm trade (Lawrence 1991); it is likely to be mediated by international banks (such as through letters of credit and other instruments that enable the firm to shift the risks and information requirements involved in international deals to banks); and in many countries it is dominated by large, specialised international trading companies.

The level of international transactions costs depends in part on past investments in physical infrastructure, information and education. Often, the investments required to reduce transactions costs involve substantial scale economies, and so transactions costs across a bilateral link will be lower in proportion to the activity across the link. For example, it is generally cheaper (per unit of output) to establish and operate a transport or telecommunications link across a high-density linkage. This is even more true for investments in information, which generate an essentially public asset, whose services can be costlessly shared by all. Interestingly, the provision of trading information was an important early objective of Japanese policies in East Asia, and is among the first objectives of APEC, the region's new forum for economic cooperation.

In still other cases, intra-bloc transactions costs will be reduced through political mechanisms. For example, a free trade agreement will be easier to negotiate among partners who already have intense linkages. Similarly, the arguments for stabilising an exchange rate will be much more compelling for countries with substantial bilateral trade than for those that are not highly interdependent. Such mechanisms presume, to be sure, that the trade linkage is valued highly by all of the bloc's countries; asymmetric trade, by contrast, may not lead to reinforcing agreements even if the (one-way) flow is very intense.

The key point is that developments that increase bilateral contacts may trigger strong, positive feedback effects through their impact on trade-facilitating investments. A shock to a bilateral link may be significantly amplified as the initial increase in contacts leads to new investments in the bilateral linkage, which in turn reduce bilateral transaction costs. In some respects, these mechanisms are similar to those that generate irreversible changes ('hysteresis') in trade flows in reaction to exchange rate changes (see, for example, Baldwin 1990).

The endogeneity of trade-facilitating investments, and thus transactions costs, suggests a simple model of bloc formation. Suppose that a relatively loosely connected group of economies becomes more interdependent due to an economic or non-economic shock. The increased intensity of contacts will make it attractive to invest further in the bilateral relationship. Bilateral transactions costs will fall, leading to further increases in the intensity of the bilateral relationship. The cycle may repeat itself over time. This story is consistent with Europe's integration process in the 1950s and 1960s. After the war, European peace and economic recovery increased the importance of European partners to each other and provided incentives for reducing intra-European trade barriers. The Common Market undertook a massive effort to eliminate trade barriers and later to reduce the volatility of EC exchange rates. These steps substantially raised the regional bias of European trade and, arguably, resulted in further efforts to reduce intra-European barriers.

If international transactions costs are endogenous, then history matters. The extent to which countries are 'shocked' into close trading relationships, and the extent to which their periods of rapid growth are parallel, affects their investments in their bilateral trade and shapes their subsequent trading relationships.

This paper will examine how various historical events have shaped East Asian interdependence. A key piece of the argument is that various 'accidents' of history — that is, close international contacts that cannot be traced to market forces alone — have changed the international pattern of transactions costs and have permanently affected East Asia's bilateral trading patterns. Three such accidents appear particularly important. First, the imperialist policies of the Western countries established an initial network of East Asian trade. Later, Japanese imperialism provided an impetus for the integration of East Asia's northern economies. As was often observed at the time, 'trade followed the flag'. Finally, the rapid growth of various East Asian countries is now making them loom increasingly large to each other and is providing a new impetus for regional integration.

East Asian interdependence before 1931

East Asia has a long history of trade, dating back to Arab and Chinese trade among East Asian countries and with Europe. The volume of East Asian trade in general, and of East Asian intra-trade as well, appears to have gained momentum with the stepped-up involvement of European powers in the nineteenth century. Subsequently, the expansion of Japan's economic sphere of influence became the main force driving interdependence.

The treaty port system

Towards the middle of the nineteenth century, prompted by British leadership, a wave of liberalisation spread through Europe. Britain sought similar objectives in East Asia: it abolished the monopoly of the East India Company and moved aggressively to obtain free access to Chinese markets. The Treaty of Nanking, which Britain concluded with China at the end of the Opium War of 1840–42, opened five ports where British subjects could carry on trade 'without molestation or restraint' and ceded Hong Kong 'in perpetuity' to Her Majesty. Export and import duties were fixed at an average of 5 per cent, and consular courts were established to keep British subjects safe from local laws.

As in Europe, Britain also included MFN clauses in this and other treaties. Thus it paved the way for 'cooperative' imperialism, with France and the United States, and eventually Russia, Prussia, Portugal, Denmark, the Netherlands, Spain, Belgium and Italy all signing treaties guaranteeing access to Chinese and other ports (Beasley 1987).

A surge of trade ensued, both regionally within East Asia, and with Europe. The profitability of this trade led to a lively competition for new ports. The United States focused on Japan, and, following Matthew C. Perry's landings, eventually concluded a treaty in 1858. Russia, the Netherlands, Britain and France followed with similar treaties of their own. Japan's early trade thus came to be oriented towards the West: silk, tea and coal were exported to France, Italy and the United States, while textiles, weapons and machinery were imported from Britain and the United States.

Thus, by the turn of the twentieth century, when relatively comprehensive regional trade data became available, the level of East Asian regional interdependence was already high. As Table 10.1 shows, by 1913 about 42 per cent of the region's trade was intra-regional, compared with 46 per cent in 1938 and 47 per cent today. Most of this trade was mediated by the great ports developed by the European powers — Hong Kong, Manila, Shanghai and Singapore. In addition to maintaining bilateral ties between the colonies and their home countries — between Malaysia and Singapore and England, Indonesia and the Netherlands, and the Philippines and the United States — the ports also played a key role in coordinating the trade of a vast region stretching from India to Japan. Roughly 70 per cent of Thailand's trade, for example, was mediated by Singapore, which sent some of Thailand's rice on to China and Japan, in exchange for Indian and British textiles.

Table 10.1   **East Asian trade as a share of total trade for different countries (exports plus imports)**

	1913	1925	1938	1955	1990
China	0.53	0.46	0.70	0.43	0.59
Indonesia	0.32	0.38	0.26	0.32	0.60
Taiwan			0.99	0.50	0.42
Japan	0.41	0.47	0.70	0.22	0.29
Korea			1.00	0.35	0.40
Malaysia	0.44	0.39	0.35	0.30	0.37
Philippines	0.18	0.15	0.11	0.17	0.43
Thailand	0.62	0.71	0.65	0.52	0.51
Simple average	0.42	0.43	0.59	0.35	0.45
Excluding Korea, Taiwan	0.42	0.43	0.46	0.33	0.47
Excluding Korea, Taiwan, and Japan	0.42	0.42	0.41	0.35	0.50

Source: League of Nations, Long-Term Economic Statistics of Japan.

Japanese expansion

A second impetus for the intensification of regional ties came from Japan's industrialisation and expanding economic influence. By the end of the nineteenth century Japan had established a role parallel to or surpassing those of other powers in Korea and China. It continued to gain economic and military power in the early twentieth century, and began to displace the exports of European powers in their own colonies.

Japan's role in the treaty port system quickly changed from host to protagonist. By 1876 Japan had itself opened three Korean ports and began competing aggressively with China to re-export Western textiles to Korea. In 1895 Japan won a major military victory over China, gaining a large indemnity, further influence in Korea, commercial privileges in China, and two important territories: the Liaotung Peninsula (including Dalien, Manchuria's most important port) and Taiwan. Japan was eventually forced to back down on the Liaotung claims, but its victory had clearly established it as a rising imperial power.

Scholars tend to agree that the conquest of Korea reflected primarily military, rather than economic, objectives — as the Japanese army's Prussian adviser put it, Korea was 'a dagger thrust at the heart of Japan' (Myers and Peattie 1984, p. 15).

In any case, Japan's military triumphs in Korea were quickly followed by investments in communications infrastructure related to bilateral trade, and eventually modifications in the Taiwanese and Korean economies that helped to make them more complementary to the Japanese economy. Meiji-style agricultural reforms, such as comprehensive land surveys, were introduced, establishing clear criteria for the ownership and taxation of land and facilitating the sale of land. A combination of these administrative measures and new agricultural technologies imported from Japan resulted in a dramatic surge of agricultural production. By the late 1920s Korea and Taiwan supplied 80 per cent of Japan's rice imports, two-thirds of its sugar, and substantial shares of other minerals and lumber (Peattie 1984, p. 32).

But it was China that was regarded as the great prize. In 1905 Japan defeated Russia in Manchuria and acquired control over the Liaotung Peninsula (known as the Kwantung Leased Territory), all of Korea, the southern half of Sakhalin Island (Karafuto), and the Chinese Eastern Railway. There followed a substantial wave of investments in communications, coordinated by the Southern Manchuria Railway Company, a quasi-public company that remained a key player also in later phases of Japanese expansion. A key objective of the company was to shape the transport infrastructure of Manchuria — that is, to ensure that the network fed into Dalien, the Japanese-controlled port (Beasley 1987, pp. 90–2).

The Japanese government also moved aggressively to improve information on the Chinese economy. The Ministry of Finance proposed a wide-ranging study of Chinese demand, exhibitions in treaty ports, visits by Japanese entrepreneurs, and new ways of disseminating information, including a China Association in Japan that would encourage businesspeople to take an interest in China.

But as Japan became good at imperialism, the Western powers began to change the rules of the game. The powers started to relax their control over their colonies by revising the treaties on foreign ports; soon after the First World War, for example, China was granted substantial tariff autonomy. At the same time, powers moved to control Japan's growing regional influence. The Washington Conference in 1921 sharply limited the size of the Japanese navy, and a period of economic and political frictions ensued.

Despite the strained political circumstances, the sphere of influence established at the turn of the century resulted in a sharp increase in Japan's regional economic role. By the late 1920s Japan had essentially caught up with Western interests in China, and by 1931 the stock of Japanese investments in China equalled those of Great Britain and exceeded those of all other countries combined (Beasley 1987, p. 133). Japanese investments reached deep into Manchuria; for example, by the end of the First World War, the Hanyehping Coal and Iron Company supplied 60 per cent of Yawata Steel's iron ore requirements (Beasley 1987, p. 137). This period of the so-called Shidehara diplomacy was characterised by frequent Japanese–Western clashes, repeated concessions on both military and trade rights, yet considerable economic gains.

Interdependence between 1931 and 1945

The era of political compromise ended in 1931. This turn of events was hastened by Chinese resistance to Japan's economic advance and by world depression. Subsequently, Japan's economic strategy dramatically changed. The colonial-style exchange of manufactures for raw materials gave way to a concerted effort to develop independent bases of industrial strength in several parts of Japan's economic empire. The new strategy led to substantial industrial investments outside Japan proper, and eventually gave rise to increasingly sophisticated economic linkages among Japan, Korea, Taiwan, and eventually China.

Military expansion

Three factors helped to replace the economic approaches of the 1920s with a strategy based on military power. The first was China's emerging nationalism. By the late 1920s, Japan's influence in China came under increased threat from the Kuomintang. In 1927, for example, the northern Chinese warlord Chang Tso-lin, under Kuomintang influence, withdrew permission for the construction of five new Japanese railway lines into northern Manchuria. A year later, Chiang Kai-shek defeated his Beijing rivals and set his sights on the north Chinese provinces dominated by Japan. Japan's Kwantung Army responded with a complex series of intrigues that eventually led to the invasion of Manchuria in 1931 (Barnhart 1987).

A second factor involved trade frictions that increasingly limited Japan's conventional access to international markets. As the world economy began to decline starting in 1929, Japan's trade relations sharply deteriorated, since many trade partners blamed Japan for the particularly large gains that it had achieved during the previous decade. For example, by 1932 Japan had displaced the Netherlands as Indonesia's largest trade partner, and had made similar inroads in Malaysia. During the 1930s Japan became embroiled in one trade dispute after another; conflicts with India, the Dutch East Indies, and Canada each resulted in a trade war or reciprocal boycott. As one contemporary writer put it, it was

> the bad fortune of the Island Empire that it has come of age industrially at a time when economic theory and, still more, economic practice have drifted far away from the ideals of Bright and Cobden . . . [Its] export trade has been considerably retarded by a multitude of economic barbed-wire entanglements in the shape of quota restrictions, high tariffs, and other measures designed to check the sweep of 'Made in Japan' products . . . More than sixty countries have imposed special restrictions on Japanese textiles; less than thirty have left the door open on equal terms (Chamberlin 1937, p. 219).

The final factor that pushed Japan towards a military strategy was a severe agricultural recession. Policies designed to generate rice surpluses in Taiwan and Korea coincided with worldwide commodity deflation. As rice prices fell, conditions in Japanese agriculture worsened, and the government rapidly shifted its colonial investments towards industry.

In any case, the 1931 invasion of Manchuria, like previous Japanese colonial moves, was followed by a large wave of public and private investments. But there was little room in this picture for non-Japanese companies; by the early 1930s Anglo-Dutch Petroleum, Standard Oil, Seimens, and Skoda had all liquidated major interests

(Jones 1949). Manchuria, Korea, and to a lesser extent Taiwan, became thoroughly transformed. In the meantime, the complementarity of the Manchurian, Korean and Japanese economies came to be based on manufacturing; for example, Nissan, a manufacturer of armaments, airplanes, automobiles, and machinery, moved its headquarters to Changchun, and its president eventually went on to direct the Manchuria Industrial Development Company (Jones 1949). Manchuria was to become a self-sufficient industrial base, supplying basic materials, including coal, iron and steel, electricity and synthetic oil, rolling stock, and ships to itself and Japan in exchange for machinery (Beasley 1987, p. 216).

Towards the end of the 1930s Japan's expansion into China became increasingly ominous and continued to accelerate. In 1937 a minor clash between Chinese and Japanese troops provided a pretext for capturing Nanking and much of the Yangtze valley. Soon afterward, Prime Minister Konoe announced a 'new order' that called for close cooperation ('co-prosperity') among China, Japan and Manchuria.

A broad southern advance also began to emerge as part of Japan's increasingly expansionist strategy. In 1939 the Showa Research Institute developed an extensive plan for an East Asian Economic Bloc (Lebra 1975, pp. 100–3), which would be self-sufficient by relying on tin, rubber, bauxite, tungsten, nickel and chromium from Thailand, the Philippines, the Dutch East Indies and Malaya (Beasley 1987, p. 225).

As the Second World War approached, the scope of Japan's sphere of influence was expanded to include Indochina in the so-called Greater East Asia Co-Prosperity Sphere (GEACS). In the event, not much economic integration took place during the GEACS period, aside from the diversion of some raw materials to Japan, because the sea-lanes were not safe to permit large-scale transport. Instead, the region suffered a deep economic decline as its trade with the West collapsed.

Legacies and parallels

Japan's role in the pre-war economy substantially increased East Asian interdependence, particularly among China, Korea, Taiwan and Japan in the 1930s. Japan's activities in these countries focused on developing transport infrastructure and information, and in the end on developing complementarities with the Japanese economy. The result, naturally enough, was a surge in Japan's regional trade, as shown in Figure 10.1. The GEACS expanded Japan's influence into Southeast Asia, but the economic connections between this region and Japan were brief and overshadowed by the imperatives of war. The Japanese occupation, however, did drive European colonial governments from Southeast Asia and laid the foundations for independence after the war. Thus the economic links that emerged after the war were more Asian than before.

Japan's intense style of imperialism has left long-lived legacies. Unlike the European imperialist powers, Japan was close to its colonies and, in Korea and Manchuria, had excellent communications with them through rail transport. Also, because it was concerned not only with the economic exploitation of the colonies but also with their

Figure 10.1   Partner composition of Japanese exports (five-year moving averages)

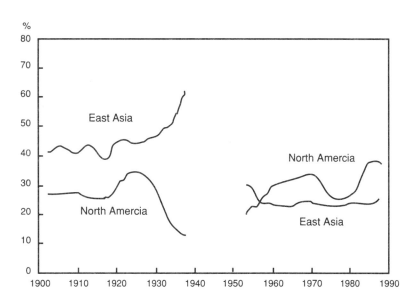

role as buffers against Russian and Western forces, Japan developed dense political and military organisations to control its empire. Finally, given rice exports as a key early objective, Japan could not restrict its economic activities to an 'enclave', but was forced to penetrate local economic structures (Ho 1984, p. 385).

By the early 1930s Japan's style of complementarity differed dramatically from that of other colonial powers; as Cumings (1984, p. 482) has observed, Japanese imperialism 'involved the location of industry and an infrastructure of communications and transportation *in* the colonies, bringing industry to the labor and raw materials, rather than vice-versa'. Although the linkage between the Japanese occupation and the subsequent spectacular development of Manchuria, Korea and Taiwan is extremely controversial, there is no doubt that powerful industrial centres developed in each of these areas and that these centres evolved along the same technological lines as Japan's own industries.

The notion of a large regional bloc that would also include Southeast Asia does not appear to have been a part of Japan's strategy until 1939. Prime Minister Konoe's 1938 announcement made no mention of southern areas, and the inclusion of Southeast Asia did not arise until the fall of France. By that time, the GEACS was clearly designed to obtain raw materials needed for war. As Peattie (1991, p. 42) has argued, the GEACS is best seen as a response to a 'sudden turn in international events . . . rather than the consequence of long-considered for widely-held interest in the co-prosperity of Asian peoples'.

Interdependence from the Second World War to 1985

The Second World War thoroughly disrupted the trade patterns established in the pre-war years. Trade flows shifted towards the United States, now the leading military power in the Pacific and the only country with its economy largely intact. Linkages between Japan and Taiwan and Korea were sharply curtailed. China's trade also collapsed as the country sank into civil war. Insurrections erupted also in Indonesia, Indochina and Malaysia. As a result, trade flows declined sharply throughout the Pacific, especially among China, Japan, Korea and Taiwan, the 'core' countries of the GEACS.

Post-war US policy recognised that this sharp dislocation in trade patterns would undermine the prospects for economic recovery in all of the countries that once formed the Japanese empire. The influential Institute of Pacific Relations, for example, concluded at its 1947 conference on the reconstruction of East Asia that, for the sake of Japan and the rest of the region, 'Japan must be actively helped to regain something of her old position as the mainspring of the Far Eastern economy as a whole' (Institute of Pacific Relations 1949). The US occupation authorities in turn began to use the leverage provided by their influence over aid and Japanese reparations to China, Korea and Taiwan, as well as in Southeast Asia, to revive these countries' trade with Japan.

The data show the magnitude of this challenge. Japan's two-way trade with East Asia fell from 73 per cent of trade around 1940 to only about 31 per cent in 1951. At the same time, the partner composition of this East Asian trade shifted from the 'core' economies of the GEACS to Southeast Asia. The decline in the importance of the East Asian countries in general, and of the core partners in particular, can be traced almost entirely to the general decline of their economies, rather than to a decline in the intensity of their trade linkages with Japan. The analysis of intensity indexes suggests that regional biases within East Asian trade remained at essentially the same high level in 1955 as they were in 1938. While East Asian linkages remained strong, they were now driven not by Japanese policy but by economic structures inherited from the pre-war period and by US policies designed to restart this group of highly interdependent economies.

The subsequent story of East Asian economic growth is well known and has been recently reviewed by Kuznets (1988), Noland (1990), Wade (1990), and others. What is of interest here is that the spectacular growth of the region's economies was accompanied by a substantial decline in their regional trade bias. As shown in Table 10.2, the intensity indexes of East Asian trade,[3] which survived the Second World War at relatively high levels, fell steadily in the following years. The pattern of decline is similar for most East Asian countries, and the few anomalies that do occur (an unusually rapid decline in the case of China, and an unusual increase in the case of the Philippines) can be understood in terms of major political changes in the countries involved.

Equally remarkable is a parallel decline in the dispersion of intensity indexes (that is, in variations in the intensity of linkages across different trade partners) in the region. As shown in Table 10.3 the standard deviations of the intensity indexes of most

Table 10.2   Trade intensity indexes of different countries and regions with East Asia

	1938	1955	1969	1979	1985	1990
Japan	4.66	3.13	2.07	2.02	1.46	1.50
North America	0.92	1.16	1.48	1.53	1.48	1.44
Australia, New Zealand	0.53	1.35	2.70	2.85	2.24	2.11
Taiwan	6.63	7.15	4.83	2.82	1.72	2.14
Korea	6.68	4.92	4.83	2.91	1.96	2.04
Hong Kong	3.96	7.55	3.72	3.22	3.09	2.96
Malaysia, Singapore	2.31	4.22	3.34	3.11	2.05	1.88
Thailand	4.34	7.36	5.38	3.64	2.69	2.61
Philippines	0.70	2.45	4.58	3.17	2.54	2.22
Indonesia	1.76	4.60	5.52	4.89	3.34	3.10
China	4.70	6.13	2.91	2.76	3.23	3.04
Western Europe	0.26	0.49	0.33	0.34	0.31	0.36
Middle East	0.46	1.05	1.39	1.84	1.36	1.33
Rest of world	0.30	0.67	0.81	0.62	0.70	0.76
Total imports	1.00	1.00	1.00	1.00	1.00	1.00
East Asia	4.48	4.45	2.97	2.64	2.05	2.09
Pacific Rim	2.61	1.95	2.05	2.08	1.77	1.80
Average	2.72	3.51	2.93	2.44	1.94	1.91

East Asian countries fell steadily during the post-war period. In effect, each country's bilateral trade pattern came to look more and more like the world's trade pattern — the importance of any particular partner to a given country came to resemble the importance of that partner in world trade as a whole. (If each partner's share of a country's trade was equal to that partner's share in world trade, then all intensity indexes would be one.) Country-specific biases became less and less important in explaining the distribution of East Asian trade, both between East Asia and other regions and across different East Asian partners.

Three types of factors help to explain the diversification and homogenisation of the region's trade. The first was the general integration of the global economy during most of the post-war period, which was spurred by several successful rounds of trade negotiations, steady progress towards convertibility, and considerable improvements in international communications and transport. All of these factors worked to pull East Asia's trade (as well as the trade of all other countries) away from its regional partners towards more global sources and destinations.

A second important factor was the rapid development of the region's economies. The expansion of each economy's overall trade provided the scale needed to justify investments in trading linkages with an increasingly large number of countries. More frequent shipping and air schedules could now be maintained; additional investments

Table 10.3   Dispersion of trade intensity indexes, by country and over time (standard deviations)

	1938	1955	1969	1979	1985	1990
Japan	5.55	4.25	2.50	1.75	1.26	1.22
North America	1.41	0.85	0.62	0.50	0.55	0.47
Australia, New Zealand	0.65	0.66	0.94	1.19	0.97	1.23
Taiwan	4.08	4.51	2.60	1.53	1.07	1.13
Korea	4.18	5.45	2.01	1.19	0.91	0.97
Hong Kong	6.81	10.22	2.79	2.61	3.36	4.02
Malaysia, Singapore	9.25	4.21	3.78	2.74	1.95	1.24
Thailand	9.59	4.92	3.14	2.18	1.80	1.26
Philippines	1.52	1.42	1.96	1.19	1.23	0.86
Indonesia	3.11	3.53	3.45	2.58	1.49	1.30
China	6.15	9.51	2.77	2.57	3.47	4.09
Western Europe	0.56	0.43	0.33	0.32	0.36	0.33
Middle East	1.12	0.68	0.74	0.63	0.41	0.49
Rest of world	0.41	0.38	0.58	0.48	0.37	0.37
Total imports	0.00	0.00	0.00	0.00	0.00	0.00
East Asia	2.28	2.52	1.68	1.15	0.88	0.80
Pacific Rim	0.97	0.76	0.77	0.64	0.49	0.46
Average	3.39	3.19	1.80	1.37	1.21	1.19

could be made in communications; and a greater stock of information could be developed to link firms and their foreign counterparts. All these trends undoubtedly contributed to the broadening of East Asian marketing efforts. These trends presumably operated in all countries, but it is likely that their effect was especially pronounced in the context of East Asia's 'miracle' economies.

A third factor driving East Asia's diversification was the similarity of East Asian development patterns. Each country rapidly shifted its output from raw materials to manufactures, and within manufactures from labour-intensive to more capital and technology-intensive sectors. These patterns have been described as the 'flying geese pattern' of development by the Japanese economists (Akamatsu 1960) and are consistent with Heckscher–Ohlin explanations of how trade patterns are likely to change with the accumulation of human and physical capital.

The similarity in development patterns is important for two reasons. First, it explains how each country acquired an increasingly sophisticated basket of exports and thus positioned itself to compete in a wider world market. Second, it explains why East Asian countries developed competitive rather than complementary economies, and thus why they had to look to outside markets, rather than regional markets, for new trading opportunities.

An important exception to this story involves linkages based on the importation of intermediate inputs and capital goods. The commonality of East Asian development trajectories has meant that each country would typically look to neighbouring countries for appropriate technology. These supply-side linkages in turn gave rise to substantial imports of machinery and components. As a result, several East Asian economies acquired asymmetrical linkages. On the one hand, they relied heavily on the region's more advanced economies — Japan, Korea, Taiwan, Singapore — for imports of machinery and components, and, on the other, they looked outside the region to sell their exports.

Interdependence today

The intensity of East Asian interdependence appears to have reached a trough in 1985–86. The turning point came at the end of a period when the real value of the US dollar was unusually high; in the preceding years, several East Asian countries had sharply shifted their trade towards the United States. In addition, the high value of the dollar permitted Japanese companies to maintain their exports despite sharply higher wages and declining competitiveness against other East Asian economies.

The large exchange rate adjustments of 1985 and 1986 affected interdependence in a complex way. Initially, the appreciation of the yen was not matched by other East Asian currencies; thus other countries became more competitive against Japan in both US and Japanese markets. For a while, East Asian imports surged in both markets, and Korea, Taiwan and other countries began to run substantial trade surpluses. These export surges also led to accelerating imports from Japan and Singapore. As a result, East Asian interdependence intensified; intra–regional trade expanded very rapidly, and the long-run decline of the region's intensity indexes ceased.

Many observers assumed at that time that the trade flow adjustments described above represented the beginning of a new historical trend towards the greater integration of the East Asian economy. This may still be the case, but the events of 1985–88 were in large part driven by the staggered adjustment of exchange rates in different East Asian countries. By the late 1980s the second phase of the exchange rate adjustments took hold, as most of the region's currencies appreciated to close the gap that had opened between them and the yen in the mid-1980s. These corrections slowed the surge of Japanese imports from East Asia and stopped the increase in the region's intensity indexes. To be sure, the absolute volume of East Asian trade continued to expand at a rapid pace due to the high growth of the region's economies.

The more significant impact of the appreciation of the yen was a sharp increase in regional investment flows (see Table 10.4). Malaysia, Thailand and Indonesia had two-thirds as much investment in 1988–89 alone as in all previous years until then. The cause of this wave is widely accepted; the exchange rate changes of the late 1980s reduced the competitiveness of Japanese firms and led firms to shift some production activities closer to markets and to countries with lower labour costs. While most of

Table 10.4   Foreign direct investment in East Asia (million US dollars)

Host/source	Total	Japan	United States	Korea	Taiwan	Hong Kong	Singapore
Thailand							
Up to 1987	11 536	2 773	1 910	9	675	445	351
1988–89	7 868	4 431	570	66	530	278	408
Malaysia							
Up to 1987	4 200	1 741	202	0	34	262	594
1988–89	3 690	967	179	49	1 314	138	231
Indonesia							
Up to 1987	17 284	5 928	1 244	222	144	1 876	299
1988–89	11 159	1 304	783	728	1 126	867	489
Philippines							
Up to 1987	2 830	377	1 620				
1988–89	275	71	98				
Korea							
1984–88	3 648	1 857	876				
Taiwan							
1984–88	4 170	1 343	1 251				
Singapore							
1984–88	6 529	2 200	2 814				
Sum (Thailand, Malaysia, Indonesia only)							
Up to 1987	33 020	10 442	3 356	231	853	2 583	1 244
1988–89	22 717	6 702	1 532	843	2 970	1 283	1 128
Shares of sum							
1987	1.000	0.316	0.102	0.007	0.026	0.078	0.038
1988–89	1.000	0.295	0.067	0.037	0.131	0.056	0.050

these investments went into the United States and other developed countries, a substantial amount also occurred in East Asia.

By the late 1980s, as the NIEs also adjusted their exchange rates and began to face competitive strains similar to Japan's, they too joined Japan as major investors in East Asia. Thus an entirely new channel of interdependence began to operate; cross-investments among a large number of East Asian countries. This is a natural result of the region's prosperity; it recalls patterns of integration that have evolved in Europe.

The investment wave of the late 1980s differed from earlier investments in developing country production facilities not just in magnitude and origin but also in structure. Japan's investments in East Asia in the 1970s, for example, were primarily focused on local markets, often encouraged by policies that sought to increase local participation in industry; for example, through the importation of automobile kits instead of assembled automobiles. The recent wave of investments, by contrast, is the product of new, global strategies by regional firms. Nearly all firms have adopted such strategies, and some have gone to some length to plan a comprehensive distribution of their activities across different regional markets.

Since the recent investment wave has been driven by production strategy rather than by market considerations, it has included a larger share of export-oriented industries. More so than in the past, the firms established in foreign locations have also been intended to serve home (for instance, Japanese) markets. At the same time, since these investments were closely tied to Japanese technologies and suppliers that have remained at home, they have typically required a higher ratio of imported inputs than earlier investments. Because of these characteristics, the recent wave of intra-East Asian investment flows has helped to intensify regional linkages by facilitating exports into Japan and other regional markets and by spreading technologies that require regional inputs and capital goods.

The market forces that have helped to intensify regional linkages through trade and investment have also been supported by government aid policies. Japan's aid program has always been oriented towards Asia, but its growing scale has made it an important factor in recent economic linkages. Japanese aid flows to East Asia have been substantial compared to private investment flows. These flows have helped to finance the infrastructure that supports private investment.

The volume of intra-regional investment has slackened somewhat but is likely to remain relatively high compared to historical levels. Some of the reasons for the slowdown are permanent: the investment wave of the late 1980s represented, in part, a one-time adjustment in corporate sourcing policies, triggered by the appreciation of the yen and the NIEs' currencies. But other reasons are temporary. As a result of the rapid inflow of capital, infrastructure bottlenecks developed in several of the receiving economies, including especially Thailand, and labour and real estate costs rose sharply due to the overheated economy. At the same time, the accumulation of Japanese firms has contributed to the development of an economic infrastructure — consisting of suppliers and service companies — that will make it easier for other firms to invest in the future.

Conclusions

This paper has explored the hypothesis that blocs are, in part, the product of historical accidents. Reinforcing mechanisms of integration can be set into motion by military force or other developments that make countries important to each other. In East Asia important initial investments in regional linkages were triggered by imperial conquest — first by the Western powers under the treaty port system, and then by Japan during its imperialist period. By the advent of the Second World War these investments had transformed East Asia into perhaps the most interdependent region in the world.

After the war the intensity of East Asian interdependence resumed its pre-war level. Subsequently, however, the region diversified its trade patterns, due to the important role of the United States in post-war Pacific relations and to the growing sophistication of the region's industries. The trend towards diversification has been reversed in the last five or so years. Since 1985, spurred in part by investment and aid, trade flows within East Asia have grown sharply and have become more regionally biased.

An interesting question is how the recent flurry of regional policy initiatives will affect these trends. It is likely that the institutions created by these initiatives will not be strong enough to liberalise regional trade. Even if growing intra-regional linkages create a demand for cooperation, the diversity of the region's policy approaches makes broad, formal agreements difficult and unlikely. So far, collaboration has focused on narrow, highly pragmatic objectives — trade cooperation in the context of Mini-Trading Areas ('growth triangles', and so on) and ASEAN, and technical cooperation in the context of APEC.

For the time being, then, much of the region's business will be conducted through bilateral rather than multilateral institutions. Japan is raising its profile in regional diplomacy as well as in economic cooperation and consultation. Japanese ministries are also developing country-specific development plans and are encouraging their implementation with aid, expert advice, infrastructure lending, and support for private investment.

The East Asian trading bloc has a long and complex history. Investments in this bloc, some made more than a century ago, proved surprisingly durable. Today's developments, likewise, may shape the pattern of East Asian trade far into the future. If there are externalities associated with investments in bilateral trade, as the evidence here suggests, then the factors and policies that affect bilateral trade deserve more attention than they usually receive.

Notes

1   The regions referred to in this paper will be North America (Canada and the United States), East Asia (China, Hong Kong, Indonesia, Japan, Korea, Malaysia, Philippines, Taiwan, Thailand and Singapore), and the Pacific Rim (North America, East Asia, Australia and New Zealand).

2   For example, the bilateral pattern of trade is indeterminate in a Heckscher–Ohlin model with more products than factors, assuming zero transport costs.

3   Petri (1993, p. 23) describes the calculation of what he calls 'double-relative measures of trading intensity' or 'gravity coefficients', but which are the intensity indexes defined in Drysdale and Garnaut (1982) (also Chapter 3, this volume).

References

Akamatsu, K. 1960, 'A theory of unbalanced growth in the world economy', *Weltwirtschaftliches Archiv*, 86(2).

Baldwin, Richard 1990, 'Some empirical evidence on hysteresis in aggregate U.S. import prices', in Peter A. Petri and Stefan Gerlach (eds), *The Economics of the Dollar Cycle*, Cambridge: MIT Press, pp. 235–73.

Barnhart, Michael A. 1987, *Japan Prepares for Total War: The Search for Economic Security, 1919–1941*, Ithaca: Cornell University Press.

Beasley, W. G. 1987, *Japanese Imperialism: 1894–1945*, Oxford: Clarendon Press.

Chamberlin, William Henry 1937, *Japan over Asia*, Boston: Little Brown and Company.

Cumings, Bruce 1984, 'The legacy of Japanese colonialism in Korea', in Ramon H. Myers and Mark R. Peattie (eds), *The Japanese Colonial Empire, 1895–1945*, Princeton: Princeton University Press, pp. 478–96.

Drysdale, Peter and Ross Garnaut 1982, 'Trade intensities and the analysis of bilateral trade flows in a many-country world', *Hitotsubashi Journal of Economics*, 22(2), pp. 62–84.

Frankel, Jeffrey A. 1993, 'Is Japan creating a yen bloc in East Asia and the Pacific', in Jeffrey A. Frankel and Miles Kahler (eds), *Regionalism and Rivalry: Japan and the United States in Pacific Asia*, Chicago: University of Chicago Press.

Ho, Samuel P. 1984, 'Colonialism and development: Korea, Taiwan, and Kwantung', in Ramon H. Myers and Mark R. Peattie (eds), *The Japanese Colonial Empire, 1895–1945*, Princeton: Princeton University Press, pp. 347–98.

Institute of Pacific Relations 1949, *Problems of Economic Reconstruction in the Far East*, New York: Institute of Pacific Relations.

Jones, F. C. 1949, *Manchuria Since 1931*, New York: Oxford University Press.

Kuznets, Paul 1988, 'An East Asian model of economic development: Japan, Taiwan, and South Korea', *Economic Development and Cultural Change*, 36(3), pp. S11–43.

Lawrence, Robert Z. 1991, 'How open is Japan?', in Paul Krugman (ed.), *Trade with Japan: Has the Door Opened Wider?*, Chicago: University of Chicago Press, pp. 9–50.

Lebra, Joyce C. 1975, *Japan's Greater East Asia Co-Prosperity Sphere in World War II: Selected Readings and Documents*, Kuala Lumpur: Oxford University Press.

Leontief, Wassily 1973, 'Explanatory power of the comparative cost theory of international trade and its limits', in H. C. Bos (ed.), *Economic Structure and Development: Lectures in Honor of Jan Tinbergen*, Amsterdam: North-Holland.

Linnemann, Hans 1966, *An Econometric Study of International Trade Flows*, Amsterdam: North-Holland.

Montgomery, Michael 1988, *Imperialist Japan: The Yen to Dominate*, New York: St Martin's Press.

Myers, Ramon H. and Mark R. Peattie (eds) 1984, *The Japanese Colonial Empire, 1895–1945*, Princeton: Princeton University Press.

Noland, Marcus 1990, *Pacific Basin Developing Countries: Prospects for the Future*, Washington, DC: Institute for International Economics.

Peattie, Mark R. 1984, 'The Nan'yo: Japan in the South Pacific: 1895–1945', in Ramon H. Myers and Mark R. Peattie (eds), *The Japanese Colonial Empire, 1895–1945*, Princeton: Princeton University Press.

_____ 1991, 'Nanshin: the "southward advance" 1931–1941, as a prelude to the Japanese occupation in Southeast Asia', Paper presented at the conference on the Japanese Wartime Empire in Asia, 1937–1945, Hoover Institution, Stanford University, 23–24 August.

Petri, Peter A. 1993, 'The East Asian trading bloc: an analytical history', in Jeffrey A. Frankel and Miles Kahler (eds), *Regionalism and Rivalry: Japan and the United States in Pacific Asia*, Chicago: University of Chicago Press, pp. 39–70.

Wade, Robert 1990, *Governing the Market: Economic Theory and the Role of Government in East Asian Industrialization*, Princeton: Princeton University Press.

11 Is world trade becoming more regionalised?

Kym Anderson and Hege Norheim

Introduction

The recent proliferation of regional integration arrangements and proposals, and the difficulty of concluding the Uruguay Round, have fuelled fears that international trade is becoming more of a regional affair in ways that will reduce global welfare. Outside Europe the concern is that the 1992 Single Market program of the EC and its European Economic Area initiative, and the possible expansion later this decade of the number of full or associate members of the EC, will lead to a more exclusive 'Fortress Europe'. The response in North America has been to negotiate a free trade area there (NAFTA), which is adding to the concerns of third countries and causing them also to propose new, or seek membership of existing, preferential trade agreements.

What evidence might be sought to test whether a welfare-reducing regionalisation of world trade is occurring? A measure of changes in the average external tariff of free trade areas (FTAs) and customs unions (CUs) will not do, even though it is the criterion enshrined in Article XXIV of the GATT concerning the admissibility of FTAs and CUs. It would not do even if it captured the tariff-equivalent of non-tariff trade distorting measures, for it misses the trade reductions caused by the *threat* of protection that contingent protectionist measures such as antidumping legislation create. For that reason commentators have examined intra-regional trade shares, pointing to the increase in the shares of industrial countries' trade that is intra-regional. During the past five decades, for example, Western Europe's intra-regional trade share rose from a half to almost three-quarters, while that of North America (including Mexico) rose from a quarter to two-fifths.

But the strengthening of regional integration agreements (RIAs) within Europe is only one of several possible contributors to that trend. The demise of colonialism, the changing importance of different regions in world trade and other contributors to the

Reprinted with permission from the *Review of International Economics*, Vol. 1, No. 2, 1993, pp. 91–109 (with deletions). Copyright © 1993 by Basil Blackwell Ltd, Oxford, UK.

geographic redirection of trade ensure that changes in the share of a region's international trade that is intra-regional do not necessarily indicate a net increase in discriminatory, welfare-reducing trade practices. Moreover, as McMillan (1993) points out, we know from the analysis by Kemp and Wan (1976) that a new RIA will not worsen welfare in the rest of the world's economies so long as the *volume* (not necessarily the share) of their trade with the RIA countries does not fall, *ceteris paribus*. But, to be welfare-improving for the economies *within* the RIA, the volume of intra-RIA trade must increase following the RIA's formation. Thus it is quite conceivable for *both* trade volumes to rise, improving welfare for insiders and outsiders, but for the latter volume to rise faster than the former — in which case the intra-RIA trade share rises and the extra-regional share falls. Despite this insight from received economic theory, levels of protection and extra-regional trade shares continue to be used to make claims about the welfare effects of RIAs, pending the development of alternative simple-to-calculate indicators.

This paper thus has two purposes. The first is to develop a simple method for disaggregating the change in the geographic distribution of a region's trade into component parts. In the process, indexes of intensity and propensity to trade intra-regionally or extra-regionally are defined. The traditional intensity index overcomes several problems associated with using trade shares as indicators of regional bias. It is defined in the case of extra-regional trade as (roughly) the share of a region's trade with the rest of the world relative to the rest of the world's share of global trade. But even this indicator ignores the possibility that the region may be trading more or less with the rest of the world because of external trade policy changes. So we define an index of propensity to trade intra-regionally or extra-regionally, which combines the effects of geographic bias (as measured by the trade intensity index) and overall 'openness' to trade (as measured by the trade-to-GDP ratio). These indexes, which have the virtue of being simple to calculate, are used in the third section of this paper to examine changes in Europe's external merchandise trade pattern since 1830 and that of various other regions since 1928.

The findings are that the index of the propensity to trade extra-regionally increased for Europe throughout the hundred years to 1928; that it fell for all regions in the 1930s; and that it has increased for virtually all regions (though least so for Europe) since then. The rise is mainly because the proportion of GDP that is traded internationally has risen substantially. That is, the tendency to trade more of one's GDP with one's own region has been accompanied also by the tendency to trade more with the rest of the world as well: regionalisation and global interdependence have grown hand in hand.

In the concluding section, we point out that the pertinent issue from the viewpoint of global welfare therefore is not whether the world's trade is becoming more or less regional as measured, for example, by intra-regional trade shares or intensities, for there are numerous reasons apart from the growth of regional integration agreements as to why regionalisation may be occurring. Rather, the key issue is simply whether world trade is becoming more or less liberal and predictable (and thereby more or less conducive to global investment and employment growth).

Components of regionalisation in international trade

Both history and geography, in addition to government policies, play fundamental roles in shaping the pattern of world trade. The very definition of national boundaries is the result of political events in history, events that are still ongoing as the recent unification of Germany and breakup of the Soviet Union and Yugoslavia testify. Through influencing the size of nations, history also influences the share of GDP traded internationally, because large economies tend to trade a smaller proportion of their GDP (Perkins and Syrquin 1989). Historical events also influence national factor endowment ratios and thereby comparative advantages and hence the commodity composition of countries' international trade. And of course they also determine national languages, customs and legal systems, which in turn affect transactions costs of doing business with other nations as compared with transacting business domestically.

Geography influences all four of those determinants of the pattern of an economy's international trade as well (its GDP, share of GDP traded, commodity composition of trade, and relative transactions costs of doing business with different countries). The output and real income of a nation can be affected directly by proximity to a more affluent economy, as shown so dramatically in the 1980s by the reductions in trade barriers between southeast China and Hong Kong. Also, a nation's trade-to-GDP ratio is lower the lower the cost of transacting business domestically compared with transacting business internationally, and this is determined by transport and communication costs. These costs, which are affected by relative language difficulties and distance, vary across trading partners as well and change over time. They thereby influence the direction of a country's trade not only directly but also indirectly through altering its inter-sectoral and intra-industry commodity composition (Krugman 1991).

Of course, government policies also alter these four determinants of the pattern of international trade (Clarida and Findlay 1992). Even a uniform international trade tax for all commodities is inherently discriminatory, in at least two respects. First, it discriminates between domestic and international trades and so is likely to lower both GDP (especially for small economies) and the nation's international trade-to-GDP ratio below their free trade levels. And second, it alters domestic producer incentives among tradeable industries because a given change in goods prices translates to differential changes in value added, especially when the value added share of output varies by industry and elasticities of substitution in production and consumption differ across commodities. In the usual case in which a government's trade taxes (and other policies) do differ across industries, these differences add to the distortions to domestic production and hence lower GDP further. But such differences also tend to reduce trade more for those trading partners whose trade with the taxing country is concentrated in the goods taxed most. Moreover, these changes to goods trade will be accentuated if the country's trade policy allows international factor flows. Thus even if a country's policies were to contain no overtly discriminatory or preferential trade arrangements such as trade embargoes, voluntary export restraints (VERs), free trade agreements, imperial trade preferences and the like, they nonetheless would have an impact on the geographic distribution of the country's trade.

For all these reasons the share of intra-regional trade in a region's total trade is a very inadequate indicator of preferential policy-induced regional trade bias. But there are two other reasons as well, based simply on arithmetic, as to why the intra-regional trade share can be misleading. They have to do with the (necessarily somewhat arbitrary) definition of a 'region'. One is that the share is affected by the number of countries in a region. To see this, consider a free trade world of five countries and two regions (three countries in one region and two in the other), each with the same value of trade and each trading the same amount with the other four countries. Despite the absence (by assumption) of any geographic trade bias, the intra-regional trade share of the first region is a half while that of the second region is a quarter. More generally, the larger the number of countries in a region, the larger the region's intra-regional trade share, *ceteris paribus*.

To overcome this problem, one might be tempted to suggest defining regions to include a similar number of countries. But that raises a second and related problem, namely that the value of countries' total trade matters. This can be seen by again considering a two-region world, this time of four countries (two per region), with three of the countries trading identical amounts and the fourth trading twice as much as the other three. If each country's trade with the other three is directly proportional to each of the others' share of world trade, this would imply no geographic trade bias. Yet in that case the intra-regional trade shares would differ: for the region without the large trader that share is a quarter, while for the other region it is two-fifths.

These two problems can be avoided, and determinants of the share of one country's trade that goes to another country or country group can be identified formally, by making use of the definition of I_{ij}, the index of intensity[1] of country i's export trade with country (or country group) j:

$$I_{ij} = x_{ij} / m_j \qquad (1)$$
$$= x_{ij} / (q_j \cdot r_j)$$

where

x_{ij} = the share of country i's exports going to country j,

m_j = the share of country j in world imports (net of country i's imports since i cannot export to itself),[2]

q_j = the share of country j in world (net of country i's) GDP, and

r_j = the 'relative openness' of country j,[3] defined as j's import-to-GDP ratio divided by the world's (net of country i's) import-to-GDP ratio.

This index (and its counterpart for import trade) has the property that if trade is not geographically biased in the sense that the share of i's trade going to j equals j's importance in world trade, then it will have a value of unity for all j. And with slight modification,[4] equation (1) also can provide an index of intensity of trade when 'country' i is a regional group, thereby avoiding the above two arithmetic problems (associated with the number or size of countries in the regions) that the trade share suffers in indicating regional bias in trade.

The intensity index does, however, still combine the effects of differences in bilateral trade complementarities and in relative transactions costs of trading with different countries. To separate them, Drysdale (1988, p. 87) suggests subdividing the intensity index into the product of a trade complementarity index and a residual trade bias index. An appropriate complementarity index (C_{ij}), derived using the 'revealed comparative advantage' index of trade specialisation suggested by Balassa (1965), is:

$$C_{ij} = \frac{\sum_k [(x_i^k / t_w^k) \cdot (m_j^k / t_w^k) \cdot t_w^k]}{\sum_k [x_i^k \cdot m_j^k / t_w^k]} \qquad (2)$$

where

$$
\begin{aligned}
x_i^k &= \text{the share of commodity } k \text{ in country } i\text{'s exports,} \\
m_j^k &= \text{the share of commodity } k \text{ in country } j\text{'s imports, and} \\
t_w^k &= \text{the share of commodity } k \text{ in world trade.}
\end{aligned}
$$

That is, C_{ij} is the weighted average of the product of i's export specialisation index and j's import specialisation index, the weights being the shares of the commodities in world trade. A transactions cost-driven index of residual bias in i's exports to j (B_{ij}) can then be defined such that $I_{ij} = B_{ij} \cdot C_{ij}$. Drysdale shows that B_{ij} is a weighted average of the intensity index for each commodity in i's exports to j, the weights being the proportional contribution of each commodity to complementarity in i's total exports to j.

By substituting $B_{ij} \cdot C_{ij}$ for I_{ij} in equation (1) and rearranging, the share of i's exports going to j can be partitioned as follows:

$$x_{ij} = q_j \cdot r_j \cdot B_{ij} \cdot C_{ij} \qquad (3)$$

And swapping x and m in the above formulae provides a similar set of relationships for i's imports from j.

Equation (3) thus identifies the four components of the geographic pattern of trade mentioned at the outset: the relative size and 'relative openness' of different trading partners' economies, the transactions costs involved in i trading with them as compared with others, and the extent to which the commodity composition of their trade complements i's. One or more of these four may be able to provide a crude idea from trade data of the trade effects of preferential trade policies, but care is needed in their interpretation. Specifically, changes in B_{ij} in the absence of changes in transport and other transactions cost differences between trading partners may be attributable to changes in preferential trade policies. If, however, there have been changes in C_{ij} and they also are due to changes in preferential trade policies[5], I_{ij} is a better indicator of the trade effects of those preference changes than B_{ij}. Moreover, calculating B_{ij} is very laborious, because it requires matrices of bilateral trade by commodity — unlike the intensity of trade index ($I_{ij} = B_{ij}.C_{ij}$), which only requires bilateral trade totals. The intensity index thus provides at a much lower cost the same information as B_{ij} if C_{ij} has not changed over the period under consideration, or superior information to B_{ij} if C_{ij} has been affected by changes in preference policies. For these reasons, reliance will be placed in what follows on I_{ij} rather than B_{ij} to identify changes in intra-regional and extra-regional trade biases.

There is one further indicator that is useful in addition to I_{ij}. It is claimed by supporters (critics) of regional integration agreements that such agreements often are accompanied by general trade policy changes which raise (lower) a country's trade-to-GDP ratio. Thus the establishment of a RIA may result in so much net trade creation that even though the index of intensity of i's trade with other regions falls, there is a rise in its propensity to trade outside its own region because of an increase in the value of its trade with other regions as a proportion of i's GDP (rather than of i's total trade). To capture the combined effect of these two changes — in 'openness' and in extra-regional trade intensity — we define the index of the propensity to export extra-regionally (P_{ij}) as:

$$P_{ij} = t_{ij}/m_j$$
$$= t_i.I_{ij} \qquad\qquad (4)$$

where

$$t_{ij} = \text{i's exports to j divided by i's GDP, and}$$
$$t_i = \text{the ratio of i's total exports to i's GDP;}$$

and similarly for i's imports from j. The aggregate index of the propensity to trade extra-regionally — used in the next section — can then be defined as the average of the export and import intensity indexes multiplied by the ratio of exports plus imports to GDP (and similarly for the aggregate index of the propensity to trade intra-regionally).

P_{ij} is an especially useful summary index for across-time comparisons for i's trade with j when t_i has been changing because of the same policy changes that have affected I_{ij}. But it needs to be kept in mind that, unlike I_{ij}, P_{ij} does not have a weighted average across all j of unity. Nor should it be used for comparing across different sized countries or regions at a point in time because t_i is necessarily dependent on the size of economy i, *ceteris paribus*.

Regionalisation of international trade since 1830

Global economic integration through extra-regional trade has been going on for centuries of course (Tracy 1991). But with the rapid decline in the cost of ocean transport in the latter nineteenth century, as iron and then steel replaced wood in ship construction and steam substituted for sails, inter-continental trade became much less costly (North 1958). That ensured, in the presence of strong imperial–colonial ties, often stronger trade complementarities between European and less-industrialised countries than among European countries, and intermittent animosities among European countries, ensured that for a hundred or so years from 1830 there was faster growth in inter-continental rather than intra-continental trade. Moreover, this extra-regional trade bias was reinforced by imperial preference policies that were strengthened in the early 1930s. It was only after the post-Second World War reconstruction period that those preferences began to be dismantled — only to be replaced by regional preferences first in Europe and now in North America. Simultaneously, the volume of intra-industry trade among high-income industrial economies in sophisticated merchandise has become more important over time than those economies' inter-sectoral trade with exporters of primary products.

What has been the net effect of these forces, together with economic growth and the influences of other policies, on the pattern of intra-regional versus extra-regional trade of different regions? This depends of course on how we define 'regions'. While there is no ideal definition, pragmatism would suggest basing the definition on the major continents and subdividing them somewhat according to a combination of criteria based on culture, language, religion, and stage of development. We begin with Europe (East and West), which for centuries has accounted for more than half of world trade and for which pertinent data are available from 1830.

Europe

According to the data compiled by Bairoch (1974, 1976a) for Europe as a whole, the share of Europe's trade that was intra-regional varied little from its average of two-thirds during the seven decades to 1900. It dropped a little in the early 1900s and stayed around 60 per cent until the early 1960s (apart from a dip associated with the late 1940s post-war reconstruction period), but then it rose steadily and is now more than 75 per cent (first row of Table 11.1). Since Europe's share of world trade also was steady during the nineteenth century, at a little below two-thirds according to Bairoch, the index of intensity of intra-European trade hovered at very little above unity throughout that century (rows 2 and 3). That is, despite the relative proximity of

Table 11.1 Trade shares and the intensity and propensity of regionalisation in Europe's merchandise trade, 1830 to 1990 (three-year averages around the years shown prior to 1928)

	1830	1840	1850	1860	1870	1880	1890	1900	1910	1928	1938	1948	1958	1968	1979	1990
Share (%) of trade[a] that is																
intra-European	67	67	65	64	69	68	67	66	64	61	61	52	61	71	72	76
Share (%) of world trade[b]	64	62	63	65	68	64	63	60	58	52	51	42	49	53	51	51
Intensity of trade index:[c]																
intra-European	1.06	1.10	1.05	0.98	1.03	1.09	1.07	1.11	1.11	1.20	1.21	1.27	1.27	1.35	1.43	1.51
extra-European	0.90	0.85	0.92	1.04	0.93	0.85	0.88	0.84	0.85	0.79	0.79	0.81	0.75	0.62	0.56	0.49
Share (%) of GDP traded:[d]																
total	9	12	15	20	24	28	28	26	29	33	24	34	31	35	46	45
extra-European	3	4	5	7	7	9	9	9	11	13	10	16	12	10	13	11
Propensity to trade index:[c]																
intra-European	0.10	0.13	0.16	0.20	0.24	0.31	0.30	0.29	0.32	0.40	0.29	0.42	0.40	0.47	0.66	0.68
extra-European	0.08	0.10	0.14	0.21	0.22	0.24	0.25	0.21	0.25	0.26	0.19	0.27	0.24	0.21	0.26	0.22

Notes:

a Throughout the table, 'trade' refers to the average of merchandise export and import shares or intensity indexes, except that the share of GDP traded and the propensity index refer to exports plus imports of merchandise. Both Western and Eastern Europe (including Russia/USSR) are included as part of Europe.

b Refers to share of world exports up to 1910, and so slightly underestimates the share of exports plus imports. The League of Nations (1945, p. 157 ff) suggests that the latter shares for Europe were 65 per cent in 1876–80, 66 per cent in 1896–1900 and 62 per cent in 1913.

c The intensity of trade and propensity to trade indexes for regions are defined following equations (1) and (4) in the text respectively.

d Refers to GNP up to 1911, and is measured at current prices.

Source: Data for the period to 1910 are from Bairoch (1976a, pp. 18, 78, 84) and supplemented with some of his unpublished data. For subsequent years, the data are from Norheim, Finger and Anderson (1993).

European countries to each other, they traded virtually no more among themselves last century than one would expect if one knew nothing more than their importance in world trade. Since the First World War, however, that intensity index has risen steadily, from 1.1 to 1.5, as the intra-regional share of Europe's trade moved up and Europe's share of world trade fell.

Correspondingly, the intensity of Europe's trade with the rest of the world has fallen gradually during the past fifty years, from around 0.8 (a little below the average level of 0.9 maintained during the eight decades to 1910) to just under 0.5 by 1990 (row 4 of Table 11.1).

Even so, this does not necessarily mean that Europe has reduced its propensity to trade with the rest of the world, because one also needs to consider changes in the extent to which European economies have been opening up to international trade. Consistent time series of data on Europe's GDP are not available for the nineteenth century, but GNP estimates are available in Bairoch (1976a, 1976b). They and more recent GDP estimates suggest that the trade-to-output ratio for Europe rose almost continuously during the hundred years to 1928, that it fell in the 1930s, but that it has since risen again to well above its previous peak and is now four times its 1830s level (row 5 of Table 11.1). The share of Europe's GDP traded with non-Europeans has shown no upward or downward trend over the past sixty years, however (row 6).

As a consequence, the index of Europe's propensity to trade within its own region has continued to rise throughout this long period, apart from a dip in the 1930s (row 7), while the index of its propensity to trade with the rest of the world — which ceased to grow at the end of last century — has at least been maintained (row 8). That is, despite the sharp decline during the post-Second World War period in the intensity of Europe's trade with the rest of the world, its effect on the European propensity to trade extra-regionally has been more or less offset by the increasing openness of those economies.

For the 1928–90 period it makes sense to examine Western and Eastern Europe (including the former USSR) as separate regions, and to compare the regionalisation of their trade with that of other regions. The relevant data are summarised in Table 11.2. They show that the share of Western Europe's trade with itself averaged around 50 per cent until the late 1950s. But, following the formation of the EC in 1958 and EFTA in 1960, and the associated dismantling of imperial trade preferences, the share of Western Europe's trade with other Western European countries grew rapidly. By the early 1970s it had risen to two-thirds, and today it is almost three-quarters (first row of part (i) of Table 11.2).

Since the importance of the region in world trade in recent years is similar to what it was in the 1920s and 1930s (part (ii) of Table 11.2), there has been a similarly rapid rate of growth in the index of intensity of Western Europe's intra-regional trade, from 1.1 in the inter-war period to 1.6 by the 1980s (part (iii) of Table 11.2).[6]

This necessarily means the West European index of intensity of extra-regional trade has declined. It has fallen from 0.9 in the inter-war years to 0.5 now (part (iv) of Table 11.2). But, because the share of Western Europe's GDP that is inter-

Table 11.2   Trade shares and the intensity and propensity of regionalisation in world merchandise trade, 1928 to 1990

	1928	1938	1948	1958	1968	1979	1990
(i) Intra-regional trade share (%)[a]							
Western Europe	51	49	43	53	63	66	72
Eastern Europe	19	14	47	61	64	54	46
Europe, Total	61	61	52	61	71	72	76
North America	25	23	29	32	37	30	31
Latin America	11	18	20	17	19	20	14
America, Total	45	44	59	56	52	47	45
Asia	46	52	39	41	37	41	48
-Japan[f]	63	68	60	36	32	31	35
- Australasia[f]	16	16	14	25	31	49	51
- Developing Asia[f]	47	55	44	47	45	48	56
Africa	10	9	8	8	9	6	6
Middle East	5	4	21	12	8	7	6
World, Total[c]	39	37	33	40	47	46	52
(ii) Share (%) of world trade[a]							
Western Europe	47	45	36	40	43	44	46
Eastern Europe	5	6	5	9	10	8	5
Europe, Total	52	51	42	49	53	51	51
North America	18	14	22	19	19	15	16
Latin America	9	8	12	9	5	6	4
America, Total	26	22	34	28	24	21	21
Asia	18	19	15	13	13	15	21
Africa	4	5	7	6	5	5	3
Middle East	1	1	2	3	3	7	3
(iii) Intensity of intra-regional trade index[b]							
Western Europe	1.13	1.14	1.21	1.38	1.51	1.57	1.60
Eastern Europe	4.36	2.61	10.22	7.62	7.30	7.88	10.88
Europe, Total	1.20	1.21	1.27	1.27	1.35	1.43	1.51
North America	2.59	2.91	2.39	3.07	3.57	3.63	3.50
Latin America	1.37	2.30	1.71	1.95	3.55	3.80	3.53
America, Total	1.76	2.00	1.77	2.07	2.21	2.29	2.26
Asia	2.61	2.83	2.74	3.15	2.84	2.77	2.31
-Japan[f]	4.17	4.65	4.29	3.28	3.81	3.08	2.33
-Australasia[f]	0.97	0.93	1.08	2.00	2.47	3.32	2.47
-Developing Asia[f]	2.66	2.96	3.10	3.56	3.37	3.17	2.64
Africa	2.37	1.73	1.27	1.38	1.91	1.24	2.48
Middle East	7.56	3.47	9.55	4.25	3.00	1.17	2.23
World, Total[c]	1.85	1.92	2.43	2.65	2.81	2.64	2.62

(*Table 11.2 continued*)

	1928	1938	1948	1958	1968	1979	1990
(iv) Intensity of extra-regional trade index[b]							
Western Europe	0.89	0.89	0.88	0.76	0.64	0.58	0.51
Eastern Europe	0.85	0.91	0.56	0.42	0.40	0.49	0.57
Europe, Total	0.79	0.79	0.81	0.75	0.62	0.56	0.40
North America	0.83	0.84	0.80	0.76	0.70	0.76	0.75
Latin America	0.79	0.89	0.91	0.91	0.86	0.84	0.90
America, Total	0.73	0.72	0.61	0.60	0.63	0.67	0.68
Asia	0.66	0.59	0.71	0.68	0.83	0.69	0.66
-Japan[f]	0.41	0.34	0.44	0.68	0.73	0.73	0.70
-Australasia[f]	1.01	1.02	0.99	0.86	0.79	0.60	0.62
-Developing Asia[f]	0.64	0.56	0.65	0.61	0.64	0.62	0.56
Africa	0.94	0.96	0.98	0.98	0.95	0.99	0.96
Middle East	0.96	0.97	0.81	0.90	0.94	0.99	0.96
World, Total[c]	0.86	0.82	0.83	0.75	0.67	0.68	0.62
(v) Share (%) of GDP traded[a]							
Western Europe	33	24	35	33	34	48	46
Eastern Europe	30[e]	25[e]	25[e]	25[e]	40[e]	40[e]	41
Europe, Total	33	24	34	31	35	46	45
North America	10	8	11	9	10	19	19
Latin America	45[e]	30[e]	30[e]	30	21	27	28
America, Total	14	10	14	12	11	21	20
Asia	32	27	25	26	21	27	29
-Japan[f]	35	29	8	19	17	20	18
-Australasia[f]	38	32	47	31	25	29	30
-Developing Asia[f]	30[e]	25[e]	25[e]	29	26	37	47
Africa	60[e]	50[e]	50[e]	58	37	56	53
Middle East	60[e]	50[e]	50[e]	46	38	48	49
World, Total	24	19	22	22	22	35	34
(vi) Index of propensity to trade intra-regionally[d]							
Western Europe	0.38	0.27	0.30	0.46	0.50	0.75	0.73
Eastern Europe	1.31	0.65	2.56	1.90	2.92	3.15	4.52
Europe, Total	0.40	0.29	0.42	0.40	0.47	0.66	0.68
North America	0.27	0.22	0.26	0.29	0.34	0.70	0.67
Latin America	0.62	0.69	0.51	0.58	0.76	1.01	0.97
America, Total	0.25	0.20	0.25	0.24	0.24	0.48	0.46
Asia	0.83	0.76	0.67	0.83	0.60	0.76	0.67
-Japan[f]	1.37	1.57	0.28	0.53	0.31	0.55	0.42
-Australasia[f]	0.39	0.21	0.43	0.57	0.71	1.03	0.89
-Developing Asia[f]	0.82	0.72	0.84	1.07	1.09	1.23	1.21
Africa	1.42	0.86	0.63	0.63	0.73	0.60	1.21
Middle East	4.53	1.74	4.77	2.47	1.12	0.66	1.19

(*Table 11.2 continued*)

	1928	1938	1948	1958	1968	1979	1990
World, Total	0.45	0.37	0.54	0.57	0.61	0.91	0.88

(vii) Index of propensity to trade extra-regionally[d]

	1928	1938	1948	1958	1968	1979	1990
Western Europe	0.30	0.21	0.31	0.26	0.21	0.28	0.23
Eastern Europe	0.25	0.23	0.14	0.11	0.16	0.20	0.24
Europe, Total	0.26	0.19	0.27	0.24	0.21	0.26	0.22
North America	0.09	0.06	0.09	0.07	0.07	0.15	0.14
Latin America	0.43	0.27	0.27	0.27	0.18	0.22	0.25
America, Total	0.10	0.07	0.08	0.07	0.07	0.14	0.14
Asia	0.21	0.16	0.18	0.18	0.15	0.19	0.19
-Japan[f]	0.14	0.10	0.04	0.13	0.12	0.15	0.13
-Australasia[f]	0.37	0.31	0.45	0.29	0.23	0.27	0.28
-Developing Asia[f]	0.25	0.21	0.18	0.20	0.22	0.30	0.35
Africa	0.56	0.48	0.49	0.45	0.37	0.48	0.47
Middle East	0.57	0.49	0.41	0.52	0.35	0.56	0.51
World, Total	0.21	0.16	0.19	0.16	0.15	0.23	0.21

Notes: a Throughout the table, 'trade' refers to the average of merchandise export and import shares or intensity indexes, except that the share of GDP traded and the propensity index refer to exports plus imports of merchandise. All values are measured in current US dollars. Eastern Europe includes the former Soviet Union as one country and the former German Democratic Republic from 1948 as another. Turkey and Yugoslavia are included in Western Europe. North America refers to Canada and the United States, and Australasia refers to Australia and New Zealand.

b The intensity of trade index for regions is defined in the text.

c The world total intensity index is the weighted average across the seven regions, using the regions' shares of world trade as weights.

d The propensity to trade index is defined as the intensity index multiplied by the ratio of exports plus imports to GDP; see equation (4) above. The world total refers to the weighted average for the seven regions, using the regions' shares of world GDP as weights.

e In the absence of reliable estimates of GDP in the interwar period for developing countries and until 1989 for Eastern Europe, 'guestimates' have been made of the trade-to-GDP ratio for those regions. Given their small weights in world trade, the aggregates for Europe, the Americas and the world nonetheless will be reasonably reliable. The ratio is estimated at current prices.

f The rows for Japan, Australasia and Developing Asia differ from the other rows in that they are treated not as regions themselves but as part of their sum which is the Asian region.

Source: Norheim, Finger and Anderson (1993). Trade data are based on the current US dollar value of merchandise exports, from League of Nations (1942) for 1928 (adjusted to include trade between Japan, Korea and Taiwan), from United Nations, *Yearbook of International Trade Statistics,* for 1938, 1948 and 1958, and from GATT (1987, 1992) for subsequent years. GDP data are from the World Bank's *World Tables* from 1968 and from the United Nations' *Statistical Yearbook,* particularly the 1954 and 1969 issues (based on official exchange rates) for years prior to 1968.

nationally traded has doubled since the 1930s (part (v) of Table 11.2), the index of Western Europe's propensity to trade extra-regionally, as defined above in equation (4), has been more or less maintained since 1928. In particular, this propensity of Western Europe's GDP to be traded with the rest of the world, after netting out the effect of changes in the latter's importance in global trade, has declined very little since the formation of the EC and EFTA and is still above its 1938 level. And this has happened despite the considerable GDP growth in, and the introduction of preferential trading arrangements among, Western Europe's economies. Only a small proportion of that increased propensity to trade outside Western Europe is accounted for by the increased intensity of the region's trade with neighbouring Eastern Europe. Despite a 50 per cent increase in that intensity index during the past three decades (from 0.41 to 0.66), the Eastern bloc's share of West European trade has been no more than 5 per cent.

Turning to Eastern Europe's own trade, half or more of the trade of European members of Comecon was with other European members of that communist trade bloc during the Cold War period (compared with less than one-fifth in the previous hundred-plus years). But since those countries accounted for one tenth or less of world trade during the Cold War, the intensity of intra-East European/Soviet trade has been extremely high. As shown in part (iii) of Table 11.2, their index of intra-regional trade intensity has been more than 7 since the 1950s, compared with an average of less than half that in the inter-war period.

Most of that change for Eastern Europe has been at the expense of its trade with Western Europe: the intensity of trade index with those neighbours fell by two-thirds between the inter-war period and the 1950s. While it has remained low since then, it has been nonetheless creeping up slowly, from 0.4 in 1958 to 0.5 in the early 1970s, 0.6 in the early 1980s and almost 0.7 in 1990. And so too has the intensity of East European/Soviet trade with the rest of the world. Thus by 1990 this region's index of propensity to trade outside Eastern Europe was as high as that of Western Europe (part (vii) of Table 11.2).

The Americas

Trade between Canada and the United States has represented about a third of North America's international trade during the post-war period. While this is higher than the inter-war share of about a quarter, it has been lower in recent years than at its peak around 1970. But since North America's share of world trade declined somewhat from the late 1960s, the intensity of its intra-regional trade rose in the 1970s before falling slightly since then, and conversely for the extra-regional trade intensity index (parts (i) to (iv) of Table 11.2). (When Mexico is included in the definition of North America, the intra-regional trade intensity indexes are a little lower but otherwise show a similar trend).

However, the share of GDP that is internationally traded has grown even faster for North America than for Western Europe (part (v) of Table 11.2). As a consequence, the index of propensity for North America to trade extra-regionally has steadily increased since the 1930s, from 0.06 in 1938 and 0.07 in 1958 and 1968 to 0.14 by 1990 (part (vi) of Table 11.2). A small part of that growth is attributable to trade with Mexico, but the share and intensity of North America's trade with other Latin American economies have actually declined.

Latin America's intra-regional trade share rose in the 1930s and 1940s as those countries adopted inward-looking national and regional trade policies, but it has steadily declined since then. The decline is not surprising given the dramatic fall in the region's share of global trade (parts (i) and (ii) of Table 11.2) — itself a consequence of their adoption of more protectionist policies. In fact, the intensity of the region's intra-regional trade has more than doubled during the post-war period (part (iii) of Table 11.2). This was boosted in large part by the formation of various regional integration agreements in the 1960s which sought to extend those countries' inward-looking import-substituting industrialisation strategies from the national to the regional level. But because the region is such a small contributor to global trade, the indexes of intensity and propensity of its extra-regional trade are little different now than they were in the early post-war years (parts (iv) and (vii) of Table 11.2).

Asia (including the Southwest Pacific)

About half of Asia's trade is intra-regional at present, as was the case in the inter-war period. But in the third quarter of the century it was barely 40 per cent. To understand why requires first examining Japan's international trade. That trade was very heavily focused on its neighbours in the inter-war period: as much as two-thirds of Japanese trade was then with other Asian economies. However, following the collapse of the Japanese empire in the mid-1940s and the decline of barriers to Japan's trade with other industrial economies between the 1950s and 1970s, the share of its trade with other Asian economies dropped to half the inter-war level (part (i) of Table 11.2). Thus the index of intensity of Japan's trade outside Asia has grown steadily, rising from a low of less than 0.4 in the 1930s to more than double that from the 1960s (part (iv) of Table 11.2).

Australia and New Zealand, by contrast, traded little with Asia before the late 1950s as most of their ties were with the United Kingdom. The latter ties gradually weakened as Commonwealth preferences eroded, as the EC's Common Agricultural Policy reduced European demand for Australasia's farm products (particularly after the United Kingdom joined the EC in 1972), as restrictions on trade with Japan were relaxed from the mid-1950s, and as industrialisation boomed first in Japan and then in a growing number of East Asia's developing countries. The net effect of these developments (aided in a small way by the RIA formed between Australia and New Zealand in the 1980s) was a trebling in the share and intensity of Australasia's trade with Asia between 1950 and 1980 (parts (i) and (iv) of Table 11.2).

The share of developing Asian economies' trade within Asia fell a little with the collapse of the Japanese empire in the 1940s, but increased again over the post-war years as the region's share of world trade grew. Throughout the period their intra-regional trade intensity has remained high (part (iv) of Table 11.2), reflecting not only relative proximity in terms of distance and culture but also strong complementarity with the more advanced economies of the region, especially Japan. But with the dramatic growth in the share of their GDP that is traded, the index of their propensity to trade extra-regionally has doubled in the post-war period (part (vii) of Table 11.2).

The aggregate effect of these changes has been for Asia's indexes of propensity to trade intra-regionally and extra-regionally to both fluctuate around a flat trend since 1928 (parts (vi) and (vii) of Table 11.2). But note that Asia's propensity to trade extra-regionally is significantly higher today than it was in the 1960s, and that this increase has occurred in spite of the deepening integration within Asia via market forces — a phenomenon that has been described as 'open regionalism' (Drysdale and Garnaut 1993).

Africa and the Middle East

The other developing countries, of Africa and the Middle East, in total account for less than one-tenth of world trade and so their impact on the extent of regionalisation in global trade is necessarily minor. Even so, it is noteworthy that for each of these regions the share of their trade that is intra-regional has declined in recent decades. In the case of Africa this is not surprising because its share of world trade has been falling. In fact it has fallen faster than Africa's intra-regional trade share, causing its index of intensity of intra-regional trade to rise (part (iii) of Table 11.2). But during the past decade or so a number of African economies have been increasing the share of their GDP that is traded. As a consequence, the indexes of their (and the Middle East's) propensity to trade extra-regionally have risen during the past two decades and are now about as high as they were in the 1930s (part (vii) of Table 11.2).

Conclusions

Several conclusions can be drawn from the above analysis. The first is that even in the absence of a computable general equilibrium model of the world economy and estimates of policy distortions to prices, it is possible to get some idea from trade data of the trade effects of discriminatory policies. But in doing so it is necessary to look beyond intra-regional and extra-regional trade shares and even trade intensity indexes. The propensity index suggested above has the virtue that it shows the combined effect of changes in bilateral trade intensities and in the share of an economy that is traded internationally.

Second, the above data suggest the world has become more interdependent in recent decades, as measured by that index of the various geographic regions' propensities to trade extra-regionally. True, that index is no higher now than it was in 1928 for the world as a whole (as a weighted average for the seven regions shown in the last row of Table 11.2), but it is substantially higher than in the 1930s or 1950s. Even though several important regional integration agreements have come into force since the Second World War, and despite the gradual dismantling of Europe's former imperial preferences that artificially encouraged North–South trade, the world's economies have been opening up sufficiently rapidly for integration between regions to continue. Indeed, that propensity index for the world has increased by an average of more than a third since the late 1950s. Certainly, it has grown faster for North America and Asia than for Europe, but even in the case of Western Europe the index has been rising during the past three decades. Thus while the European countries that vigorously fostered extra-regional trade for centuries up to the 1930s have not done so in recent decades, they at least have not done the opposite. Meanwhile, other sources of inter-regional trade growth have emerged to allow global economic integration to continue.

And third, recall from equation (4) that an increase in the propensity to trade extra-regionally largely reflects an increase in the share of GDP that is traded with other regions. And since real GDP has been growing for all regions, this finding implies that the volume of each region's trade with other regions has been growing over time. But we know from economic theory that a regional integration agreement will enhance economic welfare in the rest of the world if the RIA causes the volume of its trade with that region to grow (Kemp and Wan 1976). The trade data therefore do not vindicate the fear that RIAs have reduced welfare in other regions. This is not to deny the possibility that the world might be a better place without RIAs of course: as Bhagwati (1992, also Chapter 12, this volume) has argued forcefully, greater liberalisation of global trade may well have occurred if no new RIAs had formed in the post-war years. Rather, the point is simply that the creation of RIAs and the growth of intra-regional trade shares and intensities since the 1950s is not inconsistent with the possibility that economies excluded from those RIAs have benefitted from them — a possibility that has also not been ruled out by results from formal quantitative models (see, for instance, Lloyd 1992; and Srinivasan, Whalley and Wooton 1993).

The issue for the 1990s and beyond is whether the recent and prospective proliferation of RIAs will be accompanied by a continuation or reversal of this trend towards a more liberal and more integrated trading world. While both the West Europeans and the North Americans claim they are not and will not be raising external trade barriers, the increased frequency of use of contingent protectionist measures in recent years has given cause for concern for excluded economies — to the point that many are lining up to join one or other of those major RIAs or are discussing ways to form another one, such as in the Asian region.

Two responses to that queueing up for RIA membership are called for. One is to reduce the 'safe haven' motive for wanting to join by making it more difficult for GATT contracting parties to use contingent protectionist measures. A second helpful response would be to introduce stricter monitoring of regional agreements than is currently undertaken under GATT's Article XXIV, to determine whether the agreements are harmful to outsiders. Such monitoring would need to be undertaken not only at the signing stage but also during and after implementation of the agreement. One possibility is for this to be done systematically by the GATT Secretariat's Trade Policy

Review Division (which currently restricts itself to reviewing national trade policies). The mere existence of such a review mechanism is likely to increase the probability that the drafters and implementers of RIAs do not deviate too far from the principles and rules of the GATT. Hopefully then we could feel more confident that RIAs will contribute to world trade becoming more rather than less liberal and predictable over time. And, as Henderson (1992) suggests in his recent review of international economic integration during the past 120 years that there is still great scope for further liberalisation despite the substantial progress of recent decades.

Notes

1   The trade intensity index was first popularised by Brown (1949). For a detailed discussion of its use in bilateral trade analysis, see Drysdale and Garnaut (1982, also Chapter 3, this volume).

2   If j is a country group and country i is part of country group j, it is necessary to subtract country i's imports from j's imports not only in the denominator but also in the numerator of the m_j ratio, and likewise to subtract country i's GDP from j's GDP in the numerator of the q_j ratio.

3   The term 'relative openness' is in parentheses because the trade-to-GDP ratio should not be interpreted as a measure of the extent to which an economy is subject to trade restrictions, not least because that ratio is affected by the relative size of the economy.

4   An adjustment is necessary because when i is a region there can be international trade between the countries in the region.

5   For example, the formation or expansion of a regional customs union could induce foreign direct investment (FDI) or immigration from other regions, thereby altering different regions' comparative advantages.

6   By way of comparison, the index of intra-regional trade intensity in 1990 was 3.5 in both North and Latin America and 2.3 in Asia. Caution is needed in comparing these index values, however, for at least two reasons. First, as equations (2) and (3) make clear, the index will be lower the less complementary are the commodity compositions of neighbours' trades within regions. And second, the larger a region's share of world trade, the closer its index of intra-regional trade intensity will be to unity, *ceteris paribus*. Since Western Europe's share of world trade is more than twice that of North America or Asia, this alone gives reason to expect the index to be somewhat lower for Europe than for North America or Asia.

References

Bairoch, Paul 1974, 'Geographical structure and trade balance of European foreign trade from 1800 to 1970', *Journal of European Economic History*, 3, pp. 557–608.

_____ 1976a, *Commerce Extérieur et Développement Économique de l'Europe au XIXᵉ Siècle*, Paris: Mouton.

_____ 1976b, 'Europe's Gross National Product 1800–1975', *Journal of European Economic History*, 5, pp. 273–340.

Balassa, Bela 1965, 'Trade liberalisation and "revealed" comparative advantage', *Manchester School of Economic and Social Studies*, 33, pp. 90–124.

Bhagwati, Jagdish 1992, 'Regionalism and multilateralism: an overview', Paper presented to the World Bank–CEPR Conference on New Dimensions in Regional Integration, Washington, DC, 2–3 April.

Brown, A. J. 1949, *Applied Economics: Aspects of the World Economy in War and Peace*, London: George Allen and Unwin.

Clarida, Richard and Ronald Findlay 1992, 'Government, trade, and comparative advantage', *American Economic Review*, 82, pp. 122–7.

Drysdale, Peter 1988, *International Economic Pluralism: Economic Policy in East Asia and the Pacific*, New York: Columbia University Press.

Drysdale, Peter and Ross Garnaut 1982, 'Trade intensities and the analysis of bilateral trade flows in a many-country world', *Hitotsubashi Journal of Economics*, 22, pp. 62–84.

——————— 1993, 'The Pacific: an application of a general theory of economic integration', in C. Fred Bergsten and Marcus Noland (eds), *Pacific Dynamism and the International Economic System*, Washington, DC: Institute for International Economics.

GATT 1987, 1992 *International Trade 1986–87, 1990–91 Volume II*, Geneva: GATT.

Henderson, David 1992, 'International economic integration: progress, prospects and implications', *International Affairs*, 68, pp. 633–53.

Kemp, Murray and Henry Wan Jr. 1976, 'An elementary proposition concerning the formation of customs unions', *Journal of International Economics*, 6, pp. 95–7.

Krugman, Paul 1991, *Geography and Trade*, Cambridge, Mass.: MIT Press.

League of Nations 1942, *The Network of World Trade*, Geneva: League of Nations.

——————— 1945, *Industrialisation and Foreign Trade*, Geneva: League of Nations.

Lloyd, Peter J. 1992, 'Regionalisation and world trade', *OECD Economic Studies*, 18, pp. 7–34.

McMillan, John 1993, 'Does regional integration foster open trade? Economic theory and GATT's Article XXIV', in Kym Anderson and Richard Blackhurst (eds), *Regional Integration and the Global Trading System*, London: Harvester Wheatsheaf.

Norheim, Hege, Karl-Michael Finger and Kym Anderson 1993, 'Trends in the regionalisation of world trade, 1928 to 1990' (Statistical Appendix), in Kym Anderson and Richard Blackhurst (eds), *Regional Integration and the Global Trading System*, London: Harvester Wheatsheaf.

North, Douglas 1958, 'Ocean freight rates and economic development, 1750–1913', *Journal of Economic History*, 18, pp. 537–55.

Perkins, Dwight and Moshe Syrquin 1989, 'Large countries: the influence of size', in Hollis Chenery and T. N. Srinivasan (eds), *Handbook of Development Economics, Vol. 2*, Amsterdam: North-Holland.

Srinivasan, T. N., John Whalley and Ian Wooton 1993, 'Measuring the effects of regionalism on trade and welfare', in Kym Anderson and Richard Blackhurst (eds), *Regional Integration and the Global Trading System*, London: Harvester Wheatsheaf.

Tracy, John (ed.) 1991, *The Rise of Merchant Empires*, Cambridge: Cambridge University Press.

Part Three

Regionalism and Multilateralism

12 Regionalism and multilateralism: an overview

Jagdish Bhagwati

The question of 'regionalism', defined broadly as preferential trade agreements among a subset of nations, is a longstanding one. As with all great issues, economists have long been divided on the wisdom of such arrangements. So have policy-makers.

While this may not be evident to the many economists who are not inhibited by lack of comparative advantage from pronouncing on these matters, and whose pronouncements are a testimony to the enduring value of the theory of comparative advantage, preferential trade arrangements were debated by economists, as such, during the very formation of the GATT.

Closer to our times, CUs and FTAs, both permitted under GATT Article XXIV, became a major topic of theoretical research. The focus, however, since Jacob Viner's (1950) classic treatment, distinguishing between trade diversion and trade creation, was on showing that CUs and FTAs were not necessarily welfare-improving, either for member countries or for world welfare: in other words, the case for preferential trade arrangements was different from the case for free trade for all. The latter, enshrined in Adam Smith and Ricardo, and rigorously proved later by Samuelson (1939), Kemp (1972), and Grandmont and McFadden (1972), is a first-best case. The former, by contrast, reflects second-best considerations and was argued by Meade (1956), Lipsey and Lancaster (1956–57), Lipsey (1957), Johnson (1958a, 1958b) and others.

But if the main focus of these analyses was on disabusing the faith in regionalism as being desirable (on static immediate-impact grounds) by analogy with the different and legitimate case for multilateralism (in the sense of free or freer trade for all), and thus could be seen as reinforcing the case for multilateralism, the effect could also go the other way, and did at times. One could thus argue, from the opposite counterfactual, that if you believed that regionalism, in being discriminatory, was necessarily inferior to non-discriminatory reduction of trade barriers, then this too was wrong. As it happened, the ideas concerning regional blocs and trading arrangements remained seductive through much of the 1960s, only to be abandoned thereafter until their revival in the 1980s.

The recent revival of regionalism, which I describe as the 'Second Regionalism' in contrast to, and because it is a sequel to, the 'First Regionalism' of the 1960s, raises several of the old issues anew. But the historically changed situation which has resurrected regionalism equally provides the context in which it must be analysed, raising several new issues.

In this paper, I address these manifold questions, dividing the analysis into a discussion of six areas:

- Article XXIV of the GATT, which sanctions CUs and FTAs;

- the 'First Regionalism', briefly reviewing the factors that led to it and the reasons why, in the end, it failed;

- the 'Second Regionalism', the reasons for its revival and its differential prospects;

- the key issues that this renewed regionalism raises, distinguishing among two main questions: the first, relating to the static impact effect of regional trade blocs; and the second, concerning the dynamic time-path that regionalism offers, in itself and *vis-à-vis* multilateralism when the objective is to reach (non-discriminatory) free trade for all, so that one asks 'whether multilateralism is the best way to get to multilateralism', therefore distinguishing between 'process multilateralism' and 'outcome multilateralism'.

In the light of this analysis, I conclude by examining the current US trade policy shift to regionalism and arguing for a change in its focus from 'piecemeal' to 'programmatic' regionalism, less antithetical to reaching the 'outcome-multilateralism' objective of eventual free trade for all. Some final observations conclude the paper.

Article XXIV of the GATT: rationale

The principle of non-discrimination is central to the final conception of the GATT, signed on 30 October 1947 by representatives from 23 countries in Geneva. Article I embodies the strong support for non-discrimination, requiring (unconditional) MFN for all GATT members.

Aside from 'grandfathering' provisions, the only significant exception to MFN is made in Article XXIV, which permits CUs and FTAs and therefore sanctions preferential trade barrier reductions among a subset of GATT members, as long as they go all the way to elimination.

It is an intriguing question as to why Article XXIV was accepted, and it is a question that also has significance for some of the issues raised by the 'Second Regionalism'. It is a bit odd that an exception to MFN should be allowed as long as it is total (going all the way to 100 per cent) rather than partial (say, 20 per cent preference for one's favoured friends): it is as if your cardinal told you that petting is more reprehensible than sleeping around. In fact, the post-Vinerian theory of preferential trade areas suggests that 100 per cent preferences are less likely to increase welfare than partial preferences.

The rationale for Article XXIV's inclusion in the GATT must therefore be explained in other ways. It appears to have been threefold, as follows:

- Full integration on trade, that is, going all the way down to freedom of trade flows among any subset of GATT members, would have to be allowed since it created an important element of single-nation characteristics (such as virtual freedom of trade and factor movements) among these nations, and implied that the resulting quasi-national status following from such integration in trade legitimated the exception to MFN obligation towards other GATT members.

- The fact that the exception would be permitted only for the extremely difficult case where all trade barriers would need to come down seemed to preclude the possibility that all kinds of preferential arrangements would break out, returning the world to the fragmented, discriminatory bilateralism-infested situation of the 1930s.

- One could also think of Article XXIV as permitting a supplemental, practical route to the universal free trade that GATT favoured as the ultimate goal, with the general negotiations during the many GATT rounds leading to a dismantling of trade barriers on a GATT-wide basis while deeper integration would be achieved simultaneously within those areas where politics permitted faster movement to free trade under a strategy of full and time-bound commitment. This is an argument that is now at centre stage: is regionalism truly a building, rather than a stumbling, block towards multilateral free trade for all: in other words, will it fragment, or integrate, the world economy?

The clear determination of 100 per cent preferences as compatible with multilateralism and non-discrimination, and the equally firm view that anything less was not, meant that when Article XXIV was drafted, its principal objective was to close all possible loopholes by which it could degenerate into a justification for preferential arrangements of less than 100 per cent; paragraphs 4–10 of Article XXIV were written precisely for this purpose. But, as is now commonly conceded, their inherent ambiguity and the political pressures for approval of substantial regional groupings of preferences of less than 100 per cent have combined to frustrate the full import of the original desire to sanction only 100 per cent preferences.

This tension between intention and reality has a direct bearing on the important question of strengthening Article XXIV today beyond even what its original drafters intended. I will therefore sketch briefly the important respects in which the original intention of Article XXIV was reasonably clear but was occasionally violated in spirit, to the point where the great expert on GATT law, Professor John Jackson, has gone so far as to observe that the accommodation of the European Common Market's imperfect union in disregard of the legal requirements of Article XXIV was the beginning of the breakdown of the GATT's legal discipline. Two issues suffice to demonstrate this contention.

First, in regard to the elimination of internal barriers down to 100 per cent, there was enough scope within the language of Article XXIV, paragraph 8, for its intent to be successfully avoided. Ambiguities could be exploited on two main fronts.

The first ambiguity lay in the directive that 'duties and other restrictive regulations on commerce' were (with specified exceptions permitted under Articles XI, XII, XIII, XIV and XX) to be 'eliminated with respect to substantially all the trade between the constituent territories'. Skilful lawyers and representatives of governments could work wonders with the concept of 'substantially all the trade', and then, even if a percentage cutoff point was accepted for this purpose (for example, 75 per cent of all initial trade), important issues remained ambiguous, such as whether across-the-board (75 per cent) cuts on everything were required or whether substantial sectors could be left out altogether from the scope of the cuts — the latter being evidently at variance with the intent of those who favoured (100 per cent) CUs but opposed (less than 100 per cent) preferential arrangements. With both interpretations possible, sectorally non-uniform preferential arrangements could evidently not effectively be ruled out.

An ambiguity of equal importance arose in regard to the problem of the speed with which the '100 per cent preferences' would be implemented. Evidently, if they were stretched out over very long periods, one was *de facto* sanctioning 'less than 100 per cent' preferential arrangements. In GATT jargon, this was the problem of 'interim arrangements'. Paragraph 5 therefore addressed this issue, requiring 'a plan and schedule', and asking for the CU or FTA to be fully consummated 'within a reasonable length of time'. Paragraph 7, in turn, laid down specific procedures for such interim arrangements to be approved. Needless to say, this nonetheless left the door open for substantial laxity in conception and execution of the CUs and FTAs under Article XXIV.

Dam's (1970, p. 290) overall judgement of the outcome is perhaps too harsh, but is certainly in the ballpark:

> The record is not comforting . . . Perhaps only one of the more than one dozen regional arrangements that have come before the GATT complied fully with Article XXIV criteria. That was the recent United Kingdom/Ireland Free-Trade Area, and even in that case certain doubts were expressed before the working party. In some cases, the regional arrangements were very wide of the

mark. The European Coal and Steel Community, covering only two major product lines, could not even qualify for the special regional-arrangement waiver of Article XXIV:10 but required a general waiver under Article XXV:5. The New Zealand/Australia Free-Trade Agreement, although not purportedly an example of 'functional integration', provided for the liberalization of an even smaller percentage of intermember trade. A strong tendency has also been manifested for interim agreements to provide for an even longer transitional period and to contain increasingly fewer detailed commitments for eventual completion of the customs union or free-trade area.

The 'First Regionalism': failure in the 1960s

In any event, one can correctly assert (based on the acceptance of Article XXIV into the GATT) that regionalism, in the shape of (100 per cent) CUs and FTAs, was not generally considered, by the architects of the GATT or by the United States, which was the chief proponent of multilateralism and non-discrimination, as antithetical to the GATT and to these principles.

1   Nonetheless, the United States, long suspicious of discriminatory trade arrangements, restrained itself from resorting to Article XXIV. The formation of the EC in 1958 marked a partial watershed. The United States put its shoulder to the wheel and saw the Common Market through, negotiating around the different hoops of Article XXIV, emasculating the Articles somewhat so as to seek GATT approval of an imperfect union (especially in regard to discriminatory preferences for the eighteen ex-colonies in Africa that the Europeans insisted on retaining, requiring therefore a waiver of GATT rules), all in the cause of what it saw as a *politically* beneficial union of the original six nations that formed the Community. But despite the enthusiasm of many to follow the EC with a North Atlantic Free Trade Area, and even a Pacific Free Trade Area, centred on the United States, nothing came of it: the United States remained indifferent to such notions.

2   There was an outbreak of FTA proposals in the developing countries as well. While stimulated by the European examples, they were motivated by the altogether different economic rationale formulated by Cooper and Massell (1965a, 1965b), Johnson (1965) and Bhagwati (1968). This was that, given any targeted level of import-substituting industrialisation, the developing countries with their small markets could reduce the cost of this industrialisation by exploiting economies of scale through preferential opening of markets with one another. By the end of the 1960s, however, the attempts at forming regional FTAs and CUs along these lines had also collapsed. The problem was that, rather than use trade liberalisation and hence prices to guide industry allocation, the developing countries attempting such unions sought to

allocate industries by bureaucratic negotiation and to tie trade to such allocations, putting the cart before the horse and killing the forward motion.

Thus, while the world was indeed filled with proposals for regional FTAs in the 1960s, regionalism had virtually died by the end of the decade, except for the original EC and EFTA.

The 'Second Regionalism': revival in the 1980s

But regionalism (namely, preferential trade liberalisation) is now back. Those who do not know the history of the 'First Regionalism' are doomed to extrapolate from the current political ferment in favour of FTAs and CUs and assume uncritically that regionalism is here to stay. Those who know the history may make the reverse mistake of thinking that regionalism will again fail. I believe that careful analysis of the causes of the resurrection of regionalism suggests that regionalism this time is likely to endure.

The main driving force for regionalism today is the conversion of the United States, hitherto an abstaining party, to Article XXIV. Beginning with the FTA with Israel (a reflection of the special relationship between the two nations and hence of little general value), the FTA with Canada marked a distinct change. Now NAFTA has been negotiated with Mexico, and the Enterprise for the Americas Initiative envisages more FTAs with the nations of South America, with Chile at the head of the line.

The conversion of the United States is of major significance. As the key defender of multilateralism through the post-war years, its decision now to travel the regional route (in the geographical *and* the preferential senses simultaneously) tilts the balance of forces at the margin away from multilateralism to regionalism. This shift has taken place in the context of an anti-multilateralist ethos that has reflected alternative but nonetheless eventually reinforcing views:

- The 'Memorial Drive' school[1] holds that the GATT is dead (Thurow: Davos) or that the GATT should be killed (Dornbusch). Regionalism is then presented in effect as an *alternative* to multilateralism. This school, aptly named in view of its funeral approach to multilateralism, has influence in Democratic circles and plays to the prejudices that one finds in Congressional circles that mistakenly identify multilateralism with America's post-war altruism and regionalism (with its connotation of 'exploiting our own markets for ourselves') with the presumed current necessity finally to 'look after one's interests'.

- An alternative view is that regionalism is a useful *supplement*, not an alternative, to multilateralism. 'We are walking on only two legs' is the popular argument. That we may wind up walking on all fours is ignored.

- It is also often asserted that regionalism will not merely supplement multilateralism. It will also *accelerate* the multilateral process: the threat of going (unilateral and) regional will produce multilateral agreements that may otherwise be held up. (However, this may be an optimistic view since threats that have to be implemented and repeatedly made, as has been the case with US regionalism, are not efficient threats; and they change external perceptions about what US trade policy options are, quite regardless of what the United States asserts to be its true intentions. In fact, the taking of two roads simultaneously can affect adversely the travel down one, as I argue below at length.)

- The panic over the continuing payments deficit has also fed demands for 'quick' results on trade (although the two issues are broadly delinkable: payments surpluses and deficits are macroeconomic phenomena that are not influenced in any predictable way by trade policy changes whose impact on the difference between domestic savings and investment, if any, can come in different ways that can go in opposing directions). Associated with this has been impatience with the pace of the multilateral trade negotiating process and the *non sequitur* (examined below) that regionalism necessarily works faster.

- In addition, 'Europe 1992' and the impending integration of Eastern Europe into the EC have reinforced, as the formation of the Common Market did with many three decades ago, those in North America who feel that a countervailing bloc must be formed there as well. Indeed, the fear that European investments would be diverted to Eastern Europe, once it is integrated with the EC, was cited by President Salinas of Mexico as a factor decisively pushing him towards the Mexico–US FTA: this would, he felt, enable Mexico to get the investment needed from the United States and Japan.

- There are strong non-economic, political and cultural factors also driving Mexico towards an FTA with its northern neighbour. Just as the Turks since Ataturk have tried to seek a European rather than an Arab (or Islamic) identity, the Mexicans clearly now seek an American future rather than one with their southern neighbours. The Hispanic (economic) destiny that many in America fear from illegal immigration and integration with Mexico has its flip side in the American (economic) destiny that Mexico's reforming elite, trained in the top universities in the United States, hope for.

- The offer in June 1990 by President Bush to get more nations from South America to join the United States in a FTA, as part of a general package of economic initiatives to assist these nations, reflects the compulsions that the debt crisis there imposes on American policy to respond in a regional framework to ensure that this crisis remains manageable and does not engulf the United States, whose banks are principally endangered by it.

- Then again, the response of South American nations to the prospect of FTAs with NAFTA, and in some cases with one another first and then joining up with NAFTA, has been enthusiastic. This time around, the prospects are better than in the 1960s. Quite simply, there is now a marked shift in economic thinking towards trade liberalisation and market forces. The macroeconomic crisis of the 1980s has fed the movement to microeconomic reforms, much as it is currently doing in India.

- Finally, the conjunction of the two dramatic events, 'Europe 1992' and the Canada–US FTA, even though fortuitous and prompted by different motivations and historical circumstances, certainly has created a sense elsewhere that regionalism is the order of the day, and that others must follow suit. In the Far East, for instance, there has been a sense that a Japan-centred regional bloc may be necessary in a bloc-infested world, and Malaysia has actively sought a Japan-centred Asian bloc to rival and confront the US-led Americas bloc.

Regionalism versus multilateralism: key questions

I suspect therefore that the 'Second Regionalism' will endure: it shows many signs of strength and few points of vulnerability. But if so, those of us who see virtue in a rule-based, open and multilateral trading system must ask searching questions as to its compatibility with such discriminatory trading arrangements. In particular, two major questions must be answered:

- Is the immediate impact effect of such preferential trade blocs, whether CUs or FTAs, to reduce rather than increase world welfare?

- Regardless of the immediate impact effect, will regionalism lead to non-discriminatory multilateral free trade for all, through continued expansion of the regional blocs until universal free trade is reached, or will it fragment the world economy? And will, in any event, such a dynamic time-path show that regionalism will get us closer to the *goal* of multilateral free trade for all than multilateralism as the *process* of trade negotiation will?

In terms of Figure 12.1, starting from the initial U^0 level of world welfare with trade barriers in place, and with multilateral free trade for all implying maximal welfare at U^*, the two questions can be readily illustrated:

Figure 12.1   **Regionalism and welfare: static impact versus dynamic time-path issue**

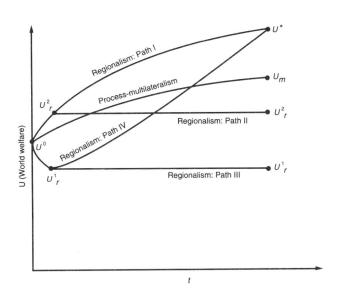

Note: Regionalism may improve welfare immediately, from U^0 to $U^2 r$ or (because of net trade diversion) reduce it to $U^1 r$. The time-path with regionalism, in either case, could be stagnant (Paths II and III), implying a fragmentation of the world economy through no further expansion of the initial trade bloc. Otherwise, it could lead (Paths I and IV) to multilateral free trade for all at U^* through continued expansion and coagulation of blocs. Under process-multilateralism, the time-path may fail to reach U^* and instead fall short at U_m because of free-rider problems. Otherwise, it may overcome them and reach U^*. As argued in the text, the regionalism and the process-multilateralism paths are interdependent. For instance, the simultaneous pursuit of both processes will affect the path and outcome of either.

• Will the static immediate impact effect of a regional bloc be to reduce welfare to U^1_r or to increase it to U^2_r?

• Will the dynamic time-path be to reach U^* through continued coagulation of blocs or will it lead to fragmentation of the world economy and lead, say, to continued stagnation of welfare at U^1_r or U^2_r each in turn *lower* than U_m, reached (with all the greater free-rider difficulties) through the multilateral process or will the multilateral process in fact override the free-rider problem and achieve U^* and dominate the regionalist outcomes?

I shall now treat each of these two important, and distinct (if at times analytically interrelated) questions in turn.

The static impact-effect question

The question of the static impact effect of preferential trade arrangements such as FTAs and CUs is, quite simply, the question raised by Viner (1950): would not such discriminatory arrangements be trade-diverting rather than trade-creating?

It is important to raise this question because, as Viner taught us, FTAs and CUs are two-faced: they liberalise trade (among members), but they also protect (against outsiders). The important issue therefore is: which aspect of an FTA or a CU is dominant? Or, to put it in the economist's language: is a particular FTA or CU trade-diverting (that is, taking trade away from efficient outside suppliers and giving it to inefficient member countries) or trade-creating (that is, generating trade from one more efficient member at the expense of another less efficient member)?

What can we say about this issue? In particular, what can we propose to ensure that, if CUs and FTAs are to flourish, they do not become trade-diversionary? Article XXIV's injunction not to raise the CU's or the FTA's average external tariff can be interpreted as a precaution against trade diversion and harm to outside GATT members, though (as argued below) this is not a satisfactory way to do it.

In essence, there are three approaches to containing the fallout of trade diversion from CUs and FTAs.

Converting preferential CUs and FTAs into (geographically) regional blocs

It is occasionally argued that we should encourage geographically proximate countries to form CUs and FTAs, discouraging geographically distant countries from doing so since the latter would be more likely to be trade-diverting. This is a misguided prescription in my view, for several reasons.

To see this, it must be first appreciated that it rests on a syllogism. The first premise is that a CU or FTA is more likely to create trade and thus raise welfare, given a country's volume of international trade, the higher is the proportion of trade with the country's CU or FTA partners and the lower is this proportion with the non-member countries. The second premise is that countries sharing borders, or closer geographically to one another, have higher proportions of trade with one another than countries further apart do.

The first premise is, of course, well known to trade economists from the early post-Vinerian theory, as developed by Lipsey (1958). But Lipsey's argument focuses on the relative sizes of imports from each source *vis-à-vis* expenditure on domestic goods as the key and decisive factor in determining the size of losses and gains from the preferential cuts in trade barriers.

While the likelihood argument is valid within the Lipsey model, it must be noted that it is only that. Thus, for specific CUs and FTAs, the *actual* welfare effects will depend not merely on the trade and expenditure shares *à la* Lipsey but also on the *substitution* at the margin between commodities. Thus, for instance, the substitution between non-member goods and domestic goods may be very high, so that the costs of discrimination would tend to be high as well, *ceteris paribus*. In short, it is important to guess at substitution elasticities among goods *as well as* trade shares, with and between members and non-members of CUs and FTAs, to arrive at a better picture of the likely effects of *specific* CUs and FTAs that may be proposed.

As for the second premise, I have problems with this too as a policy guideline. If I had access to captive research assistance and funds, I could examine whether, for all conceivable combinations of countries and distances among them and for several different time periods, the premise is valid. I do not, so I must rely on casual empiricism and *a priori* arguments. Compare, for instance, the trade throughout the 1960s between India and Pakistan with that between India and the United Kingdom or the then USSR. The former trade has been smaller than the latter. Borders can breed hostility and undermine trade, just as alliances among distant countries with shared causes can promote trade (Gowa and Mansfield 1991). The flag follows trade; and trade equally follows the flag, at least in the nineteenth-century European expansion, which was not directly across the European nations' borders. Again, even if the premise is statistically valid for any set of observations, it may be a result of trade diversion itself: proximity may have led to preferential grant of concessions such as the Generalised System of Preferences (GSP) at the expense of countries elsewhere.

In short, prescriptions to confine CUs and FTAs only to geographically proximate countries are not defensible because both premises have problems: the former is, at best, a likelihood proposition that should not be applied to specific situations where the welfare impact depends critically on other variables as well, whereas the latter does not have a firm empirical or conceptual basis.

But possibly the most damaging criticism that one can make of such a prescription is that it concentrates, at best, on the static impact-effect question and ignores the more important dynamic time-path question. By prescribing that we must rule out 'distant' country unions, as between the United States and Israel and Chile, we would make the CUs and FTAs more exclusive and less open to new members, undercutting the objective of moving speedily towards the shared objective of (non-discriminatory) multilateral free trade for all. That would be tragic indeed.

Designing disciplines to minimise trade diversion

A different, and my preferred, approach is not to pretend to find rules of thumb to exclude CUs and FTAs 'likely' to be trade diversionary but rather to examine the different ways in which trade diversion could arise and then to establish disciplines that would minimise its incidence.

Article XXIV of the GATT

In a sense, Article XXIV (paragraph 5) seeks to do this by requiring that CUs, which must have a common external tariff, should ensure that this common tariff 'shall not on the whole be higher or more restrictive than the general incidence of the duties and regulations of commerce applicable . . . prior to the formation of such a union'. For FTAs, the rule is that the 'duties and other regulations of commerce' are not to be 'higher or more restrictive' than those previously in effect.

Evidently, when tariffs change, as in CUs, and some increase and others fall, the scope for skulduggery arises again, since Article XXIV leaves the matter wholly ambiguous. As Dam (1970, p. 217) has noted:

> these ambiguities plagued the review by the CONTRACTING PARTIES to the EEC Treaty of Rome — The Six, having used an arithmetic average, refused to discuss the best method of calculation, because in their view paragraph 5 did not require any special method.

Besides, it is evident to trade economists that maintaining external tariffs unchanged is, in any event, not the same as eliminating trade diversion. What *can* be said is that, the lower the external barriers, the less is the scope for diverting efficient foreign supplies to member countries. A desirable discipline to impose on CUs and FTAs would thus be to require, for Article XXIV sanction, that one price to be paid must be the simultaneous reduction of the external tariff (implicit and explicit), *pro rata* to the progressive elimination of internal trade barriers.

Possible ways of ensuring this may be indirect disciplines. One way would be to modify Article XXIV to rule out FTAs with diverse tariffs by members and to permit only CUs with common external tariffs (CETs). With most tariffs bound, this would ensure that for the most part a substantial downward shift in tariffs would be a consequence — that, say, Argentina or Brazil would be lowering its trade barriers, *not* that the United States would be raising its trade barriers. Since regionalism is probably going to be a matter of low trade barrier hubs such as the United States and Japan, joining with their respective regional spokes, this insistence on CUs could perhaps produce excellent results.

An alternative, and surer, way would be to insist on CUs but also write into Article XXIV the requirement that the *lowest* tariff or any union member on an item *before* the union must be part of the CET of the union.

Articles VI and XIX of the GATT: AD and VERs

But none of this is enough today. For the trade economists who work in a sustained way on the problems of the world trading system are aware that protection today takes the form of unfair capture of fair trade mechanisms such as antidumping (AD) actions and VERs; countries today thus have access to selective and elastic instruments of protection. Given this reality, even the modification of Article XXIV, to ensure that the external (implicit and explicit) tariff barriers come down as a price for CUs to be allowed under GATT rules, will leave open a gaping hole that would be tantamount to an open invitation to trade diversion by these preferential arrangements. In fact, trade creation can degenerate rapidly into trade diversion, when AD actions and VERs are freely used.

Imagine that the United States begins to eliminate (by outcompeting) an inefficient Mexican industry once the FTA goes into effect. Even though the most efficient producer is Taiwan, if the next efficient United States outcompetes the least efficient

Mexico, that would be desirable trade creation (though the best course would be free trade so that Taiwan would take more of the Mexican market instead).

But what would the Mexicans be likely to do? They would probably start AD actions against Taiwan, which would lead to reduced imports from Taiwan as the imports from the United States increased, leaving the Mexican production relatively unaffected: trade diversion from Taiwan to the United States would have occurred. Similarly, the effect of Mexican competition against the United States could well be that the United States would start AD actions and even VERs against Taiwan.

My belief that FTAs will lead to considerable trade diversion (because of modern methods of protection, which are inherently selective and can be captured readily for protection purposes) is one that may have been borne out in the EC. It is well known that the EC has used AD actions and VERs profusely to erect 'Fortress Europe' against the Far East. Cannot much of this be a trade-diverting policy in response to the intensification of internal competition among the member states of the EC?

Two conclusions follow. One, if inherently discriminatory regionalism is to flourish, as seems likely, then we need greater discipline for AD actions and VERs; Article VI needs reform and Article XIX needs compliance alongside the elimination of VERs. Two, this also implies that regionalism means not the redundancy of the GATT but the need for a stronger GATT. Those who think of the two as alternatives are prisoners of defunct modes of thinking, based on the days when protection was a different beast.

Judging trade diversion case by case
While the foregoing analysis embraces a set of policy-framework and incentive creating reforms to minimise trade diversion, an alternative approach to the problem could be in terms of a case-by-case approach where the approval by the GATT of a proposed CU or an FTA would depend on the evaluation of its trade-creating and trade-diverting effects and the requirement that the net anticipated effect be trade creating.

McMillan (1991) has argued this in an ingenious paper which proposes a simple test of admissibility: 'does the bloc result in less trade between member countries and outsider countries?'. Based on the welfare economics of CU theory, this is an aggregative test and therefore has some obvious analytical problems. It is also subject to the problem of computing plausible trade outcomes. It is hard enough to apply it *ex post; ex ante,* as a test of admissibility, I see little prospect of its being effectively used to exclude any proposed CU and FTA.

Its main merit is its apparent simplicity and its better grounding in economic theory. I therefore endorse the advisability of *some* version of the McMillan test replacing in Article XXIV the current requirement not to raise the average external tariff. But I see it as doing little *in practice* to avoid trade diversion. For this, we will have to rely on changing the incentive structure, including through suitable constraints imposed by stricter discipline on selective and elastic targeting of foreign supplies. The issue of constraining trade diversion from proliferating preferential groupings is so important that it may not be a bad idea to *combine* the proposals made by McMillan and myself, rather than to treat them as alternatives.

The dynamic time-path question

The question of the dynamic time-path is particularly difficult: it is almost virgin territory.

Perhaps the theoretical approach to CU theory that appears to be most relevant to this problem is that of Kemp and Wan (1976). In contrast to the Vinerian approach, Kemp and Wan make the external tariff structure endogenously determined for the CU such that it improves the CU members' welfare while maintaining the outsiders' welfare unchanged. This restores the pre-Vinerian intuition that a CU should be welfare-improving. The problem with the operational significance of the Kemp–Wan argument is that it really is an existence argument, without any structure being put on it within the context of a specific model so that we can develop intuition about what the external tariff structure for such a Kemp–Wan CU would be. But that *any* subset of countries *could* form an unambiguously (world) welfare-improving union is definitely established by Kemp and Wan.

This also implies that the time-path to U^* in Figure 12.1, achieved under multilateral free trade as the *optimum optimorum*, can be made monotonic. But what it does *not* say is that the union will necessarily expand and, if so, in a monotonically welfare-improving manner. For *that* answer, we must turn to the *incentive structure* that any CU provides to relevant 'groups' for further expansion of the CU.

The incentives in question need not be *economic* incentives. In fact, it is hard to imagine that the arbitrary groupings of countries that seek FTAs and CUs are dependent on economic arguments as their key determinants. Often, politics seems to drive these choices of partners, as in the case of the EC, and now in the case of FTAs throughout the Americas. This also accounts for the occasional non-regionally proximate choices of partners in such blocs; such as the United States and Israel, and Pakistan, Iran and Turkey in the early 1960s. But that economic factors contribute to the incentives for such blocs to be formed is not implausible. Thus, for instance, Edward Mansfield, a Columbia University political scientist, has suggested that trade blocs will tend to be formed by security-driven allies because the gains from trade from them will accrue to friends rather than foes.

A meaningful examination of the incentives to form and to expand trade blocs will therefore have to be in the new and growing field of political economy-theoretic analysis. I believe that the models within which we investigate these issues will have to distinguish among at least three kinds of 'agents', which I will detail below with illustrations of the kinds of arguments which we would find relevant:

- *Governments of member countries:* Whether a CU will expand or not will depend partly on the willingness of the CU authorities to do so. This will be affected by ideas and ideology. Here I worry that CUs will be under pressure *not* to expand because one possible reaction to a CU will be: 'we are already a large market, so what do we really stand to gain by going through the hassle of adding more members?'. This is what I call the 'Our Market is Large Enough' syndrome. I think, as Martin Wolf has often noted, that large countries tend to be more inward-looking for precisely this type of reason.

In addition, the expansion of the CU to include any specific set of outside countries will imply differential aggregate-welfare effects for current members, implying in turn differential incentives for member countries for and against the expansion. In this context, a CU (which generally includes transfers among members) may be more expansionary (*à la* Kemp–Wan argumentation) than an FTA, though a CU that simultaneously seeks *political* integration may be less willing to expand.

- *Interest groups in member countries:* We need also to consider how interest groups, who lobby for or against CU expansion, will behave. Again, since CUs are a balance of trade-creating and trade-protecting forces, it is possible that the protectionists who profit from the diversion of trade away from efficient suppliers abroad to themselves will line up against CU expansion to include those suppliers. The problem then will be the 'These Are Our Markets' syndrome.

  This syndrome is not absent from the NAFTA scene, as many leader articles and media quotes from business groups testified during the fast-track renewal. In fact, this syndrome was also present in the Eastman Kodak pamphlet (Dornbusch et al. 1989) that I cited earlier (see note 1). It is also a sentiment that was beautifully expressed by Signor Agnelli of Fiat: 'The single market must first offer an advantage to European companies. This is a message we must insist on without hesitation' (quoted by Wolf 1989). It is, of course, fine for Signor Agnelli to express such sentiments: after all, Fiat has run for years, not on gas, but on VERs against the Japanese. But should economists also embrace such sentiments?

- *Interest groups and governments of outside countries:* The third set of 'agents' has to be the outside countries. Here, the example of a CU may lead others to emulate and seek entry. Otherwise, the fear of trade diversion may also induce outsiders to seek entry: Irwin's (1993) marvellous study on the historical experience with trade liberalisation in the nineteenth century shows that the Anglo-French Treaty may well have served this purpose. If so, this acts as an incentive to expand the CU.

This is clearly an uncharted area that is evidently the most interesting for further analysis. I might add just one empirical-econometric study, by Mansfield (1992), which takes trade data for 1850–1965, estimates an index of 'power distribution' (reflecting, among other things, trade blocs and economic power distribution) and

Figure 12.2   Concentration of power in the world and global exports

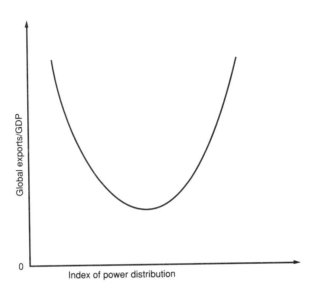

comes up with Figure 12.2. When power was centred in hegemons, during periods of British and American hegemony, and when there was 'anarchy', the world economy was relatively liberalised (in the sense that the global exports-to-GDP ratio was high); when there were a few middle-sized powers, as could happen with trade blocs, the result was a smaller ratio of trade to GDP (Figure 12.2).

If Mansfield's analysis is accepted, and if it is considered to be a reasonable approximation to the question whether CUs will have expansionist or protectionist outlooks (mapping perhaps also into their attitudes to CU expansion or stagnation), then the presumption would be that historical experience suggests that trade blocs will fragment the world economy, not go on to unify it. Of course, history does not always repeat itself. But Mansfield's work certainly suggests caution in place of the gung-ho regionalism that has been urged by the 'Memorial Drive' school.

To conclude, consider the following popular assertions by the regionalists:

* regionalism is quicker;

* regionalism is more efficient; and

* regionalism is more certain.

Is regionalism quicker?

The regionalists claim that the GATT is the 'General Agreement to Talk and Talk', whereas regionalism proceeds quicker. But is this really so?

1   Historically, at least, the 'First Regionalism' failed whereas the GATT oversaw the effective dismantling of pre-war tariffs in the OECD countries and the enlargement of disciplines over non-tariff barriers at the Tokyo Round and beyond. A little caution, to say the least, is necessary before celebrating regionalism's quickfootedness.

2   For those who believe that regionalism offers a quick route to effective trade liberalisation, Dam's analysis quoted above needs renewed attention. There is a world of difference between announcing an FTA or a CU and its implementation, and the comparison is not pleasing if you are in the regional camp.

3   As for speed, even the best example of regionalism, the EC, started almost four decades ago (1957). The 'transition' has not therefore been instantaneous any more than negotiated reductions of trade barriers under the GATT rounds. And this, too, despite the enormous political support for a united Europe.

4   Take agriculture. The record of regional trade blocs dealing with agriculture trade liberalisation is either non-existent or dismal; the CAP is not exactly the EC's crowning achievement. In fact, if it were not for multilateralism — in other words, the Uruguay Round and the coalition of the Cairns Group that crystallised around the multilateral trade negotiations (MTN) — it is difficult to imagine that the process of unravelling the CAP could even have begun.

5   The (actual or potential) exercise of the regional option can also affect the efficacy of the multilateral one. The unwillingness of the EC to start the MTN in 1982 and its largely reactive, rather than leadership, role in the Uruguay Round are in some degree a reflection of its being less hungry for multilateralism given its internal market size and preoccupations. Then again, is it not evident that, were it not for the EC, the capacity of the French (for whose political predicament one can only have sympathy, much as one deplores its consequence for the willingness to liberalise agriculture) to slow down the reform of the CAP and the liberalisation of world agriculture would have been significantly less?

6   Moreover, if regionalism is available as a realistic option, it will encourage exit rather than the seeking of voice and even the manifestation of loyalty to multilateralism:

- This may happen at the level of the bureaucrats who wind up preferring small-group negotiations among friends (code phrase: 'like-minded people') to the intellectually and politically more demanding business of negotiating with and for the larger community of trading nations.

- Or else it may happen that, just as public choice theory à la Olsen tells us in regard to the diffusion of consumer losses and concentration of producer gains that favour protectionist outcomes, the proponents of regionalism tend to be better focused and mobilised (they are often regional 'experts' and partisans who ally themselves with the preferred policy options of the countries whose FTA cause they support), whereas the support for multilateralism is often more diffused and less politically effective and therefore takes second place when regionalism is on the political scene.

- Then again, regionalism may appeal to politicians since it translates more easily into votes: the wooing of the Hispanic voters, by urging them to identify with the FTA, was quite evident during the renewal of the fast-track authority in 1991 for the NAFTA negotiations with Mexico.

- The support of business groups for multilateralism may also erode with regional alternatives because of two different reasons. One, if one can get a deal regionally, where one may have a 'great deal of trade', then one may forget about the multilateral arena. Thus, if Canada could get the United States to agree to a fairer operation of the unfair trade mechanisms, why bother to fight the battles at the Uruguay Round where the powerful American manufacturing lobbies, zeroing in with the EC against the Far East, seek instead to weaken the GATT rules? Two, again, one may get better protectionist, trade diversionary deals for oneself in a preferential arrangement than in the non-discriminatory world of the GATT: for instance, Mexico's textile interests should benefit in the NAFTA relative to Caribbean and other external competitors in the US market, weakening the Mexican incentive to push for reform in the MFA forthwith.

7   Finally, it is true that the free-rider problem looks difficult as the number of GATT members increases. Yet recent theoretical work on GATT-style trade negotiations (Ludema 1991) suggests that the free-rider problem may not be an effective barrier to freeing trade. Moreover, as Finger (1979) has pointed out, and as experience of inadequate GSP concessions underlines, developing countries have not been able to free-ride as much as their exemption from reciprocity under special and differential treatment would imply: the trade concessions on commodities of interest to them have not gone as far as the

concessions on commodities of interest to other GATT members without such an exemption. (Unconditional) MFN does not work in practice as well as it should from the free-rider's perspective.

Is regionalism more efficient?

Occasionally, one finds the regionalists arguing that regionalism is also more *efficient*: it produces *better* results. A typical argument is that, as part of the NAFTA negotiations, Mexico has accepted virtually all the US demands on intellectual property (IP) protection. A story, told in developing country circles, serves to probe this assertion critically: Ambassador Carla Hills was on a tour of South America, extolling the virtues of Mexico's 'capitulation'. At a dinner in her honour in Caracas, she apparently claimed: 'Mexico now has world-class IP legislation'. At this point, President Carlos Peretz supposedly turned to his left and remarked: 'But Mexico does not have a world-class parliament'.

The true moral of the story, however, is that, as part of the bilateral *quid pro quos* in an FTA or a CU, weak states may agree to specific demands of strong states, in ways that are not exactly *optimal* from the viewpoint of the economic efficiency of the world trading system. In turn, however, these concessions can distort the outcome of the multilateral negotiations.

This may well have happened with trade-related IP provisions (TRIPs) and trade-related investment measures (TRIMs) in the Uruguay Round. As is now widely conceded among economists, the case for TRIPs for instance is *not* similar to the case for free trade: there is no presumption for mutual gain, world welfare itself may be reduced by any or more IP protection, and there is little empirical support for the view that 'inadequate' IP protection impedes the creation of new technical knowledge significantly. Yet the use of US muscle, unilaterally through 'Special 301' actions, and the playing of the regional card through the NAFTA carrot for Mexico, have put TRIPs squarely and effectively into the MTN.

Again, a distorting impact on the multilateral trade rule from NAFTA negotiations can be feared from the fact that, as a price for the latter to be accepted by the Congress during the delicate renewal of fast-track authority, the US Administration had to accept demands for harmonisation in environment and labour standards by Mexico towards US standards. In political circles this effectively linked the case for free trade with the demands for 'level playing fields' or fair trade (extremely widely interpreted), legitimating these demands and weakening the ability of economists and of governments negotiating at the GATT (multilaterally for arm's-length free trade) to resist this illegitimate constraint on freeing trade.

Is regionalism more certain?

Much has been made, in the Mexican context, of the argument that the FTA will make trade liberalisation irreversible. But something needs to be added here:

- GATT also creates commitments: tariffs are bound. (This does not apply to concessions made under conditionality, of course, by the IMF or the International Bank for Reconstruction and Development.) Mexico *is* a member, if a recent one, of the GATT.

- Recall Dam (quoted above): Article XXIV is so full of holes in its discipline that almost anything goes. Reductions of trade barriers can be slowed down, as 'circumstances' require, other bindings can be torn up by mutual consent (an easier task when there are only a few members in the bloc but more difficult under the GATT), and so on.

- Recall, too, that regional agreements have failed (LAFTA) and stagnated (ASEAN) as well. The current mood in Canada over NAFTA is sour and the MTN looks better in consequence. The sense, however, that the United States has let Canada down and failed to live by the spirit of the FTA agreements will probably not endure. But who knows?

The United States: from 'piecemeal' to 'programmatic' regionalism

Let me conclude by considering more specifically the US shift to regionalism for the Americas in the perspective of the object of arriving at (non-discriminatory) free trade for all.

US regionalism, when presided over by Ambassador William Brock, then the US Trade Representative, was *not* geographically-circumscribed regionalism. Rather, it was truly open-ended. Brock was known to have offered an FTA to Egypt (along with the one to Israel) and to the ASEAN countries; indeed, he would have offered it to the moon and Mars if only life had been discovered there with a government in place to negotiate with. This regionalism was evidently motivated by a vision, even if flawed, of regionalism as clearly the route to multilateralism: it would go on expanding, eventually embracing many, preferably all.

By contrast, today's regionalism, confined to the Americas, lacks the 'vision thing'. In fact, when allied with former Secretary Baker's reported admonition to the Japanese not to encourage an Asian trade bloc, as suggested by Malaysia as a necessary response to the EC and US regionalism, the US policy appears to Asia also to be self-contradictory and self-serving: 'regional blocs are good for us but not for you'. And it simply will not wash, though Japan, fearing further bashing, will be deterred for a while.

If America's regionalism is not to turn into a piecemeal, world trading system-fragmenting force, it is necessary to give to it a programmatic, world trade system-unifying format and agenda. One possibility is to encourage, not discourage, Japan to line up the Asian countries (all the way to the Indian subcontinent) into an Asian FTA, with the US lining up the South Americans into the NAFTA, on a schedule, say, of ten years. Then, Japan and the United States, the two 'hubs', would meet and coalesce into the larger FTA at that point, finally negotiating with the EC and its associate countries to arrive at the Grand Finale of multilateral free trade for all in Geneva.

Only such 'programmatic' regionalism, in one of several possible variants, would ensure that US regionalism was not perceived by Asia to be hostile and fragmenting. It alone would make regionalism less harmful to the MTN and the GATT and more supportive of the cause of multilateral free trade for all.

Concluding remarks

The question of regionalism is thus both a difficult and delicate one. Only time will tell whether the revival of regionalism since the 1980s will have been a sanguine and benign development or a malign force that will serve to undermine the widely-shared objective of multilateral free trade for all.

My judgement is that the revival of regionalism is unfortunate. But, given its political appeal and its likely spread, I believe it is important to contain and shape it in the ways sketched here so that it becomes maximally useful and minimally damaging, and consonant with the objectives of arriving at multilateral free trade for all.

Note

1   The MIT Economics Department is at 50 Memorial Drive in Cambridge, Massachusetts. I obviously exclude the diaspora, including myself! If the views expressed with Dornbusch in an Eastman Kodak publication (Dornbusch et al. 1989) are a guide, Krugman may hold one of the positions described above.

References

Bhagwati, J. N. 1968, 'Trade liberalization among LDCs, trade theory and GATT rules', in J. N. Wolfe (ed.), *Value, Capital and Growth: Papers in Honour of Sir John Hicks*, Oxford: Oxford University Press.

Cooper, C. A. and B. F. Massell 1965a, 'A new look at customs union theory', *The Economic Journal*, 75, pp. 742–7.

———— 1965b, 'Towards a general theory of customs unions for developing countries', *Journal of Political Economy*, 73(5), pp. 461–76.

Dam, K. 1970, *The GATT: Law and International Economic Organization*, Chicago: University of Chicago Press.

Dornbusch, R. et al. 1989, *Meeting World Challenges: United States Manufacturing in the 1990s*, Rochester, NY: pamphlet issued by the Eastman Kodak company.

Finger, J. M. 1979, 'Trade liberalization: a public choice perspective', in R. C. Amachen, G. Haberler and T. Willett (eds), *Challenges to a Liberal International Economic Order*, Washington, DC: American Enterprise Institute.

Gowa, J. and E. Mansfield 1991, 'Allies, adversaries, and international trade', Paper presented to the American Political Science Association Meetings, Washington, DC.

Grandmont, J. M. and D. McFadden 1972, 'A technical note on classical gains from trade', *Journal of International Economics*, 2, pp. 109–25.

Irwin, D. 1993, 'Multilateral and bilateral trade policies in the world trading system: an historical perspective', in J. de Melo and A. Panagariya (eds), *New Dimensions in Regional Integration,* Cambridge: Cambridge University Press.

Johnson, H. G. 1958a, 'The gains from free trade with Europe: an estimate', *Manchester School of Economic and Social Studies.*

——————— 1958b, 'The economic gains from free trade with Europe', *Three Banks Review.*

——————— 1965, 'An economic theory of protectionism, tariff bargaining, and the formation of customs unions', *Journal of Political Economy*, 73, June, pp. 256–83.

Kemp, M. C. 1972, 'The gains from international trade', *The Economic Journal*, 72, pp. 803–19.

Kemp, M. C. and H. Wan 1976, 'An elementary proposition concerning the formation of customs unions', *Journal of International Economics*, 6, February, pp. 95–8.

Lipsey, R. G. 1957, 'The theory of customs unions: trade diversion and welfare', *Economica*, 24, pp. 40–6.

——————— 1958, *The Theory of Customs Unions: A General Equilibrium Analysis*, PhD thesis, University of London.

——————— 1960, 'The theory of customs unions: a general survey', *The Economic Journal*, 70, pp. 498–513.

Lipsey, R. G. and K. J. Lancaster 1956–57, 'The general theory of second best', *Review of Economics Studies*, 24, pp. 33–49.

Ludema, R. 1991, 'International trade bargaining and the most favoured nation clause', *Economics and Politics*, 3(1), pp. 1–41.

Mansfield, E. 1992, 'The concentration of capabilities and international trade', *International Organization*, 46(3), pp. 731–64.

McMillan, J. 1991, 'Do trade blocs foster open trade?', mimeo, University of California, San Diego.

Meade, J. E. 1956, *The Theory of Customs Unions*, Amsterdam: North-Holland.

Samuelson, P. A. 1939, 'The gains from international trade', *Canadian Journal of Economics and Political Science*, 5(2), pp. 195–205.

Viner, J. 1950, *The Customs Union Issue*, New York: Carnegie Endowment for International Peace.

Wolf, M. 1989, 'European Community 1992: the lure of the *chasse gardée*', *The World Economy*, 12(3), pp. 373–6.

13 Regionalism versus multilateralism: analytical notes

Paul Krugman

Should the rise of regional trading arrangements be welcomed, as a step on the road that will ultimately reinforce global free trade? Or should regional trading blocs be condemned, as institutions that undermine the multilateral system? Or, yet again, should they perhaps be accepted, more or less grudgingly, as the best option we are likely to get in an age of diminished expectations.

This ambivalence, and the striking extent to which reasonable analysts find themselves in sharp disagreement, are not surprising. The issue of multilateralism versus regionalism is a difficult one to get one's arms around, on at least two levels. First, even in narrowly economic terms it is a tricky area: after all, it was precisely in the context of preferential trading arrangements that the byzantine complexities of the second best were first discovered. Second, the real issues cannot be viewed as narrowly economic. International trading regimes are essentially devices of political economy; they are intended at least as much to protect nations from their own interest groups as they are to protect nations from each other. Any discussion of the international trading system necessarily thus involves an attempt to discuss not what policy ought to be but what it actually will be under various rules of the game. And the science of politics is, if possible, even less developed than that of economics.

The problem, of course, is that in spite of decades of intense research into the normative economics of trade policy, there are no widely accepted positive models of policy formation. And the multilateral–regional debate hinges crucially on how the institutions of the trading system will affect not just the consequences of given trade policies but the choices by governments of what policies actually to adopt.

The purpose of this paper is obviously not to propose a general theory of the political economy of trade policy — not only do I not have such a theory, I have no idea even where to start. Instead, it offers a set of partial analyses that try to move the discussion of the trading bloc issue a little closer to giving a realistic account of trade policy, and thus a better account of the likely economic effects.

The narrow economics of trading blocs

The pure economic theory of trading blocs is essentially part of the broader theory of preferential trading arrangements. This theory has been extensively studied. Unfortunately, it is a subject of inherent complexity and ambiguity; theory *per se* identifies the main forces at work but offers few presumptions about what is likely to happen in practice. To make any headway, one must either get into detailed empirical work or make strategic simplifications and stylisations that one hopes do not lead one too far astray. Obviously, detailed empirical work is the right approach, but it will not be followed in this paper. Instead, I continue to use the stylised approach from Krugman (1991a).

A political economy model

In my initial trading bloc model I tried to cut through the complexities of second-best analysis with a highly stylised model of a world economy. The structure of this world economy was as follows:

1   The world was assumed to consist of a large number of small geographical units ('provinces'), each specialised in the production of a distinct good.

2   The products of all provinces were assumed to enter symmetrically into world demand, with a constant elasticity of substitution between any two such products.

3   The world was assumed to be organised into a specified number of trading blocs of equal economic size, with free trade within each bloc and an *ad valorem* tariff rate charged by each bloc on imports.

4   The blocs were assumed to set tariffs non-cooperatively, in order to maximise welfare.

The unrealism of this setup is obvious. Yet it had the virtue of offering a simple way to think about regionalism versus multilateralism. One could envision a move to regional trading blocs as involving a reduction in the number of blocs. In the model, such a reduction leads to a mixture of trade creation and trade diversion. Trade creation occurs because a larger share of world trade takes place within blocs, and hence free from tariffs. Trade diversion occurs for two reasons. First, at any given tariff rate, enlarging blocs will lead to some diversion of trade that would otherwise take place between provinces in different blocs. Second, given policy assumption (4), larger blocs, which have more market power, have an incentive to levy higher tariffs than small blocs; so as the number of blocs falls, trade between blocs becomes less free.

Because of the mix of trade creation and diversion, consolidation into a smaller number of blocs has an ambiguous effect on welfare. Somewhat surprisingly, the best outcomes are with either very few or very many trading blocs. The intuition for the desirability of few blocs is obvious: when there is only one bloc, the world has achieved free trade. The converse case is perhaps less obvious: when there are many small players, each has limited market power and thus sets tariffs low — and imports are so large a share of consumption that a flat tariff has little distortive effect in any case. The worst case turns out to be for intermediate numbers of blocs, where potential inter-bloc trade is important yet tariffs distort it significantly.

The startling result is numerical: for a wide range of elasticities of substitution, the welfare-minimising number of blocs is three.

What is wrong with this model? The economic assumptions are grossly unrealistic, especially the absence of any structure of natural trading relations that defines natural blocs; we return to this point below. Even worse, however, is the description of trade politics embodied in assumption (4). Whatever it is that countries do when they set trade policy, they certainly do not choose the tariff level that satisfies the optimal tariff criterion. Even in Krugman (1991b), the problems with this assumption were acknowledged:

> The setup is clearly both too cynical and not cynical enough about the political economy of trade. The internal politics of trade are not nearly this benign: governments do not simply (or ever) maximize the welfare of their citizens. At the same time, the external politics of trade show far more cooperation than this.

In fact, the numerical results themselves are a dead giveaway that the description of politics is very wrong. For any reasonable elasticity of substitution, the model predicts tariff rates that are far higher than what large industrial countries, which are presumably the ones with the most market power, impose in fact.

But do the conclusions about the shape of the relationship between the number of blocs and world welfare hinge crucially on the unrealism of the assumed trade-policy process? In fact, they do not.

Robustness of the economics to policy description

The surprise of the basic trading bloc model is its assertion that welfare is U-shaped in the number of trading blocs, and that welfare is minimised for a small number of blocs — which suggests that current trends could indeed be adverse.

The question is whether this result depends crucially on the political piece of the model. That is, does it depend crucially on (i) the very high tariff rates predicted by the model, and (ii) the tendency of larger blocs to impose high tariffs?

One might already have guessed that (ii) was not very important to the results from the charts presented in Krugman (1991a). It turned out that predicted tariff rates did not, in fact, rise very much with reductions in the number of blocs.

The reason was basically that sufficient trade diversion takes place as the number of blocs falls so that the share of a typical bloc in foreign markets does not rise much — for example, when we move from a four-bloc to a three-bloc world, inter-bloc trade falls so much that each of the three blocs has only a slightly higher share in the external market, and hence faces only a slightly lower elasticity of demand, than each of the previous four blocs. This suggests that trade diversion at a *constant* tariff rate is doing most of the work.

The basic story about potential losses from consolidation into a limited number of trade blocs is not dependent on the specific model of tariff determination laid out in earlier papers. We may note also that this means that focusing on policy changes as a result of bloc formation may be missing the point. For example, suppose we ask whether NAFTA will hurt world trade. The participants may pledge solemnly not to raise external barriers, and may even honour that pledge. Nonetheless, this model suggests that the net effect is still one of trade diversion that could easily outweigh trade creation.

What could invalidate the story? The question is how the tariff rate depends on the number of blocs. If the tariff rate rises as the number falls, as in the case where the tariff rate is set non-cooperatively to maximise bloc welfare, then the story is simply reinforced. In order to change the story sharply, one must offer a reason why a reduction in the number of blocs might actually lead each bloc to adopt lower rather than higher external tariffs.

We will turn to (crude) models of policy below. First, however, it is necessary to repeat a caveat that plays a key role in any attempt at realistic discussion: the importance of natural trading relations.

The 'natural' trading bloc issue

If transportation and communication costs lead to a strong tendency of countries to trade with their neighbours, and if FTAs are to be formed among such good neighbours, then the likelihood that consolidation into a few large trading blocs will reduce world welfare is much less than suggested by the above discussion. The reason is straightforward: the gains from freeing intra-regional trade will be larger, and the costs of reducing inter-regional trade smaller, than the geography-free story suggests.

Imagine, for example, a world of four countries, which may potentially consolidate into two trading blocs. Suppose that these countries are all symmetric, and that external tariffs are fixed at 10 per cent. Then two blocs is the number that minimises world welfare, and hence this consolidation will be harmful. Suppose, however, that each pair of countries is on a different continent, and that intercontinental transport costs are sufficiently high that the bulk of trade would be between continental neighbours even in the absence of tariffs. Then the right way to think about the formation of continental FTAs is not as a movement from four to two, but as a movement of each continent from two to one — which is beneficial, not harmful.

In practice, the sets of countries that are now engaging in FTAs are indeed 'natural' trading partners, who would have done much of their trade with one another even in the absence of special arrangements. A crude but indicative measure of the extent to which countries are especially significant trading partners is to compare their current trade patterns (in a world of fairly low trade barriers) with 'geographically neutral' trade, in which country B's share of A's exports is equal to B's share of gross world product outside of A.

Lawrence Summers (1991) has shown that within North America, and especially within Europe, trade is much more intense than geographic neutrality would predict. The Western Pacific is less clearly a natural bloc than either of these, perhaps fitting its dubious status as a political reality as well (Summers, Chapter 15, Table 15.1).

In my policy discussion (Krugman 1991b), I argued that this correlation between the lines of emerging FTAs and those of natural trading blocs implied that the move to free trade zones is unlikely to reduce world welfare — that the main concern ought to be not global efficiency but the problems of small economies that find themselves caught out in the cold. This issue will not be pursued in this paper, however, which focuses more on the analytical issues than the practical ones.

The point of this section has been that the economic analysis of trade creation versus trade diversion in a simple trading bloc model is not dependent on taking the assumption of optimal tariff warfare literally. But this still leaves open the question of how to think about what does determine policy.

Modelling trade policy

It is one of the well-known ironies of international trade theory that the only intellectually sound basis for a tariff, the terms of trade argument, plays virtually no role in actual policy discussion, even though most empirical estimates suggest that for large countries the unilaterally optimal tariff rates are startlingly high.

Nor do modern, 'strategic' arguments play much role. Even in the midst of widespread concern about technology and new calls for a sophisticated industrial policy, when George Bush went to Japan in 1992 to demand market access he declared the purpose of his trip to be 'jobs, jobs, jobs' — and focused the political weight of his demands not on likely candidates for external economies but simply on politically visible sectors.

I have tried to summarise the apparent preferences of governments by a set of rules which can be described as 'Gatt-think' (Krugman 1991b). The essence of these rules is a desire for exports, an abhorrence of imports, but a willingness to trade off increased imports in some sectors for increased exports in others. This summary may or may not be helpful as a way to organise discussion; but in any case it does not lead on to any modelling. In this section I offer a crude further step that may prove usefully suggestive, particularly when (in the next section) we try to apply it to the issue of bargaining in trade.

An approach to trade policy

It is obvious that governments act as if they care more about the interests of producers — import-competing or exporting — than they do about consumers. This concern may in turn be rationalised as the result of the superior organisation of producers, which enables them to influence government behaviour through, say, campaign contributions. And the superior organisation of producers itself may be modelled as resulting from the role of political activity as a public good, which is more easily provided by small concentrated groups of producers than by large diffuse groups of consumers.

Modelling all these levels explicitly is, however, a difficult task. We do not have clear models either of how organised groups influence policy or of how groups get organised. Eventually we will have to devise such models. Meanwhile, however, we need a shortcut.

One such shortcut is simply to take the preference of the government for producer interests as a given. This is the 'weighted social welfare' approach. It has the disadvantage of telling us nothing about where the weights come from, but it can still give us some insights about trade-policy setting.

Consider, then, a country that is setting policy in a single market.[1] In this market, there is an upward-sloping domestic supply curve, where p is the internal price of the good. There is also a downward sloping domestic demand curve. Imports are available at a price p^*, which we take for the moment as given (that is, we assume away any domestic market power). The internal price is related to the external price by the relationship:

$$p = p^* (1 + t) \tag{1}$$

where t is the *ad valorem* tariff rate.

Suppose the government were to choose t so as to maximise the sum of producer surplus (PS), consumer surplus (CS), and revenue (R). It is straightforward to show that the optimal value of t would be zero: in the absence of market power the government would choose free trade.

What we will assume instead is that the government has a preference for producer interests. Specifically, the government's objective function is:

$$V = (1 + \pi) PS + CS + R. \tag{2}$$

In this function, π represents the premium placed on producer interests.

First, ignore the preference for producers and consider the effect of a tariff increase on welfare. A tariff increase worsens both the production distortion and the consumption distortion.

Now suppose that t is a V-maximising tariff. Then it must be the case that a small increase in t has a zero impact on the government's objective function — namely, the weighted extra payoff to producers must just offset the increase in distortions. Ultimately we find that the tariff rate that maximises the government's objective function must satisfy:

$$\frac{t}{(1+t)} = \frac{\pi}{\varepsilon u} \tag{3}$$

where u is the ratio of imports to domestic production, and ε is the elasticity of import demand.

This equation contains endogenous variables on the right-hand side as well as the left-hand side. Nonetheless, it offers a rather neat summary of the forces that should determine how much protection a given industry receives. It says that tariffs will be high in industries whose producers command an especially large premium in the government's welfare function (surprise), in industries which have a low elasticity of import demand (so that the distortionary costs of protection are less), or industries in which imports are low relative to domestic production (so a tariff is effective at transferring income to producers).

Relationship to previous analysis

Suppose that a relationship like (3), rather than optimal tariff-setting in the public interest, actually determines protection. How does the trading bloc model above hold up?

The key question is how tariffs will vary with the number of trading blocs. Recall that the basic story of trade creation versus trade diversion went through even with fixed tariffs — the rising tariffs that resulted from a reduction in the number of blocs in the original version of the model turned out not to be necessary. So what we need to ask is whether external tariffs will either rise, or at any rate not fall, as blocs become fewer in number.

We can take the preference for producers π as fixed, less out of conviction than as an application of what one of my colleagues calls the 'principle of insignificant reason'. The elasticity of import demand represents a more problematic variable. But there is a clear presumption that a larger bloc will, on average, have a smaller import share, other things being equal — that the ratio of imports to domestic production, both overall and industry by industry, will normally be lower in a large country or trading area than in a small one. And this will tend to imply that *if countries set tariffs unilaterally*, large economic units will be more protectionist than small ones.

This proposition cannot be tested by looking at modern industrial nations, which have operated under a regime of negotiated tariffs since the 1940s. In the pre-1939 era, however, a crude comparison does suggest that rates of protection were positively correlated with economic size. In particular, as Bairoch (1993) points out, the United States, the largest economy even in the early twentieth century, was notably more protectionist than any other major nation. Arguably it has also been the case that large developing countries such as Brazil and India have generally had higher rates of protection than smaller nations.

Thinking of tariff rates as set more with a view towards political pressure than as maximising national welfare does not thus, at first blush, invalidate the proposition that a move towards fewer, larger trading areas may well produce large trade diversion. This conclusion depends, however, on the assumption that tariff rates are set non-cooperatively — an assumption that was true before 1914 but has not (we hope!) been true under the GATT. So we need to turn next to the effects of negotiation on tariff-setting.

Negotiation and protection

US protection actually peaked with the Smoot–Hawley tariff, and began a forty-five-year decline during the 1930s. The basic pattern was already visible during the Roosevelt years: the United States would offer nations increased access to the US market in sectors in which it had a comparative disadvantage, in return for reciprocal access in sectors in which it had the advantage. The political economy of this method was apparent: it set the interests of US exporters as a counterweight to import-competing industries.

Trade negotiations have been highly successful in reducing trade barriers. To make sense of actual trade policy it is necessary to think in terms of a bargaining process in which there is linkage both across industries and between the trade policies of different nations.

Trade bargaining

Imagine that there are two countries and two non-residual industries. We suppose that under free trade each country would be an importer in one of these industries, and that each has a politically optimal tariff (combining the terms of trade and weighted social welfare motives) that it would choose in that industry if acting independently.

Let t_1 be the tariff charged by the first country, and t_2 the tariff charged by the second. We can then illustrate the situation with Figure 13.1. The tariff rates $t_1{}^*$ and $t_2{}^*$ are the individual optima; a few contour lines are sketched in. These contour lines reflect the fact that an increase in either country's tariff hurts the other government's objective function, both by reducing welfare and additionally by hurting exporting producers.

If the two countries set tariffs non-cooperatively, the outcome will be at point N. But as is evident from Figure 13.1, both governments prefer points to the southwest — again, this is both because they care to some extent about national welfare, and because they want to provide benefits to domestic producers.

Figure 13.1   Tariff bargaining

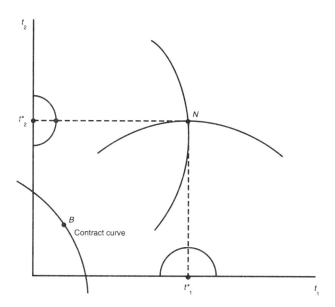

An efficient bargain *B* will lie somewhere on the contract curve between the two governments, and will involve a reduction in both tariff rates from the non-cooperative outcome.

The interesting thing about this result is that it does not depend at all on the assumption that governments are maximising national welfare. If π were zero — if governments were not subject to interest group pressures — the contract curve would pass through the origin. In that case, free trade would be an efficient bargain from the governments' point of view (although not necessarily the bargain at which they would arrive). But international negotiation will lead towards free trade, even if not necessarily all the way, even if governments are strongly affected by interest group politics.

Trade bargaining in this description is characterised by a 'prisoner's dilemma'. This dilemma arises in part from the terms of trade effect of conventional optimal tariff analysis, but also (and presumably in practice mostly) from the effect of each country's tariffs on the other country's producer interests.

Because of the 'prisoner's dilemma' characteristic of trade negotiations, we can now invoke all the usual folk theorems of repeated games to help us think about the possibilities and difficulties of reaching cooperative solutions. Trade liberalisation must be supported by the belief of countries that if they cheat they will lose from the subsequent collapse of the cooperative outcome. And to make this sanction effective, countries must be able to observe each other's trade policies, and must find each other's promises credible.

To make any sense of the issue of regionalism versus multilateralism, we need to think in terms of how the range of countries included in negotiations affects the likelihood that the conditions for successfully achieving cooperation will be met.

Regionalism, multilateralism, and bargaining

There are, I would argue, two basic issues. First, other things being equal, will the formation of regional trading blocs within a multilateral system tend to lead to lower or higher barriers to trade between blocs? Second, is the rise of regional trading blocs a second-best solution to the breakdown of a multilateral system?

Consequences of regional blocs

In the first section of this paper, I showed that consolidation of the world into a small number of trading blocs was likely, with unchanged external tariffs, to produce more trade diversion than creation — with the important practical caveat that to the extent that the blocs followed the lines of natural trading areas, the effect was likely to be more favourable. If blocs set trade policies non-cooperatively, consolidation will normally lead to higher external trade barriers, reinforcing the likelihood of adverse effects. But what if trade policies are set through negotiation?

Once upon a time, European nations came to multilateral negotiations as individual negotiators; now they come as a bloc. Does this make them more or less able and/or willing to compromise?

The answer seems to be that it can cut either way. On one side, consolidation into regional blocs could make it more likely that negotiated agreements would be reached simply because there were fewer players. A world trading system effectively run by a G-3 of NAFTA, the EC, and Japan poses far fewer problems of free-riding than one in which France or Italy are free to make independent demands and cheat on their own.

On the other side, as argued in the second section of this paper, large blocs would in the absence of cooperation tend to impose higher tariffs than small players — in other words, their temptation to protect is higher. At the same time, in the realistic case where blocs follow natural geographic lines, a collapse of free trade to non-cooperative tariff setting will probably do less harm if nations are organised into a few blocs — and therefore the prospect of such a collapse is less of a deterrent to cheating. So a consolidation into large trading blocs could undermine the sustainability of a cooperative international system.

All of this needs some careful modelling. But, overall, the answer seems to be definitely ambiguous. Regional trading arrangements could work either for or against global free trade.

Forces for regionalism

In some sense, the question of whether regional trading arrangements are good or bad is a moot point. There is nobody who is in a position to decree regional blocs either into or out of existence. So we need to ask why such blocs are in fact emerging.

This comes down to asking why nations may feel that they are able to negotiate more at a regional than at a global level. Or to put it more pessimistically, what are the problems of the GATT that lead countries to turn to their neighbourhood instead?

I would list four reasons, all of them tied to the 'prisoner's dilemma' sketched out above.

First, there is the sheer number of participants in the multilateral negotiations. As a practical matter, this changes the character of negotiations. In the early, highly productive GATT rounds, the relatively small number of players were able essentially to carry on parallel bilateral negotiations, something like playing a game of Risk. By the time of the Kennedy Round, the numbers were too great, and it was necessary to resort to formulaic tariff reductions, which inevitably find it harder to strike the right political balance. Also, once there are many players the threat that cheating will bring down the system becomes less credible — will the GATT really collapse because, say, Thailand fails to honour its rules?

Second, the changing character of trade restrictions makes monitoring increasingly difficult. The rise of the 'new protectionism' of VERs, orderly marketing arrangements (OMAs), and so on has been massively documented; it represents both exogenous bureaucratic creativity and an end run around negotiated tariff reductions. What it does is to make the negotiation space vastly more complicated than indicated in Figure 13.1, and to make monitoring of adherence extremely difficult.

Third, the decline in the relative dominance of the United States has probably made the system more difficult to run. The political theory of 'hegemonic stability' — essentially, the view that some dominant power must be there to enforce the rules of a cooperative game — is not as well founded in theory as one might suppose. Nor is it universally accepted even among political scientists. But it is certainly reasonable to argue that a dominant America, preoccupied with trade as a binding agent in a political and military struggle, may have helped the GATT to work better a generation ago than it does now.

Finally, institutional differences among major countries pose problems for the system. (This means Japan.) The reason is not that there are no gains from trade between countries with different institutions. It is that at least a shared understanding is necessary to overcome the 'prisoner's dilemma'. Suppose that a tariff reduction in country A, with its free-wheeling markets, really does open access to those markets; while a tariff reduction in country J, whose markets are governed by informal understandings and cartels, does little to open the gates. Then unless J can find something else to offer, the trade-bargaining game between the countries will break down. It may well be the case that A's welfare would be higher if it ignored this problem and simply pursued unilateral free trade. But as the GATT process itself recognises, governments do not maximise national welfare, and a successful trade regime must build in the motives governments actually have, not the ones we wish they did have.

Regional trading arrangements offer an opportunity to reconstitute the bargaining process at a level where all of these problems can be diminished. They involve smaller groups of nations; they can (as in 'EC 92') involve what Robert Lawrence has called 'deep integration', which essentially removes borders and thus the possibility of creative protectionism. Because the numbers are small, the problem of finding a hegemon is pretty much eliminated. And regional trading blocs, at least so far, avoid including nations with institutional differences large enough to undermine faith in the process.

Conclusions

We can pose two questions about the role of regional trading blocs. The normative question is, will the formation of such blocs lead to trade creation or to trade diversion? The answer is clear: more research is needed. Small numbers tend to make cooperative solutions more likely; ability of players to fare well if bargaining fails make such solutions less likely; both effects are at work.

The positive question is whether there are deep-seated reasons for a move toward regional trading blocs. Although the discussion here is loose and speculative, I would argue that the answer is yes: for a mix of reasons, the ability to support a cooperative solution at the multilateral level is declining, while at the regional level it remains fairly strong.

Note

1   An extension to a crude version of general equilibrium is considered in the full version of this paper.

References

Bairoch, P. 1993, *Economics and World History: Myths and Paradoxes*, Chicago: University of Chicago Press.

Krugman, P. 1991a, 'Is bilateralism bad?', in E. Helpman and A. Razin (eds), *International Trade and Trade Policy*, Cambridge, Mass.: MIT Press.

————— 1991b, 'The move to free trade zones', Federal Reserve Bank of Kansas City, *Review*, December.

Summers, L. 1991, 'The move to free trade zones: comment', Federal Reserve Bank of Kansas City, *Review*, December.

14 Globalism and regionalism: complements or competitors?

Soogil Young

The 1980s saw a revival of regionalism in the wake of the EC's launching of its internal market program, a trend that has been continuing in the 1990s. As a result, as of early 1992 there were about 34 RIAs and 17 prospective ones.[1] The existing ones include seven that have been founded during the last five years, the first of which was the Canada–US Free Trade Agreement.

Asia has been an exception in the formation of RIAs. Especially conspicuous is the fact that the highly trade-dependent economies of East Asia have never belonged to an RIA in their modern histories. The exception is Southeast Asia, where ASEAN unsuccessfully tried to set up a preferential tariff arrangement among its members in the late 1970s and is now making a second attempt (*The Economist*, 24 October 1992). In January 1992 it decided to launch AFTA.

The proliferation of RIAs suggests that the global economy is highly fragmented and has provoked concern that global trade may shrink as a result. This raises an intriguing question: does regionalism contribute to or interfere with the growth of global trade?

The impact of regionalism on global trade has always been highly controversial. As if to demonstrate this, there recently has been a flurry of inspiring papers on this issue, with most authors concluding that new regional arrangements will serve as 'building blocks' for an integrated global system (Lawrence 1991; Schott 1991 and 1992b; Krugman 1991; Summers 1992; de Melo, Panagariya and Rodrik 1992).

From the standpoint of East Asians, who depend heavily on trade for their economic dynamism and feel that they have been left without a bloc of their own, this is a comforting view but hardly a convincing one. In fact, their concern over new regionalism has been growing, and this is kindling their interest in a trading bloc of their own. It was out of this interest that Malaysian Prime Minister Mahathir proposed the formation of an East Asian Economic Group (EAEG) in 1990, right after the breakdown of the Brussels Ministerial on the Uruguay Round. Not having been warmly received, the proposal was later modified and renamed the East Asian Economic Caucus (EAEC). With the launching of NAFTA, however, an East Asian trading bloc has come under serious consideration in many capitals in the region.

Against this background, this paper examines the implications of new regionalism for global trade from the standpoint of East Asia, focusing on the role East Asia may play in the evolution of the global trading system.

New regionalism as viewed by East Asia

An important clue for understanding the global impact of new regionalism is the fact that the new RIAs are coalescing around either the EC or the United States and thus constitute a trend towards the emergence of two giant trade blocs. One would be the European bloc, encompassing the whole of Europe, and the other, the Western Hemisphere bloc encompassing the two American continents.

These blocs are bound to have a profound impact. Table 14.1 shows that the countries that will make up the European bloc accounted for about half of world trade in 1990. In the same year, the Western Hemisphere accounted for 20 per cent of world trade. The two poles, the EC and the United States, accounted for 40 per cent and 11 per cent of world trade, respectively. The NAFTA countries' share was 16 per cent. In contrast, East Asia accounted for 21 per cent of world trade, Japan alone accounting for 8 per cent.

Regional integration in Europe and the Western Hemisphere presents both opportunities and risks to East Asia. So long as external trade barriers of the regional countries remain unchanged, these RIAs are expected to boost economic growth in each region and stimulate external trade. But there are distinct possibilities that external barriers of these regions may be raised during integration and as a consequence of it.

This is a matter that in turn depends on the strength of multilateral trading discipline. On this matter, the present multilateral trading system based on the GATT scores rather poorly, as will be explained.

The GATT system has many loopholes and has proved to be particularly incapable of curing the proliferation of discriminatory protection in the form of so-called grey-area measures and contingency protection (Baldwin 1993). The former, especially VERs, were probably the most prominent form of NTB during the early 1980s. Of an even greater and increasing importance today for controlling trade and investment flows is contingency protection, which takes the form of unilateral actions against unfair trade practices such as dumping and export subsidies.

Hindley and Messerlin (1993) cite two ways in which contingency protection, especially the antidumping mechanism, may be, and has been, used as an instrument of protection. First, it is discriminatory by design and leads to high protection in the

Table 14.1   **Share of world trade by region, 1970 and 1990 (percentages)**

	1970	1990
East Asia	10.4	20.5
Japan	6.2	8.4
Asian NIEs	2.1	7.6
ASEAN-4[a]	1.5	2.5
China	0.5	2.0
Australasia	2.1	1.5
North America	19.5	16.0
US	13.7	11.4
Canada	5.4	3.8
Mexico	0.4	0.9
South America	5.4	3.8
European Economic Area (EEA)	44.3	46.1
EC	37.9	39.7
EFTA	6.4	6.5
Rest of world	18.2	13.0

Note: a   Singapore is included in the Asian NIEs, rather than in ASEAN.

Source: IMF, *Direction of Trade Statistics Yearbook*, 1970, 1990.

form of NTBs. Second, the threat of contingency protection may be used to introduce protection under other instruments. It is frequently used as a means of introducing or maintaining VERs or other grey-area measures. The problem with contingency protection is that it is highly susceptible to abuse, and the relevant GATT codes are ineffective in regulating it. The abuse of contingency protection is hidden in its technical details. The EC has a proven record of actively using its antidumping mechanism for this purpose (Hindley 1988, 1989; Messerlin 1989). The United States has also been a leading user of the antidumping mechanism, raising allegations of protectionist abuse.

Hindley and Messerlin (1993) argue that the perceived threat to outsiders of the EC's contingency protection in the form of antidumping action is so strong that a major advantage of full EC membership to the would-be members such as the EFTA countries and other European neighbours is that it provides insurance against this protection. Baldwin (1993) argues that an important motivation for Canada to negotiate an FTA with the United States was to bring US contingency protection against Canadian goods and services under tighter discipline.

In the presence of such loopholes in the multilateral trading system, as emphasised by Bhagwati (1992, also Chapter 12, this volume), the pressure of increased internal competition among members of RIAs that arises during integration is highly likely to spill over in the form of higher trade barriers against goods, services, and investment from non-member countries. The trade barriers against non-member countries need not take the form of grey-area measures and contingency protection. There are 'holes and loopholes' in RIAs that may impede both external and internal trade, and the area most susceptible to abuse is rules of origin (Hoekman and Leidy 1993; Palmeter 1993). The rules of origin can be designed — twisted and made complex — as an effective trade barrier against non-member countries, especially in the case of FTAs, and this seems to have happened already to a significant degree in NAFTA's case.

The fact that integration in both Europe and the Western Hemisphere will involve FTAs between developed countries and developing as well as newly marketising countries strongly suggests the possibility of increased protection against the East Asian developing economies in such products as footwear, textiles and clothing, consumer electronics, steel and automobiles — in areas in which protectionism is already strong. Should this be allowed to happen, regional integration in Europe or in the Western Hemisphere will be trade-diverting — at least with respect to the East Asian economies (Young 1993).

There is thus a strong likelihood that new regionalism will be competing with globalism unless multilateral trading discipline is tightened. This highlights an important general point: the emergence of regionalism does not dispense with the need for multilateralism. Regionalism needs a well functioning multilateral trading system in order to complement globalism (Bhagwati 1992, also Chapter 12, this volume). Accordingly, the relevant question now is whether the multilateral trading system will be strengthened.

The future of the multilateral trading system

The question of whether the multilateral trading system can be strengthened may be rephrased to ask whether the main participants in international trading — the United States, the EC, Japan, and the developing countries of East Asia — will cooperate to strengthen the system. Rephrasing the question in this way makes it immediately clear that the prospect for a stronger multilateral trading system is less than bright. The very fact that the EC and the United States themselves are the driving forces for new regionalism reveals their faltering support for the multilateral trading system.

Indeed, it is mainly this faltering support on the part of the two big powers that has prompted other countries in the respective regions to seek RIAs with their large neighbours. To many of them, the primary role of RIAs is to provide safe havens in case the multilateral trading system collapses (Srinivasan, Whalley and Wooton 1993). In contrast, the East Asian countries have so far demonstrated their reluctance to form a regionwide trade bloc.

The faltering support of the EC and the United States for multilateralism is a clear indication of their failing confidence in multilateralism as well as their dissatisfaction with the GATT system as it has been operating so far. In the case of the EC, an additional explanation is that it has all along been preoccupied with its internal integration.

A number of problems with the GATT system as viewed by the Western industrial countries explain this dissatisfaction (Baldwin 1993). The problem that is taken most seriously is these countries' sense that multilateralism has failed to provide a level playing field. This grievance arises at two levels. For one thing, they have been unhappy with the fact that developing countries have failed to offer them reciprocal market access by refusing to give up special and differential treatment. For another, the Western industrial countries believe that Japan and other East Asian countries have been engaging in unfair trade, by subsidising and dumping exports on the one hand, and by impeding foreigners' access to domestic markets with various NTBs on the other.

This perception of Japan and other East Asian developing economies as unfair traders has been a major reason for the shift by the EC and the United States to new regionalism. The same perception has also been encouraging the EC and the United States to target contingency protection and grey-area measures against the East Asian exporters (Baldwin 1993). Particularly, the United States has also pursued aggressive unilateralism against these exporters.[2]

It should be noted at this point that aggressive unilateralism has been as much a threat as contingency protection to the multilateral trading system. Because aggressive unilateralism may extract trade-diverting concessions from trade partners, it poisons the atmosphere for trade policy cooperation and undermines confidence in multilateralism. It may also lead to a trade war (Bhagwati 1991).

While the Western industrial countries' view that multilateralism has failed to curb unfair traders such as Japan and some other East Asian economies is certainly a major explanation for their dissatisfaction with multilateralism, there is another factor, a more fundamental one, which undoubtedly has reinforced this dissatisfaction. It is the exposure to inexorable competition from East Asia's dynamic exporters that multilateralism forces on the domestic industries of these countries.

The remarkable export performance of the East Asian economies for the last three decades or so has been well documented. As Table 14.1 shows, East Asia's share of world exports, due to extremely rapid export growth, doubled from 10 per cent in 1970 to 21 per cent in 1990. Most of the gain in East Asia's export share has been realised by developing economies, and the Asian NIEs in particular. Such a rapid growth of exports, nearly all of which have been manufactured products, is bound to have been highly disruptive to the importing Western industrial countries. Thus, with the extremely rapid growth of exports of low-cost manufactured products during the last three decades, the East Asian economies have been imposing a tremendous burden of adjustment on these Western industrial countries.

Facing limits to flexibility at home, these countries have not been able to make the necessary adjustment, and this failure has given rise to 'Eurosclerosis' and the US Rust Belt. Viewed from this perspective, contingency protection as well as VERs have been playing the role of blunting the competition from the East Asian manufacturers. By the same token, the EC and the United States, as well as other countries, have come to view multilateralism more as a threat than a catalyst for improved efficiency, and they see great value in regionalism as a new competitive strategy.

Unless there is a serious adverse turn of events for the East Asian economies, however, all indications are that their export dynamism is likely to continue with the same vigour as before and well into the 21st century, and the Western industrial countries' adjustment difficulties are unlikely to go away. If anything, the competitive pressure from East Asia may even increase with the accelerated industrial dynamism of China and the Southeast Asian economies. Thus, the Japan Economic Research Center (JERC) (1992) forecasts that East Asia's share of world exports will increase from 21 per cent in 1990 to 27 per cent in 2000 and to 31 per cent in 2010.

The EC and the United States have shifted to new regionalism because they wanted to supplement multilateralism with regionalism. If the East Asian economies find that multilateralism does not function well for them, should they not also supplement it with an RIA of their own? Will this be a desirable situation to East Asia? Does East Asia need an FTA or a CU of its own?

An East Asian trading bloc?

An East Asian trading bloc is an idea with considerable appeal. Its potential merit rests in the fact that, despite the unilateral trade-liberalising measures the regional countries have undertaken since the early 1980s, although to varying degrees, these countries still maintain many trade barriers. These barriers are not limited to border measures such as tariffs and import restrictions. Many instruments of industrial policy in such forms as industrial subsidies and assistance, as well as restrictions of competition, effectively serve as trade barriers. In some countries such as Japan there are also structural barriers, such as closed distribution channels and inward-oriented business practices. In principle, an East Asian trading bloc should remove all these barriers for intra-regional trade.

When these barriers are removed for intra-regional trade, trade diversion is likely to be substantial, but far more substantial will be trade creation. Accordingly, economic growth in East Asia is likely to be further stimulated.

This is so because many of the trade barriers have been erected especially against other East Asian countries for the purpose of protecting domestic industries, infant or declining, from the competing industries of other regional countries in order to pursue industrial policy objectives or to pursue 'dynamic' comparative advantage. These barriers, in turn, have had the effect of impeding the market-led integration of the regional economies.

In principle, an East Asian trading bloc could stimulate intra-regional, intra-industry trade by removing these barriers. In doing so, it would also have the critical effect of mitigating the acute adjustment pressure that East Asia has been imposing on the rest of the world. A unique feature of East Asia's development is the similarity of the pattern of industrialisation between the individual economies in the region. Similar patterns of industrialisation in East Asia have in turn aggravated the adjustment difficulties of the Western industrial countries.

The similarity in the pattern of industralisation arises from the East Asian economies' similar industrial development strategies, which have contributed to the development of the regional economies. These economies are increasingly competitive with each other rather than complementary (Petri 1992, also Chapter 10, this volume). Under this pattern of development, the regional economies have had to look to outside markets, rather than to each other, for new export opportunities. For this reason, the East Asian economies have developed a strong extra-regional orientation in their exporting (Table 14.2), and in this way, they have been intensifying the adjustment pressure on the rest of the world as well as trade frictions with industrial countries outside the region.

The adjustment problem of the Western industrial countries has been worsening as the Asian league of industrialising economies has been increasing its membership in a cascading pattern and Japan and other leading members have kept advancing. This cascading pattern of industrial development means that East Asia's market penetration has been spreading to an ever-wider range of products, from the most traditional to the increasingly more sophisticated (Anderson 1991), leaving little room for Western industrial countries to make intra-industrial adjustments in manufacturing. In this way, their problem has persisted.

There is another aspect to East Asia's trading that has exacerbated this problem, again fuelling inter-regional trade frictions: the trilateral pattern of trading under which the developing East Asian economies, especially the NIEs, rely heavily on Japan for imports of capital and intermediate goods while exporting mainly outside the region. This pattern has been aggravating the problem of trade imbalances, which the United

Table 14.2   Direction of exports by region, 1990 (percentages)

| Reporter | Partner | | | | | |
	East Asia	Australasia	North America	South America	EC	EFTA
East Asia	39.4	2.2	28.9	1.8	16.3	2.2
Australasia	45.0	10.8	12.7	1.4	14.4	2.2
North America	23.0	2.1	34.4	10.8	20.8	2.7
South America	8.8	0.4	39.8	15.0	23.1	2.4
EC	5.6	0.8	7.9	1.9	60.6	10.3
EFTA	6.8	0.9	8.1	1.7	57.8	13.6

Source: IMF, *Direction of Trade Statistics Yearbook*, 1991.

States and the EC have *vis-à-vis* Japan (Yoo 1990; Young 1993). Undoubtedly, the chronic trade deficits of these regions have been making industrial adjustment even more difficult. To the extent that it would stimulate intra-regional trade, an East Asian trading bloc would ease the balance-of-payments problem.

Expansion of the intra-regional market would make the East Asian economies less reliant on the extra-regional markets and hence less vulnerable to discriminatory protection in these markets. In this way, an East Asian trading bloc could provide a safe haven for the regional economies and, for them, supplement the weakened multilateralism.

An East Asian trading bloc could also enhance the East Asian economies' bargaining leverage *vis-à-vis* the other blocs. Indeed, Saxonhouse (1992, also Chapter 20, this volume), Krugman (1992, also Chapter 13, this volume), Summers (1992), and de Melo, Panagariya and Rodrik (1992), all argue that a trade bloc will increase the bloc's bargaining power while improving its terms of trade and that the establishment of a countervailing trade bloc in the presence of other major ones could lead to global trade liberalisation. Krugman and Summers further argue that the division of the world into large trading blocs may be conducive to global trade liberalisation because it would help eliminate the free-rider problem and also because the inter-bloc trade negotiation may be an efficient way of reorganising otherwise very complex multilateral trade negotiations. From this perspective, the tripolar division of the global economy into the European bloc, the Western Hemisphere bloc, and the East Asian bloc could contribute to global trade liberalisation. In evaluating the economic argument for an East Asian trading bloc, it should be noted that the argument is more for an Asia Pacific bloc encompassing East Asia, North America and Australasia, with a possible extension to Latin America, rather than for an East Asian trading bloc alone. The latter would only be second best to the former.

Indeed, because of the existing intense trading relationship in the Asia Pacific region, the area can be considered already highly integrated. Considering the high values of the trade intensity indexes among the three sub-regions (Table 14.3) and also that no RIA links the three, most of the economies belonging to this region may be considered to be natural trade partners. Accordingly, the East Asian trading bloc is likely to be considerably trade-diverting. Given the broad spectrum of goods in which the East Asian economies compete with North America, the East Asian trading bloc is likely to weaken the trade linkage between these two regions in particular. Conversely, an Asia Pacific trade bloc is likely to be highly trade-creating, particularly because the most important region to be excluded, Europe, has generally very weak trade linkages with the economies in the Asia Pacific region (Table 14.3). Another important advantage of an Asia Pacific trade bloc, or its expanded version including Latin America, is that, with a weight in world output and trade comparable to that of Europe, it can be a highly effective partner to Europe for negotiations of global trade liberalisation.

Table 14.3   Inter-regional trade intensity indexes,[a] 1990

	East Asia	Australasia	North America	South America	EC	EFTA
East Asia	2.29	1.55	1.62	0.47	0.41	0.34
Australasia	2.61	7.45	0.71	0.36	0.36	0.34
North America	1.34	1.44	1.92	2.82	0.52	0.41
South America	0.51	0.29	2.22	3.93	0.58	0.38
EC	0.33	0.58	0.44	0.49	1.53	1.60
EFTA	0.39	0.64	0.46	0.44	1.46	2.11

Note: a   Defined as the ratio of the partner's share in the reporting country's total exports over the partner's share in the world's total imports.

Source: International Economic Data Bank, Australian National University; IMF, *Direction of Trade Statistics Yearbook*, 1991.

This second-best nature of an East Asian trading bloc, then, raises a major reservation about it. As a corollary, an East Asian trading bloc is likely to provoke a strong reaction from North America and possibly even a trade war with the North American bloc, prompting it, if not the entire Western Hemisphere bloc, to erect retaliatory barriers against East Asia. Consequently, an East Asian trading bloc may not be feasible. In this connection, an asymmetry between an East Asian bloc and NAFTA should be noted. An East Asian bloc could be considerably trade-diverting for North America because the existing trade barriers in East Asia are considerably high. In contrast, NAFTA in itself is not expected to be seriously trade-diverting because other pre-NAFTA trade barriers among members of NAFTA are already very low (Schott 1992a).

The same point, however, validates the bargaining-leverage argument for an East Asian trading bloc. In other words, East Asian economies can use the threat to form an East Asian trading bloc as an important means of influencing the trade-policy behaviour of the North American countries. Viewed from this perspective, the Malaysian proposal of an EAEG, as well as the subsequent EAEC, by itself can be said to have served as a warning to the North American countries, and to the United States in particular.

For this reason, the Malaysian proposal should be seen as a highly significant development, and the East Asian countries should recognise value in it. For example, they can use the potential of an East Asian trading bloc to influence NAFTA, to deter the establishment of a Western Hemisphere FTA, or to force NAFTA to be opened to themselves.

The credibility of this threat can be questioned, however, because of two other problems of feasibility of an East Asian trading bloc. One is the problem of implementability. The other is the problem of weak political leadership.

An effective trading bloc in East Asia would require rather sweeping reforms of both trade and industrial policy in the cases of many of the developing economies and fundamental structural reforms in the case of Japan. A trading bloc may then be taken to mean the total surrender of industrial policy and thus be resisted by the affected developing economies. In the case of Japan, as the Structural Impediments Initiative (SII) talks demonstrated, the requisite reforms may not be easy to implement, and the effectiveness and credibility of trade liberalisation are likely to be questioned.

These considerations suggest that an East Asian trading bloc may not even be achievable, and that, even if implemented, it is unlikely to be effective. This conclusion is reinforced by consideration of the problem of political leadership. The experiences with the GATT system, as well as the cases of integration in Europe and the Western Hemisphere discussed here, demonstrate that it may not be possible to launch and maintain an effective trading arrangement, global or regional, in the absence of a strong hegemon. In East Asia, the strongest candidate for the hegemon is Japan. But Japan may not be able to become a strong and effective leader, despite its dominant influence as the main supplier of capital, technology and important intermediate goods in the region. The fear that other regional economies may have about Japan's possible domination is an often-cited rationale (Young 1992). In addition, there are other contenders for political leadership in the region. One such contender is ASEAN. Another is Korea. The third and most powerful challenger is China, which is predicted to challenge Japan's economic power within the next two decades (Perkins 1992).

There are two other, more immediate, problems that will constrain Japan's leadership role in the promotion and management of an East Asian trading bloc. One is credibility, because of the problem of effective access to Japan's domestic market in pushing for regional trade liberalisation. The other is Japan's relatively small weight as a trade partner to other regional economies. As Table 14.4 shows, the Japanese market accounts for only 11 per cent and 14 per cent in the exports of the Asian NIEs and China, respectively. Japan accounts for a larger share in the combined exports of the ASEAN countries other than Singapore, but the share still does not exceed 25 per cent. The relatively weak trade dependence on Japan of other regional economies is likely to weaken Japan's possible leadership role.

These analyses thus suggest that an East Asian trading bloc may not be a realistic idea. Would an Asia Pacific trade bloc be more realistic? Perhaps, but if so, not by a substantial degree. For one thing, whether in the context of an East Asian trading bloc or in the context of an Asia Pacific trading bloc, East Asia's trade liberalisation will suffer from the same problem of effectiveness. Also, while in the case of an East Asian trading bloc there may not be an effective leader, in the case of an Asia Pacific trading bloc, the North American trade partners may not be interested in the idea itself, as they fear East Asian competition. The question then remains — how should East Asia cope with new regionalism?

Table 14.4   Direction of exports in East Asia, 1990 (percentages)

Reporter	Partner			
	Japan	Asian NIEs	ASEAN-4	China
Japan		19.7	7.7	2.1
Asian NIEs	11.5	12.4	8.2	8.3
ASEAN-4	24.4	22.0	4.2	2.1
China	14.1	43.0	2.7	

Source: IMF, *Direction of Trade Statistics Yearbook*, 1991.

East Asia as a globalist

Two giant trade blocs are emerging, encompassing Europe and the Western Hemisphere. The characteristics of these blocs are such that, despite some trade diversion, their formation is likely to be trade-creating for their extra-regional trade partners so long as they do not raise external trade barriers. If the past trade-policy behaviours of the key regional countries are any indication, however, their external trade barriers are likely to be raised in sectors where they may experience acute adjustment difficulties, and the dynamic exporters of East Asia will be the main target. Trade barriers against these exporters may further be strengthened and the multilateral trading system further weakened as these exporters continue to grow rapidly, bringing the tremendous pressure of import competition to bear on the industries of the Western developed countries.

There is thus a legitimate concern that, because of the imperfection of the multilateral trading system, regionalism may undermine globalism in this way. The actual future of globalism will depend much on how dynamic exporters of East Asia, the ultimate source of the pressure for discriminatory protectionism, respond to regionalism in Europe and the Western Hemisphere.

They may attempt to bring the two regional blocs to agree to strengthen the multilateral trading system and to curb discriminatory protection, such as abuse of contingency protection and grey-area measures, but it is unlikely to be successful. One thing they can do is seek an RIA of their own, whether in the form of an East Asian trade bloc or in the form of an Asia Pacific trade bloc. Both can be conducive to economic dynamism of the participating economies, as well as to growth and liberalisation of global trade, although an Asia Pacific bloc will be superior to an East Asian trade bloc in a number of ways.

For the time being, however, neither bloc appears to be feasible, because of political and structural difficulties accompanying genuine trade liberalisation in East Asia. In addition, lack of effective political leadership on the part of East Asia will be a problem, as will the fact that North America may not welcome the East Asian economies as partners for free trade. What should be the trade policy agenda for East Asia under the circumstances?

First, the East Asian economies should continue to support and strengthen multilateralism. Multilateralism is necessary to discipline regionalism, and a weak multilateralism will be better than none. They should go beyond the Uruguay Round to organise new efforts to strengthen multilateralism. Given the strong outward-orientation of the North American economies and particularly the United States (Table 14.2), East Asia will find North America to be relatively more responsive to these efforts than Europe.

Given the diverse membership of the GATT, however, another GATT round is unlikely to be any more effective than earlier ones, including the Uruguay Round, in tightening up multilateral disciplines such as non-discrimination. Under such circumstances, East Asians may work with North Americans to promote a GATT-plus agreement among a subset of the like-minded members of the GATT, based on the conditional MFN principle (Baldwin 1993). The only form of a GATT-plus agreement that is compatible with the principles of the GATT — the foundation of the multilateral trading system — is an FTA (Snape, Adams and Morgan 1992). Hufbauer (1989) has already proposed an OECD Free Trade and Investment Area (FTIA). Its core members will be the members of the OECD, but the membership will be open to all willing participants. While this proposal should be taken seriously, another possible, and probably more promising, form of a GATT-plus agreement that East Asia may promote is an Asia Pacific FTA — an extended version of the NAFTA covering both North America and East Asia with an open accession clause without any geographic restriction on membership. This proposal takes advantage of the fact that the NAFTA contains a geographically non-specific accession clause (Schott 1992a). This would offer a standing invitation to the EC and other European countries to join in global trade liberalisation whenever they are ready. They may likely be eventually persuaded to join as the Asia Pacific economies, and particularly the East Asian economies, continue to grow, with ever-increasing market size.

Difficulties in the promotion of multilateral trade liberalisation, as well as a GATT-plus agreement such as an Asia Pacific FTA, have been noted already. These difficulties, however, should not prevent the East Asian economies and others from trying. A major problem that may obstruct East Asia's efforts at enhancement of globalism is the regional countries' own unwillingness and failure to liberalise trade fully. It is up to the East Asians to remove this obstacle. East Asians themselves should accept the need to liberalise trade, as well as demonstrate their willingness and ability to do so by accelerating unilateral trade liberalisation efforts in progress since the early 1980s (Drysdale and Garnaut 1993).

While trade liberalisation will help, the East Asian economies should also make independent efforts to complement it in order to reduce reliance on the extra-regional markets for the growth of their exports and economies. They need to promote intra-regional, intra-industry trade by promoting functional integration through intra-regional infrastructural investments and sub-region building (Young 1993; Drysdale and Garnaut 1993). With their continued growth, the East Asian economies should create new markets not only for themselves but for everybody, easing the burden of adjustment for others, thus addressing the ultimate source of global trade tensions.

In these and other efforts for global trade liberalisation, the East Asian economies will need the United States and other countries in the Asia Pacific region as partners. This is where the APEC forum comes in. APEC should be used as the main forum in which matters for global trade liberalisation are discussed, including the issue of macroeconomic adjustment and US–Japan frictions. APEC should be used as a source of discipline on NAFTA as well as AFTA. It is also where a GATT-plus arrangement, such as an Asia Pacific RIA, should be discussed.

The EAEC proposal should not be disregarded. It should continue to be kept on the table. As long as it remains available as an option, it can enhance East Asia's leverage for influencing the trade-policy behaviours of the United States and other partners and to maintain discipline in NAFTA.

When checks and balances exist among major trading partners, regionalism need not compete with globalism: in fact, it will complement it. It is the role of the East Asian economies to ensure that such checks and balances exist. As long as East Asia perseveres as a regional force for globalism, regionalism may serve as a complement to globalism.

Notes

1   See de la Torre and Kelly (1992) for lists of regional integration arrangements. The authors list nineteen prospective RIAs, including the EAEC and APEC. The latter two, which are discussed later in this paper, should not have been counted as RIAs, however.

2   Bhagwati (1991) defines aggressive unilateralism by the United States as imposition of the country's unilaterally defined view of unfair trade practices on others. Specifically, he refers to the use of the Section 301 and 'Super 301' provisions of the American trade legislation as revised in the 1988 act to demand negotiations from specified countries on practices that the United States finds unacceptable, regardless of whether they are proscribed by GATT or another treaty, and to seek their abolition on a tight time schedule set by the United States, using tariff retaliation by the United States if necessary. The United States has targeted its aggressive unilateralism at foreign trade and investment barriers as well as foreign infringement of US intellectual property rights. See Bhagwati (1991, p. 48).

References

Anderson, Kym 1991, 'Is an Asian-Pacific trade bloc next?', *Journal of World Trade*, 25(4), August, pp. 27–40.

Baldwin, Robert E. 1993, 'Adapting the GATT to a more regionalised world: a political economy perspective', in Kym Anderson and Richard Blackhurst (eds), *Regional Integration and the Global Trading System*, London: Harvester Wheatsheaf.

Bhagwati, Jagdish N. 1991, *The World Trading System at Risk*, Princeton: Princeton University Press.

_____ 1992, 'Regionalism and multilateralism: an overview', *Columbia University Discussion Paper Series*, No. 603, April.

de la Torre, Augusto and Margaret R. Kelly 1992, 'Regional trade arrangements', *International Monetary Fund Occasional Paper*, No. 93, March.

de Melo, Jaime, Arvind Panagariya and Dani Rodrik 1992, 'Regional integration: an analytical and empirical overview', Paper prepared for the World Bank and CEPR conference on New Dimensions in Regional Integration, Washington, DC, 2–3 April.

Drysdale, Peter and Ross Garnaut 1993, 'The Pacific: an application of a general theory of economic integration', in C. Fred Bergsten and Marcus Noland (eds), *Pacific Dynamism and the International Economic System*, Washington, DC: Institute for International Economics.

Hindley, Brian 1988, 'Dumping and the Far East trade of the European Community', *The World Economy*, December.

_____ 1989, 'The design of Fortress Europe', *Financial Times*, 6 January.

Hindley, Brian and Patrick Messerlin 1993, 'Contingent protection and regionalism', in Kym Anderson and Richard Blackhurst (eds), *Regional Integration and the Global Trading System*, London: Harvester Wheatsheaf.

Hoekman, Bernard and Michael P. Leidy 1993, 'Holes and loopholes in regional trade arrangements and the multilateral trading system', in Kym Anderson and Richard Blackhurst (eds), *Regional Integration and the Global Trading System*, London: Harvester Wheatsheaf.

Hufbauer, Gary Clyde 1989, *The Free Trade Debate: Reports of the Twentieth Century Fund Task Force on the Future of American Trade Policy*, New York: Priority Press Publications.

Japan Center for Economic Research (JERC) 1992, *The Coming Multipolar Economy: The World and Japan in 2010*, May.

Krugman, Paul 1991, 'Regional blocs: the good, the bad and the ugly', *The International Economy*, November/December.

_____ 1992, 'Regionalism vs. multilateralism: analytical notes', Paper prepared for the World Bank and CEPR conference on New Dimensions in Regional Integration, Washington, DC, 2–3 April.

Lawrence, Robert Z. 1991, 'Scenarios for the world trading system and their implications for developing countries', *OECD Technical Papers*, No. 47, October.

Messerlin, Patrick A. 1989, 'The EC anti-dumping regulations: a first economic appraisal, 1980–1985', *Weltwirtschaftliches Archiv*, 125.

Palmeter, David 1993, 'Customs unions and free trade areas: rules of origin', in Kym Anderson and Richard Blackhurst (eds), *Regional Integration and the Global Trading System*, London: Harvester Wheatsheaf.

Perkins, Dwight H. 1992, 'China's economic boom and the integration of the economies of East Asia', Paper prepared for the Korea Institute of Public Administration and the Economic Research Institute of the Daishin Group, Seoul.

Petri, Peter A. 1992, 'The East Asian trading bloc: an analytical history', *Brandeis University Working Paper*, No. 315.

Saxonhouse, Gary R. 1992, 'Trading blocs, Pacific trade and the pricing strategies of East Asian firms', Paper prepared for the World Bank and CEPR conference on New Dimensions in Regional Integration, Washington, DC, 2–3 April.

Schott, Jeffrey J. 1991, 'Trading blocs and the world trading system', *The World Economy*, 14(1), March, pp. 1–17.

_____ 1992a, 'The North American Free Trade Agreement and beyond', Statement prepared for the Subcommittees on Western Hemisphere Affairs and on International Economic Policy and Trade, Committee on Foreign Affairs, US House of Representatives, Washington, DC, 12 May.

_____ 1992b, 'Economic integration in the Western Hemisphere: the importance of regionalism and multilateralism', mimeo, Institute for International Economics, Washington, DC, July.

Snape, Richard H., Jan Adams and David Morgan 1992, *Regional Trade Agreements: Part II, Options for Australia—Interim Report*, Monash University, June.

Srinivasan, T. N., John Whalley and Ian Wooton 1993, 'Measuring the effects of regionalism on trade and welfare', in Kym Anderson and Richard Blackhurst (eds), *Regional Integration and the Global Trading System*, London: Harvester Wheatsheaf.

Summers, Lawrence H. 1992, 'Regionalism and the world trading system', Paper prepared for the World Bank and CEPR conference on New Dimensions in Regional Integration, Washington, DC, 2–3 April.

Yoo, Jung-ho 1990, 'The trilateral trade relation among the Asian NIEs, the U.S., and Japan', *Korea Development Institute Working Paper*, No. 9005, April.

Young, Soogil 1992, 'Economic development of East Asia: its impact on the Asia Pacific', *In Which Direction is the Asia Pacific Moving Towards?: Intra-Pacific Economic Competitiveness and Cooperation*, Proceedings of Kyushu University International Symposium 1992, Kyushu University, Japan.

_____ 1993, 'East Asia as a regional force for globalism', in Kym Anderson and Richard Blackhurst (eds), *Regional Integration and the Global Trading System*, London: Harvester Wheatsheaf.

15 Regionalism and the world trading system

Lawrence H. Summers

Increasing economic integration has been one of the major forces driving the world economy's impressive growth over the last forty-five years. Today, however, more than at any time since the Second World War, the future of the world trading system is in doubt, with the question of regional trading blocs increasingly to the fore.

World trade grew 3 per cent a year faster than GNP in the 1960s, 2 per cent a year faster in the 1970s, and 1 per cent a year faster in the 1980s. The good news is that integration has continued; the bad news is that it has increased ever more slowly.

Why did integration increase less rapidly in the 1980s? I think there are two important reasons. First, the technological push towards integration has slowed. Transportation and communication costs fell less quickly in the 1980s than in previous decades. Air transport, for example, is usually thought of as a dynamic industry. Yet the last major innovation was the jumbo jet, introduced nearly a generation ago. Moreover, as the total share of transportation and communication costs declines, incremental reductions have ever smaller effects; a reduction from $5 a minute to $2.50 a minute will have a greater impact on communication than a fall from 50 cents a minute to 25 cents a minute. Progress in this sense reduces the potential for future progress.

Second, the momentum of trade liberalisation has slowed as well. While sixty developing nations significantly reduced barriers to imports over the last decade, twenty of twenty-four OECD countries, including the United States, raised such barriers. The United States, which on some measures has trebled the protectionist impact of its policies, has a particularly ignominious record.

In the long run, however, it is those sixty liberalising developing countries and those that emulate them that are ultimately of greatest importance for the future development of the world trading system. Ninety-five per cent of the growth in the world's labour force over the next twenty-five years will occur in what are now developing nations. Even assuming only modest productivity performance, these demographic trends imply that these nations will be the most rapidly growing markets in the world over the next two decades. And this is a moment of historic opportunity in the developing world. There is abundant evidence — most obviously in Eastern Europe but also in large parts of Latin America; in China, where industrial production has grown at a 30 per cent annual rate over recent years; in India, where a new finance minister has pledged radical change; and even in Africa, where twenty nations are undertaking adjustment programs — of the desirability of market systems. Our top priority must be to reinforce these trends.

Trade policy not only needs to proceed on all fronts to lock in the gains that have occurred but also to provide examples that will lead to new trade gains, and even to ensure viable investment opportunities for OECD companies — GATT yes, but regional arrangements as well. I therefore assert and will defend the following principle: economists should maintain a strong, but rebuttable, presumption in favour of all lateral reductions in trade barriers, whether they be multi, uni, bi, tri or plurilateral. Global liberalisation may be best, but regional liberalisation is very likely to be good.

This position is based on four propositions: one, given the existing structure of trade, plausible regional arrangements are likely to have trade-creating effects that exceed their trade-diverting effects; two, there is a very good chance that even trade-diverting regional arrangements will increase welfare; three, apart from their impact on trade, regional trading arrangements are likely to have other beneficial effects; and four, reasonable regional arrangements are as likely to accelerate the general liberalisation process as to slow it down.

Are trading blocs likely to divert large amounts of trade? In answering this question, the issue of natural trading blocs is crucial, because, to the extent that blocs are created between countries that already trade disproportionately, the risk of large amounts of trade diversion is reduced. Table 15.1 sheds some light on the importance of natural trading blocs. It compares the ratio of observed trade for various entities to the trade one would expect if it were equiproportional to GNP. For example, the number in the upper left-hand corner indicates that the United States and Canada engaged in six times as much trade as they would if US trade with Canada were proportional to Canada's share of world, non-US, GDP. Looking at the table, I draw three conclusions:

1   Existing and many contemplated regional arrangements link nations that are already natural trading partners. Note the disproportionate share of US trade with Canada, of trade within the developing Asian countries, and of trade within industrialised Europe. If I included Mexico in the table it would have a ratio of about 7 with the United States, Korea would have a ratio of nearly 4, and even Israel would have a ratio well in excess of unity.

Table 15.1   Trading neighbours: ratio of share of trade to partnerís share of world output, 1989

| Trader | Trade with: | | | | | |
	United States	Canada	Other Americas	Japan	Developing Asia	EC
United States	-	6.06	2.38	0.87	2.34	0.61
Canada	2.63	-	0.66	0.47	0.97	0.39
Other Americas	1.13	0.63	3.16	0.31	0.57	0.67
Japan	0.95	1.15	0.75	-	4.33	0.53
Developing Asia	0.73	0.62	0.43	1.26	4.83	0.54
EC	0.22	0.30	0.42	0.17	0.63	1.75

2   There is little sense in which the United States and Canada have a natural affinity with the rest of the Western Hemisphere. American, and to an even greater extent Canadian, trade is disproportionately low, with Europe about equivalent between developing Asia and Latin America. This suggests that America should not be content with an Americas-based approach to trade reduction.

3   What is striking about the numbers in Table 15.1 is the isolation of industrial Europe, which trades disproportionately with itself. This is not an artifact of the fact that Europe is broken up into many countries; this rationalisation would fail to explain why it occupies so small a fraction of both Asian and Western Hemisphere trade.

I conclude from this exercise that most seriously contemplated efforts at regional integration involving industrialised countries cement what are already large and disproportionately strong trading relationships. To this extent they are likely to be trade-creating rather than trade-diverting. The one idea that looks bad from this perspective is that of a North Atlantic trading bloc which would be building on a weak trading relationship. Among regional groups of smaller developing countries, even trade disproportionate to GDP may constitute a small fraction of total trade and hence the argument carries less force.

It is sometimes suggested that whatever may have been true in the past, today's market is worldwide and regional arrangements are therefore more likely to be damaging than would once have been the case. Table 15.2 provides a fragment of evidence on this issue by re-doing the exercise reported in Table 15.1 for 1975. It is striking how similar the pattern of trade is. Perhaps this should not be too surprising; it is well known that intra-European trade has risen much faster than Europe's external trade.

Let me come now to my second point: trade-diverting regional arrangements may be desirable despite their trade-diverting effects. Only where trade diversion involves replacing efficient producers with inefficient producers is it a problem.

Table 15.2   Trading neighbours: ratio of share of trade to partnerís share of world output, 1975

| Trader | Trade with: | | | | | |
	United States	Canada	Other Americas	Japan	Developing Asia	EC
United States	-	6.42	2.68	0.60	1.56	0.51
Canada	2.32	-	0.90	0.37	0.58	0.36
Other Americas	1.19	0.74	2.81	0.55	0.23	0.72
Japan	0.65	1.17	1.12	-	4.70	0.26
Developing Asia	0.71	0.65	0.19	1.53	3.68	0.56
EC	0.18	0.37	0.46	0.09	0.44	1.25

I think this point has considerable force. We too often forget that more than half of US imports are either from US firms operating abroad or to foreign firms operating within the United States. And the fraction is rising rapidly. Under these circumstances, trade and investment decisions are inseparable. With many similar sites for investment by US firms producing for the US market, it is far from clear that trade diversion would have important welfare impacts.

While trade diversion is unlikely to involve large efficiency costs, trade creation is much more likely to involve real efficiency gains. First, it will help realise economies of scale which can be gained through creation but are unlikely to be lost due to trade diversion. Second, especially where agreements link developed and developing countries, or developing countries that are heavily specialised, the trade they create is likely to be substantially welfare-enhancing.

My third reason for eclectically favouring integration schemes is a reading of where the real benefits are. To the chagrin of economists, the real gains from trade policies of any kind cannot, with the possible exception of agriculture, lie in the triangles and welfare measures we are so good at calculating. Instead, they can be found in the salutary effects of competition and openness on domestic policy more generally. Pedro Aspe (1991) clearly thought more of NAFTA as a device for locking in good domestic policies and attracting investment than as a mechanism for gaining market access. To the extent that the benefits of trade integration lie in these areas, it may not be important how geographically general it is, or whether it is trade-diverting. Take the case of the Enterprise for the Americas Initiative. If the rest of Latin America desires to follow in Mexico's footsteps, a standstill on future US protection for reassurance, and the political and symbolic benefit that it can bring in promoting domestic reform, it seems almost absurd to resist them on the grounds that some trade might be diverted from some part of Asia that would produce a little more efficiently.

It is instructive to consider the breadth of the EC 1992 and GATT agendas. No small part of what is good about 1992 is the downward pressure on regulation created by mutual recognition policies. Similarly, competition for investment within the EC will have salutary effects on tax and regulatory policies. But there are diminishing returns to increasing numbers of policy competitors. A significant part of the benefits of trade liberalisation in improving domestic policy may be realisable within small groups of countries.

The fourth and final part of the case for supporting regional arrangements is their impact on the multilateral system. I do not share the view held by some that GATT is to trade policy what the League of Nations became to security policy.

But I am far from persuaded that over time regional arrangements make multilateral trade reduction impossible. The essential reason for concern is that large blocs will have more monopoly power than small ones — and will then use it. The argument is that the resulting reduced cross-bloc trade would do more harm than increased within-bloc trade would do good. This is a legitimate concern. But it is also true that three parties with a lot to gain from a successful negotiation are more likely to complete it than are seventy-one parties, each with only a small amount to gain. It may well be that a smaller number of trade blocs are more likely to be able to reach agreement than a larger number of separate countries.

This is not just a theoretical proposition. I doubt that the existence of the EC has complicated the process of reaching multilateral trade agreements. Instead, I suspect that the ability of Europe to speak with a more common voice would have helped, not hurt, over time.

Furthermore, there is the beneficial effect of successful arrangements in attracting imitation and in providing a vehicle for keeping up the momentum of liberalisation. Those concerned that the US–Mexico or possible follow-on agreements will divert attention from the multilateral trade reduction ought to consider whether they will also divert Congress' attention from the Super 301 process, or that of the business community from negotiating further import restrictions.

Even strong presumptions remain rebuttable. Obviously, some past and current proposals for regional integration would fail to satisfy the conditions. Agreements within groups of small, highly distorted, and protectionist countries that diminish momentum for greater overall liberality are clear candidates for welfare-worsening regional agreements.

But the crux of the argument is this: regional arrangements will necessarily speed up the GATT, and moving the GATT along is important if it is possible. But, holding the degree of multilateral progress constant, the world will be better off with more regional liberalisation. And the case that regional integration will slow multilateral progress is highly speculative at best.

Reference

Aspe,. Pedro 1991, 'Mexico's macroeconomic aqdustment and growth perspectives', in *Policy Implications of Trade and Currency Zones*, Federal Reserve Bank of Kansas City.

Part Four

The Idea of Open Regionalism

16 On Pacific economic integration

Ippei Yamazawa

Introduction

Following the conclusion of the Uruguay Round, it is inevitable that the contracting parties will attempt to pursue their aims by means of alternative routes — namely, through liberalisation efforts among like-minded countries in their neighbourhood. Regional integration efforts in the Pacific are no exception to this trend. However, their form and extent differ from those in Europe and North America. The word 'integration' is perhaps too strong to describe these efforts; 'cooperation' is probably a better word.

The aim of this paper is to analyse the current state of economic integration efforts in the Pacific region and to correct possible misunderstandings of its characteristics. Despite the absence of a formal framework, regional integration without a discriminatory impact on outsiders will help the region to achieve its high growth potential.

The following discussion provides an overview of the growth of the Pacific region in recent years. The discussion identifies East Asia as the core of the region's growth and evaluates the mechanisms underlying East Asia's growth. That growth is trade-oriented and needs a free trade regime to sustain it. The paper also explains how that growth has taken place in the absence of a region-wide framework for integration, with several subregional groupings characterised by informal arrangements, ASEAN being the exception. The limited achievements of the Uruguay Round have led these groupings to explore the possibility of further liberalisation. However, there seems to be a consensus in the region that it requires only a loose form of integration. The current region-wide framework — the APEC process — is analysed in this context.

An overview of Asia Pacific development[1]

Four NIEs achieved growth of 8 to 10 per cent for the 1960s and 1970s and four ASEAN countries achieved growth of 6 to 8 per cent for the 1970s. While many of these economies suffered a setback in the first half of the 1980s, they recovered quickly in the second half. The poor performances of Hong Kong and the Philippines were attributed to specific individual causes. China showed a different growth cycle from other countries for domestic reasons, but achieved steady and high growth in the 1980s.

These high growth rates of the Pacific economies contrast with the 2–4 per cent growth of the developed economies for the same period. Japan's growth rate almost halved from 10 per cent before the 1973–74 oil shock to 4 per cent thereafter — still the highest among the developed economies. In the early 1990s many developed economies recorded negative growth. Japan continued its moderate growth until 1990 but slowed down in the middle of 1991.

Table 16.1 compares the growth performance of East Asia's market economies (the NIEs, ASEAN and Japan) with those of North America (the United States, Canada and Mexico) and the EC12 in the latter half of the 1980s. The group growth rate of East Asia was maintained at 5 per cent while those of North America and the EC12 were 2–3 per cent per annum except for 1988. In 1990 and 1991 North America's growth rate was negative and that of the EC12 was down to 1–2 per cent, whilst East Asia's growth rate remained at 5 per cent.

Table 16.1   Size and growth performance of the three economic groups

	East Asia (Japan, NIEs, and ASEAN)	NAFTA (USA, Canada and Mexico)	EC12
Population (million persons)	507	362	343
GNP (1990) (billion US dollars)	37 174	62 011	57 083
Real growth rate (%)			
1986	3.9	2.6	2.7
1987	5.5	3.4	2.7
1988	6.8	4.4	4.0
1989	5.3	2.6	3.4
1990	5.6	1.0	2.8
Average 1986–90	5.4	2.8	3.1

Source: Ministry of Finance, Customs Bureau, Japan.

In terms of size, Europe and North America are roughly equivalent. The EC12 falls short of North America in both population and GNP, but if we add the six EFTA countries, Europe with a population of 376 million and a GNP of US$6,514 billion is larger than the other two. However, if the recent divergent growth performance continues, East Asia will exceed North America in 2011 and Europe in 2016.

The rapid growth of East Asia is also reflected in its trade performance. Table 16.2 gives a consolidated trade matrix for the three years 1980, 1986 and 1990. The growth of world trade shown in the bottom right-hand side of the table gives a reference rate. Total trade did not increase for the first half of the period but increased 1.6 times for the second half. Since prices of petroleum and other primary commodities fluctuated widely during the former period, these figures exaggerate changes in trade volume. The last column on the right-hand side gives total exports of individual country groups, while the bottom row gives their total imports. East Asian NIEs (EANIEs) and ASEAN recorded the highest growth rates in both exports and imports. They have been catching up with Japan in terms of total exports and imports, as shown in Table 16.3.

Imports grew more than exports in Japan, but the opposite was true in the case of China. East Asia as a whole recorded almost the same import values as North America but its exports were 25 per cent greater. This rapid expansion of East Asia's trade stimulated other groups through import growth. North America, Australia and New Zealand (ANZ), and the EC all recorded an increase in growth of exports to the EANIEs, ASEAN and Japan as rapid as that within East Asia. On the other hand, East Asia's exports increased significantly to the EC while its exports to North America and ANZ were stagnant.

How big are intra-regional trade flows in the three regions? These are shown in bold on the diagonal of the trade matrix of Table 16.2 and summarised in percentage terms in Table 16.4. Intra-regional trade is almost the same in East Asia and North America, whereas it is 50 per cent higher in the EC than in the other two. It was on the increase in all three in the 1980s.

Mechanisms underlying Pacific development

Economic relations among the countries of East Asia are different from those of the EC12 and North America. Natural resources are not distributed uniformly, and there are wide differences in industrialisation and wage levels. Exchange rate alignments are necessary to promote cross-border investment. However, technology transfers are being actively pursued, and trade patterns are moving steadily towards greater interdependence. The countries of East Asia have achieved their high growth rates because of this growing interdependence. Though the EC's Single Market and the North American free trade pact are designed to encourage Europe and North American corporations by providing access to larger markets, companies in East Asia are banking on the benefits of interdependence in an economically diverse region.

The main mechanism underlying this increasing interdependence in the Asia Pacific region is the transfer of industries, particularly manufacturing industries, from early

Table 16.2   Consolidated matrix of Asia Pacific trade, 1980, 1986 and 1990 (million US dollars)

		Japan	EANIEs	ASEAN6	China	East Asia	North America	ANZ	EC12	World
Japan	1980	-	15 434	19 069	5 078	33 581	34 309	4 069	18 025	129 542
	1986	-	25 812	12 081	9 856	47 749	87 811	6 331	30 871	209 081
	1990	-	46 487	32 066	6 145	84 698	100 132	8 134	54 045	287 678
	1986/80	-	1.67	0.92	1.94	1.42	2.49	1.56	1.71	1.61
	1990/86	-	1.80	2.65	0.62	1.77	1.14	1.28	1.75	1.38
EANIEs	1980	6 114	3 312	4 901	1 253	15 579	17 910	1 369	10 175	56 969
	1986	11 619	6 469	5 774	7 552	31 414	47 543	2 535	13 996	109 838
	1990	25 548	17 740	16 800	20 335	60 423	64 664	2 526	29 796	208 996
	1986/90	1.90	1.95	1.18	6.03	2.02	2.65	1.72	1.38	1.93
	1990/80	2.20	2.74	2.91	2.69	2.58	1.36	1.07	2.13	1.90
ASEAN6	1980	21 032	4 975	12 934	693	39 634	12 080	2 042	8 897	71 036
	1986	15 004	6 122	12 165	1 253	34 544	14 451	1 667	8 721	66 613
	1990	27 000	14 532	27 500	2 268	71 300	29 260	3 113	21 039	137 965
	1986/80	0.71	1.23	0.94	1.81	0.87	1.20	0.82	0.98	0.94
	1990/86	1.80	2.37	2.26	1.81	2.06	2.02	1.87	2.41	2.07
China	1980	4 323	4 401	1 722	-	10 447	1 362	283	2 748	18 120
	1986	5 638	10 462	2 443	-	18 543	5 682	371	4 098	31 367
	1990	9 327	26 243	3 493	-	39 063	8 132	644	6 720	66 518
	1986/80	1.30	2.38	1.42	-	1.78	4.17	1.31	1.49	1.73
	1990/86	1.85	2.51	1.43	-	2.11	1.43	1.73	1.64	2.12
East Asia	1980	31 489	28 122	32 626	7 024	**99 241**	66 660	7 763	39 845	275 668
	1986	32 281	48 865	32 463	18 661	**132 250**	155 487	10 722	57 686	416 899
	1990	61 874	105 001	79 858	28 748	**275 483**	202 188	14 417	111 600	701 157
	1986/80	1.03	1.74	1.00	2.66	**1.33**	2.33	1.38	1.45	1.51
	1990/86	1.92	2.15	2.46	1.54	**2.08**	1.30	1.34	1.93	1.68
North America	1980	24 919	12 486	9 413	4 587	51 406	**97 641**	5 317	66 148	291 431
	1986	27 440	15 523	8 700	3 963	55 626	**127 440**	6 598	57 483	301 630
	1990	57 609	38 694	20 246	6 230	120 779	**228 611**	10 674	112 132	554 520
	1986/80	1.10	1.24	0.92	0.86	1.08	**1.31**	1.24	0.87	1.03
	1990/86	2.10	2.36	2.33	1.57	2.17	**1.79**	1.62	1.95	1.84
ANZ	1980	6 109	1 500	2 082	938	10 629	3 514	1 791	4 139	27 439
	1986	6 095	2 419	1 484	1 163	11 161	3 208	1 845	4 238	27 775
	1990	11 699	5 573	4 910	1 046	23 228	6 526	3 681	6 597	48 341
	1986/80	1.00	1.61	0.71	1.24	1.05	0.91	1.03	1.02	1.01
	1990/86	1.92	2.30	3.31	0.90	2.08	2.03	2.00	1.56	1.74
EC12	1980	6 617	5 894	7 416	2 444	22 371	45 773	5 156	**381 562**	688 113
	1986	11 188	9 988	8 261	6 398	35 835	84 110	6 785	**449 592**	788 431
	1990	28 713	22 333	19 627	6 728	77 301	112 933	10 285	**889 742**	1 364 346
	1986/80	1.69	1.69	1.11	2.62	1.60	1.84	1.32	**1.10**	1.15
	1990/86	2.57	2.23	2.38	1.05	2.16	1.34	1.52	**1.98**	1.73
World	1980	139 892	63 918	63 882	20 020	287 712	327 578	25 385	768 328	1 993 312
	1986	119 424	91 009	62 232	43 247	315 912	470 533	30 471	776 627	1 973 600
	1990	235 307	205 055	159 441	55 378	655 181	668 864	48 700	1 419 062	3 332 100
	1986/80	0.85	1.42	0.97	2.16	1.10	1.44	1.20	1.01	0.99
	1990/86	1.97	2.25	2.58	1.28	2.07	1.42	1.60	1.83	1.69

Notes: EANIEs consists of South Korea, Taiwan and Hong Kong. East Asia consists of Japan, EANIEs, ASEAN6 and China.

Source: Compiled by Mr Kazubiko Yokota, Institute of Developing Economies, Tokyo, from the IDE's AIDXT (for 1980 and 1986) and the IMF's *Direction of Trade Statistics*, supplemented by Taiwan's trade statistics (for 1990).

Table 16.3   Relative size of trade of the EANIEs and ASEAN to that of Japan (= 100)

		Exports	Imports
EANIEs	1980	44.0	45.7
	1990	72.6	87.1
ASEAN	1980	54.8	45.7
	1990	48.6	67.8

Source: As for Table 16.2.

starters to latecomers. In fact, there has been a shift in the countries which have comparative advantage in mature industries such as textiles and steel — namely, from the United States and Japan to the Asian NIEs, and from the Asian NIEs to ASEAN. This is known as the 'flying geese pattern' of industrial development, and has been a catalyst for increasing interdependence. This pattern has already been extended to the stage of developing the electronics and automobile industries in ASEAN. The continued success of the flying geese pattern of industrial transfer in the future is the key to determining the future success or failure of industrialisation in ASEAN and more generally in the Pacific region.

Two types of enterprises have promoted this industrial transfer: local enterprises in the latecomer countries, which have been recipients of industrial transfer — their entrepreneurship makes them eager to acquire new technology to catch up with the early starters and thus makes them a prime mover in import substitution; and multinational enterprises (MNEs) in the early starter countries, which are sources of this industrial transfer. Which type of enterprises become the main catalyst in a given country is dependent on both the industry and the particular latecomer country receiving that new industry. For industries such as textiles and steel, which are technologically mature, it was mainly the local enterprises of the latecomer which carried out these catch-up activities. However, in industries such as electronics and fine chemicals, where new products and technologies emerge constantly, the role of

Table 16.4   Percentage shares of intra-group trade in total trade

	East Asia	North America	EC12
1980	35.2	31.5	52.4
1986	36.1	33.0	57.5
1990	40.3	37.3	63.4

Note: (intra-group trade x 2)/(total exports + total imports).

MNEs inevitably becomes more influential. Further, recipient countries with a strong entrepreneurship culture are capable of catch-up development led by local enterprises. On the other hand, when demand for new products is limited by the domestic market, export orientation is necessary from the beginning. Thus dependence on MNEs becomes necessary given their experience in overseas markets. There are also some cases where both catalysts actively work together in industrial development.

The introduction of new industries in ASEAN is striking, particularly in Malaysia, Thailand and Indonesia. In the second half of the 1980s the industrial growth rate of these three countries was the highest in the region, at 11 to 14 per cent, with the percentage of manufacturing in total domestic production expanding to 19 per cent in Indonesia, 27 per cent in Malaysia and 25 per cent in Thailand by 1990. The transfer of some new industries stands out, particularly electrical machinery and parts, precision machinery, and chemicals. Furthermore, export orientation is strong in these new products, with the percentage of industrial products in total exports reaching 46 per cent in Indonesia, 60 per cent in Malaysia and 75 per cent in Thailand. This new industry rush is characterised by the participation of MNEs, particularly in areas which are export oriented. Asian NIEs rank alongside Japan with their large share of the MNEs in ASEAN. The role of US MNEs has also begun to increase again.

The international development of these enterprises represents an attempt to confront rapid adjustments in the exchange rate, wage increases and labour shortage. They have taken advantage of the differences in development and wage levels in the region. Thus industries were transferred from the United States and Japan to NIEs first and then from NIEs to ASEAN countries. As wage levels increase in ASEAN countries, they are being attracted to countries with more abundant labour and lower wages — China and Indochina as well as South Asian countries.

It is crucial to sustain the policy environment conducive to such industrial transfer. In the NIEs of East Asia and ASEAN the industrial transfer has been encouraged by outward-looking policies. Governments have to maintain this free trade and investment stance in order to continue the process of industrial transfer. Further growth of East Asia requires trade and investment liberalisation not only within the region but also outside the region.

Development without a formal framework

The interdependent growth of East Asia was achieved without much by way of a formal integration framework. Of course ASEAN is an important exception. Indonesia, Malaysia, the Philippines, Singapore and Thailand started a formal framework for economic cooperation in 1967 and were later joined by Brunei–Darussalam. They implemented Preferential Trading Arrangements (PTAs), joint industrial projects (sharing large-scale production of heavy industrial products for the common ASEAN market), and an industrial complementation scheme (developing common parts supply networks). None of these have been very successful, however, because of limited concessions by member countries. Instead, the six countries succeeded in strengthening their bargaining position against outside developed trading partners. Intra-ASEAN trade has remained at a constant 21 per cent of total trade, of which trade between Singapore and other member countries accounts for 80 per cent (Table 16.2). In January 1992 it was agreed at the ASEAN summit meeting to reactivate their integration efforts by introducing a new AFTA. The preferential tariff reduction will be extended to fifteen selected industrial product groups in which all internal tariffs will be abolished over fifteen years. In sum, ASEAN has achieved a limited success but hardly contributed to the spectacular development of East Asia as a whole.

In addition to ASEAN the following subregional groups have developed in East Asia:

1   The 'growth triangle', centred on Singapore and including Johor state in Malaysia and Batam Island in Indonesia.

2   The Baht Zone in the border area of Thailand, Laos, Cambodia, and Vietnam.

3   The Greater South China Economic Zone, centred on Hong Kong and including China's Guandong and Fujian provinces, and Taiwan.

4   The Yellow Sea Economic Zone, which includes the coastal areas facing the Yellow Sea of North and Northeast China, North and South Korea, and Japan.

5   The Japan Sea Economic Zone, which includes the coastal areas of Northeast China, Far East Russia, South and North Korea, and Japan.

Not all of these subregional groups have been equally active. Groups (1)–(3) have developed rapidly since the mid-1980s and (4) has started only recently, whereas (5) still remains at the proposal stage. Each forms a natural economic territory, in which the neighbourhood trade has become active. In the growth triangle (1), there has long been border trade, which has been accelerated by an increase in foreign direct investment to this area since the late 1980s and limited spatial room and human resources in Singapore. The development of Batam Island was occasioned by a tacit agreement between Indonesia's President Suharto and Singapore's Deputy Prime Minister Goh Chok Tong in 1988, but has been accelerated by the same market mechanism as in the case of Johor, and its management is left to the private sectors of the two countries.

The other four have a common driving force. All are located along the borderline between market economies and socialist economies, where trade and investment exchange between the two used to be severely restricted. Since the end of the Cold War, and more open economic policies adopted by the Asian socialist countries, the natural development of trade and investment has resumed. But they can hardly be compared with the intergovernmental arrangements of ASEAN, let alone the EC, and there exist no central coordinating agents.

The real driving force of development is market driven trade and investment over the whole of East Asia. As each subregional group develops further, its coverage will be extended so as to form a greater East Asian group that happens to coincide with the geographical coverage of the East Asian Economic Group (EAEG) proposed by Malaysian Prime Minister Mahathir in December 1990, immediately after the GATT ministerial meeting failed to conclude the Uruguay Round. This quickly encountered strong criticism from the United States and Australia, which warned against the establishment of a trade bloc in East Asia that excluded those two countries. The EAEG was later renamed the East Asian Economic Caucus (EAEC) so as to emphasise its consultative role. The EAEC proposal reflected the reality of rapid economic development and trade expansion in East Asia, and its function as a consultative body met the need of its member states. But because of the absence of prior consultation among designated members on the one hand, and immediate criticism by outsiders on the other, it failed to obtain strong support from a number of member countries, including Japan, and some fellow ASEAN countries. The proposal was put on the agenda for the ASEAN summit meeting in January 1992. ASEAN leaders agreed to suspend it and launched the AFTA proposal instead.

Impediments to intra-Pacific trade

Nonetheless, many now seek a loose form of institutional framework for economic cooperation. Why do we need an institutional framework for the Pacific at this stage? In the process of rapid development for the past two decades several problems have emerged:

1   Macroeconomic imbalances result inevitably from interdependent growth. Some countries tend to incur persistent trade deficits and some persistent surpluses, and frictions will continue between the two groups. It is most evident across the Pacific.

2   There still remain restrictions to imports in the region, but more important are instruments such as VERs and OMAs to exports of manufactures to American and European markets. The region's exports of textiles and clothing have been managed tightly for individual product types and markets under the MFA. ASEAN countries have so far been given export quotas beyond their capacity and as a result have been able to expand their exports. But sooner or later their quota will be exceeded by their capacity increase and the MFA will deter further export expansion until implementation of the Uruguay Round settlement sees the weakening of MFA constraints.

3   Foreign investment and services are still subject to more regulations and restrictions than commodity trade. However, a variety of incentive measures are provided in order to make up for these regulations and reduce their net impact.

4   Rapid changes in trade and production structures have been accompanied by adjustment difficulties and frictions among trading partners. This has tended to

result in calls for foreign direct investments to replace exports, which has further promoted closer integration in the region.

5   Tacit political assurance of some form has been a prerequisite for the recent development of subregional groups along the borders between socialist and market regimes. However, tacit assurance could be withdrawn at any time, thereby deterring further development. Some form of regional framework may reduce the likelihood of political disturbance.

A consultative body is required to discuss and resolve these problems in order to mitigate disputes among trading partners. In the past this has often taken the form of bilateral arrangement between the countries concerned. The US–Japan SII talks forestalled unilateral resort by the United States to Super 301 action and thus defused tensions. However, bilateral consultation is not free from emotional conflict. Furthermore, a bilateral agreement between two parties often affects a third party. Regional consultation could help resolve disputes without unnecessary emotional confrontation and without spillover to other parties.

Elements of the loose cooperation framework desired

East Asia has not been enthusiastic about formal economic integration of the EC type. There has neither been a Rome Treaty nor a region-wide free trade agreement. East Asia has not reached that stage of integration yet. The coordination of macroeconomic policies has never been attempted among the APEC member governments. However, member economies are interdependent through trade, investment and services flows in this region, and no member economy is fully insulated from the impact of the policies of other members. It is necessary to have a regular policy dialogue to try and affect each other's policy-making in a subtle way.

As regards trade and investment policies, agreement on regional trade liberalisation is possible. In fact, many member governments in the region have recently been liberalising on a unilateral basis. All member governments supported the Uruguay Round negotiations and participated in the coordination of their interests in individual areas. 'Open regionalism' has often been mentioned by Pacific economists as the policy stance of the Asia Pacific region, but economists outside the region seem to find it difficult to understand. In contrast with globalism, regionalism focuses its policy implementation on a particular region at the expense of those outside the region. It tends to discriminate against outsiders, whether intended or not, and the expression of the 'regionalism open to outsiders' seems to involve internal inconsistency. The EC illustrates this well. Weak regionalism which does not discriminate against outsiders will not be able to activate economies within the region. However, Pacific cooperation fits into this view of weak regionalism. Despite increased intra-regional trade, East Asia remains highly reliant on trade outside the region (Table 16.4).

It is worth noting that trade is only a part of the liberalisation agenda. Nowadays, investment, services, and other forms of transactions across national borders are also important. The harmonisation of rules and the process of making national regulations transparent will encourage other member country enterprises to do business across borders while not necessarily discriminating against outsiders. Free trade agreements currently being negotiated all include harmonisation of rules and deregulation. This is much wider than the classic perception of the free trade area.

In textbook accounts, the FTA is a lower stage of liberalisation than a customs union. Internal tariffs are eliminated and external tariffs harmonised in a customs union; only internal tariffs are eliminated but different external tariffs remain in the FTA. An FTA has not been proposed for the Asia Pacific as a whole. Although an across-the-board tariff reduction was once proposed while retaining external tariffs for the Asia Pacific countries in the 1960s (PAFTA), the proposal has never been taken seriously. The modern version of the FTA is better understood as providing an environment in which goods, capital, labour and information move across borders, and enterprises are encouraged to extend their horizons and promote global operations. Tariffs and non-tariff barriers deter such business activities, but bottlenecks in transportation and communications, insufficient information, limited availability of skilled personnel, and environmental restrictions also discourage an enterprise's activities. What is evolving may be better termed an open economic association (OEA), which is not intended to discriminate against outsiders.[2]

The existing organisation which best fits the loose framework described above is the APEC ministerial meeting, which was proposed in 1989 by Australian Prime Minister Hawke and has continued its taskforce activities in close cooperation with the semi-official organisation, PECC, in many areas. It has reached the stage of establishing a small permanent secretariat within the region. It will accommodate such subregional groupings as NAFTA, ASEAN, and the Australia–New Zealand CER Agreement as well such independent trading nations as Japan and Korea. A loose framework for economic cooperation as envisaged by APEC is conducive to the continued growth of East Asia.

Notes

1   This and the following sections draw on an earlier study of mine. See Yamazawa (1992).

2   I owe this terminology to a discussion with Andrew Elek at the Australian National University in August 1992. Elek (1992) contains a similar idea regarding economic cooperation in the Pacific. I later developed this concept to analyse a practical form of regional integration in the Asia Pacific region. See Yamazawa (1993).

References

Elek, Andrew 1992, 'Pacific economic cooperation: policy choices for the 1990s', *Asian–Pacific Economic Literature*, 6(1), May.

Yamazawa, Ippei and associates 1992, *Vision for the Economy of the Asia Pacific Region in the Year 2000 and Tasks Ahead*, Report commissioned by the Ministry of Industry and International Trade, Japan; later submitted to the APEC Ad Hoc Economic Group Meeting on 10–11 August 1992.

_____ 1993, *Economic Integration in the Asia Pacific Region and Options for Japan*, Report commissioned by the Ministry of Foreign Affairs, Japan.

17 Trade policy options for the Asia Pacific region in the 1990s: the potential of open regionalism ——

Andrew Elek

Introduction

At the end of the Uruguay Round, Asia Pacific decision-makers need to select trade policy options which will advance, rather than detract from, the region's over-riding interest in a more open global trading system. The new process of APEC, launched in Australia in 1989, provides the first opportunity for regional ministers to meet regularly to identify these options and to foster the cohesion and trust needed for their progressive implementation.

APEC's twelve original participants (the six members of ASEAN, the United States, Canada, Japan, Korea, Australia and New Zealand) were joined by China, Hong Kong and Taiwan in 1991. This diverse but correspondingly complementary group of economies accounts for more than half of world GDP and almost 40 per cent of world trade. Close to 65 per cent of their exports are to each other; this is higher than the corresponding share for the EC.

APEC's guiding principles, built on the intellectual foundations laid by PECC since 1980, stipulate that cooperation should be outward-looking, building consensus on a gradually broader range of economic issues. Participation is to be open-ended, based on the strength of economic linkages; Mexico is the likely next participant. Regional trade liberalisation is to be promoted, provided it is consistent with the principles of the GATT and not to the detriment of other economies.

The last of these principles is unique. For the first time, a powerful regional group of economies has come together to promote global economic interests, rather than to defend their own narrower markets by forming a trading bloc. APEC's concept of open regionalism is radically different from the discriminatory nature of the EC.[1]

APEC was launched too late to exert real influence on the Uruguay Round but, as its perception of common interests develops, APEC can become increasingly

Reprinted with permission from the *American Economic Review*, Vol. 82, No. 2, May 1992, pp. 74–8 (with minor deletions). Copyright © 1992 by the American Economic Association, Nashville, Tennessee, USA.

effective in shaping the global economic agenda. By bridging the Pacific, APEC can provide a non-confrontational, high-level forum to identify the strong common global economic interests of East Asia and North America. APEC can also provide a convenient regional framework within which Japan can move towards a position of shared policy leadership with the United States, in buttressing and extending the GATT-based trade regime (Drysdale 1991, p. 6).

The agenda for regional trade liberalisation

Factors which impede or distort international transactions in the Asia Pacific region include:

- market access barriers, such as protection of textiles and clothing by Australia and North America;

- uncertainty, exacerbated by arbitrary and discriminatory import restrictions;[2]

- shortfalls in infrastructure, ranging from harbours to telecommunications; and

- differences in domestic policies, including divergent standards and commercial legislation.

Market access issues are well defined, but also difficult to resolve; protectionism is still well entrenched, even within the APEC region. Therefore, to generate momentum, APEC's trade liberalisation agenda should address a wider range of problems.

Reducing physical impediments to trade may be a pragmatic starting point, since the potential for mutual benefit is readily appreciated. Exchanging information about the pattern and trend of regional trade, investment and tourism can pinpoint the need for timely investments to avoid infrastructure bottlenecks. Such work has already commenced in APEC's sectoral working groups. For example, transport capacity will be boosted by APEC's electronic data interchange (EDI) project, which is to achieve total electronic exchange of trade documentation in the region. It may take some time to achieve agreement on reducing any customs duties, but worthwhile progress can be made more quickly to standardise customs documentation and clearance procedures.

APEC working groups can go on to review many of the standards being adopted by the EC; the basic principles of harmonisation and mutual recognition will also prove useful in the Asia Pacific region. Harmonising environmental standards might prove difficult, but early progress could be made on matters such as product labelling and safety standards.

Regional harmonisation will need to grapple with sometimes radical differences in legal frameworks and frequently unclear administrative procedures. A productive start could be made on investment rules, working towards a common definition of the basic rights and responsibilities of foreign investors, avoiding the need to negotiate scores of additional bilateral agreements. A more uniform approach to tax concessions offered to investors could also be considered, reducing wasteful competition for investment through subsidies.

The CER Agreement between Australia and New Zealand provides for substantial harmonisation of competition policies, leading to agreement that antidumping actions will no longer be taken between them. This example could be followed by a gradually broader group of economies, reducing uncertainty about access to markets. Another useful step to lessen uncertainty would be for APEC participants to agree to adhere strictly to the improved dispute settlement procedures and timetables which may be part of the Uruguay Round agreement. Wider access to the dispute settlement mechanism included in NAFTA could also be considered, reducing the likelihood of resort to unilateral coercion to resolve trade disputes.

Common features of the agenda considered so far are that:

- broad sets of issues can be resolved into manageable policy options and graded from less contentious to more difficult matters;

- progress can be made on each issue without any conflict with GATT principles and without detriment to others;

- it also follows that agreement on any of these matters among some APEC participants would not impose costs on others, inside or outside APEC; and

- conversely, those who do not wish to take part in any initiative would not get an obvious 'free ride'.

These important advantages hold out hope for early action on some matters. A careful, serious effort will be needed to build the widest possible consensus on any issue. APEC-wide initiatives would be strongly preferable, but none would be hurt if, ultimately, some moved faster than others on the issues discussed so far.

Improving market access

Considerable mutual economic gains would flow from reducing 'traditional' forms of border protection in the region. Drysdale and Garnaut (1989) noted that the remaining barriers to trade in the region—for instance, in agriculture, textiles, clothing and processed minerals— tend to be highest where there is greatest complementarity in terms of resource endowments and cost structures. Therefore, by far the greatest share of benefits from further non-discriminatory liberalisation by the Asia Pacific region would accrue to the region itself.

This analysis is borne out by experience. Liberalisation and deregulation contributed to the spectacular growth of trade by APEC economies during the 1980s; no attempt was made to discriminate against the rest of the world, but the relative proximity, complementarity and dynamism of Asia Pacific economies ensured that the vast majority (76 per cent) of trade growth from 1980 to 1990 was among APEC participants. Unfortunately, entrenched attitudes to trade negotiations and resentment against the small fraction of the potential benefits which would accrue to non-participants might preclude APEC-wide non-discriminatory initiatives — this is the so-called free-rider problem. Subregional agreements may be even harder to achieve, due to the greater share of potential gains accruing to free-riders.[3]

Despite these difficulties, APEC might consider non-discriminatory lowering of market access barriers in some sectors where complementarity among APEC economies is evident, the net gains from liberalisation can be estimated, the original reasons for protection have been weakened by changes in circumstances, and where natural resource endowments and transport costs limit effective competition from outside the region: an example might be trade in processed minerals, including aluminium and steel products.

APEC participants could also consider removing all remaining barriers to regional trade in tropical products. There would be considerable further gain to the region from phasing out the MFA even faster than elsewhere. APEC could also develop sectoral codes for some services of particular regional interest, such as telecommunications and transport; APEC could then promote the GATT-wide adoption of such codes or, if that proves too slow, consider adopting them initially within the region.

Even if the search for APEC-wide agreement does not lead to any early initiatives, an appreciation of the absolute and relative net gains from the potential liberalisation of trade in various goods and services would help define the region's priorities in subsequent multilateral negotiations about trade policy and institutional development.

Subregional trade liberalisation

Asia Pacific economies are evolving rapidly and there has been considerable trade liberalisation in recent years, particularly in East Asia. With a rich potential agenda for further liberalisation, individual economies or groups of regional economies can reduce impediments to trade without compromising subsequent region-wide or global liberalisation.

For the foreseeable future, most trade consultations or negotiations involving APEC participants will be on a bilateral or subregional basis. APEC ministers have noted the need for care to ensure that such negotiations do not cause internal divisions by discriminating against other APEC participants (APEC III 1991, para.18).

It is possible to promote more open global trade through bilateral or subregional negotiations. For example, following the 1988 US–Australia–Japan beef negotiations, Japanese consumers benefit from cheaper beef and all beef producers can compete for their custom. More recently, the 1990 SII talks dealt with many matters well beyond GATT's coverage. Both the United States and Japan will benefit by implementing their undertakings, but no other economy will be worse off — which is consistent with APEC principles.

FTAs are a more 'traditional' approach to trade liberalisation among pairs or groups of economies. NAFTA may include more and more of Latin America during the 1990s, so it is important to consider whether several subregional FTAs might expand or coalesce, as well as potential implications for the future of the GATT and of APEC. Although discriminatory, FTAs can be consistent with Article XXIV of the GATT, so long as most sectors are liberalised. It is more difficult to ensure that FTAs are not to the detriment of non-participants. Preferential lowering of market access barriers inevitably causes some diversion of trade: net damage to non-participants can be avoided only if this is outweighed by new trading opportunities created by the increased dynamism of FTA participants or by the simultaneous lowering of some external trade barriers.

The Australia–New Zealand CER meets both criteria. Barriers to trade in all goods and almost all services have been eliminated, while trade restrictions against the rest of the world have been liberalised substantially by both partners. The three NAFTA partners also expect that the trade-creating effects of a more integrated and efficient North American economy will outweigh any trade diversion costs. But it may prove more difficult to ensure that adding more economies to NAFTA will also be of net benefit to the rest of the world, since the potential synergy will be less than in the case of Mexico.

A potentially more important problem may be posed by the composition of an expanded NAFTA. Even if it contained accession provisions open to all others, Latin American economies would be more likely to join than any East Asian ones. If a broader Western Hemisphere FTA were accompanied by persistent threats of retaliation against imports from East Asia, APEC's positive potential would be compromised. Moreover, East Asian interest in a separate economic group would be revived, raising the risk of three increasingly defensive trading blocs dominating the world economy. Even if FTAs ultimately coalesced to encompass much of the Asia Pacific region, this would still run counter to the region's overwhelming interest in sustaining a global trading system. An Asia Pacific FTA based on discriminatory preferential trading arrangements would lead to confrontation with Europe, with serious consequences for the GATT.

Simultaneous progress in the context of APEC as well as the Enterprise for the Americas Initiative can be achieved by distinguishing carefully between the discriminatory and non-discriminatory elements of potential trade associations. Concentrating on the latter can avoid divisions and draw together a large, cooperative group of economies including both East Asian and American trading partners. Such non-discriminatory, confidence-building elements could include:

- enhanced exchange of information about trading patterns;

- increased transparency of trade policies;

- reducing uncertainty involved in international transactions; and

- harmonisation and/or mutual recognition of policies, regulations and standards.

Progress on any of these fronts can be made in carefully graduated steps. While APEC-wide moves would yield the greatest benefit, some steps can also be taken initially by a smaller group of economies, within the framework of APEC. APEC's role in such cases would be an indirect one: firstly to assess the implications of trade policy actions taken by some participants, and secondly to promote the broadest possible participation in moves to reduce impediments to regional transactions. Such a multi-faceted strategy would also increase the effectiveness and cohesion of APEC, set a positive example of open non-discriminatory regional economic cooperation, and allow APEC to set the pace of future multilateral negotiations to improve the global trading system.

Notes

1   Elek (1991) presents a more detailed account of the emergence of APEC and its guiding principles, which are contained in the Seoul APEC Declaration.

2   For China and Taiwan, these uncertainties are compounded by their lack of recourse to GATT-based mechanisms for resolving trade disputes.

3   Concern over the share of benefits accruing to outsiders has encouraged past trade liberalisation among small groups of economies to be preferential FTAs.

References

APEC III 1991, *Asia Pacific Economic Cooperation Ministerial Meeting — Joint Statement*, Seoul, November.

Drysdale, Peter 1991, 'Open regionalism: a key to East Asia's economic future', *Pacific Economic Papers*, No. 197, Australia–Japan Research Centre, Australian National University, Canberra.

Drysdale, Peter and Ross Garnaut 1989, 'A Pacific free trade area?', *Pacific Economic Papers*, No. 171, Australia–Japan Research Centre, Australian National University, Canberra.

Elek, A. 1991, 'Asia Pacific Economic Cooperation (APEC)', *Southeast Asian Affairs 1991*, Institute of Southeast Asian Studies, Singapore, pp. 33–48.

18   APEC and the world economy: a force for worldwide liberalisation

C. Fred Bergsten

Contrary to most expectations about regional economic organisations, the APEC forum is poised to become a driving force for worldwide trade liberalisation. There is already strong evidence for this conclusion: the additional liberalisation offers that APEC developed at its Seattle summit in November 1993 made an important contribution to the subsequent success of the Uruguay Round, as did the message to countries outside the Asia Pacific region that APEC represented a feasible alternative to global progress if the GATT talks were to fail. This development may be the most important of several promising initiatives launched at Seattle.

As envisioned by its Eminent Persons Group (EPG), whose proposed vision for APEC was broadly endorsed at Seattle, APEC would become neither a customs union like the European Union nor a free trade area like that covered by NAFTA. APEC would support every effort in the GATT, as it did to help achieve success in the Uruguay Round. But APEC would also try to achieve regional agreement on issues that could not yet be resolved at the global level. It would address both those that had been tried in the GATT but failed and those that had not yet found their way onto the global agenda. It would then offer to open its accords to other countries, hopefully the entire GATT membership, that were willing to accept their obligations. APEC is, in essence, considering a wholly new model of regional economic cooperation: a steady 'ratcheting up' of trade liberalisation between the regional and global levels that would confirm its dedication to 'open regionalism'.

The initiatives begun at Seattle, in addition to benefiting the Asia Pacific region, could thus be the catalysts for new global trade negotiations to maintain the momentum of liberalisation. This is crucial because extensive protectionist back-sliding marked the lengthy hiatuses after completion of the earlier GATT rounds in the late 1960s and late 1970s. The recent success of the seven-year-long Uruguay Round

Reprinted from *Foreign Affairs*, Vol. 73, No. 3, May/June 1994, pp. 20–6 (with minor editing). Copyright © 1994 by C. Fred Bergsten. All rights reserved. Reprinted with permission from the Council on Foreign Relations, Inc., New York, USA.

avoided the devastation that its failure would have wreaked on world trade and the fragile world economy. But protectionist sentiments are still quite evident in many quarters and could bloom in a vacuum, as they have done so often in the past.

APEC's uniqueness as a regional economic organisation and its potential leverage on the direction of world trade derive from the magnitude of economic activity in the region, the economic strategies of the participating nations and the attitudes of their leaders. A close look at APEC's Seattle meetings and the strategic considerations of its member states' leaders illustrate these points.[1]

Both the Asian and North American members fear that further erosion of the global trading system could undermine their strategies of export-led growth. Both groups worry about inward-looking regionalism in Europe, and Asians worry about similar trends in the Western Hemisphere as NAFTA takes effect and considers expanding southward. Asians are concerned that American withdrawal from the region could trigger instability there, and the United States, having fought three wars in Asia in the last half century, shares the goal of avoiding new regional tensions.

Both groups thus seek to avoid any division between the two sides of the Pacific. They draw the obvious conclusion that firm institutional ties could help obviate such a risk. Hence the leaders in Seattle began the process of converting APEC from a purely consultative body into a substantive international institution.

The specific results

Even more noteworthy than the repeated references in the leaders' 'vision statement' to their new Asia Pacific 'community' was the series of specific decisions made in Seattle. First, as noted, they agreed to an extensive package of additional trade liberalisation offers to help bring the Uruguay Round to successful completion. The success of the round promoted the cardinal APEC goal of restoring the credibility and effectiveness of the global trading system.

Second, the leaders in essence decided to hold annual summits. Indonesia, at the behest of all participants, offered to host a summit in 1994. Japan has publicly announced that it will probably hold one when it assumes the chair in 1995. This is a radical change from as recently as 1990, when some countries did not even want to hold annual ministerial meetings of APEC.

The decision to hold annual summits assures that the leaders will continue to focus on APEC and get to know each other better, that the President of the United States will travel to Asia at least once a year, that all APEC members will broaden their perspectives and that ministers and officials will be fully energised to carry out their leaders' instructions from Seattle.

Moreover, the leaders now have a major personal stake in the success of the APEC initiative. Hence they will take its evolution into account when making decisions on related matters. President Clinton, who made a considerable commitment to APEC at Seattle and views improving economic and political relations in the Asia Pacific region as one of his major foreign policy initiatives, has considered the implications for APEC when deciding such issues as whether to maintain tariff preferences for Indonesia. The upgrading of the APEC process should help in resolving bilateral disputes in the region; conversely, the need to resolve such disputes (such as the current United States–Japan trade wrangle) more effectively adds to the case for rapid upgrading of the process.

Institutionalising the summits should increase the momentum of community-building in the region. The Seattle sessions showed that the leaders were far more ready than their ministers, who in turn were far more ready than their senior officials, to adopt and pursue visionary goals. Heads of government can rise above the narrow and compartmentalised concerns that derail meaningful progress. Their continued engagement augurs well for the future of APEC.

Third, meetings of APEC ministers across a number of areas of responsibility began in 1994. The leaders directed their finance ministers to get together to discuss macroeconomic and monetary issues. Environmental ministers met in the (northern) spring. Trade ministers will convene to discuss the implications of the conclusion of the Uruguay Round and the future agenda of the new World Trade Organisation. Industry ministers will explore the prospects for small and medium-sized businesses. The proliferation of high-level sessions will nurture the Asia Pacific identity and a habit of cooperation.

Fourth, the ministers decided that 'those recommendations [of the Eminent Persons Group] closely linked to ongoing work should be implemented promptly'. One minister interpreted that directive to include proposals for mutual recognition of product standards and domestic testing and monitoring procedures, cooperation in national competition (including antidumping) policies, avoiding region-wide problems from rules of origin included in the various subregional agreements (including NAFTA), annual ministerial review of the entire 'trade facilitation' program, and technical cooperation in promoting infrastructure projects such as higher education and telecommunications networks. The details are to be worked out in 1994.

The leaders themselves agreed to develop an APEC investment code for adoption at their 1994 meeting. The code would initially be a set of voluntary, non-binding principles designed to protect and promote private investment in the region — one of the driving forces in its economic progress to date. The recent decline in investment flows to several Asian countries, including Indonesia and Korea, has heightened interest in such initiatives, which would enhance the attractiveness of the region to private investors. Adoption of an investment code would require APEC to make another firm decision, as it did with the trade liberalisation package endorsed in Seattle for the Uruguay Round, and thus continue its conversion into an operational body.

The summit under Indonesian leadership will likely place considerable emphasis on developmental issues of greatest concern to the group's less industrialised members. This is all to the good. The EPG recommended an extensive program of technical cooperation within APEC — what the ASEAN countries call 'resource pooling' — to improve the region's economic infrastructure and assure that all members benefit fully from its progress. New investment in human resources should be a major part of such an effort and was presaged in Seattle by the leaders' decision to create an APEC Education Program. The leaders also decided to create a Technology Transfer Exchange Centre, to facilitate the exchange of technology and technology management skills among APEC members, and an APEC Business Volunteer Program to promote human resource development.

Fifth, the leaders clearly stated that they 'welcomed the challenge . . . to achieve free trade in the Asia Pacific' (although they did not endorse the EPG recommendation to commit themselves to decide by 1996 on a plan and timetable to do so). APEC is now wrestling with the same 'broadening versus deepening' debate as the European Union and has come to the same conclusion: expanding the membership should be deferred until the organisation can decide on its substantive future. To underscore that position, APEC declared a three-year moratorium on new members (after admitting Mexico and Papua New Guinea immediately and Chile in 1994).

The future agenda

The Group of Seven (G-7) industrialised nations are supposedly highly homogeneous and have been meeting for almost twenty years. APEC includes advanced industrial countries (including the world's largest), newly industrialising economies at a middle stage of development, and less developed countries. Its leaders' conference was proposed only in July 1993 and it focused on an EPG report that was formally submitted only in October. Yet the results of Seattle compare favourably with recent G-7 summits.

To achieve these results, several serious concerns had to be dispelled. Thus the presentation of the EPG report to the ministerial meeting emphasised 'three noes'. The EPG was not proposing a community like the European Union, with extensive economic integration or even a customs union, but rather a community in the generic sense that translates into 'big family' in Chinese. Nor was it proposing a discriminatory free trade area, but rather 'free trade in the area' achieved to the maximum extent possible through multilateral liberalisation. The EPG did not recommend precipitate action, nor indeed any substantive timetable, but only that the fundamental principles be decided within the next three years.

The current period illustrates how the proposed 'ratcheting up' strategy could work. The APEC countries made a major and ultimately fruitful effort, at Seattle and subsequently at Geneva, to promote a successful Uruguay Round. But a number of key issues, such as new rules for investment and liberalisation of specific services sectors, largely fell out of the final GATT package. APEC could now address these topics and, if it could reach agreement on them, bring its pacts back to Geneva for broader adherence. Likewise, APEC could anticipate issues that will need to be addressed in GATT in the future, such as trade–environment linkages and competition policies. It could seek to develop regional agreements that would become precedents for dealing with the issues at the global level.

Rather than a stumbling block, APEC could thus be a building block — perhaps the leader — in worldwide trade liberalisation. Such collective leadership is needed in the post-Cold War period with the United States no longer willing or able to provide it alone. Both the North American and Australia–New Zealand free trade areas have already provided several useful precedents for global negotiations, and APEC could do so systematically. The successful conclusion of the Uruguay Round, by re-establishing the credibility of the GATT in regulating relations between regional arrangements, makes the world much safer for regionalism and hence for the proposed approach.

The strategy would embody the APEC mantra of 'open regionalism'. It could avoid preferential treatment altogether on some issues, perhaps including competition policy and new industrial standards. It could do so when liberalising in sectors where the APEC countries dominate world trade, such as computers. Individual APEC members could be permitted to extend their concessions to non-members, as Mexico has done with some of its investment obligations under NAFTA.

In general, however, the strategy would open APEC arrangements only to non-member countries that undertake corresponding obligations. This procedure is increasingly employed in the GATT through codes agreed to during the Tokyo Round in the late 1970s and during the Uruguay Round. It avoids 'free riding' by outsiders, including large trading entities such as the European Union, which would run afoul of domestic political realities in the United States and most other APEC members. Every subregional trade arrangement within the Asia Pacific area — including AFTA, which like NAFTA came into effect on 1 January 1994, as well as the Australia–New Zealand and North American entities — has limited all benefits to member countries and has not offered to extend them to outsiders.

Non-members would have no incentive to negotiate multilaterally if they could simply sit back and receive the benefits of APEC liberalisation without making concessions of their own. The use of 'temporarily conditional MFN' uses the negotiating leverage available to APEC because of its large economic weight to obtain maximum liberalisation around the world.

A key question is whether APEC should pursue this strategy only if all its members can agree to do so together, or whether individual countries should proceed when they are ready. One way to implement the latter approach would be to extend NAFTA to individual Asian countries or groups of countries, such as ASEAN. The EPG concluded that such a course would be inferior to progress encompassing all of APEC because it would generate new discrimination within the region during a possibly long transition period. In addition, some view it as 'imposing a North American model on Asia'.

Nonetheless, Singapore Prime Minister Goh Chok Tong announced in Seattle that his country would like to join NAFTA. Thailand has indicated its interest in studying an AFTA–NAFTA link. Korea has also sought association with NAFTA.

NAFTA is likely to open its doors to Chile and perhaps other countries in Latin America over the next few years. The upcoming Western Hemisphere summit could add impetus to this prospect. It will be essential to progress at least as rapidly towards Asia Pacific liberalisation to allay concerns that the United States is giving priority to the Western Hemisphere. Any such perception could intensify pressures for East Asia to respond with arrangements excluding North America, thereby dividing rather than uniting the Asia Pacific region. The United States must indicate its intentions in this regard when informing Congress, by 1 July 1994 under current legislative requirements, of its plans for future trade negotiations. All NAFTA and APEC members will have to address these issues in the near future.

APEC's development will be an intellectually fascinating and pragmatically critical test of whether economic interdependence can override seemingly major national differences. For example, APEC members cover virtually the entire spectrum of economic development. Japan has a per capita income of almost US$30,000 (at current market exchange rates); the United States is at about US$20,000. The newly industrialising countries of East Asia cluster at US$5,000–$10,000. Some of the developing nations of Southeast Asia (including, at market exchange rates, China and Indonesia) fall below US$1,000 per capita. Thus a successful APEC would end the 'North–South conflict', as NAFTA has begun to do and which its further extension into South America would continue.

A successful APEC would also destroy the notion that different civilisations are more likely to confront each other than to cooperate, for APEC includes at least five of Samuel Huntington's distinct groups. China and others form the core of his Confucian civilisation. Indonesia, with the world's fourth largest population, and Malaysia are Islamic. Japan is, according to Huntington, an entirely separate culture. The United States, Australia, New Zealand and Canada are Western. Mexico and Chile are Latin American. One might add that part of Canada possesses a distinct French culture.

At the centre of a new era

The historically unique current period, at the end of the Cold War and with new power configurations emerging in both the security and economic spheres,[2] offers enormous opportunities for both the United States and the Asian countries. The Asians could sharply reduce the risk of an American withdrawal, which would jeopardise both their chief export market and their national security. President Clinton, by convening the summit at Seattle and placing Asia at the centre of his foreign policy, has opened the door to creating institutional ties that would link countries across the Pacific as the post-war institutional network linked countries across the Atlantic. Such ties would provide America with access to the world's most dynamic economies and reduce the risk of future instability requiring American intervention.

At the end of the second global conflict of the twentieth century, the Second World War, Europe and the Atlantic were the focus of world events. The Atlantic nations created a series of institutional arrangements — including the North Atlantic Treaty

Organisation (NATO), the Organisation for European Economic Cooperation (OEEC), the Marshall Plan and the EEC — in an effort to preserve the newly won global peace and prosperity. Half a century later, it is clear that those arrangements were a stunning success.

We are now at the end of the third global conflict of the century, the Cold War. Asia and the Pacific are now at the centre of world affairs. Thus the time may have come to create an institutional network to link the nations on the two sides of that ocean in an effort to sustain global peace and prosperity for the decades ahead. APEC can play a major role in that process.

Notes

1   This model for APEC and the approaches described in succeeding paragraphs are developed in *A Vision for APEC*, Report of the Eminent Persons Group to APEC Ministers, October 1993. The report was unanimously agreed upon by the eleven members of the group, who were appointed by their governments but participating wholly in their individual capacities. The group includes businesspeople, economists, former government officials and political leaders.

2   C. Fred Bergsten, 'The world economy after the Cold War', *Foreign Affairs*, Summer 1990.

Part Five

An East Asian Economic Bloc?

19 Is Japan creating a yen bloc in East Asia and the Pacific?

Jeffrey A. Frankel

A debate got underway in 1991 over the advantages and disadvantages of a global trend towards three economic blocs — the Western Hemisphere, centred on the United States; Europe, centred on the EC; and East Asia, centred on Japan. Krugman (1991a), Bhagwati (1990, 1992, also Chapter 12, this volume) and Bergsten (1991) argue that the trend is, on balance, bad. Krugman (1991b) and Lawrence (1991c) argue that it is, on balance, good. Most appear to agree, however, that a trend towards three blocs is indeed underway.

There is no standardly agreed definition of an 'economic bloc'. A useful definition might be a group of countries that are concentrating their trade and financial relationships with one another, in preference to the rest of the world. One might wish to add to the definition the criterion that this concentration is the outcome of government policy, or at least of factors that are non-economic in origin, such as a common language or culture. In two out of the three parts of the world, there have clearly been recent deliberate political steps towards economic integration. In Europe, the previously lethargic EEC has burst forth with the programs of the Single Market, European Monetary Union, and more. In the Western Hemisphere, we have the Caribbean Basin Initiative and (more seriously) the Canada–US Free Trade Agreement, followed by NAFTA and the Enterprise for the Americas Initiative.

In East Asia, by contrast, overt preferential trading arrangements or other political moves to promote regional economic integration are lacking, as has been noted by others (see, for instance, Petri 1992). The ASEAN countries, to be sure, are taking steps in the direction of turning what used to be a regional security group into a free trade area of sorts. But when Americans worry, as they are wont to do, about a trading bloc forming in Asia, it is generally not ASEAN that concerns them. Rather it is the possibility of an East Asia-wide or Pacific-wide bloc dominated by Japan.

Reprinted from *Regionalism and Rivalry: Japan and the United States in Pacific Asia*, edited by Jeffrey A. Frankel and Miles Kahler, pp. 53–85 (with deletions). Copyright © 1993 by the National Bureau of Economic Research. Reprinted with permission from University of Chicago Press, Chicago, USA.

Japan is in fact unusual among major countries in *not* having preferential trading arrangements with smaller neighbouring countries. But the hypothesis that has been put forward is that Japan is forming an economic bloc in the same way that it runs its economy: by means of policies that are implicit, indirect, and invisible. Specifically, the hypothesis is that Japan operates, by means of such instruments as flows of aid, foreign direct investment, and other forms of finance, to influence its neighbours' trade towards itself (see, for example, Dornbusch 1989). This is a hypothesis that should not be accepted uncritically, but rather needs to be examined empirically.

After examining some of the relevant statistics, this paper argues that the evidence of an evolving East Asian trade bloc centred on Japan is not as clear as many believe. Trade between Japan and other Asian countries increased substantially in the late 1980s. But *intra-regional trade bias did not increase*, as it did, for example, within the EC. The phrase 'yen bloc' could be interpreted as referring to the financial and monetary aspects implicit in the words, rather than to trade flows. The second half of the paper does find a bit of evidence of Japanese influence in the Pacific via financial and monetary channels, rather than via trade flows. But it does not find evidence that the country has taken deliberate steps to establish a 'yen bloc'.

Is a trade bloc forming in the Asia Pacific?

We must begin by acknowledging the obvious: the greatly increased economic weight of East Asian countries in the world. The rapid outward-oriented growth of Japan, followed by the four East Asian NIEs and more recently by some of the other ASEAN countries, is one of the most remarkable and widely-remarked trends in the world economy over the last three decades. But when one asks whether a yen bloc is forming in East Asia, one is presumably asking something more than whether the economies are getting larger, or even whether economic flows among them are increasing. One must ask whether the share of intra-regional trade is higher, or increasing more rapidly, than would be predicted based on such factors as the GNP or growth rates of the countries involved.

Adjusting intra-regional trade for growth

The share of intra-regional trade in East Asia increased from 23 per cent in 1980 to 39 per cent in 1990. Pronouncements that a clubbish trade bloc is forming in the region are usually based on figures such as these. But the numbers are deceptive.

All three regions (East Asia, EC12, Western Hemisphere) showed increasing intra-group trade in the 1980s. The region that has both the highest and the fastest-increasing degree of intra-regional trade is not Asia but the EC, at 47 per cent in 1990.

Quite aside from the comparison with Europe, it is easy to be misled by intra-regional trade shares. The relevant concept is *intensity of trade* (see Drysdale and Garnaut, Chapter 3, this volume). Intensity of trade within East Asia grew less rapidly than trade shares, and much less rapidly than the intensity index for intra-EC trade.

A test on bilateral trade flows

The analysis should be elaborated by use of a systematic framework for measuring what patterns of bilateral trade are normal around the world: the so-called 'gravity' model. A dummy variable can then be added to represent when both countries in a given pair belong to the same regional grouping, and one can check whether the level and time trend in the East Asia–Pacific grouping exceeds that in other groupings. We do not currently have measures of historical, political, cultural and linguistic ties. Thus it will be possible to interpret the dummy variables as reflecting these factors, rather than necessarily as reflecting discriminatory trade policies. Perhaps we should not regret the merging of these different factors in one term, because, as noted, there are in any case no overt preferential trading arrangements on which theories of a Japanese trading bloc could rely.

The dependent variable is trade (exports plus imports), in log form, between pairs of countries in a given year. There are 63 countries in the data set, so that there are 1,953 data points (=63x62/2) for a given year. There are some missing values (245 of them in 1985, for example), normally due to levels of trade too small to be recorded. The possibility that the exclusion of these data points might bias the results, or that the results might be subject to heteroscedasticity because country size varies so much, is considered in Frankel and Wei (1992). The results appear to be robust with respect to these problems.

One would expect the two most important factors in explaining bilateral trade flows to be the geographical distance between the two countries and their economic size. These factors are the essence of the gravity model, by analogy with the law of gravitational attraction between masses. A large part of the apparent bias towards intra-regional trade is certainly due to simple geographical proximity. Indeed, Krugman (1991b) suggests that most of it may be due to proximity, so that the three trading blocs are welfare-improving 'natural' groupings (as distinct from 'unnatural' trading arrangements between distant trading partners such as the United States and Israel). Although the importance of distance and transportation costs is clear, there is not a lot of theoretical guidance on precisely how they should enter. We experiment a bit with functional forms. We also add a dummy 'ADJACENT' variable to indicate when two countries share a common border.

The basic equation to be estimated is:

$$\log(T_{ij}) = \alpha + \beta_1 \log(GNP_i\, GNP_j) + \beta_2 \log(GNP/pop_i\, GNP/pop_j) \\ + \beta_3 \log(DISTANCE) + \beta_4\,(ADJACENT) \\ + \gamma_1(EC_{ij}) + \gamma_2\,(WH_{ij}) + \gamma_3\,(EA_{ij}) + u_{ij}$$

The last four explanatory factors are dummy variables. The goal, again, is to see how much of the high level of trade within the East Asian region can be explained by simple economic factors common to bilateral trade throughout the world, and how much is left over to be attributed to a special regional effect.

The practice of entering GNPs in product form is empirically well established in bilateral trade regressions. It can be easily justified by the modern theory of trade under imperfect competition.[1] In addition, there is reason to believe that GNP per capita has a positive effect, for a given size: as countries become more developed, they tend to specialise more and to trade more. It is also possible that the infrastructure necessary to conduct trade — ports, airports, and so on — becomes better developed with the level of GNP per capita.

The results for 1980 and 1990 are reported in Tables 19.1 and 19.2 respectively.[2] We found all three variables to be highly significant statistically (> 99 per cent level). The coefficient on the log of distance was about -0.56, when the adjacency variable (which is also highly significant statistically) is included at the same time. This means that when the distance between two non-adjacent countries is higher by 1 per cent, the trade between them falls by about 0.56 per cent.

The estimated coefficient on GNP per capita is about 0.29 as of 1980, indicating that richer countries do indeed trade more, though this term declines during the 1980s, reaching 0.08 in 1990. The estimated coefficient for the log of the product of the two countries' GNPs is about 0.75, indicating that, though trade increases with size, it increases less than proportionately (holding GNP per capita constant). This presumably reflects the widely known pattern that small economies tend to be more open to international trade than larger, more diversified, economies.

If there were nothing to the notion of trading blocs, then these basic variables would soak up all the explanatory power. There would be nothing left to attribute to a dummy variable representing whether two trading partners are both located in the same region. In this case the level and trend in intra-regional trade would be due solely to the proximity of the countries, and to their rapid rate of overall economic growth. But we found that dummy variables for intra-regional trade *are* statistically significant, both in East Asia and elsewhere in the world. If two countries are both located in the Western Hemisphere for example, they will trade with each other by an estimated 70 per cent more than they would otherwise, even after taking into account distance and the other gravity variables (exp (0.53) = 1.70). Intra-regional trade goes beyond what can be explained by proximity.

The empirical equation is as yet too far removed from theoretical foundations to allow conclusions to be drawn regarding economic welfare. But it is possible that the amount of intra-regional bias explained by proximity, as compared to explicit or implicit regional trading arrangements, is small enough in our results that those arrangements are welfare-reducing. This could be the case if trade diversion outweighs trade creation. Inspired by Krugman's (1991a,1991b) 'natural trading bloc' terminology, we might then refer to the observed intra-regional trade bias as evidence of 'super-natural' trading blocs. The issue merits future research.

When the boundaries of the Asian bloc are drawn along the lines of those suggested by Malaysian Prime Minister Mahathir in his proposed EAEC, which excludes Australia and New Zealand (and also China, in the version tested here), the coefficient on the Asian bloc appears to be the strongest and most significant of any in the world.

Table 19.1   Gravity model of bilateral trade, 1980

Constant	GNPs	Per capita GNPs	Distance	Adjacent	EC	Western Hemisphere	ASEAN	EAEC	Asian Pacific	APEC	Pacific Rim	R²/R̄²	SEE[a]
-11.36** (.56)	.763** (.018)	.268** (.021)	-.597** (.041)	.649** (.185)	0.092 (.186)	0.449** (.157)	2.308** (.408)	-				.68/.68	1.26
-12.05** (.55)	.759** (.017)	.283** (.020)	-.538** (.041)	.775** (.180)	0.193 (.181)	0.498** (.153)		2.363** (.212)				.70/.70	1.23
-12.05** (.55)	.759** (.017)	.283** (.020)	-.538** (.041)	.772** (.181)	0.193 (.181)	0.499** (.153)	0.081 (.462)	2.341** (.247)				.70/.70	1.23
-11.97** (.54)	.753** (.017)	.287** (.020)	-.543** (.040)	.764** (.178)	0.214 (.179)	.527** (.151)			2.066** (.158)			.71/.71	1.21
-12.13** (.55)	.753** (.017)	.290** (.020)	-.532** (.040)	.770** (.179)	0.227 (.179)	0.535** (.151)	0.087 (.455)	0.730* (.332)	1.650** (.232)			.71/.71	1.21
-11.09** (.53)	.733** (.017)	.281** (.020)	-.586** (.039)	.694** (.177)	0.207 (.178)	0.503** (.150)				1.863** (.133)		.71/.71	1.21
-11.58** (.55)	.739** (.017)	.287** (.020)	-.557** (.040)	.724** (.177)	0.234 (.178)	0.526** (.150)	0.062 (.451)	0.704* (.330)	0.355 (.335)	1.319** (.248)		.71/.71	1.20
-10.83** (.56)	.762** (.018)	.259** (.021)	-.638** (.021)	.701** (.187)	0.033 (.184)	0.268 (.188)					0.018 (.014)	.68/.68	1.27
-11.55** (.55)	.739** (.017)	.288** (.020)	-.563** (.041)	.716** (.178)	0.227 (.174)	0.474** (.178)	0.062 (.452)	0.699* (.330)	0.350 (.335)	1.321** (.248)	0.0076 (.0129)	.71/.71	1.20

Notes: * and ** denote significance at the 95 and 99 per cent levels, respectively. Standard errors appear in parentheses. LHS variable (bilateral exports and imports) and first three RHS variables are in log form. All others are dummy variables.

a   Standard error of estimate.

Table 19.2 Gravity model of bilateral trade, 1990

C	GNPs	Per capita GNPs	Distance	Adjacent	EC	Western Hemisphere	ASEAN	EAEC	Asian Pacific	APEC	Pacific Rim	$R^2/\bar{R}^2$	SEE[a]
2.77** (.36)	.787** (.016)	.078** (.017)	-.589** (.038)	.732** (.166)	0.341* (.166)	0.934** (.148)	1.879** (.378)					.75/.75	1.11
2.54** (.35)	.779** (.016)	.082** (.017)	-.559** (.038)	.794** (.162)	0.412* (.163)	0.957** (.145)		1.997** (.215)				.76/.76	1.09
2.54** (.35)	.779** (.016)	.082** (.017)	-.559** (.038)	.797** (.163)	0.412* (.163)	0.955** (.145)	-0.109 (.450)	2.032** (.261)				.76/.76	1.09
2.57** (.35)	.773** (.016)	.86** (.016)	-.561** (.037)	.790** (.160)	0.437** (.160)	0.983** (.143)			1.746** (.152)			.77/.77	1.08
2.52** (.35)	.773** (.016)	.087** (.016)	-.555** (.037)	.794** (.160)	0.446** (.160)	0.86** (.143)	-0.107 (.443)	0.612†† (.331)	1.456** (.213)			.77/.77	1.08
3.02** (.34)	.756** (.016)	.083** (.016)	-.597** (.036)	.730** (.158)	0.444** (.159)	0.948** (.141)				1.597** (.128)		.77/.77	1.07
2.83** (.35)	.760** (.016)	.085** (.016)	-.579** (.037)	.750** (.159)	0.460** (.159)	0.967** (.142)	-0.144 (.440)	0.604†† (.328)	0.289 (.309)	1.194** (.231)		.77/.77	1.07
3.04** (.37)	.788** (.017)	.073** (.017)	-.619** (.040)	.780** (.167)	0.296†† (.167)	0.789** (.170)					0.015 (.013)	.75/.74	1.12
2.87** (.38)	.760** (.016)	.986** (.016)	-.584** (.038)	.743** (.160)	0.454** (.159)	0.925** (.163)	-0.143 (.440)	0.600†† (.328)	0.284 (.309)	1.196** (.231)	6.39x10⁻³ (.012)	.777/.77	1.07

Notes: ††, *, and ** denote significance at the 90, 95 and 99 per cent levels, respectively. Standard errors appear in parentheses. LHS variable (bilateral exports and imports) and first three RHS variables are in log form. All others are dummy variables.

a Standard error of estimate.

Even when the boundaries are drawn in this way, however, there is no evidence of an *increase* in the intra-regional bias of Asian trade during the 1980s: the estimated coefficient actually decreases somewhat from 1980 to 1990. The precise pattern is a decrease in the first half of the decade, followed by a very slight increase in the second half, matching the results of Petri (1991). None of these changes over time is statistically significant.

It is perhaps surprising that the estimated *level* of the intra-regional trade bias was higher in East Asia as of 1980 than in the other two regions. One possible explanation is that there has historically been a sort of 'trading culture' in Asia. To the extent that such a culture exists and can be identified with a particular nation or ethnic group, I find the overseas Chinese to be a more plausible factor than the Japanese. But there are other possible regional effects that may be showing up spuriously as an East Asian bloc, which are considered below.

Of the three trading blocs, the EEC and the Western Hemisphere are the two that show rapid intensification in the course of the 1980s. Both show an approximate doubling of their estimated intra-regional bias coefficients. As of 1980, trade within the EEC is not strong enough — after holding constant for the close geographical proximity and high incomes per capita of European countries — for the bias coefficient of 0.2 to appear statistically significant. The EEC coefficient increased rapidly in level and significance in the first half of the 1980s, reaching about 0.4 by 1985, and continued to increase a bit in the second half. The effect of two countries being located in Europe *per se*, when tested, does not show up as being nearly as strong in magnitude or significance as the effect of membership in the EC *per se*.

The Western Hemisphere coefficient experienced all its increase in the second half of the decade, exceeding 0.9 by 1990. The rapid increase in the Western Hemisphere intra-regional bias in the second half of the 1980s is in itself an important new finding. The recovery of Latin American imports from the United States after the compression that followed the 1982 debt crisis must be part of this phenomenon. The Canada–US Free Trade Agreement signed in 1988 may also be part of the explanation.

We consider a sequence of nested candidates for trading blocs in the Pacific. The significance of a given bloc effect turns out to depend on what other blocs are tested at the same time. One logical way to draw the boundaries is to include all the countries with eastern coasts on the Pacific, as in the statistics considered in the preceding section. We call this grouping 'Asian Pacific' in the tables. Its coefficient and significance level are both higher than the EAEC dummy. When we broaden the bloc search and test for an effect of APEC, which includes the United States and Canada in with the others, it is highly significant. The significance of the Asian Pacific dummy completely disappears. The EAEC dummy remains significant in 1980 and 1990, though at a lower level than the initial results that did not consider any wider Pacific groupings.

APEC appears to be the correct place to draw the boundary. When we test for the broadest definition of a Pacific bloc, including Latin America, it is not at all significant, and the other coefficients do not change (refer to 'Pacific Rim' in the tables). It remains true that the intra-regional biases in the EEC and Western Hemisphere blocs each roughly doubled from 1980 to 1990, while intra-regional biases in the Asia and Pacific areas did not increase at all. The only surprising new finding is the APEC effect: the United States and Canada appear to be full partners in the Pacific bloc, even while simultaneously belonging to the significant but distinct Western Hemisphere bloc. The APEC coefficient is the strongest of any. Its estimate holds relatively steady at 1.3 (1980), 1.0 (1985), and 1.2 (1990). The implication is that two APEC countries trade three times as much as two otherwise similar countries (exp (1.2) = 3.3).

Several further questions naturally arise. ASEAN negotiated a preferential trading arrangement within its membership in 1977 although serious progress in removal of barriers did not get underway until 1987 (Jackson 1991). In early 1992 the members proclaimed plans for an AFTA, albeit with exemptions for many sectors. Does this grouping constitute a small bloc nested within the others? We include in our model a dummy variable for common membership in ASEAN. It turns out to have a significant coefficient only if none of the broader Asian blocs are included. The conclusion seems to be that ASEAN is not in fact functioning as a trade bloc.

We know that Singapore and Hong Kong are especially open countries and engage in a large amount of entrepôt trade. A dummy variable for these two countries' trade with other Asia Pacific countries is highly significant when it is included, as shown in the first row of Table 19.3. Its presence reduces a bit the coefficient on the East Asian grouping, but does not otherwise change the results.

We also know that most East Asian countries are very open to trade of all sorts. So we added a dummy variable to indicate when *at least* one of the pairs of countries is located in East Asia, to supplement the dummy variable that indicates when both are. Its coefficient is significant. It is also positive, which appears to rule out any 'trade diversion' effects arising from the existence of the East Asian bloc: these countries trade an estimated 22 per cent more with all parts of the world, other things being equal, than do average countries (exp (0.20) = 1.22). The addition of the openness dummy reduces a bit more the level and significance of the East Asian bloc dummy. Indeed, when the APEC bloc dummy and the East Asian openness dummy are both added at the same time, the East Asian bloc term becomes only marginally significant in 1980 and insignificant in 1990. There may be no East Asian bloc effect at all!

What about bilateral trade between Asian Pacific countries and Japan in particular? Like intra-regional trade overall, trade with Japan increased rapidly in the second half of the 1980s. Most of this increase merely reversed a decline in the first half of the 1980s, however (Petri 1991). More importantly, the recent trend in bilateral trade between Japan and its neighbours can be readily explained as the natural outcome of the growth in Japanese trade overall and the growth in trade levels attained by other Asian countries overall. Lawrence (1991b) has calculated that, out of the 28 percentage point increase in the market share of Asian Pacific developing countries in Japanese imports from 1985 to 1988, 11 percentage points are attributable to improved competitiveness (as reflected in increased exports from Asia Pacific to

Table 19.3   Gravity estimates with allowance for Asian openness

	GNP	Per capita GNP	Distance	Adjacent	WH	EA	APEC	EC	JapEA	HKSEA	HKS1	EA1	Adj.R̄²/SEE	No. of observations
1980														
	.78**	.24**	-.64**	.62**	.58**	.51††	1.29**	.18	-.11		1.33**		.73/1.16	1 708
	(.02)	(.02)	(.04)	(.18)	(.15)	(.34)	(.17)	(.18)	(.16)		(.12)			
	.73**	.31**	-.66**	.63**	.65**	.31	1.22**	.18	-.12	1.06**		.52**	.72/1.18	1 708
	(.02)	(.02)	(.04)	(.18)	(.15)	(.34)	(.17)	(.18)	(.49)	(.41)		(.07)		
	.78**	.26**	-.67**	.59**	.64**	.53†	1.19**	.15	-.16	.01	1.16**	.25**	.73/1.16	1 708
	(.02)	(.02)	(.04)	(.18)	(.15)	(.34)	(.17)	(.17)	(.48)	(.42)	(.14)	(.08)		
1990														
	.80**	.04**	-.63**	.69**	.97**	.40†	1.18**	.49**	-.15		1.23**		.79/1.03	1 573
	(.02)	(.02)	(.04)	(.18)	(.13)	(.23)	(.15)	(.16)	(.14)		(.11)			
	.75**	.10**	-.66**	.69**	1.06**	.14	1.11**	.49**	-.27	1.09**		.50**	.78/1.05	1 573
	(.02)	(.02)	(.04)	(.18)	(.14)	(.30)	(.15)	(.16)	(.43)	(.37)		(.07)		
	.79**	.06**	-.67**	.65**	1.03**	.34	1.08**	.49**	-.31	.15	1.06**	.25**	.79/1.02	1 573
	(.02)	(.02)	(.04)	(.18)	(.14)	(.30)	(.15)	(.15)	(.42)	(.38)	(.12)	(.07)		

Notes: †, ††, *, and ** denote significance at the 85, 90, 95 and 99 per cent levels, respectively. Standard errors appear in parentheses. All regressions have an intercept, which is not reported here. All variables except the dummies are in logs. JapEA = trade between Japan and other East Asian countries, HKSEA = trade between Hong Kong or Singapore and other East Asian countries, HKS1 = trade between Hong Kong or Singapore and any other countries, EAI = trade involving at least one East Asian country.

worldwide markets), and 18 percentage points are attributable to the commodity mix of these countries' exports. There is no residual to be attributed to Japan's development of special trading relations with other countries in its region.[3]

We confirmed this finding by adding to our gravity model a separate dummy variable for bilateral Asian trade with Japan in particular. It was not even remotely statistically significant in any year, and indeed the point estimate was a small negative number, as is shown in Table 19.3. Thus there was no evidence that Japan has established or come to dominate a trading bloc in Asia.

To summarise the most relevant effects, if two countries both lie within the boundaries of APEC, they trade with each other a little over three times as much as they otherwise would. The nested EAEC bloc is less strong (especially if one allows also for the openness of East Asian countries), and has declined a bit in magnitude and significance during the course of the 1980s. The Western Hemisphere and EC blocs, by contrast, intensified rapidly during the decade. Indeed, by 1990, the Western Hemisphere bloc was stronger than the EAEC bloc, if one takes into account the existence of the APEC effect. There was never a special Japan effect within Asia Pacific.

In short, beyond the evident facts that countries near each other trade with each other, and that Japan and other Asian countries are growing rapidly, there is no evidence that Japan is concentrating its trade with other Asian countries in any special way, or that they are collectively moving towards a trade bloc in the way that Western Europe and the Western Hemisphere appear to be. We now turn from trade to finance.

Japan's financial influence in the region

In the case of financial flows, proximity is less important than it is for trade flows. For some countries the buying and selling of foreign exchange and highly rated bonds is characterised by the absence of significant government capital controls, transactions costs or information costs. In such cases, there would be no particular reason to expect greater capital flows among close countries than distant ones. Rather, each country would be viewed as depositing into the world capital pool, or borrowing from it, whatever quantity of funds it wished at the going world interest rate. Thus, even if we could obtain reliable data on bilateral capital flows (which we cannot), and whatever pattern they happened to show, such statistics would not be particularly interesting.

Tokyo's influence on regional financial markets

Many Asian countries still have substantial capital controls, and financial markets that are in other respects less than fully developed. Even financial markets in Singapore and Hong Kong, the most open in Asia, retain some minor frictions. Where the links with world capital markets are obstructed by even small barriers, it is an interesting question to ask whether those links are stronger with some major financial centres than with others. This question is explored econometrically below.

Information costs exist for equities, and for bonds with some risk of default. These costs may be smaller for those investors who are physically, linguistically and culturally close to the nation where the borrower resides. Proximity clearly matters as well in the case of direct investment — in part because much of direct investment is linked to trade, in part because linguistic and cultural proximity matter for direct investment. We begin our consideration of capital links by looking at direct investment.

Foreign direct investment

Table 19.4 shows the standard Ministry of Finance figures for Japanese direct investment. The steady stream of direct investment by Japanese firms in East Asia and the Pacific (including Australia) has received much attention. But the table shows that, whether measured in terms of annual flows or cumulated stocks, Japan's direct investment in the region is approximately equal to its investment in Europe, and is much less than its investment in North America (see also Komiya and Wakasugi 1991).

It has been argued that once one scales the Table 19.4 figures for GNP among the host countries, an Asian bias to Japanese direct investment might indeed appear (Holloway 1991, p. 69). But if one scales the FDI figures by the host region's role in world trade, one finds that Japan's investment in Asia and Oceania is almost exactly in proportion to their size. There is no regional bias. Its FDI in the United States and Canada, on the other hand, is more than twice what one would expect from their share of world trade. Japan's investment in Europe is about half the continent's share of trade.

Furthermore, Ramstetter (1991a, pp. 8–9; 1991b, pp. 95–6) has forcefully pointed out that the standard Ministry of Finance figures on Japanese foreign direct investment actually represent statistics on investment either approved by or reported to the government, and greatly overstate the extent of true Japanese investment in developing countries. The more accurate balance of payments data from the Bank of Japan show a smaller percentage of investment going to Asia.

Tokyo versus New York effects on Asian interest rates

Statistics also exist on Japanese portfolio investment. But, in the case of portfolio capital, looking at quantity data is not as informative as looking at price data — that is, at interest rates. For one thing, the quality of the data on interest rates is much higher than the quality of the data on capital flows. For another, the interest rate test is more appropriate conceptually. If the *potential* for arbitrage keeps the interest rate in a given Asian country closely in line with, say, Tokyo interest rates, then this constitutes good evidence of close links between the two national capital markets, even if the amount of actual arbitrage or other capital flow that takes place within a given period happens to be small.

Table 19.4 Japan's foreign direct investment, by area and country (amounts in millions of dollars)

	FY 1990			FY 1991			Cumulative total FY 1951–91		
	Cases	Amount[a]	% of total	Cases	Amount[a]	% of total	Cases	Amount[a]	% of total
United States	2 269	26 128	45.9	1 607	18 026	43.3	24 551	148 554	42.2
Canada	157	1 064	1.9	107	797	1.9	1 388	6 454	1.8
Subtotal (North America)	2 426	27 192	47.8	1 714	18 823	45.3	25 939	155 008	44.0
Latin America	339	3 628	6.4	290	3 337	8.0	7 487	43 821	12.4
Middle East	1	27	0.0	10	90	0.2	350	3 522	1.0
Europe	956	14 294	25.1	803	9 371	22.5	8 228	68 636	19.5
Africa	70	551	1.0	76	748	1.8	1 534	6 574	1.9
Australia and the South Pacific	572	4 166	7.3	394	3 278	7.9	4 351	21 376	6.1
Indonesia	155	1 105	1.9	148	1 193	2.9	2 021	12 733	3.6
Hong Kong	244	1 785	3.1	178	925	2.2	3 921	10 775	3.1
Singapore	139	840	1.5	103	613	1.5	2 662	7 168	2.0
Republic of Korea	54	284	0.5	48	260	0.6	1 895	4 398	1.2
China	165	349	0.6	246	579	1.4	1 105	3 402	1.0
Thailand	377	1 154	2.0	258	807	1.9	2 723	5 229	1.5
Malaysia	169	725	1.3	136	880	2.1	1 645	4 111	1.2
Taiwan	102	446	0.8	87	405	1.0	2 487	3 135	0.9
Philippines	58	258	0.5	42	203	0.5	892	1 783	0.5
India	7	30	0.1	9	14	0.0	176	210	0.1
Sri Lanka	9	4	0.0	7	4	0.0	126	102	0.0
Brunei	-	-	-	1	0	0.0	32	109	0.0
Pakistan	3	9	0.0	2	14	0.0	60	124	0.0
Others	26	69	0.1	12	39	0.1	166	175	0.0
Subtotal (Asia)	1 499	7 054	12.4	1 277	5 936	14.3	19 911	53 455	15.2
Total	6 589	67 540	100.0	5 863	56 911	100.0	63 236	310 808	100.0

Note: a   Million US dollars

238

Many East Asian countries have moved to liberalise and internationalise their financial markets over the last ten to fifteen years.[4] A number of studies have documented Japan's removal of capital controls over the period 1979–84 by looking at the power of arbitrage to equalise interest rates between Tokyo and New York or London.[5] Australia and New Zealand, while lagging behind Japan, also show signs of liberalisation during the course of the 1980s. Hong Kong and Singapore register impressively open financial markets, showing smaller interest differentials even than some open European countries like Germany. (Hong Kong has long had open capital markets. Singapore undertook a major liberalisation in 1978, though it has tried to segment its domestic money market from its offshore 'Asia dollar market'.) Malaysia has officially liberalised, following Singapore (Abidin 1986; Glick and Hutchison 1990, p. 45), though its covered differential has remained considerably higher.

We can apply a simple test to the hypothesis that a particular Asian country is dominated financially by Japan, versus the alternative hypothesis that ties to capital markets in the other industrialised countries are equally strong. I ran the following ordinary least squares (OLS) regression to see how the interest rate in a typical Asian country depends on interest rates in Tokyo and New York:

$$i_t^a = \alpha + \beta_1 i_t^T + \beta_2 i_t^{NY} + \varepsilon_t.$$

Under the null hypothesis that the country's financial markets are insufficiently developed or liberalised to be directly tied to any foreign financial markets, the coefficients on foreign interest rates should be zero. Under the alternative hypothesis that the country's financial markets are closely tied to those in Tokyo, the coefficient on Tokyo interest rates should be closer to 1 than to 0; and similarly for New York.[6]

Table 19.5 presents estimates for three-month interest rates in Hong Kong and Singapore, on quarterly data. For the Hong Kong interest rate, the influence of the New York market appears very strong. This is not surprising: not only does the colony have open financial markets, but its currency has since October 1983 been pegged to the US dollar, so that there is nothing to inhibit perfect arbitrage between its interest rates and US interest rates. Neither Tokyo, London nor Frankfurt has significant influence in Hong Kong on average over the sample period (from 1976 to 1989). For the Singapore interest rate, the influence of New York is again very significant; but now there is also a significant, though smaller, weight on Tokyo. The evidence suggests that both countries have had open financial markets ever since the mid-1970s, with New York having the dominant influence, but with Tokyo also having a one-quarter effect in the case of Singapore.

To see whether the influence of the foreign financial centres changed over the course of the sample period, we can allow for time trends in the coefficients, also reported in Table 19.5. For Hong Kong, it is clear that London used to have a strong influence, and equally clear that the British influence has been diminishing over time. For Singapore, there is no sign of change in New York's role, but there is weak evidence of a gradually increasing role for Tokyo.

Table 19.5   **Japanese, US, UK and German interest rate effects in Hong Kong and Singapore**

	Hong Kong		Singapore	
	Without trend	With trend	Without trend	With trend
Constant term	-2.41††	-1.70	-1.16††	-0.65
	(1.08)	(1.13)	(0.67)	(0.67)
Tokyo effect	-0.23	-0.11	0.23**	-0.36††
	(0.17)	(0.69)	(0.07)	(0.22)
Time trend in Tokyo effect		-0.00		0.02††
		(0.01)		(0.01)
New York effect	1.32**	0.61	0.75**	0.65††
	(0.15)	(0.52)	(0.09)	(0.33)
Time trend in New York effect		0.01	0.00	
		(0.01)		(0.01)
London effect	0.10	1.38**	-0.07	-0.09
	(0.11)	(0.47)	(0.06)	(0.16)
Time trend in London effect		-0.03**		-0.00
		(0.01)		(0.00)
Frankfurt effect	0.14	-1.74††	0.19	1.02††
	(0.20)	(1.13)	(0.12)	(0.54)
Time trend in Frankfurt effect		0.04††		-0.02††
		(0.02)		(0.01)
R^2	.83	.85	.87	.88
Durbin–Watson	1.50	1.61	1.53	1.92
Sample period	1976.4 to 1989.3		1974.1 to 1988.1	

Note: †† and ** denote significance at the 90 and 99 per cent levels, respectively. Standard errors appear in parentheses.

The next step is to expand the sample of countries. Some Asian countries, such as Korea and Taiwan, did not seriously begin to open their financial markets to external influence by *any* foreign centre until the late 1980s. To obtain more observations, I now switch to monthly data. Preliminary results for the period 1988–91 find a dominant role for Tokyo interest rates in Singapore and Taiwan, a dominant role for New York interest rates in Hong Kong and Australia, and apparently strong roles for both in Korea (Frankel 1991c, Table 4). Tests that also allowed a role for Frankfurt and London interest rates found apparently significant effects for the latter in Australia and New Zealand. But most of these results were tainted by high levels of serial correlation.

In Table 19.6 we use conservative standard errors, to allow for the problem created by serial correlation. We expand the set of countries still further, to a set of ten (with three alternative measures of the Korean interest rate). The time period is September 1982 to March 1992. The time trends in the coefficients tell us that New York seems to be gaining influence at the expense of Tokyo in the English-speaking countries of the Pacific Rim (Australia, Canada and New Zealand), while the reverse is occurring in a number of East Asian countries. The observed shift in influence from New York interest rates to Tokyo interest rates is highly significant in the case of Indonesia, and somewhat less so in the case of Korea. It is positive but not significant (when the conservative standard errors are used) for Hong Kong, Singapore and Malaysia.

These tests leave some important questions unanswered. Are the barriers that remain between a given country and the major world financial centres due to currency factors or country factors? Most of the Asian countries experience frequent changes in their exchange rates against the yen and the dollar. Financial markets in a country like Singapore could be very open and yet observed interest rates could differ from those in Tokyo or New York because of premiums meant to compensate investors for the possibility of changes in the exchange rate. The question of whether the yen is playing an increasing role in the exchange rate policies of East Asian countries is an important one, but it should be kept distinct from the question of whether financial links to Tokyo (irrespective of currency) are strengthening.

We can take out currency factors by using the forward exchange market. The necessary data are available for six of the countries. I simply express the foreign interest rates so as to be 'covered' or hedged against exchange risk. Doing so changes the 1988–91 results for Australia and Singapore towards a Tokyo effect that is smaller than the New York effect. Most coefficients remain significant, despite the obvious multicollinearity between covered US and Japanese interest rates (Frankel 1991c, Table 4).[7]

Returning to the longer 1982–92 time period to look for trends in the coefficients of the covered interest rates, we find that the observed upward trends for Tokyo influence in Singapore and Malaysia are not statistically significant (when conservative standard errors are used). Singapore, like Hong Kong, rather appears simply to obey a covered interest parity relationship *vis-à-vis* dollar interest rates.[8]

For six of these countries, there exists another way of correcting for possible exchange rate changes: direct data on forecasts of market participants collected in a monthly survey by the *Currency Forecasters' Digest* of White Plains, New York. One advantage of using the survey responses to measure expected exchange rate changes is that the data allow us to test explicitly whether there exists an exchange risk premium that creates an international differential in interest rates even in the absence of barriers to international capital flows. Such a differential would be compensation to risk-averse investors for holding assets that they view as risky. An advantage of the *Currency Forecasters' Digest* data in particular is that they are available even for countries like Taiwan and Korea where financial markets are less developed. A potential disadvantage is the possibility that survey data measure the expectations of market participants imperfectly.

For Singapore, the survey data corroborate the finding from the forward rate data that, once expected depreciation is eliminated as a factor, the New York effect dominates the Tokyo effect. For Korea, the survey data also show that the Tokyo effect

Table 19.6   Trends in the influence of dollar versus yen interest rates (September 1982ñMarch 1992)

	Constant	Eurodollar	Eurodollar trend	Euroyen	Euroyen trend	$\bar{R}^2$	DW	Q
Australia	8.473*	-1.992**	0.429**	3.470**	-0.539**	.52	0.409	141.47**
	(1.143)	(0.277)	(0.041)	(0.411)	(0.054)			
	[3.428]	[0.479]	[0.071]	[0.712]	[0.094]			
Canada	0.535	0.487*	0.086**	0.670*	-0.057	.79	0.477	158.12**
	(0.458)	(0.111)	(0.016)	(0.165)	(0.022)			
	[1.375]	[0.192]	[0.028]	[0.285]	[0.038]			
Hong Kong	-4.115	1.691**	-0.068	-0.353	0.104	.71	1.047	41.35**
	(0.857)	(0.208)	(0.031)	(0.308)	(0.041)			
	[2.570]	[0.360]	[0.053]	[0.533]	[0.071]			
Indonesia	14.010**	1.852**	-0.267**	-2.337*	0.410**	.33	0.700	na
	(1.483)	(0.356)	(0.053)	(0.529)	(0.070)			
	[4.449]	[0.616]	[0.091]	[0.916]	[0.121]			
Korea 1	9.094**	-0.037	-0.031*	-0.103	0.002	.82	0.488	124.18**
	(0.194)	(0.039)	(0.009)	(0.065)	(0.011)			
	[0.581]	[0.067]	[0.015]	[0.113]	[0.019]			
Korea 2	16.294**	-0.754	0.097	-0.929	0.086	.64	0.671	57.01**
	(1.087)	(0.527)	(0.077)	(0.704)	(0.091)			
	[3.262]	[0.913]	[0.133]	[1.219]	[0.158]			
Korea 3	10.079**	0.320	-0.061	-0.019	0.124*	.69	0.204	194.35**
	(0.690)	(0.143)	(0.026)	(0.231)	(0.031)			
	[2.070]	[0.248]	[0.045]	[0.400]	[0.053]			
Malaysia	5.520	-0.057	-0.072	0.700	0.016	.41	0.463	na
	(1.262)	(0.286)	(0.049)	(0.453)	(0.059)			
	[3.785]	[0.496]	[0.086]	[0.784]	[0.102]			
New Zealand	18.573**	-2.584**	0.379**	3.405**	-0.599**	.37	0.327	204.22**
	(2.063)	(0.500)	(0.074)	(0.742)	(0.098)			
	[6.291]	[0.866]	[0.129]	[1.285]	[0.169]			
Singapore	-2.768*	0.960**	-0.052*	0.174	0.056	.86	0.842	103.64**
	(0.413)	(0.093)	(0.014)	(0.142)	(0.019)			
	[1.239]	[0.161]	[0.025]	[0.246]	[0.032]			
Taiwan	-4.144	0.635	0.017	0.811	0.049	.45	0.422	109.01**
	(1.217)	(0.292)	(0.043)	(0.437)	(0.057)			
	[3.651]	[0.505]	[0.075]	[0.757]	[0.099]			
Thailand	-3.846	0.780	-0.069	1.363*	0.097	.78	0.461	na
	(1.114)	(0.232)	(0.039)	(0.363)	(0.049)			
	[3.341]	[0.402]	[0.068]	[0.628]	[0.085]			

Notes: na – Not available.

Figures in parentheses are asymptotic standard errors. Figures in brackets are standard errors assuming $N/3$ independent observations. The Q-statistic indicates the Ljung-Box Q-statistic. * and ** denote significance at the 5 and 1 per cent level, respectively, using the adjusted standard errors.

becomes smaller than the New York effect. For Australia and Taiwan, both effects largely disappear (Frankel 1991c, Table 4).[9]

The role of the yen in Asian exchange rate policies

The finding that eliminating exchange rate expectations from the calculation leaves Tokyo with relatively little effect on local interest rates in most of these countries does not necessarily mean that the Japanese influence is not strong. It is possible, rather, that much of the influence in the Pacific comes precisely through the role of the yen. If Pacific countries assign high weight to the yen in setting their exchange rate policies, then their interest rates will be heavily influenced by Japanese interest rates.

No Asian or Pacific countries have ever pegged their currencies to the yen in the post-war period. But neither are there any Pacific countries that the IMF classifies as still pegging to the US dollar. (As already mentioned, Hong Kong pegs to the dollar; but the colony is not an official member of the IMF.) Malaysia and Thailand, and a number of Pacific island countries, officially peg to a basket of major currencies and are thought to give weight to both the dollar and yen, but the weights are not officially announced.

It is interesting to estimate econometrically the weights given to the dollar, yen and other major currencies in exchange rate policies of Asia Pacific countries, especially those which follow a basket peg but do not officially announce the weights. This involves regressing changes in the value of the currency in question against changes in the value of the yen, dollar, and so on (I work in changes rather than levels, among other reasons, because exchange rates have been widely observed to behave as unit-root processes.)

There is a methodological question of what numeraire should be used to measure the value of the currencies. A simple solution is to use the SDR as numeraire. This approach suffers from the drawback that the SDR is itself a basket of five major currencies including the dollar and yen. An alternative approach is to use purchasing power over local goods (the inverse of the local price level) as the numeraire. Whatever the numeraire, under the null hypothesis that a particular currency is pegged to the dollar or yen, or to a weighted basket, the regression results should show this clearly, featuring even a high R^2. I focus here on the purchasing power measure.

Regressions of changes in the real value of the Hong Kong dollar against changes in the value of the five major currencies show highly significant coefficients on the US dollar during the periods 1974–80 and 1984–90. The weight on the dollar is statistically indistinguishable from 1 during most of the latter seven-year period, and the R^2 reaches 0.96 during the last four years. Occasional sub-periods show apparently significant weights on other currencies (the yen during 1979–81, the franc during 1983–85, and the mark during 1986–88). Overall, however, the numbers bear out Hong Kong's peg to the dollar.

Regressions of changes in the real value of the Malaysian ringgit against the five major currencies, give a large significant weight to the dollar (Frankel 1993, Table 2.9). Some sub-periods show a significant weight on the mark, and during 1986–88 even the pound is significant. But the yen is not significant during any three-year sub-period. The constant term is negative (and statistically significant), indicating a trend depreciation, and the R^2 is fairly low, indicating that the basket 'peg' was loose (even if one allows for a crawling peg).

The Singapore dollar shows significant weights (of about 0.2 each) on the US dollar and mark during the period 1974–77 (Frankel 1993, Table 2.10). The regression for 1977–79 shows a rough basket peg (= 0.83) with significant weights of 0.09 on the yen, 0.47 on the dollar, 0.25 on the mark, and 0.09 on the pound. The weight on the dollar diminishes thereafter, and the weight on the yen increases. By 1983–85, the yen weight (at a significant 0.20) has temporarily passed the dollar weight (at a significant 0.19). From 1986 to 1990 only the dollar is significant.

The results for the real value of the Thai baht show a very close peg to the dollar from 1974 to 1980, whereupon the dollar weight falls somewhat (Frankel 1993, Table 2.11). Beginning in 1986, a pattern emerges of significant weights on the yen and pound, in addition to the dollar. During the period 1988–90, the baht exhibits a close to perfect peg (= 0.99) to a basket with estimated weights of 0.82 on the dollar, 0.13 on the yen, 0.06 on the mark, and 0.02 on the pound.

Korea also claimed to have a sort of basket peg in the 1980s, but with large adjustments. Regressions of the change in the real value of the won show a statistically significant weight on the value of the dollar during the period April 1980 to March 1986, with an estimated coefficient of 0.4 to 0.5. (The Canadian dollar, which was reputed to be included in the Korean basket, also shows up with a significant coefficient of 0.2 during part of the period.) There is a significant constant term (the 'alpha') during this period: the value of the won declined during the early 1980s, whether measured by inflation or depreciation, relative to foreign currencies. The dollar, like the other major currencies, is insignificant during the period April 1985 to March 1987. Its influence re-emerges from April 1986 to March 1988. But then during the final two-year sub-period from April 1988 to March 1990, the yen (with a highly significant coefficient estimated at 0.18) suddenly eclipses the dollar (with an insignificant coefficient of 0.11) (Frankel 1992).

To summarise, there is some evidence of increased yen influence in the case of the Singapore dollar in the early 1980s and the Thai baht in the late 1980s. The only place where the yen appears to have become as important as the dollar is Korea in the period since 1988.

The role of the yen in reserves and invoicing

There is other evidence that the yen is playing an increasing role in the region. Asian central banks in the course of the 1980s increased their holdings of yen from 13.9 per cent of their foreign exchange reserve portfolios to 17.1 per cent (Frankel 1993, Table

2.12). Foreign exchange market trading in the regional financial centres of Singapore and Hong Kong, though still overwhelmingly conducted in dollars, now shows a much higher proportion of trading in yen than is the case in Europe (Tavlas and Ozeki 1992, p. 35).

The yen is also being used more widely to invoice lending and trade in Asia. The countries that incurred large international debts in the 1970s and early 1980s subsequently shifted the composition away from dollar-denominated debt and towards yen-denominated debt. The yen share among five major Asian debtors nearly doubled between 1980 and 1988, entirely at the expense of the dollar. The share of trade denominated in yen is greater in Asia than in other regions, and there was an especially rapid increase from 1983 to 1990 in the share of Asian imports denominated in yen (Frankel 1993, Table 2.13). Overall, however, it must be concluded that the role of the yen in East Asia is still not proportionate to Japan's importance in trade.

Conclusions

- The *level* of trade in East Asia, like trade within the EC and within the Western Hemisphere, is biased towards intra-regional trade, to a greater extent than can be explained naturally by distance. By way of contrast to Krugman's 'natural' trade blocs, one might call these three regions 'super-natural' blocs.

- There is no evidence of a special Japan effect within Asia.

- Although growth in Japan, the four NIEs, and other East Asian countries, is rapidly increasing their weight in world output and trade, the statistics do not bear out a *trend* towards intra-regional bias of trade and direct investment flows.

- The intra-regional trade bias did increase in Europe in the 1980s, in the Western Hemisphere in the late 1980s, and in the grouping that includes the United States and Canada together with the Asian Pacific countries, namely APEC.

- The APEC trade grouping appears to be the world's strongest, whether judged by rate of change of intra-group bias or (as of 1990) by level of bias. Far from being shut out of a strong Asian bloc centred on Japan, the United States and Canada are in the enviable position of belonging to *both* of the world's two strongest groupings.

- There is a bit of evidence of Japanese influence in East Asia's *financial markets*, as opposed to trade. Tokyo appears to have increasing influence over interest rates in Singapore, Korea and Indonesia. Overall, however, its influence is still smaller than that of New York.

- Some of Japan's financial influence takes place through a growing role for the yen, at the expense of the dollar. There has been a gradual increase in the yen's relative importance in invoicing of trade and finance in the region, and in some countries' exchange rate policies.

This still leaves a question raised at the beginning of this essay. Is Japan undertaking deliberate policy measures to increase its monetary and financial role? Gradually increasing use of the yen internationally is primarily the outcome of private decisions by importers, exporters, borrowers and lenders. It is difficult to see signs of deliberate policy actions taken by the Japanese government to increase its financial and monetary influence in Asia. To the contrary, until recently, the Japanese government has resisted whatever tendency there may be for the yen to become an international currency in competition with the dollar.

It has been the US government, in the Yen–Dollar Agreement of 1984 and in subsequent negotiations, that has been pushing Japan to internationalise the yen, to promote its worldwide use in trade, finance, and central bank policies (Frankel 1984). It has also been the US government that has been pushing Korea and other East Asian NIEs to open up their financial markets, thereby allowing Japanese capital and Japanese financial institutions to enter these countries. It has again been the US government that has been pushing Korea and Taiwan to move away from policies to stabilise the value of their currencies against the dollar (Frankel 1989; Balassa and Williamson 1990; and Noland 1990). The increasing role of the yen in the Asia Pacific may or may not be a good idea. But it is an idea that originated in Washington, not in Tokyo.

Notes

1   The specification implies that trade between two equal-sized countries (say, of size 0.5) will be greater than trade between a large and small country (say, of size 0.9 and 0.1). This property of models with imperfect competition is not a property of the classical Heckscher–Ohlin theory of comparative advantage. See Helpman (1987) and Helpman and Krugman (1985, section 1.5). Foundations for the gravity model are also offered by Anderson (1979) and other papers surveyed by Deardorff (1984, pp. 503–6).

2   For 1985 results, see Frankel (1993, Table 2.3).

3   The empirical literature on whether Japan is an outlier in its trading patterns, particularly with respect to imports of manufactures, includes Saxonhouse (1989), Noland (1991) and Lawrence (1991a), among others.

4   Frankel (1991a) presents the 1980s evidence for Japan, Australia, New Zealand, Singapore, Hong Kong and Malaysia. Faruqee (1991) examines interest differentials for Korea, Malaysia, Singapore and Thailand (*vis-à-vis* yen interest rates in London), but does not take into account exchange rate expectations.

5   These include Otani and Tiwari (1981), Frankel (1984) and Ito (1986). The interest rates in the calculations are covered on the forward exchange or Eurocurrency markets so as to avoid exchange risk. Tests that look at real or uncovered interest

differentials, rather than covered interest differentials, include Fukao and Okubo (1984) and Ito (1988).

6   It should be noted that if capital markets in Tokyo and New York are closely tied to *each other*, as they indeed are, then multicollinearity might make it difficult to obtain statistically significant estimates. But this does not mean that there is anything wrong with the test. A finding that the coefficient on the Tokyo interest rate is statistically greater than 0, or than the coefficient on the New York interest rate, remains valid.

7   The Durbin–Watson statistics improve substantially when the forward rates are included, confirming that the equation that uses covered interest rates is a more appropriate specification.

8   These results are from Tables 12a and 12b in Chinn and Frankel (1992).

9   Time trends are estimated in Tables 12a and 12b in Chinn and Frankel (1992).

References

Abidin, A. Z. 1986, 'Financial reform and the role of foreign banks in Malaysia', in Hanson Cheng (ed.), *Financial Policy and Reform in Pacific Basin Countries*, Lexington, Mass.: Lexington Books.

Anderson, James 1979, 'A theoretical foundation for the gravity equation', *American Economic Review*, 69(1) March, pp.106–16.

Balassa, Bela, and John Williamson 1990, 'Adjusting to success: balance of payments policy in the East Asian NICs', *Policy Analyses in International Economics*, 17 April, Washington, DC: Institute for International Economics.

Bergsten, C. Fred 1991, 'Comment on Krugman', in *Policy Implications of Trade and Currency Zones*, A Symposium sponsored by the Federal Reserve Bank of Kansas City, Jackson Hole, Wyoming, August, pp. 43–57.

Bhagwati, Jagdish 1990, 'Regional accords be-GATT trouble for free trade', *Wall Street Journal*, 5 December.

———— 1992, 'Regionalism vs. multilateralism: an overview', Conference on New Dimensions in Regional Integration, World Bank, Washington, DC, 2–3 April.

Chinn, Menzie and Jeffrey Frankel 1992, 'Financial links around the Pacific rim: 1982–1992', August 1992, revised April 1993; forthcoming as Chapter 2 in R. Glick and M. Hutchison (eds), *Exchange Rate Policy and Interdependence: Perspectives from the Pacific Basin*, Cambridge: Cambridge University Press.

Deardorff, Alan 1984, 'Testing trade theories and predicting trade flows', in R. Jones and P. Kenen (eds), *Handbook of International Economics, Vol. 1*, Amsterdam: Elsevier Science Publishers, pp. 467–517.

Dornbusch, Rudiger 1989, 'The dollar in the 1990s: competitiveness and the challenges of new economic blocs', in *Monetary Policy Issues in the 1990s*, Federal Reserve Bank of Kansas City.

Faruqee, Hamid 1991, 'Dynamic capital mobility in Pacific Basin developing countries: estimation and policy implications', *IMF Working Paper*, 91/115, November, International Monetary Fund.

Frankel, Jeffrey 1984, 'The yen/dollar agreement: liberalizing Japanese capital market', *Policy Analyses in International Economics*, No. 9, Washington, DC: Institute for International Economics.

_____ 1989, 'And now won/dollar negotiations? Lessons from the yen/dollar agreement of 1984', in *Korea's Macroeconomic and Financial Policies*, Seoul: Korean Development Institute.

_____ 1991a, 'Quantifying international capital mobility in the 1980s', in D. Bernheim and J. Shoven (eds), *National Saving and Economic Performance*, Chicago: University of Chicago Press, pp. 227–60.

_____ 1991b, 'The Japanese cost of finance: a survey', *Financial Management*, Spring, pp. 95–127.

_____ 1991c, 'Is a yen bloc forming in Pacific Asia?', in R. O'Brien (ed.), *Finance and the International Economy*, The AMEX Bank Review Prize Essays, Oxford: Oxford University Press.

_____ 1992, 'Liberalization of Korea's foreign exchange markets, and tests of US versus Japanese influence', forthcoming in *Seoul Journal of Economics*.

_____ 1993, 'Is Japan creating a yen bloc in East Asia and the Pacific?', in J. Frankel and M. Kahler (eds), *Regionalism and Rivalry: Japan and the United States in Pacific Asia*, Chicago: University of Chicago Press, pp. 53–85.

Frankel, Jeffrey and Shang-jin Wei 1992, 'Trade blocs and currency blocs', CEPR Conference on The Monetary Future of Europe, La Coruna, Spain, 11 December.

Fukao, Mitsuhiro and Takashi Okubo 1984, 'International linkage of interest rates: the case of Japan and the United States', *International Economic Review*, 25 February, pp. 193–207.

Glick, Reuven and Michael Hutchison 1990, 'Financial liberalization in the Pacific Basin: implications for real interest rate linkages', *Journal of the Japanese and International Economics*, 4, pp. 36–48.

Helpman, Elhanan 1987, 'Imperfect competition and international trade: evidence from fourteen industrial countries', *Journal of the Japanese and International Economies*, 1, pp. 62–81.

Helpman, Elhanan and Paul Krugman 1985, *Market Structure and Foreign Trade*, Cambridge, Mass: MIT Press.

Holloway, Nigel 1991, 'Half-full, half-empty', *Far Eastern Economic Review* December.

Ito, Takatoshi 1986, 'Capital controls and covered interest parity', *NBER Working Paper*, No. 1187; and *Economic Studies Quarterly*, No. 37, pp. 223–41.

_____ 1988, 'Use of (time-domain) vector autoregressions to test uncovered interest parity', *Review of Economics and Statistics*, 70, pp. 296–305.

Jackson, Tom 1991, 'A game model of ASEAN trade liberalization', *Open Economies Review*, 2(3), pp. 237–54.

Komiya, Ryutaro and Ryuhei Wakasugi 1991, 'Japan's foreign direct investment', *Annals of the American Academy of Political and Social Science*, January.

Krugman, Paul 1991a, 'Is bilateralism bad?', in Elhanan Helpman and Assaf Razin (eds), *International Trade and Trade Policy*, Cambridge, Mass.: MIT Press.

_____ 1991b, 'The move towards free trade zones', in *Policy Implications of Trade and Currency Zones*, A Symposium sponsored by the Federal Reserve Bank of Kansas City, Jackson Hole, Wyoming, August, pp. 7–42.

Lawrence, Robert 1991a, 'How open is Japan?', in Paul Krugman (ed.), *Trade With Japan: Has the Door Opened Wider?*, Chicago: University of Chicago Press, pp. 9–50.

_____ 1991b, 'An analysis of Japanese trade with developing countries', *Brookings Discussion Papers*, No. 87, April, Washington, DC: The Brookings Institution.

_____ 1991c, 'Emerging regional arrangements: building blocks or stumbling blocks?', in R. O'Brien (ed.), *Finance and the International Economy*, The AMEX Bank Review Prize Essays, Oxford: Oxford University Press, pp. 24–36.

Noland, Marcus 1990, *Pacific Basin Developing Countries: Prospects for the Future*, Washington, DC: Institute for International Economics.

_____ 1991, 'Public policy, private preferences, and the Japanese trade pattern', November, Washington, DC: Institute for International Economics.

Otani, Ichiro and Siddarth Tiwari 1981, 'Capital controls and interest rate parity: the Japanese experience, 1978–1981, *IMF Staff Papers*, 28, December, pp. 793–815.

Petri, Peter 1991, 'Market structure, comparative advantage and Japanese trade under the strong yen', in Paul Krugman (ed.), *Trade With Japan: Has the Door Opened Wider?*, Chicago: University of Chicago Press, pp. 51–84.

_____ 1992, 'One bloc, two blocs or none? Political–economic factors in Pacific trade policy', in Kaoru Okuizumi, Kent Calder and Gerrit Gong (eds), *The US–Japan Economic Relationship in East and Southeast Asia: A Policy Framework for Asia–Pacific Economic Cooperation*, Significant Issues Series, Vol. XIV, No.1, Washington, DC: Center for Strategic and International Studies, pp. 39–70.

Ramstetter, Eric 1991a, 'An overview of multinational firms in Asia–Pacific economies: an introduction to the commonplace ignorance', Faculty of Economics, Kansai University, Osaka.

_____ 1991b, 'Regional patterns of Japanese multinational activities in Japan and Asia's developing countries', *Economic and Political Studies Series*, No. 74, Kansai University, Osaka.

Saxonhouse, Gary 1989, 'Differentiated products, economies of scale, and access to the Japanese market', in Robert Feenstra (ed.), *Trade Policies for International Competitiveness*, Chicago: University of Chicago Press, pp. 145–74.

Tavlas, George and Yuzuru Ozeki 1992, 'The internationalization of currencies: an appraisal of the Japanese yen', *IMF Occasional Paper*, No. 90, January, Washington, DC: International Monetary Fund.

20 Trading blocs and East Asia ———

Gary R. Saxonhouse

At a time when large political and economic agglomerations like the Soviet Union, Yugoslavia and Czechoslovakia have broken up, great confidence in strong customs unions being the wave of everyone's future seems a bit misplaced. Indeed, it is possible to argue that it is the extraordinary success of small East Asian entities like Hong Kong and Singapore within the GATT-governed multilateral trading system that now emboldens Croatians, Azerbaijanis, Latvians and Slovaks to assume that political independence need not mean economic disaster. It is possible to believe that a well-functioning, open multilateral trading system makes continental superpowers that run roughshod over cultural diversity anachronistic. With the multilateral trading system capable of substituting for much of the special economic advantages of large political size, the door might be viewed as potentially open for a plethora of economically viable micro-states organised, perhaps in the East Asian image, on the basis of cultural affinity.

While liberal systems could make the world safe for cultural diversity, exclusivity does raise its ugly head. Croatians who believe that the GATT provides the economic charter for their political liberty may be in for a nasty surprise when they negotiate the terms of their access to Europe's so-called Single Market. Of course, it is the new vitality of regional arrangements such as the EC and NAFTA and prospective arrangements in East Asia, and not the obsolescence of dinosaurs like the Soviet Union, that provide the context for this paper.

In the first section of this paper, the consequences of trading bloc formation for countries left outside the bloc will be reviewed. In particular, the case where the formation of such a bloc will leave outsiders worse off will be highlighted. This can happen even without the trading bloc violating Article XXIV of the GATT. Still worse,

Reprinted from *New Dimensions in Regional Integration*, edited by Jaime de Melo and Arvind Panagariya, pp. 22–51 (with deletions). Copyright © 1993 by the Centre for Economic Policy Research. Reprinted with permission from Cambridge University Press.

such blocs can make insiders better off than the case of global free trade. In this circumstance, side payments apart, insiders will have no incentive to let in additional members, except if the formation of a rival bloc is threatened.

The case outlined in the first section of this paper reflects the concerns of the East Asian economies. Trading blocs are being formed elsewhere in the world. Even without violating existing GATT provisions such blocs can lower East Asian welfare. These trading blocs may have no incentive to expand their membership to include East Asian economies except insofar as they fear provoking the formation of an East Asian trading bloc.

The second section of this paper reviews the prospects for a regional trade regime in East Asia. Intra-East Asian trade is currently not large by historical standards. Nor does the rapid growth in intra-East Asian trade reflect very much more than the very rapid overall economic growth in this region relative to the rest of the world. Estimation of a bilateral model of intra-industry trade using a factor-endowment based version of the gravity model suggests no East Asian bias in the trading patterns of the leading economies there.

In light of this finding, the final section of this paper discusses the various proposals for East Asian and Pan-Pacific trading arrangements. Despite considerable progress on trade liberalisation by many of the East Asian economies over the past two decades, there is some indication that region-wide liberalisation could still be of considerable benefit.

New trading blocs, the consequences for members and non-members and Article XXIV

The economics literature on customs unions has come a considerable way since Haberler (1936) noted that 'Customs unions are always to be welcomed . . . the economic advantage of customs union can be proved by the Theory of Comparative Cost'. Since Viner (1950) it has been understood that the benefits for members of a trading bloc through trade creation may be less than the costs imposed on non-members through trade diversion. Indeed, many of the benefits of a trading bloc for its members may be gained precisely through a shift in the terms of trade in their favour at the expense of non-members. This can happen even if a trading bloc leaves its protective barriers against non-members unchanged. The very real possibility exists, however, that a newly formed bloc will attempt to exploit its newfound market power by raising its barriers against non-members and still further improving its terms of trade. Even without assuming such GATT-inconsistent behaviour, in a global economy where not all countries belong to a trading bloc, trading blocs can readily improve member welfare beyond what might be expected with global free trade.

By way of illustration consider a world whose basic elements are countries. There are n such countries of equal size. Following recent work by Krugman (1991), assume that each country is specialised in the production of a single good that is an imperfect substitute for the products of all other countries. Each of these countries has identical preferences and produces the same number of units of their single good. Unlike Krugman, it is assumed the global economy is divided up between members and non-members of a single trading bloc. All countries impose identical tariffs on the imports of all other countries except trading bloc members allow the free importation of member products.

The interesting question is what happens to bloc member welfare and non-member welfare as the trading bloc members allow the free importation of member products. Welfare can be assessed by considering the value of bloc member output and the value of non-member output respectively deflated by an index reflecting prices in member and non-member economies. Since countries do not differ except as to membership in the trading bloc, only two prices, P_b, the price of trading bloc member output, and P_f, the price of non-member output, are of any significance. Under these assumptions, real income of trading bloc members and non-members will be given by:

$$Y_b = \frac{\bar{s} P_b}{(n-f)P_b + f\, P_f\,(1+t)} \tag{1}$$

$$Y_f = \frac{\bar{s} P_f}{(n-f)\, P_b\,(1+t) + (f-1)P_f\,(1+t) + P_f} \tag{2}$$

where

Y_b ≡ real income of bloc member
Y_f ≡ real income of non-bloc member
n ≡ total number of countries
f ≡ number of countries outside bloc
$\bar{s}$ ≡ output
t ≡ tariff rate

If the numerator and denominator on the right-hand side of (1) and (2) are divided by the price of bloc member output and the price of non-member output respectively, we get:

$$Y_b = \frac{\bar{s}}{(n-f) + f\sigma(1+t)} = \frac{\bar{s}}{n - f[1 - \sigma(1+t)]} \tag{3}$$

$$Y_f = \frac{\bar{s}}{\dfrac{(n-f)(1+t)}{\sigma} + (f-1)(1+t) + 1}$$

$$= \frac{\bar{s}\sigma}{(1+t)[n - f(\sigma - 1)]} \tag{4}$$

where $\sigma \equiv P_f / P_b$

Equations (3) and (4) make clear that bloc member real income and non-member real income will depend on the relative importance of the bloc member output $(n - f)$ and non-member output (f) in the global market basket and on their relative prices (σ). It is by definition, that as trading bloc size increases the importance of its output in the global market basket increases. This means assessing what happens to member real income and non-member real income requires looking at σ.

The symmetry in production and preferences among all the economies being analysed here means that each economy will spend an equal share of its income on the goods of every economy except for a correction reflecting relative price differences. Under these demand conditions, as the trading bloc increases in size, the demand for tariff-disadvantaged non-member output will decline relatively and the price of non-member output will fall relative to the price of bloc member output.

The negative relationship between σ and trading bloc size means that non-member real income will decline as the trading bloc gets larger. As seen from the second and third terms in the denominator of (4), the proportion of non-member expenditure that can take place on non-discriminatory terms is falling (as f declines). By contrast, the proportion of non-member expenditure, which must take place on increasingly unfavourable terms (σ falling), is rising. This is represented by the first term in the denominator of (4).

With non-member real income declining continuously as the trading bloc increases in size, the incentive to join the bloc can be overwhelming. Note, however, real income per trading bloc member need not increase continuously as the trading bloc increases in size. Increasing the size of the trade bloc is beneficial to members both because it increases the proportion of member incomes that can be spent unburdened by trade restrictions and because it improves member terms of trade with non-members (σ declining). As seen from the denominator of equation (3), if member terms of trade with non-members are already very favourable, the real income gained from expanding the trade bloc may be less than what is lost from having fewer countries outside the trade bloc trading with members on favourable terms. In the absence of side payments, this means it will not be in the interest of members to expand the size of the trading bloc until the point where global free trade is achieved.

This finding can be made more precise. If β reflects the degree to which each economy adjusts its otherwise equiproportional spending on the goods of every economy to reflect relative price differences, then the price of non-member output to the price of member output, σ, can be given by:

$$\sigma = 1 - \frac{n - f - 1}{n} \frac{\beta t}{\bar{s} + \beta} \tag{5}$$

Substituting (5) into (3), trading bloc member income is now a function of trading bloc size:

$$Y_b = \frac{\bar{s}}{n - f + t\left(\dfrac{n - f - 1}{n}\right)\dfrac{\beta\, t}{s + \beta} - t} \tag{6}$$

As an example, suppose $s = 1.5$, $t = 0.1$, $n = 20$ and $\beta = 2$. Under these conditions Y_b, the real income for each bloc economy, will reach a maximum when half of all economies are bloc members. After this point, Y_b, real income per member, will decrease monotonically as each new member joins, up to and including the point where global free trade is achieved. Beyond $f = 6$, in this example, acting on their own, trading bloc members clearly have no incentive to expand their bloc and move on to free trade. They certainly have no incentive to admit new members on a symmetric basis. This result, which is very robust over a wide variety of parameter values, will hold only so long as outsiders do not organise themselves into a competitive trading bloc.

Nothing in the preceding analysis assumes that the trading bloc will attempt to exploit its growing market power that comes with its increasing size and raise its trade barriers against non-members. Trading bloc members can achieve real income levels better than global free trade and non-members can face continuous declines in real income as the trading bloc expands its membership, even while the trading bloc behaves consistently with GATT Article XXIV and makes no attempt to exploit its increasing market power.

The East Asian trade regime

The case just outlined captures many of the concerns of the economies on the Pacific Rim of Asia. Very comprehensive regional trading arrangements have been organised and have been greatly strengthened in North America and in Europe. The possibility that even without raising new barriers at all, the growing role of such blocs in the global economy could lower East Asian welfare is very real. The proliferation of VERs, OMAs, local content rules, new dumping regulations, and other aggressive unilateral measures against some of these economies suggests that it may even be naive to imagine that newly-created market power will not be exploited. It may be equally naive to assume that such trading blocs are the necessary waystations to a newly invigorated global trading system. Existing members are likely to be better off in a trading bloc that is exclusive. Under a wide variety of conditions, it may not make sense to continuously expand the size of a trading bloc. In particular, it is not hard to imagine East Asian economies being excluded from European or Western Hemispheric regional trading arrangements.

Exclusive arrangements will be preferred to global free trade by members of regional trading blocs only so long as there remain a non-trivial number of non-members who retain protective barriers against each other as well as against the trading bloc itself. If non-members organise their own rival trading bloc, free trade may once again become a superior outcome for all concerned. It is with this perspective that the prospect of new trading arrangements in East Asia should be examined. Intra-regional trade now accounts for 40 per cent of East Asia's total — larger than in North America (if much smaller than Europe's 70 per cent), and growing more rapidly.

These intra-regional trade trends provide some perspective on East Asia's position in a possibly regionalising global economy. Regional trade is becoming more important for East Asia. This need not reflect increasing isolation at all. Trade with East Asia is not only increasingly important for the East Asian economies themselves, it is also increasingly important for North America and for Europe. This increasing importance of East Asian trade in all regions primarily reflects the rapidly increasing economic weight of East Asia in the global economy.

Factor endowment-based gravity equations

It may be helpful to examine the issue of regional bias in trade more systematically by estimating a model of bilateral trade. The resulting structure can provide a reference point from which biases in the regional pattern of trade can be identified. The structure which will be estimated is given by:

$$X_{ik}^j = \sum_{s=1}^{K} \sum_{r=1}^{K} B_{isr} L_{sj} L_{rk}, \qquad i = 1, \ldots, N \tag{7}$$

and
$$\frac{X_{ik}^j}{\Pi_k} = \sum_{s=1}^{K} B_{isr}^* L_{sj}, \qquad i = 1, \ldots, N \tag{8}$$

where

X_{ik}^j	$\equiv$	export of variety j of good i to country k
Π_k	$\equiv$	GNP of economy k
L_{sj}	$\equiv$	endowment of factor of production s in economy j
N	$\equiv$	total number of countries

Equations (7) and (8) are derived from the standard factor endowment-based models of international trade where allowance is made for monopolistic competition. Equation (7) is a factor endowment-based version of the gravity equation, which has been used for years as a framework for estimating bilateral trade relationships. Plausibly it explains bilateral trade flows by the interaction between exporter and importer factor endowments. Equation (8), which is also closely related to traditional gravity equation formulations, states that an economy's share of its trading partner's market for a particular product is a linear function of its own factor endowments.

The structure embodied in equations (7) and (8) results from relaxing many of the strictest assumptions of the standard international trade models in order to incorporate hitherto neglected phenomena in a bilateral trade model. Still further relaxation is possible. For example, suppose that the assumption of strict factor price equalisation across countries, which is necessary to derive (7) and (8), is dropped. Suppose rather, that international trade equalises factor prices only when factor units are normalised for differences in quantity. For example, observed international differences in the compensation of ostensibly unskilled labour may be accounted for by differences in labour quality. Instead of equations (7) and (8), we get:

$$X_{ik}^{j} = \sum_{s=1}^{K}\sum_{r=1}^{K} B_{isr}a_{sj}a_{rk}L_{sj}L_{rk}, \quad i=1,\ldots,N \tag{7'}$$

and

$$\frac{X_{ik}^{j}}{\Pi_{k}} = \sum_{s=1}^{K} B^{*}_{isr}\, a_{sj}L_{sj}, \tag{8'}$$

where $a_{sj} \equiv$ quality of factors in country j.

Estimation procedures

Equations (7') and (8') can be estimated for N commodity groups and K countries using cross-country data. For example, the terms a_{sj} are not directly observable but can be estimated from equation (8'). Formally, the estimation of equation (8') with a_{sj} differing across countries and unknown is a multivariate, multiplicative error-invariable problem. Instrumental variable methods will allow consistent estimation of B^{*}_{isr}. For any given cross-country sectoral equation, a_{sj} will not be identified. In particular, for the specification adopted in equation (8'), however, at any given time there are N cross-sections that contain the identical independent variables. This circumstance can be exploited to permit consistent estimation of a_{sj}. Since the same error will recur in equation after equation owing to the unobservable quality terms, it is possible to use this recurring error to obtain consistent estimates of the quality terms. These estimates of a_{sj} can then be used to adjust the factor endowment data in equations (7') and (8') to obtain more efficient estimates of B_{isr} and B^{*}_{isr}.

Estimation of the trade model

Equations (7') and (8') are estimated with 1985 data taken from the forty-three countries for each of twenty-nine manufacturing sectors.[1] The six factor endowments used in this estimation include directly productive capital, labour, educational attainment, petroleum reserves, arable land, and transport resources. The Heckscher–Ohlin equations (7') and (8') are assumed to hold up to an additive stochastic term.

Unlike the standard Heckscher–Ohlin net trade equations, the dependent variable in these bilateral equations will never be negative, but they will occasionally be zero. As most of the twenty-nine equations to be estimated will contain some zero observations, equations (7') and (8') can be specified as a Tobit model.

Some of the results of estimating equation (7') using the a_{sj} obtained from estimating equation (8') and excluding the East Asian economies from the sample are presented in Tables 20.1 and 20.2. As noted in Table 20.1, twenty-six of the twenty-nine bilateral trade equations are statistically significant. These results mean it is possible to get a good explanation of the structure of bilateral trade when full advantage of the many available degrees of freedom is taken by including a large number of cross-country factor endowment interaction terms. Table 20.2 identifies the statistically significant role played by the interaction between exporter and importer factor endowments in explaining bilateral trade flows. The signs of these coefficients will reflect the degree of complementarity or substitutability between the various factors of production and their relative importance in the various sectoral production processes.

Is there regional bias in East Asian trade?

The results presented in Tables 20.1 and 20.2 are obtained by estimating equation (7') without using East Asian observations. Using these estimated structures and introducing East Asian observations, tolerance intervals have been constructed for East Asian regional trade and for East Asian exports to some of their major non-regional trading partners. The constructed tolerance intervals indicate, with a probability of 0.99, that 0.99 of a univariate normal population will be found within the interval. Observed exports are then compared with these tolerance intervals. Observations that fall outside these tolerance intervals are considered evidence of regional bias.

The findings for East Asian intra-regional exports compared with East Asian exports to much of North America and the EC are striking. East Asian intra-regional exports appear to be well explained by a factor endowment-based gravity equation. As seen in Table 20.3, out of a total of 2,088 trade flows only 325 are outside the tolerance interval. This relatively small number of extreme observations suggests there may be little regional bias in East Asian trade. Neither policy initiatives of one sort or another in Asia, nor very large intra-regional East Asian investment, have resulted in intra-regional distortions in East Asian trade patterns. What is true for the region as a whole is also true at the individual country level. Neither Japan, nor Korea, Taiwan, Hong Kong, Malaysia, the Philippines, Singapore, Thailand and Indonesia have more than a small number of extreme observations on their intra-regional bilateral trade flows (see Table 20.3).

By comparison, with intra-regional trade, East Asia's extra-regional trade is marked by many observations that fall outside the constructed tolerance intervals. Whereas there are an average of thirty-six extreme observations per intra-regional market, as seen from Table 20.4, for East Asian extra-regional export markets there are more than twice as many extreme observations per market. Ironically, factor endowment-based gravity equations estimated without East Asian data do a much better job of explaining the trade among East Asian economies and overall East Asian trade than they do explaining the pattern of East Asian trade with non-East Asian trading partners.

The extra-regional biases in East Asian trade are striking. Particularly interesting are the patterns of East Asian exports to the EC by comparison with East Asian exports to North America. In some 305 instances East Asian exports to the EC appear lower than what might have been expected given the economic characteristics of the various

Table 20.1   **The estimation of** $X_{ik}^{j} = \sum_{s=1}^{K} \sum_{r=1}^{K} B_{isr} a_{sj} a_{rk} L_{sj} L_{rk}$

ISIC #	Sector	R^2	$F(35, 957)$
311	Food manufacturing	0.334	13.7**
312	Other food manufacturing	0.019	0.498
313	Beverage industries	0.336	13.8**
314	Tobacco manufactures	0.323	13.0**
321	Textiles	0.195	6.6**
322	Wearing apparel, except footwear	0.515	28.5**
323	Leather products, except footwear and apparel	0.538	31.8**
324	Footwear, except rubber or plastic	0.515	29.0**
331	Wood and cork products, except furniture	0.197	5.87**
332	Furniture, fixtures, except metal	0.266	9.89**
341	Paper and paper products	0.592	39.6**
342	Printing, publishing and allied industries	0.454	22.7**
351	Industrial chemicals	0.505	27.8**
352	Other chemical products	0.011	0.331
353	Petroleum refineries	0.605	41.8**
354	Miscellaneous products of petroleum and coal	0.544	32.6**
355	Rubber products	0.283	10.8**
356	Plastic products, n.c.e.	0.013	0.383
361	Pottery, china and earthenware	0.220	7.7**
362	Glass and glass products	0.302	11.8**
369	Other non-metallic mineral products	0.283	10.8**
371	Iron and steel basic industries	0.491	26.3**
372	Non-ferrous metal basic industries	0.544	32.6**
381	Fabricated metal products, except machinery and equipment	0.389	17.4**
382	Machinery, except electrical	0.331	13.5**
383	Electrical machinery, apparatus, appliances and supplies	0.174	5.75**
384	Transport equipment	0.063	1.83**
385	Professional, scientific measuring and control equipment	0.254	9.29**
390	Other manufacturing industries	0.017	0.472

Note: ** ≡ Significant at the 0.05 level, $F(35, 957) = 1.43$.

East Asian economies. In each of these cases actual East Asian exports to the EC are below the lower limit of the tolerance interval. In only a comparatively few (fifty) cases

Table 20.2 **Number and sign of significant (0.05) coefficients on factor endowment interaction terms (B_{isr})**

LAND	CAPITAL$_{Exp}$ +	CAPITAL$_{Exp}$ -	LABOUR$_{Exp}$ +	LABOUR$_{Exp}$ -	EDUC$_{Exp}$ +	EDUC$_{Exp}$ -	OIL$_{Exp}$ +	OIL$_{Exp}$ -	TRANS$_{Exp}$ +	TRANS$_{Exp}$ -	ARA$_{Exp}$ +	ARA$_{Exp}$ -
CAPITAL$_{Imp}$	5	17	8	6	10	5	14	6	9	4	14	7
LABOUR$_{Imp}$	14	4	5	16	10	8	10	4	6	7	13	8
EDUC$_{Imp}$	15	6	12	11	7	12	11	5	8	3	9	6
OIL$_{Imp}$	7	7	7	3	9	7	4	14	5	6	7	11
TRANS$_{Imp}$	5	3	6	8	10	14	6	8	10	8	5	6
LAND ARA$_{Imp}$	11	5	17	3	12	3	5	12	7	8	8	12

Note: The rows index the factor endowments of importers. The columns index the factor endowments of exporters. The cells indicate how many significant coefficients of each sign are found for the associated interaction terms in the twenty-nine estimated equations.

are actual East Asian exports to EC markets above the upper limit of the tolerance interval. Despite very rapid growth in East Asian exports to the EC over the past two decades, still greater exports might have been expected.

As with East Asian exports to the EC, there are also a comparatively large number of extreme observations on East Asian exports to North America. By marked contrast with the extreme observations on East Asian exports to the EC, the extreme observations on exports to North America are disproportionately above the upper limit of the tolerance interval. While 85 per cent of the 355 extreme observations of exports to the EC are below the lower limit of the tolerance interval, only 19 per cent of the 195 extreme observations of exports to North America are below the lower limit of the tolerance interval. If East Asia exports are less to the EC than might be expected on the basis of global relationships, it appears to export more to North America than might be expected. While there is no intra-regional trade bias if East Asia is defined as a region, if the region is expanded to include the Pacific Basin, then intra-regional bias does become apparent.

Does Japan play a special role in East Asia? Japan's level of productivity and its industrial skills and experience remain well ahead of even the most rapidly growing economies elsewhere in East Asia. It is hardly surprising that Japan is exporting sophisticated capital goods to its East Asian trading partners, at the same time that it is importing processed raw materials, components and manufactures from them. There is at present little evidence of a regional bias in Japan's relations with the rest of East Asia that goes beyond the existing pattern of East Asian resource endowments. Out of

Table 20.3 Extreme observations on East Asian intra-regional exports

	Japan		Korea		Taiwan		Hong Kong		Malaysia		Philippines		Singapore		Thailand		Indonesia	
	+	–	+	–	+	–	+	–	+	–	+	–	+	–	+	–	+	–
Japan	–	–	1	2	1	1	1	–	–	3	2	5	3	1	3	–	–	1
Korea	2	3	–	–	2	1	–	–	4	1	3	3	–	2	2	2	3	1
Taiwan	1	2	–	4	–	–	4	–	3	4	2	2	2	3	1	1	4	2
Hong Kong	3	–	3	3	5	3	–	–	4	2	1	–	3	1	2	3	1	3
Malaysia	2	1	–	2	2	1	1	2	–	–	3	3	3	2	1	4	3	1
Philippines	2	2	4	1	2	–	3	5	3	1	–	–	3	–	4	5	5	2
Singapore	–	5	1	–	1	4	2	4	4	3	3	2	–	–	2	3	4	1
Thailand	3	1	2	6	3	1	3	5	2	1	2	4	5	4	–	–	–	–
Indonesia	3	2	2	–	4	–	3	4	–	7	3	–	6	2	5	3	–	–

Note: The rows index imports. The columns index exports. Each cell indicates the number of extreme observations: (+) indicates over-exporting and (–) under-exporting. The maximum number of extreme observations for any bilateral pair is twenty-nine. The critical value for tolerance interval T (0.99, 0.99, 957) = 2.51.

Table 20.4   Extreme observations on East Asian extra-regional exports

	Japan +	Japan −	Korea +	Korea −	Taiwan +	Taiwan −	Hong Kong +	Hong Kong −	Malaysia +	Malaysia −	Philippines +	Philippines −	Singapore +	Singapore −	Thailand +	Thailand −	Indonesia +	Indonesia −
US	9	3	11	4	14	6	8	1	12	3	6	-	12	3	7	2	4	1
Canada	11	2	9	4	11	3	12	-	7	1	4	-	9	-	6	-	5	4
Germany	-	8	2	12	3	7	4	14	4	10	2	4	2	11	4	6	2	3
Netherl.	1	6	-	4	-	3	2	6	2	7	1	3	1	8	-	2	-	4
UK	-	3	2	5	-	4	3	7	1	4	-	5	2	5	-	3	-	6
France	-	7	-	8	2	10	1	11	-	8	2	7	-	13	2	8	3	8
Italy	1	13	-	10	1	9	-	13	-	14	-	5	-	11	-	10	-	6

Note: The rows index imports. The columns index exports. Each cell indicates the number of extreme observations: (+) indicates over-exporting and (-) under-exporting. The maximum number of extreme observations for any bilateral pair is twenty-nine. The critical value for tolerance interval $T(0.99, 0.99, 957) = 2.51$.

464 instances of bilateral trade flows between Japan and the other East Asian economies only 62 extreme observations have been uncovered. These divide neatly into 16 cases of Japan over-exporting, 16 cases of Japan under-exporting, 16 cases of Japan over-importing and 14 cases of Japan under-importing.

What is particularly interesting about the regional pattern of Japanese trade is not how it differs from the rest of the countries in East Asia, but rather how similar it is. In common with the rest of the economies in East Asia, Japan exports less to the EC than might be expected and more to the United States than might otherwise be expected. While the EC appears to exhibit some negative bias against imports from East Asia and overall North America appears to exhibit considerable bias in favour, Japanese import behaviour, at least insofar as the model estimated here is concerned, appears virtually neutral with respect to the rest of East Asia.

Pricing strategies in East Asia

If there is no special intra-regional bias in East Asian trade patterns and if the growth in East Asian intra-regional trade merely reflects the growing global economic importance of East Asia, are regional initiatives superfluous except as a tactical exercise to prevent discrimination and exclusion elsewhere? Not necessarily. The absence of regional bias does not necessarily mean the absence of regional trade barriers. The estimated parameters of equation (7') may embody all manner of protective barriers. The absence of intra-regional bias simply means there is no special discrimination in favour of or against East Asian trading partners (Saxonhouse 1983, pp. 259–304). This is quite a different matter from concluding, for example, that commodity arbitrage across East Asia is near-perfect. In fact, how integrated are East Asian markets?

One helpful way to examine this issue might be to look at East Asian firms' pricing behaviour across different East Asian markets. Do East Asian firms operate as if East Asia is a single, regional market, or are each of the national markets there treated as if they were separate entities? East Asian firms will treat national markets separately if national barriers exist which make commodity arbitrage ineffective, at least on a regional basis.

East Asian firms' price responses in different markets to exchange rate changes provide a source of data on this issue. If commodity arbitrage is effective, then product prices across the region should be the same after correcting for exchange rates. If commodity arbitrage is ineffective, East Asian firms will face particular demand relationships in each East Asian market. Assuming that the price elasticity of demand varies with prices for these demand relationships, exchange rate movements among the East Asian currencies will change the relative price of a product across East Asian markets. With commodity arbitrage ineffective across markets, even after allowance has been made for lags in adjustment, there is no reason to expect 100 per cent pass-through of exchange rate changes into product prices across markets. If price elasticity varies directly with price, pass-through of exchange rate changes should be less than 100 per cent. By contrast, if price elasticity varies inversely with price, greater than 100 per cent pass-through of exchange rate changes could be an equilibrium response (Marston 1990, pp. 217–37).

The preceding analysis suggests that if movements in the real exchange rate between two East Asian economies help explain the path of relative prices of a particular product across these markets, then the integration of these markets is incomplete. Of course, any study of relative prices of particular products across markets needs to be embedded in a more comprehensive framework which also allows for lags in the adjustment of firm behaviour, cyclical demand factors and cost factors.

While such comprehensive studies remain to be done, results following this approach are available for exporters based in Japan.[2] Sectoral pass-through equations have been separately estimated for forty-seven product lines in each of six markets, including the Republic of Korea, Taiwan, Hong Kong, Singapore, Malaysia and Thailand using data from June 1984 to December 1989 (Saxonhouse 1993b, Table 12.6). Within the larger group of machinery exports, these products have been chosen on the basis of data availability for all countries in the sample; 276 relative price or pass-through equations have been estimated with the data just outlined. While the results of such estimation are broadly interesting, special interest focuses in such equations on the coefficients of the real exchange rate. In no less than 207 cases out of a possible total of 272, the coefficient on the level of the real exchange rate is statistically significantly different from zero (Saxonhouse 1993b, Table 12.7). Apparently strategic pricing is a pervasive phenomenon. Of particular interest here, Japanese machinery exporters exhibit this behaviour in the majority of their Pacific markets. Such behaviour is most pronounced in the Korean market and is practised by Japanese machinery exporters for the vast majority of the capital goods they sell in East Asia. Among types of machinery exports, machinery components, for whatever reason, seem less subject to strategic pricing than the complete machine.

Not all of the 207 statistically significant coefficients on the real exchange rate are positive. In no less than twenty cases this coefficient is negative, illustrating the case where exchange rate changes are more than passed through into foreign prices (see Saxonhouse 1993b, Table 12.8 for country distribution). These cases typically reflect the very small size of some of the overseas markets being investigated here and the resulting instability of some of the unit value indexes being used as dependent variables.

What is particularly interesting here is not just that Japanese firms practise strategic price-setting behaviour in all their East Asian markets for almost all the capital goods in this sample. Strategic price-setting behaviour varies in a statistically significant way not just across product lines but also across markets. In no less than thirty-five out of forty-seven product lines, the hypothesis that the coefficient on the real exchange rate is the same across geographic markets cannot be accepted. (Saxonhouse 1993b, Table 12.9 lists the capital goods for which this is true.) Significant barriers to commodity arbitrage in East Asia appear to exist. Considering the interest in regional trade and investment initiatives in East Asia, further investigation is clearly needed as to why pricing behaviour by exporters of the same machinery should vary so much across geographical markets. Do East Asian firms really have the capacity to effectively segregate proximate markets in Asia in the absence of host government connivance of some sort?

The results on the weakness of commodity arbitrage rest on a very simple model of international price discrimination. The limitations of this model should not be forgotten. The impact of exchange rates on strategic pricing behaviour depends critically on the price discriminator's perception of the shape of the demand function for his product. The model employed here does not contain any explanation as to why this perception should vary from market to market, and across exporters. Oligopoly theory is helpful in explaining such variation (Krugman 1986; Dornbusch 1987, pp. 93–106). Empirical versions of such models, however, are not easily employed across a large number of different product lines and markets.

Even apart from issues of specification, further evidence for other product lines and for firms operating out of other home markets needs to be examined. Despite the extraordinary growth in intra-regional trade in East Asia, the price evidence presented suggests the continuing importance of official and non-official barriers to intra-regional trade in East Asia. Are these barriers, however, significantly different from barriers to intra-regional trade in North America or Western Europe? Relative price equations have already been estimated for forty-three of the forty-seven product lines for Japanese firm behaviour in the US and Canadian markets. In less than half the cases in either the US or Canadian market is the real exchange rate coefficient statistically significant in the relative price equation (Saxonhouse 1993b, Table 12.10). Despite all the complaints about lack of Japanese pass-through exchange rate changes in the North American market, strategic pricing is far less pervasive there than in East Asia. Moreover, while there may be as many as twenty product lines in the sample examined here where US and Canadian firms do not appear well integrated with the rest of the global economy, in only half of these twenty cases do Japanese firms act as if commodity arbitrage is not an easy matter across the Canadian–US border (Saxonhouse 1993b, Table 12.11). By comparison with their behaviour in East Asia, Japanese firms appear to treat the Canadian–US market as very well integrated. This is true even for the period before the Canada–US Free Trade Agreement was ratified.

Regional initiatives in East Asia

Despite the absence of intra-regional bias in East Asian trade, evidence on the ability of East Asian firms to behave as if East Asian markets were substantially segregated from one another does suggest that important barriers to trade remain. Quite apart from the tactical benefits in global negotiations that an East Asian grouping might bring, new East Asia-wide liberalisation could still have substantial trade-creating effects within the region.

It should be no surprise that, compared with other regions, East Asia has been slow to develop region-wide initiatives. No region has enjoyed the scale of East Asia's economic success over the past two decades. As pointed out earlier, however, East Asia's success has been global in its scope, and the successful East Asian economies have been wary to take steps that might undermine the centrality of the GATT. Great variation across East Asia in both the role the government plays in the economy and in the level of development have also contributed to a dearth of formal regional initiatives. The absence of any identifiable regional bias in East Asian trade also suggests that the absence of formal arrangements in no way masked any kind of informal preferential arrangements. In particular, at least as late as the mid-1980s, there is no evidence at all of a Japanese-led informally organised regional bloc in Asia.

ASEAN is the oldest and best-known regional grouping in East Asia. While originally focused on political and security issues, this grouping, which includes Brunei, Indonesia, Malaysia, the Philippines, Thailand and Singapore, has always had an economic component. As long ago as 1977, ASEAN negotiated a preferential trade agreement. Unfortunately the amount of trade covered by this agreement has always remained small.

With renewed commitment by the ASEAN member-states to economic liberalisation in early 1992, however, agreement has been reached to transform the old preferential trade agreement into a free trade area over the next fifteen years. How much substance this new agreement will have remains to be seen. Intra-ASEAN trade remains relatively small and the ASEAN economies may be too similar for large gains in trade to develop from the projected liberalisation. The removal of intra-ASEAN barriers, however, may aid the region's efforts to attract still more investment.

While ASEAN continues to lack substance as an economic grouping, there are regional arrangements on still a smaller scale in East Asia which have the promise to exert considerable economic force. The most important of these is the Shenzhen Free Trade Zone which ties together Hong Kong and Guandong province in the PRC. Much of the extraordinary development of this part of China in recent years can be attributed directly to the institution of this trading arrangement.

The great success of the Shenzhen Free Trade Zone has triggered proposals to link the following: Singapore, Johore province of Malaysia and Batam Island of Indonesia; China, the Koreas, eastern Siberia and western Japan; Japan, Korea and the coastal province of China; Hong Kong, Taiwan and China (south of Shanghai); Hong Kong, Guangdong, Guangxi and northern Thailand, Laos and Vietnam; Thailand, Cambodia and southern Vietnam; Myanmar, Thailand and Indochina; and Thailand, northern Sumatra and northern Malaysia. While nothing may come of most of these proposals, what is characteristic of almost all of them is the joining together of parts of what were once heavily regulated non-market economies with other areas of East Asia that have long records of economic dynamism.

Notwithstanding the many Asian free trade area proposals made in the image of the Shenzhen Free Trade Zone, the most widely discussed proposals are much more comprehensive in scope. The best known of these was made by Prime Minister Mahathir of Malaysia in 1990 and called for the formation of the EAEG, consisting of Japan, the East Asian NIEs, China and the other ASEAN economies. Although the precise role that such an economic grouping might play was never set out in detail, it was clear at the outset that the EAEG was meant to be the East Asian response to emerging trade blocs in Europe and the Americas. As such, the Mahathir proposal was strongly opposed by the United States, Australia and New Zealand, all of whom wished East Asian regional cooperation undertaken rather in the context of Pacific-wide economic institutions such as APEC. Strong pressure from the United States has also led Japan to publicly oppose the EAEG. Privately, however, at least some Japanese government officials and business leaders have been more supportive (Petri 1993). Indeed, it has been suggested that Japanese encouragement may have prompted Mahathir to make his proposal in the first place.

The opposition to the original Mahathir plan has led to changes in this proposal. The EAEG is now thought of not so much as a formal grouping but rather as a periodic consultative mechanism. Whether this East Asian consultation will deal chiefly with the coordination of East Asian positions on global trade policy or whether it will extend to regional economic integration remains to be seen.

While Mahathir has been seeking an East Asian locus for regional cooperation, Australia, New Zealand and the United States have been stressing regional cooperation on a Pacific-wide basis through the development of APEC. Since 1989, the foreign ministers of twelve Pacific Rim countries including Australia, Brunei, Canada, Indonesia, Japan, Korea, Malaysia, New Zealand, the Philippines, Singapore, Thailand and the United States have agreed to meet annually to review issues of mutual interest. More recently, in a precedent-setting arrangement, China, Taiwan and Hong Kong have all been admitted to APEC.

To date, APEC's accomplishments have been extremely limited. The small secretariat that has been established has confined itself almost entirely to regional information exchange and technical cooperation. The annual APEC ministerial meetings have been used primarily as fora where resolutions stressing global economic goals have been framed and endorsed. APEC has yet to deal in a concrete way with any significant regional economic issues. It has yet to sponsor regional economic liberalisation initiatives, or harmonise regional economic policies, or resolve regional economic disputes.

Conclusion

Regional initiatives in Europe and North America have triggered considerable interest and concern in the Pacific Basin. New trade initiatives by ASEAN, the Mahathir proposal for an EAEG, the evolving APEC, now with its own secretariat, reflect, at least in part, a reaction to developments elsewhere. This is quite apart from the somewhat more familiar, smaller subregional trading zones, proposals for which are proliferating wherever there is proximity in East Asia. These proposals are not being made in the face of long dormant East Asian economic interaction: quite the contrary. In absolute terms, East Asian regional trade and East Asian cross-investment have grown very rapidly.

In the perspective of these developments this paper concludes that:

- It is certainly possible that trading blocs being formed elsewhere in the world might lower East Asian welfare. This can happen even in the absence of any explicit or implicit effort by these blocs to exploit their market power at the expense of East Asia. These trading blocs may have no incentive to expand their membership to include East Asian economies except insofar as they fear provoking the formation of an East Asian trading bloc. In the presence of a substantial group of disorganised, non-retaliating outsiders, a trading bloc even without violating GATT Article XXIV can achieve outcomes for its members that might be superior to global free trade.

- The rapid growth in intra-regional East Asian trade reflects not very much more than the very rapid growth in this region relative to the rest of the world. Estimation of a bilateral model of intra-industry trade using a factor endowment-based version of the gravity model suggests no East Asian bias in the trading pattern of the leading economies there. When the Pacific region is defined to include North America, however, substantial regional bias will likely be present. This reflects the positive bias found in East Asian exports to North America. By contrast, there is a negative bias in East Asian exports to Western Europe. From the perspective of the first section of this paper, there may be some tactical merit in an East Asian regional trading arrangement, but there is no evidence in the available trade data that this is yet happening.

- Despite the absence of intra-regional bias in East Asian exports, evidence that East Asian markets are substantively segregated from one another in ways, for example, that Canadian and US markets are not, does suggest important barriers to trade remain. While East Asian economies have benefited from substantial liberalisation in recent years, new region-wide liberalisation could still have substantial trade-creating effects within the region. Extra-regional effects remain to be analysed.

Notes

1   Since the factor endowment variables in equation (8) explain national development, there is no need to limit the sample used here to just the most advanced economies. This development-related protection is explained by changes in the levels of the factor endowments. Typically, the higher the level of factor endowments, the less the protection. The economies in this sample include Argentina, Australia, Austria, Belgium, Brazil, Chile, Denmark, Finland, France, Germany, Greece, Honduras, Hong Kong, India, Ireland, Italy, Jamaica, Japan, Korea, Malaysia, Malta, Mexico,

the Netherlands, New Zealand, Nigeria, Norway, the Philippines, Peru, Portugal, Singapore, Spain, Sri Lanka, Sweden, Switzerland, Taiwan, Thailand, Turkey, Egypt, the United Kingdom, the United States and Yugoslavia.

2   Full detail of the results discussed here is in Saxonhouse (1993a). The tables referred to are from Saxonhouse (1993b), the full version of this paper.

References

Dornbusch, R. 1987, 'Exchange rates and prices', *American Economic Review*, March.

Haberler, G. 1936, *Theory of International Trade with Applications to Commercial Policy*, London: Macmillan.

Krugman, P. 1986, 'Pricing to market when the exchange rate changes', *National Bureau of Economic Research Working Paper*, No. 1926, May.

_____ 1991, 'Is bilateralism bad?', in E. Helpman and A. Razin (eds), *International Trade and Trade Policy*, Cambridge, Mass.: MIT Press.

Marston, R. 1990, 'Pricing to market in Japanese manufacturing', *Journal of International Economics*, November.

Petri, P. 1993, 'The East Asian trading bloc: an analytical history', in J. Frankel and M. Kahler (eds), *Regionalism and Rivalry: Japan and the United States in Pacific Asia*, Chicago: University of Chicago Press.

Saxonhouse, Gary. R. 1983, 'The micro- and macroeconomics of foreign sales to Japan', in W. Cline (ed.), *Trade Policy in the 1980's*, Cambridge, Mass.: MIT Press.

_____ 1993a, 'Pricing strategies and trading blocs in East Asia', in J. Frankel and M. Kahler (eds), *Regionalism and Rivalry: Japan and the United States in Pacific Asia*, Chicago: University of Chicago Press.

_____ 1993b, 'Trading blocs and East Asia', in J. de Melo and A. Panagariya (eds), *New Dimensions in Regional Integration*, Cambridge, UK: Cambridge University Press.

Viner, J. 1950, *The Customs Union Issue*, Washington, DC: Carnegie Endowment for International Peace.

21 Changing patterns of direct investment and the implications for trade and development ————

Shujiro Urata

Introduction

Rapid export expansion contributed significantly to economic growth of the economies in the Asia Pacific, as export earnings enabled them to import important items for promoting economic development such as capital goods and foreign technology. Although foreign trade is still very important for these economies to maintain rapid growth, FDI has come to play an important role in promoting economic development in the 1980s, especially in the second half of the 1980s. FDI can contribute to economic development in various ways, since it transfers not only financial resources, which are used to expand production facilities, but also technology and management know-how, which improves technical and managerial efficiency. Moreover, it has been recognised that FDI promotes economic development by expanding marketing and information networks.

In light of the increasing importance of FDI in economic development in the Asia Pacific, this paper attempts to achieve two objectives. One is to examine the pattern of FDI in the Asia Pacific and the other is to analyse the impact of FDI on the economic development of the countries in the Asia Pacific. The final section of the paper presents some concluding comments.

Changing pattern of FDI in Asia

FDI in the world increased rapidly in the 1980s, accelerating even faster in the second half of the decade. Asia has been an active investor as well as an increasingly important recipient of FDI. This section first examines the changes in the importance of Asia in world FDI, before studying the changing patterns of FDI in Asia, focusing separately on Japan, the NIEs, ASEAN and China.

Rapid increase of FDI in Asia

Table 21.1 shows the changing patterns of both outward and inward FDI for selected Asian countries and regions in the second half of the 1980s. As investors, Japan and the NIEs increased in importance. Between 1985 and 1990 the magnitude of outward FDI for Japan and the NIEs increased 7.5 times and 16.5 times, respectively. As the rate of increase of outward FDI by Japan and the NIEs exceeded the corresponding rate for world outward FDI in the second half of the 1980s, their respective shares in world outward FDI increased respectively from 11.2 and 0.6 per cent in 1985 to 22.1 and 3.0 per cent in 1990. In 1990 outward FDI by Japan and the NIEs amounted respectively to US$48.0 and US$6.6 billion. In 1990 Japan was the world's largest investor, followed by the United States (US$33.4 billion), France (US$24.2 billion) and Germany (US$22.3 billion). In terms of cumulative outward FDI for the 1970–90 period, the United States was by far the largest investor at US$421.5 billion, followed by the United Kingdom (US$233.6 billion) and Japan (US$201.4 billion).

As a recipient of FDI, the NIEs and ASEAN countries attracted substantial amounts of FDI in the second half of the 1980s, as the magnitude of inward FDI for these two regions increased 4.3 and 5.7 times respectively during the period. Since the rate of world inward FDI increased more slowly — by 3.3 times over the 1985–90 period — the shares of the NIEs and ASEAN in world inward FDI increased from 3.3 and 2.5 per cent respectively in 1985 to 4.3 per cent each in 1990. As the relative share of developing countries in world inward FDI declined in the second half of the 1980s, the fact that the NIEs and ASEAN increased their respective shares in world inward FDI is particularly noteworthy.

Similar to other Asian countries, China was successful in attracting FDI in the second half of the 1980s, as the magnitude of inward FDI doubled in five years from US$1.7 billion in 1985 to US$3.5 billion in 1990. China is second only to Singapore in the magnitude of inward FDI.

It is to be noted that Japan's inward FDI is quite limited, not only in terms of absolute value, as shown in Table 21.1, but also in relation to the size of its economy. According to one estimate, the ratio of stock of inward FDI to GNP at the end of 1989 was a mere 0.3 per cent for Japan, while the corresponding ratios for the United States, the United Kingdom (1988) and West Germany (1988) were, respectively, 7.7, 14.1 and 3.0 per cent (Japan Development Bank 1991). A number of obstacles to undertaking FDI in Japan have been noted by foreign firms. These include tough competition, high land prices, high wages, high demand by consumers, high material costs, government regulation, and difficulty in entering *keiretsu*-dominated markets (Japan Development Bank 1991). Costs of undertaking FDI in Japan rose with the yen appreciation. It is important to note that potential Japanese entrants to the existing markets were also confronted by many of the same obstacles as the foreign investors.

Table 21.1   Foreign direct investment in Asia

	Out		In	
	Millions of US dollars	Share of world total	Millions of US dollars	Share of world total
1985				
Japan	6.4	11.1	0.6	1.2
NIEs	0.4	0.7	1.6	3.3
ASEAN	0.0	0.0	1.2	2.5
China	0.6	1.0	1.7	3.5
World	57.4	100.0	48.3	100.0
1987				
Japan	19.5	14.3	1.2	1.1
NIEs	1.1	0.8	4.2	3.8
ASEAN	0.1	0.1	1.5	1.4
China	0.6	0.4	2.3	2.1
World	136.4	100.0	110.5	100.0
1990				
Japan	48.0	22.1	1.8	1.1
NIEs	6.6	3.0	6.9	4.3
ASEAN	0.1	0.0	6.8	4.3
China	0.8	0.4	3.5	2.2
World	217.2	100.0	159.2	100.0

Source: International Monetary Fund, *International Financial Statistics*, various issues; and Executive Yuan, Republic of China, *Statistical Yearbook of the Republic of China*, various issues.

It was noted above that in the second half of the 1980s, Japan and the NIEs strengthened their position as FDI suppliers in the world, while the NIEs, ASEAN and China became relatively larger recipients of FDI among the developing countries. The next section examines the patterns of outward as well as inward FDI in Asia by focusing on Japan, the NIEs and ASEAN.

FDI in Asia: Japan, NIEs and ASEAN

Japan: an active foreign direct investor
Japanese FDI started to increase rapidly in 1986 and continued until 1989. The speed of the increase during the 1986–89 period was unprecedentedly high, as the average annual growth rate for the period was as high as 53.3 per cent. In 1990 the magnitude

of annual Japanese FDI declined from the previous year for the first time in eight years, and the declining trend continued in 1991.

Although the rapid increase of Japanese FDI was mainly led by FDI in non-manufacturing sectors such as financial services and real estate in developed countries, Japanese FDI in Asia has been increasing significantly in various sectors. The magnitude of Japanese FDI in manufacturing in Asia on an annual basis increased from US$460 million in 1985 to US$3,068 million in 1990. The substantial appreciation of the yen in the mid-1980s led Japanese firms to undertake FDI in Asian countries, especially in the NIEs, to take advantage of low production costs. In 1987, however, Japanese firms started to shift the location of FDI from the NIEs to ASEAN countries, as the NIEs lost cost advantages because of rising wages and the appreciation of their currencies. In addition, the fact that the NIEs had graduated from the US GSP scheme further reduced their attractiveness as a host to FDI.

The shift in Japanese manufacturing FDI from the NIEs to ASEAN can be seen clearly in Table 21.2, where the cumulative FDI values are shown. Between 1985 and 1987, the value of Japanese manufacturing FDI to the NIEs was increased by US$1.5 billion, significantly higher than that to the ASEAN countries at US$0.9 billion. The situation changed dramatically after 1987; over 1987–90, the value of Japanese manufacturing FDI in the NIEs rose US$2.9 billion, substantially lower than the corresponding value for ASEAN, at $5.0 billion. It is also to be noted that Japanese manufacturing FDI to China increased significantly after 1987.

As for the sectoral distribution of Japanese FDI to Asia, the share of the non-manufacturing sector is increasing in the NIEs. Within manufacturing, the electrical sector captured a large share, and one that increased significantly during the second half of the 1980s. The rate of increase was particularly notable for ASEAN and China. The share of the electrical sector in overall manufacturing FDI in cumulative value from 1951 in ASEAN and China increased from 4.9 and 10.1 per cent respectively in 1985 to 20.6 and 35.8 per cent in 1990. As the electrical sector increased its share, a number of sectors lost their shares. The textiles sector experienced a remarkable decline in the NIEs and ASEAN, while the food sector lost its share in China. The decline in the share of textiles in Japanese FDI to the NIEs and ASEAN indicates that these countries lost a comparative advantage in labour-intensive production such as in textiles because their factor endowments changed as a result of economic development. More specifically, with accumulation of physical and human capital, the capital-to-labour ratio increased rapidly in the NIEs and ASEAN, resulting in the loss of comparative advantage in labour-intensive pro-duction. A similar argument may be made for the decline in the share of the food sector in Japanese manufacturing FDI in China.

The pattern of Japanese FDI observed above was realised by the interaction of supply-side factors in Japan and demand-side factors in the recipient countries. As for the factors in Japan promoting Japanese FDI, the most important was the rapid and substantial yen appreciation, which reduced the international competitiveness of Japanese products by increasing the cost of production in Japan. To overcome the

Table 21.2   Japanese foreign direct investment in Asia

	Amount (US$b)		Share of manufacturing (%)								
	Total	Manu-facturing	Food	Textiles	Wood	Chemicals	Metals	Machinery	Electrical machinery	Transport machinery	Other
World											
1985	83.7	24.4	4.5	8.5	4.6	16.3	21.3	8.1	15.4	13.8	7.5
1987	139.3	36.0	4.3	6.5	4.1	14.6	17.5	9.1	19.9	15.7	8.3
1990	310.8	81.6	5.0	4.9	3.6	13.4	12.6	9.7	24.9	13.3	12.4
NIEs											
1985	7.6	3.3	2.4	10.7	0.9	25.4	5.8	14.4	19.0	8.6	12.9
1987	11.7	4.8	3.4	7.9	0.7	22.4	6.2	13.0	23.2	9.9	13.3
1990	23.3	7.7	9.5	7.1	0.9	18.5	6.9	10.9	24.0	8.7	13.4
ASEAN											
1985	11.2	4.0	3.8	20.4	3.9	10.7	36.8	2.3	4.9	9.2	8.2
1987	12.8	4.9	4.7	17.1	3.5	9.8	35.3	3.0	7.7	10.2	8.8
1990	20.8	9.9	3.7	11.8	4.4	11.3	22.4	7.0	20.6	9.5	9.3
China											
1985	0.3	0.1	26.7	4.4	5.1	22.3	8.3	6.0	10.1	1.1	16.0
1987	1.7	1.0	15.0	4.8	2.8	15.1	9.5	5.3	36.3	0.4	10.7
1990	2.8	2.8	8.4	7.7	1.5	7.5	6.1	15.6	35.8	1.1	16.2

Source: Ministry of Finance, Japan.

unfavourable situation, Japanese firms have adopted various strategies, including globalisation, rationalisation and diversification. Globalisation has been pursued not only through FDI but also through forming alliances with foreign firms. Alliances have taken various forms such as technology tie-up arrangements, production cooperation, original equipment manufacturing, and others.

Rationalisation is pursued to increase competitiveness by improving productive efficiency, while diversification is undertaken to increase profitability by upgrading the quality of the products and/or by moving into a new line of business where higher profitability may be realised. One of the important developments observed in the latter half of the 1980s was that a number of firms pursued these three strategies simultaneously in coherent fashion in order to facilitate industrial restructuring, in responding to dramatic changes in their environment. Such a strategy was most apparent in the electrical industry. Take colour television production, for example. A number of Japanese TV producers shifted their production of standard colour TVs, such as small and medium-sized TVs, to the NIEs and ASEAN, where production of such standardised TVs was efficiently performed with low-wage labour, while in Japan they concentrated on the production of high-quality TVs such as those capable of receiving satellite broadcasting and/or large screen colour TVs (Urata 1991).

Although there is no doubt that the significant yen appreciation precipitated globalisation of Japanese firms, there were other factors at work. The 'bubble economy' created by excessively expansionary monetary policy, which was conducted in order to deal mainly with recessionary pressures resulting from the yen appreciation, promoted domestic and foreign investment. Under the bubble economy, the prices of stocks and land in Japan skyrocketed, enabling firms with appreciated assets to obtain loans for investment. Another factor promoting Japanese FDI was the impetus that FDI undertaken by Japanese firms had in encouraging other Japanese firms to invest. There were two motivations leading to this reaction. One was to keep up with the investing rival firms in business performance; the other was to follow the investing trading partners to maintain business. Furthermore, the overseas experiences accumulated by Japanese firms also contributed to rapid FDI in the latter half of the 1980s.

As a result of the rapid increase in FDI by Japanese firms, overseas production by these firms expanded quickly. In manufacturing, the overseas production ratio — defined as the ratio of overseas production to total (overseas and domestic) production — grew from 3.0 per cent in 1985 to 5.7 per cent in 1989 (MITI 1991). Despite the notable increase, the overseas production ratio by Japanese manufacturing firms is still much lower than the corresponding ratio for firms of other developed countries, as US and German firms recorded overseas production ratios of around 20 per cent. Among the manufacturing subsectors, the overseas production ratio is particularly high for transport machinery and electrical machinery subsectors, for which the overseas production ratios in 1989 were 14.3 and 11.0 per cent. The overseas production ratios for most sectors are likely to increase in the future, as FDI projects undertaken in the latter half of the 1980s will soon be fully operational.

The NIEs: active participants in inward and outward FDI

It has already been noted that inward as well as outward FDI for the NIEs increased significantly in the second half of the 1980s.[1] It was also found that Japanese FDI in the NIEs increased during the period. The speed of increase as well as the magnitude of FDI from Japan to the NIEs was particularly notable in non-manufacturing and for the electrical industry in manufacturing. This section, therefore, examines the factors in the NIEs that attracted inward FDI and then turns to discussion of their outward FDI.

The composition of inward FDI in the NIEs changed dramatically in the second half of the 1980s. In total inward FDI, the share of non-manufacturing, especially that of services, increased, and among the manufacturing subsectors, inward FDI shifted from labour-intensive to technology-intensive sectors. Various factors promoted inward FDI in non-manufacturing in the NIEs. Demand for services increased as income levels grew with economic development. A typical example may be active FDI in commercial sectors — for example, retail services such as department stores and supermarkets — responding to increased consumer demand for a variety of products. Furthermore, deregulation and liberalisation contributed to increasing inward FDI. For example, deregulation and liberalisation in the insurance sector in Korea led to active FDI in that sector.

The shift in inward FDI in the NIEs towards technology-intensive sectors was attributable to the NIE governments' FDI promotion policies in high technology sectors. Such policies were pursued because the NIEs felt a need to improve competitive advantage in high-tech sectors to compensate for their loss of comparative advantage in low-technology products to the ASEAN countries. Policymakers in the NIEs thought foreign technology was necessary to gain competitive advantage in high-tech products, and that FDI would be an important means for importing technology.

Outward FDI has been actively undertaken by the NIEs since the mid-1980s, in particular by Taiwan. Destinations of outward FDI differ among the NIEs, but the shares of ASEAN and China have increased in recent years (Table 21.3). The key factors in the NIEs' outward FDI are similar to those observed for the rapid rise in Japanese FDI: a sharp increase in wages due to shortage of labour, appreciation of their currencies, and trade frictions with developed countries. As such, the sectors actively undertaking outward FDI are those losing comparative advantage, such as toys, apparel, sporting goods, and other labour-intensive products, and those subject to trade frictions such as electronics.

There are some similarities as well as differences in the patterns of FDI by the NIEs and Japanese firms. One important similarity is their motivation for FDI. In both cases, FDI was undertaken to promote industrial restructuring in these countries, which would lead to further economic growth. Indeed, outward FDI promotion policies have been adopted not only in Japan, but also in Korea, Taiwan and Singapore. As for the differences, one may note the difference in the size of the firms undertaking FDI in Japan and the NIEs, although there are substantial differences in this regard among NIE firms. In general, the NIE firms undertaking FDI are smaller than their Japanese counterparts, as reflected in the sectoral distribution of FDI in the NIEs and Japan. However, compared with US firms, the share of small and medium firms in total investing firms is significantly higher for Japan.

ASEAN: an increasingly attractive recipient of FDI
It was shown earlier that inward FDI in ASEAN on a balance of payments basis increased remarkably towards the end of the 1980s.[2] The same observation may be made from the statistics on an approval basis (Table 21.3). As a source of FDI in ASEAN, the NIEs expanded rapidly in importance. In 1990 Japan was the largest investor in Thailand, but in other ASEAN countries — Malaysia, Indonesia and the Philippines — the NIEs were the largest investors. Even in Thailand, the amount of Japanese FDI was only slightly greater than that of the NIEs.

This paper has already discussed the factors in investing countries — Japan and the NIEs — that led to active FDI in the ASEAN countries. As for the factors in the ASEAN countries that attracted FDI, it is important to point out the change in trade and FDI policies from inward-oriented to outward-oriented ones. For example, in order to expand exports, export-processing zones where preferential tax treatment is applied to attract FDI have been established in some ASEAN countries. The shift from the inward-looking policies to outward-looking ones such as export and FDI promotion policies by the ASEAN countries appears to have been prompted by the successful experiences of outward-oriented policies of the NIEs.

By sector, the increase in FDI is noticeable in manufacturing, hotels, commerce, and other services. Although there are substantial differences among ASEAN countries, in manufacturing, the electrical and chemical sectors attracted significant FDI in these countries. In recent years, automobiles and automobile parts sectors have experienced an increase in FDI. This is mainly due to the increased demand for automobiles in ASEAN resulting from economic development. Since the automobile market in ASEAN is virtually closed to imports because of strict protection, FDI is the only means foreign producers have of serving the local market.

FDI and economic development

The impact of FDI inflow on host countries

The impact of FDI on host countries varies widely among Asian countries. For example, the ratios of FDI to domestic capital formation are quite different among the NIEs, ASEAN and China. In 1990 Singapore and Malaysia recorded high ratios of 36.6 and 21.2 per cent, respectively, while Korea registered a significantly lower ratio of 0.8 per cent. For other countries, the ratios are between 2.5 per cent (Indonesia) and 8.3 per cent (Thailand) (International Monetary Fund 1991a, 1991b). These differences in the importance of FDI in domestic capital formation are mainly attributable to the differences in the policies towards FDI in these countries.

Table 21.3 Inward foreign direct investment in ASEAN and China from Japan, NIEs, United States, and the world, 1987–90

Recipient		Japan		NIEs		United States		World
		Millions of US dollars	Share of world total	Millions of US dollars	Share of world total	Millions of US dollars	Share of world total	Millions of US dollars
Malaysia	1987	284	34.7	236	28.9	65	7.9	818
	1988	467	25.1	607	32.6	204	11.0	1 863
	1989	993	31.1	1 335	41.8	119	3.7	3 194
	1990	657	28.5	1 100	47.8	69	3.0	2 302
Thailand	1987	965	36.6	501	19.0	172	6.5	2 634
	1988	3 045	48.7	1 684	26.9	673	10.8	6 249
	1989	3 524	44.1	2 011	25.2	550	6.9	7 996
	1990	2 706	33.7	2 696	33.6	1091	13.6	8 031
Philippines	1987	29	17.4	38	22.8	36	21.6	167
	1988	96	20.3	141	29.8	153	32.3	473
	1989	158	19.7	323	40.2	131	16.3	804
	1990	306	31.8	384	39.9	59	5.2	961
Indonesia	1987	532	36.5	172	11.8	73	5.0	1457
	1988	247	5.6	1 588	36.0	672	15.2	4 409
	1989	769	16.3	1 197	25.4	348	7.4	4 719
	1990	2 241	25.6	2 598	29.7	153	4.7	3 750
China	1987	220	9.5	1 620	70.0	263	11.4	2 314
	1988	515	16.1	2 123	66.5	236	7.4	3 194
	1989	356	10.5	2 162	63.7	284	8.4	3 393
	1990	503	14.4	1 963	56.3	456	13.1	3 487

Note: For Malaysia and Indonesia, approval data for manufacturing; for the Philippines and Indonesia, approval data for the whole sector; for China, executed data.

Source: Country official sources.

Singapore and Malaysia actively attracted FDI, while Korea limited FDI and relied on other means such as foreign borrowing and technology imports to obtain resources from foreign countries.

As for the impact of FDI on employment in host countries, Table 21.4 shows the magnitude of employment at all foreign subsidiaries and at Japanese subsidiaries in the Asian countries. The largest number of workers employed by foreign firms in Asia was in the Philippines, with more than half a million workers working for foreign firms there. The Philippines was followed by Korea at 416,000. Even the smallest number of employment at foreign firms, which was recorded in Hong Kong (only in manufacturing), was greater than 100,000. For the sample Asian countries as a whole, as many as 2 million workers were employed by foreign firms.

With respect to employment at Japanese subsidiaries, in 1988 the number of workers at Japanese subsidiaries in Asia amounted to 797,000, of which 685,000, or 86 per cent of the total were employed in manufacturing. By groups of countries, there were 456,000 workers at Japanese subsidiaries in the NIEs and 278,000 workers in ASEAN. The number of workers employed at the subsidiaries in the NIEs, ASEAN and China amounted to 764,000, or 96 per cent of total employment at Japanese subsidiaries in overall Asia. Among the NIEs, Korea and Taiwan held a large number of workers employed at Japanese firms, both recording approximately 170,000, while among the ASEAN countries, Thailand registered large employment at Japanese firms, amounting to 110,000 (Toyo Keizai Shinposha 1989).

The shares of exports by foreign firms in total exports are significantly higher than the corresponding shares for total sales in most of the sample countries, indicating the high export propensity of foreign firms (Table 21.5). This pattern is particularly notable in Singapore and in Malaysia, where foreign firms are credited with as large as 88 and 60 per cent of their respective manufactured exports. Following Singapore and Malaysia, the share of exports carried out by foreign firms in total exports is high for the Philippines, Korea, Indonesia, Taiwan and China, each registering a share greater than 10 per cent.

One apparent exception to the high export propensity of foreign firms is Thailand. In its case, the definitions of foreign firms (foreign affiliates) used in sales statistics and export statistics are different, making direct comparison difficult. The coverage of foreign firms for sales is wider than that for exports, leading to underestimation of the contribution of foreign affiliates in export sales.

Expansion of networks through FDI

Through FDI, host countries not only obtain resources such as financial capital and technology but also gain access to foreign firms' networks. For example, foreign subsidiaries may use marketing channels established by parent firms to export their products and to purchase intermediate goods as well as capital goods for their production. The contribution of foreign firms to the host economies in this respect is important, since establishing these networks entails enormous financial and human

Table 21.4   Employment at foreign subsidiaries in selected Asian countries

Country	Year	All foreign subsidiaries	Japanese subsidiaries (1988) Total	Manufacturing
Hong Kong	1988	108 032[a]	38 494	18 306
Taiwan	1986	266 837	171 851	166 424
Korea	1986	416 000	179 269	162 386
Singapore	1988	235 130	67 441	54 087
Malaysia	1988	251 823	70 324	57 456
Philippines	1982	502 835	36 183	24 414
Thailand	1985	182 635	109 831	96 115
Indonesia	na	na	61 611	52 257
China	na	na	28 775	21 283

Notes: na—Not available.
    a   Indicates manufacturing only.

Source: United Nations, *World Investment Directory 1992*, Vol. 1; and Toyo Keizai Shinposha (1989).

resources. This section examines the contribution of foreign firms to the host economies in expanding their sales and procurement networks. Because of data unavailability, analysis is confined to the case of Japanese firms, and where possible a comparison will be made to the practices of US firms.

The magnitude of sales and procurement by the Asian affiliates of Japanese manufacturing firms appeared to have increased substantially during the 1980s. Although accurate figures are not available, the sample surveys conducted by MITI (1991) indicate that manufacturing sales and procurement by these affiliates increased respectively from ¥6.1 trillion and ¥4.9 trillion in 1980 to ¥14.3 trillion and ¥11.6 trillion in 1989, indicating the expansion of sales and procurement networks of the host countries by the Japanese firms in Asia.

Turning to the changes in the destinations of the sales of the Asian affiliates in the 1980s, one finds that the share of exports in total sales remained the same, at 36.1 per cent. However, there is a notable shift in the export destinations towards Japan, as Japan's share in total manufacturing sales increased from 9.8 per cent in 1980 to 15.8 per cent in 1989. Export orientation intensified mainly in the machinery sectors over 1980–89. This tendency is particularly noticeable for the electrical machinery sector, where the export to total sales ratio increased from 48.4 per cent to 62.6 per cent over the period. The increase in the export to total sales ratio in the electrical machinery sector was attributable to rapid export expansion to the Japanese market, as the share of exports to Japan in total electrical machinery sales increased from 16.2 per cent in 1980 to 26.9 per cent in 1989. Other sectors that experienced a large increase in exports to Japan as a share in total sales include textiles, non-ferrous metals, general

Table 21.5   **Foreign firmsí manufacturing sector activities in host countries (percentage of overall activities)**

Host	Year	Employment	Sales	Exports
Korea	1986	9.5	21.5	29.0[a]
Hong Kong	1987	13.5[b]	17.5	na
Taiwan	1986	10.0	13.9	18.5
Singapore	1988	59.5	53.0	88.1
Malaysia	1988	48.7	44.8	59.6
Indonesia	1990	18.8	na	22.3[a]
Thailand	1986	8.8	48.6	5.8
Philippines	1987	27.3	40.8	34.7[a]
China	1990	0.1[a]	na	12.6[a]

Notes: na—Not available.
　　　　a   Values are for overall sectors.
　　　　b   1990 figure.

Source: United Nations, *World Investment Directory 1992*, Vol. 1; and estimates by the Sanwa Research Institute based on data from country sources.

machinery and precision machinery. Indeed, the exports from the affiliates of Japanese firms to Japan — or so-called 'reverse imports' from the viewpoint of Japan — are reported to have increased remarkably since the mid-1980s (JETRO 1990). The remarkable shift in export destinations towards Japan from the rest of the world is obviously due to the substantial yen appreciation. Furthermore, export-promotion policies by host country governments contributed to overall export expansion.

It is often asserted that expansion of exports to Japan from Asia was carried out mainly in the form of intra-firm trade; accordingly, exports to the 'closed' Japanese market are only possible through the use of Japanese distribution channels. Considering that the shares of exports by Japanese subsidiaries in total manufacturing exports from the NIEs and ASEAN to Japan are estimated to be 12.5 and 19.1 per cent respectively (see Hirata and Yokota 1991), this assertion appears to be rejected, despite the fact that the share of intra-firm trade in the Asian affiliates' exports to Japan was as high as 60 per cent. Although the importance of intra-firm trade in the Asian affiliates' exports to Japan declined substantially from 1986 to 1989, it is still much higher compared with cases in which products are sold in other markets.

An international comparison is useful to see if the Japanese firms' behaviour is exceptionally closed in their sales to the home market. Information necessary for such comparison is very limited and available only for the US firms for all affiliates (and not for those in Asia only). According to the US Department of Commerce (1990), the share of intra-firm trade in total manufacturing exports of the affiliates of US firms to the United States was 82.2 per cent in 1988, while the corresponding share for

Japanese firms in 1989 was 61.6 per cent. These findings indicate that US firms are more closed than Japanese firms in their export transactions. This is somewhat surprising because Japanese firms are frequently criticised for their close-minded business practices (Lawrence 1991). Several reasons may be noted for the high share of intra-firm trade for US firms. One is a special arrangement that the US government imposes tariffs only on the value added portion of imported products when the components used for the production at foreign affiliates are exported from the parents. This arrangement promotes intra-firm trade. Another reason may be that US imports from their foreign affiliates are more technology intensive than the Japanese counterparts, leading to high intra-firm trade for US trade, thereby avoiding market imperfections often associated with technology.

What appears to be most important for the host countries is the fact that exports are carried out, and not so much which channels of exports are used. Indeed, it is the consumers — in this case consumers in home countries — who are adversely affected by the closed channels.

Before closing the discussion on the sales pattern of foreign affiliates, it is worthwhile examining whether foreign affiliates of Japanese firms are more export oriented than those of US firms, an issue which has often been debated. Lack of information on the sales behaviour of Asian affiliates of US firms precludes comparison of the behaviour of Asian affiliates of US and Japanese firms. Instead, I compare the behaviour of all affiliates. For manufacturing, the export propensity of all affiliates of Japanese firms in 1989 was 20.6 per cent, while the corresponding value for the US firms in 1988 was significantly higher, at 37 per cent. From these findings it is clear that the affiliates of US firms have a higher propensity to export than those of Japanese firms in general. This result is extraordinary. However, before providing a conclusive statement, more careful comparison is needed, taking into account factors such as areas of operation, sectoral distribution, and length of operation.

I now turn to the pattern of procurement of intermediate goods by the Asian affiliates of Japanese firms. For the manufacturing sector, the ratio of local to total procurement increased from 42.2 per cent in 1980 to 49.8 per cent in 1989, resulting in lower dependency on foreign supply. Considering that there is a positive correlation between the length of operation and dependence on local supply, because it takes time to develop local procurement networks, and given also that a large number of Asian affiliates have a short history, one would conclude that the local supply ratio for the Asian affiliates established before the 1980s increased substantially in that decade. Over 1980–89 most of the manufacturing subsectors experienced an increase in the local-supply ratio as a result of an increase in the capacity as well as improvement in the capability of local firms in the production of intermediate goods. One exception was the electrical machinery sector, whose local-supply ratio declined over the same period. This may have been due to the physical and also the technological inability of local producers of intermediate goods to catch up with rapidly growing demand resulting from active FDI as well as rapidly advancing technological progress in that industry.

Among the foreign supply sources for the Asian affiliates, Japan has been most important. In particular, dependence on Japan for intermediate goods was high for the four machinery sectors and iron and steel, both relying on Japan for more than 40 per cent of total procurement. Coupled with the observation that the export to total sales ratio is high for electrical and precision machinery, high foreign-supply ratios for these sectors indicate that intra-industry trade, probably inter-process trade, is taking place in these sectors. Moreover, a large increase in the share of other Asian firms in sales as well as procurement in the electronics industry indicates that intra-Asia trade in electronic components expanded in the 1980s.

Intra-firm trade for the Asian affiliates of Japanese firms is more important for procurement than for sales. The share of intra-firm trade in total procurement is particularly high in procurement from parent firms in Japan. This may be understandable, as a large portion of parts and components are often produced according to specific designs shared with parent firms. It may be important, however, to point out that the importance of intra-firm procurement declined in the 1980s, leading to more open trading practices.

Finally, it is interesting to note that intra-firm trade in the procurement from the home country is significantly higher for affiliates of the US firms, compared with affiliates of Japanese firms. Concerning procurement for overall sectors, as high as 92.9 per cent of imports from the United States by the Asian affiliates are conducted in the form of intra-firm trade, while the corresponding figure for the Asian affiliates of Japanese firms is significantly lower, at 63.2 per cent in 1989. These observations once again point to the 'closed' behaviour of the US firms. Here, the same explanations apply as used with regard to the high intra-firm export ratio for the US subsidiaries earlier.

Conclusions

The substantial realignment of the currencies of the Asian countries precipitated FDI in the region in the mid-1980s. Japan and the NIEs actively undertook FDI, while the NIEs and ASEAN countries received FDI hungrily. Through FDI, Japan and the NIEs achieved industrial adjustment by relocating overseas the industries and production processes that had lost comparative advantage at home. At the same time, the NIEs attempted to promote high-tech industries by attracting FDI. By contrast, the ASEAN countries and China pursued industrialisation by attracting FDI mainly from Japan and the NIEs. Since the flow of FDI was accelerated as a result of liberalisation of trade regimes, the pattern of production in Asia realised by relocating production facilities through FDI appears to be more or less consistent with the pattern of comparative advantage of the countries in the region.

FDI contributed to economic development of host countries not only by promoting capital formation, production and employment, but also by upgrading technological capability through technology transfer. In addition, FDI contributed to export expansion by involving the host country in the sales networks of the parent firms. FDI also contributed to upgrading the industrial structure of the home countries, as relocation of industries losing comparative advantage was carried out through rationalisation and diversification in the home countries.

Notes

1   Among the NIEs, the patterns of FDI for Korea and Taiwan are analysed, respectively, by Lee and Ramstetter (1991) and Shive and Tu (1991).

2   Pangestu (1991) and Tambunlertchai and Ramstetter (1991) examine the cases of FDI in Indonesia and Thailand, respectively.

References

Hirata, Akira and Kazuhiko Yokota 1991, 'Hattentojokoku eno eikyo' [The Impact on Developing Countries], in Ippei Yamazawa and Akira Hirata (eds), *Senshinshokoku no Sangyochosei to Hattentojokoku* [Industrial Adjustment in Developed Countries and Developing Countries], Tokyo: Institute of Developing Economies, pp. 93–112.

International Monetary Fund 1991a, *International Financial Statistics Yearbook 1991*, Washington, DC: International Monetary Fund.

—————— 1991b, *Balance of Payments Statistics Yearbook 1991*, Washington, DC: International Monetary Fund.

Japan Development Bank 1991, *Chosa* [Research], No. 151, July.

JETRO (Japan External Trade Organization) 1990, *White Paper on International Trade*, Tokyo (in Japanese).

Lawrence, Robert Z. 1991, 'How open is Japan?', in Paul Krugman (ed.), *Trade with Japan*, Chicago: University of Chicago Press, pp. 9–37.

Lee, Chung H. and Eric D. Ramstetter 1991, 'Direct investment and structural change in Korean manufacturing', in Eric A. Ramstetter (ed.), *Direct Foreign Investment in Asia's Developing Economies and Structural Change in the Asia–Pacific Region*, Boulder, Co.: Westview Press, pp. 105–41.

MITI (Ministry of International Trade and Industry) 1991, *Kaigai Toshi Tokei Soran* [Statistics on Foreign Investment], No. 4, Tokyo.

Pangestu, Mari 1991 'Foreign firms and structural change in the Indonesian manufacturing sector', in Eric A. Ramstetter (ed.), *Direct Foreign Investment in Asia's Developing Economies and Structural Change in the Asia–Pacific Region*, Boulder, Co.: Westview Press, pp. 35–64.

Ramstetter, Eric D. (ed.) 1991, *Direct Foreign Investment in Asia's Developing Economies and Structural Change in the Asia–Pacific Region*, Boulder, Co.: Westview Press.

Shive, Chi and Jenn-Hwa Tu 1991, 'Foreign firms and structural change in Taiwan', in Eric A. Ramstetter (ed.), *Direct Foreign Investment in Asia's Developing Economies and Structural Change in the Asia–Pacific Region*, Boulder, Co.: Westview Press, pp. 142–71.

Tambunlertchai, Somsak and Eric D. Ramstetter 1991, 'Foreign firms in promoted industries and structural change in Thailand', in Eric A. Ramstetter (ed.), *Direct Foreign Investment in*

Asia's Developing Economies and Structural Change in the Asia–Pacific Region, Boulder, Co.: Westview Press, pp. 65–102.

Toyo Keizai Shinposha 1989, *Kaigai Shinshutsukigyo Soran* [Statistics on Foreign Subsidiaries], Tokyo: Toyo Keizai Shinposha.

Urata, Shujiro 1991, 'Globalization of Japanese electronics industry and its impact on foreign trade in electronics products', Paper prepared for OECD Development Centre project on Regionalisation and Globalisation, Paris, February.

US Department of Commerce 1990, *U.S. Foreign Direct Investment Abroad, Preliminary 1988 Estimates*, Washington, DC.

Part Six

Regionalism in the Americas

22 Implications of NAFTA for US trade policy in the Pacific Basin

Jeffrey J. Schott and Gary C. Hufbauer

US trade and the Pacific Basin

If one looks at the geographic pattern of US trade, it is clear that it does not have a regional focus. As shown in Table 22.1, the Pacific Basin accounts for about 35 per cent of total US trade, with the US regional partners in North America accounting for 26 per cent and Western Europe for 24 per cent. Shares of US exports are fairly evenly divided between the Pacific Basin (29 per cent), North America (28 per cent), and Europe (27 per cent); while shares of US imports are skewed more towards the Pacific Basin (40 per cent). Not surprisingly, the Pacific Basin is the region with which the United States runs a large trade deficit.

Table 22.2 breaks down US trade with the Pacific Basin by country. US–Japan trade dominates the regional total, accounting for 44 per cent of total US trade with Pacific Basin countries. Taiwan and China combined represent another 20 per cent. Japan, China and Taiwan together account for almost 90 per cent of the US deficit with the region, which in 1991 reached US$80.6 billion (compared with a global US trade deficit of US$87.5 billion).

One can draw three relatively simple policy conclusions from Tables 22.1 and 22.2. First, the United States has global trading interests; it thus has a big stake in maintaining and increasing access to overseas markets, and depends importantly on the multilateral trading system to both safeguard existing access to foreign markets and to promote further trade liberalisation.

Second, concerns about the United States refocusing its trade priorities towards the Western Hemisphere under the Enterprise for the Americas Initiative are exaggerated. US trade with North and South America combined only accounts for

Table 22.1   US regional trading partners, 1991

Country/ region	Share of total US trade (%)	US exports		US imports		Balance (US$ billions)
		US$ billions	%	US$ billions	%	
North America[a]	26.2	118.4	28.1	125.6	24.7	-7.2
Europe[b]	23.6	115.6	27.4	104.2	20.5	11.4
Latin America[c]	6.9	30.2	7.2	33.9	6.7	-3.7
Pacific Basin[d]	34.8	121.5	28.8	202.1	39.7	-80.6
Rest of world	8.5	36.0	8.5	43.4	8.5	-7.4
World total	100.0	421.8	100.0	509.3	100.0	-87.5

Notes: a   Canada and Mexico.
      b   EC and EFTA.
      c   Excludes Mexico.
      d   For country coverage, see Table 22.2.

Source: IMF, *Direction of Trade Statistics Yearbook,* 1992.

one-third of total US exports and imports, and it would take a substantial increase in the volume of US trade with its hemispheric neighbours to match its trade with Pacific Basin countries. Moreover, unlike Canada and Mexico, few countries or groups of countries in Latin America trade predominantly with the United States or even with their own neighbours; European and other foreign markets account for a significant share of their exports.[1] So global objectives also dominate in Latin America.

Third, US trade policy will continue to focus on the Pacific Basin, if for no other reason than the large US bilateral trade deficit. While bilateral deficits are not a good guide for economic policy, they are a leading indicator of current and potential trade friction. The large bilateral deficits with Japan, China and Taiwan will continue to generate protectionist pressures and market-opening demands by the United States with a strong regional flavour. Relations with China will also be coloured by human rights issues, GATT accession issues, and efforts to impose preemptive restrictions against Chinese exports of textiles and apparel.

NAFTA: Implications for US–Pacific Basin trade

To understand the implications of NAFTA for US trade with Pacific Basin countries, it is worth first assessing the accord in broad terms and highlighting those areas where the accord is likely to make a significant difference in existing opportunities for Pacific Basin countries to trade in the North American market. In many areas, NAFTA merely codifies the preferences already accorded to Mexican firms in the US market;

Table 22.2   US trade with the Pacific Basin, 1991

Country/region	Share of total US trade (%)	US exports		US imports		Balance (US$ billions)
		US$ billions	%	US$ billions	%	
World total	100.0	421.8	100.0	509.3	100.0	-87.5
Pacific Basin total	34.8	121.5	28.8	202.1	39.7	-80.6
Australia and New Zealand	1.6	9.4	2.2	5.6	1.1	3.8
Japan	15.4	48.1	11.4	95.0	18.7	-46.9
People's Republic of China	2.9	6.3	1.5	20.3	4.0	-14.0
Hong Kong	1.9	8.1	1.9	9.7	1.9	-1.6
Republic of Korea	3.6	15.5	3.7	17.7	3.5	-2.2
Chinese Taipei (Taiwan)	4.0	13.2	3.1	24.2	4.8	-11.0
Brunei Darussalam	0.0	0.2	0.0	0.0	0.0	0.1
Indonesia	0.6	1.9	0.4	3.6	0.7	-1.17
Malaysia	1.0	3.9	0.9	5.5	1.1	-1.6
Philippines	0.6	2.3	0.5	3.7	0.7	-1.4
Singapore	2.0	8.8	2.1	10.2	2.0	-1.4
Thailand	1.1	3.8	0.9	6.5	1.3	-2.7
ASEAN total	5.4	20.8	4.9	29.5	5.8	-8.7

Source: US Department of Commerce, 'US Merchandise Trade: December 1991', FT-900 (91–12), Exhibit 8; IMF, *Direction of Trade Statistics Yearbook,* 1992.

but, in a few sectors, the agreement may divert trade from Pacific Basin and other suppliers to the North American market.

First, it is important to emphasise that NAFTA is designed to make it harder for foreign firms to compete in the North American market — *not* because of higher barriers against third-country trade, but because of the heightened competitiveness of North American firms. As with the internal market reforms in the European Community pursuant to the 1992 process, NAFTA should promote more efficient use of natural and human resources in North America, and thus enable regional firms and workers to compete more effectively against foreign suppliers both at home and in world markets (see Hufbauer and Schott 1992a).

That said, NAFTA can be best characterised as a new, improved trilateral version of the Canada–US Free Trade Agreement. In large part, the agreement involves commitments by Mexico to trade and investment reforms comparable to those undertaken by the United States and Canada in their bilateral free trade agreement. But NAFTA goes even further, by augmenting unfinished business from the Canada–US Free Trade Agreement, including coverage of intellectual property protection; rules against distortions to investment (local content and export performance requirements); and transportation services.

NAFTA provisions provide for the phased elimination of tariff and most non-tariff barriers affecting US–Mexico and Canada–Mexico trade within ten years, although the liberalisation schedule is extended to fifteen years for a few import-sensitive sectors. In addition, NAFTA extends the innovative dispute settlement procedures of the free trade agreement to Mexico (in return for a substantial revamping of Mexican trade laws that injects more transparency into the administrative process and brings Mexican antidumping and other procedures closer to those of the United States and Canada); contains precedent-setting rights and obligations regarding services and investment; and takes an important first step in addressing cross-border environmental issues.

What impact, if any, will NAFTA have on the trade of the United States with countries in the Pacific Basin? To judge the 'additionality' of NAFTA, one needs first to understand the current state of US–Mexican trade relations, and the size and scope of the prospective changes in market access afforded by the trade pact.

To a large extent, North America has had a large integrated trading bloc for many years: it is called the United States! The US economy represents 85 per cent of the combined output of the North American economies, and 70 per cent of the combined population. Access to the US market by Canadian firms has been relatively open because of low MFN rates, the Auto Pact, and the Canada–US Free Trade Agreement.

Moreover, Mexico already enjoys relatively unfettered access to the US market as a result of recent quota expansion in textiles and steel, and generous tariff preferences under the GSP and in-bond duty drawback programs. Approximately 60 per cent of Mexican exports already enter the United States duty free. And, when imposed, effective tariff rates are generally low; for example, the average US tariff on textiles and apparel imports from Mexico is in the 6 to 8 per cent range. In addition, most quotas are not binding, although some important product categories in apparel are restricted.

Note that the main access problems in the US market are in agriculture, especially fruits and vegetables. However, even in this area, NAFTA contains notable liberalisation commitments. In particular, the accord immediately converts almost all of the major agricultural restrictions to tariff-rate quotas, provides for 3 per cent annual growth in the quotas, and sets a maximum fifteen-year period for the phase-out of the tariff surcharges — an impressive achievement considering the dismal track record of other trade talks in reducing long-standing farm trade barriers. While there is scope for trade diversion in some products (such as beef, sugar and orange juice) of interest to Pacific Basin and Latin American suppliers, the protracted liberalisation schedule is back-end loaded. By the time Mexican or US producers actually receive preferences in each other's market, the competitive climate will likely already be influenced by GATT reforms that are expected to be implemented over a faster timetable.

What this means for Pacific Basin suppliers to the North American market is that, in most cases, NAFTA preferences will not erode their markets to any significant degree. Existing barriers to the US market are quite low. The margin between the MFN rate that third countries pay, and the preferential (zero) rate applied under the free trade agreement, is very small in most sectors

Moreover, concerns about investment diversion are also to a large extent exaggerated, since pressures often arise within a free trade agreement to reduce MFN tariff rates down to the level of the low tariff country in the region to avoid potential investment diversion *within* the region. Martin Richardson (1993) provides two explanations for this behaviour. First, because of the threat of investment diversion, pressures build in high-tariff countries to reduce their MFN rates so as not to lose production to areas that charge lower duties on imported components.[2] Second, as free trade agreement preferences are phased in, less competitive industries will contract and thus over time lose political influence to lobby for the maintenance of high external tariffs. The combined result is continued support for multilateral trade liberalisation, despite its eroding effect on regional preferences.

Nonetheless, industry-specific rules of origin in NAFTA may pose problems for Pacific Basin countries. In those areas, traditional transformation tests (that establish domestic origin if local processing of the product results in a change in its tariff classification) have now been encumbered by complex value-added tests and/or arcane requirements that products not be contaminated by key components sourced abroad. NAFTA contains 193 pages on rules of origin, a clear indication that this issue has enjoyed a prolonged political massage. Moreover, the interpretation of these rules of origin will remain susceptible to political manipulation.

While in most sectors NAFTA adopts the traditional change in tariff heading approach, it institutes a hybrid approach in two industry sectors — textiles and autos — that is substantially more restrictive than other trade pacts, including the Canada–US Free Trade Agreement. In textiles, the agreement establishes a triple transformation test which makes the already protectionist rule of origin for textiles in the Canada–US Free Trade Agreement seem quite liberal by comparison. For most products, NAFTA establishes a 'yarn forward' rule, which requires an item to be produced from yarn made in a NAFTA country to qualify for regional preferences; otherwise, the high MFN barriers apply. Moreover, the intense lobbying that prompted these restrictive NAFTA rules likely presages the industry's counterattack against the proposed global reform of the MFA in the Uruguay Round of GATT negotiations.

As noted above, however, Mexico already benefits from extensive preferences. Over time, these have probably diverted some trade and investment from other areas into Mexico (primarily in the maquiladora sector). Compared with Mexican (and more recently Caribbean) companies, Pacific Basin suppliers have been discriminated against for some time; NAFTA makes their competitive position in the North American market marginally worse.

In autos, NAFTA adopts a net cost approach for origin calculations, which is an administrative improvement. However, the NAFTA value added test (62.5 per cent for autos, light trucks, engines, and transmissions; 60 per cent for other vehicles and parts) is much higher than (and supercedes) the 50 per cent requirement of the Canada–US Free Trade Agreement. Furthermore, NAFTA also includes tracing requirements for key components to ensure that engines, transmissions, and a long list of other specified parts meet the new content requirements (and to eliminate so-called 'roll-up' abuses). Together these rules substantially raise the overall local content requirements for automotive products.

Nonetheless, the restrictive origin rules for autos apply only if a producer wants to avoid MFN trade barriers, which for the United States are quite low (2.5 per cent for autos, 3.1 per cent on average for auto parts, but 25 per cent for light trucks), are a bit higher for Canada (9.1 per cent), but remain an important obstacle to the Mexican market (20 per cent for autos; 13.2 per cent for parts) along with a spate of other non-tariff barriers. As a practical matter, NAFTA will likely block access to the rapidly growing but still small Mexican auto market for foreign companies that do not meet the strict origin requirements, but will have only a small impact on their ability to sell in the much larger US and Canadian markets.

Impact of NAFTA on US trade policy towards the Pacific Basin

We believe that the United States will continue to pursue *complementary* global and regional trade initiatives, for one simple reason: in recent years, net exports of goods and services have been a major contributor to US economic growth. Trade balance improvement since 1986 has provided about 30 per cent of total US growth; and the recent recession would have been much deeper without the sustained export expansion (see Bergsten 1992, pp. 4–5). Mexico has been America's fastest growing export market, with shipments increasing from US$12.4 billion in 1986 to US$33 billion in 1991 (and running at an annual rate of about US$42 billion in 1992).

Given the constraints on US fiscal policy, the United States will perforce have to continue during the next few years at least the export-led growth strategy that has prevailed since the Plaza Accord of September 1985. This means that US trade policy will continue to be outward-oriented, so there will be little risk of 'fortress North America' or even 'fortress Western Hemisphere'.

Uruguay Round trade reforms could yield large long-term dividends for the US economy: the Council of Economic Advisers estimate that US GNP would be 3 per cent higher in the year 2000 than it otherwise would be, and that cumulative US income gains over the decade would total US$1.1 trillion (see *Economic Report of the President*, 1991).

At the same time, the United States will continue to promote the liberalisation of foreign trade barriers to US goods and services through a variety of bilateral and regional initiatives. We regard such efforts as complementary to US global objectives.

With a strong and effective multilateral trading system, regional initiatives can complement GATT reforms in several ways:

- they tend to be trade-creating since regional partnerships usually generate positive income effects that outweigh the adverse effects of the trade discrimination;

- they tend to broaden and deepen GATT trade reforms so that regional industries can take better advantage of new trading opportunities around the globe; and

- they can serve as models for strengthening multilateral disciplines (for example, the provisions of the Canada–US and Australia–New Zealand free trade agreements on services).

In most respects, regional integration reinforces existing multilateral disciplines, and provides building blocks for new global accords. Regional integration in North America should complement multilateral liberalisation and provide useful precedents (with a few notable exceptions, particularly with regard to rules of origin) for integration efforts throughout the Western Hemisphere. Indeed, the NAFTA incorporates rights and obligations comparable to — and in some ways better than — those already developed in the Uruguay Round (especially in services, intellectual property and investment).

NAFTA thus presages a continuation of bilateral and regional trade initiatives. Rather than characterise NAFTA as the 'model' for future pacts, however, it may be more accurate to say that it sets the core agenda for future trade negotiations between the United States and other countries. While we would have preferred the NAFTA to be the vehicle for the accession of other countries to a common set of rights and obligations (Hufbauer and Schott 1992a, ch. 2), too many of the industry-specific provisions were designed without reference to their possible extension to additional countries.

NAFTA does include a vague accession clause. However, the three governments merely state that 'any country or group of countries may accede to this Agreement subject to such terms and conditions as may be agreed between such country or countries and the Commission and following approval in accordance with the applicable approval procedures in each country'. In addition, NAFTA contains a 'non-application' provision that allows existing members to deny new members at the time of their accession the benefits of NAFTA in their market without blackballing the candidate country or countries entirely from the club. As crafted, the accession clause has several interesting features:

- it provides for a one-country veto of prospective new members since all three legislatures must act before new members can join the club;

- the accession negotiations will be conducted by the NAFTA Commission (comprising all existing members), which presumably will act by consensus;

- nevertheless, any member is free to form its own network of free trade agreements with other countries that do not wish to join NAFTA or are blackballed; and

- it does not include geographic limitations on the eligibility of candidate countries.

The absence of geographic limitations on the accession clause is perhaps its most notable feature. The scope of potential partners was left open by design to avoid accusations that NAFTA was seeking to build a hemispheric 'fortress'. In principle, accession is open to all countries, including important Asian trading countries such as Japan and Korea. In practice, the US Congress is unlikely to provide the US Executive Branch the authority to negotiate free trade agreements with such powerful competitors, thus limiting the prospects for large East Asian nations to join NAFTA in the near future.

Indeed, the prospects for new free trade agreement negotiations between the United States (or NAFTA as a whole) with any country or group of countries are remote in the near term, because such negotiations would require the renewal of fast-track authority in US trade law. Support for renewal of fast-track authority (particularly for bilateral or regional negotiations) does not command strong support in the Congress; President Clinton will have to spend substantial political capital to obtain new authority. Moreover, as the Congressional debate in the (northern) spring of 1991 over extension of US fast-track authority demonstrated, Congress will likely insist that US negotiators come to future trade negotiations with an increasingly broad non-trade agenda, including labour and environmental issues, and foreign policy issues (such as democratic rule and human rights enforcement) as a condition for the further extension of fast-track authority in 1993 (see Gephardt 1992).

Conclusions

We conclude with some reflections on near-term prospects for US–Pacific Basin trade relations.

US–Japan relations

US–Japan trade issues will continue to dominate US policy-making towards the Pacific Basin. Since the fundamental solution to the bilateral friction (macroeconomic imbalances) is not in sight, trade policy will continue to be used as a channel to vent the frustration of politicians who want to 'do something' about the Japan problem, but refuse to do what needs to be done.

Bilateral talks will focus on highly contentious issues regarding basic aspects of the Japanese system of capitalism, including: the strong cross-buying relationships corresponding both to cross-ownership ties and to established loyalties between major firms and their subcontractors; the relatively closed distribution system; and the designation of targeted industries. The United States will likely follow three approaches to managing the bilateral trade frictions generated by these practices: change Japan, copy Japan, and protect against Japan.

The first approach involves trying to change Japan; this was the motive behind the SII talks. The SII, started in 1989, focused on six Japanese issues identified as structural barriers to trade: exclusionary business practices, the *keiretsu* system, savings–investment patterns, pricing disparities, the closed distribution system, and high land prices. It also took the United States to task for its outsized budget deficit, its high consumer debt, and the weaknesses in its educational system. By all accounts, the SII talks have so far yielded a modest harvest of results.

The second approach is to copy Japan. This would involve, for example, relaxing US antitrust laws, providing research and development subsidies, and, in the extreme case, creating a US copy of the vaunted MITI. This approach so far has a limited following because it entails an unnaturally activist role for the US government.

The third approach is to accept the Japanese system for what it is, and try to insulate the United States from its effects. This is the approach advocated by those who contemplate a policy of managed trade that would guarantee approximately fixed shares of the Japanese market for US firms (the shares would be determined by reference to the Japanese share of the US market). The Semiconductor Accord that guarantees foreign producers a 20 per cent share of the Japanese market exemplifies this approach.

Each of these approaches poses risks for US relations with Pacific Basin countries. The first approach is the most benign, but still raises the prospect that many developing countries will be excluded from the negotiating table; the emulation approach compounds the trade and investment distortions generated by the Japanese practices; and the managed trade approach poses substantial risks for the multilateral trading system. In short, we believe that Pacific Basin countries will be sideswiped by US–Japan trade frictions.

US–China relations

Perhaps an even greater source of tension within the Pacific Basin, however, will be the deteriorating relations between the United States and China. US–Chinese trade has been subject to draconian import controls by China in the late 1980s, to trade sanctions following the Tiananmen Square massacre in 1989, to hot-and-cold negotiations regarding GATT accession, and to annual efforts by the US Congress to rescind MFN treatment for Chinese goods because of human rights concerns. The huge bilateral trade imbalance is only the tip of the iceberg; political and foreign policy concerns also colour bilateral relations.

Most of the US–China frictions will linger, and create problems for Pacific Basin relations as well. The United States will seek ways to continue to discriminate against China, both in bilateral relations and in the GATT, until its political regime becomes more democratic and its overall economy more market-oriented. Efforts to remove MFN could well be replaced by more narrowly targeted import controls pursuant to

Super 301 retaliatory authority that is likely to be reinstated in US trade law. China's accession to GATT will be clouded by parallel efforts by Taiwan (that receive strong US support) and by invocation of GATT Article XVII provisions that discriminate against non-market economies.

US–China tensions will complicate efforts to develop regional trade and investment initiatives within APEC. Because of ongoing US–China tensions, sights will need to be set lower; as a journey of a thousand miles begins with a single step, regional efforts will likely focus first on very discrete projects and consultative arrangements among governments.

Prospects for regional trade arrangements

Proposals for the negotiation of free trade agreements between the United States and East Asian countries were revived during the 1992 US election campaign. However, we regard these pronouncements more as a long-term vision than a near-term event. Congress is less than enamoured by the prospect of new free trade agreements; hence, the extension of fast-track authority to negotiate such agreements is likely to be put off for a while.

However, there is an even more fundamental reason why the bilateral and regional free trade agreement agenda is likely to be delayed. Simply put, few countries in the Western Hemisphere (and Eastern Europe) are ready to negotiate a *reciprocal* free trade agreement comparable to the pact initialled by Mexico (see Hufbauer and Schott 1992b). And for those Pacific Basin countries ready and willing to negotiate, the Congress is likely to up the ante of concessions demanded in a variety of trade and non-trade areas that may make the deal offered to Mexico seem generous by comparison.

At the same time, we do not see the development of broad regional trade arrangements in the Pacific Basin without the participation of the United States. There is little incentive for Asian countries to create their own trade cocoon: even though the volume of intra-regional trade has grown sharply over the past decade, too much of their trade still spans the Pacific for them to seriously contemplate crafting a regional bloc (see Frankel 1991). Recent efforts by the ASEAN countries to create a long-awaited free trade area are modest, with meaningful steps not scheduled for a decade or longer. Malaysia's attempt to rally support for an East Asian regional grouping has been generally regarded as politically motivated and without economic logic.

In sum, we believe that — over the near to medium term — a Pacific Basin free trade agreement comprising all APEC members is clearly beyond the pale; so, too, are more limited efforts to construct a Pacific Area OECD-like organisation. Rather, we are likely to see continued US efforts to cooperate on regional projects under the APEC umbrella, to negotiate framework agreements to improve consultations on trade and investment issues, and to coordinate approaches to multilateral trade reforms in the GATT.

This outlook lacks the sweeping vision of the Holy Roman Empire, or, on a more mundane scale, the Bretton Woods system. But just as the EC is discovering the practical virtues of multiple speeds and variable geometry, so should the Pacific Basin countries realise that, in the 1990s, different issues will be addressed among different groups of partner countries, according to different timetables.

Notes

1   Both Chile and the Mercosur countries export more to the EC than to the United States; and for those countries for which the United States is the predominant export market (the Andean Pact, Central American and Caricom countries), shipments to the EC still outweigh exports to regional neighbours.

2   This concern was evident in resisting a restrictive NAFTA origin rule for computers, and requiring a common external tariff after the ten-year transition period.

References

Bergsten, C. Fred 1992, 'The primacy of economics', *Foreign Policy*, No. 87, Summer, pp. 3–24.

Frankel, Jeffrey A. 1991, 'Is a yen bloc forming in Pacific Asia?', in Richard O'Brien (ed.), *Finance and the International Economy: 5*, London: Oxford University Press, for the Amex Bank Review.

Gephardt, Richard 1992, 'Address on the Status of the North American Free Trade Agreement before the Institute for International Economics', 27 July (processed).

Hufbauer, Gary Clyde and Jeffrey J. Schott 1992a, *North American Free Trade: Issues and Recommendations*, Washington, DC: Institute for International Economics.

_____ 1992b, 'Western Hemisphere economic integration: subregional building blocks', Paper prepared for the Inter-American Development Bank, September (processed).

Richardson, Martin 1993, 'Endogenous protection and trade diversion', *Journal of International Economics*, 34 (3/4) May, pp. 309–24.

23 Is the United States bowing out of Asia?

Peter A. Petri

US–East Asian economic relations have changed dramatically in the last fifteen years. Once dominated by US technology and capital, the market-oriented economies of the Asia Pacific region have become formidable competitors to US industry. East Asia's intra-regional trade, investment, and aid flows have surpassed similar linkages with the United States. In addition, the collapse of communism has rendered obsolete one of the principal tenets of the US–East Asian political relationship. Will these changes spell the end of the close economic relationship between the United States and East Asia? Has in fact the United States already begun to shift its attention away from the Pacific, ceding regional leadership to Japan?

Some indicators of weakening US–East Asian ties include a recent decrease in the share of the United States in foreign investment in East Asia, an increase in the importance of Japanese exports and aid flows to East Asia, and a perceived decline in US influence in the region due to diminished aid flows and growing trade friction. In the realm of trade policy, recent US initiatives have focused on Latin America rather than East Asia, and at least one widely discussed Asian integration proposal — Malaysian Prime Minister Mahathir's East Asian Economic Group (or Caucus) — has excluded the United States. The impression of a declining US role in the region has triggered widespread criticism of US policies both within and outside the United States.[1]

This paper addresses the strength of US–East Asian economic linkages by looking at facts rather than perceptions — by examining recent economic trends in the broader historical context of Pacific economic linkages. It concludes that reports of the demise of a US role in Asia are exaggerated. US industry continues to export and invest actively in East Asia and is maintaining its economic role *vis-à-vis* other developed countries, including Japan. This steady and important role of the US in East

Asia is not widely recognised, and contrasts sharply with the more tumultuous political dimension of the relationship.

Theoretical issues in US–East Asian linkages

Bilateral economic linkages are certainly interesting to political scientists and historians, but should they also interest economists and policy-makers? Conventional economic theory recognises little of economic interest in the pattern of bilateral economic linkages, such as those between the United States and East Asia. In some key theoretical models, bilateral trade flows are at best due to accidents of the distribution of endowments, but are more likely to be simply indeterminate.[2] While such models provide a theoretical basis for determining each country's overall trade patterns, they cannot explain the allocation of trade across particular partners.

In fact, bilateral trade and investment patterns are far from randomly distributed and exhibit remarkable stability over time (Woytinsky and Woytinsky 1955). This suggests large, differential transactions costs across alternative bilateral linkages. A host of factors appear to be responsible for differential transactions costs, including transportation, communication and information costs associated with working with a particular partner. Since some of these costs involve high fixed investments (for instance, in obtaining information about a partner's reputation), the choice of a trading partner has serious, long-lasting implications for nations as well as firms. This is presumably why Lawrence (1992) has recently asked the question: 'Why would the United States follow a policy in which it gained access to Latin America while leaving Asia — the world's most dynamic region — to Japan?'

In a recent paper on the origins of East Asian trade (Petri 1993, also Chapter 10, this volume), I suggested a simple model of bloc formation to explain differences in the intensities of alternative bilateral relationships. In this model, the intensity of a bilateral relationship depends on bilateral transaction costs, which in turn tends to be low when economic or political reasons have caused countries to invest heavily in their linkages. Such investments may have taken the form of low-cost transport or communication channels, agreements that help to integrate goods or capital markets across the two economies, or the accumulation of information about potential partner companies and business opportunities. In effect, a bilateral contact paves the way for — has positive spillovers on — other bilateral contacts.

One implication of this theory is that 'historical accidents' that draw countries together may be amplified and perpetuated by the linkage investments that they induce. In the East Asian context, the First and Second World Wars were important in developing a strong economic relationship between the United States and the Asia Pacific region. Today, however, the region's rapid growth is making its economies loom increasingly important to each other. In the past, historical forces worked in favour of US–East Asian economic ties; today, historical forces are helping to strengthen relationships among East Asian countries themselves. As a result, we expect to find the advantage of the United States eroding relative to the region's own economies.

A second, and potentially more important, implication is that governments may have reason to intervene in shaping bilateral economic relationships. If externalities generated by bilateral economic contacts are significant, market forces may not lead to socially desirable outcomes. Governments may wish to subsidise such contacts in general (for example, by providing marketing information through a system of commercial attachès) or they may wish to tilt the outcome — the pattern of intensification of regional linkages — in favour of partner countries that offer attractive long-term markets. Some have argued that Japan's intensive Asian aid policies are playing precisely this role.

Without knowing the size of linkage externalities, it is not possible to provide specific prescriptions for bilateral trade policy. It is useful to check, however, whether the US linkages with East Asia are weakening compared to intra-East Asian linkages. A significant 'tipping' of East Asia's economic orientation away from the United States could suggest that new policy initiatives may be required to maintain US contacts with this exceptionally dynamic region of the world. The next sections therefore examine in some detail four specific dimensions of the US–East Asian relationship, covering both directions of trade and investment flows between the United States and East Asia.

East Asia as a market for US exports

In 1990 nearly one-third of US exports went to East Asia — 14.5 per cent to Japan and 17.5 per cent to other East Asian countries. As Figure 23.1 shows, this was essentially an historical record. While the United States has been keenly interested in East Asia since the nineteenth century, its linkages with the region did not intensify until after the First World War, when the United States took over markets previously held by Europe. During the war US exports to Asia rose fourfold, and shortly after the war there was unbridled optimism about Asian opportunities. As the Irving National Bank's (1919, pp. 8–12) pamphlet, *Trading with the Far East*, put it at the time:

> . . . the Far Eastern market is capable of almost unlimited expansion. Here are literally hundreds of millions of human beings — in China alone 400,000,000 — whose standards of living are wretchedly low . . . Asia needs capital, machinery and managing ability; she offers tremendous profits in exchange . . . And could any background be more splendid than the position we now occupy before the world? We went into the war with clean hands and came out of it in the same condition. Indemnities and territorial annexations and war plunder mean nothing to us. We fought in the interest of right and humanity, and the nations of the world are glad to credit us with just these motives. From now on, to be an American, to represent an American line of goods, to have the American nation behind you, will represent substantial selling value in almost any market of the world.

Figure 23.1   Composition of US exports

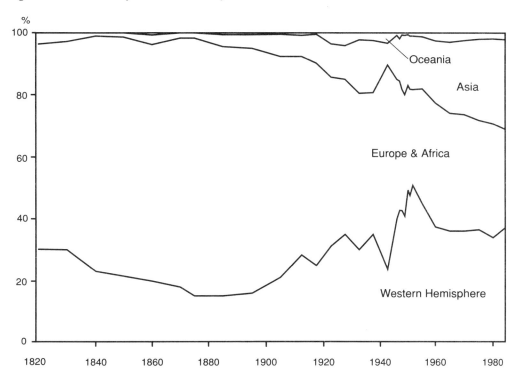

After the First World War, US exports to Asia continued to increase, particularly to Japan, until the Second World War disrupted normal trade patterns. US exports to Asia again rose sharply after that war, fuelled in part by rebuilding efforts, but at no time did Asia's share reach one-fifth of US exports.

The current role of East Asian markets in US exports is examined in Table 23.1. This table shows, in addition to export values, the share of US products in various markets. While the US holds 11.9 per cent of world export markets for manufactures, its market share in Japan is 29.7 per cent and in other East Asian countries 15.6 per cent. In this and other sectors the United States has captured a systematically higher share of the market in East Asia, and especially in Japan, than in other markets. Whatever concerns US traders may express about East Asian markets, these markets continue to play a central role in US international trade.

The penetration of East Asian markets is high across the full spectrum of products exported by the United States. The last two columns of Table 23.1 show trade intensity indexes for US exports to Asia — essentially the ratio of US market shares in Asia to US market shares worldwide.[3] These ratios are particularly high in intermediate goods sectors such as pulp and paper, chemicals and coal and oil

Table 23.1   Indicators of US exports to East Asia, 1990

Product	Sales to (US$m)			Market shares in (%)			Trade intensity indexes	
	World	E. Asia	Japan	World	E. Asia	Japan	E. Asia	Japan
Merchandise trade	362 418	63 535	52 700	11.5	15.8	22.8	1.4	2.0
Manufacturing by sector	307 663	54 387	38 996	11.9	15.6	29.7	1.3	2.5
Resource-based manufactures	44 281	8 736	10 753	9.5	17.2	27.9	1.8	2.9
Light manufactures	16 821	2 192	2 120	4.6	4.5	8.9	1.0	1.9
Heavy manufactures	61 252	12 045	7 461	10.5	14.7	27.9	1.4	2.7
Machinery	185 309	31 414	18 663	15.8	18.9	44.3	1.2	2.8
Manufacturing by subsector								
Food	10 798	1 929	3 293	8.0	16.3	27.5	2.0	3.4
Animal feeds	2 310	295	394	13.3	16.9	31.5	1.3	2.4
Beverages	808	51	295	3.7	3.9	13.5	1.1	3.6
Tobacco	2 518	920	999	36.2	50.0	95.0	1.4	2.6
Textiles	4 580	695	347	4.5	2.9	6.8	0.6	1.5
Apparel	1 415	65	305	1.3	0.8	3.5	0.6	2.7
Leather products	865	307	95	4.2	7.2	5.9	1.7	1.4
Footwear	407	78	45	1.6	4.2	5.3	2.6	3.3
Wood products	4 494	303	1 585	11.2	9.1	25.9	0.8	2.3
Furniture	1 288	75	221	5.2	7.6	17.4	1.5	3.3
Pulp and paper	8 968	1 884	1 415	11.8	26.8	45.5	2.3	3.9
Printing, publishing	3 518	269	281	17.0	22.4	41.3	1.3	2.4
Industrial chemicals	31 991	8 234	4 079	14.6	22.5	37.2	1.5	2.6
Other chemicals	9 847	1 330	1 586	13.0	17.0	36.1	1.3	2.8
Petroleum refining	4 363	1 326	332	6.0	10.8	30.3	1.8	5.1
Coal and oil products	478	70	58	8.1	13.0	47.6	1.6	5.9
Rubber	2 461	169	277	9.5	10.2	28.4	1.1	3.0
Plastics	2 881	336	255	7.7	7.8	18.2	1.0	2.4
Pottery, ceramics	350	62	36	4.1	7.7	12.6	1.9	3.1
Glass	1 668	173	242	9.8	10.7	32.1	1.1	3.3
Other mineral products	1 160	151	101	6.0	6.8	8.9	1.1	1.5
Iron and steel	3 943	627	283	3.8	3.5	6.0	0.9	1.6
Non-ferrous metals	6 494	869	1 831	8.4	10.1	17.5	1.2	2.1
Metal scrap	3 050	1 088	550	26.0	46.6	48.1	1.8	1.9
Fabricated metals	6 951	963	600	9.0	11.3	28.0	1.3	3.1
Non-electrical machinery	68 077	10 997	6 498	16.8	18.5	47.2	1.1	2.8
Electrical machinery	39 140	10 612	4 840	13.6	16.7	45.2	1.2	3.3
Transport equipment	60 782	7 575	4 969	15.3	25.5	40.7	1.7	2.7
Precision instruments	17 310	2 231	2 355	19.7	16.3	43.7	0.8	2.2
Misc. manufactures	4 747	702	826	7.2	8.7	14.7	1.2	2.0

Note: Excludes the Philippines. Trade measured by importing countries.

Source: UN trade data.

products, as well as in more advanced manufacturing sectors, including fabricated metals, machinery, electrical machinery and transport equipment. In these sectors the

Table 23.2   Share of imports by supplier (per cent)

Importer/supplier	1965	1970	1975	1980	1985	1990
World						
United States	16.1	15.3	13.5	12.1	12.2	11.5
Japan	4.2	5.6	6.0	6.5	9.3	8.9
East Asia	4.1	4.0	5.1	7.1	9.7	12.1
Others	75.6	75.0	75.5	74.4	68.8	67.5
East Asia (excl. Japan)						
United States	16.0	17.7	18.3	17.4	16.6	15.8
Japan	21.4	29.2	26.0	23.6	22.9	22.4
East Asia	19.8	15.1	15.6	20.7	25.5	30.4
Others	42.9	37.9	40.0	38.3	35.0	31.4
Japan						
United States	29.0	29.5	20.1	17.5	20.3	22.8
Japan						
East Asia	12.5	12.0	16.5	22.4	25.9	26.9
Others	58.5	58.5	63.4	60.1	53.8	50.3

Source: UN trade data.

market share of the United States is 3 to 5 times as high in Japan as worldwide, and 1.5 to 2.5 times as high in other East Asian countries as worldwide.

Not only is the US share of East Asian markets high, but it also shows no signs of decline in the longer term. There have been fluctuations in market shares in East Asia over time, but in 1990, the US share of East Asian (excluding Japan) markets was 15.8 per cent, only slightly below the 16 per cent share of 1965 (Table 23.2). The United States has experienced much smaller losses than Japan, which held 29.2 per cent of East Asian markets in 1970 against 22.4 per cent today. And both Japan and the United States have done much better than the rest of the world, whose market share fell from 42.9 per cent to 31.4 per cent over the last 25 years. The sole gainer has been the region itself, with its own-market share increasing from 19.8 to 30.4 per cent.

Developments in Japanese markets have been only slightly less favourable to the United States. Here US market shares have declined from 29.5 per cent of imports in 1965 to 22.8 per cent today. This decline occurred almost entirely between 1970 and 1975 (in part due to the oil shocks) and the United States has gained market share since then. In Japanese as in other East Asian markets, the biggest story has been the increase in the share of East Asian suppliers at the expense of countries other than the United States.

The relative performance of the United States in East Asia (that is, US performance in East Asia compared to US performance in other markets) has been especially strong. As Table 23.3 shows, US market shares in East Asia were one per cent smaller than US market shares worldwide in 1965 (16.0 per cent versus 16.1 per cent,

Table 23.3   Relative success of suppliers in East Asia and Japan (trade intensity indexes)

Import market/supplier	1965	1970	1975	1980	1985	1990
East Asia (excl. Japan)						
United States	0.99	1.16	1.36	1.44	1.36	1.37
Japan	5.07	5.17	4.37	3.67	2.46	2.50
East Asia	4.83	3.78	3.09	2.92	2.63	2.52
Others	0.57	0.51	0.53	0.51	0.51	0.47
Japan						
United States	1.80	1.92	1.49	1.45	1.66	1.98
Japan						
East Asia	3.07	3.00	3.27	3.17	2.67	2.23
Others	0.77	0.78	0.84	0.81	0.78	0.75

Source: Table 23.2.

yielding an intensity index of 0.99), while in 1990 they were 37 per cent higher than US market shares worldwide (15.8 per cent versus 11.5 per cent). By contrast, neither Japan nor other East Asian countries have managed to increase their shares in East Asian trade as fast as they have in other markets.

There are obviously complex country stories behind these aggregates. In some countries, such as Korea and Taiwan, the United States lost market share rapidly in the late 1960s as its political involvement diminished, but then held its share since. In others, such as Indonesia, Malaysia and Singapore, it has steadily improved its position. In still others, including Hong Kong and Thailand, its role has diminished. But overall, there is no evidence for a pullback in these export data.

In sum, the United States has remained actively involved in East Asian markets, despite setbacks in its domestic economy, and despite the extraordinary development of Japan and the region's own economies. Indeed, the remarkable story is that the US economy has managed to shift resources into export industries — that is, to open its economy — rapidly enough to maintain its share of a market that has grown substantially more rapidly than its home economy.

East Asia as a source of US imports

East Asia's exceptional strides in penetrating US markets are well known (Figure 23.2). Between 1965 and 1990 Japan and other East Asian countries more than doubled their share of US imports from 17.3 to 37 per cent (Table 23.4). Their role is especially important in light manufactures, where East Asia excluding Japan supplies more than half of US imports, and in machinery where Japan alone supplies

Figure 23.2   Composition of US imports

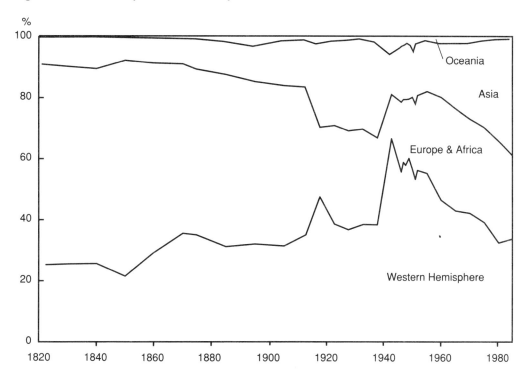

more than one-third of US imports. Rapid gains in these shares took place between 1975 and 1985, from both Japanese and other East Asian suppliers. Since 1985 overall East Asian shares in US markets have been roughly constant, but a substantial part of these shares has shifted from Japan to other East Asian economies.

But if US performance in East Asia is insufficiently appreciated, then East Asia's reliance on US markets is easily overstated. The changes cited above are not so dramatic when viewed from the perspective of East Asia's rapidly growing economies. East Asia's export growth was not especially focused on the United States. The share of East Asian exports (excluding Japan) going to the United States increased by only one percentage point from 1965 to 1990 — from 21.2 to 22.5 per cent. The share of Japanese exports going to the US grew by only two percentage points — from 29.7 to 31.7 per cent. Both of these ratios had been substantially higher in 1985 than they were in 1990; since 1985, the surge of intra-East Asia trade has again diminished the importance of the American market to overall post-war averages.

US markets have played a crucial role in East Asia's economic development, but East Asia's spectacular export growth was *not* due to an increasing US preference for East Asian goods. Table 23.5 shows that East Asia always enjoyed better access

Table 23.4   Market shares in US imports (per cent)

Type of import/supplier	1965	1970	1975	1980	1985	1990
Merchandise trade						
Japan	11.3	14.7	11.8	13.1	20.2	18.0
East Asia	6.0	7.4	9.9	12.4	16.0	19.0
Others	82.7	77.9	78.3	74.5	63.9	63.0
Manufactures						
Japan	13.6	17.6	16.4	20.0	24.3	21.4
East Asia	5.3	7.8	11.0	14.9	17.1	21.5
Others	81.1	74.6	72.6	65.0	58.6	57.1
Resource-based manufactures						
Japan	1.7	2.5	1.4	1.9	2.1	1.7
East Asia	5.6	7.2	8.5	8.7	8.6	7.0
Others	92.7	90.3	90.1	89.4	89.3	91.4
Light manufactures						
Japan	22.5	19.9	9.4	6.3	6.7	6.7
East Asia	14.3	24.3	35.4	46.7	50.0	51.4
Others	63.2	55.8	55.2	47.0	43.3	41.9
Heavy manufactures						
Japan	29.9	31.9	30.2	22.3	18.2	14.9
East Asia	1.8	5.3	7.4	11.9	17.3	20.5
Others	68.3	62.8	62.4	65.8	64.5	64.6
Machinery						
Japan	21.0	24.3	25.6	35.2	38.9	33.5
East Asia	1.2	3.6	7.6	11.1	11.8	17.0
Others	77.8	72.1	66.8	53.7	49.4	49.5

Source: UN trade data.

to US markets than to markets in third countries—Japan and other East Asian countries have steadily held roughly twice as high a market share in the United States as worldwide. This factor of preference has fluctuated some, but remained largely unchanged between 1965 and 1990. Japan and other East Asian countries have enjoyed still more favourable access to each other's markets, with market shares 3–4 times as high as worldwide. The preference indexes for intra-East Asian trade, however, have generally declined, suggesting some global diversification of the region's exports.

In sum, East Asia is a vital and increasingly important supplier of US products. US buyers have always been more receptive to East Asian products than to those from other regions of the world. The constancy of this preference, however, indicates that East Asia's export growth has not been disproportionately targeted at US markets.

Table 23.5   **Relative success of exporters in East Asia and Japan (trade intensity indexes)**

Exporter/destin. markets	1965	1970	1975	1980	1985	1990
East Asia (excl. Japan)						
United States	1.69	2.02	2.22	1.85	1.69	1.56
Japan	4.10	3.78	4.03	3.40	3.61	2.85
East Asia	2.98	2.93	2.65	2.77	2.46	2.79
Others	0.63	0.50	0.49	0.50	0.45	0.45
Japan						
United States	2.37	2.25	1.78	1.94	1.98	2.19
Japan						
East Asia	4.41	4.27	4.23	3.60	2.92	2.67
Others	0.63	0.60	0.73	0.67	0.56	0.56

Source: Table 23.4.

East Asian export market shares have grown roughly at the same rate in the United States as worldwide.

US investment in East Asia

The factor most often cited as signaling US decline in East Asia is the surge of Japanese and East Asian direct investment within the region; since 1987 Japanese investment in East Asia has been two to three times as high as US investment (Table 23.6). The investment boom has been especially vigorous in China, Indonesia, Malaysia and Thailand, where Japan and the NIEs have found ideal locations for relocating labour-intensive industries (Guisinger 1992; Sakurai 1992).

The first point to note is that Japan has nearly always held a lead in regional investment. The only time it did not was for a short period in the early 1980s, just before the Japanese and NIE investment surge, when US investments in East Asia were more than twice as high as Japan's (Table 23.6). But this was an historical aberration. Over the 1951–82 period, the United States invested only 78 per cent as much as Japan in East Asia, despite the fact that United States had a much larger economy over this period. Since then, America's relative size advantage has diminished. In the late 1980s US investments fell slightly, but the factor making the difference was the sudden explosion of Japanese and then NIE investment flows.

The key question is whether these flows represent a temporary surge or a new trend. No definitive answer is possible for now, but recent data suggest declining outflows from Japan and some NIEs. There are also strong theoretical reasons for expecting the recent East Asian investment wave to be temporary. The critical factor

Table 23.6   **US and Japanese direct investment in East Asia (US$ million)**

	1951–82	1983	1984	1985	1986	1987	1988	1989
	Cumulative							
US investment								
Japan	6 636	678	777	988	1 107	1 150	1 801	
East Asia	11 400	4 133	3 222	2 757	2 528	2 472	2 762	
Hong Kong	2 928	482	428	443	342	266	301	
Indonesia	2 281	2 051	1 337	1 176	1 178	999	758	
Malaysia	1 199	498	440	357	336	541	491	
Philippines	1 308	194	156	114	126	119	140	
Singapore	1 745	282	243	245	226	246	416	
Korea	641	88	105	76	78	74	185	
Taiwan	521	125	140	154	147	133	254	
Thailand	777	413	373	192	95	94	217	
Japanese investment								
World					22 320	33 364	47 022	67 540
United States	13 970	2 565	3 360	5 395	10 165	14 704	21 701	32 540
East Asia, nes	14 639	1 768	1 490	1085	2 084	3 610	5 230	7682
Hong Kong	1 825	563	412	131	502	1 072	1 662	1898
Indonesia	7 267	374	374	408	250	545	586	631
Malaysia	765	140	142	79	158	163	387	673
Philippines	721	65	46	61	21	72	134	202
Singapore	1 612	322	225	110	302	494	747	1 902
Korea	1 312	129	107	134	436	647	483	606
Taiwan	617	103	65	114	291	367	372	494
Thailand	520	72	119	48	124	250	859	1 276
China					226	1 226	296	438
Ratio: US to Japan								
East Asia, nes	0.78	2.34	2.16	2.54	1.21	0.68	0.53	
Hong Kong	1.60	0.86	1.04	3.38	0.68	0.25	0.18	
Indonesia	0.31	5.48	3.57	2.88	4.71	1.83	1.29	
Malaysia	1.57	3.56	3.10	4.52	2.13	3.32	1.27	
Philippines	1.81	2.98	3.39	1.87	6.00	1.65	1.04	
Singapore	1.08	0.88	1.08	2.23	0.75	0.50	0.56	
Korea	0.49	0.68	0.98	0.57	0.18	0.11	0.38	
Taiwan	0.84	1.21	2.15	1.35	0.51	0.36	0.68	
Thailand	1.49	5.74	3.13	4.00	0.77	0.38	0.25	

Note: nes—Not elsewhere specified.

Source: Guisinger (1992) and Ministry of Finance, Japan.

behind the surge was a huge appreciation of the yen and other NIE currencies against the dollar and the currencies of the other countries. These changes suddenly undermined the profitability of entire industries in Japan and the NIEs. Due to the rapidity of these changes, firms producing labour-intensive products such as electronic components, shoes and garments could not scale back their activities gradually, but rather turned to foreign investment as a way to salvage existing assets.

In this rapidly changing environment, many Japanese and NIEs firms found themselves with strong, up-to-date assets in technology, marketing and management, on the one hand, and highly adverse domestic cost conditions, on the other. This combination created just the right environment for foreign investment, that is, for moving marketing and technological assets to sites with low-cost labour. The mismatch between assets and cost conditions that existed in the late 1980s is likely to diminish as firms return to the usual process of shifting assets gradually out of declining industries. In a more predictable setting, there will be much less incentive to invest abroad than there was over the last five or so years.

The recent East Asian investment surge aside, US investment has *not* been overshadowed by investment from Japan or other sources. Table 23.7 shows that the share of the United States in foreign direct investment stocks in East Asia rose between 1975 and 1980, and rose again (slightly) between 1980 and 1988. US shares were below those of Japan and other East Asian countries in 1988 (21.3 per cent for the United States versus 26.5 per cent for Japan and 22 per cent for other East Asian countries), but not by nearly the same margin as they had been in 1975. The data do not yet show the recent surge of investment by the NIEs, which took place largely after 1988. Up to that time, the shares of other East Asian investors were relatively constant. As in the trade data, the losers in East Asia were countries from outside the Pacific Rim.

The investment trends vary a great deal across countries. Both the United States and Japan have increased their share of Singapore's foreign direct investment stock. The United States lost ground relative to Japan in Hong Kong and Thailand, but gained ground in Indonesia and Korea. Interestingly, in all of these cases the changes have tended to level some sharp initial advantage by one or the other of these two investing countries. Thus, in nearly all East Asian countries, US and Japanese influences are now more nearly matched.

US subsidiaries in East Asia have varied missions: those in Japan penetrate the Japanese market (and perhaps acquire technology), while those in other East Asian countries export to the United States and third countries (Table 23.8). Subsidiaries in Japan sell roughly 90 per cent of their output in Japan; other East Asian subsidiaries (for example, in manufacturing) sell only 37.6 per cent of their output locally, and export 37.1 per cent to the United States and 25.2 per cent to third markets. Over the 1980s subsidiaries in Japan as well as manufacturing subsidiaries in other East Asian countries have become more export oriented (Yamashita 1991). At the same time, the local sales of US subsidiaries in other East Asia have risen overall, because of compositional shifts — increasing investments in the service sector. But on the whole,

Table 23.7   Foreign direct investment stocks

Host	Inward FDI stock (US$m)	Shares by investor (%)			
		North America	Japan	East Asia	Others
East Asia					
1975	15 829	14.3	24.2	25.2	36.2
1980	31 899	20.5	25.3	19.3	35.0
1988	97 666	21.3	26.5	22.0	30.2
China					
1982	1 048	28.3	4.9	38.8	28.0
1984	2 653	18.9	5.8	56.2	19.1
1987	7 015	16.9	7.2	63.9	12.0
Hong Kong					
1975	362	47.2	15.4	6.4	31.1
1984	3 691	54.1	21.1	6.1	18.7
1989	11 771	32.1	29.9	14.9	23.1
Indonesia					
1975	4380	3.9	42.4	16.8	36.9
1980	10 274	4.9	37.5	16.2	41.5
1988	32 656	8.8	27.7	23.1	40.4
Korea					
1976	651	21.0	62.7	1.8	14.5
1980	1 238	20.1	61.8	2.1	16.0
1988	3 701	28.2	52.8	3.9	15.1
Malaysia					
1981	6 288	6.7	17.6	38.2	37.5
1987	7 509	7.3	20.1	37.9	34.6
Philippines					
1975	373	57.1	23.5	2.3	17.1
1980	1 240	58.6	16.8	5.2	19.4
1987	1 429	58.9	13.3	7.4	20.4
Singapore					
1975	2 326	15.7	9.4	18.9	56.0
1980	6 065	29.6	16.7	8.0	45.7
1989	26 012	33.2	30.7	4.4	31.7
Taiwan					
1980	3 326	35.0	18.6	26.3	20.1
1988	7 356	32.1	26.8	17.1	23.9
Thailand					
1975	506	40.3	27.1	16.8	15.8
1980	988	32.3	28.9	20.3	18.6
1988	3 854	24.5	36.7	22.4	16.4

Source: UN, *World Investment Directory 1992*.

Table 23.8   Sales of US subsidiaries by type of market (per cent of total sales)

	Location of subsidiary		
	World	Japan	Other Asia
Sales to local market			
All industries			
1983	64.8	91.1	40.8
1990	66.7	88.6	51.6
Manufacturing			
1983	64.9	85.3	39.9
1990	60.9	83.2	37.6
Sales to United States			
All industries			
1983	10.9	3.6	26.4
1990	10.4	5.3	21.4
Manufacturing			
1983	11.6	6.2	44.0
1990	12.0	8.0	37.1
Sales to third markets			
All industries			
1983	24.4	5.3	32.8
1990	22.9	6.1	27.0
Manufacturing			
1983	23.6	8.4	16.2
1990	27.1	8.8	25.2

Source: Calculated using Department of Commerce data.

US firms in East Asia seem to engage in what Professor Kojima has called 'Japanese style' direct investment — investment aimed at developing exporting capabilities — to a greater extent than Japanese firms.

In sum, the United States remains an important investor in East Asia. Its stock of investments rose as a share of all foreign investments in East Asia between 1975 and 1988, nearly eliminating Japan's large initial lead in investments in the region. In the late 1980s Japanese investments and also NIE investments accelerated, due to the appreciation of the yen and NIE currencies. These inflows are likely to diminish as industrial structures throughout East Asia adjust to the new currency alignments, leaving the US in a leading position in East Asia's rapidly growing markets.

East Asian investment in the United States

East Asian investment in the United States is a relatively recent phenomenon, but its rapid growth adds a new dimension to expanding US–East Asian economic linkages.

Table 23.9   East Asian foreign investment abroad

Investor	Av. annual outflows 1987–89 (US$m)	Shares by host country (%)		
		North America	East Asia	Others
China	640	14.8	26.3	59.0
Hong Kong	2 891			
Korea	239	43.8	22.7	33.4
Malaysia	137			
Philippines	2			
Taiwan	4 151	60.5	23.6	15.9
Thailand	82	23.1	75.2	1.7

Source: UN, *World Investment Directory 1992*.

Between 1977 and 1990 Japan's share of the total stock of foreign investments in the United States rose from 5 per cent to 21 per cent (Graham and Krugman 1991). This is partly the product of rising Japanese foreign direct investment, and partly of changes in its composition. In 1980, 31.8 per cent of Japan's foreign investment went to the United States and 25.4 per cent to Asia; by 1990 the share of the United States had increased to 45.9 per cent, while that of Asia had fallen to 12.4 per cent. Investment in the United States by other East Asian countries is small compared to total US inward investment stocks, but still represents a large share of the outward investment flows of several countries (Table 23.9).

In sum, the United States is an increasingly important target for East Asian investments. These investments represent a surge in the diversification of East Asian assets, and probably also efforts to escape potential protectionist measures by the United States. East Asian investments in the United States are now slowing. In the meantime, however, several East Asian countries have built large stakes in the US economy. These investments provide further incentives for the United States and its East Asian partners to maintain a strong US–East Asian relationship.

Conclusions and implications for policy

Notwithstanding the powerful image of the American flag being lowered over Subic Bay for the last time, this study has shown that the United States remains actively involved in the dynamic economies of East Asia. In particular:

- exports have held their relatively high market shares in East Asia over the last twenty-five years, while the market shares of Japan and other countries outside the region have declined;

- East Asian countries have increased their relatively high share of US imports, at roughly the same rate as they increased their market shares worldwide;

- firms have increased their shares of foreign investments in East Asia over the last twenty-five years, although a recent (and most likely temporary) surge of investments from Japan and the East Asian NIEs has partly reversed these gains; and

- East Asian direct investments in the United States have surged in recent years, sharply raising their share of US inward investments stocks.

Other types of connections, not examined in this paper, including educational ties, tourism and portfolio ownership, also show intense and strengthening linkages. In virtually all dimensions of economic contact, the trends point to steadily stronger economic linkages between the United States and East Asia.

The critical challenge for US and East Asian policies is to maintain the international framework that has permitted such rapid gains in the past. The task of developing a common policy framework, however, has been complicated by several factors.

First, despite the fact that international economic ties have developed rapidly, the Pacific Rim's economies differ enormously in economic development and organisation. The region includes some of the world's richest countries and some of its poorest, as well as some of its largest and smallest. There are also large differences in resource endowments and technology, and in fundamental aspects of firm behaviour and industrial structure. Thus, similar policies can have very different effects in different countries. A tariff reduction, for example, may have a large effect on Thai trade, which is relatively competitive and free of non-tariff distortions, and a small effect on Japanese trade, where complex institutional barriers make it difficult to introduce foreign products. Because of such issues, it is difficult to launch discussions among countries with widely differing economic systems.

Second, the region's economies also differ in their approaches to economic policy-making. Some countries tend to implement policies using explicit legal and regulatory systems, while others rely on informal interactions between government and industry. Either of these systems can provide an effective way for reaching government objectives in the right context, but neither provides an acceptable basis for a common, regional policy framework.

Third, the region's complex political structure and varied obligations to other, outside trade partners create a difficult backdrop for economic negotiations. It took several years of negotiations, for example, to work out a formula for admitting some of the regions most important economies — China, Hong Kong and Taiwan — into APEC, the main forum for regional dialogue. Although ASEAN is now committed to a free trade area, its own economic negotiations were long stalled by political frictions. At the same time, the United States has felt compelled to pursue closer economic ties with its troubled Latin American neighbours outside of its East Asian dialogue.

These factors make a 'large' trade agreement along the lines of NAFTA or the EC highly unlikely in the Pacific Rim (Petri 1992). The concept of a PAFTA has been discussed in Japan and other East Asian countries since the 1960s. However, many policy makers in the United States as well as other countries fear that even if an agreement were reached, it would not change government and business behaviour enough to overcome informal, invisible barriers to international trade and investment. Thus countries with important informal barriers might gain at the expense of others who are able to commit genuine concessions.

At the same time, the urgency of a large agreement is tempered by the fact that economic integration is occurring rapidly, even without formal, regional negotiations. The competitive impact of private sector activities is continuously forcing countries to harmonise regional policies — for example, by liberalising and modernising their international trade and investment regimes. Especially large gains have been made in the region's 'special economic zones', which permit economic integration across national borders within certain geographical constraints.

But while a large agreement may not be urgent, there is a need for improved economic dialogue and dispute resolution. APEC was designed to create a forum to address these requirements. APEC has not, so far, taken any high profile steps towards liberalising the trade and investment environment, but it has created a forum for regular inter-governmental discussions at a high level. It is now developing a permanent secretariat and may become an influential centre for information gathering and policy discussion. Some ideas on trade liberalisation are also being explored. Part of the responsibility for the slow progress of APEC lies with the United States, which has vigorously defended APEC against alternative institutions, such as the EAEG, but has not used APEC to address sensitive trade questions, such as the design and future enlargement of NAFTA.

Because APEC includes most of the region's economies, it represents, in effect, the low common denominator of regional interests in economic integration. Other institutions may be more effective in accelerating the pace of regional integration. The successful implementation of NAFTA and AFTA could play such a role. Also, since the huge and complex US–Japanese economic relationship is critical to any integration effort, an effective bilateral dialogue between the United States and Japan would go a long way towards improving East Asian economic prospects in general. Along these lines, a recent US–Japan study group recommended that the United States and Japan pursue parallel commitments to APEC and to high-level, bilateral negotiations to solve their bilateral frictions (Okuizumi, Calder and Gong, 1992).

A still more aggressive approach was suggested in a speech by President Bush, which emphasised that NAFTA was not merely restricted to Mexico, but was intended to 'develop a strategic network of free-trade agreements with Latin America, with Poland, Hungary and Czechoslovakia, and with countries across the Pacific' (*Far Eastern Economic Review* 1992a). Any East Asian country willing to meet NAFTA's standards would be able to join and, according to a senior US government official, Australia, Hong Kong, New Zealand, Singapore and Taiwan might be early candidates.

A two-continent NAFTA grouped around the United States could turn out to be as exclusive as Malaysian Prime Minister Mahathir's EAEG. If Japan is excluded on the ground that its economic system contains implicit trade barriers, a sharp and divisive competition might emerge between Japan and the United States for regional markets. It is difficult to predict whether this competition would encourage the splintering of the Pacific Rim economy, or make all parties better appreciate the importance of maintaining 'open regionalism' and strengthening APEC.

What the United States needs to do is to pursue its Asian policies more visibly and vigorously. Concerns about declining US economic ties with Asia are not borne out by facts, but are nevertheless widespread. Concerns about increasing US protectionism also tend to obscure the continuing vigorous role of US markets to East Asian exporters. Countering these concerns should become a central objective of US policy. The visibility of US public and private sector commitments to East Asian ties should match the strength of the underlying economic linkages.

Notes

1   The lead article of a recent issue of the *Far Eastern Economic Review* (1992b, p. 15), for example, was devoted to the theory that President Clinton, 'preoccupied with domestic economic problems, may turn his attention to Asia only when a crisis erupts'. A similar theme served as the common denominator for two articles in a recent issue of *Economic Insights*, a magazine published by the influential Institute for International Economics in Washington, both of which essentially counselled 'Don't Forget Asia' (Drysdale 1992; Lawrence 1992).

2   For example, the bilateral pattern of trade is indeterminate in a Heckscher–Ohlin model with more products than factors, assuming zero transport costs.

3   Petri uses the term 'gravity coefficients' in the original version of this paper, which is equivalent to the trade intensity indexes defined in Drysdale and Garnaut (1982) (also Chapter 3, this volume).

References

Drysdale, Peter 1992, 'Advice to the US: don't forget Asia', *Economic Insights*, III(6), November–December, pp. 10–13.

Drysdale, Peter and Ross Garnaut 1982, 'Trade intensities and the analysis of bilateral trade flows in a many-country world', *Hitotsubashi Journal of Economics*, 22, February, pp. 62–84.

Far Eastern Economic Review 1992a, 'After Mexico and Canada, Who?', 5 November, p. 54.

_____ 1992b, 'Clinton's Asia: Not All Pacific', 19 November.

Graham, Edward M. and Paul R. Krugman 1991, *Foreign Direct Investment in the United States*, Washington, DC: Institute for International Economics.

Guisinger, Stephen E. 1992, 'Foreign direct investment flows in East and Southeast Asia: policy issues', in Kaoru Okuizumi, Kent E. Calder and Gerrit W. Gong (eds), *The US–Japan Relationship in East and Southeast Asia*, Washington, DC: Center for Strategic and International Studies, pp. 71–98.

Irving National Bank 1919, *Trading with the Far East*, New York: Irving National Bank.

Lawrence, Robert Z. 1992, 'The US–Asian pillar: a new initiative', *Economic Insights*, III(6), November–December, pp. 7–9.

Okuizumi, Kaoru, Kent E. Calder and Gerrit W. Gong (eds) 1992, *The US–Japan Relationship in East and Southeast Asia*, Washington, DC: Center for Strategic and International Studies.

Petri, Peter A. 1992, 'One bloc, two blocs or none? Political–economic factors in Pacific trade policy', in Kaoru Okuizumi, Kent E. Calder and Gerrit W. Gong (eds), *The US–Japan Relationship in East and Southeast Asia*, Washington, DC: Center for Strategic and International Studies, pp. 39–70.

—————— 1993, 'The East Asian trading bloc: an analytical history', in Jeffrey A. Frankel and Miles Kahler (eds), *Regionalism and Rivalry: Japan and the United States in Pacific Asia*, Chicago: University of Chicago Press.

Sakurai, Makoto 1992, 'Japanese foreign direct investment and Asia', in Kaoru Okuizumi, Kent E. Calder and Gerrit W. Gong (eds), *The US–Japan Relationship in East and Southeast Asia*, Washington, DC: Center for Strategic and International Studies, pp. 99–114.

Woytinsky, W. S. and E. S. Woytinsky 1955, *World Commerce and Governments: Trends and Outlook*, New York: Twentieth Century Fund.

Yamashita, Shoichi (ed.) 1991, *Transfer of Japanese Technology and Management to the ASEAN Countries*, Tokyo: University of Tokyo Press.

Part Seven

Southeast Asian Regionalism

24 The ASEAN Free Trade Area: the search for a common prosperity

Lee Tsao Yuan

ASEAN entered the decade of the 1990s faced with two new political challenges. The fall of the Berlin Wall in 1989 and the end of the Cold War meant that security issues would, in most parts of the world, no longer be of paramount importance. Instead, economic issues have moved to the top of the global agenda. At the same time, the signing of the Peace Accord in Paris in 1991 heralded the impending solution to the Cambodian problem, which had dominated discussions in ASEAN capitals and in New York for more than a decade. These two factors led to a fundamental rethinking of strategy for ASEAN cooperation. The search began for a new glue which would be the focal point for ASEAN unity.

While it is now widely acknowledged that, in the 1970s and 1980s, the *raison d'être* for ASEAN cooperation was political, a consensus began to develop that the new *raison d'être* for ASEAN cooperation in the 1990s and beyond had to be economic. In addition to the political factors mentioned above, developments on the economic front, both external and domestic, also contributed towards this change of mindset.

Externally, the prolonged delay in concluding the Uruguay Round of GATT negotiations which had begun in 1986 created a climate of uncertainty over continued global trade liberalisation and market access. In this environment, the creation of the European Single Market and negotiations towards NAFTA raised the spectre of a protectionist world divided into trading blocs. At the same time, two new sources of competitive challenge to ASEAN emerged in the form of the possible diversion of investments away from ASEAN. The first was Mexico, because of NAFTA and its free access to the United States, ASEAN's largest export market. The second was the marketisation of the socialist economies of China and Vietnam, which, together with their low-cost labour and land, made these economies attractive, both as production locations for export and for the domestic market.

Economically, therefore, ASEAN faced two new challenges. The first was that of sustaining ASEAN's economic competitiveness, and the second, of ensuring continued market access to ASEAN's major markets in the United States, Japan and Europe. Both were essential for sustained rapid economic growth in ASEAN.

Internally, the rapid economic development that had been achieved since the mid-1980s gave the ASEAN countries a newfound confidence that they could meet the competitive challenges that came with increased liberalisation. Indeed, it was these very same liberalisation, deregulation and privatisation measures that attracted the wave of foreign, especially Asian, investment, sparked off an unprecedented growth in the manufacturing and financial sectors, and resulted in ASEAN becoming the fastest growing region in the world. The old fears that Singapore, the most developed of the ASEAN countries, would gain most from intra-regional trade liberalisation subsided as Singapore began to compete in the higher cost, higher value added market segments, and more successful local companies emerged in the other ASEAN countries.

The coincidence of factors, external and internal, political and economic, made the timing right for the Fourth ASEAN Summit Meeting in Singapore in January 1992. The Heads of Government/State signed an historic declaration to achieve an ASEAN Free Trade Area within fifteen years. Considering that economic cooperation efforts in ASEAN had never made much headway in the past, the agreement to proceed with AFTA constituted a milestone in ASEAN economic cooperation.

The CEPT scheme

AFTA is to be effected by means of the Common Effective Preferential Tariff (CEPT) scheme,[1] with the goal of reducing tariffs on all intra-ASEAN trade in manufactured and processed agricultural goods to 0–5 per cent within fifteen years. There are two programs of tariff reduction: the Fast Track and the Normal Track.

The Fast Track Program

There are two aspects to the Fast Track Program: tariffs above 20 per cent will be reduced to 0–5 per cent within ten years (by 1 January 2003); and tariffs at 20 per cent and below will be reduced to 0–5 per cent within seven years (by 1 January 2000). The Fast Track Program covers fifteen product groups: vegetable oils, chemicals, fertiliser, rubber products, pulp and paper, wooden and rattan furniture, gems and jewellery products, cement, pharmaceuticals, plastics, leather products, textiles, ceramics and glass products, copper cathodes, and electronics.

The Normal Track Program

Similarly, the Normal Track Program is bipartite: tariffs above 20 per cent will be reduced in two stages: to 20 per cent within five to eight years (by 1 January 2001), and subsequently to 0–5 per cent in seven years according to an agreed schedule ending on 1 January 2008; and tariffs of 20 per cent and below will be reduced to 0–5 per cent within ten years (by 1 January 2003). In order to promote commonality of tariff rates, three tranches have been agreed upon: year 2003 — 15 per cent; year 2005 — 10 per cent; and year 2008 — 0–5 per cent.

The CEPT scheme covers all manufactured products including capital goods and processed agricultural products, with temporary exclusions at the detailed Harmonised System 8/9-digit level. Unlike the PTA scheme of the past, which was on a product-by-product basis, the CEPT scheme is on a sectoral basis at the HS 6-digit level. The CEPT Products List released by the ASEAN Secretariat in November 1993 covers about 41,000 tariff lines (about 88 per cent of the total tariff lines in ASEAN), and accounts for about 84 per cent of intra-ASEAN trade. About 36,000 tariff lines (or about 87 per cent) of the Products List will reach 5 per cent or less within a period of ten years, earlier than the fifteen-year target. Tariff reduction for about 10,000 items started to come into effect in January 1994.

There are three conditions for eligibility; that is, for a product to enjoy the CEPT concessions in an importing country: the product has to be on the Inclusion Lists of both the exporting and importing country; it must have an approved tariff reduction schedule, except for products with tariffs already at or below 5 per cent; and it has to be an ASEAN product, with a local content requirement of 40 per cent, on a single country or on a cumulative ASEAN basis. In addition, there is a condition for the exchange of concessions: products that have tariff rates at and below 20 per cent in the exporting country are eligible for all the concessions of these products in the importing country; and products that have tariff rates above 20 per cent in the exporting country can enjoy the concessions on these products in the importing country only if the tariff of these products is also above 20 per cent.

Exclusions from the CEPT scheme

There are three categories of exclusions from the CEPT scheme: temporary exclusions, which will be reviewed after eight years; general exceptions, on the grounds of national security, public morals, and so on; and unprocessed agricultural products. Only a small number of products are involved: about 7 per cent of the total tariff lines are excluded under the first category, and 5 per cent under the other two categories.

The CEPT scheme also includes agreements to eliminate quantitative restrictions, such as prohibitions, quotas and restrictive licensing, once the product enjoys CEPT concessions, and to eliminate other NTBs gradually within five years after the enjoyment of concessions.

There is, in addition to the trade liberalisation border measures of the CEPT scheme, an agreement to explore further measures on non-border areas of cooperation, such as the harmonisation of standards, reciprocal recognition of tests and certification of products, removal of barriers to foreign investments, macroeconomic consultations, rules of fair competition, and promotion of venture capital. Discussions have begun in some of these areas. For example, products beyond the HS 6-digit level are being reviewed to ensure comparability of product nomenclature. An ASEAN Consultative Committee on Standards and Quality has been established and has started work on harmonisation of standards, testing and accreditation of laboratories, conformity assessment and technical information. The First Consultative Forum on Foreign Direct Investment in ASEAN countries was convened in February 1993, and will meet on a regular basis to exchange views as to how to improve the investment climate in ASEAN.

An assessment of the CEPT scheme

There are two features of the CEPT scheme which are worthy of note. It is a long-term scheme, the effects of which are likely to be noticeable only a number of years in the future, after a significant degree of tariff reduction. More importantly, AFTA is unusual as a free trade arrangement in that it not only has the objective of establishing a larger domestic consumer market (comprising 330 million people), which is the primary objective of most other free trade areas, but it also seeks to promote greater efficiency as an export production location. Indeed, official statements declare that the 'ultimate objective of AFTA is to increase ASEAN's competitive edge as a production base geared for the world market' (ASEAN Secretariat 1993, p. 1). This is in recognition of the fact that, in contrast to other groupings where intra-regional trade is high, intra-ASEAN trade comprises less than 20 per cent of total ASEAN trade.[2] ASEAN's major markets are in the United States, Japan and Europe. Although the domestic ASEAN consumer market will increase with greater prosperity, this external orientation is likely to continue for some time to come. In other words, in an increasingly integrated world where countries and regions are competing for investment capital, the goal of AFTA is to create an economically borderless, integrated ASEAN, in order to achieve greater global competitiveness.

There are pros and cons to this long-term approach. On the positive side, the announcement of the schedule of tariff reductions which will occur in the future will give businesses time to adjust and to restructure. It will also make the CEPT scheme more politically palatable in those member countries with higher average levels of protection. On the negative side, the current fifteen-year time frame may be too slow in light of the rapid economic developments in the emerging economies in Asia — notably China, Vietnam and, most recently, India — and the challenges that these developments pose for ASEAN's continued competitiveness. Indeed, the fall in foreign investment commitments in 1992 and 1993 in Indonesia and Malaysia has been attributed to investment diversion to China, and to a lesser extent, Vietnam. In their bilateral meeting, Singapore Prime Minister Goh Chok Tong and Thai Prime Minister Chuan Leekpai have agreed that the implementation of AFTA should be speeded up (*Business Times*, 28 December 1993).

Second, in order for firms to consider ASEAN as a borderless production region where production processes can be rationalised to take advantage of each country's comparative advantage, AFTA would need to go beyond tariff reduction to the liberalisation of regulations governing investment, and other NTBs. There is some evidence that quantitative restrictions and other NTBs do constitute a serious constraint to intra-ASEAN trade. For example, Kumar (1992) found from fifteen private sector interviews, that NTBs were the single most important deterrent to increased trade among ASEAN countries. This was also the experience of the Nestlé ASEAN Industrial Joint Venture project (Santos 1993). Not only did the company face many obstacles and bureaucratic red tape in pursuing the approval process, many NTBs continued to hamper the implementation, such as voluminous and tedious import documentation and procedures and other administrative requirements that unreasonably delay the flow of goods.

Furthermore, Imada and Naya (1992) have pointed out that the implementation of a free trade area also involves the establishment of other administrative systems, such as rules of competition, rules of origin (cf. Pearson 1993), duties (and drawbacks on duties) on imported goods, government supports, procurement procedures, treatment of revenue tariffs and dumping; and some form of dispute settlement mechanism.

In short, in order to achieve the goals of AFTA, ASEAN would need to go beyond tariff reduction to include non-border issues ranging from NTBs to investment policies, industrial cooperation and macroeconomic consultation — in other words, what is needed is not AFTA *per se*, but an 'AFTA-plus'.

Third, the regional production-oriented approach is necessarily dynamic, and not static, in nature. This has implications for research on the effects of AFTA. In particular, the methodology employed, although more difficult and messy, should focus on the dynamic nature of investment competitiveness, production efficiency and industrial restructuring, and the effects of these on income and employment. A static approach would, in view of the low percentage of intra-ASEAN trade, yield positive but small trade creation effects of tariff reduction, as has been obtained by Imada, Montes and Naya (1991).

AFTA: the challenges ahead

ASEAN faces major challenges ahead with regard to AFTA. The CEPT scheme needs to be implemented efficiently and expeditiously. The original intention, announced at the Singapore summit, was for implementation to begin on 1 January 1993. There have, however, been some delays. The AFTA Council of Ministers, established during the summit to oversee the implementation of the CEPT scheme, did not hold its inaugural meeting until September 1992, and by its third meeting in December 1992, one month before the 1 January 1993 implementation date, only tentative lists of product inclusion and temporary exclusions were exchanged. Although some countries did reduce tariffs in early 1993, the CEPT Products List was released only in

November 1993 after confirmation by the ASEAN Economic Ministers Meeting in October 1993. This delay has caused some degree of disillusionment.

There is some cause for optimism. The ASEAN Economic Ministers Meeting in October 1993 has put AFTA firmly back on track, and some real progress in implementation has been achieved. All countries have begun to offer concessions beginning on 1 January 1994. The Inclusion Lists account for a large majority, 78–98 per cent, of the total tariff lines of member states, including some agricultural products, although these are not strictly in the CEPT scheme. Moreover, the conditions for exchange of concessions build in an incentive to lower tariffs quickly to 20 per cent and below in order to automatically enjoy tariff concessions by other countries.

Nevertheless, much more needs to be done in terms of broadening the product coverage, speeding up the time frame of tariff reductions, and achieving concrete results in the reduction of NTBs. For example, automobiles, a sector which has good production potential and the ability to create a network of supporting industries, is on the Temporary Exclusion List of all member countries. Although the CEPT scheme does provide for the elimination of NTBs by member countries on a gradual basis within a period of five years after the enjoyment of concessions applicable to the CEPT products, concrete progress in this area, including schedules of reductions, is urgent.

Since AFTA's objective is to improve the investment competitiveness of the ASEAN region, details regarding the CEPT scheme and AFTA as a whole need to be widely circulated, particularly to the business communities, in ASEAN as well as in the rest of the world. In other words, just as individual countries have active and focused investment promotion programs domestically and abroad, a similar ASEAN investment promotion program, to highlight the opportunities available with AFTA, would be very useful in helping to achieve the objective of increased investments.

AFTA in the context of ASEAN cooperation

Where does AFTA fit in the broader context of ASEAN cooperation? In the 1990s, I believe that ASEAN cooperation has broadened to comprise a two-track approach. Political and security issues are still important, and constitute the first track. The ASEAN Regional Forum is an important first step in the search for a collective security arrangement in this region. In light of a decreased US military involvement and the potential flash points that still exist, there will, no doubt, be more confidence-building measures. The second track comprises economic cooperation, the centrepiece of which is AFTA. Although there have been a number of economic cooperation measures in the past, the CEPT scheme is, by far, the most comprehensive and the most important. There are, in addition, other economic cooperation measures, the most notable of which are the sub-regional arrangements such as the Johor–Singapore–Riau Growth Triangle and the Indonesia–Malaysia–Thailand Growth Triangle (Lee 1991; Toh and Low 1993). Since the beneficial effects of AFTA are likely to be felt only in the long term, the 'growth triangles', which are smaller and hence more easily implemented, are likely to have more immediate positive effects.

There is some discussion as to whether free trade areas, which, by definition, lower trade barriers on a preferential, discriminatory basis, are becoming outmoded and less desirable as a trading arrangement.[3] This argument is based on the view that unilateral liberalisation on a non-discriminatory, MFN basis is first-best. Furthermore, it was unilateral liberalisation that provided the impetus for the growth spurt in ASEAN since the mid-1980s. Free trade areas also have trade creation/trade diversion effects, and non-ASEAN countries may worry about the effects of intra-ASEAN trade liberalisation on their ASEAN markets. While there is a strong case for this view, the answer in defence of AFTA is that it should be seen as an intermediate step in the process of gradual liberalisation. This intermediate phase, where internal tariffs are lowered at a faster pace than external tariffs, affords ASEAN businesses some degree of protection while at the same time increasing the competition from other ASEAN businesses. This encourages the development of ASEAN businesses, along infant industry lines, on a regional scale. AFTA can also be viewed as a source of additional external pressure on individual member countries to adopt accelerated liberalisation programs. The CEPT–AFTA scheme is GATT-consistent in the sense that it is outward-looking and does not seek to raise trade barriers against non-ASEAN economies. ASEAN has notified GATT of this scheme, in accordance with Article IV on trade and development (ASEAN Secretariat 1993, p. 9).

In a world which is increasingly focused on economics, AFTA can give ASEAN renewed credibility in global and regional forums, provided substantive progress is achieved. For example, in the APEC forum, ASEAN as a grouping can provide a useful counterweight to the economic giants, the United States and Japan, and in future, China. The idea of the linking of two free trade areas, NAFTA and AFTA, has also been floated, as a means of enabling ASEAN products to have continued access to the important US market.[4]

Conclusion

For the first twenty-five years of its existence, ASEAN cooperation has been mainly on political issues. The preservation of regional political stability has been ASEAN's *raison d'être,* and countries have pursued economic goals largely on an individual basis. Now, for the first time, ASEAN is embarking on the search for a common prosperity. There is now the recognition that regional economic cooperation can constitute a vital complement to measures taken by individual countries, to increase the attractiveness of the region as a whole, and hence individual countries, as a location for investment. This will help ASEAN meet one of the crucial challenges of the 1990s, that of sustaining its economic competitiveness. AFTA therefore augurs well for the economic development of ASEAN, now and in the future.

Notes

1   The best source of details regarding the CEPT scheme is the *AFTA Reader* (see ASEAN Secretariat 1993).

2   In contrast, intra-NAFTA trade and intra-EC trade comprised 39 and 60 per cent respectively of their total trade in 1992 (computed from the International Monetary Fund, *Direction of Trade Statistics Yearbook*, 1993).

3   See, for example, Professor Mohamed Ariff's inaugural lecture on 'AFTA — Another future trade area?', reported in the *New Straits Times*, 4 February 1994. See also Elek (1992).

4   Remarks attributed to Dr Supachai Panichapakdi, Deputy Prime Minister of Thailand (*Business Times*, 28 December 1992).

References

ASEAN Secretariat 1993, *AFTA Reader, Vol. 1*, November.

Elek, Andrew 1992, 'Pacific Economic Cooperation: policy choices for the 1990s', *Asian–Pacific Economic Literature*, 6(1), pp. 1–15.

Imada, Pearl, Manuel Montes and Seiji Naya 1991, *A Free Trade Area: Implications for ASEAN*, Singapore: Institute of Southeast Asian Studies.

Imada, Pearl and Seiji Naya 1992, 'The long and winding road ahead for AFTA', in Pearl Imada and Seiji Naya (eds), *AFTA: The Way Ahead*, Singapore: Institute of Southeast Asian Studies, pp. 53–66.

International Monetary Fund 1993, *Direction of Trade Statistics Yearbook,* Washington, DC: International Monetary Fund.

Kumar, Sree 1992, 'Policy issues and the formation of the ASEAN Free Trade Area', in Pearl Imada and Seiji Naya (eds), *AFTA: The Way Ahead*, Singapore: Institute of Southeast Asian Studies, pp. 71–94.

Lee Tsao Yuan (ed.) 1991, *Growth Triangle: The Johor–Singapore–Riau Experience*, Singapore: Institute of Southeast Asian Studies.

Pearson, B. 1993, 'Rules of origin', *Asian–Pacific Economic Literature*, 7(2), pp. 14–27.

Santos, J. B. 1993, 'ASEAN/AFTA: A corporate perspective', Paper presented to the Pacific Rim Forum, September, Bali, Indonesia.

Toh, Mun Heng and Linda Low (eds) 1993, *Regional Cooperation and Growth Triangles in ASEAN*, Singapore: Times Academic Press.

25 The political economy of the ASEAN Free Trade Area

Narongchai Akrasanee and David Stifel

The emerging economic environment and the ASEAN Free Trade Area

Confidence in ASEAN economic cooperation is growing. Yet data suggest that ASEAN is fighting an uphill battle in its attempt to form a free trade area. Much seems to be going against it. First, as Table 25.1 illustrates, intra-ASEAN trade has been insubstantial. In 1988 it accounted for just over 18 per cent of total ASEAN exports. This figure was actually lower than the 21.4 per cent of 1970. Although intra-ASEAN trade is high relative to the intra-regional trade of other developing country groups,[1] if Singapore — a large centre for entrepôt trade — is excluded, the share of intra-ASEAN trade drops to only 4 per cent of the region's total exports. Second, the ASEAN-4 countries (excluding Brunei and Singapore) have relatively similar production structures and compete for the same export markets. There is a greater degree of complementarity between the ASEAN economies and the industrial and newly industrial economies than between the ASEAN countries themselves. Although these economies are moving upstream and are producing greater quantities of light manufactured goods, natural resources and agricultural goods continue to account for large shares of their exports. For example, in 1990, 64 per cent of Indonesia's exports consisted of primary commodities, two-thirds of which included oil exports. Similar figures for the other ASEAN-4 states are: Malaysia (59 per cent), the Philippines (36 per cent), and Thailand (36 per cent) (World Bank 1992). Finally, the levels of development in ASEAN differ significantly. With such extremes as Indonesia with a per capita income of US$560 in 1990, and Singapore (US$11,245) in the same group, market sharing is difficult at best. The less developed countries in the region are reluctant to open their economies to competition from the more advanced countries.

Table 25.1   ASEAN export matrix (percentage of total exports)

To \ From	ASEAN	Brunei	Indonesia	Malaysia	Philippines	Singapore	Thailand	ASEAN[a]
1970								
World (US$m)	6 254	101	1 108	1 687	1 043	1 605	710	4 649
Asia Pacific	72.0	100.0	80.5	68.0	89.8	58.8	67.5	63.9
Australia	2.4	11.9	3.6	2.2	0.5	3.3	0.5	2.1
Canada	0.9	na	0.0	1.0	0.3	1.2	0.1	0.8
Japan	23.7	1.0	40.8	18.3	40.1	7.4	25.5	29.3
New Zealand	0.3	4.0	0.0	0.5	0.0	0.4	0.1	0.3
United States	17.0	0.0	13.0	13.0	41.6	10.7	13.4	19.2
NIEs[b]	5.6	1.0	2.0	5.4	6.1	5.0	13.0	5.8
ASEAN	21.4	83.2	21.1	25.4	1.2	29.4	14.9	-
Brunei	0.6	-	0.0	0.6	na	1.6	na	0.2
Indonesia	1.3	0.0	-	0.6	0.2	3.2	2.3	0.6
Malaysia	8.0	82.2	3.3	-	0.0	21.2	5.6	3.4
Philippines	1.0	na	2.3	1.7	-	0.3	0.1	1.2
Singapore	9.5	1.0	15.5	21.6	0.7	-	6.9	12.8
Thailand	1.1	0.0	0.0	0.9	0.3	3.2	-	0.4
ASEAN[a]	-	82.2	5.6	3.8	0.5	29.4	8.0	5.9
China	0.7	na	0.0	1.3	0.0	1.4	0.0	0.5
European Community	13.8	0.0	14.9	20.3	8.0	16.8	19.3	12.7
1988								
World (US$m)	105 651	1 987	19 376	21 125	7 034	40 137	15 992	65 514
Asia Pacific	74.0	86.2	83.1	75.0	76.9	72.4	62.2	63.7
Australia	2.2	0.6	1.5	2.4	1.6	2.7	1.9	1.9
Canada	1.0	na	0.5	0.7	1.5	0.9	1.8	1.0
Japan	19.0	51.9	41.7	16.9	20.1	8.5	15.9	25.4
New Zealand	0.2	na	0.2	0.2	0.2	0.3	0.2	0.2
United States	20.7	1.4	16.2	17.3	35.7	23.3	20.0	19.1
NIEs[b]	10.3	17.5	9.8	11.1	10.0	10.8	7.8	10.0
ASEAN	18.1	14.5	10.7	24.4	6.9	23.0	11.6	-
Brunei	0.5	-	0.0	0.3	0.0	1.0	0.1	0.1
Indonesia	1.1	0.1	-	3.1	0.4	2.0	0.5	0.6
Malaysia	5.8	0.1	0.9	-	1.7	13.3	3.0	1.2
Philippines	1.0	1.6	0.4	1.5	-	1.3	0.4	0.8
Singapore	6.9	5.1	8.5	19.3	3.1	-	7.7	11.1
Thailand	2.8	7.7	0.8	2.0	1.8	5.3	-	1.3
ASEAN[a]	-	9.4	2.2	5.1	3.8	23.0	4.0	3.9
China	2.5	0.3	2.5	2.0	0.9	2.9	3.0	2.2
European Community	14.3	11.7	11.1	14.4	17.7	12.7	20.7	15.3

Notes: na—Not available
      a   Not including Singapore.
      b   Hong Kong, South Korea and Taiwan.

Source: Naya and Plummer (1991).

Similarly, the more advanced countries tend to be unwilling to enter exclusive arrangements with the inefficient industries of their developing neighbours.

Traits of this sort have led many observers to conclude that economic cooperation is neither viable nor desirable. Yet, despite these conditions and the constraints discussed earlier, the ASEAN countries have agreed to establish AFTA within fifteen years (from 1 January 1993). Why is this so? The reasons lie more in the recent developments of the ASEAN economies, which have changed to cope with the new international trade and investment trends, rather than in the desire to expand intra-ASEAN trade.

What is clear is that the real changes that have taken place in the international arena and within ASEAN have altered the calculus of national interest for countries in the region. The evolving nature of the costs and benefits associated with economic cooperation has undoubtedly affected the support being lent to AFTA by member countries.

The first of these changes is embodied in the transformations sweeping through the ASEAN countries. The ASEAN leaders have been compelled to adopt economic reforms as a result of hardships suffered from external circumstances in the early 1980s. General liberalisation policies, as well as the adoption of outward-oriented industrialisation strategies, have strengthened the economies in ASEAN. Their improved competitiveness stemming from these policies has instilled a sense of conviction in ASEAN national leaders. Domestic industries have gained significantly from international competition and trade, and many officials are dedicated to enhancing these gains. Barriers to trade need to be reduced further and membership in the GATT strengthened. Cooperation within ASEAN, in the form of a free trade area, is seen as a first step in the process of reducing tariff and non-tariff barriers on an MFN basis. This gradualist approach allows for domestic industries to be subjected to greater competition from within ASEAN before being exposed to the rigours of the international marketplace. The strength concomitant with the dynamism and flexibility of the ASEAN economies has boosted confidence among many national leaders that, although certain inefficient industries will fold under greater international competition, the economies themselves have the capacity to withstand adjustments and to benefit in the long run. Furthermore, ASEAN liberalisation policies have been predicated on the assumption of an open international market. ASEAN solidarity as exemplified in AFTA — especially now that a general commitment has been made — will allow the group to have a greater say in the international community and to address its concerns over the trading system.

The second change is related to the growth strategies adopted by the ASEAN governments in the 1990s. These policies stress the need to attract foreign direct investment which has already contributed to the economic growth and the relatively rapid rates of industrialisation in ASEAN. In light of the competition from Indochina, China, Eastern Europe and Mexico (as a result of NAFTA) for increasingly scarce capital, an effort has been made to maintain these inflows. A multitude of incentives have been offered to foreign investors throughout the region. Incentives, however, are not the primary factor influencing the decisions of foreign investors. The general investment climate is a far more important determinant of an economy's attraction. This climate is not only positively affected by sound macroeconomic management, economic growth, a developed structure, and political and economic stability, but also by the size of the market. The establishment of AFTA will form a single enlarged market with 325 million people, instead of six individual markets. This undoubtedly will be attractive to foreign investors who are looking to gain from economies of scale by producing for the region or by manufacturing truly regional products for export. Officials involved in the negotiations leading up to the summit meeting in Singapore admit that this capability of attracting foreign investment was one of the most compelling arguments for the free trade area.

Third, the introduction of international production networks is beginning to affect the way business is done in ASEAN. The consequence of technological advances which have lowered the costs of transportation and improved telecommunications networks, has been that locations of production are more sensitive to production cost differentials, including those of wages. Following the foreign investment boom in the late 1980s, when, for example, investment in Thailand grew by over 500 per cent, the ASEAN countries were exposed to these new technologies. Taking advantage of such technologies to develop production networks can help ASEAN businesses lower their costs of production and become more competitive.

Although this was the basic idea behind the ASEAN Industrial Complementation (AIC) scheme, its success was limited by time-consuming approval processes and red tape, and because it was an idea ahead of its time. The enthusiasm among foreign automobile manufacturers for the Brand-to-Brand Complementation (BBC) scheme suggests that a more diverse production base — including all six ASEAN economies — will be attractive to firms producing on a global scale. The successful implementation of AFTA will eliminate the barriers to intra-firm trade and trade in intermediate inputs — an essential ingredient needed to facilitate intra-regional production networks — on a broader scale than has been seen with the AIC and BBC schemes. This will not only help to strengthen ASEAN firms but will also attract foreign investors who plan to produce regional goods.

Finally, the emerging shape of the international economic environment is affecting the outlook of ASEAN officials *vis-à-vis* regional economic cooperation. The development of economic blocs in Europe and North America has heightened the apprehensions of leaders in the developing world. These two blocs continue to represent significant markets for the ASEAN countries; 35 per cent of ASEAN exports in 1988 were destined for these markets, and 39 per cent of ASEAN imports originated from these countries (United Nations 1991). Furthermore, delays in the completion of the Uruguay Round of talks — which will affect more than ASEAN's trade with these two blocs — are primarily a result of disputes between the major industrialised economies. The international economic environment is being shaped largely by the OECD countries, and since the ASEAN countries are relatively trade-dependent, they need to assure that their interests — maintaining open international markets — are not ignored. AFTA can show the world that ASEAN is more than just a political club, and that it is a force to be reckoned with. Greater solidarity will bolster the bargaining power of ASEAN, but an *esprit de corps* is not enough. Genuine conviction for economic cooperation is important because it will not only show the commitment of the region's leaders to ASEAN but will also enhance the group's bargaining power by reinforcing the dynamism of each individual economy. The experiences of other regional groupings of developing countries have shown that a group's strength in the international arena is highly dependent on the performance of each individual economy (Langhammer 1987). The cumulative bargaining power of the group will be much stronger if an outcome of the formation of AFTA is greater competitiveness in each of the ASEAN economies.

The ASEAN Free Trade Area

AFTA, which is to be formed within fifteen years by means of the CEPT scheme, is a manifestation of the fundamental changes in the global and regional economies. Despite the commitment of the regional leaders, sceptics still insist that ASEAN's track record and the potential loopholes that exist do not bode well for the plan. The architects of CEPT have been responsive to this and adapted its design to overcome the past weaknesses and to minimise the loopholes.

One means used to assuage scepticism and to maximise the likelihood of AFTA's effectiveness is to include as broad a range of goods as possible in the initiative. According to the agreement signed in Singapore, 'all manufactured products, including capital goods, processed agricultural products and those products falling outside the definition of agricultural products . . . shall be in the CEPT scheme'.[2] Instead of specifically defining, at the HS 7-digit level, which goods are included in the scheme, as was the custom with the PTAs, inclusions for CEPT are made on a 'sectoral basis' — at the HS 6-digit level. This tactic, along with the requirement that exclusions be made at the HS 8/9-digit level, is designed to avoid excluding significant numbers of traded goods from the agreement. This was a lesson learned from the experiences encountered in the PTAs; the list of goods eligible for preferences under the PTAs has grown significantly, yet it accounts for only a small fraction of total intra-ASEAN trade. In classifying goods by sector, the architects of the CEPT scheme have attempted to discourage the use of gimmicks such as padding the inclusion list. Questions, however, arise over the classifications for exclusions at the 8/9-digit level since there is no accepted standard among the ASEAN nations. A solution acceptable to all parties must be reached before the exclusion list is determined.

Another means employed to improve the effectiveness of AFTA is the agreement to reduce tariffs according to a predetermined schedule. Tariffs on products included in the CEPT scheme are to be lowered to a range of 0 to 5 per cent by the year 2008. Tariffs rates on goods presently exceeding 20 per cent shall be lowered to 20 per cent within five to eight years. Subsequent reductions of tariffs to between 0 and 5 per cent are to be made within another seven years. Minimum rates of reduction during this period have been set at 5 per cent. Similarly, each ASEAN state will design tariff reduction schedules for goods with existing rates of protection less than 20 per cent in order to lower these rates of protection to a minimum of 5 per cent within fifteen years. The agreement allows for two or more countries to accelerate tariff reductions for specific products. Quantitative restrictions on products under the CEPT scheme are to be eliminated when the tariff rates reach 20 per cent — while other non-tariff barriers are to be gradually eliminated.

The benefit of adopting a pre-set schedule for tariff reduction is that the stakes of AFTA will have been raised which assures a greater chance for success. Since ASEAN's reputation for rhetoric without concomitant action would be reinforced if one of the states does not meet its obligations within the CEPT framework, the motivation to participate will be strong. Stalling tariff reductions is much easier during the process of negotiation than when a commitment has already been made. The repercussions of delays for the whole group tends to be negative, rather than neutral. With hazards of this sort, there are incentives for each ASEAN state to abide by the tenor of the CEPT scheme.

An issue that will not be easily overcome as ASEAN officials work to implement AFTA will be the enforcement of rules of origin. As Table 25.2 illustrates, tariff protection based on published rates (actual rates may be lower) in ASEAN varies significantly. Among the seven sectors from the list of fifteen for accelerated tariff reduction selected in the table, tariff rates range from levels of zero per cent in Singapore to as high as 100 per cent for certain apparel and leather products in Thailand. These disparities mean that strict rules of origin must be enforced to avoid

Table 25.2   ASEAN tariff rates in seven selected sectors, 1990 (per cent)

	Brunei[a]	Indonesia	Malaysia	Philippines	Singapore	Thailand
Wood and wood products	20	0–60	0–60	10	0	1–70
Leather and leather products	0	0–60	0–40	10	0	0–100
Apparel products	10	40–60	0–55	na	na	10–60
Precious stones and jewellery	10	0–50	0–55	10	0	0–60
Fertiliser	0	0–5	0–5	10	0	0–30
Cement	0	30	0–55	na	0	0–50
Electrical parts	na	0–60	20–55	10	0	5–80

Notes: na—Not available.
            a   1987.

Source: Ministry of Commerce, Ministry of Finance, Thailand.

the deflection of extra-regional imports through low-tariff countries such as Singapore and Brunei to high-tariff countries such as Thailand, Indonesia and Malaysia. As it stands now, a product is considered to be an ASEAN good if 40 per cent of its content originates in ASEAN, but how the 40 per cent is to be calculated has not been agreed to. Rules such as this are sensitive because they open up a multitude of opportunities for corruption and falsification of documents. Furthermore, despite the fact that the CEPT Agreement specifically declares that 'Member States shall not nullify or impair any of the concessions as agreed upon through the application of methods of customs valuation, any new charges or measures restricting trade . . .'[3] a dispute over the origin of an import can be used as a pretext for stalling its delivery — this is equivalent to a non-tariff barrier.

In response to the difficulties and costs inherent in enforcing fair rules of origin in ASEAN, scholars have proposed various hybrids of customs unions (see Rieger 1986, pp. 58–9). This, however, in the eyes of the ASEAN leaders, is much more difficult to achieve than a free trade area and has supranational characteristics which are unacceptable.

Prospects for the ASEAN Free Trade Area

The new political and economic environment in Asia and the Pacific created by the changes which have taken place over the past few years has stimulated the pursuit of greater economic cooperation within ASEAN. Although sincere economic cooperation is no longer the political liability it once appeared to be, the parochial views of government officials with interests in 'sensitive' sectors means that AFTA is not a forgone conclusion. While there is significant support for the free trade area from the private sector in each of the ASEAN economies, enough powerful private interests are at stake to threaten the initiative if the participating governments do not approach it with enthusiasm.

Given the lethargic pace at which endeavours proceed in the consensus-based group, the zealous leadership of at least one ASEAN country is vital to the success of AFTA. The experience of the ASEAN Industrial Joint Venture (AIJV) initiative shows that ardent support by a given group can facilitate the establishment of the cooperation mechanism. The submission of schedules for tariff reductions by each of the ASEAN governments by 1 January 1993 constitutes the first test of the group's will to proceed with the initiative. But the negotiation process has been hindered by the vague strategy for implementing the CEPT. At the senior ministerial levels of the ASEAN governments, endorsements have been forthcoming. However, at the director-general level — those responsible for implementation — the lack of a defined procedure to complete the CEPT has given rise to scepticism. Since there is no clear approach to the selection of sectors to be included in the scheme, the directors general have increasingly adopted a product-by-product mentality, betraying the sector-by-sector spirit of AFTA. They have also become bogged down in other technicalities such as questions of rules of origin. Without a concerted effort on the part of this group, AFTA is sure to fall to the vices of avoidance. An impetus is needed to keep them directed and to avoid unnecessary hesitation.

Although intra-ASEAN trade is minimal, AFTA is a mechanism which can place mutual group pressure on each of the participants to continue with the measures already taken to liberalise their trade regimes. Constructive outside pressure can tip the balance of interests within the domestic debates over the effects of unilateral liberalisation in favour of reform. This is especially the case for Indonesia, the Philippines and Thailand where tariff rates are relatively high and certain sectors will be visibly affected. By assuring a *quid pro quo* in which the other regional countries liberalise their trade regimes in a similar fashion, the elimination of tariff and non-tariff barriers can more easily be achieved. This outside pressure, however, is contingent on the full participation of the ASEAN members. The withdrawal of one member will undermine the dynamic of mutual group pressure. Leadership by an ASEAN country needs to be taken to assure the commitment of each member country to maintain the pressure. Ideally, this helmsman should be either Indonesia, the Philippines or Thailand — the countries with the greatest short-term sacrifices to make. As we shall see, Thailand is the best suited among these three to play the role. Uncertainties over the Thai government's dedication to AFTA, however, make joint leadership between Malaysia and Thailand a more plausible scenario.

The first question we must ask is why it is inappropriate for Singapore and Brunei to actively advocate the implementation of AFTA. Singapore is the economy with the most to gain, which also makes it the member most resented and questioned over its motives. Singapore's efforts to initiate regional cooperation mechanisms have often been met with suspicion. While the island republic can hardly be expected to pursue an initiative which it will not benefit from, ASEAN's less developed countries — Indonesia and Malaysia in particular — question Singapore's motives when they perceive the gains to be unevenly distributed. Although all those involved in the Singapore–Johor–Riau Growth Triangle are benefiting from the scheme, Malaysia has vocally questioned the disproportionate gains accruing to Singapore. Such opposition to the growth triangle has not stopped the three countries from proceeding with the initiative, but it does illustrate the sensitive position that the Singaporean leaders occupy in ASEAN. Although they are extremely eager for greater liberalisation of intra-ASEAN trade, Singapore government officials have clearly adopted a position of passive support; there is an understanding of the degree to which excessively active endorsement on their part could be counterproductive.

Brunei is in a position similar to Singapore. Sensitivity to the interests of other ASEAN countries has encouraged the sultanate to maintain a low profile. With its dependence on oil revenues and small domestic market, freer trade within the region will assist Brunei to diversify its economy and maintain its economic security. Just as in the case for Singapore, Brunei's policy on AFTA is based on the principle that the best means of achieving its objectives is to not aggressively pursue them, but rather to count on the initiative of the less developed economies in the region.

Second, despite their commitments to implementing the CEPT scheme within the fifteen-year time frame, why are Indonesia and the Philippines unlikely to be the countries to stimulate and maintain pressure on the others? With a GDP in 1990 of US$100 billion — the largest in ASEAN — Indonesia should ideally be the country to take the helm to assure the success of AFTA. The CEPT was, after all, an Indonesian proposal reflecting their awareness of the positive impact of trade liberalisation on growth. Aside from rhetoric, however, the enthusiasm of the Suharto government for the initiative, as indicated by implementation efforts, has been ambivalent. The support shown by the President and his ministers has not been clearly reflected among their subordinates who remain uncertain about how AFTA is to be achieved.

The selection of a new cabinet in 1993 also gives rise to questions about the future of ministerial support. As one cabinet minister stated, 'the composition of the next cabinet will be crucial in determining how the economy fares for the rest of the decade'. The future of certain pro-AFTA cabinet members is far from certain and some of their potential replacements are either ambivalent towards AFTA or are 'not of the free trade mode'.[4] This is a manifestation of the two camps which are emerging in the Indonesian political scene. The free marketers who have been largely responsible for the liberalisation program begun in the latter half of the 1980s, are being partially eclipsed by a faction with designs of basic import substitution. Whilst the tenor of this group is far from the more stringent inward-oriented policies of the pre-reform era, their posturing clouds the commitment of the Indonesian officials towards AFTA. Pressure from within ASEAN can provide the necessary balance and impetus for the government to proceed with its liberalisation policies.

Despite its enthusiasm for AFTA, the Philippines is not in a position to make the voluntary concessions needed to set the pace for the rest of ASEAN. Domestic economic problems confront the government of Fidel Ramos and many of the administration's resources will need to be diverted to handle them. High levels of international debt (around US$5.3 billion) accumulated since 1986 have forced the central bank to maintain a strong peso — resulting in a loss of export competitiveness. Similarly, treasury bills issued to cover accumulated central bank losses of US$12.7 billion have hindered growth by pushing interest rates up to 20 per cent and crowding out private investors. Central bank officials play down the seriousness of the issue for fear that it reflects a poor performance on their part. Senator Alberto Romulo, who introduced a bill to Congress in 1991 to help the central bank straighten out its finances, has been frustrated by the lack of backing he received: 'I've been trying to emphasize to [central-bank governor Jose] Cuisia that the problem didn't arise under his watch, so he doesn't have to be defensive about it' (Tiglao 1992, p. 46). A resolution to these problems is not in clear sight.

Along with conflicts over social issues such as family planning in a predominantly catholic country, the Ramos administration's capability to overhaul the trade regime is being constrained by the stagnating economy. The disadvantages that Philippine industrialists face as a result of an overvalued exchange rate, high interest rates, brown-outs, and a weak infrastructure, have resulted in incentives for interest groups to fight for protection. Poor economic performance provides fertile ground for those seeking protection (and rents), thus making it difficult for government officials to ardently pursue reductions in tariff and non-tariff barriers. Furthermore, with taxes on international trade transactions accounting for 21.5 per cent of total government revenue in 1988, and difficulties in raising revenues through income or sales taxes, the Philippine government is confronted by another constraint to liberalising its tariff regime for the region. Pressure from the other developing economies — particularly Indonesia and Thailand — through the mutual reduction of tariff and non-tariff barriers, can counter the protectionist pressures and compel the Philippine government to liberalise its trade regime in the spirit of the CEPT.

Finally, why is the joint leadership of Thailand and Malaysia the most plausible means of ensuring a relatively exclusion free implementation of the CEPT? Thailand, under the leadership of Prime Minister Anand Panyarachun, initiated the AFTA proposal as it exists today and followed through with behind-the-scenes promotion. Thailand's commitment was enhanced by the Prime Minister's pledge at the Singapore summit of 1992 to reduce all of Thailand's tariffs on imports from ASEAN countries to a maximum of 30 per cent by the beginning of 1993. The Anand government, which has put Thailand in a position in which it cannot undermine AFTA without losing prestige, was temporary. The uncertainty surrounding the policies of the future Thai government means that ASEAN cannot depend solely on Thai leadership, although the government of Prime Minister Chuan Leekpai confirmed its full support of the AFTA agreement.

The new Thai government will undoubtedly be confronted by the resistance of affected trade associations. The doubts raised by this, along with the potential for parochial behaviour on the part of the newly elected officials, casts doubt on the leadership capabilities of Thailand. The support of powerful private interest groups suggests that the adjustment process resulting from lowering barriers to trade in sensitive sectors will not be unnecessarily difficult. Nevertheless, the assistance of another ASEAN country — Malaysia — could prove essential to providing the leadership necessary to maintain the spirit of AFTA.

Although Prime Minister Datuk Seri Mahathir Mohamad neglected to discuss AFTA in his opening address to the Singapore summit and instead defended his proposal for an EAEC, Malaysian support for the initiative has been strong. AFTA has indeed received much attention from Malaysian officials and intellectuals. With a per capita income of almost US$2,300 in 1990, second only to Brunei and Singapore in ASEAN, and one of the most dynamic economies in the world, Malaysia is well positioned to gain from AFTA. Yet government energies in regional economic cooperation have been primarily devoted to the EAEC. While this is indeed worthy of attention, Mahathir and his ministers could do well to redirect some of their energy to assure the successful implementation of AFTA. Otherwise the effectiveness of the EAEC could be undermined by a weak ASEAN. It is in Malaysia's interest to assure the implementation of AFTA, and this can be achieved through the pioneering of trade concessions.

Malaysian motives, unlike those of Singapore and Brunei, are not questioned by other members of ASEAN since Malaysia's economy remains less developed. This places Kuala Lumpur in a unique position in which it has domestic support for further liberalisation of its trade regime, and is able to influence the other ASEAN countries without creating resentment. By working together, Malaysia and Thailand can help to shape and maintain not only the explicit agreement between all members of ASEAN to implement the CEPT, but also the implicit agreement to maintain mutual pressure on each other to continue with their respective liberalisation policies by ensuring a *quid pro quo*.

Conclusion

The new environment in Southeast Asia is altering the way regional governments and private sectors perceive the costs and benefits of economic cooperation in ASEAN. The adoption of liberalisation policies, the turn to growth strategies based on attracting FDI, and the emergence of economic blocs in Europe and North America are the primary factors which make AFTA possible today. The past constraints to cooperation have diminished in light of these changes. Yet, they have not disappeared. The success of AFTA will not be assured unless visionary action is taken in ASEAN. The cards as they are played now suggest that Thailand and Malaysia are in the position to accept the challenge and to lead ASEAN into a new era of closer cooperation in AFTA.

Notes

1   The average share for all intra-group exports among developing countries, including ASEAN, was less than 10 per cent in 1988 (see Imada, Montes and Naya 1991, p. 4).

2   *Agreement on the Common Effective Preferential Tariff (CEPT) Scheme for the ASEAN Free Trade Area (AFTA)*, Singapore, 28 January 1992, Article 2.

3   *Agreement on the Common Effective Preferential Tariff (CEPT) Scheme for the ASEAN Free Trade Area (AFTA)*, Singapore, 28 January 1992, Article 5, Section D.

4   Mari Pangestu, Institute of Strategic and International Studies, Jakarta, telephone interview, 30 July 1992.

References

Imada, Pearl, Manuel Montes and Seiji Naya 1991, *A Free Trade Area: Implications for ASEAN*, Economic Research Unit, Institute of Southeast Asian Studies, Singapore.

Langhammer, Rolf 1987, 'Fallacies of transposition: what ASEAN should learn from other integration efforts', in Noordin Sopiee, Chew Lay See and Lim Siang Jin (eds), *ASEAN at the Crossroads: Obstacle, Options and Opportunities in Economic Co-operation*, Secretariat of the Group of Fourteen, Institute of Strategic and International Studies, Kuala Lumpur, pp. 535–50.

Naya, Seiji and Michael G. Plummer 1991, 'ASEAN economic cooperation in the new international economic environment', *ASEAN Economic Bulletin*, 7(3), March.

Rieger, Hans Christoph 1986, 'ASEAN: a free trade area or a customs union?', *Far Eastern Economic Review*, 1 May, pp. 58–9.

Tiglao, Rigoberto 1992, 'A nettle to grasp: remedies may be politically unpalatable', *Far Eastern Economic Review*, 23 July.

United Nations 1991, *International Trade Statistics Yearbook 1991*, United Nations.

World Bank 1992, *World Development Report, 1992*, World Bank.

Part Eight

Australia and New Zealand: CER Regionalism

26　The future of the CER Agreement: a single market for Australia and New Zealand ———

P. J. Lloyd

Closer economic relations

The CER Agreement came into effect on 1 January 1983. It replaced the New Zealand–Australia Free Trade Agreement, which had come into effect on 1 January 1966. In terms of the usual economists' classification of regional trading agreements, the CER denotes a free trade area, whereas its predecessor, although formally recognised by GATT as a 'free trade area', was restricted to freeing trade in products of the forest products sector and a quite limited range of manufactures.

The objectives of the CER Agreement, as stated in Article 1, are:

(a)　to strengthen the broader relationship between Australia and New Zealand;

(b)　to develop closer economic relations between the member states through a mutually beneficial expansion of free trade between Australia and New Zealand;

(c)　to eliminate barriers to trade between Australia and New Zealand under an agreed timetable and with a minimum of disruption; and

(d)　to develop trade between New Zealand and Australia under conditions of fair competition.

Objectives (b) and (c) state unmistakeably that the trade objective is ultimate free trade. The first objective, and the preamble to the Agreement, declare that the free trade provisions are part of a more basic desire to maintain closer economic relations, and the preamble refers to 'strengthening and fostering links and cooperation in such fields as investment, marketing, movement of people, tourism and transport'.

The CER Agreement was a major accomplishment, given the long history of failed attempts at freeing trade between the two countries and the climate of opinion at the time.

The Ministerial Review of the Agreement in June 1988 reached agreement on a 'comprehensive package of arrangements designed to accelerate the implementation of the full free trade area and open a new chapter in the closer economic relationship between the two countries'. Free trade in commodities was achieved on 1 July 1990, by which time all tariffs, import licensing and quantitative restrictions, and export incentives restricting trade between the two countries were removed. This was five years ahead of the date specified in the Agreement. The other principal features of this important review were the extension of Australian state preferences to trans-Tasman government purchasing, an agreement on trade in services which freed trade in services except those specified by 1 January 1989, the termination of antidumping measures from 1 July 1990, the agreement on avoiding industry assistance policy which impacts on competition within the free trade area, and the agreement to harmonise policies and practices in a number of areas. The areas of harmonisation included business law, customs policies and procedures, quarantine administration, and technical barriers to trade. In the important area of competition policy it was agreed that competition policies in each country should be amended so that dominance was defined as a dominant position in the market of either country or the combined market. This review was another notable and praiseworthy achievement in bilateral trading relations.

As a result of the procedures agreed to in the 1988 review there has been further progress in removing impediments to trade. In particular, a comprehensive review of the scope for harmonisation of business laws identified a number of areas where harmonisation would be beneficial to the business communities (Steering Committee of Officials 1990). To implement the 1988 agreement on dominance in competition policy, both Australia and New Zealand in May–June 1990 altered the laws relating to enforcement of orders and judgements to allow their courts to sit in each other's jurisdictions to determine competition law cases. Also an Agreement on Standards, Accreditation and Quality was signed by the two governments in October 1990.

The CER has been accompanied by a rapid expansion of trade between Australia and New Zealand. Table 26.1 contains series of imports into Australia and New Zealand from the Tasman partner for the period immediately preceding the CER until the latest available year. It also includes 1965, the year New Zealand–Australia Free Trade Agreement was introduced, and five-yearly intervals until 1980 for comparison.

These trade statistics are in current price US dollars. Most of the increase in trade throughout the period of the New Zealand–Australia Free Trade Agreement and the CER is due to inflation rather than to increases in the volume of trade. Nevertheless, trade in real terms has increased steadily, particularly since the formation of the CER.

Table 26.1   AustraliañNew Zealand commodity trade, 1965ñ93

| | Australian imports from NZ | | NZ imports from Australia | |
	Total US$m	% total imports	Total US$m	% total imports
1965	55.99	1.51	199.98	18.36
1970	117.60	2.35	247.04	19.38
1975	288.01	2.62	600.01	19.05
1980	761.24	3.41	1 011.36	18.48
1981	853.50	3.27	1 079.36	18.81
1982	803.23	3.03	1 102.58	19.02
1983	753.52	3.54	1 028.79	19.29
1984	963.42	3.75	1 252.38	20.38
1985	1 052.09	4.08	1 025.67	17.25
1986	1 010.16	3.86	980.14	16.33
1987	1 220.78	4.13	1 474.63	20.28
1988	1 608.98	4.41	1 587.46	21.60
1989	1 827.95	4.09	1 829.93	20.96
1990	1 886.84	4.40	1 930.55	20.19
1991	1 947.73	4.59	1 848.81	22.02
1992	2 064.30	4.63	1 941.13	21.19
1993	2 225.08	4.93	2 003.72	21.68

Note: This table replaces that in the original source, which provided local currency data up to 1990.

Source: International Economic Database, Australian National University, Canberra.

Another indication of the effects of a preferential reduction in trade barriers is the change in the percentage of trade which is with the CER partner. The New Zealand share of Australian imports has steadily increased for New Zealand throughout the period of the New Zealand–Australia Free Trade Agreement and CER but the Australian share of New Zealand imports has been roughly constant. New Zealand seems to have gained more from the trade agreements than Australia.

The CER is a successful and far reaching trade liberalisation agreement. It is a more advanced form of trade liberalisation than the Canada–US Free Trade Agreement of 1989, which has a number of exclusions and exceptions that substantially limit the extent to which trade in both goods and services will be freed. It is second only to the EC in terms of the range of measures which relate to or bear upon trade that is covered.

Yet there is still no free trade in a number of important services, notably shipping between the two countries and entry into Australia for New Zealand exports of civil aviation and telecommunications; there is no common external tariff, no common commodity taxes/subsidies, and a number of domestic policies relating to technical standards and business laws inhibit trade in goods and services. Furthermore, the CER

Agreement is unique among regional trading arrangements around the world in that it has freed completely trade in all goods and most services, and there is free movement of residents of both countries under the long-standing Trans-Tasman Travel arrangements, but there are still significant restrictions on capital movements, especially from New Zealand to Australia.

Another feature of the restrictions on trade which remain between the two countries is that the Australian restrictions on imports of goods and services and capital flows are (at the time of writing) in 1991 more comprehensive in extent than the New Zealand restrictions on imports from Australia. This is especially true in services where the New Zealand exemptions are less than the Australian, in agriculture (where trade is still inhibited by regulations on trade across state borders) and in the area of capital flows. It is the reverse of the situation which prevailed throughout the period of the New Zealand–Australia Free Trade Agreement and it is the result of the extensive and rapid liberalisation of trade and the removal of assistance for agricultural producers and manufacturers which New Zealand began in 1984 with its global trade liberalisation program, and the deregulation of the service sector in New Zealand.

However, this difference in the extent of barriers does not imply that imports into New Zealand from Australia are restricted more in value than Australian imports from New Zealand as the effects of freeing trade bilaterally depend on the *margins of preference* for all goods and services. When bilateral trade has been freed totally the margins of preference are measured simply by the difference between the rates for the rest of the world countries and the zero rate for the partner. Unfortunately, it is not possible to compare the structure of industry assistance *vis-à-vis* third countries. In Australia, the Industry Commission (and before it the Industries Assistance Commission and the Tariff Board) has prepared an annual set of estimates for all commodity groups, including in recent years agricultural and mining industries (see Industry Commission 1990a, Appendixes 9–11) and there are estimates for some service industries. Unfortunately, there is no comparable series in New Zealand. The first set of measures in New Zealand of assistance to producers which were comprehensive in covering all manufacturing and agricultural production were in Syntec Economic Services (1988). These revealed that in 1987–88 for the manufacturing sector the average effective rate of industry assistance, which is the best single summary measure of the assistance, was 26 and 18 per cent for manufacturing and pastoral agriculture respectively. The comparable figures for Australia in the same year were 19 and 49 per cent respectively.

Since 1987–88 the New Zealand rates have fallen in the manufacturing sector under the trade liberalisation program. The reductions will end in 1996, by which time the maximum tariff will be 10 per cent. Post-1992 the average rates of assistance to domestic producers *vis-à-vis* third countries in New Zealand will be lower than that in Australia for the agricultural and service sectors and possibly for the manufacturing sector too. This means that the margins of preference which New Zealand enjoys because of the freeing of bilateral trade will in the future be greater on average than those which the Australian producers receive.

The last feature of the CER Agreement that should be noted is that the freeing of trade between the two countries since 1983 has been accompanied by a significant liberalisation of trade *vis-à-vis* third countries over the same period. This is especially true of New Zealand but it is also true of Australia.

This fact has two important implications. It means that the standard dangers of welfare losses to the two countries, given that the preferences divert import (and export) trade from the lowest cost sources of supply and deflect trade because of differences in the nominal rates of protection for materials and other inputs, are reduced. It also means that the Agreement is outward looking in the sense that the discrimination against third countries has been reduced and the total trade with these countries has been expanded by global assistance reductions. Indeed, in the case of New Zealand, the bilateral freeing of trade was only undertaken by the smaller country because it adopted this strategy of avoiding the cost of increased trading with a country that is a high cost supplier of many commodities. The CER was a part of a larger set of trade liberalisation strategies.

Trends in world trade

Both governments have expressed the view that the CER should be an outward-looking agreement which should not restrict the trade with third countries. Both have expressed the view that the CER should provide a base for the development of enterprises which are competitive on the global marketplace. This is a reflection of the growing concern of both the Australian and New Zealand governments that they have been losing competitiveness in world markets which are becoming increasingly competitive and more closely integrated. They share this concern with other countries such as the United States. This concern was also a fundamental factor behind the EC movement to the measures of the EC '92.

The added feature of the Australian and New Zealand economies that needs to be considered is that, on the world stage, these two nations are two small and peculiar trading economies. Their peculiarity is that they are high-income countries with a specialisation in primary commodities.

This pattern of commodity trade is an oddity among developed market economies. Unfortunately, it is a specialisation in markets which have the features that the world demand for the products has grown less rapidly than that for manufactures and services and the world markets are more heavily restricted. The pattern has been exacerbated historically by remoteness, which is not easily changed, and by the highly protectionist policies towards manufactures in the two countries, which are changeable and have recently been changing rapidly. The central question for both economies is how they can become more closely linked to the markets which are growing more rapidly. The governments of both countries are strongly in favour of a multilateral approach to those barriers to world trade which result from border protection and are strong supporters of GATT.

A comparison of the CER with the EC Single Market

In order to appreciate what the establishment of a single market across Australia and New Zealand would imply, Table 26.2 compares the (1991) CER with the Single Market measures in EC '92. A +(-) sign indicates that the measures in the EC have, or at least will have, by 1992, progressed further (less) towards a single market than the corresponding provisions of the CER, provided the measures are implemented by all EC members. An = sign indicates that the progress is roughly equal in the EC '92 and in the CER. An ± sign indicates approximate equality of single-marketness, some features in the EC being more single and some less single than in the CER. The measures in the EC relating to road transport are not applicable to the CER because of the separation by the Tasman Sea. One should also note that the single market features of a common external tariff and freedom of movement of capital do not appear in this table as they were achieved in the original Treaty of Rome.

There is a preponderance of = or ± signs, indicating that in many respects the degree of single-marketness in the CER is about equal to that of the EC. However, the EC '92 has progressed further towards a single market than the CER in a number of areas, notably the common market for all services, the common excise and value added taxes, and freedom of movement of capital. In two significant areas the CER has progressed further than the EC '92. These areas are the important area of subsidies and bounties to producers ('state aids' in the EC terminology) and 'Proposals for Cooperation in Training and Education'. The first reflects the agreement reached in the 1988 Ministerial Review of the CER under which the two governments agreed to avoid the adoption of industry-specific measures which have an adverse effect on competition between industries in the free trade area. This was based on the principle that 'bounties and subsidies providing long-term competition can no longer be regarded as viable instruments of industry policy' in a free trade area. The second is the result of cooperation between the two governments in recognising the qualifications of professionals trained in the other country which precedes the CER but has been recognised as a principle in the Agreement.

Overall, the general conclusion is that the CER experience parallels that of the EC in many respects but that the EC is advancing more rapidly than the CER towards a single market.

From the point of view of the future development of the CER one sees that the CER is an advanced form of regional trading arrangement with many features of a single market. In a few ways the CER is very advanced; these include the abolition of export incentives affecting bilateral trade, the agreement to abolish subsidies and bounties which affect bilateral trade, and in the area of business law generally but particularly in competition policy with the extension of dominance to the single trans-Tasman market and the legislation to allow the courts to sit in the jurisdiction of the other

Table 26.2 A comparison of the EC í92 and CER internal market measures

Market measures	Goods	Services	Labour	Capital
Removal of Border Protection and Restrictions	+ (Abolition of Frontier Controls) = (Liberalisation of Public Procurement) Not Applicable (Abolition of Quotas at Border [road transport])	(Liberalisation of Public Procurement)	+ (Abolition of Intra-EC Frontier Controls on Individuals) = (Elimination of Obstacles to the Movement and Residence of Migrant Workers and Unemployed)	+ (Monitoring of Exchange Controls and Restrictions on Capital Movements)
Removal of Discriminatory Non-Border Taxes/and Discriminatory Subsidies/Regulations	+ (Fiscal Approximation) – (State Aids) + (Harmonisation of Standards in Sectors)	+ (Common Market for Transport) + (Common Market for New Technologies and Services) + (Harmonisation of Income Tax Transactions in Securities)	+ (Right of Establishment for Professionals with Higher Education Diplomas based on Mutual Recognition) = (European Vocational Training Card) + (Harmonisation of Income Tax Provisions for Migrants)	= + (European Company Statute) + (European Interest Grouping) ± (Proposals on Cross-Border Mergers and Takeovers)
Measures to Improve Single Functioning Single Activities	± (Company Law Framework) ± (Harmonisation of Intellectual and Industrial Property Law) ± (Company Policy)	± (Company Law Framework) ± (Harmonisation of Intellectual and Industrial Property Law) ± (Company Policy)	– (Proposals for Cooperation in Training and Education)	± (Company Law Framework) ± (Harmonisation of Intellectual and Industrial Property Law) ± (Company Policy)

country. On the other hand, there are some areas in which current taxes/subsidies/ regulations fall significantly short of a single market; these include the absence of a common external tariff, the absence of a common market for some services, inter-country differences in commodity and value added tax rates, and the absence of an agreement on capital flows.

The advantages and disadvantages of a single market

The appeal of a single market is that it removes all differences between the member countries in the rates of taxes/subsidies/regulations which discriminate between producers or consumers according to their location. Since the time of Adam Smith at least, economists have known that all such differences distort the choices of consumers and producers. This simple but powerful idea applies to distortions in all markets, that is, to the markets for goods and services and factors alike.

As examples, consider two of the measures of the EC '92 which go beyond the traditional concern of free trade areas and customs unions with that subset of discriminatory instruments which apply at the border. These are the harmonisation of standards and the 'approximation' of tax rates.

The loss of efficiency in production due to inter-country differences in standards applying to industrial safety, health, transport, goods specifications, labelling, and so on is obvious. The primary loss is the distortion due to differences in costs. The costs of meeting the different standards will differ between the two countries and thus consumers will buy the products at different prices in the two countries. These costs include the costs due to the loss of consumer welfare because the standards may prohibit the sale of goods in one country but not in the other.

Now there may be a justification for standards which, say, protect the consumer from products which are unsafe in ways which the consumer cannot perceive as a buyer. In such cases, however, there is no reason in general to expect that the standards should differ between countries. Either they are too stringent in one or too lax in the other or both too stringent or too lax but by differing degrees. Both producers and consumers will benefit if the standards are harmonised, provided of course that the harmonisation moves in the direction of the country with the better standards (or, more generally, the optimal standards).

The second general source of welfare loss is that differences in standards between jurisdictions impose extra costs of compliance. Harmonisation which results in simplification will yield benefits by reducing the costs of production.

The second example is the equalisation of commodity tax rates. Inter-country differences in tax rates on a commodity or group of commodities distort the pattern of consumption and trade in these commodities because they lead to differences in relative consumer prices between the countries concerned as tax differences are passed on to consumers/users, and usually to the same extent in different countries as the elasticities of demand and supply which determine the incidence will not in general differ systematically between countries. Article 99 of the Treaty of Rome specifically provided for the approximation of indirect taxes. Accordingly, in 1967 the EC member states decided that the existing turnover taxes must be replaced by a value added tax levied on a common basis, and the broad principles of the harmonised common tax base were laid down in 1967. Indeed, the White Paper stated that 'It is clear . . . that the harmonisation of indirect taxes has always been regarded as an essential and integral part of achieving a common market' (Commission of the European Communities 1985, p. 42). However, the Commission lacked the means of enforcing common value added tax rates. In 1989 there were wide differences of many percentage points among the twelve members for each of the three rates permitted — the normal rates, the reduced rates and the high rates (see Siebert 1990, p. 55). These will be eliminated by 1992 under the European Single Market.

Another advantage of a single market is that it would increase competition. Commodity trade liberalisation by itself will increase competition. A study by Australia's Bureau of Industry Economics (1989) indicated that the gains from trade liberalisation are likely to be much greater than previously estimated because of economies of scale and increased competition effects. The full extent of potential competition can only be reached if all barriers due to non-border restrictions, standards, and the territorial limitation of competition law and other business laws are removed.

The disadvantages of a single market relate to the fact that the equalisation of rates (or equivalent) rates of taxes or subsidies across the members of the area will generally result in the creation of new differences between the rates which apply within the area on the one hand and the rates which apply to trade with other countries outside the area on the other. This is exemplified by the classic problem of trade diversion when the rates of taxes are due to tariffs at the border. The gains due to the equalisation of rates within the area for some commodities will be offset by losses due to the differentiation of the rates between the member countries and the non-member countries on other commodities where the discriminatory tariff reductions induce some countries within the area to substitute imports from members for imports from other countries which produce them at a lower real cost ex-tariff. Such trade diversion may apply to export trade as well as import trade, and to capital flows when the source or destination of investment flows are distorted by trade preferences.

Precisely the same problem arises with other equalisations in a single market which create new differences between the members and non-members. Perhaps the most important such case which would be involved if Australia and New Zealand were to form a single market is that of a common external tariff. All of these are examples of the theory of the second best which arises with any piecemeal reforms.

In the case of equalisation of rates of *non-border* taxes/subsidies such as excise or value added rates, the creation of a single market with a single rate for each commodity across the whole area would not create new differences between the rates at which the goods are traded across borders. But it would create new differences in the rates across commodities which give rise to analogous gains and losses. However, the danger of losses can be reduced by various strategies of harmonisation.

It is likely that the gains from the formation of a single market would be greater for New Zealand simply because it joins with a larger market with more market opportunities and more suppliers. It is also true that the greater orientation of the Australian economy towards trading with third countries means that the potential gains from increased trading with third countries may be proportionately larger for New Zealand. Nevertheless, the gains will not be negligible for Australia. If it is to progress with trade liberalisation and industry deregulation it is better to do so in the context of a single market and to gain the benefits of a simultaneous improvement in market access and efficiency of production with the trading partner.

Implementing a single market for Australia and New Zealand

The argument for a common market for services is a standard case of establishing a common market for any commodity. The fact that a market is for a service rather than a commodity does not change the gains and losses of trade liberalisation. The CER has accepted the merits of freeing trade in all physical commodities and many services and the remaining services are an anomaly that should be corrected. The exemptions on the Australian and New Zealand lists are all industries or commodity groups which are highly regulated in the exempting country. The freeing of international trade in commodities which are subject to domestic regulation is more complicated and requires more legislative changes but one should note that many of the physical commodities for which trans-Tasman trade was liberalised in July 1990 had been subject to industry plans or other forms of regulation including state trading monopolies (for example, the former New Zealand Wheat Board). These commodity groups were put in Annex E of the Agreement for special negotiation and a delayed timetable but this did not prevent the freeing of trade. Free trade tends to undermine domestic regulations and bilateral freeing of trade therefore requires a large measure of deregulation. Those interest groups which gain rents from the present national regulations will protest vigorously at suggestions to free trade and deregulate the markets concerned but the fundamental case for free trade is not essentially different from that of non-regulated commodities.

The absence of free trade in capital is also an anomaly in the factor markets. There was no provision for free trade in capital in the CER, unlike the Treaty of Rome for instance. During the CER negotiations the question of investment policy arose but it was considered inappropriate. The essential argument for free movement of the factor capital is based on the increase in factor productivities. The elimination of barriers to the movement of capital will allow capital to move to the location in the free trade area where it can earn the highest rate of return (allowing for possible differences in risk). In the absence of distortions, this is the location where the marginal productivity of the factor capital is greater. The liberalisation of commodity trade within a free trade area itself changes factor productivities and creates incentives to reallocate production between as well as within the two countries. This reallocation of production requires takeovers, joint ventures, mergers and other inter-company stock transactions to rationalise the location of plants. These can only be realised in full if there is free movement of capital within the area.

Since both countries still restrict capital movements into their markets from all foreign countries, the freeing of capital within the free trade area would give a capital preference to the capitalists in the other member country over all other third countries. To enforce the preferences, the governments would have to introduce a content rule similar to that which governs trade within free trade areas in order to prevent the preference being received by investors of third countries through entering the country with the less restrictive barriers and then reinvesting in the second country.

The Australian government has repeatedly stated that the Nara Treaty between Australia and Japan prevents the introduction of investment policies which diminish Japan's MFN status. The obvious resolution of this problem is to approach it in the same way as the GATT treats discriminatory tariff reductions in free trade areas; namely, to ensure that the agreement on foreign investments does not impose new restrictions on the investments from third countries and is outward-looking in encouraging investment flows.

The real difficulty is not one of law but of the possibility that the freeing of capital which is bilateral and therefore discriminatory will, like that of commodity trade, produce new distortions that result in a net loss associated with capital movements. For example, it might encourage investment in New Zealand by some Australian company to take advantage of the new opportunities when this company is techno-logically inferior and a higher cost producer than some other producer from a third country. As both countries have liberalised capital flows greatly in recent years this danger has been greatly reduced. Where it might occur, the obvious action is to reduce restrictions on capital inflows from all countries.

The absence of a common external tariff and differences in commodity tax rates are two examples of the issue of harmonisation of policy instruments which affect the bilateral trade flows indirectly. Articles 12 and 14 of the CER Agreement recognised some of these. Article 12 declared that member states shall 'examine the scope for taking action to harmonise requirements relating to such matters as standards, technical specifications and testing procedures, domestic labelling and restrictive trade practices . . .'. Agreements were reached to begin harmonising standards on foods, consumer products and other standards and labelling. Article 14 recognised the 'intermediate goods problem' which arises because of the absence of a common external tariff on intermediate goods.

The CER did not recognise the generality or the extent of the harmonisation issue. Subsequently, there has been considerable debate in Australia and especially in New Zealand about the meaning of harmonisation. This has arisen in several contexts, including external tariffs, taxation, business laws, standards, and exchange rates (see, especially, Holmes et al. 1986). The problem is, however, a universal one which applies to all areas of government intervention in the economies which impinge on bilateral trade. In all areas of policy the two countries as sovereign states have made policies which differ in at least some material respects.

The view which is predominant in New Zealand seems to be that 'harmonisation' of a policy instrument should not mean 'uniformity' or 'replication'. Sir Frank Holmes and his colleagues at the Institute of Policy Studies opted for 'approximation rather than unification of policy' (Holmes et al. 1986, p. 91). Similarly, Professor Farrar (1989), in his commentary on the harmonisation of business laws which is proceeding under the 1988 Memorandum of Understanding between the two governments, argues that 'harmonisation is simply a means to an end' and cites other legal authorities who believe that harmonisation does not mean necessarily the adoption of identical policies. Indeed, the Memorandum of Understanding is quite explicit in stating under Article 8 that 'both governments recognise that effective harmonisation does not require replication of laws, although that may be appropriate in some cases'. The former Prime Minister of New Zealand, Mr Geoffrey Palmer, cited these views with approval (Palmer 1990).

It is true that harmonisation is a means to an end, that end being efficient production and exchange. It should, therefore, mean what is in the best interests of the economies rather than a dogma. However, there is a very strong logic based on efficiency of production and exchange which implies the two economies should move towards unification or approximation of the major policies which impinge upon bilateral trade.

As the first example, consider the common external tariff; that is, a common external tariff on all items. It is useful to consider the tariffs on two sets of goods, those on intermediate inputs and those on final goods.

The existence of differences in tariffs or tariff equivalents on raw materials, components and capital equipment gives the producers of the country which imposes the lower tariffs or tariff equivalents upon the input goods an advantage in bilateral competition. Under the CER this is regarded by industries in which it occurs as unfair competition but we shall see that the real issue is efficiency of production.

Article 14 provides for several responses — a common external tariff, compensating export duties, compensating input duties or countervailing subsidies, variation of area content requirements, cancellation of drawback or tariff concession, or acceleration of trade liberalisation — on the items concerned. Of these, the only instrument which completely and permanently removes the advantage is the common external tariff.

The objection that has been raised in New Zealand to the common external tariff is that it would result in New Zealand having to accept the higher Australian tariff levels for many intermediate goods (see Holmes et al. 1986, pp. 71–7; and Australia–New Zealand Business Council 1990, Session Four). This is so because more intermediates and capital goods enter New Zealand at zero or low concessional rates of duty than in Australia. It is also based on the premise that the harmonisation would proceed by averaging the rates or at least would result in some rates which are higher than their lower pre-harmonisation levels. The GATT rules require that the common tariff be no higher than the pre-harmonisation trade weighted average.

This objection can be overcome. The obvious method of overcoming it is to harmonise in such a way that the post-harmonisation level is lower than the simple average of the pre-harmonisation levels of the tariffs on an item. This method shifts the adjustment to the country with the higher pre-harmonisation level. It is likely to encounter the objection in that country that the harmonisation in the trading arrangement is undermining the level of protection given by the general tariff rate. While this is true, it is a merit of the common external tariff, and in any case the levels of tariffs are generally falling in both countries.

There is a second variant of this strategy. That is to reduce the tariffs on all intermediates in both countries from all sources to zero. Such a reduction would automatically harmonise the rates (at zero) and remove the discrimination *vis-à-vis* third countries for these imports. The justification for this policy is that efficient production requires that there be no distortion of input prices (Diamond and Mirrlees 1971). Any tariffs or other taxes on inputs result in a loss of aggregate production. This powerful theorem means that there should be no tariffs on inputs.

This proposition is neither as novel nor as radical as it seems at first. Both the Australian Tariff through its by-laws and commercial tariff concessions and the New Zealand Tariff through Part II and other end-user concessions have long allowed duty free or concessional entry for intermediates not produced in the country. These concessions have always been based on the realisation that tariffs on inputs increase the real costs of production. Numerical simulations of the Australian economy done by the Industry Commission indicate that these concessions do provide significant benefits to the Australian economy by reducing industries' costs of production (Industry Commission 1990b, Appendix F).

The common external tariff on final goods avoids another distortion in the economies. If there is a difference between the (effective) rate of assistance on a final commodity between the two countries, there is another violation of Pareto efficiency in the regional trading area as a whole. Consequently, the elimination of this difference would permit an increase in the aggregate production of the region. This argument has already been recognised loosely in the CER provision under Article 13 that a common external tariff on the outputs as well as the inputs may be used to promote rationalisation in an industry. The argument holds generally for all industries.

For most final goods tariff items, the establishment of a common external tariff would not have a major impact because the differences in rates are small or the tariffs are protective in only one of the two countries. However, there are a small number of industries in both countries which are heavily protected by tariffs. In Australia these are the group of clothing, textile and footwear, passenger motor vehicles and tobacco products; and in New Zealand the same groups less tobacco products. Even if the area continues to protect these groups heavily, production within the area should be efficient; that is, minimise the real costs of area production. This requires a common tariff. As with the difference on intermediate inputs, it is best if the rates are harmonised downwards.

Thus there should be a common external tariff on the tariff items for all traded goods. Once tariffs were harmonised it would then be essential to harmonise other forms of assistance which inhibit trade or efficiency. It would also mean that future changes in tariff rates and other forms of assistance would have to be decided by both countries jointly. While this was seen as a disadvantage by the Australia–New Zealand Business Council (1990), it is really an advantage because it would in practice act as a form of rate binding which would inhibit future rate increases but not decreases.

The second issue of the harmonisation of commodity and value added taxes poses very similar issues. Consider excise taxation as a form of commodity taxation that is common to both countries and which, indeed, has a common historical origin in British excise taxation, which was transplanted to the colonies in the nineteenth century. The nature of the harmonisation problem in this area and its relationship to the harmonisation of tariffs is best appreciated if we regard an excise tax as a tax levied on the unit of production of the commodity at an administratively convenient stage of manufacturing production, such as the brewery or distillery for alcoholic beverages, or the refinery for petroleum products. In Australia and New Zealand excise taxes are specific duties but the *ad valorem* equivalent can be easily calculated.

An excise tax is a negative subsidy on production, expressed in *ad valorem* equivalent terms. As with a subsidy, part of the tax is passed forward to the buyer or backward to the supplier, depending on market conditions, in the usual way. Thus the system of excise taxation discourages the production of excisable commodities in precisely the same way as the use of subsidies and bounties encourages the production of the subsidised commodities. The argument for harmonising the rates of excise within a free trade area is precisely the same as the argument for harmonising subsidy and bounty rates, namely to avoid distortions of production within the area which move the economies away from efficient production.

The case for harmonising other commodity taxes such as wholesale sales taxes, the goods and services tax or financial services duties is precisely the same as that of harmonising excise tax rates.

Furthermore, we can relate the issue of harmonising production taxes/subsidies to the issue of harmonising tariffs by using the familiar equivalence relation in tax theory. An *ad valorem* tariff is equivalent to the combination of an *ad valorem* subsidy on the production of the commodity and an *ad valorem* tax on the consumption of the commodity, provided all of the tax rates are levied at the same rate and under very general conditions. The first component affects production in precisely the same way as the *ad valorem* subsidy on production. This is the protective effect of the tariff. Again we see that the essential argument for harmonising excise taxes and other taxes levied directly on commodities and subsidies/bounties is the same as that for harmonising tariffs (and all other forms of border protection).

This argument can readily be extended to value added taxation. At the present time New Zealand has a value added tax, the Goods and Services Tax (GST). Australia does not have a value added-type tax but the desirability of introducing a broad-based commodity tax and quite possibly a value added tax has been canvassed repeatedly since the Tax Summit of 1985. Value added taxes use as a base of the tax the value added rather than the volume of production at each stage of production but inter-country differences in rates of value added taxation distort production within a free trade area in the same way as differences in production taxes or subsidies/bounties. Therefore, there is an argument for their harmonisation.

In all of the four areas of harmonisation discussed so far — the common markets for services and capital, the common external tariff, and harmonisation of commodity tax rates — the argument for harmonisation of the relevant instruments has also produced an argument for unification or replication. This is essentially due to the nature of these instruments, all of which are expressible in terms of *ad valorem* rates of assistance (in the case of services and the external tariff) or subsidy/taxation. Inter-country differences in tax/subsidy rates give an incentive for producers to change the location of production or for consumers to change their consumption choices and these differences are removed if and only if the rates are equated. In the case of capital flows the incentive comes directly from the restrictions on capital flows.

The feature of unification is not inevitable and general. An important counter-example is standards. The experience of the EC is germane here. For many years the Community attempted to eliminate technical barriers through harmonisation, by which was meant the adjustment of national regulations to conform to a single common Community standard. The process proved to be slow, bureaucratic and time con-suming. The 'new approach' to harmonisation of standards in the White Paper is based on the principle of 'mutual recognition' of each other's standards. The Cassis de Dijon decision of the European Court in 1976 ruled that a product which was brought legally into the market of one member country can enter without restriction the markets of the other member countries. This made a policy of mutual recognition enforceable. However, harmonisation in the form of agreed community standards will still be required for two types of standards, those for 'essential requirements' and those in high technology areas where the inter-operability of equipment is necessary for the rational development of new products and the maintenance of free competition.

The reason for the preference for a non-uniform approach in the area of standards lies in the difficulty of comparing standards and the need to trade off the desirability of uniformity with the costs of negotiating and enforcing 'uniformity' when the standards are not readily comparable. Moreover, the Community is seeking to avoid the creation of new barriers by requiring member states to notify the Commission in advance of proposals for new regulations. This will lead to a high degree of uniformity in the long run.

The method of 'mutual recognition' may also be applicable in other areas. For example, the EC has also used this method in the area of recognition of professional training for certification in professional bodies. As a result of the Australian Prime Minister's initiative on cooperative federalism in 1990, the Commonwealth and State governments agreed to adopt mutual recognition of regulations. The New Zealand government wishes to be involved in this process, which could see mutual recognition of regulations extended throughout the area.

A single market will also require ultimately the harmonisation of other policies. One obvious example is income tax regimes. Substantial differences between countries in either the tax base or the tax rate payable on an income will provide a distortion of economic activities. Perhaps the clearest way of seeing this is to regard the labour income after tax of an income taxpayer as the price of leisure foregone. Differences in the tax base and/or tax rates lead to a differential in the price of leisure and, therefore, violate the 'law of one price'.

The final area of harmonisation I shall consider is the idea of a common currency. This has been discussed by Holmes et al. (1986, Section 3.8), Lloyd (1990) and the Australia–New Zealand Business Council (1990, Session Three). Sir Frank Holmes and his colleagues recommended against a common currency and the Australia–New Zealand Business Council recommended that this be put on the agenda of the 1992 review of the CER. The issue of a common currency or, more generally, of exchange rate policy is undoubtedly a very important one that has been debated since the formation of the New Zealand–Australia Free Trade Agreement. However, a common currency is not conceptually a part of a single market. It is an aspect of a larger set of issues concerning macroeconomic policy coordination between the governments of a free trade area or simply between any governments. It involves a trade-off of the gains from the elimination of exchange rate risk and the reduction in transactions costs against the losses in the form of the loss of an instrument of macroeconomic policy. The theory of optimal currency areas suggests that the primary consideration should be the extent to which the two national economies are subject to similar or dissimilar shocks from the rest of the world (see Kawai 1987).

This list of measures which may be harmonised is not exhaustive. In a single market it would also be necessary to examine other areas of economic policy which restrict efficiency of production in the area such as transport and energy policies, technology development, other taxes, and labour market policies.

The inevitability of greater unification

Market forces will inexorably drive the two economies towards a greater degree of unification and ultimately towards complete unification of the major policies which impinge on trade between the two countries.

The first set of market forces stems from the pressures which will be put on governments to unify policies between the two economies by the removal of all border barriers for traded commodities. For example, the freeing of tariffs on final commodities has quickly led to pressures to remove non-tariff barriers. The freeing of all trade in final commodities has shown that truly free competition between two producers who add value in the two countries requires in addition equal access to raw materials and components and other intermediate inputs. Complete freedom of trade for all commodities including intermediates demonstrates that assistance by means of bounties/subsidies and other non-border assistance also has a significant effect on the competitiveness of country producers. The awareness of the importance of these differences then leads the producers in the disadvantaged country to lobby their politicians for equality of opportunity and fair competition.

This sequence of discovery is evident in the progress made under the New Zealand–Australia Free Trade Agreement and the CER, and in the progress of the EC. The most dramatic expression of it was the realisation in the EC that a 'common market' was not an integrated single market because of the existence of other domestic impediments. Indeed, the whole history of free trade areas which have progressed to a substantial freeing of trade is a realisation that the freeing of trade in one area of potential trade reveals that other policies which were not previously thought to be important are now a more important impediment which prevents the full realisation of potential trade.

The second way in which harmonisation of policies can come about is through the incentives which the differences give to the governments themselves to make the change because the government is losing fiscal revenue or business or the migration of its citizens which induces the governments to act. The essential ingredient is the arbitrage of firms and households as consumers and factor suppliers and asset-owners. In response to price differentials due to differences in tax/subsidy rates or regulations or conditions for market entry, agents will respond by shifting their purchases or sales or assets to the market with the more favourable conditions.

Consider, for example, differences in a commodity or value added tax. If the goods are freely tradeable after taxes are paid, arbitrage will occur in many forms such as direct mailing or purchases on tourist or business travel. This then leads to competition between the governments fixing the tax rates. A similar process can occur in the regulation of industries via licensing or other regulations, leading to the phenomenon known as 'regulatory competition'. The phenomenon applies broadly to differences in all policies where there is some scope for agents to avoid the higher taxes or the more restrictive regulations by arbitraging. Siebert (1990) has called it *ex post* harmonisation.

Arbitrage requires that the agents are free to contract. Hence, in a particular market, development of inter-government competition may require the removal of barriers which restrict commodity trade and other forms of contracting. The importance of the adoption of the policy of 'mutual recognition' of standards is that it permitted trade which had been banned.

The phenomenon of arbitrage followed by convergence of policies between jurisdictions is observable for some policy differences among the Australian states. Trade across the border of neighbouring states occurs when there are significant differences in the level of state taxation of commodities such as alcoholic beverages or when gambling is prohibited in one state but permitted in a neighbouring state. The most dramatic example in Australia occurred when the former Premier of Queensland, Sir Joh Bjelke-Petersen, abolished death duties in Queensland. Within a short time all other Australian states were forced to follow suit because of the flow of migration of elderly citizens to avoid the duties in their home states.

A similar process has occurred in the CER when differences in the treatment of some items of income for corporate tax assessment led to a large loss of revenue to the Australian government. In both Australia and New Zealand there is a long practice of travellers returning to their country of residence loading themselves up with duty-free goods.

The phenomenon has another fundamental implication in that it provides an alternative route to harmonising some policies by government negotiation and agreement. The alternative is to remove the barriers to arbitrage and allow competition to produce convergence in the longer run rather than the governments trying to agree upon the level of the instruments and all other legislative change required to enforce them. The conspicuous example is the EC policy of 'mutual recognition' of standards. A similar policy could be applied in other areas.

An important example is the possibility of the establishment of an Australasia without a frontier, parallel to the Europe without frontiers. A single market requires the abolition of all restrictions on travellers and on the transport of goods within the area; that is, the abolition of the customs controls at the frontier. There can be little doubt that the removal of trans-Tasman restrictions on the transport of dutiable goods and all duties on goods transported across the Tasman would increase this form of arbitrage. An obvious example is the transport of automobiles that would occur between the two countries with differential commodity taxes. For tax instruments the abolition of the frontier would require the substitution of the country-of-origin basis of taxation (where the tax is levied in the country of origin and paid to the government in this country) for the country of destination basis, as in the example of commodity taxes above.

This approach to harmonisation could even be applied to a common currency. In this instance the governments would only have to legislate to declare that the currency of each member country is legal tender throughout the free trade area. Currency substitution may then result in individuals declaring a distinct preference for one currency.

A policy of *ex post* harmonisation could not, however, be applied in all areas. It would not be applicable to competition policy, which is designed to ensure competition among all producers, or to areas such as environmental problems, which involve spillover effects from one country to the next.

This policy of *ex post* harmonisation has several advantages over the traditional choice of *ex ante* negotiation of common or harmonised levels or regulations. It avoids protracted government negotiations, can take place over a longer time, reduces considerably the cost of the bureaucracy, and may in some cases be more responsive to the preferences of the economic agents or decision-makers and less responsive to the pressure of industry lobbies. It also avoids the necessity of courts or other agencies to enforce arbitrary area-wide standards and thereby avoids the infringements on the sovereignty of the two countries This method of harmonisation is gaining more proponents in the EC (see Siebert 1990; Pelkmans 1990; Lal 1990), including the United Kingdom.

Conclusions

The existing CER is a far-reaching and highly successful trade agreement. The two economies are approaching the status of a free trade area though there are still some exceptions to free international trade, notably in the markets for services and capital.

This paper concludes that there is a strong case that Australia and New Zealand should proceed to form a single market; that is, that the two countries should remove all impediments to trade and competition and harmonise major policies that impinge on trade and competition across the Tasman. We should unashamedly emulate in general (though not in all detail) the policies of the Single European Market. These measures include a common market for all services, a common market for capital, a common external tariff and a common regime for commodity taxation. They also include an Australasia without a frontier.

The essential justification for these measures is that they are required if the two economies are to realise the full potential gains from the freeing of trade under the CER. A second advantage is that the increase in efficiency and in competition that will occur throughout the single market will improve the competitiveness of the two economies in global markets.

An additional substantial argument in favour of the adoption of the concept of a single market is that it provides a standard by which to evaluate alternative proposals and positions during negotiations. Without such a standard there is a considerable danger that the negotiations will be *ad hoc* and directionless.

The harmonisation of instrument levels will require in some cases, such as the common external tariff and the common market for services, the unification of instruments or measures. However, in other cases where the instruments are not easily expressible in terms of percentage rates or other measurements, harmonisation will mean approximation rather than unification. This applies to measures such as standards and the recognition of professional and educational qualifications and industry regulations.

Harmonisation may occur either by the negotiation of common tax/subsidy regimes and regulations or the convergence of tax/subsidy rates and regulations as a result of competition between governments in pursuit of the welfare of their citizens. The two governments should consider the extension of the EC principle of 'mutual recognition' to standards and other areas of policies.

The issue of a common currency is not a part of a single market but it should be addressed by the two governments.

The process of forming a single market could begin with the compilation of a list of measures needed for implementation, like the list compiled by the Commission of the European Communities (1985) in its White Paper. It is not necessary that the single market be achieved by a single date. A common target date could be set for the achievement of measures which require *ex ante* harmonisation. For those measures which are subject to 'mutual recognition' and evolution towards a common level, the progression towards a single market could take place over a longer time.

The single market would require new institutional arrangements for some measures such as the abolition of the frontier and the institution of common trade policies *vis-à-vis* third countries. These need careful attention.

The formation of a single market involves many complex issues which have scarcely been debated in either country. The two governments should promote a debate in the community at large which extends beyond consultations with the main industry associations and unions as the extension of the CER will substantially affect all residents of both countries.

References

Australia–New Zealand Business Council 1990, *Proceedings of the Annual Conference*, 14–15 November.

Australian Minister for External Trade Relations 1990, Speech at the Opening of the Australia–New Zealand Business Council Annual Conference, Christchurch, 14 November.

Bureau of Industry Economics 1989, *Trade Liberalisation and Australian Manufacturing Industry: The Impact of the Australia–New Zealand Closer Economic Relations Trade Agreement*, Research Report No. 29, Canberra: Australian Government Publishing Service.

Commission of the European Communities 1985, *Completing the Internal Market: White Paper for the Commission to the European Council*, Luxembourg: Office for Official Publications of the European Communities.

Diamond, P. A. and J. A. Mirrlees 1971, 'Optimal taxation and public production — production efficiency', *American Economic Review*, 61, pp. 8–27.

Farrar, J. H. 1989, 'Harmonisation of business law between Australia and New Zealand', *Victoria University of Wellington Law Review*, 19, pp. 435–63.

Holmes, Sir Frank et al. 1986, *Closer Economic Relations with Australia: Agenda for Progress*, Wellington: Victoria University Press.

Industry Commission 1990a, *Annual Report 1989–90*, Canberra: Australian Government Publishing Service.

_____ 1990b, *The Commercial Tariff Concession and By-Law System, A Draft Report*, Canberra: Industry Commission.

Kawai, M. 1987, 'Optimal currency area', in J. Eatwell et al. (eds), *The New Palgrave: A Dictionary of Economics*, Vol. 3, London: Macmillan.

Lal, D. 1990, 'Comment', in H. Siebert (ed.), *The Competition of the Internal Market*, Tubingen: J. C. B. Mohr.

Lloyd, K. 1990, 'An Australia–New Zealand currency union?', *Policy*, 6, Winter, pp. 9–12.

Palmer, G. 1990, 'International trade blocs: New Zealand and Australia: beyond CER', Address to the Ninth Commonwealth Law Conference, Auckland.

Pelkmans, J. 1990, 'Regulation and the single market: an economic perspective', in H. Siebert (ed.), *The Competition of the Internal Market*, Tübingen: J. C. B. Mohr.

Siebert, H. 1990, 'The harmonization issue in Europe: prior agreement or a competitive process?', in H. Siebert (ed.), *The Competition of the Internal Market*, Tübingen: J. C. B. Mohr.

Steering Committee of Officials 1990, *The Harmonisation of Australian and New Zealand Business Law*, Canberra and Wellington.

Syntec Economic Services 1988, *Industry Assistance Reform in New Zealand*, Syntec Economic Services.

Part Nine

Subregionalism in the Asia Pacific

27 Subregional economic zones in Southeast Asia

Chia Siow Yue and Lee Tsao Yuan

This paper examines one manifestation of the intensified intra-regional investment flows and the accompanying trade flows in the Asia Pacific region, namely the phenomenon of subregional economic zones (SREZs). After outlining the conceptual framework underlying this phenomenon, a case study of one established SREZ — the Singapore–Johor–Riau Growth Triangle — is presented. The concluding section discusses the broader issues of the effects and implications of, and prospects for, SREZs in the Asia Pacific region.

The emerging phenomenon of subregional economic zones

A newly emerging category of economic grouping is that of SREZs. SREZs transcend political boundaries but do not always involve entire national economies. Instead, each SREZ involves only the border areas of at least one of the economies involved. For example, the Great South China Economic Zone comprises the economies of Hong Kong, Macau and Taiwan but only two of the coastal provinces of southern China — Guangdong and Fujian. The Singapore–Johor–Riau Growth Triangle comprises Singapore, the state of Johor in peninsular Malaysia, and the Riau province in Indonesia. In addition to these two already-established SREZs, four others are on the drawing board: the Northern Growth Triangle, involving southern Thailand, north-western Malaysia, and western Sumatra; the Tumen River Delta Area project, involving eastern Russia, China, Mongolia, and South and North Korea; the Yellow Sea Economic Zone, involving Japan, South Korea, and northern China; and the Japan

Sea Economic Zone, involving Japan, eastern Russia, northeastern China, and South and North Korea.

Growth triangles in Southeast Asia

In ASEAN, the growth triangle concept has caught interest in recent years. The idea of an economic zone linking Singapore and adjacent areas in Malaysia and Indonesia was officially proposed in December 1989 by Singapore's then-Deputy Prime Minister Goh Chok Tong, as a new form of subregional economic cooperation in ASEAN through cooperation in investment rather than through trade. There was concern over the slow pace of trade cooperation and liberalisation and the difficulty of always having to achieve consensus among the six member countries of ASEAN. Various names have been given to the growth triangle that has since developed in the area: SIJORI (coined by Indonesian Minister B. J. Habibie), the Johor–Singapore–Riau (JSR) Growth Triangle (popular in Singapore), and Nusa Tiga, which means 'three areas' and was coined by Chief Minister Muhyiddin of Johor. There has been official endorsement of increased cooperation at the highest levels of all three governments, but there is as yet no formal trilateral agreement. There are only two formal documents, signed by Singapore and Indonesia and not directly related to the growth triangle as a whole, outlining Singapore's role in the development of the Riau province and Indonesia's undertaking to supply water to Singapore as well as guaranteeing investments in Indonesia.

Following the success of SIJORI, there are proposals for more growth triangles within ASEAN. Of these, the furthest advanced is the Malaysian proposal for a Northern Growth Triangle encompassing the contiguous subregions of northwestern Malaysia (4 states), southern Thailand (14 provinces), and western Indonesia (2 provinces in Sumatra), to jointly develop infrastructure, natural resources, and industries (Salleh 1992). The triangle covers an area of 230,000 square kilometres, with an estimated population of 26 million.

At its fourth summit in Singapore in January 1992, ASEAN agreed to form a free trade area, within a time frame of fifteen years. The growth triangle approach was endorsed as a parallel and supportive mechanism of regional economic cooperation. There is also the possible emergence of a Baht Economic Zone in Indochina, with Thailand (whose currency is the baht) as the hub.

Categorisation of SREZs

One can identify five driving forces behind the emergence of SREZs, which may be present with varying degrees of importance in different SREZs: economic complementarity, geographical proximity, the political and economic policy framework, infrastructure, and market access. A categorisation of different types of SREZs can be determined, depending on the relative importance of each of the various driving forces mentioned above.

SIJORI is an example of a category reflecting 'metropolitan spillover into the hinterland'; essentially a growth pole spillover phenomenon in a transnational context. The driving forces here are economic complementarity, geographical proximity, and a policy framework more favourable to foreign investment in the less developed countries. Economic complementarity is what motivates the cross-border movement of capital, after an initial change in the policy framework in favour of foreign capital. Geographical proximity comes into its own as an economic factor that lowers transaction costs, but also because of cultural and kinship factors. McGee and MacLeod (1992) term this concept the 'extended metropolis region', while Scalapino (1992) calls them 'natural economic territories'.

Within this category, further differences exist between those SREZs that are market driven and those that have a greater degree of specific government facilitation or political motivation other than a general relaxation of investment rules. The Singapore–Johor link of SIJORI is market driven, with relatively little government participation. On the other hand, government has had greater involvement with the Singapore–Batam link of SIJORI. Not only have there been investment and water agreements signed between Indonesia and Singapore, but two investment missions to Northeast Asia to promote SIJORI have been organised with ministerial participation. The Batam Industrial Park, the first industrial estate to be built on Batam, is jointly owned and managed by an Indonesian conglomerate as well as two Singapore government-linked companies.

Metropolitan spillovers are primarily investment driven. At the moment, both SIJORI and the Great South China Economic Zone are export platforms, or the equivalent of transnational export processing zones, for exporting to other countries. However, the market potential of the SREZ itself as well as the countries whose areas are involved in the SREZ could increase.

The Singapore–Johor–Riau Growth Triangle

SIJORI has an area of 20,000 square kilometres and a population of 5 million (Table 27.1). Annual per capita GDPs in the constituent areas ranged from over US$3,000 in Johor and possibly less than US$1,000 in Batam to nearly US$13,000 in Singapore. There are concerted trilateral efforts to promote SIJORI, particularly the Singapore–Johor and Singapore–Riau links. SIJORI remains mainly a bilateral rather than a trilateral arrangement, with Singapore as the growth pole. In that sense, the term 'triangle' is a misnomer. The Johor–Riau side of the triangle is the least developed, and the economic linkages between Johor and Riau remain limited, because the two areas appear to be more competitive in resources than complementary, and factor price differentials in land and labour appear insufficient to induce investment flows.

Until recent years, economic linkages in SIJORI were limited. A common history and geographical proximity led to strong economic linkages between Singapore and

Table 27.1   Basic indicators for the SIJORI Growth Triangle

Indicator	Johor	Singapore	Riau	Total
Area (square kilometres)	18 914	639	3 300[a]	22 853
Population (millions)	2.2[b]	2.8[c]	0.1[c,d]	5.1
GDP (million US dollars)[e]	4 300[b]	34 600[b]	45[d,f]	38 945[g]
Per capita GDP (US dollars)	3 954[b]	12 940[b]	500[d,f]	
Growth rate of GDP (percentages)	9.0[c]	6.7[c]	na	

Notes: na— Not available.
        a   Includes only Batam, Bintan, Bulan, Singkep, Rempang, Galang and Barelang.
        b   1990.
        c   1991.
        d   Batam only.
        e   At current prices.
        f   1988.
        g   Figure is approximate.

Source: Johor State Economic Development Corporation, *Johor Investment Guide* 1991; Department of Statistics, *Yearbook of Statistics Singapore 1991*; World Bank, *World Development Report 1992*; Sakura Institute of Research, *Pacific Business and Industries*, vol. II, 1992; *Asiaweek*, 31 July 1992, p. 57; Batam Industrial Development Authority, *Statistics on the Manufacturing Sector in Malaysia, 1985–1990*; Pangestu (1991).

Johor. However, with the separate political development of Malaysia and Singapore since the mid-1960s, economic ties were gradually eroded. Nonetheless, movements of people and goods remained at a high level, in spite of immigration restrictions on both sides and the Malaysian government's desire to reduce the amount of external trade routed via Singapore. In spite of their geographical proximity, Singapore had negligible economic linkages with the islands of Riau province, because of separate political histories, the Indonesian government's restriction on foreign investment, and the relatively underdeveloped infrastructure in Riau. Economic linkages in SIJORI have increased significantly since the mid-1980s.

Rationale for SIJORI

The economic rationale for the promotion of SIJORI is that it makes possible the joint development of the subregion, capitalising on the resource complementarity and geographic proximity of the three component areas.

SIJORI offers the investor the whole range of business requirements: land, infrastructure, workers and skills. However, economic complementarity can only be exploited when there is a favourable political and policy environment and available infrastructure to facilitate the movement of goods, people and capital.

Political commitment and policy changes

It may be argued that SIJORI has been proposed largely in response to market forces, and that official cooperation has merely facilitated the already-growing economic linkages undertaken by the private sector. While this may be true of Singapore–Johor, official policy was decisive in promoting the Singapore–Riau side of the triangle, where market forces were weak.

SIJORI would not be what it is today without political commitment at the highest levels. The Indonesian Minister of State for Research and Technology, B. J. Habibie, who has responsibility for the development of Batam Island, first discussed the concept of interlinked development of the area with then-Singapore Prime Minister Lee Kuan Yew in 1979. He proposed that, like balloons, Singapore and other economies of the area could only continue to expand without bursting by being linked to each other. He further proposed an arrangement similar to those that link the Benelux countries, with free entry and exit of people, goods, and services (Habibie 1992). This idea of interlinked development between Singapore and Batam was discussed at a meeting between Indonesia's President Suharto and Lee Kuan Yew. This was crucial to the subsequent relaxation of Indonesian regulations governing foreign direct investment on Batam, and the growth in economic relations. In June 1990, when Suharto visited Malaysia, both heads of government endorsed the growth triangle concept.

Policy changes by Indonesia to attract investments to Batam include the following:

- 100 per cent foreign equity ownership is allowed for the first five years, after which there must be a 5 per cent divestment; no further divestment is required if the company is 100 per cent export-oriented (this condition is different from other parts of Indonesia, where divestment must reach at least 51 per cent within fifteen years).

- Investment applications can be processed in Batam itself rather than at the Investment Board (BKPM) in Jakarta.

- The private sector is allowed to set up industrial estates in Indonesia; this relaxation of the rules led to the establishment of the Batam Industrial Park as a joint venture between the Indonesian private sector and Singapore state organisations and enterprises.

These major policy changes, and the strong support of the Singapore government, were instrumental in overcoming the earlier reluctance of Singaporean investors and foreign multinationals based in Singapore, and led to a surge in Singapore investments in Batam, which had earlier been designated as a duty-free zone. For example, the Japanese multinational firm Sumitomo was the first to commit itself to becoming a tenant in the Batam Industrial Park and cited the urging of the Singapore government as one important reason for the investment move (Lee 1992b). Two high-level Indonesia–Singapore joint investment promotion missions were also organised to promote investment opportunities available in Batam (and Bintan): the first travelled to Osaka in December 1990, and the second to Hong Kong, South Korea and Taiwan in September 1991.

In August 1990 Singapore and Indonesia signed two bilateral agreements providing the framework for the joint development of Riau. The Agreement on Economic Cooperation in the Framework of the Development of the Riau Province is an enlargement of the Batam Economic Cooperation Agreement of 1980. The Agreement on the Promotion and Protection of Investments supplements the ASEAN Investment Guarantee Agreement. A third bilateral agreement in June 1991 provided for the joint development by Indonesia and Singapore of water resources in Riau, under which Singapore is guaranteed water supply from the Riau island of Bintan for at least fifty years. A joint committee at the ministerial level was set up to coordinate development efforts in Riau. There are ongoing efforts to coordinate and harmonise regulations and procedures. One example is cooperation on immigration procedures, which has helped to streamline commuting between Singapore and Batam; computerised processing of immigration procedures through the use of smart cards (plastic cards containing information on a microprocessor) was introduced in October 1991.

Although Malaysia's Prime Minister Mahathir had endorsed the growth triangle concept, Malaysian federal support for Johor's participation is not as enthusiastic as Indonesian central government support for Riau has been. However, the Johor state (provincial) government is a strong advocate of promoting bilateral Johor–Singapore economic linkages. Johor has benefited from its proximity to Singapore as well as from the Malaysian relaxation of foreign investment rules and regulations in recent years. Johor also has an Export Processing Zone at Pasir Gudang, which enables the duty-free importation of raw materials and intermediate inputs used in export production.

Economic complementarity

SIJORI as an integrated subregion is more attractive to investors than its separate parts. Each of SIJORI's three nodes has specific comparative advantages. Singapore's advantage lies in its managerial and professional expertise and its well-developed financial, transportation, and telecommunications infrastructure. Riau and Johor can offer land and labour at lower cost than can Singapore. Together they can produce a competitive business environment. However, while economic complementarity in the Singapore–Johor and Singapore–Riau sides of the growth triangle is obvious, that between Johor and Riau is less apparent, and helps to explain why this side of the triangle remains relatively less developed.

Participation in SIJORI will help Singapore achieve the following objectives: economic restructuring; becoming a high-value-added service economy and a hub city; promoting the regionalisation and internationalisation of Singaporean enterprises; providing leisure areas in proximity; achieving a secure water supply; and helping promote the economic advancement of the ASEAN region out of enlightened self-interest.

Singapore's per capita GNP reached US$13,240 in 1991 after a quarter century of rapid economic growth. The city-state, with its resident population of 2.7 million and a minuscule land area of 639 square kilometres, is faced with labour and land shortages, rising wages, and rising real estate costs. There are obvious limits to the importation of foreign workers before they pose a political and social problem. The relocation of labour-intensive industries and processes and land-intensive activities to Johor and Riau will enable the Singapore economy to shift to new areas of comparative advantage in high-value-added manufacturing and service activities, and to become a regional hub for trade, finance, transportation, telecommunications, and information, and the regional headquarters of multinational corporations. SIJORI enables multinationals based in Singapore to relocate their labour-intensive manufacturing processes outside of Singapore while remaining within the region; Singapore benefits from the retention in Singapore of the service functions attached to those industries, such as management, finance, marketing, communication and transport.

The Singapore economy has become a net capital exporter. Hitherto this exportation of capital has mainly taken the form of government portfolio investment, usually in developed countries. Increasingly, the large state enterprises and private companies are being urged to move into the international marketplace with the aim of promoting home-grown multinationals. Small and medium-sized Singapore enterprises are also encouraged to invest offshore to overcome factor scarcities in Singapore and to secure markets. Johor and Riau represent opportunities for Singapore's state enterprises and banks to internationalise their activities and for small and medium-sized enterprises to expand offshore to gain experience for eventual internationalisation.

The rising affluence of Singapore has led to a growing demand for leisure and recreational facilities in close proximity to the city-state. The strength of the Singapore dollar *vis-à-vis* the Malaysian ringgit provided an added attraction for Singapore tourist spending in Johor. With the tourism boom in Southeast Asia, Singapore, as the transportation hub of the region, has become an increasingly important tourism gateway for Johor. Both Johor and Riau are developing leisure and tourist facilities to attract Singaporeans, foreigners based in Singapore, and the tourist traffic through Singapore.

Singapore is critically dependent on Johor for its water supply, and this vulnerability has been highlighted whenever bilateral relations with Malaysia reach an ebb. Economic cooperation with Johor through SIJORI has as a major objective the improvement of bilateral relations. However, it is anticipated that because of Johor's own growing needs as well as the needs of other Malaysian states for water, Singapore cannot continue to depend on Johor water for its growing future needs. Thus, to ensure an adequate supply of water for the future, Singapore entered into an agreement with Indonesia to help develop the Riau islands.

Singapore also sees SIJORI as a vehicle to promote ASEAN regional economic cooperation and ensure Singapore's economic future. Progress in intra-ASEAN trade liberalisation and industrial cooperation has been painfully slow. SIJORI enables more like-minded members of ASEAN to cooperate at a faster pace. Through the relocation to Johor and Riau of some of the activities of Singapore-based multi-nationals and Singapore-owned enterprises, and through joint missions to promote inward foreign investment, Singapore hopes to help promote investment and technol-ogy transfer in neighbouring countries, in the firm belief that a more prosperous ASEAN will also mean a more peaceful and stable ASEAN.

Similarly, Johor and Riau also have motivations for cooperating within the growth triangle framework. Their policies are explicitly aimed at twinning their investment attractions with those of Singapore to take advantage of Singapore's infrastructure. Proximity to Singapore will enable investors in Batam and Johor to be more efficient and competitive in production and distribution. It is to be noted that there is no over-abundance of labour in Batam, and also more recently in Johor, and these two areas are dependent on immigration from other parts of Indonesia and Malaysia, respec-tively. The point of SIJORI is not so much that there is abundant cheap labour in these areas, but that labour is available near Singapore. In fact, given the limited supply of labour in Johor and Batam, investors from Singapore (both foreign multinationals and Singapore enterprises) are venturing beyond these two areas into the other Malaysian states north of Johor, and into the other Riau islands.

Table 27.2 shows relative land and labour costs in the constituent areas of SIJORI. There is no significant difference in land cost between Singapore and Johor, while the cost of land in Batam is much lower. Labour costs in Johor are about half to two-thirds those in Singapore, while labour costs in Batam are about half to two-thirds those in Johor. On the basis of land and labour costs alone, Batam would appear to be a more attractive investment location than Johor. In both areas real estate prices are rising rapidly in response to demand from Singapore investors. In 1990 some 85 per cent of Singapore investment in Batam was in tourism and housing (Pangestu 1991).

Availability of infrastructure

The provision of infrastructure and industrial facilities such as industrial estates facilitates private-sector investments. Johor has a relatively well-developed infra-structure for industries, including port and airport facilities, industrial estates, and free trade zones. Government resources are able to provide for further infrastructural expansion. As such, Singapore's participation in infrastructural development is limited, except for the development of water supply and the proposed construction of a second causeway linking Johor with Singapore. In contrast, the Riau islands are much less developed than Johor, and the Indonesian government lacks adequate financial resources to allocate to Riau's development. Thus, two features were introduced for infrastructural development, namely private-sector participation and joint ventures between countries. The largest joint infrastructural projects are the Batam Industrial Park (BIP) and the Bintan Integrated Development Project (BIDP). The BIP is a S$600 million, 500 hectare joint venture between an Indonesian

Table 27.2   Costs of land and labour in Johor, Singapore and Batam, 1989

	Land (US dollars per square metre)	Labour (US dollars per month)		
		Unskilled	Semi-skilled	Skilled
Johor	4.08	150	220	400
Singapore	4.25	350	420	600
Batam	2.30	90	140	200

Source: Mann (1990, p. 50).

conglomerate (the Salim group) and Singapore state enterprises. The BIP provides investors with a one-stop business centre to minimise the formalities of setting up production. The BIDP is a joint venture between the Indonesian and Singapore private sectors to develop the Bintan Beach International Resort and the Bintan Industrial Estate. Work started in March 1991. The Bintan Beach International Resort will cover 19,000 hectares and cost S$3.5 billion to develop. The Bintan Industrial Estate is being developed along the same lines as the Batam Industrial Park. It will complement BIP, which is intended for electronics-based industries, by providing facilities for light and medium industries, such as textiles and garments, woodwork, footwear, food processing and packaging, toy manufacturing, and electronics.

Impact of SIJORI

At the macroeconomic level, Singapore will benefit from the reduced pressure on land and labour, and these scarce resources can then be put to more productive use. Johor and Riau in turn will gain from the increased investment inflows, with their attendant positive effects on GDP and employment growth, as well as from the training, technology transfer, and export marketing expertise that normally accompany foreign direct investment. The land-abundant areas of Johor and Riau could also specialise in tourism and agribusiness. At the microeconomic level, firms in the SREZ are able to rationalise their resources and production and distribution through vertical specialisation and division of labour. For those firms engaged in manufacturing, labour-intensive processes could be located in areas with abundant labour resources, while activities requiring knowledge and skill inputs, such as engineering development, marketing, supply acquisition, and finance, as well as newer and more complex production lines, could be based in Singapore. Intra-regional effects on Singapore and on Johor are not so large that structural adjustments can be attributed to the formation of the SREZ, as distinguished from other general factors affecting Singapore and Malaysia. It is otherwise for the Riau islands of Batam and Bintan.

Effect on Singapore

The impact of the SIJORI Growth Triangle on Singapore to date can be seen mainly in the outward investment and relocation of industries in Johor and Batam. Lee (1992a) reported two surveys that sought to determine the extent of relocation of labour-intensive activities from Singapore to the neighbouring region. A survey in January 1992 by the Singapore Manufacturers' Association of its members, 270 of whom responded, showed that 40 per cent have either moved or intend to relocate part of their business to neighbouring countries (not necessarily Johor or Riau) to cope with rising labour costs, although only 3.8 per cent said they would relocate their entire operations. Other measures to cope with rising labour costs in Singapore were training, automation, and upgrading to higher-value-added activities; some businesses were even contemplating abandoning manufacturing altogether. A second mail questionnaire survey, by Yeoh et al. (1992), of 310 respondents showed that 47.7 per cent already had offshore production facilities: 45.9 per cent had facilities in Johor and 10.8 per cent in Batam. Respondents who indicated plans to invest in Johor and Batam were mainly engaged in manufacturing, involving both expansion as well as relocation of certain processes. Although biases in responses may be expected, the survey results do point to significant relocation of labour-intensive activities offshore.

Relocation of production facilities to Johor and Riau appears to have no significant impact on Singapore's industrial structure and employment. The manufacturing sector's share of GDP in 1988–91 remained at 27 to 28 per cent, largely unchanged from the level of 1980–81. Likewise, the manufacturing sector's share of employment remained at 28 to 29 per cent of the national total, and the absolute number employed in manufacturing has risen from under 300,000 in 1986 (a recession year) to nearly 430,000 in 1991.

Trade linkages between Singapore and Johor and Riau have increased, but their magnitudes cannot be ascertained in the absence of published statistics.

Effect on Johor

Johor covers 19,000 square kilometres and has a population of 2.2 million. There is intensive movement of people and goods between Johor and Singapore, resulting in serious traffic congestion at the causeway linking the two areas during peak hours. Unfortunately, there are no published statistics on the number of people and volume of goods moved across the causeway. A second causeway is being planned, and an extension of Singapore's mass rapid transit system into Johor has also been mooted.

Johor is now Malaysia's second most important industrial region and investment destination (after Selangor). Its share of approved FDI in Malaysia has been rising, to 20 per cent in 1989 (Kumar and Lee 1991). There was a sharp jump in FDI to Johor after 1987. The main investors are from Japan and the Asian NIEs. Singapore is not the lead investor, although there was a quantum jump in investment approvals from Singapore in 1990. FDI in Johor is wide-based, ranging from proposed multi-billion dollar Taiwanese and Korean steel mills to small Singaporean textile and plastics factories.

The inward surge of FDI is rapidly transforming the physical landscape and the labour and property markets. Labour shortages have emerged in certain critical areas, and wages as well as land and property prices are rising rapidly. The increased investments as well as the surge of visitors from Singapore, taking advantage of the exchange rate and lower prices in Johor, have contributed to a sharp rise in retail prices and the cost of living of Johor residents.

Effect on Riau

To date, the biggest impact of SIJORI has been on the Riau islands. These islands have long been on the periphery of Indonesian development and are only now emerging as a possible major growth centre. Linkages between Singapore and the Riau islands, particularly Batam, have grown rapidly in recent years. This is reflected in the growth of ferry services between Singapore and the Batam Industrial Park; and the introduction of smart cards for commuting between Singapore and Batam.

Development of Batam

Batam Island is part of Indonesia's Riau province and has an area of 415 square kilometres, two-thirds the size of Singapore, from which it is separated by only a thirty to forty-minute ferry ride. A 1970 presidential decree designated Batam as the logistics base for the Indonesian oil industry. In 1978 Batam was declared a duty-free zone. The Batam Industrial Development Authority (BIDA) is responsible for development of the island. Batam has been growing rapidly since 1988 in population, employment, GDP, tourism, trade, and shipping as a result of the foreign investment boom. The population has grown from 7,000 in the early 1970s to over 100,000. Employment grew from around 6,000 in the mid-1980s to nearly 23,000 in 1991. Workers are brought in from other parts of Indonesia, mainly Java, on a contract basis. Batam's GDP increased by 14 per cent annually during 1988–90, much faster than the national average. Batam accounts for 3.5 per cent of Riau GDP and 16 per cent of its manufacturing sector. Exports from Batam increased tenfold in five years: from US$20.9 million in 1986 to US$210.3 million in 1991. Tourist arrivals (mainly from and through Singapore) increased tenfold from about 60,000 in 1985 to over 600,000 in 1991. Batam has surpassed Bali as the number two tourist entry point in Indonesia after Jakarta (Pangestu 1991; Ahmad 1992).

Investment in Batam boomed following changes in Indonesian foreign investment policy and the establishment of the Batam Industrial Park. Data from BIDA show that by end-1991 total cumulative investments in Batam amounted to US$3.3 billion, of which 19.2 per cent is government investment in basic infrastructure; foreign investment accounts for 32.2 per cent, domestic private investment for 18.3 per cent, and non-facility investment for 30.4 per cent (non-facility investment is investment made without prior application to the Indonesian Investment Coordinating Board, and which thus does not receive investment incentives). Most of the companies with non-facility investment are small in scale or engaged in agriculture. Private-sector investments are concentrated in manufacturing (48.6 per cent), followed by tourism and hotel development (17.1 per cent) and real estate (18.5 per cent). Within manufacturing, the electronics industry is the fastest growing. Investments in residential property and tourism facilities are targeted at the Singapore market. Investments from Singapore (including multinationals based in Singapore) are the major source of FDI in Batam, accounting for over half the foreign companies. More than 90 per cent of present Singapore investments in Batam were undertaken in 1989–91. Singapore's share of Batam FDI was US$532 million or 50.5 per cent. Investments from Malaysia (including the Johor mode of SIJORI) were negligible.

Development of Bintan and other Riau islands

Bintan island is located 42 kilometres, or less than an hour's ferry ride, from Singapore. It has a land area almost double that of Singapore and a population of 130,000. Bintan will be developed for industry and tourism as well as a water supply project to cater to the needs of Singapore and Bintan itself. The development cost is estimated at about US$7 billion. The private sector is expected to participate heavily in these three basic infrastructure projects, with the Indonesian government under-taking the provision of infrastructure outside these project areas (Ahmad 1992).

For industrial development in Bintan, a Singapore–Indonesia joint venture with partners from the Indonesian private sector and Singapore's state-owned Jurong Town Corporation will develop a 4,000 hectare bonded industrial estate at Tanjung Uban at an estimated cost of US$800 million. Construction is expected to be completed by 1995. The industries planned include aluminium processing, oil refining, downstream petroleum-based products, textiles, garments, electronics, wood-based products, metal components, and agri-based industry. Development of a tourist resort is being undertaken by a consortium of Indonesian and Singapore companies, with the intention of catering to both Singaporean and other foreign tourists. The resort will cover 23,000 hectares. The project is estimated to cost S$3 billion to S$5 billion. Work started in 1991 and will take ten years to complete. The water supply project will cost about S$1 billion and involves construction of five dams and a water treatment plant. The project is designed to operate for fifty years and will produce 121 million gallons of water per day. A construction contract was signed in March 1992 between Singapore's Public Utilities Board and an Indonesian private-sector group. The entire project will take fifteen years to complete.

There are also plans for the joint development with Singapore of the other Riau islands, particularly Bulan (where there are already pig and orchid farms) and Karimun (where a giant shipyard and oil processing centre is being proposed).

Effects, implications and prospects of SREZs

The case study of SIJORI in this paper has highlighted many effects and issues related to the emergence and development of subregional economic zones. Some of these are outlined below.

Growth, employment and structural change

There are many positive effects arising from the metropolitan spillover version of the SREZ for its participating members. For the less developed areas of the SREZ there are the usual positive growth, employment, and technology transfer effects arising from accelerated inflows of foreign investment and increased domestic investment for infrastructural development and directly productive activities. The presence of export-oriented foreign investors and the ready availability of export infrastructure (finance, transportation, telecommunications and trade networks) enable these areas with limited experience to have a jump-start in export manufacturing. As the initial areas become more developed in terms of infrastructure, industry and employment, the effects of economic development spread to an ever-widening zone, so that these areas themselves become secondary growth poles.

For the urban metropolis, outward investment, relocation of industries, and outward processing to the less developed areas facilitate the process of industrial restructuring towards higher-value-added manufacturing and service activities, with consequent improvements in resource allocation and gains in productivity. The Singapore experience suggests that there have been no major relocation costs or negative effects from the hollowing out of its industry. Instead, the high-value-added functions are retained or are attracted to the metropolis. At the same time, outward investment to a geographically proximate area provides the domestic firms with the learning experience for eventual internationalisation.

Political, distributional and social issues

The SREZ as a transnational phenomenon involves relations at multiple levels and different perceptions of the benefits and costs of participation. These may be differentiated into relations and effects between the central government and provinces not in the SREZ and the province in the SREZ, between participating areas, and between economic and social groups within the SREZ.

Since a SREZ involves parts of different countries, there is the possibility of perceived conflicts of interest between the participating province and its central government and other provinces within the country. For example, there are already indications of unhappiness in some quarters in Malaysia and Indonesia over the perception that areas of these countries are coming 'under the influence' of Singapore. In Malaysia, the economic advantage that Johor enjoys with SIJORI has introduced a new element in federal–provincial and inter-provincial relations. In Jakarta, some have questioned the utility and equity of large government infrastructure expenditures on the Riau islands of Batam and Bintan, which are perceived to be benefiting only a small elite group, especially when there are strong contending claims for development funds in other parts of Indonesia. Some argue that the SREZ increases FDI in the Riau islands, but possibly at the expense of other parts of Indonesia, due to the investment diversion effect.

Relations between the more developed and less developed areas of a SREZ are akin to metropolis–hinterland or centre–periphery relations within a single country. However, when the urban centre and the hinterland are located in different countries, and where there are ethnic overtones, the political sensitivities are much greater. In the urban metropolis, adjustment costs have fallen on those workers who have lost their jobs with the relocation of industries; for unskilled workers of mature age, finding a new job can be difficult. Small and medium-sized enterprises also worry about loss of business when their multinational customers relocate offshore and they have difficulties in maintaining business links. For Singapore, such adjustments do not pose a serious political, social and economic problem. In the less developed areas, on the other hand, there are social problems of massive immigration, particularly of young female workers. Infrastructural bottlenecks in housing and transportation could develop, and traffic congestion and environmental pollution could rise noticeably. Consumer groups in Johor have been vocal about some adverse effects of the Singapore connection, manifested in a higher cost of living, escalation in real estate values, traffic congestion, and a rise in socially undesirable activities. In Batam and Bintan there are issues of unfair compensation for community and private land acquired for infrastructural, industrial, tourism and commercial development.

These political, social and distributional issues arise as a result of accelerated economic growth within the SREZ. In order to ensure continuing integration and growth, the political economy of SREZs needs to be handled with care. Rapid economic growth and its attendant consequences for economic and social adjustments will always upset those who wish to maintain the status quo. Governments (and politicians) have a role to play in managing the political overtones, inasmuch as they have a role in liberalising investment regulations and facilitating infrastructural development and hence the process of economic integration.

Prospects

Notwithstanding political sensitivities and distributional issues, the economic forces of complementarity, comparative advantage, and division of labour have led to the development of SREZs. What are the prospects for SIJORI for the remainder of the 1990s? What is the likely evolution of SREZs? To what extent are SREZs replicable elsewhere?

As SIJORI evolves, its character will change. Both Johor and Batam are experiencing shortages of skilled workers, which are expected to worsen as investments in the pipeline come into commercial production. The fact of an emerging scarcity of labour is discouraging new investments in Johor. In Batam, industrial estates such as Batam Industrial Park are assisting investors in recruiting workers from Java and other parts of Indonesia. Nonetheless, the present subregional division of labour cannot be sustained. There are limits to the relocation of 'sunset' and 'residual' industries from Singapore to the less developed areas. And both Batam and Johor are pressing for more FDI with higher value added, skills, and technology. The Malaysian Minister of Trade and Industry, Datuk Seri Rafidah Aziz, recently reiterated that Malaysia had graduated out of the 'cheap labour country club' and would like Singapore investors to look at Malaysia as a location for non-labour-intensive investments (*Straits Times*, 7 August 1992).

Investments in Johor and Riau are already diversifying away from labour-intensive industries. Newer investments include infrastructural projects, resource-based and tourism projects, and property development; these are not the labour-intensive and low-value-added investments that typify export platforms.

There is also evidence that SREZs are extending beyond their original geographical boundaries. Developments in the Indonesian part of SIJORI started with Batam but have since extended to other Riau islands such as Bintan, Bulan and Karimun. And as Johor experiences labour shortages and rising property prices, investors have gone further north to Malacca and elsewhere. In other words, the initial 'hinterlands' of SREZs could themselves develop into growth poles, generating spillover effects into ever-widening contiguous areas.

The replication of SREZs in the Asia Pacific region is contingent on the presence of the same key factors that promoted their growth in SIJORI: namely economic complementarity, geographical proximity, infrastructure availability, and government commitment to facilitate the cross-border movements of capital, people and goods. The success of SIJORI has a demonstration effect and could encourage formation of other growth triangles in ASEAN, although not all of the proposed SREZs will have the same favourable conditions. The emergence of multiple and overlapping growth triangles may lead to their eventual merger under the umbrella of AFTA.

With a growing number of countries in the Asia Pacific region pursuing FDI to promote economic development, the intensified competition will lead to the formation of more SREZs to maximise attractions for investors. Geographic competition for FDI will increasingly take the form of competition among SREZs rather than among individual countries. There may be eventual specialisation among SREZs as each seeks its own niche in the regional and international division of labour (Wong 1992).

Although they are currently export platforms, it is conceivable that, with rapid economic growth and newfound affluence, SREZs will also evolve into consumption centres, much like other metropolitan areas around the world. SREZs would then be a truly major motive force and an engine of growth in the Asia Pacific.

References

Ahmad, Mubariq 1992, 'Economic cooperation in the southern growth triangle: an Indonesian perspective', Paper presented at the Conference on Regional Cooperation and Growth Triangles in ASEAN, organised by the National University of Singapore, Singapore, 23–24 April.

Habibie, B . J. 1992, 'Technology and the Singapore–Johor Growth Triangle', Speech delivered at the Tripartite Meeting and Seminar on Economic Development in the Growth Triangle and Its Environment Impact, Batam, 8 May.

Kumar, Sree and Lee Tsao Yuan 1991, 'A Singapore perspective', in Lee Tsao Yuan (ed.), *Growth Triangles: The Johor–Singapore–Riau Experience*, Institute of Southeast Asian Studies and Institute of Policy Studies, Singapore.

Lee Tsao Yuan 1992a, 'Regional economic zones in the Asia–Pacific: an overview', Paper presented at the Conference on Regional Cooperation and Growth Triangles in ASEAN, organised by the National University of Singapore, Singapore, 23–24 April.

_____ 1992b, 'Growth triangles in ASEAN', *PITO Economic Briefs*, 10, East–West Center, Honolulu.

McGee, T. G. and Scott MacLeod 1992, 'Emerging extended metropolitan regions in the Asia–Pacific urban system: a case study of the Singapore–Johor–Riau Growth Triangle', Paper presented at the Workshop on the Asian Pacific Urban System: Towards the 21st Century, held at the Chinese University of Hong Kong, 11–13 February.

Mann, Richard I. (ed.) 1990, *Batam: Step-by-Step Guide for Investors*, Toronto: Gateway.

Pangestu, Mari 1991, 'An Indonesian perspective', in Lee Tsao Yuan (ed.), *Growth Triangles: The Johor–Singapore–Riau Experience*, Institute of Southeast Asian Studies and Institute of Policy Studies, Singapore.

Salleh, Ismail Muhd 1992, 'Economic cooperation in the northern triangle', Paper presented at the Conference on Regional Cooperation and Growth Triangles in ASEAN, organised by the National University of Singapore, Singapore, 23–24 April.

Scalapino, Robert A. 1992, 'The United States and Asia: future prospects', *Foreign Affairs*, Winter, pp. 19–40.

Wong, Poh Kam 1992, 'Economic cooperation in the southern growth triangle: a long term perspective', Paper presented at the Conference on Regional Cooperation and Growth Triangles in ASEAN, organised by the National University of Singapore, Singapore, 23–24 April.

Yeoh, Caroline, Lau Geok Theng and G. Ray Funkhouser 1992, 'Summary report: business trends in the growth triangle', mimeo, Faculty of Business Administration, National University of Singapore, Singapore.

28 The economic integration of Hong Kong, Taiwan and South Korea with the mainland of China

Yun-Wing Sung

China's inauguration of its open-door policy in 1979 coincided with the need of the East Asian NIEs to change their economic structures. Wages had been rising rapidly in the NIEs, forcing a shift from labour-intensive manufacturing to capital-intensive and skill-intensive activities. The East Asian NIEs have taken advantage of China's open-door policy through international trade and investment channels. Hong Kong and Taiwan, for their part, have moved their labour-intensive processes to the mainland on a large scale.

This paper focuses on the economic integration of the three NIEs of Hong Kong, Taiwan and South Korea with mainland China. The fourth of the NIEs, Singapore, is excluded since it is more closely integrated with the ASEAN group than with China by virtue of geography.

The strength of economic ties between mainland China and the three NIEs can be gauged from commodity trade, investment and tourism statistics. Hong Kong and the mainland are each other's foremost trading partner and investor. Taiwan trades with the mainland mainly through Hong Kong, but direct trade (illegal from Taiwan's standpoint) as well as indirect trade through other third parties is also substantial. However, reliable statistics exist only for Taiwan's indirect trade through Hong Kong. According to rough estimates, direct trade, and indirect trade through other third countries, amounted to at least one-third of the indirect trade in both exports and imports. On these estimates, in 1990 Taiwan was China's fifth largest trading partner, accounting for at least 4.5 per cent of China's trade, while South Korea was China's seventh largest trading partner, accounting for 3.2 per cent of its trade. Taiwan's imports from China were quite small, though its exports to China had grown rapidly, accounting for at least 5.8 per cent of its total exports in 1990. South Korea's trade with China has also grown rapidly, constituting 3.1 per cent of total trade in 1990.

Reprinted from *Economic Reform and Internationalisation: China and the Pacific Region*, edited by Ross Garnaut and Liu Guoguang, pp. 141–81 (with deletions). Copyright © 1992 by the Australian National University. Reprinted with permission from Allen & Unwin Pty Ltd, Sydney, Australia.

Hong Kong accounts for roughly 60 per cent of foreign investment in China. Taiwan's investment in China has grown extremely rapidly since 1989; according to Beijing's figures, Taiwan's cumulative pledged investment stood at US$100 million at the end of 1987, growing to US$520 million by 1988, US$1 billion by 1989, and US$2 billion by 1990. Taiwan's pledged annual flow for 1990 was thus US$1 billion or 14 per cent of China's total, giving it a ranking of second after Hong Kong. In terms of cumulative stock, Taiwan's investment was 4.4 per cent of the total, ranking fourth in size after that of Hong Kong, the United States and Japan, with Taiwan expected to overtake Japan in 1991–92. By comparison with Hong Kong and Taiwan, South Korea's investment in China has been very modest. According to figures from the Bank of Korea, 66 projects at a cost of US$81 million had been approved (by the bank) at the end of 1990, while 43 projects valued at US$36 million had commenced operation. However, growth in the value of approved projects was rapid, trebling in 1989 and again in 1990.

In 1990, 27 million tourists visited China, from which the industry earned US$2,220 million. Hong Kong visitors numbered 18 million, accounting for roughly 66 per cent of the total. Taiwanese visitors numbered 950,000, or 3.5 per cent of the total, giving Taiwan a ranking of third after Hong Kong and Macau.

Trade and investment flows between the mainland and the three NIEs are very large. Economic ties between the mainland and the NIEs are qualitatively different from China's ties with developed countries. China's commodity trade with the developed countries includes mostly inter-industry trade, whereas its trade with the three NIEs includes substantial intra-industry trade, because China's level of development is closer to that of the NIEs than the developed countries. The three NIEs have less advanced technology than the developed countries, but their level of medium technology may be better suited to China's stage of development and could enhance the latter's bargaining power in acquiring technology from the developed countries. The three NIEs tend to invest in export-oriented processing and assembling operations, whereas Japan and the United States tend to invest in import substitution. Investment by the three NIEs is thus a significant factor behind China's successful export drive.

The first section of this paper discusses the three NIEs' degree of economic integration with China. A second section briefly surveys changes in government policies leading to closer economic ties, while sections three, four and five examine, respectively, commodity trade, services trade, and investment between the three NIEs and the mainland. A final section offers some concluding remarks.

The degree of economic integration between China and the three NIEs

There is a sense in which it can be argued that China is more closely integrated with most other economies than with Taiwan and South Korea. Taiwan still prohibits investment from the mainland, and trade between the two is mostly carried out indirectly through Hong Kong due to the absence of direct official and commercial links. Though China and South Korea established trade promotion offices in each other's capital in early 1991, the lack of diplomatic relations remains an obvious obstacle to closer ties.

However, the rapid growth in trade and investment between Taiwan, South Korea and the mainland shows that the lack of direct official and commercial links has not been an insurmountable barrier to business. Hong Kong has been able to offer highly efficient intermediary services that have helped to overcome the lack of direct official and commercial ties. It is interesting to note that the greater part of China–South Korea trade is still carried out through Hong Kong, even though direct shipping between China and South Korea commenced in 1988.

Besides the lack of diplomatic and commercial ties, the three important barriers to economic integration often listed in textbooks are tariffs, controls on factor movements, and exchange risks. That being so, the barriers to economic integration between the mainland and the three NIEs are very high. Take, for instance, the case of the mainland and Hong Kong. Even though China is scheduled to resume sovereignty over Hong Kong in 1997, the Sino-British Agreement on Hong Kong specifies that Hong Kong will remain a separate customs territory and continue to have its own currency. Migration from China to Hong Kong will be strictly controlled. It can be argued, therefore, that Hong Kong and the mainland are less integrated than Greece and Ireland, which are both members of the EC and between which there is complete freedom of movement of goods and factors. Since China is not a member of the GATT and its currency is not convertible, it can also be argued that Hong Kong is more closely integrated with most of the world's market economies than with China. The above arguments also apply to Taiwan and South Korea.

Though economic theory concentrates on tariffs, controls on migration, and exchange integration, the effect of geographical and cultural distances may be even more important. Hong Kong is only half-an-hour's train ride from China, and Taiwan and South Korea are also geographically close to China. The importance of cultural affinity is quite evident. People in Hong Kong have their ancestral roots in Guangdong province, and Guangdong has received the bulk of Hong Kong's investment in China. Taiwan's investment is similarly concentrated in Fujian province. In South Korea's case, its surge of investment in Shandong and Liaoning appears to be related to the abundance of ethnic Koreans in those two provinces.

It should be noted that geographic and cultural proximity enable businesspeople to evade the formal barriers that exist to trade and investment. Tariffs can be evaded through smuggling, which is rampant from Hong Kong and Taiwan to China. Movement of people from Hong Kong and Taiwan to China is relatively free though movement in the opposite direction is highly controlled. However, illegal immigrants from the mainland are relatively common in Hong Kong and Taiwan as the labour markets of the two economies are extremely tight. While the Chinese yuan is not convertible, the Hong Kong dollar circulates widely (and unofficially) in Guangdong province, especially in the SEZ in Shenzen. The amount has been estimated at HK$6,300 million (US$808 million) or 16 per cent of Hong Kong's total currency supply (*Hong Kong Economic Times*, 21 March 1991).

China has tailored its open-door policy towards closer links with Hong Kong, Taiwan and South Korea. In 1979 Guangdong and Fujian provinces were given authority to form SEZs, with special autonomy in trade and investment. Guangdong operates the three SEZs of Shenzhen and Zhuhai — which are adjacent to Hong Kong and Macau, respectively — and Shantou, which has close links to overseas Chinese populations, including a community in Hong Kong that originated in Shantou. Fujian operates the Xiamen SEZ, which lies opposite Taiwan and is only a few miles from the two coastal islands controlled by Taiwan. The Liaoning and Shandong peninsulas were designated as open areas in 1988, partly to improve economic ties with South Korea. During his 1988 presidential election campaign, South Korea's Roh Tae Woo unveiled a 'Western Coast Development Concept' to develop economic relations with China. Construction of industrial parks, harbours and highways along Korea's west coast has already commenced. In addition, a 'Yellow Sea Economic Region' linking Korea's west coast and the Bohai coast of China is likely to emerge in the future.

It should be noted that there are significant differences among the three NIEs in terms of their degree of economic integration with the mainland. Of the three, Hong Kong shows the highest degree of integration due to lack of political, cultural and geographical barriers. Political barriers exist in the cases of Taiwan and South Korea, which also have significant geographical barriers since they are not connected by land to China. Transportation costs from Taiwan to the mainland are not very different from Taiwan to the ASEAN countries. ASEAN is thus a strong competitor with the mainland for Taiwanese investment. A recent survey shows that wages in China are comparable to those in the ASEAN countries, and that China's only advantage over ASEAN lies in consignment processing, the simplest part of all production (Watanabe 1990, p. 11). In Hong Kong's case, the investment advantage of the mainland over ASEAN is considerable due to land access as well as kinship and cultural links.

Of the three NIEs, the degree of integration with the mainland is lowest for South Korea. This is partly due to cultural differences, but firm size also plays a part — the Hong Kong and Taiwanese economies are dominated by small firms, whereas large firms figure prominently in South Korea. While small firms lack the ability to overcome the barriers to overseas investment, cultural and geographical proximity have enabled small firms in Hong Kong and Taiwan to invest in the mainland. The large firms in South Korea have the ability to overcome high barriers and have more investment options overseas.

Policy changes leading to closer ties

Economic relations between Hong Kong and the mainland

Before the communists came to power in 1949, Hong Kong had been an important entrepôt for China. While China could have taken Hong Kong by force in 1949, it chose to leave it in British hands. This suggests how high a value Beijing placed on Hong Kong as China's 'window' to the outside world. Following China's entry into the Korean War in 1951, the United Nations imposed an embargo on strategic materials sales to China, and the United States banned all imports from China. However, strategic materials were smuggled from Hong Kong into China on a large scale, which Hong Kong failed to halt. Due to China's isolation, the value of Hong Kong as China's 'window to the world' was thereby enhanced.

Hong Kong's entrepôt trade nevertheless declined, partly as a result of the UN embargo and the US ban, and partly because Beijing placed international trade in the hands of the state and redirected China's trade to the Comecon bloc. The greater part of China's trade in the 1950s was state-to-state, handled directly by the government's foreign trade corporations, and bypassing Hong Kong. China's imports from Hong Kong dwindled to negligible amounts, but while its exports to Hong Kong also declined, they were substantial enough to earn it the hard currency it required, particularly after the Sino-Soviet rift of the late 1950s. However, before 1979 a mere one-quarter to one-third of China's exports to Hong Kong were re-exported, with the rest being retained in Hong Kong for internal use.

With the decline in its entrepôt trade, Hong Kong was deprived of its main means of livelihood. Refugee capital and labour from China, however, worked to transform Hong Kong into an industrial city — a dazzling example of success achieved through an export-oriented strategy. Hong Kong became a lucrative market in the 1960s and 1970s and China's exports to Hong Kong grew rapidly, food being the major item of trade, accounting for over half of China's exports to Hong Kong. China's trade surplus with Hong Kong was around one-fifth of its total exports, and it used the hard currency thus earned to finance its imports of grain, industrial raw materials and capital goods from the developed countries.

Since China's adoption of economic reforms and its open-door policy in 1979, economic relations between Hong Kong and China have changed dramatically — Hong Kong re-emerged as a major entrepôt for China, while China also became a major market for Hong Kong products. Hong Kong investment in China led to rapid growth in intra-industry and intra-firm trade. Hong Kong developed into a services centre, exporting industrial, financial and business services to China.

Hong Kong's importance as a 'window' for China grew after the latter's adoption of its open-door policy. The Chinese promise in the Sino-British joint declaration of 1984 to preserve the capitalist system in Hong Kong for fifty years after 1997 — an extraordinary arrangement of 'one country, two systems' — appears to reflect Beijing's awareness of Hong Kong's importance to its open-door policy.

Needless to say, Hong Kong is even more dependent on the mainland than vice versa for the simple reason that the mainland economy is much larger and more diversified. The mainland supplies over half of Hong Kong's potable water and around one-quarter of its food requirements. Despite a chronic labour shortage and soaring wages, Hong Kong manufacturing has been able to maintain its competitiveness by moving its labour and land-intensive processes to the mainland. In this study, however, it is appropriate to concentrate on the economic importance of Hong Kong to the mainland, rather than the opposite case, since Hong Kong is the key to China's open-door policy.

With the inauguration of economic reforms and its open-door policy, Beijing called for the establishment of 'three links' (mail, travel and trade) and 'four exchanges' (science, culture, sports and arts) with Taiwan on 1 January 1979. On the same day, the United States established diplomatic relations with the mainland and broke off its long-standing diplomatic relations with Taiwan.

Faced with diplomatic isolation, Taiwan nevertheless adhered to its original schedule of liberalisation and lifted its ban on overseas travel for tourist purposes. Though Taiwan responded to Beijing's overture with a reaffirmation of the old 'three noes' policy — no contact, no negotiations and no compromise — its relaxation of tourist travel constituted a 'known loophole' in the policy of no contact. Taiwanese can meet their mainland relatives in third countries or even secretly visit their relatives on the mainland via Hong Kong or other places. Before November 1987, when the ban on travel to the mainland was lifted, around 10,000 Taiwanese visited the mainland secretly every year (Wakabayashi 1990, p. 6).

Beijing took more steps to promote exchanges with Taiwan in 1980. A mission to Hong Kong purchased US$80 million of Taiwanese goods, and the mainland's imports from Taiwan in 1980 increased 11.5 times over 1979 levels. China also abolished the tariff on Taiwanese goods in 1980, but the concession was short-lived. Taiwanese goods, and Hong Kong goods claiming to be Taiwanese, flooded the mainland market, and China levied an 'adjustment tax' on those goods from 1983.

On 30 September 1981, Ye Jianying, Chairman of the Standing Committee of the National People's Congress, announced a 'Nine-Point Proposal' calling for peaceful reunification through negotiation and allowing Taiwan to maintain its capitalist system and an army. Under the proposal, Taiwan would enjoy a high degree of autonomy as a 'special administrative region' of China. In January 1982 Deng Xiaoping announced that the formula of 'one country, two systems' would apply to Taiwan as well as Hong Kong.

Taiwan gradually softened its interpretation of the 'three noes' policy to cope with the reality of increasing contacts and thriving indirect trade. In July 1985 it indicated that it would not interfere in indirect exports as it could not control them. Indirect imports, however, would still be subject to control. Import controls on mainland products were gradually liberalised from 1987. By the end of 1990 indirect import was permitted of a total of 92 items, including all agricultural and industrial raw materials. In July 1987 Taiwan eased its foreign exchange controls, and indirect investment on the mainland grew rapidly. In November that year Taiwan lifted its ban on the visiting of mainland relatives. Two years later in October 1989, Taiwan promulgated regulations sanctioning indirect trade, investment and technical cooperation with China.

On 23 February 1991 Taiwan promulgated a policy on national reunification — it would abandon its policy of 'three noes' and establish official contacts with the mainland providing that the latter softened its drive to isolate Taiwan diplomatically and abandoned its threat to use force against Taiwan. It made it clear that in the absence of these gestures it would continue to shun official contacts with the mainland. However, policy allowed for the gradual development of unofficial exchanges with the mainland. Bilateral issues were to be dealt with by the Straits Exchange Foundation, a semi-official body established by Taipei.

On 1 May 1991 Taiwan officially terminated the 'period of communist rebellion' on the mainland, declaring an end to four decades of civil war across the Taiwan Straits. This action enabled it to adopt a more pragmatic policy towards the mainland. At the same time, a delegation from the Straits Exchange Foundation visited Beijing for the first time and requested its cooperation in solving problems such as piracy in the Taiwan Straits and the entry of illegal immigrants into Taiwan from the mainland.

Taiwanese businesspeople are now pressuring Taipei to lift its ban on direct trade and investment, which it wants to use as a lever to gain political concessions from Beijing. Whether the ban will be lifted depends on Beijing's response to Taipei's overtures as well as on the outcome of the tug-of-war between Taiwanese business-people and bureaucrats.

Though it is unlikely that Beijing and Taipei will be able to settle their political differences in the near future, economic ties across the Taiwan Straits will continue to grow. Taiwan is eager to expand its presence in Hong Kong to handle the thriving business with the mainland. In April 1991 it established the Taipei Centre in Hong Kong to help Taiwanese investors establish paper companies in Hong Kong for investment in the mainland.

Economic relations between South Korea and China

Enmity between South Korea and China continued for two decades after the Korean War. Following the re-establishment of relations between China and the United States in 1972, South Korea announced its intention to improve relations with communist countries in 1973, though North Korea actively opposed contacts between China and South Korea. Indirect trade commenced between South Korea and China in 1979 following China's adoption of economic reforms and its open-door policy. Chinese duties on South Korean products are higher than those on other countries because political limitations prohibit a bilateral trade agreement. South Korea applies a uniform tariff to all countries. In 1985 the two countries agreed to set up a temporary channel of communication in Hong Kong through the South Korean Consulate and the China News Agency. Relations improved in 1986 when China sent a huge delegation to the Asian Games in Seoul, despite objections from North Korea. In 1988 the South Korean government actively pursued its 'North policy' to improve economic ties with communist countries. In that year, cargo transport routes were established between China and South Korea, with the proviso that vessels be registered in, and fly the flags of, third countries. In 1988, also, China's Shandong province was designated an open area to attract South Korean investment. In the following year, South Korea gave selected Korean banks permission to enter into correspondent bank agreements with the Bank of China, thereby facilitating foreign exchange transactions. A direct passenger service by sea between China and South Korea commenced in 1990, and the two countries established Overseas Trade Promotion Offices in each other's capitals in 1991. In July that year negotiations on direct flights between South Korea and China were reported to be underway and China confirmed that it hoped to sign a trade and investment protection agreement with South Korea by the end of the year.

Commodity trade between the mainland and the three NIEs

As a large fraction of China's trade is conducted via Hong Kong in the form of entrepôt trade, statistics on China's trade by country are very misleading. In trade statistics, exports are classified by country of immediate destination, whereas imports are classified by country of ultimate origin. For example, in US–China trade, both countries regard their exports to each other through Hong Kong as exports to Hong Kong and thus understate their exports to each other. Imports are not understated, however, as they are traced to the country of origin. Both countries thus overstate (understate) their bilateral trade deficits (surpluses). In 1990, according to US statistics, the United States had a deficit of US$11.5 billion in its trade with China, whereas China claimed it had a trade deficit of US$1.4 billion with the United States! Though both claims are biased, US statistics are less misleading because over 64 per cent of China's exports to the United States were re-exported through Hong Kong in 1990, whereas the corresponding percentage for the United States was only 19 per cent. After taking into account indirect trade through Hong Kong, the US deficit would have been US$10.3 billion, and China's surplus US$7 billion (Sung 1991a).

As South Korea and Taiwan trade with China largely through Hong Kong, they take indirect trade through Hong Kong into account in their official statistics. Hong Kong's re-exports of South Korean (Taiwanese) goods to China, recorded in Hong Kong trade statistics, are regarded as indirect exports by South Korea (Taiwan) to China. Hong Kong's re-exports of Chinese goods to South Korea (Taiwan) are similarly regarded as indirect imports by South Korea (Taiwan) from China. However, such a procedure is unsatisfactory since it ignores the re-export margin — the very substantial one earned by Hong Kong. The re-export margin includes profits and costs of transportation, storage, insurance, packaging and minor processing that are not substantial enough to confer country of origin. The re-export margin for Chinese goods is estimated to be 25 per cent, but 14 per cent for that of non-Chinese goods. The re-export margin for Chinese goods is much higher because many Chinese goods are packaged or processed in Hong Kong before export.

In this paper, all statistics on China's trade by region include direct trade as well as indirect trade via Hong Kong. The re-export margin is netted out of indirect exports because exports should be reported on an f.o.b. (free on board) basis. For instance, the data on Taiwan's indirect exports to China given in this study are lower than

Taiwan's estimates by the amount of the re-export margin. However, the re-export margin is not netted out of indirect imports because imports should be reported on a c.i.f. (cost, insurance, and freight) basis. The procedure used here should provide the most accurate estimates of trade with China.

It is well known that statistics on bilateral trade flows obtained from the import side usually exceed those obtained from the export side because of transportation and insurance. In the case of China, the discrepancy is especially large because statistics obtained from the import side include the re-export margin, whereas the data on the export side exclude the re-export margin.

China's statistics on trade with Hong Kong are particularly misleading since a considerable portion of China's imports of third country goods via Hong Kong is attributed to Hong Kong instead of to the country of origin. To remedy the deficiency of these statistics, this study uses Hong Kong statistics to calculate China's trade with Hong Kong. Time lags and differences between f.o.b. and c.i.f. prices are ignored, though these differences are quite minor due to the geographical proximity of the mainland and Hong Kong.

In 1990, China's trading partners, in order of importance, were the United States, Japan, Hong Kong, West Germany, the Soviet Union, Taiwan and South Korea. In order of importance, China's major markets were the United States, Japan, Hong Kong, West Germany, Singapore, the Soviet Union and South Korea. Its major suppliers were Japan, the United States, Hong Kong, Taiwan, West Germany, the Soviet Union, France and South Korea. China regards Hong Kong as its largest market as well as largest supplier since its indirect trade via Hong Kong is categorised in its statistics as trade with Hong Kong.

China's commodity trade with Hong Kong

Prior to 1979, most of China's exports went to Hong Kong; its imports from Hong Kong were negligible. China–Hong Kong trade was transformed in the post-reform period, with the re-exported portion of China's exports to Hong Kong growing rapidly, to the point that they exceeded the retained portion by 1986. The share of Chinese exports re-exported via Hong Kong rose from about 6 per cent in 1977 to almost 40 per cent in 1990. China's imports from Hong Kong also grew rapidly. Between 1977 and 1990 China's imports via Hong Kong and imports of Hong Kong origin grew 374 times and 869 times, respectively. The share of indirect imports in China's total imports rose from 0.5 per cent in 1977 to almost 27 per cent in 1990. Hong Kong re-emerged thereby as a major entrepôt for China, and China also became a major market for Hong Kong products.

Hong Kong was the largest final market in the late 1960s and early 1970s for Chinese exports (excluding Chinese exports via Hong Kong) but was overtaken by the Japanese and US markets in 1973 and 1987, respectively. The Hong Kong market accounted, nevertheless, for 8 per cent of China's exports in 1990 and is still regarded by China, which ignores the substantial re-exports of Chinese products via Hong Kong in its trade statistics, as its largest market. Domestic exports of Hong Kong to China have grown from negligible amounts to US$6,086 million in 1989. In 1984 Hong Kong became the third largest supplier of goods to China after Japan and the United States. Part of the reason for its rapid growth of domestic exports is due to its investment in processing and assembling operations in China. Hong Kong firms supply these operations with the required raw materials and components, part of which are produced in Hong Kong. It should be noted that China viewed Hong Kong as its largest supplier from 1987 onwards — its trade statistics list a substantial part of the re-exports of Hong Kong to China as imports from Hong Kong.

China's exports retained in Hong Kong have stagnated since 1987 and their share of China's total exports has declined sharply. China has been unable to capture the higher end of Hong Kong's market, which is dominated by Japan. Given the increasing affluence of Hong Kong, and the Japanese dominance in vehicles, capital goods and quality consumer durables and goods, the prospects for Chinese products in Hong Kong do not appear very bright (Sung 1991b, p. 119).

China's indirect trade through Hong Kong

Since the inauguration of its open-door policy, China has established numerous direct links with the rest of the world, including diplomatic, commercial and transportation ties. Paradoxically, Hong Kong's role as a middleman is becoming more prominent, and an increasing share of China's commodity trade is handled through Hong Kong. To explain this paradox, a theory of intermediation, with its strong predictions for entrepôt trade and services trade, is helpful.

It is important to distinguish trans-shipment from entrepôt trade. Trans-shipment means that goods are consigned directly from the exporting country to a buyer in the importing country, though the goods are transported via an entrepôt and may be stored there for onward shipment. Trans-shipped goods are not regarded as part of the trade of the entrepôt and they do not clear customs because they only represent goods in transit.

Unlike trans-shipment, entrepôt trade is part of the trade of the entrepôt. Imports for re-export are consigned to a buyer in the entrepôt and the buyer takes legal possession of the goods after clearing customs. These imports may then be processed before being re-exported as long as the processing is not substantial enough to confer country of origin status.

The usual explanation of entrepôt trade in terms of transportation costs is faulty because it ignores the importance of transaction costs. It is useful to classify re-exports into processed and pure re-exports. Processed re-exports refer to re-exports that have been physically treated (packaged, sorted and so on), whereas pure re-exports have not been changed in any physical way.

Pure re-exports are difficult to account for theoretically because re-exports involve higher costs than trans-shipment (other things being equal) owing to two factors: one, re-exports have to clear the customs of an entrepôt twice, whereas trans-shipped goods do not have to clear the customs of the entrepôt at all, so fewer delays and lower storage costs for trans-shipment are involved; and two, trans-shipped goods are insured and financed just once, whereas re-exports have to be insured and financed twice — when they are imported into the entrepôt, and when they are re-exported. While transportation costs determine trans-shipment, pure re-exports are determined by both transportation and transaction costs, and processed re-exports involve processing costs as well.

Since China's adoption of its open-door policy in 1979, it has been easier for other countries to trade directly with China. The transaction costs of establishing direct trade links have fallen and this should lead to a rise in direct trade relative to indirect trade. However, China began decentralising its foreign trade system in 1979, replacing vertical channels of command with horizontal ones. The number of trading partners and trade links multiplied rapidly, creating a huge demand for intermediation. Before 1979 the establishment of trade links with ten state trading corporations would have ensured a complete coverage of China trade. The number of trading corporations increased to over 1,000 by 1984, and it is very costly for an individual firm to establish trade links with the growing number of Chinese trading corporations. Intermediation emerged to economise on the cost of establishing trade links, and the demand for intermediation was channelled to Hong Kong on account of its comparative advantage in trade. Decentralisation of China's foreign trade came in three waves — in 1979, 1984 and 1988 — with an increase in China's trade share through Hong Kong on each occasion.

The market composition of China's indirect trade via Hong Kong and the change over time of these markets in dependency on Hong Kong's entrepôt trade confirm the overwhelming importance of trade decentralisation to intermediation (Sung 1988, pp. 199–202). Countries that have long histories of trading with China have found it worthwhile to pay for the fixed cost of establishing trade links, and are less dependent on Hong Kong than new entrants. Political recognition and trade pacts also lower dependency on Hong Kong. However, the decentralisation of China's trading system in 1979 and 1984 increased the dependency of both old and new entrants on Hong Kong's entrepôt trade. For instance, the dependence of Canada and the United States on Hong Kong for China's exports decreased in the early 1970s when the two countries established political and commercial links with China, but this trend was reversed in 1979. From 1984 dependency on Hong Kong for China's exports increased substantially among all of China's major markets — Japan, the United States, Singapore, West Germany, the United Kingdom, Canada and Australia. Similarly, from 1979, all of China's major suppliers — Japan, the United States, West Germany, the United Kingdom, France, Italy and Singapore — became more dependent on Hong Kong for their exports to China.

China's commodity trade with Taiwan

Besides its indirect trade through Hong Kong, China also trades with Taiwan through Singapore, Japan and other third countries. There is also direct trade, including smuggling, and 'minor trade' that takes place in designated coastal mainland ports managed by customs offices. Taiwanese can participate in 'minor trade' through the use of Taiwanese vessels of under 100 tons. From Taiwan's viewpoint, 'minor trade' also constitutes smuggling. With respect to Taiwan's imports from China, direct imports were estimated to be one-third of indirect imports via Hong Kong. No reliable estimates exist of Taiwan's direct exports to China, though, in addition to smuggling, it is known that Taiwanese businesspeople have illegally trans-shipped goods to the mainland via Hong Kong on a large scale. Such goods are reported on the bill of lading as being destined for Hong Kong buyers on departure from Taiwan. However, the documents are switched mid-voyage, and the goods trans-shipped via Hong Kong to the mainland. Such goods do not go through Hong Kong customs since they are reported as being destined for mainland buyers on arrival in Hong Kong and the Taiwanese exporters save on the costs and delays of going through customs. The risk of such trade is that, in the event of an accident on the Hong Kong–mainland leg of the voyage, the insurance company can refuse compensation on the grounds of illegality.

The magnitude of this trade can be detected by comparing Taiwan's and Hong Kong's statistics on bilateral trade flows. In 1990 Taiwan's exports to Hong Kong exceeded Hong Kong's imports from Taiwan by US$1 billion, which represented Taiwan's direct exports to the mainland in the form of trans-shipment via Hong Kong. Such exports constituted over one-third of Taiwan's indirect exports to China through Hong Kong in 1990. For both exports and imports in Taiwan's trade with the mainland, it is possible to conclude that direct trade amounted to at least one-third of indirect trade through Hong Kong. As reliable statistics are not available for direct and indirect trade through ports other than Hong Kong, this study relies largely on indirect trade data through Hong Kong. In 1979 Beijing started wooing Taiwan by importing Taiwanese products, and the mainland's customary trade surpluses changed into deficits from 1980. Between 1979 and 1990 China's imports from Taiwan via Hong Kong grew 154 times and China's exports to Taiwan 14 times. The growth was fast but bumpy as China's indirect imports from Taiwan declined in 1982–83 as well as 1986 due to China's stabilisation policies. However, despite retrenchment in 1988 and the Tiananmen incident in 1989, growth was not interrupted. China's exports to Taiwan grew slowly until 1987, as Taiwan restricted imports largely to Chinese herbal medicine. With the liberalisation of Taiwanese controls from 1987, China's exports to Taiwan have grown faster.

The major commodities in Taiwan's exports to China in 1990 were synthetic fabrics (33 per cent of the total) and non-electric machinery (8 per cent). The major commodities in China's exports to Taiwan in 1989 were Chinese herbal medicine (23 per cent), textile fabrics (11 per cent) and clothing (6 per cent). The cross flow in textile fabrics indicates that intra-industry trade is starting to supplement the traditional inter-industry trade.

The mainland suffers a massive deficit in its trade with Taiwan that may be a drag on the development of their trade in the long run. The deficit is partly due to Taiwanese import restrictions, but the lack of competitive products on the mainland may be a more basic problem. However, intra-industry trade is expected to develop rapidly with the surge in Taiwanese investment in the mainland. Moreover, China has a large surplus with Taiwan in tourism, gifts and remittances, and investment. The payments balance across the Taiwan Straits is thus quite even.

China's commodity trade with South Korea

The Tiananmen incident stalled the fast growth of China's trade with South Korea in the 1980s, though recovery began in 1990. Korea's major imports from China include raw materials such as chemicals, coal and non-ferrous metals as well as finished goods such as textile fabrics. South Korea's main exports to China include chemical fertilisers, plastics, television monitors, steel, medical equipment, household appliances, electrical goods and textile fabrics. As in the case of Taiwan, intra-industry trade exists in textile fabrics.

The share of indirect trade through Hong Kong in South Korea's imports from China has declined from 75 per cent in 1987 to 45 per cent in 1990, whereas that for exports to China has declined from 69 per cent in 1988 to 59 per cent in 1990. This seems to be a natural result of the commencement of direct shipping between South Korea and China in 1988.

Services trade between the mainland and the three NIEs

Services trade between the mainland and Taiwan is restricted to Taiwanese tourists visiting China. After Hong Kong and Macau, Taiwan ranks third as a source of tourists for the mainland, accounting for 3.5 per cent of tourist arrivals in 1990. The Taiwanese share of tourist expenditure in China is probably two to three times higher than its share in tourist arrivals because, on a per capita basis, Taiwanese visitors spend much more than the short-term visitors from Hong Kong and Macau. Of the 950,600 Taiwanese visitors to China in 1990, 920,000 entered through Hong Kong.

Services trade between the mainland and Hong Kong is extremely important. Conceptually, the re-export margin that Hong Kong earns through entrepôt trade is in fact representative of export of services. However, such services are embodied in the goods sold and are usually recorded in trade statistics as export of goods rather than export of services.

With respect to tourist services, Hong Kong visitors accounted for 66 per cent of all visitors to China in 1990; Hong Kong is also an important gateway for other visitors to China. In addition, Hong Kong exports transportation, trading, construction, financial and business services to China. However, except for entrepôt trade and tourism, little data exist for shipping, trading and financial services, while reliable data is lacking for the other categories.

Hong Kong's contribution to China's tourism accounts for around 70 per cent of tourist arrivals and expenditure. Though mainland tourists visiting Hong Kong have also increased rapidly, their numbers are quite small in comparison with Hong Kong residents visiting China. Such trips are usually paid for by the Hong Kong relatives of the mainland tourists.

Hong Kong is also the foremost gateway for foreigners touring China, many of whom join package tours organised in Hong Kong. Though China has established many more direct air links with other countries since 1979, the percentage of foreign tourists leaving (visiting) China via Hong Kong has increased since 1982, rising to 55 (44) per cent in 1987. This paradox can again be explained by the theory of intermediation, as China decentralised part of the authority to organise China tours from the China Travel Service to provincial and local authorities in the early 1980s.

In commodity trade, Hong Kong is an important entrepôt as well as trans-shipment centre for China. The value of trans-shipped goods is not available as the goods do not go through customs, though their weight is known. From 1983 to 1989 trans-shipment of goods to (from) China via Hong Kong increased 13.2 (2.7) times. In 1989 trans-shipment of goods to (from) China represented 21 (31) per cent of China's imports (exports) from (to) Hong Kong. If the value of trans-shipment to (from) China per ton is assumed to be the same as China's imports (exports) from (to) Hong Kong, trans-shipment of goods to (from) China via Hong Kong would amount to 10 per cent of China's imports (exports) by value in 1989. Hong Kong trading firms also perform an important brokerage role for China's direct trade, accounting for US$15 billion or 7 per cent of China's total trade in 1988 (Hong Kong Trade Development Council, 1988). The shares of China's exports for the four categories of consumed, re-exported, trans-shipped and intermediated by Hong Kong were 10 per cent, 37 per cent, 10 per cent and 7 per cent respectively in 1988–89, making a total of 64 per cent. Though some overlap is likely in the last two categories, it is possible to conclude that Hong Kong plays an important role in close to two-thirds of China's exports. On the import side, the shares of China's imports produced, re-exported, trans-shipped and intermediated by Hong Kong were 9 per cent, 22 per cent, 10 per cent and 7 per cent in 1988–89, making a total of 49 per cent. One can thus conclude that Hong Kong plays an important role in close to half of China's imports.

Though Hong Kong's exports of construction services and business services to China are undoubtedly important, there is very little data to go by. Hong Kong is the foremost base for China-related consultancy services. According to *Intertrade* (October 1984, p. 2) half of the foreign law firms in Hong Kong provide legal advice on China's trade. China's foremost trading corporation in Hong Kong, China Resource Co. Ltd, set up a consultancy firm in 1983 — China Resources Trade Consultancy Co. Ltd (CRTC) — for both foreigners and Chinese export firms. The China International Trust and Investment Corporation (CITIC) has also established a subsidiary in Hong Kong to provide consultancy services.

Services trade between South Korea and China is relatively minor and is thus omitted from this discussion.

Investment on the mainland by Hong Kong, Taiwan and South Korea

Hong Kong is the foremost source of direct investment and loans for the mainland while Taiwan is a significant source of direct investment. If South Korea continues its current pace of investment, it will soon become a significant source of direct investment as well.

South Korean investment in China

There was rapid growth of South Korean investment in China between 1985 and 1990. According to the Korean Overseas Trade Association, by the end of 1990 the South Korean government had approved 66 projects worth US$81 million. According to Chinese statistics, China had approved 82 South Korean-funded projects with a total pledged investment of US$108 million by the end of 1990 (*South China Morning Post*, 19 July 1991). The bulk of South Korean investment tended to be in small-scale labour-intensive operations producing electronics, toys, processed foods, apparel and household items. However, South Korean investment is increasing in size and sophistication. For instance, more recent proposed South Korean projects involve Hyundai's US$4 million project to manufacture tungsten products in Jiangxi, and Tong-Il's US$10 million car-parts joint venture in Qingdao (*The China Business Review*, November–December 1990, p. 38). Though South Korea cannot compare with Hong Kong or Taiwan in terms of size of investment, it has the most sophisticated industrial technology of the three, and is also geographically close to China's northeast region, the heartland of China's heavy industry. South Korean investment therefore has a significance far beyond its size.

Taiwanese investment in China

Despite the explosive growth of Taiwanese investment on the mainland in recent years, the total stock of contracted Taiwanese investment at the end of 1990 was only 7 per cent of that of Hong Kong. This indicates that there is considerable potential for further expansion of the Taiwanese share. Taiwan's investment was largely in small-scale labour-intensive operations producing light manufactures for export, including textiles, footwear, umbrellas, travel accessories and electronics. Projects were concentrated in Fujian and Guangdong provinces, particularly in the Xiamen region of Fujian. However, as in the case of South Korea, Taiwanese investment is also increasing in size and sophistication, with an increasing number of more technology-intensive projects such as chemicals, building materials, automobiles and electronic products and components. Investment has diversified from manufacturing into real estate, finance, tourism and agriculture, and the location of that investment has spread inland from the coast.

A 1989 State Council decree gave Taiwanese investors favourable treatment over other external investors. Most of the special concessions are fairly insignificant, except for one which allows Taiwan to invest in industries that are off-limits to other foreign investors; for example, in the labour-intensive footwear industry. Over 80 per cent of Taiwan's footwear industry has moved to the mainland. These special concessions have led to complaints from domestic producers whose exports have been displaced by those of Taiwanese investors. It must be stressed that economic concessions that favour one group over others are likely to be distortionary, leading to economic inefficiencies.

The surge of Taiwanese investment in the mainland has raised fears that such investment will lead to a 'hollowing out' of Taiwanese industry and create threats to security. In July 1990 the Taiwan government tried to halt the mainland investment boom by improving the investment environment in Taiwan and steering investment away from the mainland to ASEAN. A variety of means was used to prevent Formosa Plastics from implementing its proposal to build a gigantic naphtha cracking plant in Xiamen. To control the mainland investment boom, Taiwan authorised 3,319 products for indirect investment in September 1990, mostly labour-intensive products involving low degrees of processing. Authorisation is not granted for investment in industries that are still competitive in Taiwan, including naphtha, catalysts, knitwear, synthetic leather, sheet glass and glass fibre. Moreover, the Taiwan government also backed away from a proposed bill, 'Provisional Law on Relations Between the Peoples of Taiwan and the Mainland', which would have liberalised private relations between the mainland and Taiwan. Though the draft bill was completed in February 1989, its passage was stalled. The Taiwan government is trying to guide the mainland investment boom rather than reverse it. Taiwan's indirect trade and investment with the mainland continued to grow rapidly in early 1991.

Hong Kong investment in China

Between 1979 and 1989 contracted direct foreign investment by Hong Kong totalled US$22.4 billion, accounting for 59 per cent of total contracted direct foreign investment in China. Hong Kong's large share in China's direct foreign investment conceals the important middleman role it plays. In China's statistics, investment from Hong Kong includes investment by subsidiaries of foreign companies incorporated in Hong Kong. Because Hong Kong has the expertise, many multinational companies prefer to test the Chinese investment environment through their Hong Kong subsidiaries. If such investment is successful, then the parent company will also invest in China.

Hong Kong investment in China is highly diversified, ranging from small-scale labour-intensive operations to large-scale infrastructural projects. Though manufacturing in Hong Kong is not as sophisticated as in South Korea and Taiwan, Hong Kong has considerable expertise in service industries, including construction, hotels and financial services.

The share of Hong Kong in China's external loans was small in the early 1980s but rose from 0.6 per cent in 1983 to 9.4 per cent in 1989. The share was low partly because Hong Kong does not extend official loans to China. However, China-backed companies began to raise funds in Hong Kong's stock market through share placements in 1987 (*South China Morning Post*, 18 June 1987) and there are signs that China may in the long term make more use of Hong Kong's stock market.

Loan syndication, which is one of Hong Kong's important middleman functions, raises 80 per cent of China's syndicated loans. The share of China's external loans syndicated in Hong Kong rose from 6 per cent in 1979–82 to 31 per cent in 1987, before declining to 14 per cent in 1989. Such changes can be explained by the theory of intermediation. The rapid jump in the share of China's loans syndicated in Hong Kong in 1987 was related to the decentralisation in 1986 of the power to raise foreign loans to selected provincial governments and enterprises. The rapid decline in the share of China's loans syndicated in Hong Kong since 1988 lay with the 1988 recentralisation of power to borrow foreign loans as part of the retrenchment program. In commodity trade, tourist trade and financial services, decentralisation has a decisive influence on intermediation.

Conclusions

Despite the formidable political barriers separating the mainland from Taiwan and South Korea, the efficiency of Hong Kong in intermediation has enabled a significant degree of economic integration to emerge between the mainland and the three NIEs, and they all share many common economic interests as a consequence. For example, China's MFN status in the United States is important not only for China but also for the other three. If the United States were to revoke China's MFN status, China would suffer since the US market accounts for a considerable portion of China's exports (21 per cent in 1990). However, Hong Kong would suffer most (Sung 1991a, p. 15.8), as it accounts for around 60 per cent of foreign investment in both 'foreign-invested enterprises' and processing and assembling operations, which respectively accounted for 41 and 13 per cent of China's exports in 1990 (Sung 1991c, p. 19). Foreign investment is involved, therefore, in the production of 54 per cent of China's exports. If the United States were to revoke China's MFN status, Hong Kong investors would lose heavily. Hong Kong would also lose the re-export margin, and its service exports that support China's trade and investment would also suffer. As Taiwan has invested heavily in processing and assembling operations on the mainland, Taiwan would also be hard hit. While South Korea is more immune than either Taiwan or Hong Kong, given the small size of its investment and the fact that a substantial share of its investment is in import-substitution activities, if Sino-US relations were to turn sour over the MFN issue, it would also lose considerably.

Hong Kong is the key to China's open-door policy since its intermediary role is crucial in the latter's economic ties with Taiwan, South Korea and a number of other countries as well. If the dynamism of the Hong Kong economy can be preserved beyond 1997, the economic integration of Guangdong and Fujian with Hong Kong and Taiwan will continue to develop, and a prosperous south China region should emerge. It is also probable that a 'Yellow Sea Economic Region' linking Korea's west coast and the Bohai coast of China will emerge.

However, Hong Kong's future prosperity is by no means assured. The Tiananmen incident sorely tested the confidence of the Hong Kong community. Taiwan is closely watching the situation in Hong Kong since the formula of 'one country, two systems' is meant to apply to both countries. If the Hong Kong economy stagnates due to a crisis of confidence about 1997, the repercussions for China's open-door policy will be severe, with very little chance then of Taiwan's encouraging a greater degree of economic integration with the mainland.

China has sought to entice Taiwan with special economic concessions, but these are not only economically inefficient, they will also prove politically counter-productive in the long run. Taiwanese businesspeople are given favoured treatment over others on the ground that Taiwan is a part of China. However, while Hong Kong is also a part of China, Hong Kong businesspeople are not given the same treatment. The mainland Chinese, for their part, receive the worst treatment of all. It appears then that the only reason Taiwanese businesspeople receive such favoured treatment is because Taiwan's reunification with the mainland is not yet assured, unlike Hong Kong's. Taiwanese businesspeople will thus try to maintain Taiwan's political separation from the mainland in order to retain these special economic concessions. In this way, the mainland's policy runs contrary to the goal of national reunification.

As already noted, Beijing abolished tariffs on Taiwanese goods in 1980 on the grounds that Taiwan was a part of China. However, Hong Kong goods received no tariff exemptions even though Hong Kong was also a part of China. This policy proved to be unsustainable and Beijing was obliged to levy 'adjustment taxes' (they could not be called tariffs) on Taiwanese goods in 1983 to stem their flow, and that of Hong Kong goods disguised as Taiwanese goods. Due to the special concessions given to Taiwanese investors in 1989, Beijing is beginning to have problems with investors adopting Taiwanese 'disguise'.

In the long run, Beijing will need to adopt national treatment for all if it is to realise economic integration. However, given that its economy contains many distortions, this goal will only be achieved in many stages.

References

Hong Kong Trade Development Council 1988, 'Survey on Hong Kong re-exports: summary report', mimeo, November.

Sung, Yun-Wing 1988, 'A theoretical and empirical analysis of entrepôt trade: Hong Kong and Singapore and their roles in China's trade', in Leslie V. Castle and Christopher Findlay (eds), *Pacific Trade in Services*, Sydney: Allen & Unwin, pp. 173–208.

_____ 1991a, 'Foreign trade and investment', in Kuan Hsin-chi and Maurice Brosseau (eds), *China Review*, Hong Kong: Chinese University of Hong Kong Press, pp. 15.1–22.

_____ 1991b, *The China–Hong Kong Connection: The Key to China's Open Door Policy*, Cambridge, UK: Cambridge University Press.

_____ 1991c, 'Explaining China's export drive: the only success among command economies', *Hong Kong Institute of Asia Pacific Studies Occasional Paper*, No. 5, The Chinese University of Hong Kong.

Wakabayashi, Masahiro 1990, 'Relations between Taiwan and China during the 1980s, viewed from the Taiwan perspective', *China Newsletter*, No. 87, July–August.

Watanabe, Toshio 1990, 'Bringing China out of its shell: the Asian NIEs', *China Newsletter*, No. 87, July–August.

29 Prospects of trade expansion in the SAARC region

Mangat Ram Aggarwal and Posh Raj Pandey

The South Asian Association for Regional Cooperation (SAARC) — comprising the seven countries of Bangladesh, Bhutan, India, the Maldives, Nepal, Pakistan and Sri Lanka — was formed with the signing of its charter by the Heads of State/ Government at Dhaka in December 1985. The association was set up to accelerate the process of economic, social and cultural development, and to promote and strengthen collective self-reliance through joint action in certain agreed areas of cooperation (SAARC Secretariat n.d.).

The idea of regional cooperation in the South Asian region is not new. The countries of the region have worked together on bilateral and multilateral bases under the Economic and Social Commission for Asia and the Pacific (ESCAP), the Non-Aligned Movement, and within the Commonwealth. Realising that the existing efforts have not fully exploited the vast potential of regional cooperation that exists (SAARC 1988), a fresh initiative in this regard was expressed in November 1980 by Bangladesh. Thereafter, a series of meetings among the foreign secretaries of the members of the region took place for the formation of a regional group. An 'Integrated Program of Action' through the adoption of a Declaration on South Asian Regional Cooperation (SARC) was formally launched by the foreign ministers in 1983, and in 1985 SAARC came into existence. The broad areas of cooperation which have been identified so far are: agriculture and forestry, health and population activities, meteorology, rural development, telecommunication, transportation, science and technology, postal services, sports, arts and culture, women in development, drug trafficking and abuse, anti-terrorism, control of environment degradation and disaster management, food security, and audiovisual exchange. However, the vital areas of 'trade and industry' have been excluded. These have been the major areas for cooperation in ASEAN, a neighbouring and comparatively mature regional organisation. In particular, the basic

Reprinted with permission from *The Developing Economies*, Vol. 30, March 1992, pp. 3–23 (with deletions). Copyright © 1992 by the Institute of Developing Economies, Tokyo, Japan.

aims of ASEAN, as defined in the ASEAN Concord (1967) and the PTA concluded in 1977, are the expansion of intra-regional trade, particularly in basic manufactures through the reduction of tariff and non-tariff barriers on a product-by-product basis over a period of time; short and long-term bilateral and multilateral trade agreements within and outside the region; and the creation of industrial complementarity, particularly through the setting up of joint industries and/or projects involving two or more countries.

Slow path to industrialisation

Table 29.1, which provides the basic economic and trade indicators of SAARC member countries, shows that the level of per capita GNP of the region as compared with the industrialised nations is extremely low, and its growth rate between 1980 and 1987 has been below expectations. Figures for Bangladesh, Nepal and Sri Lanka have been particularly disappointing (below 3 per cent), chiefly because of the high rate of population growth, which has ranged between 1.5 to 3.2 per cent. However, the relative performance of the region and the countries individually (except Bangladesh) as measured by the growth of GDP has been quite satisfying. This growth has ranged between 4.6 and 12.5 per cent, and the share of the industrial sector in total GDP for all the countries (except Bhutan) has increased significantly, ranging between 13 and 30 per cent in 1987. This indicates that the region has been gradually undergoing a process of structural transformation, but the slow rate of change does not raise expectations of an early restructuring of the economies in the region. The importance of trade in the economies of the region as revealed by the ratio of total trade to GDP is quite high, ranging between 32 and 149 per cent, except in India and Bangladesh, where it was 16 and 19 per cent respectively in 1987. Though the trade performance of the region and the countries individually has been quite impressive (they achieved far higher rates of export growth during the 1980–87 period than the developed countries), they have experienced huge and progressively increasing trade deficits, which may be explained partly by their inability to create export surpluses and partly by a weak world growth environment. However, within the region, India and Pakistan have had continuously increasing trade surpluses, while Sri Lanka, Bangladesh, Nepal and the Maldives have had continuous sizeable deficits.

Table 29.2 presents the direction of trade for the region during the period 1980–87. It reveals the following four points.

One, the magnitude of intra-regional trade was very low, 2.98 per cent in export trade and 1.79 per cent in import trade, and was below 10 per cent in 1987 in all the countries, except for the Maldives in exports and Nepal in both exports and imports.

Two, intra-regional trade has continuously declined, except for minor deviations, showing that the countries of the region have been moving away rather than coming together in their economic relations. The high magnitude of regional trade for Nepal and the Maldives gives a distorted picture. Nepal is importing 22 per cent of its total

Table 29.1   Basic economic and trade indicators of SAARC member countries, 1987

	GDP (US$m) (1987)	Rate of growth of GDP (1980–87)	GNP per capita (US$) (1987)	Average annual growth rate of per capita GNP (1980–87)	Share of industry in GDP(%) (1987)	Total trade as a % of GDP (1987)	Balance in current account (US$m) (1987)
Bangladesh	17 600	3.8	160	1.6	13	19	-1 0413
Bhutan	250	6.1	150	3.9	6	61	-84.1
India	220 830	4.6	300	3.1	30	16	-5 027.0
Maldives	87[a]	12.5	300	9.0	13[a]	149	-9.1
Nepal	2 560	4.7	160	2.0	14	36	-196.9
Pakistan	31 650	6.6	350	3.7	28	32	-967.2
Sri Lanka	6 040	4.6	400	2.9	27	56	524.4
SAARC region[b]	279 017	4.8	260	3.9	28	19	-7 765.9
Developed countries	10 780 345[a]	2.5	13 552	2.7	30[a]	33	na

Notes: na—Not available.
   a   1986.
   b   Figures for SAARC region are weighted average.

Source: World Bank, *World Development Report, 1989*; United Nations, *Handbook of International Trade and Development Statistics, 1988*; United Nations, *Economic and Social Survey of Asia and the Pacific, 1988*; Bhutan, Planning Commission, Central Statistical Office, *Statistical Yearbook of Bhutan, 1988*.

Table 29.2   Direction of trade of SAARC member countries, 1980 and 1987 (per cent)

From To	Bangladesh		India		Maldives		Nepal		Pakistan		Sri Lanka		SAARC region	
	1980	1987	1980	1987	1980	1987	1980	1987	1980	1987	1980	1987	1980	1987
Bangladesh														
Exports	-	-	26.09*	25.56	n	n	4.62*	0.19*	33.17*	55.41*	5.43*	14.42*	12.31*	7.72*
Imports	-	-	5.71*	12.12	n	n	0.58*	4.66*	61.06*	52.93*	2.27*	0.14*	16.49*	20.39*
India														
Exports	11.66*	24.83*	-	-	n	n	74.87*	90.28*	42.87*	13.07*	46.54*	16.92*	41.14*	44.61*
Imports	57.80*	63.64*	-	-	68.75*	5.41*	98.95*	93.98*	3.13*	12.57*	73.31*	60.03*	24.00*	17.27*
Maldives														
Exports	n	0.23*	0.87*	0.39*	-	-	n	n	0.18*	0.18*	1.63*	12.12*	0.38*	0.75*
Imports	n	n	n	n	-	-	n	n	0.40*	n	1.44*	3.55*	0.82*	1.29*
Nepal														
Exports	0.73*	11.51*	33.91*	39.45*	n	n	-	-	0.24*	0.98*	n	0.19*	3.49*	9.32*
Imports	1.04*	0.17*	15.00*	53.54*	n	n	-	-	3.22*	1.17*	0.30*	3.26*	14.76*	20.57*
Pakistan														
Exports	80.61*	62.98*	1.74*	4.30*	19.05*	n	18.46*	1.87*	-	-	46.40*	56.34*	29.50*	28.53*
Imports	36.28*	31.91*	52.86*	24.24*	4.17*	4.05*	0.46*	1.44*	-	-	22.67*	33.02*	21.31*	16.38*
Sri Lanka														
Exports	6.99*	0.45*	37.39*	29.30*	80.95*	100.00*	2.05*	7.66*	23.53*	30.36*	-	-	13.18*	9.06*
Imports	4.88*	4.28*	26.43*	10.10*	27.08*	90.54*	n	n	32.18*	33.33*	-	-	23.98*	24.09*
SAARC region														
Exports	8.71	4.11	2.91	2.06	29.17	18.14	34.57	32.11	6.30	3.93	7.09	3.81	4.50	2.98
Imports	3.68	4.28	1.04	0.48	26.67	7.44	43.07	23.90	2.32	1.61	6.48	6.50	2.46	1.79
Industrial countries														
Exports	36.04	65.82	57.59	59.28	70.83	18.14	54.26	65.31	36.41	58.58	39.57	63.54	50.24	59.80
Imports	48.10	44.82	48.50	60.83	65.56	26.06	45.52	50.39	50.13	58.26	45.35	43.28	48.52	57.56

Notes: *— Represents the share of the country in its intra-regional exports/imports to the concerned members.
n— Negligible.

Source: IMF, *Direction of Trade Statistics*, various issues.

imports from, and exporting 29 per cent of total exports to, a single trading partner — India. The situation is similar for the Maldives, which sent 18 per cent of its total exports in 1987 to Sri Lanka.

Three, the region's trade has been directed more towards the industrial countries, whose share in the region's exports and imports in 1987 stood at 59.8 and 57.6 per cent respectively. India and Pakistan are the major exporters within the region, together contributing 73 per cent of the region's export trade. On the other hand, 65 per cent of the region's imports have been absorbed by Sri Lanka, Nepal and Bangladesh, making them the region's major importers. The extremely low share for the Maldives shows that it has still not entered into the intra-regional trade.

Four, India's major importers are Nepal, Sri Lanka and Bangladesh; Pakistan's are Bangladesh and Sri Lanka. The chief exporters to Bangladesh and Sri Lanka continue to be India and Pakistan; the chief exporter to Nepal is India.

In terms of the product structure, the share of 'food items' dominates intra-regional trade and is followed by 'other manufactures', 'agricultural raw materials', 'machinery and equipment', and 'chemical products'. Around 70 per cent of intra-regional trade in 1985 was accounted for by the first three broad commodity groups; little change over the situation in 1980. But the composition of intra-regional product trade is not symmetrical. Bangladesh, Nepal and Sri Lanka export relatively more 'food items' and 'agricultural raw materials' commodities. The reverse is true for both India and Pakistan. Within the region, India's share in the export of 'food items' is the highest, followed by Nepal; India is also the highest in the export of 'machinery and equipment' and 'other manufactures', followed by Pakistan. Pakistan is the highest exporter of 'agricultural raw materials' and 'chemical products', followed by India. On the other hand, Pakistan dominates in the import of 'food items' and 'agricultural raw materials' and Bangladesh in 'machinery and equipment'.

There are two inescapable inferences from the above analysis. One, the region is on the path of industrialisation, as revealed by the increased share of the industrial sector and manufactured exports to GDP. India, Pakistan, and Sri Lanka are relatively more attuned to the process of development when measured in terms of the level and real growth in per capita and total GDP and the manufacturing sector. Two, despite the fact that all the countries are saddled with huge and growing current account deficits *vis-à-vis* the outside world, there exists enormous scope for mutual trade expansion in the region. This can be done by restructuring and redistributing the region's trade through intra-regional understanding and arrangements for action, internally as well as in relation to the outside world. Intra-regional trade is bound to increase considerably if India and Pakistan (which have continuously maintained their high share in the intra-regional export trade and have had trade surpluses within the region) undertake to accept additional responsibility by opening up their markets more liberally to the other members and grant full or partial non-reciprocity; and if Sri Lanka, Nepal, and Bangladesh (the major importers which have absorbed a major share of intra-regional imports and have faced continuous intra-regional trade deficits) are assured by the rest of the members, in particular the surplus ones, of fair access to their markets, keeping in view each country's level of development, export capabilities, and mutuality of interests. In addition, there is the need to harmonise production and investment plans, particularly in the export sectors (taking into account the actual and potential comparative advantages or disadvantages); to gradually reduce tariff and non-tariff barriers; to undertake bilateral and/or multilateral long-term commodity agreements between the deficit and surplus countries of the region and with the outside world; to pool financial resources for maintaining buffer stocks in the major commodities on a regional or subregional basis; to set up joint projects in the basic and heavy goods sectors at the regional level and the allocation of their production to different areas; and to carry out joint marketing policies coupled with payment arrangements. Development in these areas would go a long way towards diversifying the structure and pattern of trade within the region and with the rest of the world.

Trade intensity analysis

In current literature, the degree of competitiveness and complementarity in the production and trade structures of member countries within a CU has assumed a central place when judging whether the CU will be trade creating or not. The wider the difference in cost ratios (high complementarities), the greater the prospects for trade expansion in a CU. In the remainder of this paper, we will use the following indexes: trade intensity, complementarity, and country bias to assess the degree of 'existing' and 'potential' complementarity in order to evaluate the prospects for trade expansion in general and to identify the products in the broad sectors where intra-regional trade could be expanded.

The trade intensity index (I_{ij}) measures the extent to which one country's share in another country's exports (imports) is large or small in relation to the former country's share in world trade (Brown 1949; Kojima 1964; Wadhva 1987). The value of more (or less) than unity of this index indicates that a country is exporting more (or less) to another country than might be expected from the country's share in world trade.

High values of this index during the period 1965–87 reveal that the intensity of trade for the countries within the region is very high, except for India–Pakistan, the Maldives–Bangladesh, the Maldives–India, the Maldives–Nepal, Nepal–Bangladesh, Nepal–the Maldives, Sri Lanka–India and Sri Lanka–Nepal in export trade, and Bangladesh–the Maldives, India–the Maldives, the Maldives–India, the Maldives–Nepal, Nepal–the Maldives, Nepal–Sri Lanka, Pakistan–India and Sri Lanka–Bangladesh in import trade, where the values of the indexes are less than unity. The magnitude of bilateral trade orientation is the highest between the Maldives–Sri Lanka followed by India–Nepal, Bangladesh–Pakistan and Pakistan–Sri Lanka. However, the degree of intensity between each of the countries within the region has fallen between 1975 and 1985, largely due to the adoption of vigorous inward-looking policies by the members to spearhead the drive for rapid overall development.

The trade intensity index can be decomposed into two indexes, complementarity and country bias, in order to assess the contribution of complementarity and other factors influencing the intensity of trade. Whereas the complementarity index measures the extent to which one country's export pattern matches another country's import pattern more closely than it matches that country's import pattern for world imports, the country bias index measures the extent to which one country's exports have more or less favourable access to another country's market than might be expected from both countries' share in world trade (Drysdale 1969; Drysdale and Garnaut 1982, also Chapter 3, this volume; Anderson 1983).

The values of the complementarity index (obtained by disaggregating six major commodity groups — food items, agricultural raw materials and mineral ores, fuels, chemical products, machinery and equipment, and 'other manufactures' goods, and thereafter summing) show that the level of complementarity in the bilateral trade structure of the member countries as well as within the region as a whole is not only low, but also that it has not risen substantially during the period 1965–85. In other words, the high intensity of trade between the member countries cannot be attributed to the level of complementarity in their trade structure. One of the plausible explanations for the low and nearly stable level of complementarity is the dramatic increase in trade barriers and protectionism by the members to intra-regional trade. For example, the average *ad valorem* tariff rate in 1983–84 was more than 71 per cent, except for Sri Lanka, where it was 41 per cent, and the average tariff-frequency ratio was more than 80 per cent in the countries of the region (DeRosa 1986). Hence, the cause of the very high intensity in the trade pattern between the member countries can be largely explained by country bias trading relationships as the values of this index are significantly high (although showing a declining trend when compared with 1965, except for India–Pakistan, Pakistan–Nepal, Sri Lanka–India and Sri Lanka–Nepal in export trade, and vice versa in import trade). The magnitude of the country bias trading relationship is the highest in India–Nepal trade followed by Sri Lanka–Pakistan and Bangladesh–Pakistan in both export and import trade. The extremely high country bias trading relations might have resulted from, *inter alia*, geographical proximity, bilateral trade agreements, and the availability of market information. On the other hand, the low intensity of trade among some of the countries is clearly due to the low magnitude of the country bias index, possibly resulting from continuous hostile political relations, several discriminatory trade practices against co-members, and an information gap about trading and investment opportunities rather than the low level of complementarity.

Conclusion

The major conclusion emerging from the foregoing analysis is that the fundamental cause for the existing low level of intra-regional trade is the presence of the low degree of complementarity in the production and trade structures of the countries of the region. This is largely the direct outcome of the imposition of trade and other barriers by the member countries on their intra-regional trade and the pursuit of import substitution and self-sufficiency policies in light manufactured goods and consumable items in order to attain self-sustaining growth or self-support as soon as possible. This conclusion implies that the countries of the region can increase mutual trade substantially if they immediately make prodigious and outstanding efforts to expand and explore potential complementarity through gradual market opening; to introduce a phased program to reduce tariffs and non-tariff barriers on a 'product-by-product' basis and to reduce 'other interventionist' measures in the different sectors of their production structure; to conclude bilateral and multilateral long-term commodity agreements between the deficit and surplus countries within and outside the region; to set up 'regional industries' involving two or more countries; to introduce government procurement preferences *vis-à-vis* the outside world (as has been done by ASEAN); and to establish regional trade information and promotion centres in order to identify the prospective buyers and their demands in relation to technical standards, quality, design and payment arrangements. The countries of the region also need to harmonise their production, investment and export plans at the regional level, keeping in view their actual and potential comparative advantages and disadvantages and the long-term economic interest of the less developed areas of the region.

References

Anderson, K. 1983, 'Prospects of trade growth among Pacific Basin countries', *Developing Economies*, 21(4), December.

Brown, A. J. 1949, *Applied Economics: Aspects of World Economy in War and Peace*, London: George Allen and Unwin.

DeRosa, D. A. 1986, 'Trade and protection in the Asian developing region', *Asian Development Review*, 4(1).

Drysdale, P. 1969, 'Japan, Australia, New Zealand: the prospect for Western Pacific economic integration', *Economic Record*, 45(3), September.

Drysdale, P. and R. Garnaut 1982, 'Trade and intensities and the analysis of bilateral trade flows in a many-country world: a survey', *Hitotsubashi Journal of Economics*, 22(2), February.

Kojima, K. 1964, 'The pattern of international trade among advanced countries', *Hitotsubashi Journal of Economics*, 5(1), June.

SAARC (South Asian Association for Regional Cooperation) Secretariat n.d., 'South Asian Association for Regional Cooperation' (brochure), Kathmandu: SAARC Secretariat.

SAARC (South Asian Association for Regional Cooperation) 1988, *From SARC to SAARC: Milestones in the Evolution of Regional Cooperation in South Asia (1980–1988)*, Vol. 1, Kathmandu: SAARC.

Wadhva, C. D. 1987, 'India: 1. Trade relations', in C. D. Wadhva et al., *Regional Economic Cooperation in Asia*, Ahmedabad: Allied Publishers.

Part Ten

China: The Region's Emerging Giant

30 China's reforms in international context

Ross Garnaut

This paper examines some of the policy conditions for modern economic growth in China, drawing on the comparative experience of other, especially East Asian, economies. It relates the lessons of analysis and experience to the conditions of China, seeking to draw conclusions about the process of change and reform that will be necessary for rapid economic growth to be sustained.

The comparative context of China's reforms

The East Asian context

The East Asian phenomenon of sustained, rapid growth in the period since the Second World War is now well known (Ariff 1991). China shares some characteristics with East Asian economies like Japan, Korea, Taiwan, Hong Kong and Singapore, which have sustained rapid growth over long periods. It differs markedly in other characteristics that are relevant to economic performance.

The characteristics that China shares with its rapidly growing neighbours include location in an economically dynamic region, some economically relevant history of social organisation and values, relative resource endowments in the early stages of growth, and, recently, a pattern of interaction with the international economy. These similarities together hold out positive prospects of rapid growth in the East Asian style when viewed alongside Chinese economic performance in the reform era.

Location in an economically dynamic region has influenced growth in one small way, and one large. The small way is the cost advantage that proximity provides for economic transactions. Location alongside Hong Kong has been particularly important, and proximity to Taiwan is becoming so. Larger has been the effect of proximity through the transmission of ideas and ambitions. For China, the demonstration effects of adjacent Chinese communities in Hong Kong and Taiwan have been especially powerful.

Chinese coastal provinces share one structural feature with all of the high-growth East Asian economies: an exceptionally low per capita endowment of land and, at an early stage of their development, capital as well. With appropriate policies, this leads to large economic gains from strong specialisation in exports of labour-intensive manufactured goods while incomes remain low, with mostly favourable implications for the political economy of development and income distribution in the course of development. Interestingly, despite the huge price distortions and controls in China's factor and goods markets, which some observers have argued could prevent China's trade specialisation from being consistent with comparative advantage (Hsu 1989), both the commodity specialisation and the rate of growth of China's exports have been similar to successful East Asian economies at comparable stages of development. Other structural similarities include unusually high rates of savings and investment and, since the greater use of markets in the reform period in China, a high capacity to transform rapidly the industry composition of production.

There is much dispute about the relevance to economic performance of the shared East Asian cultural traditions. For familiar reasons, we are wise to be cautious. One cannot help but notice, however, the long time-horizons in East Asia, when other conditions arc favourable to them, which support high rates of savings and investment, including in education. The East Asian polities, too, have found it easier than developing economies elsewhere to build social and political cohesion around the goal of rapid economic growth. China seemed to be sharing this characteristic early in the reform period. More recently, there have been doubts about the capacity of the Chinese Leninist state to adjust enough to the changes in hopes, values, knowledge and individual self-confidence that accompany rapid economic growth. This is an important question, but one that is not addressed in this paper.

The biggest difference relevant to long-term growth between China and the East Asian economies that have been growing rapidly over a long period is the communist legacy — not so much the profession of commitment to distributional equity or to public ownership of business enterprises, both of which have been important elsewhere in East Asia, but the particular legacies of the Leninist political organisation (democratic centralism) and the Stalinist system of central planning. These place constraints on growth that are difficult to reform.

The context of liberalising inward-looking Pacific economies

China in the process of reform shares problems and experience with inward-looking Pacific economies undergoing reform. The parallels are closest with heavily regulated economies with authoritarian governments, including Korea, Taiwan and Indonesia in the 1960s, and several Latin American economies, notably Chile, in recent years.

Internationally-oriented reform of inward-looking liberal democracies, including Australia and New Zealand in the 1980s, is also instructive on a few points.

There is a growing literature on reform of inward-looking economies, swelled recently by an explosion of interest in the experience with reform in centrally planned economies. The Latin American experience, in particular, has produced some generalisations about the desirable sequencing of reform: that reforms of the real economy should precede the financial, and that domestic reforms should precede international reforms. There has also been inconclusive discussion of the lessons of experience, on whether rapid reform was more or less likely to be successful than gradual reform. The reality does not lend itself to confident generalisations, since much depends on the institutional constraints on policy choice, and the settings of policies in other spheres (for example, the budget balance).

Every case of reform has its own transitional problems. These problems are often associated with the particular institutions and histories of individual economies. The few general lessons that are drawn here are applied to China with caution in later sections of this paper. China is further into some aspects of internationally-oriented reform than many other inward-looking economies, and so has much domestic experience from the past decade to compare with that of others.

The positive lesson from the Pacific experience, including in China, is that the efficiency gains from internationalisation are large, rather larger than traditional economic analysis suggests (Krueger 1991). The removal of controls on foreign exchange quickly expands international economic transactions of many kinds. The Indonesian experience of the late 1960s is the most radical — there the efficiency gains were enhanced by the emergence of a less egregiously corrupt and more economically-oriented political economy. Foreign exchange and trade liberalisation, and the reduction of domestic costs relative to international prices with which they were commonly but not universally associated, promoted rapid diversification and expansion of exports in many Pacific economies, easing fears of balance of payments weakness (Garnaut 1991a).

The most important transitional costs of liberalisation were suffered in economies which experienced periods of severe misalignment in the real exchange rate. This occurred principally when tight monetary policies were applied for anti-inflationary purposes before fiscal deficits had been brought under control (Chile, New Zealand), and were most severe when financial deregulation was well in advance of real trade liberalisation.

In Chile, the high real exchange rate in the process of liberalisation occurred with a currency that was fixed in value to the US dollar as part of a strategy of radical disinflation (Hachette 1991). The episode can now be seen as having delivered major long-term real economic gains, but the short-term costs to producing tradeable goods, reflected in high unemployment, were greater than would be tolerable in most political systems.

In New Zealand, and to a lesser extent Australia, misalignment occurred under floating exchange rate regimes, as the authorities sought to correct the inflationary and external payments effects of excessive monetary expansion in the process of financial deregulation (Bollard and Buckle 1987). Continuing fiscal deficits made the real costs greater in New Zealand. A general lesson, with echoes in the Taiwan and ASEAN economies, concerns the need to strengthen prudential supervision of trading banks in the process of domestic and international financial deregulation.

In Hong Kong, the combination of foreign exchange liberalisation and the absence of effective controls on monetary expansion supported a devastating spiral of currency depreciation and inflation. It was brought to a halt only with the pegging of the Hong Kong dollar against the US dollar in 1983 (Garnaut 1991b). The Hong Kong experience since then, like Indonesia from the late 1960s and Singapore from the late 1970s, demonstrates that a fixed exchange rate — in Indonesia adjusted from time to time in an attempt to maintain international competitiveness after periods of domestic inflation, and in Singapore to insulate the economy from international inflation — is consistent with freedom from controls when accompanied by prudent fiscal policy (Garnaut 1991b).

External trade and payments liberalisation was usually part of wider reform programs encompassing many aspects of the domestic economy. It was rare for a comprehensive program to be defined in advance and followed systematically, although Korea kept the earlier time-path of Japanese development closely in mind. Chile was the nearest to having a blueprint for reform, and, as it turned out, experienced the greatest transitional pain.

It was much more common for economic leaders to have in mind a general model of a more liberal and internationally-oriented economy, and to take *ad hoc* steps towards it in response to opportunities for progress in one area or another. Opportunities often came at times of macroeconomic crisis, where trade and payments liberalisation was associated with exchange rate depreciation, as in China late in 1990. The determinant of the success of the transition was the strength of the instinct towards market-oriented solutions to problems as they arose.

In Taiwan, the region's most far-reaching and successful case of internationalisation and development, economic leaders without a blueprint but with instincts favouring internationalisation and liberalisation groped their way towards what became a brilliantly successful strategy (Li 1988).

It is inevitable that there will be uneven progress on policies that are necessary to maintain growth in a huge backward country like China. The keys to success are the consistency of the responses to opportunity, and the preparedness to take large steps in a liberalising direction when major barriers to progress are identified.

The market and the state

East Asian lessons

The success of many economies in East Asia over recent decades has generated much heated discussion, in the region and elsewhere, about the role of the state in their development. At one extreme, Friedman (1981) has argued that Singapore and Hong

Kong demonstrate the case for a minimal economic role for government. Singapore had done well, he said, because it had relied upon the free market, and Hong Kong better because it had relied more on the market.

Other theologians of capitalism have not been so sure. Berger (1986), for example, states as one of his 'fifty propositions about prosperity, liberty and equality' that the 'East Asia evidence falsifies the idea that a high degree of state intervention in the economy is incompatible with successful capitalist development'.

Jones (1988) looks back over a thousand years and asks why China, in Song times having generated many of the inventions later thought to be essential to the industrial revolution in Europe, and enjoying high and rising productivity levels, did not sustain economic growth in the later style of Europe. Growth can occur, he concluded, only within an 'optimality band', where 'factor and commodity markets are freed and the government is neither too grasping nor too weak'.

Not much can be said about the overall effect of government intervention on East Asian economic development. It depends on the nature of the intervention and of the society and polity within which it operates. Government must be strong enough to deliver a range of services that are essential for development and must allow markets to operate in some important spheres.

The provision of relatively stable macroeconomic conditions, a stable system of law and order, and of the institutions of the market itself, represent the irreducible minimum of state intervention for economic growth to proceed. In these days of economic integration across international orders, the irreducible minimum must also be defined to include an adequate contribution to the institutions of an international market. The state must be strong enough to remove private incentives to corrupt the legal basis of market exchanges. These are not trivial conditions, as the failure of development in many developing countries attests. It was their provision within imported legal systems in Singapore and Hong Kong that unlocked the potential for great economic dynamism in those Chinese communities.

Everywhere in high-growth East Asia except Hong Kong, the state has been active in promoting growth-oriented ideology. The state's definition and assertion of the national interest in economic growth, and close interaction between political and business leaders (although the latter less in Hong Kong), have created a favourable environment for accepting market outcomes, including the inconvenience of structural change. These factors have also reduced business uncertainty, by generating shared perspectives on the directions of structural change in the course of economic growth.

The negative role of government in distorting market prices has been demonstrated to be greatly damaging to development. Rapid economic growth requires far-reaching structural change. It is not possible to introduce the required flexibility beyond the earliest stages of economic development unless markets are used extensively to allocate goods, services and factors of production, and to set the prices which govern exchanges. East Asian economies which have sustained high growth have, relative to other countries, low degrees of price distortion (World Bank 1983, pp. 57–63).

The most important prices to get right are those governing incentives for production for export, relative to production for home markets. Hong Kong and Singapore have achieved the required balance with free trade. Korea and Taiwan early in their rapid industrialisation achieved this outcome with assistance to exports to offset the assistance that protection provided for import-competing production. All of the rapidly growing East Asian economies which had earlier relied on balancing protection with export incentives found it expedient to move towards free trade as productivity and incomes increased.

Open foreign exchange policies and regimes have been important in getting the foreign trade prices right.

It seems that economic development becomes increasingly demanding over time of flexibility, free communications and openness to ideas and technologies from the international economy, all of which depend on extensive use of effective markets with undistorted prices. Growth can get under way with distorted prices, as with the early experience of central planning in China, North Korea and the former Soviet Union. But growth with highly distorted prices drifts into stagnation, and eventually economic and political instability — hence the 'shifting bottleneck' described by Krueger (1991), in which liberalisation of economic institutions is required to go further and further over time if growth is to be sustained.

Another aspect of the role of government relates to the share of national output provided directly to the community through government administrative structures, or sold through state-owned enterprises.

Direct spending on administrative and other non-commercial services has tended to be relatively low in East Asian economies, and this has been associated with relatively low taxation shares of national income. But the high-growth economies have not skimped in the provision of public education or economic infrastructure, although the efficiency with which the latter is provided has been enhanced in several cases by potential and realised competition from private investors. In the more advanced economies in recent years, there has been a trend towards sale of infrastructure into the private sector.

The role of state-owned commercial enterprises has varied through East Asia, being prominent in Singapore and Taiwan, and relatively unimportant in Hong Kong and Japan. The keys to successful performance have been the quality of recruitment into public enterprises, and the establishment of a strong commercial orientation, often with competition from other, sometimes international, enterprises, and with high expectations of commercial performance.

The state in East Asia has concerned itself with equitable income distribution. This has been important to maintaining social cohesion around high growth in the face of massive strains associated with rapid structural change. Tough action by a strong state, sometimes externally imposed, was important to establishing conditions for equitable distribution early in the process of rapid growth: land reform; a hard, competitive and high quality public education system; and, in several economies, minimum standards of housing.

Overall, the role of the state in the rapidly growing economies of East Asia has varied considerably but has been strong enough to deliver a substantial minimum of public goods, and focused enough to allow a considerable role for exchange of a wide range of goods, services and factors through markets at relatively undistorted prices. Ironically, one of the problems of Chinese development has been weakness in provision of a range of public goods and services that elsewhere in East Asia are provided efficiently by governments. The problem of the role of the state in China is as much the poor direction and low effectiveness of government efforts as it is the excessive strength of government.

Reform for international economic integration

The partial reforms of the 1980s supported strong growth in exports, consistently with China's comparative advantage in labour-intensive production. They also supported absolutely large gains from direct investment and financial flows from abroad, although these were of modest scale in the context of China's economic size.

The growth in external trade is remarkable, given the myriad bureaucratic controls in foreign trade and payments, the irrational prices and the foreign reactions, especially in the United States, to Chinese trade distortions. The substantial reduction of these distortions would ensure that the strong trade growth since the late 1970s would continue, and probably accelerate, underwriting one of the key conditions for sustained, rapid growth in China.

In some months in late 1990 and in 1991 domestic exports from China were larger than from any Western Pacific economy other than Japan, having increased significantly faster than exports from Korea and Taiwan over recent years. This remarkable growth derived from use of a relatively small part of the potential gains from trade. Exports have been drawn heavily and increasingly from non-state enterprises in a few coastal provinces, and from relations with or through neighbouring East Asian economies. Non-convertibility of the renminbi, the controls on trade, the partial monopolies of state trading cooperations, the quantitative controls on export and import trade, the random and contradictory bureaucratic interventions, and the differential trade subsidies systematically diminished the participation in international trade of state enterprises, inland provinces, and enterprise whose potential gains were mainly in trade with the West or which lacked informal ties with Hong Kong and, of increasing importance from 1987, Taiwan.

There are obviously large and economically inefficient variations in assistance across industries and enterprises, although these cannot be measured precisely in the environment of distorted prices. The variations in assistance have no obvious relationship to any possible economic or political strategy that might be thought to favour some forms of production over others. For example, official policy continues to favour high levels of self-sufficiency in food, especially rice, and yet the subsidies on agricultural inputs and food consumption, currency overvaluation, protection and subsidised credit to heavy industry, and controls on trade have almost certainly combined to reduce food production and, in the short term, to increase net food imports above what they would be with free trade linked to free domestic markets. Official policy is meant to favour incomes growth from inland provinces, but controls and price distortions in domestic trade diminish income gains in these provinces from trade with internationally-oriented coastal provinces. (At the same time, these controls and distortions diminish the international competitiveness of both inland and coastal production.) Official policy is meant to favour production in state enterprises, but the system of trade controls blocks the direct contact between these enterprises and their customers that could contribute much to improvement in competitiveness. The exchange controls affect state enterprises most. Official policy is meant to favour direct investment and trade which strengthens capacities in industries that use advanced technology; yet the overall system of incentives allows, wisely, relatively free access to gains from trade with East Asian developing economies applying standard technologies, but, without good reason, creates barriers to trade and investment with technologically advanced economies.

The development of non-plan enterprises in East and South China and the informal business relations with neighbouring, especially Chinese, communities has been responsible for much of the success of the open policies over recent years. The success is considerable, and the first objective of continuing reform for strengthening international integration should be the preservation and enhancement of these gains. There is now a considerable danger, however, that international reactions to distortions in China's trade-related policies will tangle the foreign trade of Hong Kong and, to a lesser but increasing degree, Taiwan, in ways that damage China's economic relations with these adjacent economies.

Hong Kong's specialisation in international trade has been transformed since 1984, from integrated export-oriented manufacturing to the supply of high-value business services overwhelmingly related to the economic relationship with the mainland. Hong Kong's manufacturing employment has fallen by a third in recent years, to 700,000, while employment in Hong Kong related manufacturing enterprises in Guangdong province has increased rapidly to over 2 million. Two-way Hong Kong–China trade, including re-exports, at US$50 billion in 1990, and growing rapidly, is one of the largest bilateral relationships in the Pacific region. Exports from Taiwan nominally to Hong Kong, but in reality in unknown proportions to Hong Kong and the mainland, have grown even more rapidly since the legalisation of indirect trade with the mainland in 1987. Exports to Hong Kong and China now account for 15 per cent of Taiwan's total exports, and in the early months of 1991 were one-third larger than the year before.

The three Chinese economies together are now major participants in the Pacific and world economies, with combined exports two-thirds as large as Japan, and three-quarters the total for all other Western Pacific economies. The growing politicisation and pressures for official management of advanced economies' trade with China, justified in terms of Chinese trade distortions, is thus a substantial problem for trade relations in the whole Pacific region.

A few years ago, China's currency overvaluation and inconvertibility, and the export subsidies that were allocated unevenly to compensate for balance of payments disequilibrium, represented the most important barrier to utilisation of potential gains from international trade and investment. Recent reforms have greatly diminished the importance of this barrier: the introduction in 1987 and the progressive liberalisation of access to legal foreign exchange 'swap markets' at floating rates; the series of devaluations of the official exchange rate; the large reductions in central export subsidies; and the stronger control of domestic demand. The differential between 'swap market' and official exchange rates has fallen from over 100 per cent during the inflationary boom of 1988 to around 10 per cent in early 1991.

The experience of liberalising Pacific economies cautions against proceeding rapidly to full integration of the 'swap market' and official foreign exchange markets. There would be dangers in allowing uncontrolled convertibility of the renminbi into foreign exchange by government agencies and state enterprises, pending the completion of financial reforms, including effective independence and prudential supervision of trading banks, and the range of reforms necessary to enforce macroeconomic discipline and hard budget constraints on a continuing basis. Priority should be given to consolidating and extending gains from recent foreign exchange reforms, including prevention of the re-emergence of a large differential between market and official exchange rates through domestic demand restraint and timely official devaluation.

The continued limitation on the free participation of state enterprises and agencies in foreign exchange transactions has efficiency costs, which can be removed safely only when domestic reform has made more progress.

The increasing friction in trade relations with Western economies, especially the United States, is an unfortunate development for the whole Pacific community. Among other costs, it is extending to China, and inevitably Hong Kong, pressures to bilateralism, to the exclusion of efficient trading relations with other Pacific economies. While unfortunate, the friction is also predictable and inevitable, given the increasing politicisation and official management of US trade in general, the closer focus on human rights that flows from more intimate contact between Chinese and foreign communities under the open policies, the diminution of perceptions of international interest in China's open policies now that they are well established and taken for granted, and the removal of strategic imperatives in US–China relations with the end of the Cold War.

China, like Japan in the mid-1950s, can most effectively limit damage from the proliferation of trade discrimination by accepting and appealing to internationally agreed rules of liberal trade. GATT membership has become important and urgent. Acceptance of China into the GATT requires further progress in reform of the Chinese trade system and the domestic economy. This is consistent with implicit and explicit Chinese policy and interest. Chinese membership of GATT would facilitate

Taiwan membership, which in itself is important for the international system. Early, full APEC membership of China, Chinese Taipei and Hong Kong would allow discussion of, and place some constraints on, problems for the wider Pacific community arising out of pressures for bilateral resolution of US–China trade frictions.

In the best of circumstances, China's participation in the international economy will for many years be characterised by many and large divergences between international and domestic prices, and by variations in levels of domestic assistance and penalty across industries. If the general framework of foreign exchange management and participation in the international trading rules is sound, this can be consistent with rapidly increasing gains from trade, and a gradual approach to continuing reform. The consistency depends, however, on China making transparent to itself, if not to the international community, the effects on prices and industry assistance of official interventions in price determination and resource allocation. This will require the generation, assembly and analysis of much data that is not currently available in China. If this condition is met, there is a chance that continuing *ad hoc* reform in the East Asian and Pacific style will lead to consistent movement in a liberalising direction, allowing China to remain ahead of the 'shifting bottleneck' that accompanies successful development (Krueger 1991).

Priorities in domestic and international reforms

This paper's discussion of the East Asian and Pacific experience with economic development and reform suggests that the imperatives of domestic and international reform are consistent with each other.

China shares with other East Asian economies an opportunity for sustained, rapid, internationally-oriented growth. The East Asian experience tells us that the absence of a comprehensive reform blueprint is not in itself a barrier to sustained growth, so long as there is commitment to market and international orientation, and so long as immediate threats to progress are removed by reform that is consistent with the necessary directions of change. The presence of strong government is not in itself a barrier to growth, although there are currently problems with the focus of government strength in China, and we do not yet know whether it is possible to change large enterprises established within the framework of central planning into effective commercial entities in a market environment. The experience of reforming communist economic systems, including the recent Chinese experience, warns us that macroeconomic instability in the process of reform is the greatest immediate threat to sustained growth. Pending deeper reform of the domestic system, this requires direct controls on bank lending to state agencies and enterprises, at substantial economic cost, especially to the efficiency and growth of the enterprises themselves. This need not threaten the continuation of strong growth in the large parts of the Chinese economy outside the state sector.

Realisation of Communist Party ambitions for a continued large role for state enterprises in a rapidly growing economy depends on effective systemic reform, so that these enterprises are operating with commercial cultures within a market framework. The development of the required culture poses a great challenge, and at best will take a number of years. In the meantime, the relative position of large state enterprises in the economy will continue to decline, if rapid economic growth continues.

The greatest immediate threat to continued expansion of gains from the open policies is the increasing friction in relations with advanced Western economies, especially the United States. The most difficult steps required to manage this threat are coincident with the steps that are necessary in domestic reform: substantial progress in price and enterprise reform, so that China can participate in the international trading system under agreed rules.

The study of the experience of others can help to avoid some pitfalls in reform. Radical financial deregulation needs to be accompanied by the building of a firm framework of macroeconomic control, prudential supervision and market-enforcing institutions. Hard budget constraints for state enterprises need to be introduced in an environment of macroeconomic stability. Meanwhile, the pressures of transition can be eased in China by the dynamism of non-plan production, which was not available to reform governments in the former Soviet Union and parts of Eastern Europe.

If the basic framework can be established along these lines, there will be time to implement gradually the reforms in the wider environment, and to build the institutions of a market-oriented economy that are necessary to extend economic growth and rising living standards through China's huge population.

But if these basic steps prove to be too hard in the current political context of China, the prognosis is not favourable for the 'socialist commodity economy'. Macroeconomic instability would soon find its way into political instability. Even the dynamism of the non-plan economy would be damaged, including through the entanglement of the People's Republic and its immediate neighbours in intractable international trade frictions.

Chinese economic reform over the past dozen years has much success to its credit. The expansion of production and trade that has already occurred has proven many early critics wrong.

Some years ago Deng told Takeshita, then in Beijing as Chairman of the LDP, that reform was like the challenge facing Guan Yu in the Chinese classics. Guan had to cross five passes and cut down six generals before he achieved success. Now further into its journey, China has, at least, a clearer view of the passes still to be crossed.

References

Ariff, Mohamed (ed.) 1991, *The Pacific Economy: Growth and External Stability*, Sydney: Allen & Unwin.

Berger, P. L. 1986, *The Capitalist Revolution*, Hants: Wildwood House.

Bollard, Alan and Robert Buckle 1987, *Economic Liberalisation in New Zealand*, Wellington: Allen & Unwin and Port Nicholson Press.

Friedman, Milton 1981, 'The invisible hand in economics and politics: inaugural Singapore lecture 1980', Singapore: Institute of Southeast Asian Studies.

Garnaut, R. 1988, 'China: Asia's giant', *Australian Economic Papers*, 27(51).

_____ 1991a, 'Economic stability and growth in the Pacific: an overview', in Mohamed Ariff (ed.), *The Pacific Economy: Growth and External Stability*, Sydney: Allen and Unwin.

_____ 1991b, 'Exchange rate regimes in East Asia and the Pacific', *Asian–Pacific Economic Literature*, 5(2).

Hachette, Dominique 1991, 'Chile: trade liberalisation since 1974', in Geoffrey Shepherd and Carlos Geraldo Langoni (eds), *Trade Reform: Lessons from Eight Countries*, San Francisco: International Center for Economic Growth.

Hsu, John C. 1989, *China's Foreign Trade Reforms: Impact on Growth and Stability*, Cambridge, New York and Melbourne: Cambridge University Press.

Jones, E. L. 1988, *Growth Recurring: Economic Change in World History*, Oxford: Clarendon Press.

Krueger, A. O. 1991, 'Pacific growth and macroeconomic performance: models and issues', in Mohamed Ariff (ed.), *The Pacific Economy: Growth and External Stability*, Sydney: Allen & Unwin.

Li, K. T. 1988, *The Evolution of Policy Behind Taiwan's Development Success*, New Haven and London: Yale University Press.

World Bank 1983, *World Development Report*, Washington, DC: World Bank.

Abbreviations

AD	Antidumping
AFTA	ASEAN Free Trade Area
AIJV	ASEAN Industrial Joint Venture (Scheme)
APEC	Asia Pacific Economic Cooperation
ASEAN	Association of South East Asian Nations
CAP	Common Agricultural Policy
CEPT	Common Effective Preferential Tariff (Scheme)
CER	Closer Economic Relations (Agreement)
COMECON	Council for Mutual Economic Assistance
CU	Customs Union
EAEC	East Asian Economic Caucus
EAEG	East Asian Economic Group
EANIES	East Asian NIEs
EC	European Community
ECSC	European Coal and Steel Community
EEC	European Economic Community
EFTA	European Free Trade Association
EPG	Eminent Persons Group
ESCAP	Economic and Social Commission for Asia and the Pacific
FDI	Foreign Direct Investment
FTA	Free Trade Area
FTIA	Free Trade and Investment Area
GATT	General Agreement on Tariffs and Trade
GEACS	Greater East Asia Co-Prosperity Sphere
GSP	Generalised System of Preferences
HS	Harmonised System
IMF	International Monetary Fund
IP	Intellectual Property
JERC	Japan Economic Research Center

LAFTA	Latin American Free Trade Association/Area
LDP	Liberal Democratic Party
MFA	Multifibre Arrangement
MFN	Most-Favoured-Nation
MITI	Ministry of International Trade and Industry (Japan)
MNEs	Multinational Enterprises
MTN	Multilateral Trade Negotiations
NAFTA	North American Free Trade Agreement
NATO	North Atlantic Treaty Organisation
NIEs	Newly Industrialising Economies
NTBs	Non-tariff Barriers
OEA	Open Economic Association
OECD	Organisation for Economic Cooperation and Development
OEEC	Organisation for European Economic Cooperation
OLS	Ordinary Least Squares
OMAs	Orderly Marketing Arrangements
OPEC	Organisation of Petroleum Exporting Countries
OPTAD	Organisation for Pacific Trade and Development
PAFTA	Pacific Free Trade Area
PAFTAD	Pacific Trade and Development (Conference)
PBEC	Pacific Basin Economic Council
PCC	Pacific Cooperation Committee
PECC	Pacific Economic Cooperation Conference
PTAs	Preferential Trading Arrangements
RIAs	Regional Integration Agreements
RTAs	Regional Trading Arrangements
SAARC	South Asian Association for Regional Cooperation
SDRs	Special Drawing Rights
SEZs	Special Economic Zones
SII	Structural Impediments Initiative
SREZs	Subregional Economic Zones
TRIMs	Trade-related Investment Measures
TRIPs	Trade-related Intellectual Property Provisions
VERs	Voluntary Export Restraints

Index ———————————————————————————

Development 163
International Monetary Fund (IMF) 43, 164
International Trade Organisation 12
Investment 198, 213; codes 220; flows 119, 120–1, 373, 381; policies 40, 122, 291; rules 214, 290 *see also* TRIMs
Iran 158
Israel 150, 155, 158
Italy 94, 110 176, 267

Japan 2, 59, 77, 78, 80, 84, 110, 116, 188, 228, 267 *see also* Tokyo; and APEC 85, 212, 219; and ASEAN 86, 104, 322; and Australia 27, 80, 351; and China 114, 207; and East Asia 107, 111, 112, 114, 116, 122, 188, 227–46, 259, 266, 307, 308; and Korea 111–12, 207, 365; and Russia 207, 365–6; and the United States 4, 104, 164, 213, 294–5, 305, 311–12; and the Western Pacific 40; economic growth 101, 102, 111–12, 202, 223; inward FDI 270; overseas investments 270–6; trade liberalisation 4, 48; trade policies 183, 227–46
Japan Economic Research Centre (JERC) 79, 81, 184
Japan Institute of International Affairs (JIIA) 81
Japan Sea Economic Zone 366
Japan–Australia Business Cooperation Committee 80
Java 53, 375
Johor 90, 95, 96, 97, 207, 265, 324, 365, 367, 370, 371, 372, 374–5, 377, 378
Johor–Singapore–Riau (JSR) Growth Triangle *see* SIJORI

Kajima, Morinosuke 79
Karimun island 376, 379
Khoman, Thanat 106
Kojima, Kiyoshi 79, 80, 81, 82
Korea 84, 85, 114, 115, 116, 267 *see also* North Korea, Republic of Korea, Seoul; and APEC 212; and China 5; and East

Asia 111, 114; and Japan 111–12; and NAFTA 222; economic growth 120; foreign investment 308; trade liberalisation 4, 48
Kurimoto, Hiroshi 79, 80

Labour issues 119, 195, 309, 347, 371, 372, 374, 379
Labour markets 93, 115, 383
Laos 207, 265
Latin America 3, 6, 30, 31, 59, 92, 104, 186, 413; and NAFTA 216, 222, 314; protectionism 3; trade policies 195, 288; trade shares 134–6, 138, 288
Latin American Free Trade Association 92, 164
Lee Kuan Yew 369
Leekpai, Chuan 322, 336
London 14, 239, 240
Los Angeles 14

Macau 365, 384, 393
Mahathir, Datuk Seri 96, 180, 208, 230, 266, 298, 315, 336, 370
Malacca 379
Malaysia 68, 84, 95, 152, 164, 239, 263, 267 *see also* Johor, Penang; and ASEAN 265, 322, 334, 336–7; and East Asia 111, 114, 308; and Indonesia 365, 366 *see also* SIJORI; and Japan 113; economic growth 4, 86, 120; industrialisation 206; trade liberalisation 48, 58, 334
Maldives 400, 401, 404
Manchuria 111, 112, 113, 114, 115
Manila 82, 107, 110
Manufacturing 117, 272, 302, 320, 374, 376 adjustments 185, 344
Market integration 2, 13, 38, 52–4, 99, 350–6
Marshall Plan 224
Medan 95
Mexico 59, 84, 85, 92, 137, 151, 156–7, 162, 267; and APEC 212, 221; and NAFTA 3, 288, 290, 319, 329

measures
TRIPs *see* Trade-related IP provisions
Tumen River Delta Area project 365
Turkey 151, 158, 268

United Kingdom 30, 93, 94, 155, 268 *see also* London; and China 110
United Kingdom–Ireland Free Trade Area 148
United Nations Centre for Regional Planning 90
United Nations Economic Commission for Latin America 92
United Nations Regional Commission *see* Economic and Social Commission for Asia and the Pacific (ESCAP)
United States of America 2, 18, 59, 80, 83, 84, 85, 107, 149, 155, 177, 268 *see also* New York, Washington; and APEC 6, 85, 98, 212, 219, 223; and ASEAN 164, 208, 288, 319, 322; and Canada 4, 57, 150; and China 287, 295–6, 388; and East Asia 119, 266, 298–315; and Israel 158; and Japan 40, 98, 104, 209, 220, 287, 294–5, 312, 314; and Korea 4; and Mexico 156–7, 290; and multilateralism 182; and NAFTA 287–97; and Taiwan 4, 156, 287, 386; and the Philippines 4; and the United Kingdom 110; and Vietnam 5; payments deficit 151; per capita income 223; trade imbalances 51, 197, 287, 288; trade policies 150–2, 164, 194, 287–97

Uruguay Round 125, 161, 162, 163, 180, 201, 208, 214, 218, 291, 319
USSR *see* Soviet Union

Vietnam 3, 207, 319, 322
Voluntary export restraints (VERs) 128, 156–7, 177, 180, 208

Washington 98
Washington Conference *1921* 112
Western Europe 23, 49, 50, 80, 101, 133–7, 140
Western Pacific 4, 5, 40, 106, 171; discriminatory practices 59; economy 51
World Trade Organisation 7, 220
World War II *see* Second World War

Yamazawa, Ippei 28
Yellow Sea Economic Zone 207, 365, 384
Yen bloc 227, 228
Yugoslavia 90, 127, 250, 268